A Core Collection

for Young Adults

SECOND EDITION

Rollie James Welch

Neal-Schuman Publishers, Inc.

New York   London

Published by Neal-Schuman Publishers, Inc.
100 William St., Suite 2004
New York, NY 10038

Printed and bound in the United States of America.

The paper used in this publication meets the minimum requirements of American National Standard for Information Sciences—Permanence of Paper for Printed Library Materials, ANSI Z39.48-1992.

Library of Congress Cataloging in Publication Data

Welch, Rollie James, 1957-
    A core collection for young adults. — Second edition / Rollie James Welch.
        p. cm. — (Teens @ the library series)
    Includes bibliographical references and indexes.
    ISBN 978-1-55570-692-0 (alk. paper)
    1. Teenagers—Books and reading—United States. 2. Preteens—Books and reading—United States. 3. Young adults' libraries—United States—Book lists. 4. Young adult literature—Bibliography. I. Title.

Z1037.J66 2011
011.62'5—dc22

                                                    2010046693

Contents

Appendixes

Foreword

When Charles Harmon, vice president of Neal-Schuman Publishers, mentioned to me that he wanted an update to the first edition of *A Core Collection for Young Adults* by Patrick Jones, Patricia Taylor, and Kristin Edwards, my first and only recommendation was Rollie Welch. Of all the amazing, talented, creative young adult librarians I have been fortunate to meet over the past decade, he stood out as the most dedicated young adult book reader, with the largest retention of book details stored in his head, and who could talk about any title on the spot. Too many times when someone asks me if I read a book, I have to refer to my Goodreads list and read about it to remember, so someone who remembers titles and authors and plots and characters so readily makes a real impression upon me.

I met Rollie at Ohio library conferences and regional workshops, first listening to him talk about young adult books and then getting to know him in person. I sat in on several of the Best Books for Young Adults (BBYA) sessions at American Library Association Annual and Midwinter Conferences when he was on the committee, and then when he was chairing the committee. People who know Rollie and have worked with him enjoy his company and appreciate his dedication to the profession. His knowledge and evaluation of the many, many books he read for BBYA was insightful, humorous, and on target.

He and BBYA cohort Elsworth Rockefeller of the DC Public Library system became coauthors of a regular column in *Voice of Youth Advocates* (*VOYA*) magazine, called "Man Up!," that addresses the reading and library service needs of teen boys. Rollie's personality comes through in his writing style with serious information delivered with a fun sense of humor. Rollie's love of young adult literature, his practical experience as a young adult librarian, his expertise in readers' advisory with a diverse range of teens, along with his librarian sensibilities of what you need to know to develop a young adult collection came together to make him the perfect choice to create this indispensable professional guide.

The revised and updated *Core Collection for Young Adults* has some of the best features of the first edition but, like all good revisions, adds more to the picture with organization that will make it even more useful as a readers' advisory tool as well as a collection development tool. The categories of books fall in line with today's teen requests and current trends, including Dystopian thrillers and super-natural beings, while keeping the new classics we hope to see on the shelves for many years. Thorough listings of editions available will help the reader make the most of the young adult collection budget. The inclusion of sequels and series titles ensures that your collection is complete, and the grade ranges for teen readers are helpful for readers' advisory, but also for building suggested reading lists for teachers. Rollie's annotations tell a bit about the plot, setting, and char-acters, but he also gives an evaluation, a recommendation for type of reader, and points out important elements that might limit the book's appeal.

After seeing Rollie tackle this huge project with dedication and perseverance while maintaining a busy work schedule that includes reviewing, book selection committee work, collection management for Cleveland Public Library, not to mention reading, along with being a husband and father, I am still positive that Rollie Welch was the best person for this job and I hope his readers will think so, too.

RoseMary Honnold
Editor-in-Chief
Voice of Youth Advocates (*VOYA*)

Preface

A Core Collection for Young Adults, Second Edition, and its companion CD-ROM, the Young Adult Core Collection Builder, is intended to give new and reassigned librarians who work with teens a launching point for developing a thriving collection of appealing books for young adults. Experienced teen librarians can also use the book and CD-ROM for retrospective collection development and for revitalizing particular sections of their collections. This core collection-building resource can also serve as a reader's advisory tool.

WHO IS THE INTENDED AUDIENCE FOR THIS BOOK?

Many libraries lack the luxury of having a specific group of staff members to work with teens, a result of staff reductions due to current economic conditions. Teen duties are now often part of a split position, with the librarian working in two areas simultaneously, such as services for both adults and teens or for both children and young adults. Thus, the primary audience for this core collection is anyone who is not specifically proficient in young adult literature.

Another group who will benefit from this resource includes full-time librarians who work with teens but may not have the time to read the latest young adult titles. Balancing programming, customer service, and collection development leaves little time to read from the wide range of titles published each year. Even teen librarians with a solid knowledge of YA literature may face a shrinking pool of titles and can use this book and CD-ROM as a tool to "freshen up" their collections.

Graduate students enrolled in library science classes will find this book helpful as well. It is also hoped that this edition will be embraced by instructors seeking to help students explore newer titles that may have more appeal to twenty-first-century teens.

Last, it is hoped that library administrators will be interested in this title and recommend it to staff working with teens. Progressive libraries often provide quality service to teens and this title may be used to keep teen book collections fresh and lively, thus enhancing the mission of the library: providing quality collections for all community members.

WHAT IS A YOUNG ADULT CORE COLLECTION?

The concept of a core collection initially sounds simple, but a working definition is less obvious. Does the word "core" suggest that every library serving teens should have these titles on their shelves? Should a public library and a school library share the same core collection? Should a middle school library and high school library duplicate titles? The crucial focus when selecting a core collection is the demographics of the audience that collection is intended to serve.

In compiling this second edition of *A Core Collection for Young Adults*, I considered a wide age range of young adults, gender, ethnicity, and economic factors both when making initial selections and when composing annotations. My work on the Young Adult Library Services Association's (YALSA) Best Books for Young Adults (BBYA) committee was a microcosm sorting exercise similar to what I did for this book. From the 1,000-plus titles published during the committee's eligibility time frame, the BBYA whittles down more than 200 titles to around 80 for a final list. Nobody can possibly read all of the titles published in any given year, so this work attempts to separate the "chaff from the wheat" by identifying high-quality titles with above-average interest to teen readers.

WHO ARE YOUNG ADULTS AND WHAT DO THEY READ?

YALSA defines the young adult age range as ages twelve to eighteen. However, very few titles have enough universal appeal to attract both sixth graders and high school seniors. Some titles will always appeal more to males than females and vice versa. Mix in the age factor and you can see that a book with high appeal for a twelve-year-old boy may not be of interest to an eighteen-year-old girl. When economic status is considered the book that appeals to a wealthy African American girl living in a gated community may not resonate with a Caucasian boy living in Section 8 housing.

This book follows a simple rule of thumb that helped me in my booktalking years to connect teens with books; it has two basic principles:

1.   Teens want to read about someone with whom they identify in some way.
2.   Teens want to read about someone who shares their life experiences.

At its simplest, this basic rule can be illustrated by the ethnic and economic makeup of the reader and the book. An example: I once spoke to an African American teenaged girl during a visit to a juvenile detention center. She craved realistic fiction and abhorred fantasy, telling me, "I don't want to read a fairy that doesn't mean anything anybody" [*sic*]. Consequently, well-reviewed fantasy titles did not accompany me to this detention center, which housed primarily African American teens on the low end of the socioeconomic scale.

This illustrates how the literary likes and dislikes of teens are often tied to their home life—both where they live and how they live. Understanding what teens read includes factoring in the influence of both regional differences and pop culture. For this reason, *A Core Collection for Young Adults* strives to include as much variety in setting as possible.

After reading dozens of books, the trends of any particular publishing year easily stand out, with almost identical locations repeated over and over—Seattle's coffeehouses, Manhattan's Upper East Side, and Florida's beaches—all have provided backdrops for numerous teen novels. But do the duplicated settings alienate teens unfamiliar with those locations? Perhaps, and perhaps not, as it can be argued that a teen living on a Midwestern farm might be attracted by the glamour of New York City. Still, I think that revisiting the same location in book after book wears thin for every reader, particularly for teens who seek new and novel experiences. Diversity, always an important element of young adult literature, is one factor driving the selections in this book.

Another factor influencing the selections in this book is popularity among teens. A quick walk through any chain bookstore will reveal what's "hot" in books for teens, a trend fueled by a spike in retail sales of YA literature. Rather than, as in the past, just a couple of shelves of the basic series titles (Hardy Boys, Nancy Drew, Fear Street) in one section at the back of the store, bookstores now feature numerous and varied young adult titles in key display locations, often near the front entrance or check-out lines, where patrons are sure to notice them.

It is evident that pop culture drives book sales. Consider, for instance, Stephenie Meyer's *Twilight* series, which has launched a seemingly endless number of vampire spin-offs, and Rachel Cohn and David Levithan's *Nick and Norah's Infinite Playlist*, whose appeal is enhanced by its connection to currently cool and hip tunes. Books linked to pop and rock music or movies, especially the tie-ins with graphic novels, now dominate bookstore shelves. The covers of movie tie-in paperback editions are much more visually attractive to teen shoppers because they often include photographs of actors playing the book's characters.

Selection committees, especially the Best Books for Young Adults committee (renamed Best Fiction for Young Adults in 2011), constantly wrestle with balancing popularity and literary quality. A general statement that sums it all up is this: If teenagers are not interested in reading a title, why should libraries shelve it in teen sections?

WHAT SELECTION CRITERIA ARE USED?

Much of the legwork on title selection came from my experience on YALSA's selection committees. During my stints with Quick Picks and Best Books for Young

Adults—which covered six consecutive years, three on each committee—I evaluated hundreds of current titles from all genres and with potential appeal to a wide variety of teens of either gender and different ages. Thus, both the Quick Picks and Best Books for Young Adults lists contributed significantly to my initial culling. I tried to include titles that were field-tested "hits" from my own booktalks, favorite titles from booklists produced by teen librarians who presented workshops, and titles from "best choices" lists from different review journals.

The Internet played a role in selection as well. Reviewing website and blog postings of both teens' and professionals' opinions of titles helped me to assess a title's teen appeal and quality and, most important, brought to my attention titles I might otherwise not have considered. Publisher presence on the Internet made it fairly easy to ensure that I considered the newest titles for inclusion, and Amazon's customer feedback proved a quick source for checking titles' popularity with teens.

Reviews in professional journals, especially those offering starred or "best of" selections, were of utmost importance in final selections. *Booklist, Kirkus, Publishers Weekly, School Library Journal,* and *VOYA* were the major print review sources consulted. *The New York Times* and *Publishers Weekly* best-seller lists provided additional verification of titles' popular appeal among teens.

The section on classics was problematic because certain titles once considered classic may fade from use over time or across regions. A list of classics that supports one urban, suburban, or rural school district's curriculum may very well differ from another similar district's classics list, and the recommended reading lists in schools may differ from those in public libraries. The selections in this book reflect both "traditional" classic titles and "new" classic titles with appeal to diverse readers.

The titles included in *A Core Collection for Young Adults* were greatly informed by choices made by the following selection committees, whose charges are included here to clarify their connection to the core collection presented in this book:

Alex Awards

- This committee selects from the previous year's publications ten books written for adults that have special appeal to young adults ages twelve to eighteen.

Best Books for Young Adults

- This is a general list of fiction and nonfiction titles selected for their proven or potential appeal to the personal reading tastes of young adults.

- Such titles should incorporate acceptable literary quality and effectiveness of presentation.
- Fiction titles should feature characterization and dialogue that is believable within the context of the novel or story.
- Nonfiction titles should have an appealing format and readable text.

Great Graphic Novels

- This is a general list of graphic novels, both fiction and nonfiction, selected for proven or potential appeal to the personal reading tastes of teens.
- For the purpose of the committee, graphic novels are defined to include trade compilations and original works published in a sequential art format. Such titles should incorporate acceptable literary and artistic quality with effectiveness of presentation.

John Newbery Medal

- The Newbery Medal is the grandfather of youth book selection, dating back to 1922, and recognizes the most distinguished contributions to American literature for children.
- Many titles considered classics have won the Newbery Medal, but it is interesting to see which titles were awarded honor status. Many honor books are titles most remembered by parents and grandparents.

Michael L. Printz Award

- The committee selects from the previous year's publications the best young adult book ("best" being defined solely in terms of literary merit).

Quick Picks for Reluctant Young Adult Readers

- This list features titles for young adults ages twelve to eighteen who, for whatever reasons, do not like to read. The purpose of this list is to identify titles for recreational reading, not for curricular or remedial use.

These summaries of the YALSA committees' charges underscore the wide scope of young adult literature.

In addition to these selection lists, I consulted other award lists to glean titles that may not have been acknowledged by the various YALSA committees. For example, *VOYA* annually produces Top Shelf for Middle School Fiction and Top

Shelf for Middle School Nonfiction lists, both of which were consulted for this edition of *A Core Collection for Young Adults.*

WHAT DOES THIS CORE COLLECTION INCLUDE AND HOW DO I USE IT?

This second edition of *A Core Collection for Young Adults* recommends 1,386 titles. Of these, 877 are fully annotated and 509 additional sequels or other titles are mentioned in the bodies of the annotations. The appendixes list 871 titles, some covered in the core collection and some not.

This edition differs in arrangement from the first edition. Instead of one long alphabetical list, the titles are divided into thirteen sections:

1. Adventure Tales
2. Cautionary Novels
3. Classic Literature
4. Coming-of-Age Stories
5. Fantasy Novels
6. Graphic Novels
7. Historical Fiction
8. Humorous Novels
9. Inspirational Fiction
10. Problem Novels
11. Readable Nonfiction
12. Romance Novels
13. Science Fiction

Each of these sections begins with a brief introduction, describing the draw of that type of book and the general age and gender of the targeted audience. To ensure that each section is diverse and representative of different authors and writing styles, only a sampling of titles by an author appears in any one section.

No attempt was made to list all titles in a complete series; only sample titles from a series are listed. Thus, L. A. Meyer's Bloody Jack series is introduced in the "Adventure Tales" section but not all six titles are annotated. Several series with a significant number of individual titles have only the initial title annotated, with the remaining titles listed under "Other Titles in the Series" at the end of the annotation.

Titles by authors who are prolific in one genre are handled in a similar fashion, with no attempt to provide a comprehensive list of all of their titles in that genre; this information is available from any number of sources, such as Amazon and *Books in Print.* Thus, sample titles of Tamora Pierce's many fantasy titles and Will Hobbs's outdoor adventure yarns are included, but the listings are not meant to be exhaustive.

Each of the 877 main entries follows a similar content format: author (last name first), title, number of pages, and a listing of a title's various formats, each followed by publisher, ISBN, publication date, and price; here's an example:

Salisbury, Graham. *Eyes of the Emperor.* 240 p. TR. Random House Children's Books. 978-0-385-72971-0. 2005. $15.95. RE. San Val, Incorporated. 978-1-4177-6903-2. 2007. $17.20. PB. Random House Children's Books. 978-0-440-22956-8. 2007. $6.99. CD. Recorded Books, LLC. 978-1-4193-8486-8. 2006. $49.75. CASS. Recorded Books, LLC. 978-1-4193-8481-3. 2006. $39.75. EB. Recorded Books, LLC. 978-1-4237-6882-1. N/A. $1.00.

Eddie Okubo feels the pull of patriotism and is anxious to join the military to help his country. He is a Japanese-American youth living in Hawaii at the time of the Pearl Harbor attack. Eddie and his friends join the United States Army and they're upset by having to endure forced marches and perform unskilled labor tasks. Salisbury relates the shocking experiment where the Japanese-American soldiers are forced to hide from military dogs that are being trained to attack when smelling the so-called Japanese body odor. This novel relates a little-known ugly racial practice during the grim days on the World War II homefront.

GRADES: 7–10

REVIEWS: *Booklist* 5/15/05, *Publishers Weekly* 9/05/05, *SLJ* 9/05, *VOYA* 8/05

Each title was checked against *Books in Print* for all available formats of the title. Each available format is listed in the bibliographic information section at the beginning of each main entry. To save space, the following format abbreviations are used:

TR   Trade
PB   Paperback
LB   Library Binding
RE   Reinforced Binding
LP   Large Print
CD   Book on CD
CASS Book on Cassette
PLAY Playaway
EB   E-book

Like the bibliographic information, the annotations have a similar structure. The opening sentence introduces the main character(s) and states the primary conflict. A brief plot summary follows. The final sentence is an evaluation and recommendation of audience. Where appropriate, I have noted excessive profanity, sexual encounters, and violence.

A recommended reading level by school grade follows the narrative annotation. Because I find wide age-range recommendations to provide little actual help for selectors, especially those professionals working on a limited budget in a public or school library, I opted to steer away from vague general recommendations such as "for ages 12–18" or "for ages 12 and up." Thus, the recommended levels are my own shorthand and are not gleaned from review sources or vendor websites.

Each annotation ends with a list of review sources for that title. I consulted *Books in Print*, publishers' websites, and vendor databases to find review citations and narrowed the list to these five journals:

- *Booklist*
- *Kirkus*
- *Publishers Weekly*
- *School Library Journal*
- *VOYA*

If a book was reviewed in any of these journals, I listed it. Some of the older titles did not have reviews listed, and it was interesting to see the increase in reviews of young adult titles as the twenty-first century developed.

Annotations for titles that have been honored by major YALSA awards include this information last. Several titles received multiple awards. Professionals interested in acquiring award-winning titles for their young adult collections should consult the appendixes of award-winning title lists at the end of this book.

WHAT IS ON THE YOUNG ADULT CORE COLLECTION BUILDER CD-ROM?

The CD-ROM on the inside back cover includes all bibliographic information for all formats for all 1,386 titles featured in the book in several Excel files:

- The entire collection listed by chapter, with a separate tab for each of the thirteen genres and arranged alphabetically by author
- The entire collection as one list arranged alphabetically by author
- The entire collection as one list arranged alphabetically by title
- The entire collection as one list arranged by recommended grade level

The benefit of the Excel format is that the information can be electronically sorted to compare publishers, prices, available formats, and so forth. Savvy librarians will electronically search the files to locate favorite authors or titles. The alphabetical author list will quickly show if an author is prolific, with many titles recommended in this work, or if this writer is simply a "one-hit wonder." The CD-ROM can also be used as an ordering tool when a title is lost or needs to be replaced due to wear and tear. A simple sorting of the files can show titles arranged by price, format, or even ISBN to see if a work with a particular ISBN is still in print. The files can also be arranged by publisher to determine the best choice for direct-ordering purposes.

Part of creating a collection is not only adding new titles but also evaluating existing works parked on the shelves. Should a title with a copyright date of 40 years ago be discarded? Should it be replaced if worn? The CD-ROM, with just a few keystrokes, will inform librarians if an updated version is available. Of course, the coinciding problem is that many tried-and-true titles have dozens of paperback versions available and those lengthy listings became too cumbersome to include in the CD-ROM.

The thirteen sections in this second edition of *A Core Collection for Young Adults* include more than 1,300 titles. A typical library shelf holds about thirty books. If starting from scratch and using all of the titles listed in this work, a collection would need at least forty-three shelves. Most young adult spaces in public libraries do not provide that much shelf space, but even so, I urge you to consider these recommendations if only as a starting point for building your young adult collection.

Now that you know what is in *A Core Collection for Young Adults*, turn the page to start exploring the many wonderful recent young adult titles and older classic titles that have retained their appeal for decades.

Acknowledgments

It's appropriate that I begin this work by introducing readers to an important collaborator for this book. The task of checking for in-print formats quickly became overwhelming for me. It was a very slow process to check all formats currently in print for each title, then copy and paste that information from the Excel spreadsheet into a Microsoft Word document and then finally write the annotation. I sent a plea for help to friends working at Kent State School of Library and Information Science. I am a 1992 graduate of that school and still maintain contact with faculty members. I asked (no, pleaded) if any interns or students about to graduate might be interested in performing research for the titles.

Immediately the name Angela Wojtecki was mentioned. Angela has just recently completed her master's degree and was anxious for some hands-on experience in the young adult book world. I provided my password to the online version of *Books in Print* and told her to have at it. I was extremely pleased with her efficiency and promptness in completing the checks for titles currently in print and in all formats. Angela took it upon herself to cross-check for titles already included in previous sections and that saved embarrassment regarding title duplication.

Angela is currently employed as a school librarian in a suburban middle school in northeastern Ohio. I am quite positive her school administration values her and undoubtedly the students worship her. I do feel her talents are so polished that her future in the library profession is limitless. Without her work ethic and skill, this edition of *A Core Collection for Young Adults* would still be in the planning stage. Thank you, Angela.

I also thank my colleagues throughout thirty-plus years of librarianship who suggested books to me and also were patient when I either ranted or raved about titles. Finally, a big shout to people I served with on YALSA (Young Adult Library Services Association) selection committees (Quick Picks, Best Books for Young Adults, and Printz). We went through the wars together; we survived, and the experiences were special to me.

Annotated Core Collection

1

Adventure Tales

Adventure stories enable readers to immerse themselves in a situation that may very well be life threatening. However, the reader is safe in a favorite reading area while the characters may fend off flesh-eating piranhas, survive a raging blizzard, or climb massive mountains.

Marked by fast-moving action, adventure stories are more likely to be plot driven rather than dominated by a single character's inner emotions. Readers of adventure tales do care about the characters and worry about their safety, yet the story's appeal usually stems from a series of challenges for those characters. Their bravery and courage arise when a conflict blocks them from achieving their goals. That grace under pressure keeps readers coming back. Robert Louis Stevenson set the bar at a high mark with his classic adventure tale, *Treasure Island*. It contains all the elements of a crackling good adventure: evil criminals, a boy trapped in a situation he must escape by using his wits, danger, death, and a challenging outdoor environment.

Adventure may take place in a jungle, outer space, or on the concrete streets of an urban setting. Often the conflict is man against nature, or possibly man against man, or both. The characters must confront the situation, solve the problem, and move on. The knack of quick thinking and resourcefulness is a draw for teenage boy readers, but many adventure tales also enthrall girl readers. All adventure readers love to imagine how they would handle the threats. As they project themselves into the situation, readers pause to wonder if they would display as much bravery as the imaginary characters.

Selections were chosen for this area by the dominance of a conflict against nature, or a situation where natural elements impede the teen character's progress in resolving the conflict. Action scenes, often death threatening to the characters, which lead to a struggle to survive, also became criteria for selection of titles. Nature's barriers can spring up in a fantasy novel, a realistic fiction story, or a historical fiction novel, thus many traditional genres gain representation in this section. You'll notice that many of the titles concentrate more on fast-moving plots rather than developing characters, a trait that will gives them teen male reader potential.

Bradbury, Jennifer. *Shift.* 256 p. TR. Simon & Schuster Children's Publishing/Atheneum. 978-1-4169-4732-5. 2008. $17.99.

A two-month cross-country bicycle adventure turns out to be more than just battling fatigue and challenges of the road for best friends Chris and Win. Pulling hills, getting drenched in rainstorms, and suffering under the broiling sun becomes secondary as the boys' tight friendship unravels. Alternating flashbacks let readers know something happened during the journey and only one of the travelers returned home. *Shift* features an intricate plot with characters learning about idealism.

GRADES: 9–12

REVIEWS: *Kirkus* 5/01/08, *Publishers Weekly* 5/05/08, *SLJ* 5/08, *VOYA* 6/08

Burroughs, Edgar Rice. *Tarzan of the Apes.* Page count varies with edition. There are significant formats currently available in print.

Imagine growing up an orphan without knowledge of being descended from royalty. Your immediate family is vastly different in talent and appearance from yourself. However, your intellect and courage separate you from the others and you become their dominant leader. Oh yes, and you have a scar on your forehead from a battle with your arch enemy. Harry Potter? No, this story line is from the original Tarzan yarn, first appearing in book form in 1914. Tarzan's parents were killed by apes and the young man, Lord Greystroke, was raised by Kala, a mother ape of the tribe. Tarzan's thrilling adventures against other beasts and men have been popular for almost a century. Readers and educators should be aware that the sanitized movie scripts do not include the underlying racism for Africans that can be read into the original work.

GRADES: 8–12

Collins, Suzanne. *The Hunger Games.* 384 p. TR. Scholastic. 978-0-439-02348-1. 2008. $17.99. CD. Scholastic. 978-0-545-09102-2. 2008. $39.95. PLAY. Findaway World. 978-1-60640-682-3. 2008. $64.99.

The future dystopian society, Panem, has replaced the United States. Each year a boy and a girl from each of the country's twelve districts are selected by lottery to take part in the Hunger Games. Enclosed in an outdoor forest environment and constantly monitored by television cameras, the twenty-four teenagers must use their skill and wits to battle to the death while surviving harsh weather conditions. Katniss is a sixteen-year-old with outstanding bow and arrow skills, but her biggest challenge may be with Peeta. During the slaughter, she develops an emotional attachment with the guy from her district also competing in the Games. Several gruesome death scenes may have sensitive readers shielding their eyes, but this title remains hugely popular with both middle school and high school teens. Other titles in the series are *Catching Fire* and *Mockingjay.*

GRADES: 6–12

REVIEWS: *Booklist* 9/01/08, *Kirkus* 9/01/08, *Publishers Weekly* 11/03/08, *SLJ* 9/08, *VOYA* 10/08

AWARDS: BBYA Top Ten, Teens' Top Ten

Crichton, Michael. *Jurassic Park.* 416 p. TR. Knopf Doubleday. 978-0-394-58816-2. 1990. $32.95. LB. Perma-Bound. 978-0-7804-6158-. 1990. $14.99. RE. San Val/Turtleback. 978-0-8335-8934-7. 1991. $18.40. PB. Random House. 978-0-345-01954-7. 1991. $6.99.

The adventure here stems from man tinkering with nature. Bioengineers have cloned species of dinosaurs and have enclosed them in an island theme park for tourists. Of course science has stepped into an area where it has no business and should leave well enough alone. Soon the huge beasts begin to assert themselves over the humans with deadly results. It is up to a group of youngsters and a guide trapped on the island to bring a halt to the madness and killing. This tension-packed story linking science with horrific adventure may be too intense and complicated for middle school readers.

GRADES: 9–12

REVIEWS: *Publishers Weekly* 9/28/90, *SLJ* 3/91

Farmer, Nancy. *A Girl Named Disaster.* 320 p. TR. Scholastic/Orchard Books. 978-0-531-08889-0. 1996. $20.99. LB. San Val. 978-0-613-07863-4. 1998. $14.15. LB. Perma-Bound. 978-0-605-36530-8. 1996. $13.99. PB. Penguin/Puffin. 978-0-14-038635-6. 1998. $7.99. PB. Scholastic/Orchard 978-0-531-09539-3. 1996. $19.95. CASS. Recorded Books. 978-0-7887-1342-2. 1997. $77.75. LP. Thorndike. 978-0-7862-8037-7. 2005. $10.95.

Nhamo, an eleven-year-old Shona girl, flees her village rather than marry a cruel man to satisfy an avenging spirit. Her escape by boat to Zimbabwe has peril at every turn. She speaks to spirits for guidance but also must deal with a constant struggle for survival in the wilderness. Finally arriving to her father's family, she is shunned. Mixing in dealings with supernatural spirits with day-to-day survival may bewilder younger readers, making this title more suitable for older teen readers.

GRADES: 9–12

REVIEWS: *Kirkus* 9/96, *Publishers Weekly* 10/28/96, *SLJ* 10/96, *VOYA* 12/96

AWARDS: Newbery Honor

George, Jean Craighead. *My Side of the Mountain.* 176 p. (Only the most recent of the many in-print editions of formats are listed.) TR. Penguin/Dutton. 978-0-525-46346-7. 1999. $16.99. LB. Perma-Bound. 978-0-8479-9431-1. 1988. $13.99. RE. San Val/Turtleback. 978-1-4177-0489-7. 2004. $17.20. PB. Scholastic. 978-0-439-57277-4. 2003. $4.99. CD. Recorded Books. 978-0-7887-9522-0. N/A. $39.00. LP. Thorndike. 978-0-7862-7359-1. 2005. $10.95.

Although originally published in 1959, twenty-first-century teens will still be engaged with the thirst for independence and resourcefulness of teen Sam

Gribley. Sam leaves his home in New York City and runs off to the Catskill Mountains, wishing to live by himself in the woods. Determined to survive his self-imposed adventure, he learns how to live off the land, builds a home in a huge tree, and trains a peregrine falcon named Frightful. Teens in tune with the wilderness will immediately connect with Sam's ingenuity to not only survive, but thrive in the forest. Other titles in the series are *On the Far Side of the Mountain*, *Frightful's Mountain*, *Frightful's Daughter*, and *Frightful's Daughter Meets the Baron Weasel*.

GRADES: 6–8

AWARDS: Newbery Honor

Hautman, Pete. *Rash.* 256 p. TR. Simon & Schuster. 978-0-689-86801-6. 2006. $16.99. RE. San Val/Turtleback. 978-1-4177-9697-7. 2007. $20.85. PB. Simon & Schuster/Simon Pulse. 978-0-689-86904-4. 2007. $9.99. CD. Recorded Books. 978-1-4281-1103-5. 2006. $66.75. CASS. Recorded Books. 978-1-4281-1098-4. 2006. $39.75. EB. Recorded Books. 978-1-4294-1259-9. 2006. $1.00. LP. Thorndike. 978-0-7862-9312-4. 2007. $22.95.

Bo Marsten, a sixteen-year-old who has trouble controlling his emotions, lives in a future society where it is illegal to run without protective gear. His anger lands him in an arctic factory where he's forced to make pizzas sixteen hours a day. Once entrenched in the facility, he suggests he has poisoned another student who has developed a rash. Through a series of artificial intelligence workings, Bo finally gains his release, but he must cross a tundra populated by hungry bears. This satire of corporate influence on society features Bo using his wits and strength to survive. The wry humor is a better fit for high school teens.

GRADES: 9–12

REVIEWS: *Booklist* 5/15/06, *Kirkus* 6/01/06, *Publishers Weekly* 5/08/06, *SLJ* 8/06, *VOYA* 6/06

Hobbs, Will. *Beardance.* 197 p. LB. Perma-Bound. 978-0-7804-8508-2. 1991. $13.50. RE. San Val/Turtleback. 978-0-8335-9198-2. 1996. $13.55. PB. Random House/ Laurel Leaf. 978-0-440-22673-4. 1995. $6.99.

While prospecting for gold, Cloyd Atcity, a member of the Ute Indian nation, helps Ursa find the last grizzlies in Colorado, a mother and three cubs. The mother bear and a cub perish in an accident and Cloyd stays with the two remaining cubs throughout the winter. His survival is challenged by both nature's wrath and human interference. Middle school teens seeking a story about Native American culture and the wilderness will find it in *Beardance*.

GRADES: 6–10

REVIEWS: *Kirkus* 9/93, *SLJ* 12/93

Hobbs, Will. *Downriver.* 224 p. LB. Perma-Bound. 978-0-7804-8508-2. 1991. $13.50. RE. San Val/Turtleback. 978-0-8335-9198-2. 1996. $13.55. PB. Random House/ Laurel Leaf. 978-0-440-22673-4. 1995. $6.99.

A group of problem teens have been sent to Discovery Unlimited, a camp where they are to be helped in overcoming their issues. After trying mountain climbing, the teens feel compelled to steal the camp leader's van and equipment and raft the raging Colorado River. The inexperienced teens' adventure on the river is a journey with exciting twists and turns, much like the river itself. This title is an easy fit for reluctant readers who favor plot over character-driven novels.

GRADES: 6–10

REVIEWS: *SLJ* 3/91

Jaramillo, Ann. *La Linea.* 144 p. TR. Roaring Brook Press. 978-1-59643-154-6. 2006. $16.95. PB. Square Fish. 978-0-312-37354-2. 2008. $7.99.

It's now Miguel's turn to leave Mexico and cross over into the United States. His journey will be a harsh one as he plans to cross the desert with the help of some shady adults. Miguel's efforts become more difficult when he realizes his younger sister, Elena, has followed him. Their journey becomes one of battling to survive, and moments during the adventure become absolutely heartbreaking. Fair warning; not all of the characters attempting to cross the border will survive.

GRADES: 7–10

REVIEWS: *Booklist* 3/15/06, *Kirkus* 3/15/06, *SLJ* 4/01/06, *VOYA* 4/06

Key, Watt. *Alabama Moon.* 304 p. TR. Farrar, Straus & Giroux. 978-0-374-30184-2. 2006. $16.00. PB. Square Fish. 978-0-312-38428-9. 2008. $6.99. CD. Recorded Books. 978-1-4281-3392-1. 2007. $87.75. CASS. Recorded Books. 978-1-4281-3387-7. 2007. $67.75.

Although he is only ten years old, Moon has a complete distrust of the government, an anger he learned from his survivalist father. But his father has died leaving last instructions for the boy to head for Alaska where he can live free without hassles. Early in his journey, Moon is tossed into a detention center but the resourceful boy leads a mass escape and works his way back to his family's cabin hidden in the wilderness. Moon's can-do spirit and know-how of handling himself in the woods will engage middle school readers. The sequel is called *Dirt Road Home.*

GRADES: 6–9

REVIEWS: *Booklist* 11/01/06, *Kirkus* 8/15/06, *Publishers Weekly* 10/02/06, *SLJ* 9/06, *VOYA* 10/06

King, Stephen. *The Stand.* 1168 p. TR. Knopf Doubleday. 978-0-385-19957-5. 1990. $50.00. RE. San Val/Turtleback. 978-0-88103-722-7. 1999. $19.65. PB. Penguin/Signet. 978-0-451-16953-2. 1991. $8.99. CASS. Books on Tape. 978-0-7366-1248-7. N/A. $184.00. EB. Knopf Doubleday. 978-0-385-52885-6. 2008. $50.00.

A superflu epidemic wipes out most of the world's population within days. Death is agonizing from the disease that goes by the street name Captain Trips. However, a handful of people find themselves to be immune and are drawn to the comfort of an ancient black woman, Mother Abigail. Their epic cross-country journey pits Mother Abigail's kindness against Randall Flag, the Walking Dude, a being of nightmarish evil. Horror, science fiction, and situations drawing on their courage are mixed in with the issues King's characters face while attempting to re-establish the world. This is not romanticized adventure, but a gruesome yarn combining nature and the supernatural to present a deadly challenge for a noble group of humans.

GRADES: 10–12

REVIEWS: *Publishers Weekly* 4/05/91

Lawrence, Iain. *B for Buster.* 321 p. LB. Perma-Bound. 978-0-605-01368-1. 2004. $12.99. PB. Random House/Laurel Leaf. 978-0-307-43315-2. 2007. $5.99. CASS. Recorded Books. 978-1-4193-5474-8. 2005. $54.75. EB. Recorded Books. 978-1-4237-9715-9. N/A. $1.00

Sixteen-year-old Kat seeks adventure and lies about his age to enter the Canadian military. He's assigned to be a radio operator on a British long-range bomber during World War II. Kat's fear and his mates' fatalism about their chances of surviving are sharply contrasted with their dedication to service and fear of being labeled cowards. Laced with intriguing details of air battles, Lawrence's work is an outstanding example of grim adventure found during war. Targeted to a male audience, this title will resonate with teens familiar with World War II details. Several violent death scenes make this title more suitable for upper middle school readers.

GRADES: 8–10

REVIEWS: *Booklist* 6/01/04, *Kirkus* 5/15/04, *Publishers Weekly* 7/05/04, *SLJ* 7/04, *VOYA* 8/04

Lisle, Janet Taylor. *Black Duck.* 240 p. TR. Penguin/Philomel. 978-0-399-23963-2. 2006. $16.99. PB. Penguin/Puffin. 978-0-14-240902-2. 2007. $6.99. CD. Random House. 978-0-7393-4875-8 2007. $45.00. CD. Random House/Listening Library. 978-0-7393-4882-6. 2007. $35.00. EB. Random House. 978-0-7393-5516-9. N/A. $38.25.

Set in the Prohibition era, this title has a distinct historical feel, but is also a fine adventure yarn. Two boys find a body washed up on their Rhode Island beach; he's a rumrunner with one half of a fifty dollar bill in his wallet. Easy cash has corrupted the town, but the bootlegging crew of the Black Duck may push their luck too far once out in the open sea. Middle school boys will be drawn to the gangster scenario created by Lisle and the multi-generational slant marks it as a solid choice for a wide range of grade levels.

GRADES: 7–10

REVIEWS: *Booklist* 5/01/06, *Kirkus* 4/01/06, *Publishers Weekly* 5/01/06, *SLJ* 5/06, *VOYA* 6/06

Marsden, John. ***Tomorrow When the War Began*** **(*Tomorrow* series).** 288 p. TR. Houghton Mifflin. 978-0-395-70673-2. 1995. $16.00. TR. Perfection Learning. 978-0-7569-7236-3. 2001. $16.65. RE. San Val/Turtleback. 978-1-4177-7005-2. 2006. $19.65. PB. Scholastic. 978-0-439-82910-6. 2006. $8.99. CD. BBC Audiobooks America. 978-1-4056-5557-6. 2006. $69.95.

Upon returning from a camping trip in the desert, a group of Australian teens finds nobody remains in their neighborhood, the electrical power has been cut off, and their pets are starving. Their country has been invaded and everyone has been taken prisoner. The teens band together and attempt to make a stand and survive. Grim violence in this title pushes it toward the high school crowd. Other titles in the series are *The Dead of The Night, The Third Day, The Frost, Darkness, Be My Friend, Burning for Revenge, The Night Is for Hunting* and *The Other Side of Dawn.*

GRADES: 9–12

REVIEWS: *SLJ* 6/95

McKernan, Victoria. ***Shackleton's Stowaway.*** 336 p. RE. San Val. 978-1-4177-5956-9. 2006. $16.60. PB. Random House. 978-0-440-41984-6. 2006. $6.50. EB. Random House. 978-0-307-54566-4. 2008. $6.50.

In 1914, eighteen-year-old Perce Blackborrow joins Shackleton's Antarctic expedition as a stowaway. The young man doesn't realize the hardship that lies ahead of him. Shackleton's ship, *The Endurance,* gets caught in the ice hundreds of miles from help. The crew must survive hardship over the course of months with incredible courage. The true story of Shackleton's voyage is a legendary adventure tale and McKernan's fictional account brings it to life. Scenes of amputation may be too much for younger middle school readers.

GRADES: 7–10

REVIEWS: *Booklist* 2/15/05, *Kirkus* 01/01/05, *SLJ* 2/05, *VOYA* 4/05

McNamee, Graham. *Bonechiller.* 304 p. TR. Random House/Wendy Lamb. 978-0-385-74658-8. 2008. $15.99. LB. Random House/Wendy Lamb. 978-0-385-90895-5. 2008. $18.99.

The brutal cold of the Canadian backwoods sets the backdrop for this creepy thriller. A supernatural soul-stealer is feasting on small-town teenagers, making them disappear. Danny gets stung by the creature and realizes he has only a narrow window of time to destroy the beast or he will die. His friends band together in a fight to the finish, but the creature may be immune to the below-zero temperatures. With more thrills than gross outs, both boys and girls will be enthused by *Bonechiller's* fast pace.

GRADES: 7–12

REVIEWS: *Booklist* 11/01/08, *Kirkus* 8/15/08, *SLJ* 1/09

Meyer, L. A. *Bloody Jack: Being an Account of the Curious Adventures of Mary Jacky Faber, Ship's Boy.* 336 p. TR. Harcourt. 978-0-15-216731-8. 2002. $17.00. RE. San Val/Turtleback. 978-0-613-71640-6. 2004. $15.25 LB. Perma-Bound. 978-0-8479-1019-9. 2002. $13.95. PB. Houghton Mifflin/Sandpiper. 978-0-15-205085-6. 2004. $7.95. CD. Listen & Live Audio. 978-1-59316-094-4. 2007. $29.95. EB. NetLibrary. 978-1-4294-7194-7. N/A. $29.95.

Mary Faber escapes the mean streets of eighteenth-century England and by her wits talks her way on board a sailing ship. She's taken steps to disguise herself as a boy and now goes by the name "Jacky." The effervescent girl soon emerges as a leader of other ship's boys and sailors as her mettle is tested in the harsh ocean-going world and also in bloody battles. Jacky is a winning role model for middle school girls, but some of her encounters may not sit well with the squeamish.

GRADES: 6–10

REVIEWS: *Booklist* 11/15/02, *Kirkus* 8/01/02, *Publishers Weekly* 10/07/02, *SLJ* 9/02, *VOYA* 12/02

Meyer, L. A. *Curse of the Blue Tattoo: Being an Account of the Misadventures of Jacky Faber, Midshipman and Fine Lady.* 496 p. TR. Houghton Mifflin. 978-0-15-205115-0. 2004. $17.00. RE. San Val/Turtleback. 978-1-4177-0596-2. 2005. $18.40. LB. Perma-Bound. 978-0-605-50426-4. 2004. $13.95. PB. Houghton Mifflin/Sandpiper. 978-0-15-205459-5. 2005. $7.95. CD. Listen & Live. 978-1-59316-134-7. 2008. $29.95. PLAY. Findaway World. 978-1-60640-633-5. 2008. $39.99. EB. NetLibrary. 978-1-4356-4996-5. N/A. $29.95.

In this second installment of the series, Jacky Faber abandons her disguise as a ship's boy and as Mary finds herself landlocked in Boston's Lawson Peabody School for Young Girls. She finds it impossible to rein herself in to be a lady and yearns for adventure. To satisfy her thirst for thrills, she sneaks out at night to dance and play her pennywhistle in a local tavern. Her bold behavior makes many enemies who would like to have this charismatic scamp removed from the school. She rights many wrongs and the end of the story has Jacky once again back at sea. Middle school girls will nod in agreement with Mary's fussing at being held up to society's expectations.

GRADES: 6–10

REVIEWS: *Booklist* 5/15/04, *Kirkus* 6/01/04, *Publishers Weekly* 6/21/04, *SLJ* 7/04, *VOYA* 8/04

AWARDS: Teens' Top Ten

Meyer, L. A. *Under the Jolly Roger: Being an Account of the Further Nautical Adventures of Jacky Faber.* 528 p. TR. Houghton Mifflin. 978-0-15-205345-1. 2005. $17.00. PB. Houghton Mifflin Harcourt Trade. 978-0-15-205873-9. 2007. $6.95. CD. Listen & Live Audio. 978-1-59316-141-5. 2008. $29.95. EB. NetLibrary. 978-1-4356-7825-5. N/A. $29.95

Now fifteen, Jacky arrives in London intent on finding her beloved Jaimy in this third installment of the series. Once again disguised as a boy, her plan backfires when she's abducted by a press gang and forced aboard a British warship. Of course, this girl's never-say-die attitude carries her through the tough times and she'll always come out on top, even though she is accused of piracy. An almost rape scene makes this volume a bit more serious than the more lighthearted earlier tales. Other titles in the series are *In the Belly of the Bloodhound*, *Mississippi Jack*, *My Bonny Light Horseman* and *Rapture of the Deep*.

GRADES: 6–10

REVIEWS: *Booklist* 8/01/05, *Kirkus* 7/01/05, *Publishers Weekly* 9/05/05, *SLJ* 9/05, *VOYA* 8/05

Mikaelsen, Ben. *Touching Spirit Bear.* 256 p. TR. HarperCollins. 978-0-380-97744-4. 2001. $16.99. TR. Perfection Learning. 978-0-7569-1099-0. N/A. $13.45. LB. HarperCollins. 978-0-06-029149-5. 2001. $17.89. LB. Perma-Bound. 978-0-605-23961-6. 2001. $13.99. PB. HarperCollins. 978-0-605-23961-6. 2002. $5.99.

Cole Matthews has trouble controlling his inner rage and hate. After brutally assaulting another boy, he is given a chance at an alternative path of justice. He's isolated on a remote island with no way to leave (he unsuccessfully tries to swim to the mainland). His anger sparks and he burns down his only shelter. Helpless, he is attacked by a ferocious bear, the Spirit Bear of the title. Mauled almost to death, Cole now must discover if he has the will to survive. The sequel is called *Ghost of Spirit Bear.*

GRADES: 9–12

REVIEWS: *Booklist* 1/01/01, *Kirkus* 1/01/01, *SLJ* 2/01, *VOYA* 6/01

Monninger, Joseph. *Baby.* 173 p. TR. Boyd's Mills/Front Street. 978-1-59078-502-7. 2007. $16.95.

Baby has been passed around a series of foster care homes and her last stop is with an older couple who raises competition sled dogs. Baby figures she'll put in an appearance for a short time and then hook back up with her boyfriend, allowing them to do what they want. Baby's issues could easily justify putting this title in the problem novel section, but working in unison with the dogs and the struggle to survive a disastrous accident in the freezing cold marks this title as a thrilling adventure story.

GRADES: 9–12

REVIEWS: *Booklist* 9/01/07, *Kirkus* 9/01/07, *SLJ* 11/07

AWARDS: BBYA Top Ten

Naylor, Phyllis Reynolds. *Blizzard's Wake.* 224 p. TR. Simon & Schuster/Atheneum. 978-0-689-85220-6. 2002. $16.95. LB. Perma-Bound. 978-0-605-01994-2. 2002. $12.99. RE. San Val/Turtleback. 978-0-613-73409-7. 2004. $16.00. PB. Simon & Schuster/Simon Pulse. 978-0-689-85221-3. 2004. $5.95. LP. Thorndike. 978-0-7862-5815-4. 2003. $22.95.

During 1941, Kate Sterling is alone in her farmhouse waiting for her father to finish his tour of home doctor visits when a huge blizzard hits. Not only are her father and brother stranded, but a released convict, Zeke Dexter, is also caught in the storm. Kate ties a rope to her waist and pulls her father and brother through the huge drifts to safety. Kate also rescues Zeke but quickly identifies Zeke as the man who killed her mother. Surviving the horrific snowstorm is only the beginning of Kate's trials. Although no modern-day social taboos are in this work, it still packs a load of tension.

GRADES: 7–10

REVIEWS: *Booklist* 10/15/02, *Kirkus* 9/15/02, *Publishers Weekly* 10/28/02, *SLJ* 12/02, *VOYA* 10/02

Oppel, Kenneth. *Airborn.* 355 p. TR. HarperCollins. 978-0-06-053180-5. 2004. $17.99. LB. San Val/Turtleback. 978-0-606-33347-4. 2005. $15.64. RE. San Val/Turtleback. 978-1-4176-7482-4. 2005. $18.40. LB. Perma-Bound. 978-0-605-01394-0. 2004. $14.99. PB. HarperCollins. 978-0-06-053182-9. 2006. $7.99. CD. Full Cast Audio. 978-1-934180-04-4. 2007. $44.95. PLAY. Findaway World. 978-1-60252-492-7. 2007. $54.99. LP. Thorndike Press. 978-0-7862-8367-5. 2006. $10.95.

Matt Cruse signs on as a cabin boy for the huge airship *Aurora.* Matt's small size comes in handy when he saves a dying balloonist who asks if Matt saw "the flying beasts." Air pirates, science, and suspense all come together in this crackling tale set in the clouds where nature's gravity is all powerful. Although it contains elements of fantasy, this title is well paced and middle school readers will identify with Matt, an underdog who becomes a hero. This thrilling adventure is enhanced by an innocent flirtation between Matt and passenger Kate de Vries.

GRADES: 6–10

REVIEWS: *Booklist* 6/01/04, *Kirkus* 5/15/04, *Publishers Weekly* 4/26/04, *SLJ* 7/04, *VOYA* 6/04

AWARDS: BBYA Top Ten, Printz Honor

Oppel, Kenneth. *Skybreaker.* 384 p. TR. HarperCollins. 978-0-06-053227-7. 2005. $16.99. RE. San Val/Turtleback. 978-1-4177-8130-0. 2007. $17.20. PB. Harper Collins. 978-0-06-053229-1. 2007. $6.99. PLAY. Findaway World. 978-1-60514-608-9. 2008. $54.99.

This sequel to *Airborn* finds Matt Cruse and Kate de Vries continuing their platonic relationship in Paris. But Matt is training on the airship *Flotsam* and they cross paths with the legendary *Hyperion*, a ghost ship rumored to be full of gold. Matt boards the haunted ship with a team of rescuers. They fail to find gold, but learn the ship contains mummified corpses and squid-like beasts with deadly tentacles. Struggling to survive high above the clouds, oxygen begins to run scarce.

GRADES: 6–10

REVIEWS: *Booklist* 11/15/05, *Kirkus* 12/01/05, *SLJ* 12/05, *VOYA* 12/05

Paulsen, Gary. *Dogsong.* 192 p. TR. Simon & Schuster/Atheneum/Richard Jackson Books. 978-0-689-83960-3. 2000. $17.99. LB. Perma-Bound. 978-0-8000-2251-8. 1985. $12.99. PB. Simon & Schuster/Simon Pulse. 978-1-4169-3919-1. 2007. $6.99. PB. HarperCollins. 978-0-06-147381-4. 2010. $7.99. CD. Harper Collins. 978-0-06-176103-4. 2009. $27.99. EB. HarperCollins. 978-0-06-185818-5. 2009. $16.99.

Russel Suskit, a thirteen-year-old Eskimo, feels the pull of the old ways and embarks on a journey of self-discovery. By driving his village's last remaining dog sled team on an epic 1,400-mile journey, he learns how to survive in the bitter cold of the wilderness and put his trust in his dogs. Dogs, a boy, the wild—all the makings of an adventure tale—are mixed into this title.

GRADES: 6–10

Paulsen, Gary. *Hatchet.* 192 p. (Only most recent of the many in-print editions of formats are listed.) TR. Simon & Schuster. 978-1-4169-2508-8. 2007. $19.99. LB. Perma-Bound. 978-0-8000-5226-3. 1987. $13.99. LB. San Val/Turtleback. 978-1-4177-6883-7. 2007. $17.20. PB. Simon & Schuster/Aladdin. 978-1-4169-3647-3.

2007. $6.99. CASS. Random House. 978-0-676-31628-5. 1986. $21.33. LP. Thorndike. 978-0-7862-2845-4. 2000. $21.95.

Brian Robeson is thirteen but when the single-engine plane he's flying in crashes in the Canadian wilderness, he is forced to instantly grow up. His thin windbreaker offers little protection and his only useful item is the hatchet his mother gave to him as a present. But Brian has no time to worry; his immediate concern is survival. This title is one of the all-time great man-against-nature conflicts in young adult literature and is appropriate for a wide range of both male and female teens.

GRADES: 6–10

Rollins, James. *Jake Ransom and the Skull King's Shadow.* 416 p. TR. Harper Collins. 978-0-06-147379-1. 2009. $16.99. LB. HarperCollins. 978-0-06-147380-7. 2009. $17.89. CD. Random House. 978-0-307-20723-4. 2005. $32.30. CASS. Random House. 978-0-307-20722-7. 2005. $30.00. EB. Random House/Wendy Lamb. 978-0-375-89054-3. 2004. $7.99. EB. Random House Audio. 978-0-7393-4486-6. N/A. $32.30.

Jake and his sister Kady find themselves whisked to a parallel world inhabited by dinosaurs and humans. Arriving at a weird village inside a dormant volcano, they mingle with Egyptians, Romans, Vikings, American Indians, and Sumerians—remnants of lost tribes. Middle school boys will want to be like Jake. He's smart, practices tae kwon do, and normally loathes his sister's cheerleading squad. But in this strange otherworld, he must prove resourceful in battling the Skull King, an evil demigod who commands killer half-human, half-pterodactyls. This one's all adventure, all the time.

GRADES: 6–9

REVIEWS: *Booklist* 3/15/09, *Kirkus* 4/01/09, *Publishers Weekly* 5/18/09

Rosoff, Meg. *how i live now.* 194 p. TR. Perfection Learning. 978-0-7569-6617-1. 2006. $15.65. LB. Perma-Bound. 978-0-605-01380-3. 2004. $23.95. RE. San Val/Turtleback. 978-1-4177-6922-3. 2006. $18.40. PB. Random House/Wendy Lamb. 978-0-553-37605-0. 2006. $7.99. CD. Random House Audio. 978-0-307-20723-4. 2005. $32.30. CASS. Random House. 978-0-307-20722-7. 2005. $30.00. EB. Random House. 978-0-375-89054-3. 2004. $7.99. EB. Random House Audio. 978-0-7393-4486-6. N/A. $32.30.

Leaving New York City, fifteen-year-old Daisy arrives in England to stay with her aunt and cousins and escape her pregnant stepmother. She bonds with her extended family, but a terrorist attack plunges the country into war. Determined to battle the odds of surviving in the ravaged country, the once self-centered Daisy now struggles with keeping a younger cousin alive. War carnage and a sex scene with an older cousin shifts this title to the older high school reader's bracket.

GRADES: 10–12

REVIEWS: *Booklist* 9/01/04, *Kirkus* 7/15/04, *Publishers Weekly* 7/05/04, *SLJ* 9/04, *VOYA* 12/04

AWARDS: Printz Winner

Smelcer, John. *The Trap.* 170 p. TR. Henry Holt. 978-0-8050-7939-5. 2006. $15.95. PB. Square Fish. 978-0-312-37755-7. 2007. $7.99

An elderly Native American steps into his own steel trap and is unable to free himself as the Alaskan temperature drops and wolves move in. His grandson senses disaster and travels the trapline's length to rescue his dying grandfather. The classic man against nature conflict is deftly written as the old man devises ways to survive as the clock ticks down. Older teens, and teachers suggesting this title for upper-level English classes, will appreciate the trap as an extended metaphor for modern Native American culture.

GRADES: 10–12

REVIEWS: *Kirkus* 8/15/06, *SLJ* 10/06, *VOYA* 10/06

AWARDS: BBYA Top Ten

Smith, Andrew. *Ghost Medicine.* 368 p. TR. Feiwel & Friends. 978-0-312-37557-7. 2008. $17.95. CD. Random House . 978-0-7393-7243-2. 2008. $44.00. EB. Feiwel & Friends. 978-1-4299-1804-6. 2008. $17.95.

Distraught following his mother's death, Troy Stotts heads to a cabin in the mountains, but his crush girl, Luz, encourages him to return to his ranch life. Tommy Buller, Troy's lifelong friend and Gabey, Luz's weak younger brother, form a relationship in an area where rattlesnakes and mountain lions can attack at any time. The teens grow into men after a tragic attack happens when they are isolated far up in the mountains. Their potential rescue is hampered by the terrain and violent weather. Older male readers will thrill at the toughness these young men display. Several scenes of drinking and discussions of sex make this title more suited for high school teens.

GRADES: 9–12

REVIEWS: *Kirkus* 8/01/08, *Publishers Weekly* 9/22/08, *SLJ* 9/08, *VOYA* 2/09

Smith, Roland. *Peak.* 256 p. TR. Houghton Mifflin Books for Children. 978-0-15-202417-8. 2007. $17.00. PB. Houghton Mifflin/Sandpiper. 978-0-15-206268-2. 2008. $6.95. CD. Recorded Books. 978-1-4281-6356-0. 2007. $66.75. CASS. Recorded Books. 978-1-4281-6351-5. 2007. $51.75.

Fourteen-year-old New Yorker Peak Marcello is given probation after being caught climbing a city skyscraper. His probation re-connects him with his famous mountaineering father, a guy too busy to be at home. Soon, his old man's goal is for Peak to become the youngest to scale Everest. Freezing cold that may cause frostbite and oxygen deprivation is the main challenge for Peak in this adventure about confronting nature's harshest environment.

GRADES: 7–12

REVIEWS: *Booklist* 4/01/07, *Kirkus* 6/01/07, *Publishers Weekly* 6/04/07, *SLJ* 6/07, *VOYA* 4/07

Takami, Koushun. *Battle Royale.* 624 p. TR. Viz Media. 978-1-56931-778-5. 2003. $15.95.

In a future dystopian society, a classroom of Japanese ninth-grade students find themselves drugged and kidnapped. Upon awakening they are all fitted with collars and are told they are part of a bizarre reality television contest. They are give a map and a random weapon and told to fight to the death until one teen remains alive. The collars? If any student breaks a contest rule, it will explode. This is a story of raw, gruesome, bare-bones survival with only a hint of hope. Violent death makes this title every bit as rough as any controversial video game, but teens requesting a thriller will love it. This title has been adapted into a manga series that is also extremely bloody and violent. It has without a doubt earned its "M" for mature rating.

GRADES: 10–12

Tullson, Diane. *Red Sea.* 169 p. PB. Orca Books. 978-1-55143-331-8. 2005. $7.95.

Libby is sullen and rebels with major attitude toward her mother and stepfather. She hates the year-long family bonding journey of sailing a small boat through various locales. However, in the Red Sea, they are attacked by modern-day pirates, her stepfather is murdered, and her mother is seriously injured. It is up to problem child Libby to fix the craft and find help while keeping her mother alive. A plot seemingly pulled from current twenty-four-hour news channels, Tullson's story is tension packed and teens will want to help Libby find a way to survive. The murder scene might be too gripping for younger middle school teens.

GRADES: 8–12

REVIEWS: *Booklist* 9/01/05, *Kirkus* 10/01/05, *SLJ* 1/06, *VOYA* 2/06

Twain, Mark. *The Adventures of Huckleberry Finn.* Page count varies with edition. There are significant formats currently available in print.

Many of today's young adult realistic novels can trace their roots back to Twain's classic tale of a young man and an escaped slave floating on a raft down the Mississippi River. During Huck and Jim's adventure they meet both lowlifes and noble people from various parts of society. The natural dangers of the mighty river's water become a constant background challenge, but humans are the foremost danger to the pair. Be advised, this title is a deceiving story. Folksy dialogue and wry humor cloak serious and often deadly issues involving class wars and racism. Several racial words have become taboo since Twain's day and may shock twenty-first-century readers. Through it all, Huck emerges as a winner although the deck is stacked against him.

GRADES: 8–12

Twain, Mark. *The Adventures of Tom Sawyer.* Page count varies with edition. There are significant formats currently available in print.

It is difficult to totally appreciate *The Adventures of Huckleberry Finn* without having read *The Adventures of Tom Sawyer.* Tom Sawyer is a dreamer and charismatic young man who manipulates adults and other teens in his Missouri town. He exhibits typical teen behavior such as spying on adults, falling in love with Becky Thatcher, and roaming through graveyards in the dead of night. His adventures have become legendary, but his challenge against nature comes about when Becky and he become lost in a cave and cannot find their way out. Huck Finn is an intriguing secondary character in this book, which sets the stage for Huck's own adventure. This title does not contain the harsh reality of *The Adventures of Huckleberry Finn* and contains some degree of whimsy.

GRADES: 6–12

White, Robb. *Deathwatch.* 224 p. LB. Perma-Bound. 978-0-8479-9184-6. 1972. $13.50. RE. San Val. 978-0-8085-1407-7. 1973. $17.20. PB. Dell. 978-0-440-90033-7. 1993. $3.99. PB. Random House/Laurel Leaf. 978-0-440-91740-3. 1973. $6.99. CASS. Recorded Books. 978-0-7887-3082-5. 1999. $48.24.

Ben is hired to act as a wilderness guide for an executive named Madec who is hunting for bighorn sheep in a remote region of the desert. A misjudged shot leaves a hermit dead and Medec demands Ben lie to cover up the killing. Ben refuses and the deranged adult forces him to strip and set off into the desert without food or water. Using his wits, Ben seems to have a chance at surviving until Medec begins to hunt him as if Ben were a wild animal. This young adult classic tale of wilderness survival continues to engage readers, especially older middle school boys.

GRADES: 8–10

Wilson, Diane Lee. *Black Storm Comin'.* 304 p. TR. Simon & Schuster/Margaret K. McElderry. 978-0-689-87137-5. 2005. $17.99. LB. Perma-Bound. 978-0-605-01992-8. 2005. $12.99. PB. Simon & Schuster/Aladdin. 978-0-689-87138-2. 2006. $5.99.

During a wagon train journey west, twelve-year-old Colton Wescott is determined to keep his family alive, but his heritage is mixed race, which leads to several instances of prejudice. Worse yet, his father abandons the family and his siblings have fallen ill. The only way to make money is to become a rider for the Pony Express. Colton endures incredible hardship to earn his money and a riveting scene of Colton caught in a blizzard will thrill readers. An added bonus, his horse steals scenes and becomes absolutely heroic. Grim and violent in certain sections, this title does not paint a romanticized view of the western expansion.

GRADES: 7–10

REVIEWS: *Booklist* 8/01/05, *Kirkus* 6/15/05, *SLJ* 7/01/05, *VOYA* 10/05

2

Cautionary Novels

During the teenage years circumstances happen at an extremely rapid pace. Physical changes, emotional changes, and becoming aware of the world around them are adjustments every teen undergoes. Young people may use this time of life to explore their limitations. They are also eager to find out where figurative boundaries put in place by adults, or by society, are set. It is not uncommon for teens to make the choice of being adventurous and ignoring these boundaries. The limits can be stretched or broken in one aggressive act.

These years of growth can be described as times of making decisions and realizing there are consequences for actions.

Young adult novels have long included tales of teens making somewhat iffy choices and then undergoing an emotional change when the consequences become known.

This section offers a list of fiction titles that can be called cautionary tales. The word cautionary seems to suggest the teens are making wrong decisions and the harsh consequences will make them pay. This is not necessarily true. Didactic stories of what teens should have done and the proper decisions that should have been made are thankfully being weaned out of titles recently published.

It's true that lessons must be learned, but the top works show rather than tell what situations confront teens, what decisions they make, and what ultimately happens. At times adult intervention and judging occurs, but for the most part, teen characters work themselves out of a jam. Authors relish leaving cautionary tales open-ended, allowing readers to decide for themselves what the ultimate resolution will be.

The stories here often involve serious issues: first-time sex, teen pregnancy, anorexia, drug and alcohol use, crime, and other situations that become society's problems. The teen's situation is often one initiated by a decision or a series of decisions made by the character. In other words, the young people make a decision, carry out the act and then (perhaps unforeseen) the consequences are brought forth.

Also referred to as morality tales, these titles attempt to show the right way to lead a life. Teen readers are often drawn to these titles due to the edgy situations presented. These titles are often page-turners and readers connect to the fact that fictional characters may very well be undergoing situations far worse than the teenagers' own lives. Selections were made toward avoidance of titles with heavy didactic statements that wrap up the story. I included titles that show rather than tell the folly of the teens' actions.

A criterion for placing these titles in this section requires the work to involve a decision or act done by the teen. This situation may have been made before the book's opening scene. The decision or act comes packaged with consequences, usually very serious in nature. The initial decision or act is done in normal human society; there are no supernatural solutions nor has a mystical being cursed the teen to create the problem.

The difference between cautionary tales and realistic stories in this edition of *A Core Collection for Young Adults* is that a lesson is presented as part of the resolution in the cautionary tales. The realistic stories may not always result in an acceptable solution. For this work, realistic fiction will most likely contain edgier titles featuring harsh dialogue and more graphically detailed scenes...but the cautionary tales have some kick to them also.

Almond, David. *The Savage.* 80 p. TR. Candlewick. 978-0-7636-3932-7. 2008. $17.99.

> Blue Baker is suffering at the hands of a bully and his pent-up emotions are set to explode. Instead of taking an eye for an eye, Blue develops a story of what an alter ego figure would do under the same pressure. Almond blurs the perception between reality and imagination and readers are not quite sure what is really happening. The part-graphic novel technique features edgy illustrations relaying Blue's inner turmoil and teases readers about the possibility of a violent resolution. This is an important book that educators may utilize for lessons about alternatives to violence.

GRADES: 8–12

REVIEWS: *Booklist* 9/15/08, *Kirkus* 9/15/08, *SLJ* 12/01/08, *VOYA* 10/01/08

Anderson, Laurie Halse. *Wintergirls.* 288 p. TR. Penguin/Viking. 978-0-670-01110-0. 2009. $17.99. CD. Brilliance Audio. 978-1-4233-9186-9. 2009. $29.99. CD. Brilliance Audio. 978-1-4233-9189-0. 2009. $39.97. EB. Brilliance Audio. 978-1-4233-9190-6. 2009. $24.99.

> Lia's former best friend, Cassie, has been found dead in a cheap motel room. Lia now harbors extreme guilt that perhaps if she had returned any of the thirty-three last-ditch phone calls from Cassie, things may have turned out differently. Lia becomes caught in the spiral of anorexia, hiding her weight loss from her parents and stepparents. Anderson writes with a sharp pen, holding nothing back about the grim reality of young girls starving themselves. The harsh reality and intensity of this novel may be too much for middle school teens.

GRADES: 9–12

REVIEWS: *Booklist* 12/15/08, *Kirkus* 2/01/09, *LJ* 4/20/09, *Publishers Weekly* 1/26/09, *SLJ* 2/1/09, *VOYA* 4/01/09

Anderson, M. T. *Feed.* 320 p. RE. San Val/Turtleback. 978-0-613-99702-7. 2004. $18.40. PB. Candlewick. 978-0-7636-2259-6. 2004. $7.99. CD. Random House. 978-0-8072-1773-3. 2004. $38.25. CD. Random House. 978-0-7393-5620-3. 2008. $30.00. CASS. Random House. 978-0-8072-1654-5. 2004. $30.00. EB. Random House. 978-0-7393-4439-2. N/A. $38.25.

> Readers will know they're in for a different experience from Feed's opening sentence, "We went to the moon to have fun, but the moon turned out to completely suck." Titus is one of several youths looking for fun in the future, a place where everyone has an implant in his head that allows a steady feed of advertisements and other information. But it's all about control and following the media's push of what is popular. At times hilarious and other times poignant, this cautionary tale will make older readers pause about who, or what, really is in control. Drug use, sex, and profanity mark this title best suited for older teens.

GRADES: 10–12

REVIEWS: *Booklist* 10/15/02, *Kirkus* 9/01/02, *Publishers Weekly* 7/22/02, *SLJ* 9/02, *VOYA* 12/02

AWARDS: BBYA Top Ten

Asher, Jay. *Thirteen Reasons Why.* 320 p. TR. Penguin/Razorbill. 978-1-59514-171-2. 2007. $16.99. CD. Random House Audio. 978-0-7393-6122-1. 2007. $45.00. CD. Random House Audio. 978-0-7393-5650-0. 2007. $35.00. EB. Random House Audio. 978-0-7393-6123-8. N/A. $38.25.

> Clay Jensen comes home from school to find a package has been delivered containing cassette tapes. The tapes were recorded by Hannah Baker, a girl from his class who had recently committed suicide. Her haunting voice emerges from the tapes prompting Clay to travel back and forth across his town trying to discover why Hannah decided to kill herself and who is to blame. Teens will be intrigued by realizing how even a casual comment can lead to a serious consequence and although the topic is grim, this title handles suicide with respect.

GRADES: 8–12

REVIEWS: *Booklist* 9/01/07, *Kirkus* 9/01/07, *Publishers Weekly* 10/08/07, *SLJ* 11/07, *VOYA* 2/08

Bechard, Margaret. *Hanging on to Max.* 204 p. TR. Perfection Learning. 978-0-7569-1479-0. 2001. $14.65. LB. Perma-Bound. 978-0-605-01276-9. 2002. $13.99. LB. San Val/Turtleback. 978-0-613-70821-0. 2003. $15.30. PB. Simon & Schuster/Simon Pulse. 978-0-689-86268-7. 2003. $6.99.

Sam Pettigrew becomes a father at age seventeen. His girlfriend wanted to give the baby away, but Sam is determined to prove himself a good father for Max. Bechard realistically portrays high school attitudes about suddenly having to become mature. Sam's conflict of switching from typical high school football player to the sobering responsibilities of being a father is especially well constructed. As one of the few teen books dealing with teenage pregnancy from the boy's viewpoint, this title is suitable for a wide range of maturity levels. It proves there are no easy answers when dealing with another life.

GRADES: 9–12

REVIEWS: *Booklist* 5/01/02, *Kirkus* 4/15/02, *Publishers Weekly* 6/03/02, *SLJ* 5/02, *VOYA* 4/02

Brooks, Martha. *True Confessions of a Heartless Girl.* 192 p. TR. Farrar, Straus & Giroux. 978-0-374-37806-6. 2003. $16.00. LB. Perma-Bound. 978-0-7804-6037-9. 2003. $13.99.

Noreen Stall is a mess. She robbed her boyfriend of his truck and money and has hit the road. She lands in a tiny village in Manitoba where nothing seems to be happening. The irresponsible teen can't get anything right and alienates the young mother and two elderly women who step up to help her. Teens will bond with Noreen, a girl who wants out of a lousy situation mostly created by her own poor decisions. Honest and open situations about pregnancy and sexuality will make this title a perfect fit for older teens.

GRADES: 10–12

REVIEWS: *Booklist* 4/01/03, *Kirkus* 2/15/03, *Publishers Weekly* 2/17/03, *SLJ* 2/01/03, *VOYA* 6/03

AWARDS: BBYA Top Ten, Teens' Top Ten

Budhos, Marina. *Ask Me No Questions.* 176 p. TR. Simon & Schuster/Atheneum. 978-1-4169-0351-2. 2006. $16.95. TR. Perfection Learning. 978-0-7569-8114-3. 2007. $16.95. PB. Simon & Schuster/Simon Pulse. 978-1-4169-4920-6. 2007. $8.99.

Fourteen-year-old Nadira, originally from Bangladesh, has been living in New York City with her family. Their visas have expired and when the September 11 attacks occur, as Muslims, the family feels unwelcome. They are turned away at the Canadian border and Nadira's father is imprisoned. The cautionary theme here is to avoid judging people by their appearance and personal faith. Teens will become aware of their possible misconceptions about the immigrant experience.

GRADES: 9–12

REVIEWS: *Booklist* 12/15/05, *Kirkus* 12/15/05, *Publishers Weekly* 2/06/06, *SLJ* 4/01/06, *VOYA* 2/06

Conner, Leslie. *Waiting for Normal*. 304 p. TR. HarperCollins. 978-0-06-089088-9. 2008. $16.99. LB. HarperCollins. 978-0-06-089089-6. 2008. $17.89. CD. Recorded Books. 978-1-4361-0644-3. 2008. $66.75. CASS. Recorded Books. 978-1-4361-0639-9. 2008. $51.75. EB. Recorded Books. 978-1-4356-6728-0. N/A. $1.00. EB. HarperCollins. 978-0-06-188167-1. 2009. $16.99.

Addie has become the responsible person in her family. Her mother loves to party and can disappear at any time. Her stepfather, Dwight, feels he should be more active in supporting Addie, but following a divorce from Addie's mom, he remains distant. Addie is dyslexic and has trouble focusing, but with help from neighbors, she is able to function alone until a disaster strikes their shabby trailer. The cautionary message is that with optimism and perseverance, a person can beat the odds. This happy-ending story is suitable for all young adult age levels.

GRADES: 6–12

REVIEWS: *Booklist* 4/01/08, *Kirkus* 12/15/07, *Publishers Weekly* 2/18/08, *SLJ* 2/08, *VOYA* 2/08

AWARDS: BBYA Top Ten

Doctorow,, Cory. *Little Brother*. 382 p. TR. Tom Doherty Associates. 978-0-7653-1985-2. 2008. $17.95. CD. Random House Audio. 978-0-7393-7287-6. 2008. $70.00. EB. Tom Doherty Associates. 978-1-4299-3744-3. 2008. $17.95.

Marcus, a.k.a "w1n5t0n," knows how to handle technology and get ahead at his San Francisco area high school. When a terrorist attack destroys a bridge, Marcus and his friends are rounded up by the Department of Home Security and tossed in jail. Tortured and released, Marcus harnesses the power of technology to form a revolt. Based on George Orwell's Big Brother concept, this tale cautions about what can happen when absolute power controls the mainstream population. Sexual situations and torture scenes make this possibly too rough for middle school readers.

GRADES: 10–12

REVIEWS: *Booklist* 4/01/08, *Kirkus* 4/01/08, *Publishers Weekly* 4/14/08, *SLJ* 5/08, *VOYA* 4/08

Draper, Sharon M. *The Battle of Jericho.* 304 p. TR. Simon & Schuster/Atheneum. 978-0-689-84232-0. 2003. $17.95. LB. Perma-Bound. 978-0-605-01963-8. 2003. $13.99. RE. San Val/Turtleback. 978-1-4176-4425-4. 2005. $17.20. PB. Simon & Schuster/Simon Pulse. 978-0-689-84233-7. 2004. $6.99. CD. Recorded Books. 978-1-4025-8741-2. N/A. N/A. EB. Recorded Books. 978-1-4237-1472-9. N/A. $68.00.

Jericho is thrilled that both he and his cousin, Joshua, have been invited to pledge for their school's honor fraternity, The Warriors of Distinction. But before becoming complete members of the organization, they must endure rigorous hazing that spins out of control with tragic consequences. Jericho finds himself battling the decision to do what is what right versus what he most wants, a cautionary theme that will ring true with teens. Draper's work is hard-hitting without falling into sexual themes or extended profanity. The sequel is called *Just Another Hero.*

GRADES: 8–12

REVIEWS: *Booklist* 6/01/03, *Kirkus* 6/01/03, *Publishers Weekly* 6/09/03, *SLJ* 6/03, *VOYA* 8/03

Felin, M. Sindy. *Touching Snow.* 240 p. TR. Simon & Schuster/Atheneum. 978-1-4169-1795-3. 2007. $16.99.

Karina is trying to navigate the usual teen issues of school and home life. But her situation is horrifying due to the extreme physical abuse her stepfather doles out to Karina and her siblings. Felin outlines the challenges of an immigrant family in the United States but compounds their issues with the seemingly no-way-out abuse. Teen readers will be alternatively appalled and hopeful that Karina will take action following beatings that are extremely disturbing. The cautionary theme here is abuse can be cleverly guarded by a variety of people involved with the situation.

GRADES: 9–12

REVIEWS: *Booklist* 5/15/07, *Kirkus* 5/15/07, *Publishers Weekly* 6/04/07, *SLJ* 9/07, *VOYA* 4/07

Flake, Sharon G. *Bang!* 320 p. TR. Hyperion. 978-0-7868-1844-0. 2005. $16.99. RE. San Val/Turtleback. 978-1-4177-7952-9. 2007. $18.40. PB. Hyperion. 978-0-7868-4955-0. 2007. $7.99. CD. Random House Audio. 978-0-7393-3124-8. 2006. $45.00. CD. Random House Audio. 978-0-7393-3115-6. 2006. $35.00. CASS. Random House Audio. 978-0-7393-3126-2. 2006 $35.00. EB. Random House Audio. 978-0-7393-6005-7. N/A. $42.50.

Thirteen-year-old Mann is withdrawn following his younger brother's death from a random drive-by shooting. His father believes he will make Mann outgrow his depression by calling on an African tradition of placing the son outside a village and making his own way back. The cautionary plot warns of problems that teens, especially African American teens, have in maturing through their teenage years without a solid father figure. Several violent scenes may be too graphic for younger teen readers.

GRADE: 8–12

REVIEWS: *Booklist* 7/01/05, *Kirkus* 7/15/05, *Publishers Weekly* 10/24/05, *SLJ* 10/05, *VOYA* 12/05

Flake, Sharon G. *Who Am I Without Him? A Collection of Stories about Girls and the Boys in Their Lives.* 176 p. TR. Hyperion. 978-0-7868-0693-5. 2004. $15.99. PB. Hyperion. 978-0-7868-1504-3. 2005. $5.99. PB. Hyperion. 978-1-4231-0383-7. 2007. $7.99.

Sharon Flake presents a set of short stories about girls and boys and the conflict that naturally arises when romance begins. Each story poignantly shows girls becoming so involved with the boys that what the boy does begins to dominate their lives. The author has an ear for authentic dialogue of inner-city teens. Girls will be especially drawn to female characters struggling to understand interaction with boys while balancing their own self-respect.

GRADES: 8–12

REVIEWS: *Booklist* 4/15/04, *Kirkus* 4/15/04, *Publishers Weekly* 7/05/04, *SLJ* 5/04, *VOYA* 6/04

AWARDS: Quick Picks Top Ten

Flinn, Alex. *Breathing Underwater.* 272 p. RE. San Val. 978-0-613-60383-6. 2002. $19.65. LB. Perma-Bound. 978-0-605-01218-9. 2001. $14.99. PB. HarperCollins. 978-0-06-447257-9. 2002. $8.99. PLAY. Findaway World. 978-0-8072-0686-7. 2004. $30.00. EB. Random House. 978-0-7393-8069-7. N/A. $32.30.

Nick Andreas leads two different lives. On one side he is very smart, handsome, wealthy and popular. On the other side of his life, he guards the abuse his controlling father smothers him with each day. His girlfriend Caitlin seems to be an anchor he can use to stabilize his life, but Nick follows the pattern of abuse and becomes truly threatening to Caitlin. Flinn deftly establishes the repeated abuse a son copies from his father. The scenes where Nick bullies and puts Caitlin in harm's way are extremely intense.

GRADES: 9–12

REVIEWS: *Booklist* 8/01/01, *Kirkus* 4/14/01, *Publishers Weekly* 4/16/01, *SLJ* 5/01, *VOYA* 6/01

AWARDS: BBYA Top Ten

Frank, E. R. *Wrecked.* 256 p. PB. Simon & Schuster/Simon Pulse. 978-0-689-87384-3. 2007. $9.99.

Anna is suffering from deep emotional problems. She was the driver that swerved into another lane, creating a head-on collision with another car. That car was driven by her brother's girlfriend, who died at the scene. Anna undergoes therapy sessions to ease her guilt. Teens will be drawn to Anna, who deals with her controlling father and her brother's anger. The cautionary message is that whatever life throws at you, it can be handled with help. The car wreck is a scene featuring highly charged intense writing. That, along with the sophistication of the therapy session, may be lost on younger teens.

GRADES: 9–12

REVIEWS: *Booklist* 12/01/05, *Kirkus* 9/01/05, *Publishers Weekly* 11/14/05, *SLJ* 11/05, *VOYA* 12/05

Frank, Hillary. *Better Than Running at Night.* 272 p. TR. Houghton Mifflin. 978-0-618-10439-0. 2002. $17.00. LB. Perma-Bound. 978-0-605-47205-1. 2002. $17.00. RE. San Val/Turtleback. 978-0-613-90721-7. 2002. $18.40. PB. Houghton Mifflin. 978-0-618-25073-8. 2002. $7.99.

Ellie embraces her freshman year at an art college and takes a walk on the wild side by dirty dancing with a costumed devil at a party. The devil is really Nate, a guy she is attracted to and they enter a friends-with-benefits relationship. Trying to balance her course load with late-night bedroom rendezvous puts a strain on Ellie. Her instructor criticizes her art and she discovers she's being used as Nate's other woman. His real girlfriend visits on the weekends, so Ellie can only be with Nate during weeknights. Sexual scenes and a blunt look at on-campus life makes this story a great fit for older high school students curious about what is in store for them post-high school.

GRADES: 10–12

REVIEWS: *Booklist* 10/01/02, *Publishers Weekly* 8/05/02, *SLJ* 1/01/03, *VOYA* 2/03

George, Madeleine. *Looks.* 240 p. TR. Penguin/Viking. 978-0-670-06167-9. 2008. $16.99. PB. Penguin/Puffin. 978-0-14-241419-4. 2009. $7.99.

Two outcasts from the popular high school crowd enter an unsteady friendship. Meghan Ball is an elephantine girl who somehow doesn't record a blip on the school radar. She meets Aimee Zorn in the nurse's office and Meghan realizes Aimee is suffering from anorexia. Together they learn to rely on each other for support. The strength of George's story is in the total reality of how cruel and damaging comments can be, even if they are throwaway lines. This book is targeted toward younger teen girls regarding the importance of acceptance.

GRADES: 9–12

REVIEWS: *Booklist* 9/15/08, *Kirkus* 5/01/08, *SLJ* 5/08, *VOYA* 10/08

Giles, Gail. *Shattering Glass.* 224 p. LB. Perma-Bound. 978-0-605-98108-9. 2002. $14.99. RE. San Val/Turtleback. 978-0-613-73394-6. 2003. $18.40. PB. Simon & Schuster/Simon Pulse. 978-0-689-85800-0. 2003. $7.99. CASS. Random House. 978-0-8072-1640-8. 2004. $30.00.

Charismatic Rob Haynes comes up with a plan to do a makeover for nerdy loser Simon Glass. What they don't count on is that Simon is pretty wise and actually has a lot going for himself, but that doesn't stop the popular crowd from messing with him. Early on readers know that a killing happens and Giles sets the stage for a series of events that lead up to that death. By showing rather than telling about the potential tragic consequences of manipulating another person, this story will shake up readers until the final page. A powerful, violent climax marks this title as more suitable for high school readers.

GRADES: 9–12

REVIEWS: *Booklist* 3/01/02, *Kirkus* 2/01/02, *Publishers Weekly* 2/11/02, *SLJ* 4/02, *VOYA* 6/02

Going, K. L. *Fat Kid Rules the World.* 224 p. TR. Penguin/Putnam. 978-0-399-23990-8. 2003. $17.99. LB. Perma-Bound. 978-0-7804-5732-4. 2003. $13.99. RE. San Val/Turtleback. 978-1-4176-3906-9. 2004. $17.20. PB. Penguin/Puffin. 978-0-14-240208-5. 2004. $6.99. CD. Random House Audio. 978-1-4000-9116-4. 2004. N/A. CASS. Random House Audio. 978-0-8072-1695-8. 2004. $32.00. EB. Random House Audio. 978-0-7393-6003-3. N/A. $45.00.

Going sets this intriguing story of a mismatched friendship in the Lower East Side of Manhattan. There, grossly overweight Troy Billings is set to step off a subway platform and commit suicide. Curt MacCrae, a down-and-out guitar legend, intervenes. Together the two teens form a relationship that results in Troy becoming the drummer in Curt's new punk band. Troy's self-doubt drips from practically every page until he battles his stage fright and triumphantly bangs on the drums. Drug use is mentioned and rough profanity is laced throughout the storyline. More of a high school book, but Troy's story is so cool and will be hard for middle school readers to resist.

GRADES: 10–12

REVIEWS: *Kirkus* 5/01/03, *Publishers Weekly* 6/23/03, *SLJ* 5/03, *VOYA* 6/03

AWARDS: Printz Honor

Going, K. L. *Saint Iggy.* 272 p. TR. Houghton Mifflin. 978-0-15-205795-4. 2006. $17.00. PB. Houghton Mifflin/Sandpiper. 978-0-15-206248-4. 2008. $6.95. CD. Books on Tape. 978-0-7393-3782-0. 2006. $32.30. EB. Random House Audio. 978-0-7393-4839-0. N/A. $32.30.

Sixteen-year-old Iggy Corso is searching for something good in his life. Iggy is suspended from school and nobody cares. His drug-addicted parents could not care less about what is going on around them. He seeks support from Mo, a neighbor who sometimes tutors, but most often smokes pot. Looking for money to score more dope, Mo makes a reckless deal that Iggy feels compelled to straighten out. This title for older teens contains a realistic representation of the drug world with an underlying message about finding religion.

GRADES: 10–12

REVIEWS: *Booklist* 9/15/06, *Kirkus* 9/15/06, *Publishers Weekly* 10/30/06, *SLJ* 9/06, *VOYA* 10/06

Green, John. *Looking for Alaska.* 160 p. TR. Penguin/Dutton. 978-0-525-47506-4. 2005. $15.99. LB. Perma-Bound. 978-0-605-64015-3. 2005. $14.99. LB. San Val/Turtleback. 978-1-4177-2915-9. 2007. $11.87. PB. Penguin/Puffin. 978-0-14-241221-3. 2008. $9.99. CD. Brilliance Audio. 978-1-4233-2447-8. 2006. $39.25. CD. Brilliance Audio. 978-1-4233-2444-7. 2006. $29.95. PLAY. Findaway World. 978-1-60640-598-7. 2008. $59.99. EB. Brilliance Audio. 978-1-4233-2449-2. 2006. $39.25.

Miles Halter leaves Florida and enters a boarding school in Alabama. He sets about trying to discover his purpose. His roommate is "The Colonel," a lively but weird dude who's always ready for a prank or mischief. The story's focal point centers on the mysterious and sexy Alaska, a girl who has achieved legendary status among the male students. Green sets his story into a tailspin with a tragedy at its midpoint. Following this unfortunate death, Miles must discover his feelings and determine what is ultimately important. This is one of the top high school titles for the first decade of the twenty-first century.

GRADES: 10–12

REVIEWS: *Booklist* 2/01/05, *Kirkus* 3/01/05, *Publishers Weekly* 2/07/05, *VOYA* 4/05

AWARDS: BBYA Top Ten, Printz Winner, Teens' Top Ten

Hautman, Pete. *Godless.* 208 p. TR. Simon & Schuster. 978-0-689-86278-6. 2004. $15.95. LB. Perma-Bound. 978-0-605-01377-3. 2004. $14.99. RE. San Val/Turtleback. 978-1-4177-2544-1. 2005. $19.65. PB. Simon & Schuster/Simon Pulse. 978-1-4169-0816-6. 2005. $8.99.

Jason Bock scoffs at religious beliefs and is fed up with over-the-top worshipping, so he invents a new god—the town's water tower. Meant to be a lark, his buddies hang out under shade from the ten legs of the tower. But Shinn latches onto writing his version of their religion's Bible and becomes obsessed to the point of insanity. Hautman's allegory cautions readers about abandoning all things to worship an abstract concept, a situation that turns dangerous and then deadly. This title's deep religious themes will be better appreciated by high school readers.

GRADES: 10–12

REVIEWS: *Booklist* 6/01/04, *Kirkus* 5/01/04, *Publishers Weekly* 6/28/04, *SLJ* 8/04, *VOYA* 10/04

Hautman, Pete. *Invisible.* 160 p. TR. Simon & Schuster. 978-0-689-86800-9. 2005. $16.99. LB. Perma-Bound. 978-0-605-00027-8. 2005. $14.99. RE. San Val/Turtleback. 978-1-4177-6426-6. 2006. $18.40. PB. Simon & Schuster/Simon Pulse. 978-0-689-86903-7. 2006. $7.99. CD. Recorded Books. 978-1-4193-8456-1. 2006. $44.75. CASS. Recorded Books. 978-1-4193-8451-6. 2006. $29.75. EB. Recorded Books. 978-1-4294-7847-2. N/A. $1.00.

Doug Hanson is fixated on his elaborate model train layout, which is set up in his basement. He obsessively constructs a bridge out of matchsticks, but first separates the striking part...and saves the heads. His best friend is Andy Morrow, a star athlete at the high school. Doug and Andy talk things over at night as their bedroom windows face each other. They are different people and Doug tells us they both had a bit of trouble with fire some time back, but they are much more careful now. Hautman has created a fascinating case study of a teen embedded in his own sense of reality. High school teens will become cautious about the murky truth of what is really going on in Doug's life. A weird voyeuristic scene pops up in Doug's narrative and may disturb some readers.

GRADES: 9–12

REVIEWS: *Booklist* 6/01/05, *Kirkus* 05/15/05, *Publishers Weekly* 6/27/05, *SLJ* 6/05, *VOYA* 8/05

Hautman, Pete. *Sweetblood.* 192 p. TR. Simon & Schuster. 978-0-689-85048-6. 2003. $16.95. LB. Perma-Bound. 978-0-605-01337-7. 2003. $12.99. RE. San Val/Turtleback. 978-1-4176-7575-3. 2004. $17.20. PB. Simon & Schuster/Simon Pulse. 978-0-689-87324-9. 2004. $6.99.

Hautman teases readers with this story about sixteen-year-old Lucy Szabo, a girl obsessed with the undead. It may seem to be a vampire goth tale, but ends up being much more. Lucy has a theory that the vampire legend evolved from ignorance about medieval diabetics, people who develop uncontrollable thirst, have long teeth, and pale skin. Lucy is a diabetic and tests her theory in a chat room where she becomes involved with Draco, who offers to introduce her to real vampires. The caution here is that legendary evil beings may be safer than creeps found online.

GRADES: 9–12

REVIEWS: *Booklist* 5/01/03, *Kirkus* 6/01/03, *Publishers Weekly* 6/02/03, *SLJ* 7/03, *VOYA* 10/03

Hiaasen, Carl. *Flush.* 272 p. TR. Random House. 978-0-375-82182-0. 2005. $16.95. LB. Perma-Bound. 978-0-605-02204-1. 2005. $23.95. RE. San Val/Turtleback. 978-1-4177-8924-5. 2007. $19.65. LB. Random House. 978-0-375-92182-7. 2005. $18.99. PB. Random House/Knopf. 978-0-375-84185-9. 2007. $8.99. CD. Random House Audio. 978-0-307-28070-1. 2005. $30.00. PLAY. Random House Audio. 978-0-307-28289-7. 2005. $35.00. EB. Random House. 978-0-375-83752-4. 2005. $8.99. EB. Random House Audio. 978-0-7393-4482-8. N/A. $38.25. LP. Thorndike. 978-0-7862-7908-1. 2005. $23.95.

Hiaasen revisits his Florida setting and this time the nesting area of loggerhead turtles is threatened. It seems a casino boat is illegally dumping raw sewage into the bay and damaging the beach where the turtles lay their eggs. Noah's dad tried to halt the dumping, but he was arrested and tossed into jail. It is up to Noah to figure out how to turn the tables on the bad guys and this twelve-year-old proves to be equal to the challenge. Hiaasen writes a funny yet important cautionary tale about carelessly damaging sections of the wildlife environment.

GRADES: 6–12

REVIEWS: *Booklist* 8/01/05, *Kirkus* 8/01/05, *Publishers Weekly* 6/27/05, *SLJ* 9/05, *VOYA* 10/05

Hiaasen, Carl. *Hoot.* 304 p. TR. Random House. 978-0-375-82181-3. 2002. $15.95. LB. Perma-Bound. 978-0-8479-0955-1. 2002. $13.50. RE. San Val/Turtleback. 978-0-613-99982-3. 2004. $19.60. PB. Random House. 978-0-375-82916-1. 2004. $8.95. CD. Random House Audio. 978-0-8072-1595-1. 2004. $42.50. PLAY. Findaway World. 978-0-7393-7489-4. 2006. $39.99. CASS. Random House Audio. 978-0-8072-0923-3. 2004. $32.00. EB. Random House. 978-0-375-89027-7. 2002. $8.95. EB. Random House Audio. 978-0-7393-4443-9. N/A. $42.50. LP. Thorndike. 978-0-7862-5014-1. 2003. $25.95.

Roy Eberhardt is puzzled by the weird folks he meets upon his relocation in a small Florida town. He notices a barefoot boy running down the street faster than anyone else. His classmates bully him each day and he resigns himself to not being part of the popular crowd. Then Roy forms a protest movement about the destruction of burrowing owls' nests. Marked with Hiaasen's offbeat humor and a story chock full of quirky characters, this title is geared to middle school readers concerned about the environment but younger high school age readers will also get a chuckle.

GRADES: 6–10

REVIEWS: *Booklist* 10/15/02, *Kirkus* 7/15/02, *Publishers Weekly* 6/24/02, *SLJ* 8/02, *VOYA* 10/02

AWARDS: Newbery Honor

Hiaasen, Carl. *Scat.* 384 p. TR. Random House. 978-0-375-83486-8. 2009. $16.99. LB. Random House. 978-0-375-93486-5. 2009. $19.99. CD. Random House. 978-0-7393-7128-2. 2009. $40.00. EB. Random House. 978-0-375-89167-0. 2009. $16.99. EB. Random House Audio. 978-0-7393-7131-2. N/A. $51.00. LP. Thorndike. 978-1-4104-1277-5. 2009. $23.95.

Mrs. Bunny Starch, the most feared biology teacher ever, was last seen during a field trip to Black Vine Swamp. Soon, Nick and Marta fear that something is terribly amiss. It seems an oil drilling company is taking over land in a shady deal. The land happens to be the habitat of the all-but-extinct Florida panther. It's a race against time for Nick and Marta to rescue their strict teacher, throw a monkey wrench into the drilling operation, and save the panther. All in a day's work, right? Once again, Hiaasen offers an ecological mystery that warns about greedy businessmen and will appeal to both male and female readers.

GRADES: 6–10

REVIEWS: *Booklist* 11/01/08, *Kirkus* 11/15/08, *Publishers Weekly* 10/27/08, *SLJ* 1/09, *VOYA* 4/09

Hornby, Nick. *Slam.* 204 p. TR. Penguin/Putnam. 978-0-399-25048-4. 2007. $19.99. PB. Penguin/Riverhead Trade. 978-1-59448-345-5. 2008. $14.00.

Sam is gobsmacked to learn that his ex-girlfriend, Alicia, is pregnant. The sixteen-year-old has nobody to offer him sound advice, so he consults his skateboarding hero, Tony Hawk. Can Tony actually communicate with Sam through a wall poster? Sam and Alicia are teens on the lower end of the economic ladder, but that doesn't mean they are not above hurting each other. Sam, as a teen guy on track to become a father, wants to find a way out of his dilemma. There may not be an easy answer. Hornby has created a sympathetic character in Sam, and teen readers will feel his pain. Blunt discussions about sex mark this book for older high school readers.

GRADES: 10–12

REVIEWS: *Booklist* 8/01/07, *Kirkus* 9/15/07, *SLJ* 10/07, *VOYA* 10/07

Jenkins, A. M. *Damage.* 192 p. TR. Perfection Learning. 978-0-7569-1890-3. 2001. $16.65. LB. Perma-Bound. 978-0-605-97564-4. 2001. $13.99. RE. San Val. 978-0-613-62741-2. 2003. $19.65. PB. HarperCollins. 978-0-06-447255-5. 2003. $8.99.

Austin Reid is out of sorts and unable to shake a feeling of being unworthy. Jenkins builds tension as her work progresses when readers discover Austin is suffering from depression. Even his lofty status as high school football star fails to bring him around. Being a rough-and-tumble guy, Austin is reluctant to reach out for help and readers will become fascinated with his inner emotional turmoil. The author's literary plant of a straight razor is absolutely chilling. The heavy issues presented mark this title for more introspective high school readers.

GRADES: 9–12

REVIEWS: *Kirkus* 10/15/01, *Publishers Weekly* 4/28/03, *SLJ* 10/01, *VOYA* 10/01

AWARDS: BBYA Top Ten

Jenkins, A. M. *Out of Order.* 256 p. LB. Perma-Bound. 978-0-605-01330-8. 2003. $13.99. LB. HarperCollins. 978-0-06-623969-9. 2003. $16.89. PB. HarperCollins. 978-0-06-447374-3. 2005. $6.99.

Colt Trammel lives for baseball and could not care less for anything else in his high school, including girls. At first blush this story seems to be about a self-centered jock, but it is much more. Colt deals with his girlfriend leaving him, but when he learns he's on the brink of athletic ineligibility he needs help, and fast. When Colt enters tutoring sessions with Corrine, an avant-garde girl with green hair who is a whiz at biology, he meets his match. She doesn't buy his "I'm great so worship me" cover-up for his insecurities. Jenkins's story cautions readers to dig beneath the surface of anyone's outward personality and not make rushed judgments.

GRADES: 9–12

REVIEWS: *Booklist* 9/01/03, *Kirkus* 8/01/03, *SLJ* 9/03, *VOYA* 10/03

Johnston, Tony. *Bone by Bone by Bone.* 192 p. TR. Roaring Brook. 978-1-59643-113-3. 2007. $17.95.

Realistic details of 1940s' racism packs a powerful punch in this slim work. Set in small-town Tennessee, Dr. Franklin Church pushes his son David to become a doctor. David's father is totally dedicated to his practice outside the home. But once inside the house a totally different personality emerges, one of an extreme racist. This story, as seen through David's eyes, centers on the friendship of David and his friend Malcolm, who is African American. David's father informs him that he will kill Malcolm if David invites him into their house. The cautionary message is the power of tolerance over hate, but the harsh racial tension makes this title more applicable to high school teens.

GRADES: 9–12

REVIEWS: *Booklist* 8/01/07, *Kirkus* 7/15/07, *Publishers Weekly* 8/20/07, *SLJ* 10/07, *VOYA* 10/07

Koertge, Ron. *Stoner & Spaz.* 176 p. LB. Perma-Bound. 978-0-605-51731-8. 2002. $13.99. RE. San Val/Turtleback. 978-0-613-74820-9. 2004. $17.20. PB. Candlewick. 978-0-7636-2150-6. 2004. $6.99. CASS. Listening Library. 978-0-8072-1246-2. 2003. $23.00.

Ron Koertge creates two characters caught up in an opposites attract love story. But at the same time it is a cautionary tale about breaking the cycle of drug abuse. Sixteen-year-old Ben Bancroft—a kid with mild cerebral palsy—is Spaz. He meets drugged-up Colleen Minou in an old movie theater. She's Stoner. They enter a relationship, each encouraging the other to make something better of their lives. Only one will succeed. The interesting contrast is a handicap by birth that cannot be controlled and a "handicap" of drug use that is willingly embraced. Language and straightforward descriptions of sex and drug use place this work squarely in the high school arena.

GRADES: 10–12

REVIEWS: *Booklist* 5/01/02, *Kirkus* 4/01/02, *Publishers Weekly* 4/22/02, *SLJ* 4/02, *VOYA* 4/02

Lyga, Barry. *Boy Toy.* 416 p. TR. Houghton Mifflin Harcourt. 978-0-618-72393-5. 2007. $16.95. PB. Houghton Mifflin Harcourt/Graphia. 978-0-547-07634-8. 2009. $8.99.

Josh Mendel has been separated from almost all other teenagers because of his past, or more accurately, what happened to him at age twelve. During that time, he entered a sexual relationship with Eve, his sexy teacher. Five years later Josh harbors mixed feelings about the relationship and is confused about how to act around Rachel, a girl who at one time was his best friend. Older teens will be riveted to Josh's story and how he now feels about reconnecting with Eve, who spent time in prison for her actions. The cautionary message is that not all authoritative adults are stable and nurturing.

GRADES: 10–12

REVIEWS: *Booklist* 9/01/07, *Kirkus* 9/01/07, *Publishers Weekly* 9/03/07, *SLJ* 10/07, *VOYA* 10/07

Lynch, Chris. *Inexcusable.* 176 p. TR. Simon & Schuster/Atheneum. 978-0-689-84789-9. 2005. $16.95. RE. San Val/Turtleback. 978-1-4177-7780-8. 2007. $18.40. PB. Simon & Schuster/Simon Pulse. 978-1-4169-3972-6. 2007. $6.99.

Talented football star Keir Sarafian honestly believes he is one of the "good guys." He loves Gigi and would never intentionally harm her. But Gigi contends that Keir has done something to her, something awful. Flashback chapters show that Keir is living in a world of denial, that he truly thinks he is good, but readers learn his actions are otherwise. The cautionary tale is about respect for the opposite sex and viewing girls as something other than objects to conquer. Situations of date rape and blunt discussions of its aftermath mark this title for a high school audience.

GRADES: 10–12

REVIEWS: *Booklist* 9/15/05, *Kirkus* 10/15/05, *Publishers Weekly* 10/17/05, *SLJ* 11/05, *VOYA* 12/05

AWARDS: BBYA Top Ten

Mackler, Carolyn. *The Earth, My Butt, and Other Big Round Things.* 256 p. TR. Candlewick. 978-0-7636-1958-9. 2003. $15.99. LB. Perma-Bound. 978-0-605-01304-9. 2003. $15.99. RE. San Val/Turtleback. 978-1-4176-7488-6. 2005. $19.65. PB. Candlewick. 978-0-7636-2091-2. 2005. $8.99. CD. Recorded Books. 978-1-4193-1817-7. 2003. $48.75. CASS. Recorded Books. 978-1-4193-0306-7. 2004. $45.75.

Her oversized body has fifteen-year-old Virginia Shreves immersed in a huge inferiority complex. She is pushed by her Type A mother to be perfect, but would rather zone out in front of the TV armed with snack food. When her "perfect" brother messes up and shows feet of clay, Virginia feels it's time to stand up on her own. Mackler's story illustrates a conflict between mother and teenage daughter but also sends a warning about living up to someone else's ideal. This is an important book for teenage girls entering their adolescent years who are searching for ways to "be themselves."

GRADES: 8–12

REVIEWS: *Booklist* 9/01/03, *Kirkus* 6/15/03, *Publishers Weekly* 7/23/03, *SLJ*, 9/03, *VOYA* 10/03

AWARDS: Printz Honor, Teens' Top Ten

Manning, Sarra. *Guitar Girl.* 217 p. LB. Perma-Bound. 978-0-605-55795-6. 2004. $13.99. RE. San Val/Turtleback. 978-1-4176-7634-7. 2005. $17.20. PB. Penguin/Puffin. 978-1-4176-7634-7. 2005. $6.99.

Seventeen-year-old Molly Montgomery is into her guitar and loves rock. But when her band, The Hormones, hits the charts, fame and fortune comes to her fast and furiously. Her innocence is tested by screaming fans on the road, a sleazy manager, and love. Molly is about to discover that the road to the fast life and wealth isn't all it's cracked up to be. With more layers than fluff, this tale cautions readers to keep everything in perspective, even when temptation is around every corner.

GRADES: 9–12

REVIEWS: *Booklist* 5/01/04, *Kirkus* 3/01/04, *Publishers Weekly* 3/08/04, *SLJ* 4/04, *VOYA* 6/04

Mazer, Norma Fox. *The Missing Girl.* 288 p. TR. HarperCollins/HarperTeen. 978-0-06-623776-3. 2008. $16.99. LB. HarperCollins. 978-0-06-623777-0. 2008. $17.89.

The five Herbert sisters—Beauty, Mim, Stevie, Fancy, and Autumn— are being watched by an unnamed character. When his voice emerges in alternating chapters, it is disturbingly creepy. Mazer cranks up the tension by showing this guy deliberately pondering which of the girls he would like to abduct. There is an interesting contrast with the innocence lives of the sisters disrupted by a stalker with decidedly warped issues. The caution is that one never knows what is going on in the mind of others. Be careful of what may be lurking in your own neighborhood.

GRADES: 9–12

REVIEWS: *Booklist* 12/15/07, *Kirkus* 1/15/08, *Publishers Weekly* 12/17/07, *SLJ* 2/08, *VOYA* 4/08

McCormick, Patricia. *Cut.* 168 p. TR. Boyds Mills Press. 978-1-886910-61-4. 1996. $16.95. LB. Perma-Bound. 978-0-605-01244-8. 2000. $13.99. RE. San Val. 978-0-613-49394-9. 2002. $18.40. PB. Scholastic/PUSH. 978-0-439-32459-5. 2002. $7.99. CASS. Random House Audio. 978-0-8072-0523-5. 2004. $25.50. EB. Random House Audio. 978-0-7393-4988-5. N/A. $25.50. LP. Thorndike. 978-1-4104-1277-5. 2009. $23.95.

Callie is a fifteen-year-old girl housed at a residential treatment center, a place where she has been sent because she cuts herself. Callie obviously has issues that occurred before the book's opening that have caused her to mutilate her body, and those reasons are gradually revealed. The secrecy with which Callie searches for a sharp object to continue cutting will fascinate readers. Written in 1996, this remains one of the best novels on the topic of cutting. Readers will leave with the thought that help is available for anyone and there is no need to isolate yourself with your problems.

GRADES: 10–12

REVIEWS: *Booklist* 1/01/01, *Kirkus* 11/01/00, *Publishers Weekly* 10/23/00, *SLJ* 12/00, *VOYA* 2/01

AWARDS: Quick Picks Top Ten

Murray, Jaye. *Bottled Up.* 224 p. LB. Perma-Bound. 978-0-605-50616-9. 2003. $12.99. RE. San Val/Turtleback. 978-1-4176-2689-2. 2004. $16.40. PB. Penguin/Puffin. 978-0-14-240240-5. 2004. $6.99. EB. Random House Audio. 978-0-7393-4482-8. N/A. $38.25. LP. Thorndike. 978-0-7862-7908-1. 2005. $23.95.

Pip sees no problem with mouthing off to teachers, skipping out of school, and blazing up to get high. At home he has to deal with an alcoholic father, but observing both their father and Pip is younger brother Mikey. Pip grudgingly attends rehab, but figures that it is just something to do between highs. What he doesn't see, almost before it's too late, is his responsibility to Mikey.

Pip's convincing teenage voice carries this cautionary tale about teens thrust into being role models for younger siblings in a dysfunctional family.

GRADES: 9–12

REVIEWS: *Kirkus* 6/01/03, *Publishers Weekly* 6/16/03, *SLJ* 6/03, *VOYA* 8/03

Myers, Walter Dean. *Autobiography of My Dead Brother.* 224 p. TR. HarperCollins/Amistad. 978-0-06-058291-3. 2005. $15.99. LB. Perma-Bound. 978-0-605-01945-4. 2005. $13.99. RE. HarperCollins/Amistad. 978-0-06-058292-0. 2005. $16.89. PB. HarperCollins/Amistad. 978-0-06-058293-7. 2006. $7.99. CD. Recorded Books. 978-1-4193-8476-9. 2006. $49.75. CASS. Recorded Books. 978-1-4193-8475-2. 2006. $49.75.

Myers sets this cautionary tale in what could be any inner-city neighborhood. Random violence does not play favorites, a fact well know to fifteen-year-old Jesse and his blood brother Rise. Jesse pursues his goal of becoming an artist and sets upon sketching and writing the story of Rise. However, Rise is running with a gang and although the reader realizes from the title that this will become a tragedy, the violence confronting African American males remains stunning. Can a childhood bond be strong enough to overcome street violence?

GRADES: 8–12

REVIEWS: *Booklist* 6/01/05, *Kirkus* 7/01/05, *Publishers Weekly* 9/19/05, *SLJ* 8/05, *VOYA* 10/05

Myers, Walter Dean. *The Beast.* 192 p. LB. Perma-Bound. 978-0-8000-7738-9. 2003. $13.99. PB. Scholastic. 978-0-439-36842-1. 2008. $6.99.

Anthony Witherspoon, called Spoon by his friends, accepts the opportunity to leave one world and enter a completely different environment. He enrolls in an elite prep school, distancing himself from the streets of Harlem. Left behind is Gabi, Spoon's poetic girlfriend. Upon his return at Christmas, Spoon discovers Gabi has been running with a crowd that dabbles in heroin. Teens will be engaged in Spoon's search for the missing Gabi. Myers' message is how the power of love comes into play to rescue someone trapped in the cycle of drug use.

GRADES: 7–12

REVIEWS: *Booklist* 10/01/03, *Kirkus* 9/15/03, *Publishers Weekly* 12/01/03, *SLJ* 12/03, *VOYA* 10/03

Myers, Walter Dean. *Dope Sick.* 192 p. TR. HarperCollins/Amistad. 978-0-06-121477-6. 2009. $16.99. LB. HarperCollins/Amistad. 978-0-06-121478-3. 2009. $17.89. EB. Random House Audio. 978-0-7393-4443-9. N/A. $42.50.

This realistic portrayal of street life is combined with a mystical feeling. Seventeen-year-old Lil J has seen a drug deal go south, shot a cop, is wounded himself, and is coming off a drug high. After entering an abandoned warehouse, Lil J stumbles upon Kelly. The eerily calm vagrant is merely sitting in a chair watching television. But the television is able to replay scenes from Lil J's life. Myers writing will encourage at-risk teens to ask the age-old question: what in your life would you do differently if given the chance?

GRADES: 9–12

REVIEWS: *Booklist* 11/15/08, *Kirkus* 01/01/09, *Publishers Weekly* 01/19/09, *SLJ* 4/09

AWARDS: Quick Picks Top Ten

Myers, Walter Dean. *Monster.* 288 p. TR. HarperCollins. 978-0-06-028077-2. 1999. $16.99. LB. Perma-Bound. 978-0-605-66925-3. 1999. $14.99. RE. San Val. 978-0-613-35985-6. 2001. $19.65. PB. HarperCollins/Amistad. 978-0-06-440731-1. 2001. $8.99. CD. Random House. 978-0-7393-5556-5. 2007. $19.95. CASS. Random House. 978-0-8072-8363-9. 2004. $29.00. EB. HarperCollins. 978-0-06-178288-6. 2008. $9.99.

Walter Dean Myers' ground-breaking novel is formatted as if he were shooting a script for a film. That is because Steve Harmon had a goal of becoming a famous movie director until he was pulled into being a lookout for an armed robbery at a convenience store. The crime goes terribly wrong and Steve finds himself on trial for murder. To counteract his fears of being in prison for life, Steve observes the scenes in court and in jail as if he were filming a documentary. Myers' powerful words stress how one poor decision may affect an entire life.

GRADES: 9–12

REVIEWS: *Booklist* 5/01/99, *Kirkus* 5/01/99, *Publishers Weekly* 4/05/99, *SLJ* 7/99, *VOYA* 8/99

AWARDS: BBYA Top Ten, Printz Winner

Nelson, Blake. *Rock Star, Superstar.* 224 p. TR. Penguin/Viking. 978-0-670-05933-1. 2004. $16.99. LB. Perma-Bound. 978-0-605-01365-0. 2004. $13.99. RE. San Val/Turtleback. 978-1-4177-2954-8. 2006. $17.20. PB. Penguin/Puffin. 978-0-14-240574-1. 2006. $6.99. EB. Brilliance Audio. 978-1-4233-2449-2. 2006. $39.25.

Pete is happiest when playing his Fender bass guitar. Nothing matters, not girls or prestige; he's there for the music. He hooks up with the Carlisle brothers, a group with a dedicated following. Pete is shocked that these guys can barely play, but grudgingly joins The Tiny Masters of Today. Soon there is a chance at stardom, and Pete ponders if he is a sellout for his music. This is a great cautionary tale about temptation and the realization that talent may not be everything. Teens into music will not be disappointed with the authentic details of life in a rock-and-roll band.

GRADES: 9–12

REVIEWS: *Booklist* 11/01/04, *Kirkus* 8/01/04, *Publishers Weekly* 9/20/04, *SLJ* 10/01/04, *VOYA* 10/04

Nolan, Han. *Born Blue.* 284 p. TR. Perfection Learning. 978-0-7569-1602-2. 2001. $14.60. LB. Perma-Bound. 978-0-605-89422-8. 2001. $13.95. RE. San Val. 978-0-613-59882-8. 2003. $17.15. PB. Houghton Mifflin/Sandpiper. 978-0-15-204697-2. 2003. $6.95. EB. Random House Audio. 978-0-7393-4839-0. N/A. $32.30.

Readers will be pulled into the first-person narrative of Janie, a troubled teen who has not been given even the glimmer of a life break. Abandoned by her mother, neglected by her foster parents and later kidnapped and sold to a drug dealer, Janie feels content only when she copies the singing voices of famous blues singers. This grim tale follows the self-destructive path of Janie, a girl who clings to her unrealistic expectations about fame. Rape, drug use, and pregnancy all are intertwined in Janie's life, making this strictly a high school tale. The cautionary theme in question is that of trusting someone when there is no longer a reason to do so.

GRADES: 10–12

REVIEWS: *Booklist* 9/15/01, *Kirkus* 9/15/01, *Publishers Weekly* 10/08/01, *SLJ* 11/01, *VOYA* 10/01

Northrop, Michael. *Gentlemen.* 256 p. TR. Scholastic. 978-0-545-09749-9. 2009. $16.99. EB. Random House Audio. 978-0-7393-6003-3. N/A. $45.00.

This story paralleling Dostoevsky's *Crime and Punishment* is set in a dismal town in the eastern United States. Each day, sophomore Micheal Benton—he hates his name's odd spelling—and his friends Tommy, Mixer, and Bones drag themselves to Mr. Haberman's 10R English class. The R stands for remedial. One day, Tommy overturns his desk, storms out of class, and disappears. The next day, a covered barrel containing something heavy is rolled into class. Could Haberman be a murderer? Northrop captures the voice of a rebellious teen unable to accept respect when it is offered. The cautionary aspect of this novel is friends may not be as loyal as they claim to be.

GRADES: 10–12

REVIEWS: *Booklist* 5/01/09, *Kirkus* 3/01/09, *Publishers Weekly* 4/06/09, *SLJ* 8/09, *VOYA* 6/09

Oates, Joyce Carol. *Big Mouth & Ugly Girl.* 288 p. LB. Perma-Bound. 978-0-605-01269-1. 2002. $14.99. RE. San Val. 978-0-613-62725-2. 2003. $19.65. PB.

HarperCollins. 978-0-06-447347-7. 2003. $8.99. PLAY. Findaway World. 978-1-60252-953-3. 2008. $54.99. CASS. HarperCollins. 978-0-06-008969-6. 2002. $25.00. EB. HarperCollins. 978-0-06-118729-2. 2002. $13.50.

Matt Donaghy (Big Mouth) cracks a joke in his school cafeteria that targets him as troublemaker. Yanked out of study hall by plainclothes policemen, he learns that he's suspected of plotting to bomb the school. Nobody steps up to his defense except basketball star Ursula Riggs (Ugly Girl), a girl who is rude and intolerant of anyone she feels is beneath her status. Matt and Ursula form a got-your-back relationship as classmates begin to take sides. Oates' story warns about jumping to conclusions concerning throwaway remarks that are meant to be harmless.

GRADES: 9–12

REVIEWS: *Booklist* 05/15/02, *Kirkus* 4/15/02, *Publishers Weekly* 4/22/02, *SLJ* 5/02, *VOYA* 8/02

Orwell, George. *1984.* Page count varies with edition. TR. 1st World Publishing. 978-1-59540-432-9. 2004. $15.95. TR. Penguin/Plume. 978-0-452-28423-4. 2003. $15.95. RE. San Val/Turtleback. 978-0-88103-036-5. 2003. $20.85. PB. Penguin/Signet. 978-0-451-52493-5. 1950. $9.99. CD. Books on Tape. 978-0-7366-8768-3. 2002. $72.00. CASS. Books on Tape. 978-0-7366-8767-6. 2002. $56.00. EB. 1st World Publishing. 978-1-59540-482-4. 2004. $4.00.

Orwell created the most widely known dystopian society in this title that added many phrases to pop culture, specifically the omnipresent Big Brother. Winston Smith, a Londoner disgusted with his oppressed life, joins an underground movement to counteract the totalitarian control of Big Brother. However, he learns after being tortured, that he can offer no resistance to the authorities and must learn to embrace Big Brother. This is a story of love, rebellion, and ultimately, tragedy. Often appearing on required reading lists, this classic work warns about unquestioning acceptance of total government control over a society.

GRADES: 8–12

Orwell, George. *Animal Farm.* Page count varies with edition. TR. Akasha Publishing. 978-1-60512-061-4. 2008. $21.99. PB. Akasha Publishing. 978-1-60512-161-1. 2008. $10.99. PB. Penguin/Signet. 978-0-451-52634-2. 1996. $9.99. CD. Blackstone Audio. 978-1-4332-1039-6. 2008. $14.95. CASS. Books on Tape. 978-0-7366-8812-3. 2002. $24.00. EB. Akasha Publishing. 978-1-60512-261-8. 2008. $9.99.

Napoleon, a pig, assumes leadership of a farm that has rebelled against its human owners. Hoping to make the farm something of a great society that is run only by animals, the area is re-named Animal Farm. However, greed takes over as Napoleon becomes ruthless in his quest for total power. At the end of the story, the pigs in charge confer with humans and the worker animals have trouble determining who is who. This classic cautionary tale is a commentary on a totalitarian society deceiving its workers and how greed corrupts even the most noble intentions. This title is a long-standing staple on required reading lists.

GRADES: 8–12

Pratchett, Terry. *Nation.* 504 p. TR. HarperCollins. 978-0-06-170913-5. 2008. $16.99. TR. HarperCollins/HarperTeen. 978-0-06-143301-6. 2008. $16.99. LB. HarperCollins/HarperTeen. 978-0-06-143302-3. 2008. $17.89. CD. HarperCollins. 978-0-06-165821-1. 2008. $29.95.

In Pratchett's futuristic, or possibly parallel world, a tsunami hits islands in a vast ocean much like the Pacific. At first we believe there are only two survivors. One is Mau, a boy who is the only one of his people, the Nation, to survive. The other survivor is Ermintrude, a girl from somewhere like Britain in a time like the nineteenth century, who survives her ship's thrilling wreck but reinvents herself as Daphne. Mau and Daphne begin to help stragglers from other islands, but conflicts soon arise. Prachett writes a humorous and cautionary tale about mixing religion and different cultures. The tone is often deceivingly light, but sophisticated readers will grasp Prachett's layered message.

GRADES: 7–12

REVIEWS: *Booklist* 8/01/08, *Kirkus* 8/15/08, *Publishers Weekly* 8/11/08, *SLJ* 10/08, *VOYA* 10/08

AWARDS: BBYA Top Ten, Printz Honor

Reinhardt, Dana. *How to Build a House.* 240 p. TR. Random House/Wendy Lamb. 978-0-375-84453-9. 2008. $15.99. LB. Random House/Wendy Lamb. 978-0-375-94454-3. 2008. $18.99. CD. Random House Audio. 978-0-7393-6412-3. 2008. $45.00. CD. Random House Audio. 978-0-7393-6410-9. 2008. $35.00. EB. Random House. 978-0-7393-8069-7. N/A. $32.30.

Harper Evans is shaken by her father and stepmother's divorce and leaps at the opportunity to participate in a summer program in Tennessee. In a small town, Harper and other high school students band together to build a new house for a family whose home was destroyed by a tornado. Planning to bury herself and forget her problems in physical labor, Harper doesn't count on falling in love with Teddy. Reinhart's story cautions against wallowing in self-pity and will encourage teen readers to evaluate their situation while comparing it to others who may be worse off.

GRADES: 9–12

REVIEWS: *Booklist* 4/15/08, *Kirkus* 4/15/08, *Publishers Weekly* 4/7/08, *SLJ* 6/08, *VOYA* 8/08

Shusterman, Neal. *The Schwa Was Here.* 240 p. TR. Penguin/Dutton. 978-0-525-47182-0. 2004. $16.99. LB. Perma-Bound. 978-0-605-56553-1. 2004. $12.99. PB. Penguin/Puffin. 978-0-14-240577-2. 2006. $6.99. CD. Random House Audio. 978-0-7393-7237-1. 2008. $50.00. EB. Random House Audio. 978-0-7393-6005-7. N/A. $42.50.

Calvin Schwa seems to be practically invisible because nobody really notices him. This trait greatly impresses Anthony "Antsy" Bonano and his friends. They wish to parley The Schwa's talent in a moneymaking scheme involving stealing a reclusive millionaire's dog's water bowl. They are caught by Mr. Crawley and their community service involves walking Crawley's fourteen Afghan hounds and escorting his blind granddaughter, Lexie. Schusterman's quirky characters and plot cloak the subtle message of accepting others and discovering the actual person behind a first impression.

GRADES: 8-10

REVIEWS: *Booklist* 12/01/04, *Kirkus* 10/01/04, *SLJ* 10/04, *VOYA* 10/04

Sonnenblick, Jordan. *Notes from the Midnight Driver.* 265 p. TR. Scholastic. 978-0-439-75779-9. 2006. $16.99. RE. San Val/Turtleback. 978-1-4177-9950-3. 2007. $17.20. PB. Scholastic. 978-0-439-75781-2. 2007. $6.99.

Following a poor decision to drive drunk, which resulted in a crash into a garden gnome, sixteen-year-old Alex is ordered to perform weeks of community service. His passion is playing guitar and his service is to work with Solomon Lewis, a curmudgeon who was once a jazz musician. Told through Alex's eyes, the story progresses with Alex slowly accepting Solomon's prickly nature. The cautionary message here is trying on adult behaviors too soon and being forced to accept responsibility. Language and the opening realistic drunken spree make this title suitable for high school students. Sonnenblick's climactic scene simply soars.

GRADES: 9–12

REVIEWS: *Booklist* 10/01/06, *Kirkus* 9/15/06, *Publishers Weekly* 9/18/06, *SLJ* 10/06, *VOYA* 10/06

St. James, James. *Freak Show.* 304 p. TR. Penguin/Dutton. 978-0-525-47799-0. 2007. $18.99. PB. Penguin/Puffin. 978-0-14-241231-2. 2008. $8.99.

Billy Bloom is one of the most charismatic young adult protagonists in recent years. He's also gay and totally flamboyant. Billy has been transferred to an out-of-the-way Florida high school where he first endures verbal abuse that quickly escalates into physical violence. His reaction? To launch a campaign for him to be crowned prom queen. James St. James' wickedly fast paced and over-the-top characterization of Billy may distract from the serious message of acceptance that is subtlety woven throughout Billy's narrative. Language issues and a brief sexual encounter mark this title for older teens.

GRADES: 10–12

REVIEWS: *Kirkus* 5/01/07, *SLJ* 6/07, *Publishers Weekly* 3/19/07, *VOYA* 6/07

Strasser, Todd. *Can't Get There from Here.* 208 p. TR. Simon & Schuster. 978-0-689-84169-9. 2004. $16.95. LB. Perma-Bound. 978-0-605-00208-1. 2004. $12.00. RE. San Val/Turtleback. 978-1-4176-8939-2. 2005. $17.20. PB. Simon & Schuster/Simon Pulse. 978-0-689-84170-5. 2005. $6.99. EB. Recorded Books. 978-1-4237-1472-9. N/A. $68.00.

Using fake names, a band of runaways relies upon each other to survive on the streets of New York City. Narrated by fifteen-year-old "Maybe" (her usual answer to any question), their lives are conveyed with a sense of hopelessness and weird pride. They would rather take their chances on the streets than return to abusive homes. Rejecting help from even the basic homeless shelter, they find that obtaining essential survival needs like food and clothing is a daily challenge. By showing the harsh treatment average people give to runaways, this hard-hitting story will have teens thinking twice about the often overlooked plight of street teens.

GRADES: 9–12

REVIEWS: *Booklist* 3/15/04, *Kirkus* 2/15/04, *Publishers Weekly* 4/26/04, *SLJ* 3/04, *VOYA* 6/04

Tashjian, Janet. *The Gospel According to Larry.* 240 p. TR. Henry Holt. 978-0-8050-6378-3. 2001. $16.95. LB. Perma-Bound. 978-0-605-01226-4. 2001. $12.99. RE. San Val/Turtleback. 978-0-613-72333-6. 2003. $17.20. PB. Random House/Laurel Leaf. 978-0-440-23792-1. 2003. $6.99. CD. Random House Audio. 978-1-4000-8618-4. 2004. $45.00. CASS. Random House Audio. 978-0-8072-2305-5. 2004. $32.00. EB. Tom Doherty Associates. 978-1-4299-3744-3. 2008. $17.95.

Seventeen-year-old Josh Swensen is frustrated when a girl steers away from him to one of the school jocks. Adopting the persona of Larry, Josh constructs a website (www.thegospelaccordingtolarry.com) on which he posts a running commentary against consumer culture and its obsession with celebrities. Larry offers pictures of his meager belongings, and soon everyone becomes obsessed about Larry's true identity. The cautionary theme of gushing over trite celebrities and ignoring people of substance will continue to ring true with every generation of teenagers. High school readers will embrace Larry's snarky blasting of mindless consumerism.

GRADES: 10–12

REVIEWS: *Booklist* 11/01/01, *Kirkus* 10/15/01, *Publishers Weekly* 12/03/01, *SLJ* 10/01, *VOYA* 12/01

Tharp, Tim. *The Spectacular Now.* 304 p. TR. Random House/Knopf. 978-0-375-85179-7. 2008. $16.99. LB. Random House/Knopf. 978-0-375-95179-4. 2008. $19.99. EB. HarperCollins. 978-0-06-188167-1. 2009. $16.99.

Sutter Keely spends his last high school days on a perpetual drunk. He is the life of the party and girls want to be near him, until they realize he always loses interest in them. The alcohol covers the pain of an absentee father, and outcast geek Aimee seems determined to love Sutter in spite of his flaws. Sutter's voice is on every page and he is a clown with an outside persona that cloaks his emotional pain and loneliness. The cautionary theme of course is that constant drinking will not make any situation better, but just bury the user into deeper despair. Adult themes of sex and alcoholism have this title firmly geared to high school readers.

GRADES: 10–12

REVIEWS: *Booklist* 11/15/08, *Kirkus* 10/15/08, *Publishers Weekly* 11/17/08, *SLJ* 12/08

Vaught, Susan. *Trigger.* 292 p. TR. Bloomsbury. 978-1-58234-920-6. 2006. $16.95. PB. Bloomsbury. 978-1-59990-230-2. 2007. $8.95.

Jersey Hatch has spent the past year recovering from a gunshot wound to his head. The once charismatic teen pulled the trigger in a suicide attempt. He arrives home not fully recovered but has scenes looping in his brain. Unable to control his thought process, he blurts out gibberish. Haunting dreams and memories cause him to seek the forgotten reason he tried to kill himself. The cautionary message is that suicide does not just affect the single person, but the attempt will resonate through all other people connected to him. Vaught offers a vastly different take on the basic teen suicide theme.

GRADES: 10–12

REVIEWS: *Booklist* 12/01/06, *Kirkus* 9/01/06, *Publishers Weekly* 11/13/06, *SLJ* 11/06, *VOYA* 10/06

Volponi, Paul. *Black and White.* 192 p. TR. Penguin/Viking. 978-0-670-06006-1. 2005. $15.99. LB. Perma-Bound Books. 978-0-605-01035-2. 2005. $13.99.

Marcus and Eddie are best friends and top high school basketball players in New York City. Marcus is black and Eddie is white, but they are past that being an issue. Deciding they need cash, the friends begin a series of armed robberies. One goes completely wrong and Marcus is arrested. The problem is that Marcus is innocent, but Eddie cannot bring himself to do the right thing and help his friend. This cautionary tale about loyalty and a rushed decision that leads to more serious problems will hit home with a wide variety of teens, especially inner-city males.

GRADES: 9–12

REVIEWS: *Booklist* 9/01/05, *Kirkus* 4/15/05, *Publishers Weekly* 6/20/05, *SLJ* 6/05, *VOYA* 6/05

AWARDS: Quick Picks Top Ten

Vrettos, Adrienne Maria. *Skin.* 240 p. TR. Simon & Schuster/Margaret K. McElderry. 978-1-4169-0655-1. 2006. $16.95. PB. Simon & Schuster/Simon Pulse. 978-1-4169-0656-8. 2007. $6.99.

In the opening scene of Skin, fourteen-year-old Donnie tries to revive his sister Karen. He is unsuccessful and by the fourth page Karen is dead. The rest of Vrettos' story is told in flashbacks as readers learn of Karen and Donnie's dysfunctional family and how Karen plunged into anorexia. Donnie's voice is poignant and rings true about the helplessness of a young man powerless to stop the train wreck of his battling parents and his beloved sister beginning to starve herself. The details of anorexia, told not by the victim but by an outsider, makes Donnie's narrative that more powerful.

GRADES: 9–12

REVIEWS: *Booklist* 3/01/06, *Kirkus* 3/15/06, *Publishers Weekly* 4/24/06, *SLJ* 6/06, *VOYA* 6/06

Weeks, Sarah. *So B. It.* 256 p. TR. HarperCollins/Laura Geringer. 978-0-06-623622-3. 2004. $16.89. LB. Perma-Bound. 978-0-605-01367-4. 2004. $13.99. RE. San Val/Turtleback. 978-1-4176-9442-6. 2005. $17.20. LB. HarperCollins/Laura Geringer. 978-0-06-623623-0. 2004. $16.89. CD. HarperCollins/HarperChildren's Audio. 978-0-06-075481-5. 2004. $25.95. EB. Random House Audio. 978-0-7393-6123-8. N/A. $38.25.

Twelve years after baby Heidi and her mother appeared at Bernadette's apartment building, they have established a strange but loving household. Heidi's mother is still in the picture, but she has a vocabulary of only 23 words. Bernadette lives next door, but is agoraphobic and stays inside. Heidi is curious to discover the meaning behind her mother's few words, especially "soof." A cross-country journey brings her to the alarming truth. The cautionary theme is simple: love can manifest itself in many ways and never should be taken for granted. This sweet and moving tale connects on many age levels.

GRADES: 7–12

REVIEWS: *Booklist* 6/01/04, *Kirkus* 5/15/04, *Publishers Weekly* 5/31/04, *SLJ* 7/04, *VOYA* 12/04

AWARDS: BBYA Top Ten

Westerfeld, Scott. *So Yesterday.* 240 p. TR. Penguin/Razorbill. 978-1-59514-000-5. 2004. $16.99. LB. Perma-Bound. 978-0-605-66672-6. 2004. $14.99. RE. San Val/Turtleback. 978-1-4176-9945-2. 2005. $18.40. PB. Penguin/Razorbill. 978-1-59514-032-6. 2005. $7.99. CD. Random House Audio. 978-0-307-28457-0. 2006. $35.00. CD. Random House Audio. 978-0-307-28458-7. 2006. $42.50. EB. Random House. 978-0-7393-4439-2. N/A. $38.25.

Seventeen-year-old Hunter Braque is as one with the cool culture of Manhattan. Paid by huge corporations, he's in constant search of styles that will become new trends. He hits the mother lode by stumbling upon a cache of vintage sneakers in pristine condition. His hip girlfriend is fellow trend-watcher Jen. Together they uncover clues about a plot to subvert a consumer system that determines what is cool and turns humongous profits. Being slave to the fashion industry is the caution here, and Westerfeld holds an intervening mirror up to teens who must have the latest and greatest thing.

GRADES: 9–12

REVIEWS: *Booklist* 9/15/04, *Kirkus* 8/01/04, *Publishers Weekly* 10/04/04, *SLJ* 10/04, *VOYA* 10/04

Woodson, Jacqueline. *After Tupac and D Foster.* 160 p. TR. Penguin/Putnam. 978-0-399-24654-8. 2008. $15.99. EB. Brilliance Audio. 978-1-4233-9190-6. 2009. $24.99.

An unnamed narrator and her friend Neeka meet the newcomer to their Queens, New York, neighborhood. D Foster has seen some of the world, but the three girls thrill to Tupac's lyrics as they ponder what their "Big Purpose" in life will be. Woodson nails teenspeak but avoids falling into stereotypical street slang. D Foster is covering her past, and the other girls at first misjudge her, a cautionary point Woodson quietly weaves into her story. This well-constructed story will have wide appeal to girls of various backgrounds.

GRADES: 8–12

REVIEWS: *Booklist* 2/01/08, *Kirkus* 12/01/07, *Publishers Weekly* 12/10/07, *SLJ* 4/08, *VOYA* 2/08

AWARDS: Newbery Honor

Yang, Gene Luen. *American Born Chinese.* 240 p. TR. Roaring Brook. 978-1-59643-373-1. 2007. $19.95. TR. Roaring Brook. 978-1-59643-208-6. 2006. $29.95. RE. San Val/Turtleback. 978-1-4177-5449-6. 2006. $30.55. PB. Roaring Brook. 978-1-59643-152-2. 2006. $17.95. PB. Square Fish. 978-0-312-38448-7. 2008. $8.99. EB. Roaring Brook. 978-1-4299-6936-9. 2006. $17.95.

Yang weaves three stories that come together in a finale that illustrates the dilemma of all teens feeling out of place in their environments. By incorporating the fable of The Monkey King, Yang introduces readers to Jin Wang, an Asian boy who doesn't fit in with his white classmates. The Monkey King tries to be something he is not, as does Jin. Cousin Chin-Kee is a racial stereotype who makes Jin ponder if he is abandoning his past. Presented in graphic novel format, this tale about being true to oneself is an important addition to all young adult collections, but the layered message requires astute readers to grasp its meaning.

GRADES: 9–12

REVIEWS: *Booklist* 9/01/06, *Publishers Weekly* 6/12/06, *SLJ* 9/06, *VOYA* 10/06

AWARDS: BBYA Top Ten, Printz Winner, Great Graphic Novels for Teens (Top Ten)

3

Classic Literature

Classic literature, whether it originates from Great Britain or the United States, will spark debate. Are there certain titles all teenagers should aspire to read? Does a hierarchy exist in which some works are considered stepping stones for readers in the search for quality literature?

To be considered a classic, should a book stand the test of time? Does popularity come into play? What are the criteria for classics? I have heard a short definition of "Classic Literature" as merely titles that are old and important to individuals such as teachers or librarians. These pointed questions are worthy of debate at another time and in another professional development title.

The following list includes classic titles that have long been included on recommended reading lists for both high school and college classes. Titles long considered classics appear in other chapters. For example, *The Adventures of Huckleberry Finn* has been placed with the Adventure Titles. Authors instantly recognized are included such as Shakespeare, Dickens, and Brontë. As stated in the Introduction, this list is common to school-assigned reading. I've included many titles common to inner-city school districts that serve predominately African American neighborhoods.

Alcott, Louisa May. *Little Women.* Page count varies with edition. There are significant formats currently available in-print.

> Four sisters in the March family, Meg, Jo, Beth, and Amy, struggle to overcome their own character flaws as they deal with becoming young women rather than girls. Jo especially deals with nineteenth-century society's restrictions on girls. Teenage girls who read *Little Women* will be very interested to discover that teenage situations of 100 years ago continue to vex girls of the twenty-first century.

GRADES: 6–10

Angelou, Maya. *I Know Why the Caged Bird Sings.* Page count varies with edition. There are significant formats currently available in print.

In this autobiography that includes writing techniques used in fiction, Maya Angelou explores her youth while incorporating themes common to African American women, especially racism in the South. On the controversial side of the work, the author also explores subjects such as identity, rape, literacy, lesbianism, and pregnancy. This powerful work deserves a place on all teen area shelves, especially in schools where African American teens are confronted with the same issues.

GRADES: 9–12

Armstrong, William H. *Sounder.* Page count varies with edition. There are significant formats currently available in print.

A young African American boy is distraught because his father is jailed for stealing food for his family, and he struggles to comprehend the situation with his devoted dog, Sounder. Comparisons are easily made between Sounder and the father, but this novel geared to a middle school audience also illustrates the courage to stand up against racism as well as exhibiting the courage and loyalty to die for others.

GRADES: 6–9

AWARDS: Newbery Winner

Austen, Jane. *Pride and Prejudice.* Page count varies with edition. There are significant formats currently available in print.

Set in nineteenth-century England near London, Austin's story continues to enchant teenage readers two centuries after being published. Girls feel themselves side by side with Elizabeth Bennet as she deals with issues of manners, her upbringing, morality, education and marriage. Many adult readers trace their love of reading to Austin's work, especially Elizabeth's interaction with the aloof Mr. Darcy. Growing up in the twenty-first century mirrors Austin's world.

GRADES: 9–12

Avi. *Nothing But the Truth.* N/A. LB. San Val, Incorporated. 978-0-606-12300-6. 2010. $17.20. PB. HarperCollins Publishers. 978-0-380-71907-5. 1993. $6.99.

Presented in documentary form this title includes memos, letters, and a diary. It also shows an African American teenager, Phillip Malloy, who has a conflict with his English teacher who has assigned him a "D" in her class. To annoy her, Phillip sings along with the national anthem, an act that earns him a suspension. By using the "factual" items in the text, Avi illustrates how the truth is viewed differently by a variety of people. The theme of persecution will connect with older teens who also believe their school has autocratic teachers.

GRADES: 9–12

REVIEWS: *Kirkus* 10/91, *Publishers Weekly* 9/06/91, *SLJ* 9/91

AWARDS: Newbery Honor

Babbitt, Natalie. *Tuck Everlasting.* Page count varies with edition. There are significant formats currently available in print.

Winifred "Winnie" Foster stumbles onto the Tuck family, living in a wooded area, who are immortal after drinking from a spring more than a century ago. When one of the Tucks kills a man, they are sentenced to be hanged for the crime. Winnie intervenes, helps the family escape, and is found in their cell. This work will prompt discussion on mortality and love and has wide appeal for many age levels.

GRADES: 8–12

Banks, Lynne Reid. *The Indian in the Cupboard.* Page count varies with edition. There are significant formats currently available in print.

A young boy named Omri, living with his family in London, England, discovers a magical cabinet that can bring plastic toy figures back to life. By simply turning the cabinet's key, Omri brings a plastic Indian (Little Bear) to life. This act launches a series of events that quickly spirals out of control as Little Bear becomes demanding. The message of leaving things alone is learned as Omri struggles to control the various figures he brings to life. Other titles in the series are *The Return of the Indian, The Secret of the Indian, The Mystery of the Cupboard,* and *The Key to the Indian.*

GRADES: 6–10

Blume, Judy. *Are You There God? It's Me, Margaret.* Page count varies with edition. There are significant formats currently available in print.

This book, one of the cornerstones of teenage literature, is about a girl in sixth grade who, in addition to questioning her religious background, also confronts problems of growing up. Margaret's mother is Christian and her father is Jewish, which becomes the catalyst for questioning her religion. Margaret also deals with buying her first bra and having her first period. This classic work is a go-to title for young girls who worry about their future.

GRADES: 6–9

Brontë, Charlotte. *Jane Eyre.* Page count varies with edition. There are significant formats currently available in print.

The first-person narrator of the title character progresses through stages from childhood to become a young woman. Jane Eyre leaves behind the physical and emotional abuse of her childhood to acquire an education at Lowood School. As governess of Thornfield Manor, she falls in love with Edward Rochester. Later she finds herself receiving a proposal from her clergy-man cousin but ultimately does reunite with Rochester. There are many instances of social criticism in the story along with a strong sense of right and wrong. Many teenage girls consider Jane Eyre their personal hero.

GRADES: 8–12

Brontë, Emily. *Wuthering Heights.* Page count varies with edition. There are significant formats currently available in print.

The narrative tells the tale of the all-encompassing and passionate, yet thwarted, love that happens at Wuthering Heights, a Yorkshire manor on the moors. The love between Heathcliff and Catherine Earnshaw remains unresolved but their passion eventually leads to tragedy and sorrow for all those around them. Themes of love beyond death and revenge will engage older teenage readers.

GRADES: 9–12

Cervantes, Miguel de Saavedra. *The Ingenious Gentleman Don Quixote of La Mancha.* Page count varies with edition. There are significant formats currently available in print.

Alonso Quixano is an older gentleman who becomes obsessed with books of chivalry and knighthood. He embarks on a quest to be a knight and reality be-comes blurred in his mind as he attacks windmills thinking they are giants. More widely known as simply Don Quixote, this classic title considers the theme of nobly following your dreams, but also warns about attempting to be someone you are not.

GRADES: 10–12

Chaucer, Geoffrey. *The Canterbury Tales.* Page count varies with edition. There are significant formats currently available in print.

This set of tales relates the journey of a pilgrimage to the shrine of Saint Thomas Becket at Canterbury Cathedral. To pass the time, the pilgrims share stories that mask Chaucer's criticism of English society and particularly the Church. Rarely is the whole work assigned as a school read, but teachers pick and choose single tales. Tales from The Wife of Bath, The Parson, and The Knight have all been used in schools during my tenure as a teen librarian.

GRADES: 10–12

Davis, Sampson, George Jenkins, and Ramick Hunt. *The Pact: Three Young Men Make a Promise and Fulfill a Dream.* 272 p. TR. Penguin Group (USA) Incorporated. 978-1-57322-989-0. 2003. $15.00. TR. Perfection Learning Corporation.

978-0-7569-9067-1. 2003. $21.65. CD. HighBridge Company. 978-1-56511-651-1.
2002. $32.95.

As teenagers, three friends make a pact to always stick with each other and to
find a way out of their harsh lives in Newark, New Jersey. They have done so
and this nonfiction work is told by alternating voices of all three young men
who are now employed as doctors. The idea of following one's dreams, helping each other through tough times and making life-changing decisions are
powerful lessons for today's African American teenagers who should view
these three successful men as role models.

GRADES: 7–12

REVIEWS: *Booklist* 5/01/02, *Publishers Weekly* 4/22/02, *SLJ* 1/03, *VOYA* 10/02

DiCamillo, Kate. *Because of Winn Dixie.* 184 p. TR. Book Wholesalers, Incorporated. 978-0-7587-6512-3. 2002. $13.83. TR. Candlewick Press. 978-0-7636-0776-0.
2000. $15.99. RE. San Val, Incorporated. 978-0-613-39503-8. 2001. $16.00. PB.
Candlewick Press. 978-0-7636-4432-1. 2009. $6.99. PB. Candlewick Press. 978-0-
7636-2558-0. 2004. $5.99. CD. Random House Audio Publishing Group. 978-1-
4000-9149-2. 2004. $19.99. CD. Random House Audio Publishing Group. 978-0-
8072-1162-5. 2004. $20.40. CASS. Random House Audio Publishing Group.
978-0-8072-8856-6. 2004. $23.00. EB. Candlewick Press. 978-0-7636-4945-6. 2009.
$6.99. EB. Random House Audio Publishing Group. 978-0-7393-4437-8. 2006.
$20.40. LP. Thorndike Press. 978-0-7862-7366-9. 2005. $10.95.

Ten-year-old India Opal Buloni moves to a tiny town in Florida. At first she's
lonely but she finds a stray dog that she names Winn-Dixie. Together young
girl and dog meet a variety of quirky characters who populate the town. India
also learns the story behind her mother who left the family when India was
three. DiCamillo mixes moments of hilarity with poignancy as the winning
pair discovers different forms of friendship. This is an excellent title for introducing young teens to how a large cast of characters play their roles in a story.

GRADES: 6–9

REVIEWS: *Booklist* 5/01/00, *Kirkus* 4/01/00, *Publishers Weekly* 8/06/01, *SLJ* 6/00

AWARDS: Newbery Honor

Dickens, Charles. *A Christmas Carol.* Page count varies with edition. There are
significant formats currently available in print.

This story has been adapted into various movies that have placed a humorous
spin on the tale. However the original plot is one of possible redemption.
Ebenezer Scrooge is a greedy businessman with no place in his life for com-
passion. He is visited by Ghosts of Christmases Past, Present, and Yet to Come
who each show Scrooge scenes in hope that the old man will transform. Steal-

ing scenes are employee Bob Cratchit and his frail son, Tiny Tim. Teachers often assign this work to be read in December, which makes perfect sense.

GRADES: 7–12

Dickens, Charles. *A Tale of Two Cities.* Page count varies with edition. There are significant formats currently available in print.

Against the backdrop of the French Revolution themes of love and sacrifice are woven throughout this work. Dickens contrasts two societies, the brutality of the revolution in France with many parallels with life in London during the same time. Sydney Carton is a British barrister who wishes to redeem his life out of love for Lucie Manette, the wife of Charles Darnay, a French aristocrat who has been captured during the frenzy of the Revolution. Older teens will be engaged with the intricate workings of Dickens' plot.

GRADES: 10–12

Doyle, Arthur Conan. *The Complete Sherlock Holmes.* Page count varies with edition. There are significant formats currently available in print.

The famous detective's adventures will attract young readers. Many of today's modern detective tales can trace their roots to Arthur Conan Doyle's creation. Although adults are familiar with the stories, teens may very well be fascinated as to how Holmes manages to solve crimes in such tales as *The Redheaded League, The Hound of the Baskervilles,* and *The Adventure of the Speckled Band.*

GRADES: 7–10

Draper, Sharon. *Darkness Before Dawn.* 240p. TR. Simon & Schuster Children's Publishing. 978-0-689-83080-8. 2001. $18.99. RE. San Val, Incorporated. 978-0-613-53804-6. 2002. $17.20. PB. Simon & Schuster Children's Publishing. 978-0-689-85134-6. 2002. $6.99. EB. Recorded Books, LLC. 978-1-4237-0896-4. N/A. $68.00. LP. Thorndike Press. 978-0-7862-8364-4. 2006. $10.95.

The third installment of the Hazlewood High trilogy focuses on the problems of Keisha, a high school senior who has endured several tragedies. Her ex-boyfriend committed suicide and a good friend was killed in a car crash. She begins to date her track coach, an older guy she feels attracted to, but after a date he attempts to rape her. Many issues are laced throughout this story: suicide, anorexia, divorce, and death. Teens don't seem to mind and the three books in Draper's Hazlewood High will still be read years from now.

GRADES: 6–12

REVIEWS: *Booklist* 01/01/01, *Kirkus* 12/01/00, *SLJ* 2/01, *VOYA* 8/01

AWARDS: Quick Picks Top Ten

Draper, Sharon. *Forged by Fire.* 160 p. TR. Follett Library Resources. 978-0-7587-0354-5. 2002. $16.09. TR. Simon & Schuster Children's Publishing. 978-0-689-80699-5. 1997. $16.95. RE. San Val, Incorporated. 978-0-613-05000-5. 1998. $17.20. PB. Simon & Schuster Children's Publishing. 978-0-689-81851-6. 1998. $6.99. EB. Recorded Books, LLC. 978-1-4237-1799-7. N/A. $41.00. LP. Thorndike Press. 978-0-7862-8358-3. 2006. $10.95.

Gerald Nickelby, a minor character in *Tears of a Tiger,* emerges full-fledged and courageous in this companion story. Gerald lives with his aunt while his mother is in prison for child neglect. His mother returns with her daughter, Angel, and a new husband Jordan. Gerald learns that Jordan is sexually abusing Angel and he takes risks to intervene. This second title in the Hazlewood High trilogy continues with Draper's strong voice about social issues confronting inner-city teenagers.

GRADES: 6–12

REVIEWS: *Booklist* 2/15/97, *Kirkus* 12/01/96, *SLJ* 3/97

Draper, Sharon. *Tears of a Tiger.* N/A. TR. Simon & Schuster Children's Publishing. 978-0-689-31878-8. 1994. $18.99. RE. San Val, Incorporated. 978-0-7857-7677-2. 1996. $17.20. PB. Simon & Schuster Children's Publishing. 978-0-689-80698-8. 1996. $6.99. CASS. Recorded Books, LLC. 978-1-4025-0925-4. 2003. $28.00. CASS. Recorded Books, LLC. 978-1-4025-0926-1. 2003. $24.95. EB. Simon & Schuster Children's Publishing. 978-1-4169-2831-7. 2006. $6.99. EB. Recorded Books, LLC. 978-1-4237-1475-0. N/A. $37.00. LP. Thorndike Press. 978-0-7862-8361-3. 2006. $10.95.

Draper's first tale in her Hazlewood High trilogy packs a wallop in the opening pages. A star basketball player dies in a fiery wreck and Andy experiences survivor guilt because he was behind the wheel. Many voices appear in the story and Draper constructs her story through poetry, conversations, police reports, newspaper reports, and letters. Many teachers encourage young teens to read by introducing them to Draper's work, which has a direct bearing on their lives. The Hazlewood High trilogy is quickly becoming a classic read for African American teens.

GRADES: 6–12

REVIEWS: *Booklist* 11/01/94, *Publishers* 10/31/94, *SLJ* 2/95

Fisher, Antwone Q. *Finding Fish: A Memoir.* 352 p. TR. HarperCollins Publishers. 978-0-06-052792-1. 2002. $13.95. TR. HarperCollins Publishers. 978-0-06-000778-2. 2001. $13.99. PB. HarperCollins Publishers. 978-0-06-053986-3. 2002. $7.99. LP. Thorndike Press. 978-0-7862-5493-4. 2003. $29.95.

Antwone Fisher's autobiography relates his rise, first from poverty and then abuse at the hands of a foster family. Born in Cleveland to an underage mother sentenced to prison for murder, Fisher lived with a family that took him in and sold themselves as being ultra-religious. He finally escapes their abuse in his later teen years and finds himself in the military. Older teens will be interested in Fisher's determination to make something of himself regardless of the odds against him.

GRADES: 9–12

REVIEWS: *Kirkus* 12/15/00, *Publishers Weekly* 11/27/00, *VOYA* 10/01

Frank, Anne. *The Diary of a Young Girl.* Page count varies with edition. There are significant formats currently available in print.

The story of a teenager caught in the horrifying reality of the Holocaust has been used extensively in both middle and high schools as a work to illustrate teenage hope for the future. Anne Frank's diary tells in her own words how the family must stay hidden from Nazis who will ship them to a concentration camp if discovered. Despite her hopes and dreams of a future, Anne and her family are found. Anne and her sister Margot died at Bergen-Belsen. This is one of the primary sources for Holocaust studies.

GRADES: 7–12

Gaines, Ernest. *The Autobiography of Miss Jane Pittman.* Page count varies with edition. There are significant formats currently available in print.

Jane Pittman tells of her life from when she was a young slave girl in the South, to the end of the Civil War and finally culminating with her joining the American civil rights movement in 1962 at the age of 110. Along the way the story relates instances of racism in the South and the dangers of speaking out. The work shows teenagers the importance of being emotionally strong in the face of adversity and in the role of community leader.

GRADES: 9–12

Gaines, Ernest. *A Gathering of Old Men.* Page count varies with edition. There are significant formats currently available in print.

In the opening of Gaines's story, a white woman, Candy, discovers that a Cajun man has been shot by a black man. In order to protect this man from a horrible fate, Candy enlists the help of every other black man nearby. They are told to come to the house where the killing happened with a shotgun and one empty number-five shell so the sheriff will not be able to prosecute the correct murderer. A sense of community and friendship in the presence of racial hatred marks this work and will prompt discussion on right versus wrong.

GRADES: 9–12

Gantos, Jack. *Joey Pigza Swallowed the Key.* 196 p. TR. Perfection Learning Corporation. 978-0-7569-0177-6. 2000. $13.65. TR. Farrar, Straus & Giroux. 978-0-374-33664-6. 1998. $16.99. RE. San Val, Incorporated. 978-0-613-28228-4. 2000. $16.00. PB. HarperCollins Publishers. 978-0-06-440833-2. 2000. $5.99. CD. Random House Audio Publishing Group. 978-0-8072-2003-0. 2004. $30.00. CASS. Random House Audio Publishing Group. 978-0-8072-8165-9. 2004. $23.00. CASS. Books on Tape, Incorporated. 978-0-7366-9006-5. 2000. $18.00. EB. Farrar, Straus & Giroux. 978-1-4299-3626-2. 1998. $16.00. EB. Random House Audio Publishing Group. 978-0-7393-3042-5. 2007. $25.50. LP. Thorndike Press. 978-0-7862-2912-3. 2000. $21.95.

Joey is the kind of guy who gets in trouble at school. Who can blame him? His mother and father have divorced and he's being raised by his grandmother and his life is dangerously close to being out of control. Joey is formally diagnosed with ADHD and he is placed in special education classes. This is the go-to series for librarians and adults wishing to connect teens with ADHD to a fictional character who may be just like them. Other titles in the series are *Joey Pigza Loses Control* (Newbery Honor), *What Would Joey Do?*, and *I am Not Joey Pigza.*

GRADES: 6–8

REVIEWS: *Publishers Weekly* 1/10/00

Gipson, Fred. *Old Yeller.* Page count varies with edition. There are significant formats currently available in print.

Travis is the man of the house in this story set in the years following the Civil War. His father is on a cattle drive and a stray dog happens upon the property. Travis initially tries to reject the dog, but after Old Yeller saves Travis and his younger brother, the boy and dog become inseparable. The incredibly sad ending has Travis growing to make a mature decision after Old Yeller is infected with rabies. Teens in rural areas will do well to read about the loyalty of a dog. The sequel is called *Savage Sam.*

GRADES: 6–9

AWARDS: Newbery Honor

Golding, William. *Lord of the Flies.* Page count varies with edition. There are significant formats currently available in print.

This title has been required reading for both middle and high school students since the late 1950s. A group of British schoolchildren are stranded on an island without adult supervision. A struggle for group dominance ensues with Ralph and Jack battling to ascend to the leadership role. The descent from cooperation to social disorder and death has been dissected over and over in schools. Teenagers will find the chaos and primitive actions of the characters fascinating, especially as they witness climbing of the social structure in their own school.

GRADES: 7–12

Griffin, John Howard. *Black Like Me.* Page count varies with edition. There are significant formats currently available in print.

To experience racism in the South, journalist John Howard Griffin darkened his skin to pass as an African American traveling throughout racially segregated states in 1959. His aim was to bring to light the difficulties facing African Americans in different areas in the South. Griffin found that black communities seemed run-down and defeated. In Montgomery, however, the black community is charged with determination and energy by the example of one of its leaders, a preacher named Marin Luther King, Jr. This title has become an important piece of history leading up to the civil rights movement.

GRADES: 9–12

Hamilton, Virginia. *The House of Dies Drear.* Page count varies with edition. There are significant formats currently available in print.

Taking place in 1961, this novel is about Thomas Small, a 13-year-old African American boy who moves into a house that was once part of the Underground Railroad. Strange things begin to happen and the malicious family next to them seems to want them to leave. Part mystery, part history lesson, this title is about a young boy becoming aware of both the world he lives in and the history that contributes to his life.

GRADES: 6–9

Hamilton, Virginia. *M. C. Higgins, the Great.* Page count varies with edition. There are significant formats currently available in print.

M. C. Higgins's family lives on Sarah's Mountain, a place to where his great-grandmother escaped as a runaway slave. His father built a 40-foot pole—a gift for swimming the Ohio River—and M. C. gazes at the rolling hills stretching out in front of him. Behind him is a huge pile of dirt and debris from aggressive strip mining. This story shows a young boy conflicted to hold on to his heritage while also wanting to move his life forward.

GRADES: 9–12

AWARDS: Newbery Winner

Hansberry, Lorraine. *A Raisin in the Sun.* Page count varies with edition. There are significant formats currently available in print.

This play focuses on the Youngers, an African American family living on the South Side of Chicago sometime between World War II and the 1950s. When the play opens, the Youngers are about to receive an insurance check for $10,000, money from the deceased Mr. Younger's life insurance policy. The conflict is that each adult member of the family has different dreams of how to use the money. Each dream shows the social conflict confronting African Americans from being loyal to their neighborhood to attempting to immerse themselves into white society. Older teenagers will connect with the pressure of trying to make it financially versus sticking with traditional values.

GRADES: 10–12

Hawthorne, Nathaniel. *The Scarlet Letter.* Page count varies with edition. There are significant formats currently available in print.

Hawthorne's work describes the events surrounding a very twenty-first-century situation taking place in seventeenth-century Boston. Hester Prynne walks from prison with her infant daughter in her arms and on the breast of her gown is red cloth made into the shape of the letter "A." It represents her act of adultery and is a badge of shame for all to see. The question is, who is the father? Teen readers will instantly connect with the theme of persecution and rush to judgment that Hester endures. *The Scarlet Letter* has been a classic read for high school students for decades.

GRADES: 9–12

Hemingway, Ernest. *The Old Man and the Sea.* Page count varies with edition. There are significant formats currently available in print.

The Old Man and the Sea recounts an epic battle of wills between an old, experienced fisherman and a giant marlin said to be the largest catch of his life. Santiago is the fisherman enduring a streak of bad luck. His companion is Manolin, a boy who discusses baseball with Santiago. Confident his luck will soon change, Santiago ventures far out into the gulf where he hooks the marlin. Conflicts of man versus nature and man against self are evident in this story often used as a recommended read in high schools.

GRADES: 9–12

Henry, O. *The Best Short Stories of O. Henry.* Page count varies with edition. There are significant formats currently available in print.

Short stories are handy items to interest teenagers in reading without burdening them with overbearingly intricate works that take forever to read. O. Henry set the bar high and his stories are staples for literature studies. Highlighted by his signature "twist in the tale" these works will keep teens guessing the outcome. Included here are such famous stories as "The Ransom of Red Chief" and "The Gift of the Magi."

GRADES: 6–12

Hughes, Langston. *The Collected Poems of Langston Hughes.* Page count varies with edition. There are significant formats currently available in print.

Langston Hughes gained fame as an influential poet during the Harlem Renaissance, a part of his life that can be incorporated in lessons crossing over in the curriculum from English to History. For my service area of northeastern Ohio there is the added bonus that Hughes grew up in Cleveland where he attended high school. His poetry stressed the African American experience in the United States, a trait coming through in his poems "The Negro Speaks of Rivers" and "Let America Be America."

GRADES: 9–12

Hunt, Irene. *Across Five Aprils.* Page count varies with edition. There are significant formats currently available in print.

This historical fiction classic work is set in Illinois and opens before the Civil War begins. Jethro Creighton grows into manhood as his brothers and a beloved teacher leave home to fight for the Union and Confederate armies. The split loyalties stir tension in the town and Jethro becomes aware of the ugly side of political situations. Over the course of the war, Jethro grows up while observing how the conflict has changed the townspeople. His loss of innocence is the central theme of the story, thus making it an important book for families sending sons and daughters to war.

GRADES: 9–12

AWARDS: Newbery Honor

Hurston, Zora Neale. *Their Eyes Were Watching God.* Page count varies with edition. There are significant formats currently available in-print.

An African American woman in her early forties, Janie Crawford, tells the story of her life and journey via an extended flashback to her best friend, Pheoby. In turn Pheoby tells Janie's story to the nosy community on her behalf. Janie is not without controversy in her life, which came in stages coinciding with three marriages. Her final marriage ended in a murder and her new neighbors are curious about Janie's past. Strong themes of racism and Hurston's use of different dialects initially alienated prominent African American authors of the Harlem Renaissance. Older teens involved in African American studies should acquire this title.

GRADES: 10–12

Kesey, Ken. *One Flew Over the Cuckoo's Nest.* Page count varies with edition. There are significant formats currently available in print.

Set in a mental hospital, this story is narrated by "Chief" Bromden, who has pretended to be a deaf mute for years. Rebellious Randle Patrick McMurphy is the focus of the work and his main antagonist is Nurse Ratched. McMurphy's charismatic personality places him as a leader for other inmates, a situation that puts him in a power struggle with Nurse Ratched. Themes of standing up for oneself and challenging authority will attract older teen readers.

GRADES: 10–12

London, Jack. *The Call of the Wild.* Page count varies with edition. There are significant formats currently available in print.

The hero of this classic work is Buck, a huge and powerful dog snatched from his ranch home in California to work as a sled dog in Alaska. He learns how to survive in the harsh environment and emerges as a leader of other dogs. Buck is traded off to various owners, some abusive and some dangerous. He finally comes under the watch of John Thornton, an experienced outdoorsman. Buck's loyalty to Thornton is the focus of the story that can only end tragically. Younger readers fascinated by a dog's loyalty to a man will be thrilled by this classic adventure yarn. A companion novel by London is called *White Fang.*

GRADES: 6–9

Myers, Walter Dean. *Hoops.* Page count varies with edition. There are significant formats currently available in print.

One of Walter Dean Myers' early novels will still hit home with teen readers of today. Seventeen-year-old Lonnie Jackson works out with his team, which is preparing to win the city basketball Tournament of Champions. He hears advice from his coach, Cal, who knows what it takes to be a professional player, one of Lonnie's goals. Gambling enters the picture with heavy bettors hoping to throw the game. Is Cal crooked? Will Lonnie do the right thing? This is an excellent sports story for teenagers who enjoy their own hoops magic.

GRADES: 7–12

Paterson, Katherine. *Bridge to Terabithia.* Page count varies with edition. There are significant formats currently available in print.

Fifth-grader Jess Aarons becomes friends with neighbor Leslie Burke and their friendship transforms Jess into letting go of his frustrations. However, the two lonely children create a magical forest kingdom that they can cross over by swinging on a rope. When Leslie tries to cross over by herself, a tragedy occurs and Jess is devastated. This title has been targeted by censors due to the strong religious tone but remains hugely popular with middle school readers.

GRADES: 6–9

AWARDS: Newbery Winner

Pelzer, David. *A Child Called It*. Page count varies with edition. There are significant formats currently available in print.

In this autobiographic work, Pelzer relates his youth growing up in an abusive home and suffering at the hands of his alcoholic mother. The abuse is stunning, ranging from starvation to beatings and other instances that come close to killing Pelzer. The young boy finally discovers help and authorities step in. This title is a strong work to include with outreach to incarcerated teenagers, many of whom have suffered abuse from their own caregivers. Companion novels to the work are *The Lost Boy* and *A Man Named Dave*.

GRADES: 6–12

Raskin, Ellen. *The Westing Game*. Page count varies with edition. There are significant formats currently available in print.

Whoever solves the mystery put forth in self-made millionaire Sam Westing's will and testament collects his $200 million fortune. Sixteen individuals are divided into eight pairs and each set is given a different group of clues. The heirs' challenge is to solve the mystery of which of them killed Mr. Westing. To spice up the challenge, each heir is given 10,000 dollars to play the game. Teens seeking a good whodunit may wish to start with this classic title.

GRADES: 7–10

AWARDS: Newbery Winner

Shakespeare, William. *Hamlet*. Page count varies with edition. There are significant formats currently available in print.

Shakespeare's plays are must-have items in a teen collection, especially in service areas where his works are studied annually. The following three plays are commonly taught in many high schools. In Hamlet, teens will be enthused with the concept of revenge but may become frustrated with Hamlet's caution before taking action. Still, Yorick's skull is cool and there's death, ghosts, and lots of swordplay.

GRADES: 9–12

Shakespeare, William. *Macbeth*. Page count varies with edition. There are significant formats currently available in print.

Macbeth is a play that shows teenage readers how creepy the human mind can be when unchecked by moral constraints. Greed and the desire to seize power result in a murder, which in turn results in guilt and paranoia. The reality of the evil deeds becomes blurred among the characters fulfilling the witches' chant in the beginning, "Fair is foul and foul is fair." Teens will either love or hate Lady Macbeth and the constant washing of her hands.

GRADES: 9–12

Shakespeare, William. *Romeo and Juliet.* Page count varies with edition. There are significant formats currently available in print.

Even teens who are not serious students are familiar with the basic outline of this play, for it is the most famous love story in the history of English literature. Plus, Romeo and Juliet are teenagers themselves. In every high school there are instances of euphoria, tenderness, and violence when dealing with love. These traits also mark Shakespeare's play as the characters also deal with rash, spur-of-the-moment decisions.

GRADES: 9–12

Shelley, Mary. *Frankenstein.* Page count varies with edition. There are significant formats currently available in print.

The work that birthed the horror novel continues to fascinate teen readers. The boldness to create human life and the pursuit of knowledge are underlying concepts in this classic tale. Teens may be more familiar with twentieth-century adaptations of the story that have appeared in film, but the original work shows how as Victor Frankenstein attempts to create life, he actually destroys everyone dear to him. Teens may see themselves in this self-destructive behavior.

GRADES: 9–12

Sinclair, Upton. *The Jungle.* Page count varies with edition. There are significant formats currently available in print.

Teens frustrated over the lack of trust for the government or capitalistic businesses will connect to the Upton Sinclair masterful book. Written in 1906, *The Jungle* exposed the horrors of the unregulated meatpacking industry. It also examined corruption and the plight of the working class struggling to grind out an existence and rise from poverty. Corruption, unregulated industries, and the working class remain social topics in the twenty-first century.

GRADES: 9–12

Speare, Elizabeth George. *The Witch of Blackbird Pond.* Page count varies with edition. There are significant formats currently available in print.

Kit Tyler has left her sunny home in the Caribbean and now is a member of the 1687 Connecticut Colony. She is out of step with the strict Puritan community and feels lonely. While roaming the meadows, she meets and befriends an old Quaker woman, Widow Tupper, who is also known as the Witch of Blackbird Pond. The suspicious community falls back on its fear of the unknown and accuses Kit of witchcraft. This novel, the Newbery Medal winner of 1959, details the hysteria prevalent in the time leading up to the Salem witch trials.

GRADES: 6–9

AWARDS: Newbery Winner

Steinbeck, John. *Of Mice and Men.* Page count varies with edition. There are significant formats currently available in print.

George Milton and Lennie Small are two migrant field hands moving from job to job throughout California during the Great Depression. Lennie has enormous strength and size but limited mental capabilities. George is the brains of the pair. Together they dream of having a place of their own where Lennie can tend to his beloved rabbits. Their dreams never come true due to harsh reality and Lennie's fatal flaw of not being able to control his strength while petting something soft. Themes of loyalty and betrayal will led to rousing discussions when teens in school read this work as a group.

GRADES: 9–12

Walker, Alice. *The Color Purple.* Page count varies with edition. There are significant formats currently available in print.

Walker's controversial work involves female relationships, racism, and sexism. Set in Georgia during the 1930s, the story shows that African Americans suffered mistreatment from white people and felt they were doomed to live in a racist society. Main characters Celie and Sofia form a relationship that involves love and sharing, a direct contrast from their often violent heterosexual relationships. Ultimately this is a story of hope but critics have stated that the story reaffirms old racist stereotypes about pathology in black communities and of black men in particular.

GRADES: 10–12

Wiesel, Elie. *Night.* Page count varies with edition. There are significant formats currently available in print.

Told in the voice of Eliezer, a Jewish teen, this work shows the sobering plight of Jews caught up in the Holocaust. The Jews sent to concentration camps are stripped, shaved, disinfected, and treated with almost unimaginable cruelty. Throughout the work Wiesel highlights recurring themes of disgust with mankind and loss of faith in mankind. Eventually the captives are marched from Birkenau to Auschwitz. When the war finally ends, Eliezer has survived but is a shell of a human. *Night* must be included in all curriculum studies of the Holocaust.

GRADES: 9–12

Woodson, Jacqueline. *Miracle's Boys.* 144 p. TR. Book Wholesalers, Incorporated. 978-1-4046-0953-2. 2002. $13.19. TR. Penguin Group (USA) Incorporated. 978-0-399-23113-1. 2000. $15.99. RE. San Val, Incorporated. 978-1-4177-3489-4. 2006. $16.00. CASS. Random House Audio Publishing Group. 978-0-8072-0525-9. 2004. $23.00. EB. Random House Audio Publishing Group. 978-0-7393-4824-6. 2007. $20.40.

Following the death of their mother, three brothers feel they will be separated into foster homes. Lafayette is the youngest, a seventh grader, and the story is told through his eyes. The pressure is on the middle brother, Charlie, who has just returned from jail. Oldest brother Ty'ree feels he must keep the brothers together but their loyalty to each other comes under a severe test. Gang violence and inner-city poverty are realistically portrayed in this story about taking care of family.

GRADES: 7–12

REVIEWS: *Publishers Weekly* 12/03/01

Wright, Richard. *Native Son.* Page count varies with edition. There are significant formats currently available in print.

Twenty-year-old Bigger Thomas is an African American living in poverty in Chicago's South Side in the 1930s. A troubled youth, Bigger receives a job at the home of the Daltons, a wealthy white family. He accidentally kills a white woman, runs from the cops, rapes and kills his girlfriend, is arrested and tried. More of an antihero than a hero, Wright suggests Bigger is a result of the poverty in which he was raised. Inner-city teens will instantly recognize situations in this story that are prevalent in their own world.

GRADES: 10–12

X, Malcolm. *The Autobiography of Malcolm X.* Page count varies with edition. There are significant formats currently available in print.

With the assistance of Alex Haley, this work was written in 1965 based on long discussions Haley had with Malcolm X leading up to his assassination in February of that year. The work includes Malcolm X's youth, his maturing years in Boston and New York, his time in prison, and his conversion to Islam. His words include his deep concerns about the African American existence. This title is a solid recommendation for African American teenagers questioning their future purpose in life.

GRADES: 10–12

Zindel, Paul. *The Pigman.* Page count varies with edition. There are significant formats currently available in print.

Two teenagers, John Conlan and Lorraine Jensen, are sophomores who like to make prank phone calls. Lorraine picks out Mr. Pignati's number and pretends to be calling for a charity. The lonely man befriends the teens and a certain trust forms. However John invites his friends to Mr. Pignati's home and a drunken party breaks out and his late wife's collection of porcelain pigs is smashed. Themes of betrayal and the fragile existence of life are explored through the teens' actions.

GRADES: 7–10

4

Coming-of-Age Stories

Any attempt at creating a list of young adult books about characters coming of age will most likely result in something of a catch-all grouping. A trademark of young adult fiction is having a teen character encounter a conflict and grow from the experience. From that viewpoint, almost any teen novel can be considered a coming-of-age story. However, in this section titles feature characters making discoveries about their inner core that helps them establish their self-worth.

Another factor in choosing titles for this section required characters to become aware of the world around them. As the plot moves forward, the teen characters shift away from the belief that everything centers on them. Family and friends play roles and become important components to the story.

Several titles considered classics and pillars of young adult literature are listed in this section. These titles often appear on recommended reading lists for schools. I often come upon teachers and school librarians who seek "safe" books, meaning no swearing or sex. With all the advances in the teen book world, many adults working with teen readers believe that books should send a message or teach a lesson, yet the teens I encountered wanted no such lesson or message from their reading. They were more interested in a powerful story.

With those thoughts in mind, I made selections that tried to convey a character becoming aware of his world and the author presenting that situation wrapped around a powerful story.

Almond, David. *Kit's Wilderness*. 240 p. TR. Random House Children's Books. 978-0-385-32665-0. 2000. $16.99. LB. Perma-Bound Books. 978-0-605-00992-9. 1999. $12.50. RE. San Val, Incorporated. 978-0-613-36836-0. 2001. $16.60. PB. Random House Children's Books. 978-0-440-41605-0. 2001. $6.50. CASS. Random House Audio Publishing Group. 978-0-8072-8215-1. 2004. $30.00. CASS. Books on Tape, Incorporated. 978-0-7366-9017-1. 2000. $24.00. EB. Adobe Systems, Incorporated. 978-1-59061-390-0. 2001. $3.99. EB. Random House Audio Publishing Group. 978-0-7393-6001-9. N/A. $34.00.

Thirteen-year-old Kit Watson moves to an old coal-mining town to help take care of his elderly grandfather. He begins a pseudo friendship with John

Askew, the son of a drunk who is unable to take care of his family. The boys enter a game called "Death" in a wilderness area near their town. Kit and other friends lie alone in an abandoned mine waiting for visions of children who died there long ago. Almond's story shows the importance of friendship and the role of magic in our lives. Kit comes of age by helping John reconnect with his family and also keeps the memory of his grandfather alive following his death. The complicated plot with sophisticated prose works better with older readers.

GRADES: 10–12

REVIEWS: *Booklist* 1/01/00, *Kirkus* 12/15/99, *Publishers Weekly* 2/21/00, *SLJ* 3/00, *VOYA* 4/00

AWARDS: Printz Winner

Barnes, John. *Tales of the Madman Underground (An Historical Romance 1973)*. 480 p. TR. Penguin Group (USA) Incorporated. 978-0-670-06081-8. 2009. $18.99. EB. Penguin Group (USA) Incorporated. 978-1-101-08109-9. 2009. $18.99.

Set in 1973, Barnes' lengthy tale features high school senior Karl Shoemaker who just wants to be normal. For years he has been part of the Madman Underground, a group of students assigned to therapy. Karl earned the name "Psycho" after cutting up a classmate's rabbit. In his small Ohio town, Karl deals with all sorts of quirky characters and his drunken, hippie mom. Karl's misfits suffer from abuse and neglect but are fiercely loyal to each other. Karl works several jobs and although he wants to escape his dead-end town, he defends his buddies and connects with his mother. R-rated dialogue marks this title for the upper end of young adult readership.

GRADES: 10–12

REVIEWS: *Booklist* 5/01/09, *Kirkus* 4/01/09, *Publishers Weekly* 6/01/09, *SLJ* 7/09, *VOYA* 6/09

AWARDS: Printz Honor

Brashares, Ann. *The Sisterhood of the Traveling Pants*. 294 p. TR. DIANE Publishing Company. 978-0-7567-6771-6. 2003. $15.00. TR. Random House Children's Books. 978-0-385-72933-8. 2001. $15.95. LB. Perma-Bound Books. 978-0-605-01243-1. 2001. $13.99. RE. San Val, Incorporated. 978-1-4177-4718-4. 2005. $17.20. PB. Random House Children's Books. 978-0-553-49479-2. 2005. $6.99. PB. Random House Children's Books. 978-0-440-22970-4. 2004. $6.99. CD. Random House Audio Publishing Group. 978-0-7393-5681-4. 2007. $19.99. CD. Random House Audio Publishing Group. 978-0-307-24327-0. 2005. $30.00. CASS. Random House Audio Publishing Group. 978-0-8072-0590-7. 2004. $32.00. EB. Random House Audio Publishing Group. 978-0-7393-4460-6. N/A. $42.50.

Brashares' wildly popular story about a pair of worn, thrift-shop jeans that magically fit four best friends is a charming tale. But underneath the hook of the jeans that are passed from friend to friend during a single summer, there are teenagers dealing with serious life-changing issues. The story is filled with joy, sorrow, living, and dying as Carmen, Lena, Bridget, and Tibby find their way to adulthood. Teenage readers will identify with at least one if not all of the characters as they deal with boys, romance, and adults behaving badly with divorce. Targeting a female audience, this story crosses a wide range of age levels. Other titles in the series are *The Second Summer of the Sisterhood* (Teens Top Ten), *Girls in Pants: The Third Summer of the Sisterhood* (Teens' Top Ten), *and Forever in Blue: The Fourth Summer of the Sisterhood.*

GRADES: 6–12

REVIEWS: *Booklist* 8/01/01, *Kirkus* 8/01/01, *Publishers* 7/16/01, *SLJ* 8/01, *VOYA* 10/01

AWARDS: BBYA Top Ten

Brooks, Kevin. *Martyn Pig.* 230 p. TR. Perfection Learning Corporation. 978-0-7569-7217-2. 2003. $15.65. TR. Scholastic, Incorporated. 978-0-439-29595-6. 2002. $16.95. RE. San Val, Incorporated. 978-0-613-64813-4. 2003. $18.40. PB. Scholastic, Incorporated. 978-0-439-50752-3. 2003. $7.99.

Martyn Pig lives in a rundown English town with his abusive alcoholic father. His mother left years ago and he feels his life cannot get any worse. That is, until his father rushes at him in a drunken rage, stumbles and hits his head on the fireplace wall. He dies, but Martyn decides to not notify the police, instead enlisting the help of Alex, a girl who helps him dispose of the body. While cleaning up the house he discovers evidence of a blackmail scheme about his father's inheritance. This title can easily be classified as a mystery with black humor, but it has elements of a coming-of-age story as Martyn becomes aware of Alex's intent to betray him. The layered plot featuring many twists is a nice fit for high school readers.

GRADES: 9–12

REVIEWS: *Kirkus* 4/01/02, *Publishers Weekly* 5/27/02, *SLJ* 5/02

Brooks, Martha. *Mistik Lake.* 207 p. TR. Farrar, Straus & Giroux. 978-0-374-34985-1. 2007. $16.00. CD. Random House Audio Publishing Group. 978-0-7393-6472-7. 2008. $38.00. EB. Random House Audio Publishing Group. 978-0-7393-6473-4. N/A. $32.30.

Odella is a seventeen-year-old girl caught in a family that hoards many secrets. Her mother, Sally, drinks way too much. Could the reason be that Sally is haunted by the tragic automobile accident she survived as a teenager? Odella finds herself shouldering the responsibility of raising her younger sisters when her mother leaves the family for another man. Told from various points of view, this novel depicts women in Odella's family showing all their flaws. Throughout the story some dreams are followed and others are ignored, and Odella observes how lives are intertwined. The complex emotions and family dynamics in this story are perfect for older teen readers.

GRADES: 9–12

REVIEWS: *Booklist* 9/01/07, *Publishers Weekly* 9/03/07, *SLJ* 9/07, *VOYA* 8/07

Brown, Chris Carlton. *Hoppergrass.* 240 p. TR. Henry Holt & Company. 978-0-8050-8879-3. 2009. $17.99. EB. Henry Holt & Company. 978-1-4299-3666-8. 2009. $17.99.

A teen can come of age in different settings, and county jail is where fifteen-year-old Bowser finds himself. Ever streetwise, Bowser soon figures out who has his back and who wants a piece of him. His has an uneasy friendship with Nose, a tough black kid who plays off being Bowser's rival. The adult characters are nasty and Bowser becomes aware of a porn and prostitution ring. This is a story of a tough kid taking on issues outside his own personal space and figuring out the right thing to do. The backdrop of a county jail and the late 1960s setting may not resonate for all readers, but older teens seeking a gritty tale will appreciate Bowser's voice.

GRADES: 9–12

REVIEWS: *Booklist* 4/15/09, *SLJ* 7/09, *VOYA* 8/09

Cameron, Pete. *Someday This Pain Will Be Useful to You.* 240 p. TR. Picador. 978-0-312-42816-7. 2009. $13.00. TR. Farrar, Straus & Giroux. 978-0-374-30989-3. 2007. $16.00. CD. Random House Audio Publishing Group. 978-0-7393-7289-0. 2008. $39.00. CD. Random House Audio Publishing Group. 978-0-7393-7253-1. 2008. $50.00. EB. Random House Audio Publishing Group. 978-0-7393-7254-8. N/A. $42.50.

On the surface eighteen-year-old James Sveck seems to have it all. He's been accepted to Brown University and his wealthy Manhattan parents seem to have the bucks to sketch out a nice life for James. But he's not sure if he wants to enter college and dreams of owning a house in a bucolic small town in the Midwest. James also finds himself attracted to his mother's male assistant. James's life and voice are both poignant and sophisticated. His trials of navigating his way to adulthood alternate between funny and sad with a touch of tenderness mixed in. This book is a nice fit for any older teen struggling to decide about his or her future.

GRADES: 10–12

REVIEWS: *Booklist* 9/01/07, *Publishers Weekly* 10/08/07, *SLJ* 11/07, *VOYA* 10/07

Carvell, Marlene. *Who Will Tell My Brother?* N/A. RE. San Val, Incorporated. 978-0-613-63006-1. 2004. $16.00. PB. Hyperion Books for Children. 978-0-7868-1657-6. 2004. $5.99.

Evan Hill is a part-Mohawk high school senior, who protests against his school's use of Indian mascots. Told in free-verse vignettes, Evan expresses his hurt and anger against his view of racist attitudes shrugged off as school spirit. He has picked up the torch of his older brother who also protested the school's racial emblem. Carvell's story reflects instances her own sons endured while teenagers. Evan stands tall in the face of prejudice and bullying from his peers. His coming-of-age journey is one of a young man taking on a huge issue by himself. Carvell's writing is suitable for all ages.

GRADES: 9–12

REVIEWS: *Booklist* 7/01/02, *Kirkus* 7/01/02, *SLJ* 7/02, *VOYA* 6/02

Chambers, Aidan. *Postcards from No Man's Land.* 320 p. Penguin Group (USA) Incorporated. 978-0-525-46863-9. 2002. $19.99. LB. Perma-Bound Books. 978-0-605-34145-6. 1999. $14.99. RE. San Val, Incorporated. 978-1-4176-2046-3. 2004. $18.40.

Intending to honor his grandfather, a British soldier who fought and died in Holland in 1944, seventeen-year-old Jacob Todd enters Amsterdam. Jacob's coming-of-age journey is paralleled by the story of Geertrui van Riet, his Dutch grandmother. Geertrui is old now and dying of cancer, and she wants Jacob to know her story, which is also the story of his grandfather. Chambers's work is a rich, complex story that tackles big themes: time, death, happiness, love, sex, war, and the meaning of life. Jacob meets a sexy woman who turns out to be a man and is helped by an older woman. Jacob comes to realize his life is tied to his past. This is a very sophisticated and hefty volume and will be a challenge for all but the best older readers.

GRADES: 10–12

REVIEWS: *Booklist* 5/15/02, *Kirkus* 4/15/02, *Publisher Weekly* 4/29/02, *SLJ* 7/02, *VOYA* 8/02

AWARDS: Printz Winner

Cisneros, Sandra. *The House on Mango Street.* 160 p. TR. Knopf Doubleday Publishing Group. 978-0-679-43335-4. 1994. $24.95. TR. McGraw-Hill Higher Education. 978-0-07-009429-1. 1996. $17.19. LB. Perma-Bound Books. 978-0-8000-5260-7. 1984. $17.95. LB. San Val, Incorporated. 978-0-8335-6852-6. 1991. $18.75. PB. Spark Publishing Group. 978-1-4114-0256-0. 2005. $5.95. CD. Random House Audio Publishing Group. 978-0-7393-2279-6. 2005. $14.99.

Esperanza Cordero is a young girl growing up in the Latino section of Chicago. She recollects her life living on Mango Street and all the people she meets while there. Mango Street represents her heritage and upbringing. Esperanza tells the tales of all the people and experiences she has with her little sister, Nenny. Esperanza is advised by her sisters to remember where she came from. Cisneros's work explores a teen accepting her roots and discovering what defines her. This title with an historical backdrop is a staple of reading lists and could easily also be deemed a classic coming-of-age story.

GRADES: 9–12

REVIEWS: *Publishers Weekly* 3/08/91

Clarke, Judith. *One Whole and Perfect Day.* 250 p. TR. Boyds Mills Press. 978-1-932425-95-6. 2007. $16.95. CD. Brilliance Audio. 978-1-4233-6664-5. 2008. $29.99.

Seventeen-year-old Lily is sure something is mixed up about her family. Not one of them is stable and her mother continues to bring old people home from the senior day-care center. Lily's grandmother, Nan, talks to an imaginary friend. Lily feels stuck in this household and views herself as the sensible one. She is saddled with cleaning the house, cooking meals, and other chores. To overcome her situation, Lily decides to fall in love. Clarke's story is about acceptance of one's family. Teens may be put off by Australian idioms but if they stick with the story they will see a likeable character in Lily.

GRADES: 9–12

REVIEWS: *Booklist* 5/01/07, *Publishers Weekly* 3/12/07, *SLJ* 8/07, *VOYA* 6/07

AWARDS: Printz Honor

Coman, Carolyn. *Many Stones.* 158 p. TR. Perfection Learning Corporation. 978-0-7569-1937-5. 2002. $14.15. TR. Boyds Mills Press. 978-1-8869-1055-3. 1996. $15.95. LB. San Val, Incorporated. 978-0-613-45291-5. 2002. $14.15. LB. Perma-Bound Books. 978-0-8479-0404-4. 2000. $12.99. CASS. Random House Audio Publishing Group. 978-0-8072-0518-1. 2004. $30.00.

Berry's older sister, Laura, was murdered while working in South Africa. She travels to that country with her father to present money to the school where Laura worked. Coman has deftly woven together the themes of death, grieving, and reconciliation through the characters and setting of this elegant novel. Berry is at odds with her father and she sees him as a shameless and shallow flirt. The title comes from stones Berry gathers and sets on her chest to gain the feeling of being grounded. Berry's emotional journey is part coming of age and part tragedy. *Many Stones* shows a teen dealing with the large emotional topic of grief.

GRADES: 8–12

REVIEWS: *Booklist* 11/01/00, *Kirkus* 10/15/00, *Publishers Weekly* 10/30/00, *SLJ* 11/00, *VOYA* 2/01

AWARDS: Printz Honor

Compestine, Ying Chang. *Revolution Is Not a Dinner Party.* 256 p. TR. Henry Holt & Company. 978-0-8050-8207-4. 2007. $16.95. TR. Henry Holt & Company. 978-1-4287-5704-2. 2007. N/A. PB. Square Fish. 978-0-312-58149-7. 2009. $7.99. CD. Random House Audio Publishing Group. 978-0-7393-6161-0. 2007. $38.00. EB. Random House Audio Publishing Group. 978-0-7393-6162-7. 2007. $32.30. LP. Thorndike Press. 978-1-4104-0726-9. 2008. $23.95.

Ling tells her story of growing up in 1972 China. She is the daughter of two doctors and lives in a warm and loving household. But under the regime of Chairman Mao, Ling's father is jailed and Comrade Li, an officer of the Communist Party, moves into the family's apartment. Ling and her mother struggle through periods of starvation and see their books burned. Despite the troubles, Ling remains spunky and fights to keep her long hair, a trait she believes to be a symbol of independence. Set against the backdrop of an oppressive government, this work is about a young girl dealing with large issues beyond her control.

GRADES: 7–10

REVIEWS: *Booklist* 8/01/07, *Publishers Weekly* 7/09/07, *SLJ* 8/07, *VOYA* 10/07

Cormier, Robert. *Beyond the Chocolate War.* N/A. TR. Peter Smith Publisher, Incorporated. 978-0-8446-7140-6. 2000. $23.00. TR. Perfection Learning Corporation. 978-0-8124-4763-7. 1986. $14.65. LB. Perma-Bound Books. 978-0-8479-1776-1. 1985. $13.99. PB. Random House Children's Books. 978-0-440-91278-1. 1996. $6.99. PB. Random House Children's Books. 978-0-440-90580-6. 1986. $13.55.

This sequel continues the story a few months after *The Chocolate War* ends. Carter and Obie, leading members of the ruthless secret society, The Vigils, are not concerned about the future but are focused on destroying the leader, Archie Costello. A Vigil stunt ruins Obie's relationship with Laurie Gundarson. He's out for revenge. But Archie is slick and wiggles away from blame by handing over leadership of the Vigils. The secret society begins to use physical force rather than psychological force. Behind the scenes is Archie. The sequel is a fine companion to the first work. Both titles are geared to older teens with the exploration of psychological and social issues.

GRADES: 8–12

REVIEWS: *SLJ* 4/85

Cormier, Robert. *The Chocolate War.* 253 p. TR. DIANE Publishing Company. 978-0-7567-6585-9. 2003. $25.00. TR. Book Wholesalers, Incorporated. 978-0-7587-4778-5. 2002. $13.94. PB. Random House Children's Books. 978-0-375-82987-1. 2004. $8.95. PB. Random House Children's Books. 978-0-440-94459-1. 1975. $7.99. CD. Random House Audio Publishing Group. 978-0-7393-5015-7. 2007. $26.00. CD. Random House Audio Publishing Group. 978-1-4000-8996-3. 2004. $38.25. CASS. Random House Audio Publishing Group. 978-0-8072-7221-3. 1988. $32.00. EB. Random House Audio Publishing Group. 978-0-7393-4507-8. 2007. $38.25.

> Jerry Renault refuses to participate in Trinity High's annual candy sale. By taking that stance he pits himself against his fellow students and the school's administration. Cormier's work shows the struggle of an innocent freshman who pays a terrible price for confronting the system. Readers will be stunned at how Jerry's peers plot to make him conform to their will. This story is universally considered a classic piece of young adult literature. It has also been banned many times for anti-religious statements and anti-administration statements. The intricate story and heavy issues included in the plot mark this work a solid choice for older teens. It has been evaluated and dissected making it a good choice for informal or school discussions.

GRADES: 8–12

REVIEWS: *Booklist* 5/01/89

Corrigan, Eireann. *Splintering.* 192 p. TR. Scholastic, Incorporated. 978-0-439-53597-7. 2004. $16.95. LB. Perma-Bound Books. 978-0-605-01391-9. 2004. $14.99. RE. San Val, Incorporated. 978-1-4176-6866-3. 2005. $18.40.

> When a violent assault strikes a family, each member of that family is changed. Told in hard-hitting free verse with alternating voices, Corrigan shows readers how fifteen-year-old Paulie and her younger brother Jeremy are haunted by the crime. A deranged man breaks into their house wielding a knife. Paulie cannot let go of the fear she experienced and Jeremy feels ashamed about his fleeing to the safety of the basement. Paulie is a teen who has an instant life-changing moment and she discovers that her family has deeper problems than suffering from a random attack. Teens interested in psychological stories will be engaged by Corrigan's snapshot of a dysfunctional family.

GRADES: 9–12

REVIEWS: *Booklist* 4/01/04, *Publishers Weekly* 4/19/04, *SLJ* 7/04, *VOYA* 8/04

Dowd, Siobhan. *Bog Child.* 336 p. TR. Random House Children's Books. 978-0-385-75169-8. 2008. $16.99. LB. Random House Children's Books. 978-0-385-75170-4. 2008. $19.99. CD. Random House Audio Publishing Group. 978-0-7393-8538-8. 2009. $39.00.

The conflict between Northern Ireland and the Irish Republic is the focus of Dowd's unique storytelling. Eighteen-year-old Fergus McCann crosses the border to steal peat for his uncle to sell as fuel. What he digs up is a body, a victim of violence buried in the bog. Archeologists believe the body is ancient and they flock to the hillside. A side story has Fergus' brother, an imprisoned IRA member, joining a hunger strike. Fergus is an innocent caught up in events larger than his own and he may not be able to juggle all the situations. What interests him is the lead archeologist's daughter. This is a fine story about a young man coming of age in a world of political chaos.

GRADES: 9–12

REVIEWS: *Booklist* 8/01/08, *Kirkus* 7/15/08, *Publishers Weekly* 7/28/08, *SLJ* 8/08, *VOYA* 12/08

AWARDS: BBYA Top Ten

Dowd, Siobhan. *A Swift Pure Cry.* 320 p. TR. Random House Children's Books. 978-0-385-75108-7. 2007. $16.99. LB. Random House Children's Books. 978-0-385-75109-4. 2007. $19.99. PB. Random House Children's Books. 978-0-440-42218-1. 2008. $8.99.

Fifteen-year-old Shell Talent lives in Ireland during 1984. Her life is not easy and she's trapped with her distracted and alcoholic father. He has left his job to serve the Lord leaving Shell and her siblings with no real means to support themselves. Shell hopes to escape the extreme poverty and pins her hopes on their new priest, Father Rose. Shell finds herself in bigger issues than poverty and her life is, on the surface, one of hopelessness as she attempts to find a degree of solace. Sobering scenes of childbirth mark this book more suitable for older readers.

GRADES: 9–12

REVIEWS: *Booklist* 4/01/07, *Publishers Weekly* 3/19/07, *SLJ* 4/07, *VOYA* 4/07

Downham, Jenny. *Before I Die.* 336 p. TR. Random House Children's Books. 978-0-385-75155-1. 2007. $15.99. LB. Random House Children's Books. 978-0-385-75158-2. 2007. $18.99. PB. Random House Children's Books. 978-0-385-75183-4. 2009. $9.99. CD. Random House Audio Publishing Group. 978-0-7393-6288-4. 2007. $34.00. CD. Random House Audio Publishing Group. 978-0-7393-6290-7. 2007. $50.00. EB. Random House Audio Publishing Group. 978-0-7393-6291-4. 2007. $59.50. LP. Thorndike Press. 978-1-4104-0776-4. 2008. $23.95.

Before I Die offers a different take on the coming-of-age story. Tessa narrates her story, which takes place during her sixteenth year. She is dying from a rare form of leukemia. Her death is imminent but she is determined to live out her list of ten things to do before she dies. Her goals may raise eyebrows: having sex, committing a crime, and falling in love. Told in a first-person voice, Tessa will tug, no grab, onto reader's hearts and squeeze out every ounce of sympathy. Her family tries to remain strong for her, but all cave to her tragedy. The writing here is shockingly straightforward and readers are not let down gently. Although her situation is terminal, Tessa learns about what is really important and that message is truly one about coming of age. Harsh situations and language place this title into the older readers' group.

GRADES: 9–12

REVIEWS: *Booklist* 11/15/07, *Kirkus* 9/01/07, *Publishers Weekly* 8/06/07, *SLJ* 11/07

AWARDS: BBYA Top Ten, Teen's Top Ten

Flake, Sharon G. *Money Hungry.* N/A. RE. San Val, Incorporated. 978-1-4177-9314-3. 2003. $18.40. PB. Hyperion Books for Children. 978-1-4231-0386-8. 2007. $7.99.

Raspberry Hill has a money problem: she loves it too much. Greed is her driving force and she abandons friendships and her mother's love in search of ways to obtain more money. Her father fell into the drug trap and Raspberry and her mother lived on the streets for awhile. Now they have a place of their own, but everybody in the projects has issues. Raspberry Hill, although only thirteen, must make decisions a more mature person would struggle with. Sharon Flake creates a character all too human and readers will care that Raspberry finds her way. A wide range of teen readers will be drawn to this story. The sequel is called *Begging for Change*.

GRADES: 6–9

REVIEWS: *Booklist* 6/15/01, *Kirkus* 5/01/01, *Publishers Weekly* 6/18/01, *SLJ* 7/01, *VOYA* 2/02

Fogelin, Adrian. *The Big Nothing.* 224 p. TR. Peachtree Publishers. 978-1-56145-326-9. 2004. $14.95. PB. Peachtree Publishers. 978-1-56145-388-7. 2006. $6.95.

Justin Riggs is a quiet boy and slightly pudgy. The thirteen-year-old has a lot to tell readers. His father has left home and his mother is so shell-shocked by his put downs and arguments, she withdraws to the imagined safety of her bed. Justin's older brother, Duane, has left home, enlisted in the army, and was sent to Iraq. Justin handles his situation by mentally withdrawing to a state of silence he calls "The Big Nothing." Jemmie is a girl who cares for him and will not let him stew in silence. Jemmie's grandmother encourages Justin to learn piano and the young man dreams of a relationship with Jemmie. This quiet and unassuming novel is a perfect fit for middle school students who want to read about a guy unsure how to cope with adult problems.

GRADES: 7–10

REVIEWS: *Booklist* 12/15/04, *SLJ* 12/04

Frank, E. R. *America.* 224 p. TR. Simon & Schuster Children's Publishing. 978-0-689-84729-5. 2002. $18.00. LB. Perma-Bound Books. 978-0-605-95420-5. 2002. $14.99. RE. San Val, Incorporated. 978-0-613-66476-9. 2003. $18.40. PB. Simon & Schuster Children's Publishing. 978-0-689-85772-0. 2003. $8.99. CASS. Recorded Books, LLC. 978-1-4025-2889-7. 2002. $40.00. EB. Recorded Books, LLC. 978-1-4175-8880-0. N/A. $1.00. LP. Thorndike Press. 978-0-7862-6484-1. 2004. $21.95.

Born to a crack-addict mother, America was raised by kindly Mrs. Harper. Before he is slated to start kindergarten, he visits his biological mother in New York City and she abandons him in a run-down apartment. Years later he is returned to Mrs. Harper, but his life is not the best. He swears constantly and inside he believes that he's bad. E. R. Frank's story is about the failings of adults and how a youngster will progress in coming of age in his own way. The startling language and mature situations mark this title for the upper end of young adult readership.

GRADES: 10–12

REVIEWS: *Booklist* 2/15/02, *Kirkus* 12/01/01, *Publishers Weekly* 1/07/02, *VOYA* 2/02

AWARDS: BBYA Top Ten, Teens' Top Ten

Griffin, Paul. *The Orange Houses.* 160 p. TR. Penguin Group (USA) Incorporated. 978-0-8037-3346-6. 2009. $16.99.

Opening with an apparent hanging, this story then retraces the preceding month's events of Jimmi Sixes, a disturbed eighteen-year-old veteran and street poet/junkie, back in the Bronx after his discharge from the army. Fifteen-year-old Tamika, who goes by Mik, lives in the projects called the Orange Houses. She's hearing-impaired but likes turning off her hearing aids and texting rather than speaking. The third figure is Fatima, an illegal refugee who has just arrived from Africa. The trio tries to help each other but Jimmi ends up caught by a vigilante group. This story is one of hope set against harsh conditions. All three characters grow to learn what is important. The tension and rough situations will be most appreciated by older teens.

GRADES: 9–12

REVIEWS: *Booklist* 5/01/09, *Publishers Weekly* 6/22/09, *SLJ* 6/09, *VOYA* 10/09

AWARDS: BBYA Top Ten

Gruen, Sara. *Water for Elephants.* 335 p. TR. Algonquin Books of Chapel Hill. 978-1-56512-499-8. 2006. $23.95. CD. HighBridge Company. 978-1-61573-036-0. 2009. $14.99. CD. Penguin/HighBridge. 978-1-59887-062-6. 2006. $34.95. EB. Algonquin Books of Chapel Hill. 978-1-56512-585-8. 2007. N/A. LP. Thorndike Press. 978-1-59413-200-1. 2007. $13.95.

This title, marketed as an adult title, will interest older teens seeking a more intricate and challenging story. Jacob Jankowski's parents have been killed in a car accident. Distraught, Jacob abandons his veterinary studies and essentially runs off with a Depression-era traveling circus. There he learns the harsh life behind the scenes of the "Most Spectacular Show on Earth." Animals and humans are exploited and Jacob discovers a certain nobility of the performers as they bond together against the cruel dealing of the business manager. Dominating the setting is Rose, an elephant with a personality and a secret. Although Jacob is not a teenager, his time spent with the circus definitely brings about many changes in his life.

GRADES: 10–12

REVIEWS: *Booklist* 4/15/06, *Publishers Weekly* 3/06/06, *VOYA* 10/06

AWARDS: Alex Award

Hautman, Pete. *How to Steal a Car.* 176 p. TR. Scholastic, Incorporated 978-1-56512-499-8. 2009. $16.99.

While chilling on summer vacation, Minneapolis suburbanite Kelleigh knows she is a good girl. The fifteen-year-old doesn't smoke, drink (except a little), do drugs, or do anything bad. Yet she has a slightly dangerous habit of stealing cars. She doesn't exactly seek out her criminal career; her first boost happens when a guy drops his keys in the mall parking lot. Kelleigh keeps them as a "souvenir" and then learns the guy lives close to her home. By a set of circumstances, she's then recruited to steal expensive luxury cars. The coming-of-age theme deals with the thrills of stealing contrasted with Kelleigh's deteriorating home life. Her father is having an affair, her mother drinks, and the suburban life seems boring. Pete Hautman shows readers a teen girl making life-changing choices, and often wrong ones. The gritty topic is presented at a brisk pace and will appeal to both boys and girls of many age levels.

GRADES: 8–12

REVIEWS: *Booklist* 8/09, *Publishers Weekly* 9/14/09, *SLJ* 11/09

Herlong, M. H. *The Great Wide Sea.* 288 p. TR. Penguin Group (USA) Incorporated. 978-0-670-06330-7. 2008. $16.99.

Just two months after the death of his mother in a car accident, Ben Byron discovers his dad has sold their house and used the money to buy the *Chrysalis,* a thirty-foot sailboat. Ben and his two younger brothers embark on a yearlong tour of the Bahamas. Despite the harsh onboard conditions, things go fairly smoothly. But one morning everything changes—their father disappears and the boat heads into a terrible storm. Ben must save his brothers in a tension-filled story of survival. Beginning the book as an angry fifteen-year-old, Ben matures into a responsible young man who makes life-altering decisions.

Conflicts between Ben and his father ring true and this outdoor survival tale has broad appeal and fits nicely in both public libraries and school libraries.

GRADES: 7–12

REVIEWS: *Booklist* 11/15/08, *SLJ* 3/09

AWARDS: BBYA Top Ten

Hidier, Tanuja Desai. *Born Confused.* 432 p. Scholastic, Incorporated. 978-0-439-35762-3. 2002. $16.95. LB. Perma-Bound Books. 978-0-605-01271-4. 2002. $14.99. RE. San Val, Incorporated. 978-0-613-72235-3. 2003. $20.85. PB. Scholastic, Incorporated. 978-0-439-51011-0. 2003. $9.99. CD. Blackstone Audio, Incorporated. 978-0-7861-7564-2. 2006. $29.95. EB. Blackstone Audio, Incorporated. 978-0-7861-5398-5. N/A. $49.95.

Just when she thinks things could not get more complicated, Dimple's parents introduce her to Karsh, a suitable boy. Dimple is seventeen years old and tries hard to fit in. However in India, she is too American. In America her parents are determined to educate and involve her in Indian culture. But Dimple's involvement with Karsh would make him an unsuitable boy in her parents' eyes if they only knew about the teens' tricky situations. Dimple experiences the awkwardness of growing up trying to assimilate into two vastly different cultures.

GRADES: 9–12

REVIEWS: *Booklist* 12/15/02, *Kirkus* 9/15/02, *Publishers Weekly* 10/28/02, *SLJ* 12/02, *VOYA* 2/03

Hijuelos, Oscar. *Dark Dude.* 448 p. TR. Simon & Schuster Children's Publishing. 978-1-4169-4804-9. 2008. $16.99. PB. Simon & Schuster Children's Publishing. 978-1-4169-4945-9. 2009. $9.99. CD. Blackstone Audio, Incorporated. 978-1-4332-5111-5. 2008. $19.95. CASS. Blackstone Audio, Incorporated. 978-1-4332-5109-2. 2008. $44.95.

Rico Fuentes, age fifteen, is undergoing a series of problems. Set in New York City during the 1960s, Rico doesn't fit in due to his light Cuban skin. He's hassled by guys in his neighborhood and his father drinks heavily. Rico and his friend Jimmy decide to escape Jimmy's dive into the drug culture. They hit the road, hitchhiking to Wisconsin to meet up with Gilberto, another neighborhood guy gone off to college and now living on a hippie farm. Rico saves Jimmy's life and finds acceptance—by others first and, ultimately, of himself. The protracted narrative is by turns sentimental, humorous, and sad, but Hijuelos creates a memorable character who will resonate with readers wrestling with their own identity issues. This is a great multicultural book for older teens.

GRADES: 10–12

REVIEWS: *Booklist* 11/01/08, *Publishers Weekly* 9/01/08, *SLJ* 11/08, *VOYA* 10/08

Hosseini, Khaled. *A Thousand Splendid Suns.* 384 p. TR. Penguin Group (USA) Incorporated. 978-1-59448-888-7. 2009. $29.95. TR. Penguin Group (USA) Incorporated. 978-1-59448-950-1. 2007. $25.95. CD. Simon & Schuster Audio. 978-0-7435-5443-5. 2007. $29.95. CD. Simon & Schuster Audio. 978-0-7435-5445-9. 2007. $39.95. LP. Center Point Large Print. 978-1-60285-033-0. 2007. $33.95.

This title is marketed as an adult book but the topic is timely and will have broad appeal for older teens. Covering three decades of anti-Soviet jihad and Taliban tyranny, the lives of two women are brought to focus. Mariam, the illegitimate daughter of a wealthy businessman, is scorned by society. At age fifteen, she is forced to marry forty-year-old Rasheed who becomes brutal when she fails to produce a child. Eighteen years later, Rasheed takes another wife, fourteen-year-old Laila. Mariam and Laila become allies standing against the beatings and violent attitudes toward women. The two women each undergo a huge life change in their teens. The multicultural slant shows how teenage girls in another culture undergo a completely different set of challenges. The grim topic fits best for older teens.

GRADES: 10–12

REVIEWS: *Booklist* 3/01/07, *Publishers Weekly* 2/26/07

Jenkins, A. M. *Night Road.* 368 p. TR. HarperCollins Publishers. 978-0-06-054604-5. 2008. $16.99. LB. HarperCollins Publishers. 978-0-06-054605-2. 2008. $17.89. EB. HarperCollins Publishers. 978-0-06-196486-2. 2009. $16.99

Night Road could be called a road novel or a vampire novel. But many elements of Jenkins' story can be adapted into a coming-of-age novel. Cole and Sandor are vampires who leave the comfort of their Manhattan colony. Their goal is to train a new vampire, Gordon, and Cole becomes the glue keeping the trio on track. Sandor is reckless and Gordon is needy, but readers discover things about Cole's own troubled past. Details of vampire lore keep the pages turning, but this story is about teenagers, albeit vampires, maturing to take care of each other. The vampire slant will bring in many readers of a variety of ages.

GRADES: 9–12

REVIEWS: *Booklist* 5/15/08, *Kirkus* 4/15/08, *Publishers Weekly* 6/23/08, *SLJ* 9/08, *VOYA* 8/08

Johnson, Angela. *Bird.* 133 p. TR. Perfection Learning Corporation. 978-0-7569-6660-7. 2006. $13.65. TR. Penguin Group (USA) Incorporated. 978-0-8037-2847-9. 2004. $16.99. LB. Perma-Bound Books. 978-0-605-56531-9. 2004. $12.99.

RE. San Val, Incorporated. 978-1-4177-2900-5. 2006. $16.00. CD. Random House Audio Publishing Group. 978-1-4000-9926-9. 2004. N/A. CASS. Random House Audio Publishing Group. 978-1-4000-9925-2. 2004. N/A.

Bird, is a thirteen-year-old runaway. She's left her Cleveland home and journeys to rural Alabama to find her stepfather, Cecil, and bring him home. Once in Alabama, Bird finds Cecil but also learns that Ethan—Cecil's nephew—is adjusting to life after receiving a heart transplant. Observing the interaction, Bird also comes to know Jay, the brother of the boy whose heart is now in Ethan's body. Johnson's characters interact but are often at odds with their own individual problems. What begins as a simple and self-centered task grows into a more complex situation as Bird understands that many lives are connected in ways not seen at first glance. This gentle story has a place in all libraries.

GRADES: 7–10

REVIEWS: *Booklist* 9/01/04, *Publishers Weekly* 10/18/04, *SLJ* 9/04, *VOYA* 2/05

Johnson, Louanne. *Muchacho.* 208 p. TR. Random House Children's Books. 978-0-375-86117-8. 2009. $15.99. LB. Random House Children's Books. 978-0-375-96117-5. 2009. $18.99. CD. Random House Audio Publishing Group. 978-0-7393-8597-5. 2009. $28.00.

Eddie Corazon is a high school junior. He lives with his Mexican-American family in a rough town in New Mexico, a place where the drug business rules and nobody should be left by themselves on the streets. Eddie's cousin Enrique is showing Eddie the ropes of the drug trade but a violent shooting makes Eddie reconsider his life's path. He is placed in an alternative school and there his secret passion for reading springs forth. Eddie is caught in a struggle to find his true self and he escapes through literature. This is both a coming-of-age tale and a message story. The dialogue and scenes inside the alternative school are spot on, but Johnson's message may be lost on younger readers.

GRADES: 9–12

REVIEWS: *Booklist* 9/01/09, *SLJ* 9/09

Johnson, Maureen. *13 Little Blue Envelopes.* 317 p. TR. Perfection Learning Corporation. 978-0-7569-7830-3. 2006. $16.65. TR. HarperCollins Publishers. 978-0-06-054141-5. 2005. $16.99. LB. HarperCollins Publishers. 978-0-06-054142-2. 2005. $17.89. RE. San Val, Incorporated. 978-1-4177-6438-9. 2006. $19.65. PB. HarperCollins Publishers. 978-0-06-054143-9. 2006. $8.99. EB. HarperCollins Publishers. 978-0-06-182520-0. 2009. $9.99.

Seventeen-year-old Ginny's Aunt Peg has died of brain cancer. Peg was a free-spirited artist who marched to her own drummer and was known to disappear for months, the last time in Europe. Peg arranged for Ginny to follow her own adventures and left a plane ticket to London. Once in Great Britain, Ginny follows instructions planted in thirteen envelopes. During her journey Ginny discovers the hidden truth behind Peg but also has the opportunity to find her own compass. Her journey includes romance, several weird escapades and a chance to interact with other teens. Jaunting across Europe is the ultimate life-changing experience and Ginny is a winning character.

GRADES: 9–12

REVIEWS: *Booklist* 9/15/05, *Publishers Weekly* 9/05/05, *SLJ* 10/05, *VOYA* 10/05

AWARDS: Teens' Top Ten

Jones, Lloyd. *Mister Pip.* 272 p. PB. Random House Publishing Group. 978-0-385-34107-3. 2008. $12.00. EB. Recorded Books, LLC. 978-1-4356-2884-7. 2008. $1.00.

In this novel marketed for adults, thirteen-year-old Matilda is struggling to understand the violence brought to her Pacific island. The conflict prompts all the teachers to flee, but one white man stays behind, the eccentric Mr. Watts. He takes over as teacher and reads to the class from his favorite novel, Charles Dickens' *Great Expectations.* Matilda identifies with the orphan Pip in the story and Victorian England becomes real to her and her classmates. What seems to be a quirky novel becomes one of harsh realism when the soldiers return and the violence again erupts. Matilda comes of age against a backdrop of imperialism and witnesses the redemptive power of storytelling and art. The story's violence is sobering and this title will be best appreciated by mature readers.

GRADES: 10–12

REVIEWS: *Booklist* 6/01/07, *Publishers Weekly* 5/28/07

AWARDS: Alex Award, BBYA Top Ten

Jordan, Hillary. *Mudbound.* 328 p. TR. Algonquin Books of Chapel Hill. 978-1-56512-569-8. 2008. $22.95. TR. Algonquin Books of Chapel Hill. 978-1-56512-677-0. 2009. $13.95. EB. Algonquin Books of Chapel Hill. 978-1-56512-637-4. N/A. $22.95. LP. Thorndike Press. 978-1-4104-0738-2. 2008. $31.95.

Part historical fiction, part epic storytelling, *Mudbound* includes many themes that ring of the coming-of-age experience. Following World War II, two families find themselves thrust together on a Mississippi delta farm. The black sharecroppers, the Jacksons, work for the white owners, the McAllans. Each family has a member returning from the war. Jamie McAllan is haunted by what he witnessed and Ronsel Jackson returns as a hero but is confronted by extreme racism. The two families have members sharing powerful voices, and the harsh reality of the South in the 1940s is distinct. Themes of becoming aware of racism and social classes dominating each other are distinct as young men Jamie and Ronsel find their friendship leads to tragedy. The intricate plot and multiple voices make this story one best appreciated by older readers.

GRADES: 10–12

REVIEWS: *Booklist* 11/15/07, *Publishers Weekly* 11/05/07

AWARDS: Alex Award

Kidd, Sue Monk. *The Secret Life of Bees.* 320p. TR. Penguin Group (USA) Incorporated. 978-0-670-03237-2. 2002. $24.95. TR. Penguin Group (USA) Incorporated. 978-0-14-303640-1. 2005. $15.95. LB. San Val, Incorporated. 978-0-613-58386-2. 2003. $23.45. LB. Perma-Bound Books. 978-0-605-01288-2. 2002. $21.00. CD. HighBridge Company. 978-1-59887-918-6. 2009. $14.99. CD. HighBridge Company. 978-1-59887-829-5. 2008. $34.95. PLAY. Findaway World, LLC. 978-1-59895-648-1. 2006. $44.99.

Against a backdrop of racism and violence, fourteen-year-old Lily begins to understand the world around her. She has fled her abusive father and teamed up with Rosaleen, a black woman who has escaped from jail after insulting the town's racists. They land in Tiburon, South Carolina, and are sheltered by three sisters, May, June, and August who are African American and are beekeepers. The sisters are also keepers of the truth. Under their watchful eye, Lily learns about her mother and herself. Monk's book is a staple of adult reading groups and will have wide appeal for older teens who will become involved with Lily's reactions to the world surrounding her.

GRADES: 10–12

REVIEWS: *Booklist* 12/01/01, *Kirkus* 11/15/01, *Publishers Weekly* 11/12/01, *SLJ* 5/02, *VOYA* 8/02

King, Stephen. *The Body: A Novella in Different Seasons.*

Originally published in King's 1982 collection *Different Seasons* this coming-of-age story involves a journey to view a corpse. Vern Tessio tells his three friends that he knows the location of the body of Ray Brower, a boy who has gone missing. The boys begin their journey walking along railroad tracks. At night they discuss their thoughts about each of their futures. They wonder about living in a small town and the chances of escaping their dead-end existence. A confrontation with older teens at the site of the body adds tension to the story. King adds a fast forward to see if the boys' predictions come true. This novella is all about boys discovering themselves against a backdrop of an outdoor journey and coming to grips with death and destiny.

GRADES: 9–12

REVIEWS: *SLJ* 11/82

Knowles, John. *A Separate Peace.* Page count varies with edition. There are significant formats currently available in print.

John Knowles' coming-of-age novel has appeared on required and recommended school reading lists for decades. The story describes a combination
of friendship, rivalry, and possible betrayal. Gene Forrester is the story's narrator. He relates events from 15 years in the future after attending a private
school in New England during World War II. Gene's closest friend is Phineas,
a daring young man admired by the school's students. Gene is the opposite, a
quiet and intellectual guy. Their complex friendship is very competitive and a
tragedy occurs when Phineas falls from a tree and breaks his leg. Questions
about betrayal are unanswered making this title a good choice for discussion
in school groups.

GRADES: 9–12

Koertge, Ron. *Shakespeare Bats Cleanup.* 116 p. TR. Perfection Learning Corporation. 978-0-7569-6571-6. 2006. $13.65. RE. San Val, Incorporated. 978-1-4176-
9493-8. 2006. $16.00. PB. Candlewick Press. 978-0-7636-2939-7. 2006. $5.99.

Presented as a novel in verse, this is the story of fourteen-year-old Kevin
Boland who is confined to bed with a bout of mononucleosis. He begins to
write poems with the help of a book loaned to him by his father. Topics include the recent death of his mother, his love of baseball, and make-out sessions with girls. Kevin's writing becomes more sophisticated by using free
verse, haiku, sonnets, and ballads. What springs forth is the voice of a teenage
boy on the cusp of manhood. This is an excellent choice of a work used to
teach and enjoy poetry.

GRADES: 7–10

REVIEWS: *Booklist* 4/01/03, *Publishers Weekly* 2/17/03, *SLJ* 5/03, *VOYA* 8/03

Korman, Gordon. *Jake, Reinvented.* N/A. LB. Perma-Bound Books. 978-0-605-
01324-7. 2003. $12.99. PB. Hyperion Books for Children. 978-0-7868-5697-8.
2005. $5.99. CASS. Recorded Books, LLC. 978-1-4025-7030-8. 2004. $28.00.

This retelling of *The Great Gatsby* takes place in the class-conscious F. Scott Fitzgerald High. The new kid is Jake Garrett who wins over the popular crowd
with great parties at his house. When Todd Buckley suspects Jake of going after his best girl, Didi, he explores Jake's background and comes up with an
ugly secret: Jake was once a nerd. The parallels to *The Great Gatsby* are obvious
but Korman's story gives a fresh slant on a teen coming-of-age novel. The high
school backdrop of beer parties and following the herd rings true as the char-

acters cope with the power of image and who is popular. *Gatsby* scenes of murder and suicide are removed making Korman's work suitable for middle school readers.

GRADES: 7–10

REVIEWS: *Booklist* 12/01/03, *Publishers Weekly* 10/06/03, *SLJ* 2/04, *VOYA* 6/04

Lee, Harper. *To Kill a Mockingbird.* Page count varies with edition. There are significant formats currently available in print.

One of the top novels of the twentieth century must be included in this edition of *A Core Collection for Young Adults*. Scout and Jem Finch are growing up in their Alabama town, Maycomb. Atticus, their lawyer father, takes on a case of interracial rape. Times are hard in the Great Depression and to pass the time the children strike up an odd relationship with Boo Radley, the neighborhood recluse. Atticus' case does not go well and Scout and Jem are thrust onto center stage as the building racism explodes. Harper Lee writes of childhood innocence derailed by larger and serious adult situations. *To Kill a Mockingbird* rightfully is placed on many reading lists covering a wide range of ages.

GRADES: 7–12

Levithan, David. *Love Is the Higher Law.* 176 p. TR. Alfred A. Knopf Incorporated. 978-0-375-83468-4. 2009. $15.99. LB. Alfred A. Knopf Incorporated. 978-0-375-93468-1. 2009. $18.99.

Three teens' lives are only loosely connected when the World Trade Center is struck by two planes on September 11. The teenagers learn their lives are interconnected and deeper friendships are formed. Two of the characters are gay, but the story's focus is on the tragic events rather than homosexuality. The coming-of-age theme fits as the teenagers find out more about themselves in the face of a national tragedy. This story is perhaps more of a regional choice as New York City is featured with pop culture.

GRADES: 9–12

REVIEWS: *Booklist* 6/01/09, *Publishers Weekly* 8/03/09, *SLJ* 9/09, *VOYA* 6/09

Lipsyte, Robert. *The Contender.* N/A. RE. San Val, Incorporated. 978-0-88103-014-3. 2003. $17.20.

One of the first groundbreaking teen novels of the 1960s, *The Contender* remains a powerful story for twenty-first century readers. Alfred Brooks is a high school dropout living in Harlem, New York. His dead-end job at a grocery store is a drag, but he finds himself in Donatelli's Gym after running from street punks. Alfred begins training as a boxer and matures by gaining respect and confidence in his ability. His coming-of-age lesson is that it's the effort, not the win that makes a man. Although gritty in tone, this title is a quality snapshot of inner-city life that continues to resonate for teens.

GRADES: 7–12

Lynch, Chris. *Freewill.* 148 p. TR. DIANE Publishing Company. 978-0-7567-9869-7. 2006. $16.00. TR. Perfection Learning Corporation. 978-0-7569-1934-4. 2002. $16.65. LB. San Val, Incorporated. 978-0-613-56380-2. 2002. $15.30. LB. Perma-Bound Books. 978-0-605-01225-7. 2001. $13.99. PB. HarperCollins Publishers. 978-0-06-447202-9. 2002. $8.99.

Written in second person, seventeen-year-old Will is actually talking to himself. Will is a disturbed young man who usually expresses himself through wood carving. Often lonely, he makes friends with Angela, a girl in his woodworking class. Before he gains confidence to open up, his carvings begin to show up near dead bodies of teenagers from his community who've committed suicide. Lynch captures Will's confusion and his slow rise to understanding the situation with sensitivity and tenderness. Lynch's sophisticated writing and story make this work a better fit for older teens.

GRADES: 10–12

REVIEWS: *Booklist* 5/15/01, *Kirkus* 1/15/01, *Publishers Weekly* 1/29/01, *SLJ* 3/01, *VOYA* 8/01

AWARDS: Printz Honor

Magoon, Kekla. *The Rock and the River.* 304 p. TR. Simon & Schuster Children's Publishing. 978-1-4169-7582-3. 2009. $15.99.

It's 1968 and thirteen-year-old Sam Childs is growing up in Chicago. His dignified father is a civil rights activist and Sam is often involved with peaceful demonstrations. When he and his almost-girlfriend Maxie witness the police brutally beating one of their friends, Sam's world swiftly changes. His seventeen-year-old brother brings home a gun and is involved with the Black Panther Party. Magoon's story shows the tension in society while conflict and anger boil in the Childs' household. A stunning climactic scene shifts Sam into adulthood and his coming-of-age moment is one of violence. The engrossing story will work well with middle and younger high school students.

GRADES: 7–10

REVIEWS: *Booklist* 2/01/09, *SLJ* 2/09, *VOYA* 10/09

Maynard, Joyce. *The Usual Rules.* 400 p. TR. St. Martin's Press. 978-0-312-28369-8. 2004. $14.95. EB. St. Martin's Press. 978-0-312-70971-6. N/A. $24.95.

Wendy did not speak to her mother on the morning of 9/11; the mother and daughter had a fight. Wendy went to school and her mother went to work on the 84th floor of the World Trade Center. Following the tragedy, her step-father is in a daze and Wendy relocates to California to live with her biological father. In California, Wendy takes advantage of lack of parenting and be-comes involved with a homeless skateboarder, a bookstore owner, and his autistic son. Wendy begins a second chance with her life and gains an appreci-ation of people around her. Marketed as an adult novel, this title has older teen appeal featuring a character coping with an enormous tragedy.

GRADES: 10–12

REVIEWS: *Booklist* 1/01/03, *Kirkus* 12/01/02, *Publishers Weekly* 1/27/03, *SLJ* 7/03, *VOYA* 6/03

AWARDS: BBYA Top Ten

McCormick, Patricia. *Sold.* 272 p. TR. Hyperion Press. 978-0-7868-5171-3. 2006. $15.99. RE. San Val, Incorporated. 978-1-4178-1810-5. 2008. $19.65. PB. Hy-perion Press. 978-0-7868-5172-0. 2008. $8.99.

Coming of age is a difficult moment for any teenager, but Patricia McCormick shows how horrible life can be for a teenage girl in another culture. Thir-teen-year-old Lakshmi is leading a normal life on her family's Nepal farm. That is until her stepfather arranges for her to leave their village and move to Calcutta. Believing she will work as a maid, Lakshmi is shocked to realize her stepfather sold her into prostitution. Her formative years are spent enduring repeated rapes and the bleakness of forced sexual slavery. The content, al-though skillfully written, is intense and may be best suited for more mature readers.

GRADES: 9–12

REVIEWS: *Booklist* 9/15/06, *Publishers Weekly* 8/28/06, *SLJ* 9/06, *VOYA* 12/06

AWARDS: BBYA Top Ten

McDonald, Joyce. *Swallowing Stones.* N/A. LB. Perma-Bound Books. 978-0-605-46516-9. 1997. $13.99. RE. San Val, Incorporated. 978-0-613-19465-5. 1999. $17.20. PB. Random House Children's Books. 978-0-440-22672-7. 1999. $6.99.

A bizarre Fourth of July accident leaves the father of fifteen-year-old Jenna Ward dead. Three other teens have their lives changed by the accident. Sev-enteen-year-old Michael MacKenzie unknowingly fired the shot. Witness Joe Sadowski is Michael's loyal buddy, and Amy Ruggerio is a teen with a "loose" reputation. The psychological turmoil involves grief, guilt, and anxiety. The police edge closer to the truth and the characters' reactions are authentically teen. The coming-of-age theme involves loyalty and deception that test the strength of friendships.

GRADES: 9–12

REVIEWS: *Booklist* 10/15/97, *Kirkus* 7/01/97, *Publishers Weekly* 9/22/97, *SLJ* 9/97

Moore, Perry. *Hero.* 432 p. PB. Hyperion Press. 978-1-4231-0196-3. 2009. $8.99.

The coming-of-age story meets its superhero in Thom Creed. Patterned after plots in graphic novels, this prose story features Thom, the son of a disgraced superhero who made a huge mistake while trying to save the world. Thom's own super powers begin to emerge but he also realizes he is gay. He wishes to hide his sexuality from his blue-collar tough dad, but he is having trouble corralling his powers. The metaphor of having two personas, with a mask and without, is intriguing. The climactic scene has Thom emerging as a hero and his life changes in an epic showdown worthy of any graphic novel. Authentic and blunt homosexual situations steer this work to more mature readers.

GRADES: 10–12

REVIEWS: *Booklist* 8/01/07, *Publishers Weekly* 9/10/07, *SLJ* 9/07, *VOYA* 10/07

Naylor, Phyllis Reynolds. *Cricket Man.* 208 p. TR. Simon & Schuster Children's Publishing. 978-1-4169-4981-7. 2008. $16.99.

Eighth-grader Kenny Sykes is socially inept and more of an observer than a doer. He notices that Jodie Poindexter, his sixteen-year-old neighbor, is unhappy. Kenny forms a hero in his mind, an alternate persona he calls Cricket Man after his task of deciding the fate of crickets that fall into the family pool. Kenny's world is upper middle class with seemingly no real worries. His friendship with Jodie introduces him to situations beyond his years. Kenny has noble genes but he doesn't realize it until Jodie reaches out for his help. If it is possible to have a coming-of-age change in one night, Kenny does so. This quiet novel packs an unexpected punch and will please readers who like to read about other teens with problems. The serious topic is tastefully presented and *Cricket Man* is a solid choice for readers of many ages.

GRADES: 7–12

REVIEWS: *Booklist* 8/01/08, *SLJ* 10/08

Oaks, J. Adams. *Why I Fight.* 240 p. TR. Simon & Schuster Children's Publishing. 978-1-4169-1177-7. 2009. $16.99.

Wyatt Reaves, twelve years old at the beginning of this troubling story, relates his teen years. Wyatt is something of a victim as he was manipulated by his uncle who lacked a moral compass. Uncle Spade is a womanizer with an eye for a quick buck. He pushes Wyatt, who is big for his age, to become a bare knuckle fighter. The young man grows into a huge physical presence, but is emotionally just a kid. What he can do is fight ferociously if insulted, comparing himself to the Incredible Hulk. Dialogue without quotation marks gives this story a movie-script feel and pulls readers into Wyatt's confusion as he matures over six years. This title is a strong candidate for older male readers who crave violent brawls and brutality in their reading.

GRADES: 9–12

REVIEWS: *Booklist* 4/15/09, *Kirkus* 3/15/09, *SLJ* 7/09, *VOYA* 6/09

Pearson, Mary E. *The Adoration of Jenna Fox.* 272p. TR. Henry Holt & Company. 978-0-8050-7668-4. 2008. $16.95. PB. Square Fish. 978-0-312-59441-1. 2009. $8.99. CD. Macmillan Audio. 978-1-4272-0443-1. 2008. $29.95. EB. Square Fish. 978-1-4299-5205-7. 2009. $8.99.

Jenna Fox is seventeen years old and awakens from an eighteen-month coma. Her memory is blank and she watches videos of her childhood trying to piece together her past. There is an air of mystery as Jenna can recite passages from Thoreau but cannot remember having any friends. There is a mix of science fiction horror as Jenna comes of age, finally realizing what her parents have done. Parental manipulation is revealed as part of Jenna's awareness, especially her father, an expert in biotechnology. The intriguing mix of science and parental involvement will engage readers, especially girls who may also be annoyed by parents controlling their lives.

GRADES: 8–12

REVIEWS: *Booklist* 3/01/08, *Publishers Weekly* 3/03/08, *SLJ* 5/08, *VOYA* 8/08

Peters, Julie Anne. *Luna.* N/A. LB. Perma-Bound Books. 978-0-605-01381-0. 2004. $14.99. RE. San Val, Incorporated. 978-1-4176-9404-4. 2006. $18.40. PB. Little, Brown Books for Young Readers. 978-0-316-01127-3. 2006. $7.99. EB. Little, Brown Books for Young Readers. 978-0-316-03989-5. 2008. $7.99.

Two teens, a brother and sister, discover things about themselves in Julie Anne Peters' powerful novel about a transgender teen. Regan narrates the story about Liam, her brother who is determined to change from a boy to a young woman. He is Liam by day, but by night she becomes Luna. Regan has put her own life on hold, instead focusing on defending her sibling. Regan worries about her brother's double life becoming known and is fearful of her parents' potential reaction. This is a bold novel on a topic that in some regions may be viewed as controversial, yet the writing is beautiful and Regan emerges as a powerful character.

GRADES: 9–12

REVIEWS: *Booklist* 7/01/04, *Publishers Weekly* 5/17/04, *SLJ* 5/04, *VOYA* 6/04

Plum-Ucci, Carol. *What Happened to Lani Garver.* 328 p. TR. Houghton Mifflin Harcourt Trade & Reference Publishers. 978-0-15-216813-1. 2002. $17.00. LB. Perma-Bound Books. 978-0-605-48765-9. 2002. $13.95. RE. San Val, Incorporated. 978-1-4176-1830-9. 2005. $17.20. PB. Houghton Mifflin Harcourt Trade & Reference Publishers. 978-0-15-205088-7. 2004. $6.99.

Claire McKenzie is a sixteen-year-old with issues. The cheerleader is also a musician and a leukemia survivor who has dark visions that her cancer has returned. Lani Garver enters the picture as a new student at her high school. The student body cannot determine if he's a guy or a girl because of his pale skin, longish hair, and seductive walk. He is intelligent and is the one person to whom Claire can talk about her darkest dreams and fears. As Claire discovers her true self, prejudice, homophobia, friendship, tolerance, and the possibility that something spiritually bigger than everyone rules this universe are wonderfully woven into this powerfully told story. The intricate plot will appeal to mature readers.

GRADES: 9–12

REVIEWS: *Booklist* 8/01/02, *Kirkus* 9/01/02, *Publishers Weekly* 8/19/02, *SLJ* 10/02, *VOYA* 12/02

Powell, Randy. *Three Clams and an Oyster.* 216 p. TR. Perfection Learning Corporation. 978-0-7569-8184-6. 2006. $14.60. RE. San Val, Incorporated. 978-1-4177-6087-9. 2006. $17.15. PB. Farrar, Straus & Giroux. 978-0-374-40007-1. 2006. $6.95.

Best friends Rick Beaterson and Dwight Deshutsis combine with Cade Savage (who hikes the ball) to form their flag football team. The three eleventh graders are searching for a fourth member for their squad. Cade, who is increasingly into drinking and drugs, blows off practices and games, forces the three friends to set up tryouts with three possible players, including a girl. The dialogue, which mostly takes place as they drive around the Seattle area, rings of authenticity. There's lots of humor, mostly focusing on guy-to-guy insults. The coming-of-age awareness concerns whether they are too set in their ways and if they should be more open to new friends and experiences.

GRADES: 8–10

REVIEWS: *Kirkus* 3/15/02, *Publishers Weekly* 3/11/02, *SLJ* 3/02, *VOYA* 8/02

Rapp, Adam. *Punkzilla.* 256 p. TR. Candlewick Press. 978-0-7636-3031-7. 2009. $16.99.

Jamie, a.k.a. Punkzilla, due to his affection for punk rock, approaches his fifteenth birthday and embarks on another journey. Earlier he tried to quietly escape from Buckner Military Academy to Portland, Oregon. This second trip is also a secret, a secret he shares with his dying brother Peter, a playwright living in Memphis. Rapp adopts a letter-writing style of novel as Jamie communicates his feelings through the written word. Jamie is struggling to find himself and is sidetracked by using meth and living on the streets. This novel includes many grim and alarming situations, but also packs a powerful punch about teens growing up alone and trying to survive day by day.

GRADES: 10–12

REVIEWS: *Booklist* 4/15/09, *Publishers Weekly* 5/25/09, *SLJ* 7/09, *VOYA* 8/09

AWARDS: Printz Honor

Reinhardt, Dana. *A Brief Chapter in My Impossible Life.* 256 p. PB. Random House Children's Books. 978-0-375-84691-5. 2007. $8.99. CD. Random House Audio Publishing Group. 978-0-307-28566-9. 2006. $38.25. CASS. Random House Audio Publishing Group. 978-0-307-28565-2. 2006. $35.00. EB. Random House Audio Publishing Group. 978-0-7393-4461-3. 2006. $38.25.

Simone Turner-Bloom has always known she was adopted but has avoided asking questions about her past. At age sixteen she ponders about Rivka, her birth mother. When Rivka calls suggesting that mother and daughter meet, it comes as a shock to Simone. What she doesn't count on is becoming immersed with her biological mother's life. Simone learns of her Orthodox Jewish roots and becomes familiar with a new culture. At the same time she becomes involved with a boy who evolves into a guide during this period of Simone's self-discovery. Reinhardt's work connects on levels of adoption and religion as Simone uncovers new layers of her own life.

GRADES: 9–12

REVIEWS: *Booklist* 1/01/06, *Publishers Weekly* 1/02/06, *SLJ* 3/06, *VOYA* 4/06

Salinger, J. D. *The Catcher in the Rye.* N/A. TR. Book Wholesalers, Incorporated. 978-0-7587-7857-4. 2002. $13.19. LB. Perma-Bound Books. 978-0-8479-1220-9. 1951. $13.99. RE. San Val, Incorporated. 978-1-4176-4639-5. 2000. $25.75. PB. Little, Brown & Company. 978-0-316-76948-8. 1991. $6.99.

Salinger's classic work may be the link to all coming-of-age teen novels. Holden Caulfield is the narrator who relates his experiences in New York City following expulsion from a college prep school in Pennsylvania. Holden is fed up with the students and faculty of his former school. He considers them superficial or "phony." Holden spends a total of three days in the city trying to find his life's direction. During the novel Holden is lonely and drinks often; he pictures himself in a large field of rye, catching running children trying to prevent them from plunging off a cliff. Decades after being published, Salinger's work remains controversial due to language and sexual issues. However, the story is powerful and will connect with many older teen readers.

GRADES: 9–12

Selvadurai, Shyam. *Swimming in the Monsoon Sea.* No formats available in print.

Fourteen-year-old Amrith De Alwis is trying to distance himself from his parents' death that happened eight years ago. Amrith is being raised in 1980 Sri Lanka by his Aunt Budle (who is actually his mother's best friend) and her husband Uncle Lucky. He is startled by the arrival of his real uncle and his sixteen-year-old male cousin, Niresh. He develops a crush on Niresh, but becomes jealous when the boy pays more attention to Aunt Budle's daughters. Amrith experiences a coming-of-age period by dealing with his newfound cousin, his lingering grief, and his awakening sexuality.

GRADES: 9–12

REVIEWS: *Booklist* 9/15/05, *Kirkus* 9/01/05, *SLJ* 11/05

Shepard, Jim. *Project X.* N/A. TR. Knopf Doubleday Publishing Group. 978-1-4000-3348-5. 2005. $14.00. RE. San Val, Incorporated. 978-1-4176-7599-9. 2005. $24.45.

Edwin Hanratty feels stuck at the bottom of the eighth-grade pecking order. He's beaten, mocked by bullies, disliked by his teachers, and unconnected with his exasperated parents. He shares his loneliness with his even more isolated friend Flake. The two boys' anger is presented in the pitch-perfect dialogue of teens existing outside the popular crowd. Their disturbed minds create a frightening take on the social order of high school and they hatch a plan of vengeance. Shepard does not try to create a positive coming-of-age tale. Instead his characters are dysfunctional and grow in a way that is alien to the majority of teenagers. Rough language and extreme violence mark this title for older high school readers.

GRADES: 10–12

REVIEWS: *Booklist* 1/01/04, *Publishers Weekly* 11/24/03, *SLJ* 5/04, *VOYA* 6/04

AWARDS: Alex Award

Smith, Andrew. *In the Path of Falling Objects.* 336 p. TR. Feiwel & Friends. 978-0-312-37558-4. 2009. $17.99. CD. Random House Audio Publishing Group. 978-0-7393-8652-1. 2009. $44.00.

Set in the late 1960s, this story is about brothers Jonah and Simon who are ages sixteen and fourteen. They've been abandoned by their mother and have only a dead horse and a gun as they hitchhike across the blazing New Mexico desert. Fate has them sharing a ride with Mitch and his girlfriend Lily. Mitch is an unstable murderer and the boys are powerless to deal with his insanity. This is a grim novel, but Jonah matures to help his younger brother survive Mitch's trap. Fair warning: there is plenty of blood and gore as several key characters do not survive the final scene. Older readers will be fascinated reading about how the brothers go about escaping Mitch's control.

GRADES: 10–12

REVIEWS: *Booklist* 11/01/09, *Publishers Weekly* 10/12/09, *SLJ* 11/09

Smith, Betty. *A Tree Grows in Brooklyn.* Page count varies with edition. There are significant formats currently available in print.

This coming-of-age novel is the narrative of three generations in a poor American family and details urban life at the beginning of the twentieth century. Eleven-year-old Francie Nolan and her younger brother Neeley collect scraps of junk to sell for a few pennies. They try to save money and Francie's bank becomes the symbol of the Nolan family's struggle for self-reliance and also their dreams. Francie's mother works hard scrubbing floors in the hope that her daughter can achieve a better life, possibly even college. This classic work shows a girl coming of age under harsh economic conditions. *A Tree Grows in Brooklyn* is another title that has consistently appeared on school recommended reading lists.

GRADES: 9–12

Smith, Sherri L. *Lucy the Giant.* No formats available in print.

Lucy Otsego is six feet tall and lives in Alaska with her drunken father. By adopting a stray dog, Lucy attempts to pull herself out of her emotional slump. When the dog dies, she ditches school and without thinking takes off to Kodiak where fishing crews hire workers. She manages to land a job on a crabbing ship and the dangerous work is always in the background. Lucy is a teen trying to become self-reliant and better herself in one of the world's harshest environments. This title is out of print, but if copies are on your shelves, hang on to them. Lucy's voice is powerful and engaging and has appeal for many readers.

GRADES: 9–12

REVIEWS: *Booklist* 2/15/02, *Kirkus* 12/01/01, *Publishers Weekly* 12/24/01, *SLJ* 1/02

Southgate, Martha. *The Fall of Rome.* 224 p. TR. Simon & Schuster. 978-0-7432-2721-6. 2002. $14.00. PB. Simon & Schuster. 978-0-7434-8256-1. 2003. $6.99.

Three distinct voices relate the series of events occurring in an upscale New England prep school. Jeremy Washington is the erudite African American academic whose carefully constructed world begins to collapse with the simultaneous arrival of Jana Hansen, a high-spirited, divorced English teacher, and Rashid Bryson, one of the few African American students at the elite Chelsea

School. Washington feels his place is to continue the tradition of the school, not to make waves. Rashid and Jana feel the time for rebellion about the status quo is long overdue. Themes of discipline and challenging authority clash with high emotions between the three characters. Rashid is a teen coming of age in a different setting from where he grew up. His relationship with his teachers involves both conflict and support. This title is a great read for older teens, especially in a group setting discussing racism.

GRADES: 9–12

REVIEWS: *Booklist* 10/15/01, *Kirkus* 11/15/01, *Publishers Weekly* 10/10/01, *SLJ* 8/02

AWARDS: Alex Award

Stork, Francisco X. *Marcelo in the Real World.* 320 p. TR. Scholastic, Incorporated. 978-0-545-05474-4. 2009. $17.99. CD. Random House Audio Publishing Group. 978-0-7393-7989-9. 2009. $40.00. CD. Random House Audio Publishing Group. 978-0-7393-7991-2. 2009. $60.00.

Seventeen-year-old Marcelo Sandoval marches to the beat of a different drummer—literally. He perceives internal music in his head; he is obsessed with religion; he has difficulty interacting with others—behaviors that place him at the high-functioning end of the autism spectrum. His father insists he come to work in the mailroom of his law offices. There Marcelo is happy with the routine of work, but he has trouble coping with office politics. He is an innocent with a strong moral compass, but as he adjusts to the "real world" he finds things do not happen in a linear fashion. The powerful writing will work best for older teens accepting the challenge of a layered story.

GRADES: 10–12

REVIEWS: *Booklist* 4/01/09, *Kirkus* 1/15/09, *Publishers Weekly* 1/05/09, *SLJ* 3/09, *VOYA* 6/09

AWARDS: BBYA Top Ten

Thomas, Rob. *Rats Saw God: A Comic Emotionally Charged Tale.* N/A. LB. San Val, Incorporated. 978-0-613-00115-1. 1996. $13.00. RE. San Val, Incorporated. 978-1-4177-8055-6. 2007. $17.20. PB. Simon & Schuster Children's Publishing. 978-1-4169-3897-2. 2007. $6.99. EB. Recorded Books, LLC. 978-1-4237-1975-5. N/A. $59.00.

Senior Steve York has moved from Houston to live with his mother and her new husband in San Diego. He's often stoned and with his 4.0 GPA plummeting, he's now in danger of not graduating. Steve reflects on recent occurrences and his life in general. He meets Dub (a.k.a. Wanda) in his art study group, a connection that leads to first kiss, first sex, and first betrayal. Steve's coming of age is a series of explosive changes in relationships. The edginess of this title makes it almost a perfect read for older teens questioning their life's direction.

GRADES: 9–12

REVIEWS: *Booklist* 6/01/96, *Kirkus* 4/01/96, *Publishers Weekly* 6/10/96, *SLJ* 6/96, *VOYA* 6/96

Thompson, Kate. *Creature of the Night.* 256 p. TR. Roaring Brook Press. 978-1-59643-511-7. 2009. $17.95. EB. Roaring Brook Press. 978-1-4299-1973-9. 2009. $17.95.

There is an undercurrent of fantasy and mystery in Thompson's coming-of-age tale set in Ireland. Fourteen-year-old Bobby is entering a time in his life where he is easily influenced by the wrong crowd. His mother hopes to remove him from Dublin's rough crowd and mother and son relocate to an old farmhouse in the country. There Bobby learns of a murdered child and believes he sees a weird faerie woman lurking around the house. As Bobby tries to understand the strange happenings, he also discovers his mechanical talent and grows to become responsible. This nifty combination of thriller and a coming-of-age story will have broad appeal.

GRADES: 9–12

REVIEWS: *Booklist* 4/01/09, *SLJ* 8/09

Tucker, Todd. *Over and Under.* 288 p. TR. St. Martin's Press. 978-0-312-37990-2. 2008. $23.95. EB. St. Martin's Press. 978-1-4299-8933-6. 2008. $23.95. LP. Thorndike Press. 978-1-4104-1515-8. 2009. $30.95.

Tom and Andy are fourteen-year-old boys whose last names are Kruer and Gray, respectively. They live in southern Indiana during the summer of 1979 and their friendship is about to be tested. The Borden Casket Company, where their fathers both work, is going on strike, and Andy's dad is management, while Tom's dad is labor. Acts of vandalism go fatally wrong and the young boys are involved. This is an outdoors tale with Tom and Andy shooting guns and "having each other's back" as they become aware of adults that manipulate the truth and will go to no ends to cover up wrongdoing. The boys are heroes and there is much to like about this novel marketed as an adult read. It has much teen appeal, especially in rural service areas.

GRADES: 9–12

REVIEWS: *Booklist* 6/01/08, *Publishers Weekly* 5/26/08, *VOYA* 10/08

AWARDS: Alex Award

Vaught, Susan. *Stormwitch.* No formats available in print.

In 1969 a girl calls on the magic of her African ancestors to fight racism. Sixteen-year-old orphan Ruba moves from Haiti to coastal Mississippi. There her grandmother Jones thinks Ruba's spells and dances are Satan's tools. Ruba uses her powers to fight Klansmen and even a hurricane powered by an uncaring spirit. The twenty-first century tragedies following Katrina in New Orleans and also Mississippi and the earthquake in Haiti make this story a fascinating blend of magic and history. It also features a young girl becoming empowered against racism and violence.

GRADES: 8–10

REVIEWS: *Booklist* 2/15/05, *SLJ* 5/05, *VOYA* 2/05

von Ziegesar, Cecily. *Gossip Girl.* N/A. RE. San Val, Incorporated. 978-0-613-98315-0. 2003. $17.20. PB. Little, Brown Books for Young Readers. 978-0-316-02456-3. 2007. $10.99. PB. Grand Central Publishing. 978-0-446-61315-6. 2003. $6.99. CASS. Hachette Audio. 978-1-58621-570-5. 2003. $16.98. EB. Little, Brown Books for Young Readers. 978-0-316-02016-9. 2007. $10.99.

This series has its share of controversy as it is populated by hard-drinking and sex-crazed poor little rich kids in New York City. Blair Waldorf deals with her stoned hottie of a boyfriend, Nate, and her former best friend, Serena, who is just expelled from a boarding school. Parties, clothes, and shallow people are all fascinating, like watching a train wreck about to happen. Overseeing all the shenanigans is the omniscient narrator, Gossip Girl. Oh, the things she can dish about. This series offends many adults, but they also fly off of young adult shelves. This series is a must-have for public libraries. Other titles in the series include *You Know You Love Me, All I Want Is Everything, Because I'm Worth It, I Like It Like That, You're the One That I Want, Nobody Does It Better, Nothing Can Keep Us Together, Only in Your Dreams, Would I Lie to You?, Don't You Forget About Me, It Had To Be You, I Will Always Love You.*

GRADES: 9–12

REVIEWS: *Kirkus* 4/15/02, *Publishers Weekly* 2/21/02, *SLJ* 6/02, *VOYA* 6/02

AWARDS: Quick Picks Top Ten

Wallace, Rich. *One Good Punch.* 128 p. TR. Random House Children's Books. 978-0-375-81352-8. 2007. $15.99. PB. Random House Children's Books. 978-0-440-42260-0. 2009. $5.99.

Michael Kerrigan is all about being in great shape and is pumped to start his senior year, especially his last season on the track team. His talent is of state championship caliber. To keep occupied he writes obituaries for the local newspaper. All is well until a friend stashes four joints in his school locker, which are found in a random drug sweep. Michael has a decision to make. Should he rat out his friend? Or should he accept the punishment that will probably end his athletic career? This coming-of-age story shows how one mistake can lead to serious backlash. The drug-use slant to the story is fairly tame, which makes this title suitable for a wide range of readers.

GRADES: 9–12

REVIEWS: *Booklist* 9/01/07, *VOYA* 10/07

Weaver, Will. *Memory Boy.* N/A. RE. San Val, Incorporated. 978-0-613-62395-7. 2003. $17.20. PB. HarperCollins Publishers. 978-0-06-440854-7. 2003. $6.99.

Following a massive natural disaster, a suburban family must cope with the breakdown of society. Two years after Mount Rainier exploded, the rain of ash has caused huge environmental issues and strict anti-pollution laws. Cars and trucks are virtually banned, electric power heavily rationed, fresh food is almost nonexistent. Sixteen-year-old Miles constructs a wind-driven vehicle made from bicycles and a sailboat. His cleverly constructed craft helps his family navigate the dangerous country full of refugees and bandits. Miles is a teen lacking physical power but his intellect allows him to solve problems and become a hero. This is a great middle school group read for both school and public libraries.

GRADES: 7–10

REVIEWS: *Booklist* 2/01/01, *Kirkus* 1/01/01, *Publishers Weekly* 1/22/01, *SLJ* 6/01, *VOYA* 8/01

Wilson, Martin. *What They Always Tell Us.* 304 p. TR. Random House Children's Books. 978-0-385-73507-0. 2008. $15.99. LB. Random House Children's Books. 978-0-385-90500-8. 2008. $18.99.

Two brothers tell this story in alternating chapters. James is a popular, smart senior who is on track to be accepted to Duke. He's in the process of breaking up with Alice, whose only attraction for him was their sexual relationship. His brother Alex is a junior who recklessly swallows Pine-Sol at a party. Nathan, who is a friend of James, steers Alex to running but what Alex really wants is Nathan, who returns the attention. Wilson's writing relates young men making decisions that will change their lives as they try to help each other, along with a mysterious neighbor boy. The complex story line is a better fit for older teens.

GRADES: 10–12

REVIEWS: *Booklist* 11/15/08, *Kirkus* 7/15/08, *Publishers Weekly* 7/28/08, *SLJ* 9/08, *VOYA* 12/08

Zusak, Markus. *I Am the Messenger.* 368 p. TR. Random House Children's Books. 978-0-375-83099-0. 2005. $16.95. RE. San Val, Incorporated. 978-1-4177-0023-3. 2006. $19.60. PB. Random House Children's Books. 978-0-375-83667-1. 2006.

$8.95. CD. Random House Audio Publishing Group. 978-0-7393-3729-5. 2006. $45.00. CD. Random House Audio Publishing Group. 978-0-7393-3692-2. 2006. $46.75. EB. Random House Audio Publishing Group. 978-0-7393-4844-4. 2007. $46.75.

Ed Kennedy is nineteen years old and works as a cabbie. His dad died of alcoholism and now he has little to do except share a run-down apartment with his shaggy and smelly dog. Then, after he stops a bank robbery, Ed begins receiving anonymous messages marked in code on playing cards in the mail. The cab driver next begins a series of missions, which may be simple or dangerous. He saves a woman from her husband's nightly rape, but he also brings a congregation to an abandoned church. Ed's search for the meaning of his tasks prompts him to complete each one and they could very well be a series of mysteries that makes or breaks his life. The older character and Zusak's intricate plot make this title a nice selection for older teens.

GRADES: 10–12

REVIEWS: *Booklist* 1/01/05, *Kirkus* 1/01/05, *Publishers Weekly* 1/17/05, *SLJ* 2/05, *VOYA* 2/05

AWARDS: BBYA Top Ten, Printz Honor

5

Fantasy Novels

Every so often I run into adults not totally in tune with the young adult publishing world. At those times I've heard comments like, "Aren't all young adults books just fantasy and horror?" From a casual glance, one may believe that to be true. Bookstore displays and library shelves can be dominated by fantasy titles that emphasize the supernatural or magical realms. Of course, many of the more dedicated young adult readers thrive on fantasy novels.

For this section there is a loose association of fantasy titles that include works that may seem to be more science fiction, horror, or historical fiction. However, in my opinion, each title has some element of fantasy in its makeup.

Fantasy can be marked by use of magic in its plot or setting. Other titles feature characters that can morph into supernatural forms enabling them to move to alternate worlds. Wands shoot out spells, fantastic creatures cooperate (or not) with humans, or vampires stalk the countryside seeking to impose their will on others. There can be leaps of logic as magic trumps science in fantasy tales.

The fantasy world may appear to be similar to ours, but there are subtle and not so subtle differences. Parallel worlds may open with a medieval feel but closer look may reveal rudimentary technology being used. Animals may talk and become anthropomorphic allies to human characters. A story's base may be rooted in legend or myth such as the tales surrounding the King Arthur legend.

Regardless of setting or characterization, danger is prevalent throughout fantasy. The main character often embarks on a quest to seek truth or to save his homeland. Along the way are hardships either formed by nature or roadblocks constructed by villains. Accompanying the main characters on this hero's journey may be a group of loyal friends, or a creature sworn to protect the hero. The role of protector is often filled by dragons. This is the boiled down essence of Tolkien who set the bar high with his *Lord of the Rings* trilogy, a work whose theme has been adapted throughout the fantasy genre.

But not all works are set in a parallel medieval-like world. Urban fantasy is fast becoming a popular subgenre. Here the magic often goes awry leading to horrifying results that bring peril to the main character. Supernatural beings roam through the modern urban settings, emphasizing the gritty poverty of decaying urban centers.

Whatever the setting, or however magic is incorporated into the story, fantasy remains one of the more popular styles in young adult literature. The wild success of J. K. Rowling's *Harry Potter* series pumped a huge interest into fantasy, making it more of a mainstream user-friendly genre. Undoubtedly, more wonderful stories will continue to be written.

Many titles listed here are parts of a lengthy series as readers seem to be comfortable with the characters and wish to read more of their adventures. At the end of each annotation I've included other titles in the series. From the wide range of story lines in fantasy, it's obvious all libraries should acquire a working knowledge of titles and authors that are offered in this section.

Adams, Richard. *Watership Down.* 496 p. TR. Simon & Schuster. 978-0-7432-7770-9. 2005. $16.00. PB. HarperCollins Publishers. 978-0-380-00293-1. 1976. $7.99. CASS. Literate Ear, Incorporated. N/A. 1993. $10.80. EB. Simon & Schuster. 978-1-4391-7612-2. 2009. $16.00.

A traveling group of rabbits copes with many dangers on their journey in search of a new home. Fiver, a young rabbit who is a seer, has a vision showing his warren's imminent destruction. He convinces his brother Hazel they need to leave and Hazel becomes the leader of the group. Along the way they encounter many dangerous situations, especially their stay at Cowslip's Warren, which they learn is a human farm designed to harvest the rabbits. Eventually the rabbits arrive at Watership Down, a safe place where they are reunited with rabbits from their original home. This classic tale features anthropomorphic animals but also offers a subtle commentary on society.

GRADES: 7–10

Alexander, Lloyd, ed. *Firebirds: An Anthology of Original Fantasy and Science Fiction.* 432 p. PB. Penguin Group (USA) Incorporated. 978-0-14-240320-4. 2005. $9.99.

Some of the top writers of fantasy and science fiction present offerings in this collection of 16 short stories. The prolific group of authors includes Nancy Springer, Garth Nix, Diana Wynne Jones, and Megan Whalen Turner. The stories contain a morality play framework and end with readers saying "hmmm." Each work leans to the more mature and thoughtful reader, but these stories will appeal to imaginative young adults of many ages.

GRADES: 9–12

REVIEWS: *Booklist* 10/15/03, *Kirkus* 8/01/03, *Publishers Weekly* 9/01/03, *SLJ* 10/03, *VOYA* 12/03

Alexander, Lloyd. *Westmark.* 184 p. TR. Perfection Learning Corporation. 978-0-8124-0105-9. 2002. $14.65. LB. Perma-Bound Books. 978-0-8479-9903-3. 1981. $5.99.

A young printer's apprentice goes on the run after his master is murdered in the fictional kingdom of Westmark. Times are complicated in this society that resembles situations that occurred in the eighteenth century during the French Revolution. The king is ineffective due to his deteriorating mental condition and anyone challenging authority is subject to punishment and prison. Young Theo finds himself in trouble after he attacks a soldier that results in the murder of Anton, his master. Although Alexander does not use magic in this work, the setting is in a world that is not historical in nature. Other titles in the trilogy are *The Kestrel* and *The Beggar Queen.*

GRADES: 7–10

Anthony, Piers. *On a Pale Horse.* 336 p. PB. Random House Publishing Group. 978-0-345-33858-7. 1986. $7.99.

In the late twentieth century, Zane is living a pathetic life without money or employment. When a magic gem merchant cheats Zane out of an opportunity for romance, Zane decides to take his own life. As he starts to pull the trigger, he sees Death advancing on him. Startled, he pulls the gun from his own head and shoots Death. Now he learns he must take the position of the man he killed, thus becoming the New Death. He's instructed in his new duties, which involve balancing good and evil and determining if souls are sent to heaven or hell. Complicated situations may be too deep for younger readers.

GRADES: 9–12

Atwater-Rhodes, Amelia. *Demon in My View* (*Den of Shadows* **series**). N/A. LB. San Val, Incorporated. 978-0-613-69052-2. 2000. $13.00. PB. Random House Children's Books. 978-0-440-22884-4. 2001. $6.99.

Atwater-Rhodes sets her novel in the fictional town of Ramsa, New York, and details the story of teenager Jessica Ashley Allodola. Jessica is gorgeous, dark black hair with green-eyes, pale skin, and a perfect body. She seems immune to adolescent awkwardness and people are afraid of her because they believe her to be a witch. A boy named Alex arrives at school. He seems to be very similar to Aubrey, the most powerful vampire in the world of Jessica's books. An interesting and dangerous world where witches are vying for ultimate power swirls around Jessica and she wonders what is going and how she will survive. This title is the sequel to *In the Forests of the Night.* Other titles in the series are *Shattered Mirror, Midnight Predator,* and *Persistence of Memory.*

GRADES: 9–12

REVIEWS: *Publishers Weekly* 9/24/01

Barker, Clive. *Abarat.* 431 p. TR. Perfection Learning Corporation. 978-0-7569-3248-0. 2004. $14.65. TR. HarperCollins Publishers. 978-0-06-440733-5. 2003.

$14.99. LB. HarperCollins Publishers. 978-0-06-051084-8. 2002. $26.89. RE. San Val, Incorporated. 978-1-4177-3607-2. 2005. $23.30. PB. HarperCollins Publishers. 978-0-06-059638-5. 2006. $7.99. CASS. HarperCollins Publishers. 978-0-06-051075-6. 2002. $39.95.

Candy Quackenbush skips out of school, the accumulating act of her being tired of her humdrum existence. Wandering to an empty field, she finds herself transported to Abarat, a magical realm of 25 islands. Candy finds herself in the middle of a power struggle for control of the islands, each of which represents one hour of the day with the extra designated for Time Outside of Time. Candy realizes that she has become the deciding factor in either the survival or destruction of the island chain. Candy's journey to the frightening world is suitable for high school readers.

GRADES: 9–12

REVIEWS: *Booklist* 9/01/02, *Kirkus* 9/01/02, *Publishers Weekly* 6/24/02, *SLJ* 10/02, *VOYA* 10/02

Barron, T. A. *Child of Dark Prophecy* (*The Great Tree of Avalon*: Book One). 432 p. TR. Penguin Group (USA) Incorporated. 978-0-399-23763-8. 2004. $19.99. RE. San Val, Incorporated. 978-1-4177-4602-6. 2005. $18.40. CASS. Random House Audio Publishing Group. 978-1-4000-9100-3. 2004. $50.00. EB. Random House Audio Publishing Group. 978-0-7393-7223-4. 2008. $63.75.

Seventeen-year-old Tamwyn fears he is the Dark Child destined to destroy Avalon. Barron re-imagines the legendary world of Avalon as a gigantic tree, with a separate realm located on each of its seven roots and stars hanging in the unseen branches far atop its trunk. In Avalon's year of 1002, the only hope of saving Avalon lies in finding Merlin's true heir. A crippling drought has brought the realm to the verge of warfare, and Tamwyn seeks the advice of the fabled Lady of the Lake. The lengthy story incorporates humor with high fantasy and will appeal to readers willing to tackle an epic tale. The other titles in the Great Tree of Avalon series are *Shadows on the Stars* and *The Eternal Flame*.

GRADES: 7–10

REVIEWS: *Booklist* 9/01/04, *Kirkus* 9/15/04, *Publishers Weekly* 10/25/04, *SLJ* 10/04, *VOYA* 12/04

Bass, L. G. *Sign of the Qin* (*Outlaws of Moonshadow Marsh*). N/A. LB. Perma-Bound Books. 978-0-605-55789-5. 2004. $7.99. EB. Random House Audio Publishing Group. 978-0-307-24597-7. N/A. $42.50. EB. Random House Audio Publishing Group. 978-0-7393-4950-2. 2007. $42.50.

Fantasy themes abound when a volcanic eruption releases a demon sealed away for centuries. Shortly following the eruption, the Emperor's first son is born marked with the sign of the Qin, which is the brand of the outlaw. The child may be the new Starlord come to restore justice to the land. The emperor decides to kill his heir, but before the assassination is completed, a mysterious monk whose tattoos foretell the future foils the plot. Fast-moving action and intricate plotting mark this story that adds an Asian slant to the fantasy world.

GRADES: 7–10

REVIEWS: *Booklist* 4/15/04, *Publishers Weekly* 3/29/04, *SLJ* 4/04, *VOYA* 6/04

Beddor, Frank. *The Looking Glass Wars.* 384 p. TR. Penguin Group (USA) Incorporated. 978-0-8037-3153-0. 2006. $17.99. RE. San Val, Incorporated. 978-1-4177-8744-9. 2005. $19.65. CD. Scholastic, Incorporated. 978-0-439-89825-6. 2006. $34.95. PLAY. Findaway World, LLC. 978-1-60252-616-7. 2007. $54.99.

Beddor mines the traditional Alice in Wonderland tale by introducing Alyss Heart, the heir to the Wonderland throne. After her vicious Aunt Redd murders her parents, the King and Queen of Hearts, Alyss escapes to Victorian London. She represses her memories until her wedding when the royal bodyguard Hatter Madigan crashes the ceremony. He's determined to start another war for Wonderland's throne. Other titles in the series are *Seeing Redd* and *ArchEnemy.*

GRADES: 7–10

REVIEWS: *Booklist* 9/01/06, *Publishers Weekly* 8/14/06, *SLJ* 10/06, *VOYA* 10/06

Bell, Hilari. *The Goblin Wood.* 371 p. TR. Perfection Learning Corporation. 978-0-7569-3253-4. 2004. $14.65. EB. HarperCollins Publishers. 978-0-06-189098-7. 2009. $9.99.

When the story opens, twelve-year-old Makenna has just witnessed the murder of her mother, the local hedgewitch. A priest of the Hierarchy ordered the killing and it was carried out by the villagers whom Makenna's mother had always helped. Angry and bitter, the grieving girl seeks revenge on the village and runs away into the woods, where she befriends the goblins. Five years later she meets Tobin, a knight who wishes to capture the sorceress who leads the goblins, which of course is Makenna. Bell offers insight on the grey areas between good and evil that are not always easily determined. Middle school readers will be interested in her mythical world.

GRADES: 6–9

REVIEWS: *Booklist* 6/01/03, *Publishers Weekly* 3/24/03, *SLJ* 7/03, *VOYA* 8/03

Bell, Hilari. *The Last Knight.* 368 p. TR. HarperCollins Publishers. 978-0-06-082503-4. 2007. $16.99. PB. HarperCollins Publishers. 978-0-06-082505-8. 2008. $8.99. EB. HarperCollins Publishers. 978-0-06-189748-1. 2009. $6.99.

This story relates the misadventures of a sarcastic seventeen-year-old ex-con and his idealistic employer, who is just one year older. Sir Michael Sevenson is a knight-errant who saves the narrator, Fisk, from a lengthy jail sentence by hiring him on as his squire. The unlikely duo rescues an imprisoned damsel in distress from a tower—only to discover that they've freed a woman suspected of murdering her husband. This magic-filled adventure has moments of downright hilarity, especially scenes involving Tipple, the alcoholic horse. Younger teens will be drawn to Bell's mix of fantasy and humor.

GRADES: 9–12

REVIEWS: *Booklist* 10/01/07, *Publishers Weekly* 9/24/07, *SLJ* 9/07, *VOYA* 10/07

Black, Holly. *Tithe: A Modern Faerie Tale.* 320 p. TR. Simon & Schuster Children's Publishing. 978-0-689-84924-4. 2002. $17.99. LB. Perma-Bound Books. 978-0-605-01295-0. 2002. $8.99. RE. San Val, Incorporated. 978-0-613-73456-1. 2004. $19.65. PB. Simon & Schuster Children's Publishing. 978-0-689-86704-0. 2004. $8.99. EB. Simon & Schuster Children's Publishing. 978-1-4391-0662-4. 2008. $8.99.

Sixteen-year-old Kaye has a rock singer for a mother and hangs out with a group of faeries who have been her friends since childhood. When she rescues a gorgeous knight, the act of mercy throws her into a terrifying otherworld war between two rival faerie kingdoms. Holly Black combines the gritty setting of industrial New Jersey with the horror of the faerie worlds. Many subplots in the story involve sexual situations, but the totally creative edginess of the story will have broad appeal for older readers of fantasy. A companion title is *Ironside: A Modern Faery's Tale.*

GRADES: 9–12

REVIEWS: *Booklist* 2/15/03, *Kirkus* 9/01/02, *Publishers Weekly* 10/28/02, *SLJ* 10/02

AWARDS: Teens Top Ten

Black, Holly. *Valiant: A Modern Tale of Faerie.* 320 p. TR. Simon & Schuster Children's Publishing. 978-0-689-86822-1. 2005. $17.99. RE. San Val, Incorporated. 978-1-4177-7994-9. 2006. $19.65. PB. Simon & Schuster Children's Publishing. 978-0-689-86823-8. 2006. $8.99. CD. Random House Audio Publishing Group. 978-0-7393-3598-7. 2006. $50.00. CASS. Random House Audio Publishing Group. 978-0-7393-3597-0. 2006. $40.00. EB. Simon & Schuster Children's Publishing. 978-1-4169-3451-6. 2006. $8.99. LP. Thorndike Press. 978-0-7862-8226-5. N/A. $21.95.

Seventeen-year-old Valerie Russell walks in on her boyfriend having sex with her mother, so she bolts from Jersey to Manhattan. There she falls in with some creepy homeless teens living on an abandoned subway platform. The drugs they shoot are faerie drugs and Val joins her fellow teens as couriers for

Ravus, a troll who plays the role of the Beast in this takeoff on the Beauty and the Beast plot. Val is soon addicted to the drugs but also becomes involved with the conflicted politics between rival faerie courts. Language and sexual issues are laced throughout this story that will appeal to fans of urban fantasy.

GRADES: 9–12

REVIEWS: *Booklist* 7/01/05, *Kirkus* 6/01/05, *Publishers Weekly* 8/01/05, *SLJ* 6/05, *VOYA* 8/05

Bradbury, Ray. *Something Wicked This Way Comes.* 304 p. TR. HarperCollins Publishers. 978-0-380-97727-7. 1999. $18.99. PB. HarperCollins Publishers. 978-0-380-72940-1. 1998. $7.99. CD. Blackstone Audio, Incorporated. 978-1-4332-1079-2. 2007. $24.00. CD. Blackstone Audio, Incorporated. 978-1-4332-1080-8. 2007. $19.95. CASS. Blackstone Audio, Incorporated. 978-1-4332-1078-5. 2007. $22.95. CASS. Recorded Books, LLC. 978-1-4025-2492-9. 1999. $24.95. EB. Blackstone Audio, Incorporated. 978-1-4332-8626-1. 2007. $19.95. LP. Center Point Large Print. 978-1-58547-020-4. 2000. $26.95.

William Halloway and Jim Nightshade are almost fourteen when they encounter a stranger selling lightning rods who warns them a storm is coming their way. Soon the boys find a handbill advertising Cooger & Dark's Pandemonium Shadow Show, a traveling carnival that is both enthralling and dangerous. Will's father also is interested in the show, especially when they watch Mr. Cooger riding backward on the carousel (while the music plays backward), and when he steps off, he is twelve years old. Bradbury's classic story ushers readers into a dark and thrilling setting that on the surface seems joyfully innocent.

GRADES: 7–10

Bradley, Marion Zimmer. *The Mists of Avalon.* 912 p. TR. Random House Publishing Group. 978-0-345-35049-7. 1987. $18.00. CASS. Recorded Books, LLC. 978-1-55690-917-7. 1993. $70.00. EB. Adobe Systems, Incorporated. 978-1-58945-945-8. 2001. $15.00.

In this retelling of the Arthurian legend, Morgaine witnesses the rise of Uther Pendragon to the throne of Camelot. She is given in a fertility ritual to a young man she will later learn is Arthur, her half-brother. Morgaine also conceives a child, Gwydion, or "bright one," later called Mordred, or "evil counsel" in the Saxon tongue. When the Knights of the Round Table of Camelot leave to search for the Holy Grail, Arthur's and Mordred's armies square off. *The Mists of Avalon* is an essential work that stands out from the many versions of the Arthurian tale.

GRADES: 9–12

REVIEWS: *Booklist* 1/01/90

Bray, Libba. *Going Bovine.* 496 p. TR. Random House Children's Books. 978-0-385-73397-7. 2009. $17.99. LB. Random House Children's Books. 978-0-385-90411-7. 2009. $20.99. CD. Random House Audio Publishing Group. 978-0-7393-8557-9. 2009. $50.00. CD. Random House Audio Publishing Group. 978-0-7393-8559-3. 2009. $75.00.

Cameron Smith, age sixteen, learns he has contracted mad cow disease. It is a death sentence. After he's hospitalized, he meets a perky angel, but readers are not sure if the angel has actually appeared or Cameron is undergoing vivid hallucinations. His journey to find a cure involves a neurotic dwarf, a Norse god disguised as a yard gnome and of course his angel, Dulcie. With direct comparisons to Don Quixote, Cameron is chasing his own impossible dream, which is his hope to survive. Along the way, Libba Bray inserts satire about religion, materialism, and education. The journey to other worlds is fantastic and the destination is sobering. Language and the complicated plot make this work best suited for high school readers.

GRADES: 9–12

REVIEWS: *Booklist* 8/01/09, *Publishers Weekly* 8/03/09, *SLJ* 9/09, *VOYA* 10/09

AWARDS: Printz Winner

Bray, Libba. *A Great and Terrible Beauty (Gemma Doyle Trilogy).* 416 p. TR. Random House Children's Books. 978-0-385-73028-0. 2003. $16.95. LB. Perma-Bound Books. 978-0-605-01321-6. 2003. $9.99. PB. Random House Children's Books. 978-0-385-73231-4. 2005. $9.99. CD. Random House Audio Publishing Group. 978-0-8072-2376-5. 2007. $44.00. CD. Random House Audio Publishing Group. 978-1-4000-8621-4. 2004. $60.00. CASS. Random House Audio Publishing Group. 978-0-8072-2067-2. 2004. $50.00. EB. Random House Audio Publishing Group. 978-0-7393-4463-7. 2006. $59.50. LP. Thorndike Press. 978-0-7862-6504-6. 2004. $23.95.

On her sixteenth birthday, Gemma Doyle witnesses the murder of her mother on the streets of Bombay, India. She envisioned a dark shape enveloping her mother and now Gemma has been whisked off to Britain's Spence Academy. There Gemma's visions intensify and she learns she has the ability to move between two worlds. An old tragedy at Spence, the plight of teenage girls forced to marry older men, and a fantastic journey to a parallel world all come together in Bray's complicated tale. Teenage girls will love the mix of fantasy and historical fiction mixed with romance. Other titles in the series are *Rebel Angels* (Teens' Top Ten) and *The Sweet Far Thing* (Teens' Top Ten).

GRADES: 8–12

REVIEWS: *Booklist* 11/15/03, *Publishers Weekly* 12/08/03, *SLJ* 2/04, *VOYA* 4/04

AWARDS: Teens' Top Ten

Brennan, Sarah Rees. *The Demon's Lexicon.* 336p. TR. Simon & Schuster Children's Publishing. 978-1-4169-6379-0. 2009. $17.99. CD. Simon & Schuster Audio. 978-0-7435-8198-1. 2009. $34.99. EB. Simon & Schuster Children's Publishing. 978-1-4169-9492-3. 2009. $17.99.

Two brothers must protect each other's back in this gruesome tale that involves hunting down demons and killing them. Nick is a hunky guy who has a dark and brooding air. His older brother Alan is physically weaker, but knows how demons will attack them. Together they are on a quest to help two teen siblings who have been marked by demons. The raw emotions of loneliness and loyalty are set against the truly horrifying attacks by demons sent by evil magicians. The complicated plot comes together in a thrilling climactic scene not to be missed, and several scenes include horrifying deaths that are not for the squeamish. Brennan's tale has wide appeal for both boys and girls. The sequel is called *The Demon's Covenant.*

GRADES: 8–12

REVIEWS: *Booklist* 4/15/09, *SLJ* 7/09

AWARDS: BBYA Top Ten

Bujold, Lois McMaster. *The Warrior's Apprentice (Vorkosigan Saga).* 320 p. TR. New England Science Fiction Association, Incorporated. 978-1-886778-27-6. 2002. $25.00. CD. Blackstone Audio, Incorporated. 978-0-7861-7691-5. 2005. $81.00. CD. The Reader's Chair, Incorporated. 978-1-885585-14-1. 1999. $29.95. CASS. Blackstone Audio, Incorporated. 978-0-7861-3677-3. 2005. $65.95. CASS. The Reader's Chair, Incorporated. 978-1-885585-02-8. 1997. $54.00. EB. Blackstone Audio, Incorporated. 978-0-7861-5057-1. 2007. $49.95.

Seventeen-year-old Miles Vorkosigan fails to qualify for the Barrayaran Service Academy after breaking both legs during a run over an obstacle course. Not to be kept down, on a visit to Beta Colony, he obtains a ship, a pilot, and a smuggling mission, running guns to a beleaguered government. Representing himself as "Admiral Naismith," commander of the nonexistent Dendarii Mercenaries, he ushers the crew through improvisation, sheer audacity, and luck. This fantasy tale mines the theme of the underdog character challenging a huge empire and winning. Under Naismith's brilliant leadership, the Dendarii eventually take over the rest of the Oseran fleet and win the war. Other titles included in the series are *The Vor Game, Barrayar, Mirror Dance, Falling Free, Memory, A Civil Campaign, Shards of Honor, Dreamweaver's Dilemma,* and *Ethan of Athos.*

GRADES: 9–12

Bunce, Elizabeth. *A Curse Dark as Gold.* 400 p. TR. Scholastic, Incorporated. 978-0-439-89576-7. 2008. $17.99.

Charlotte takes over the family mill following her father's death, but a curse lingers over the business. When Charlotte is unable to pay the mill's mortgage, her younger sister Rosie conjures up Jack Spinner, an odd little man promising to spin straw into gold . . . for a price. There are elements of historical fiction in this tale set in England during the early years of the Industrial Revolution, and with the nod to Rumpelstiltskin, there is obvious fantasy involved. Teenage girls will also be drawn to Charlotte's romantic love life.

GRADES: 8–12

REVIEWS: *Booklist* 5/01/08, *SLJ* 5/08, *VOYA* 8/08

Cabot, Meg. *Avalon High*. 304 p. TR. HarperCollins Publishers. 978-0-06-075586-7. 2006. $16.99. LB. HarperCollins Publishers. 978-0-06-075587-4. 2006. $17.89. PB. HarperCollins Publishers. 978-0-06-075588-1. 2007. $8.99. CASS. Random House Audio Publishing Group. 978-0-307-20664-0. 2005. $35.00. EB. Harper Collins Publishers. 978-0-06-118728-5. 2005. $12.95. EB. Random House Audio Publishing Group. 978-0-7393-4469-9. 2006. $42.50.

Ellie starts her junior year at Avalon High and her parents are medieval scholars who named her for Lady Elaine, a.k.a. the Lady of Shalott. Her high school math teacher Mr. Morton belongs to a secret society dedicated to the return of Arthur and believes the Round Table will be reenacted in Ellie's school, a place where high school teens are remarkably similar to Camelot's characters. Cabot delivers a clever modern American high school take on Arthurian legend. Her effort will draw both fans of her other titles plus fantasy readers seeking a lighter take on the legend of King Arthur.

GRADES: 7–12

REVIEWS: *Booklist* 2/01/06, *Publishers Weekly* 1/23/06, *SLJ* 1/06, *VOYA* 2/06

Carey, Janet Lee. *Dragon's Keep*. 320 p. PB. Houghton Mifflin Harcourt Trade & Reference Publishers. 978-0-15-206401-3. 2008. $7.95. CASS. Recorded Books, LLC. 978-1-4281-8312-4. 2008. $61.75. EB. Recorded Books, LLC. 978-1-4356-3439-8. 2008. $1.00.

Princess Rosalind Pendragon is meant to fulfill a 600-year-old prophecy from Merlin that she will restore her family's good name and end a war. Rosalind was born with a finger that is a dragon talon, which is kept secret by her constantly wearing gloves. When Rosalind reveals her claw to Lord Faul, a dragon that has been terrorizing the island, her destiny is set in motion. Rosalind begins a journey that has her being a nursemaid to the dragon's children, but also a journey that enables her to find inner peace. The creative characterization of the dragon interacting with Rosalind will excite fans of dragon tales.

GRADES: 7–12

REVIEWS: *Booklist* 2/01/07, *Publishers Weekly* 5/07/07, *SLJ* 4/07, *VOYA* 4/07

Cashore, Kristin. *Fire.* 480 p. TR. Penguin Group (USA) Incorporated. 978-0-8037-3461-6. 2009. $17.99. CD. Penguin Group (USA) Incorporated. 978-0-14-314511-0. 2009. $39.95.

Fire is a "monster-woman" with the fundamental elements of her kind, which is breathtaking beauty that inspires nearly irresistible sexual attraction. She also has dual powers of reading thoughts and bending another's will to her purposes. However Fire struggles to use her powers for good to veer away from her father's practice of using his power to control the kingdom for evil purposes. Eventually Fire finds herself caught in the dilemma to use or not use her powers on the behalf of the royal family. The alternate world is fascinating, but the strength of this prequel to Cashore's *Graceling* is the tough-as-nails heroine who is all too human as she falls in love.

GRADES: 7–12

REVIEWS: *Booklist* 9/15/09, *Publishers Weekly* 7/20/09, *SLJ* 8/09, *VOYA* 10/09

Cashore, Kristin. *Graceling.* 408 p. TR. Houghton Mifflin Harcourt Trade & Reference Publishers. 978-0-15-206396-2. 2008. $17.00. LB. San Val, Incorporated. 978-0-606-07993-8. 2009. $20.85. PB. Houghton Mifflin Harcourt Trade & Reference Publishers. 978-0-547-25830-0. 2009. $9.99. CD. Full Cast Audio. 978-1-934180-89-1. 2009. $39.95. EB. Houghton Mifflin Harcourt Publishing Company. 978-0-547-35127-8. 2008. $17.00.

In this alternate word "Graced" means to be gifted in a particular way. These special people are marked with eyes that are different colors. Katsa's "Grace" is that she is a hardened fighter and is invincible. She is under the control of her uncle, a king of one of the seven kingdoms. Katsa is sent out to torture subjects who have committed infractions against her uncle. But the world-weary girl finds hope in Prince Po, who has his own special "Grace." Together they partner to undertake a dangerous mission to rescue a prisoner who has been unjustly abducted. Cashore's story is one of incredible creativity and readers will discover a very likable hero in Katsa.

GRADES: 7–12

REVIEWS: *Booklist* 10/01/08, *SLJ* 10/08, *VOYA* 10/08

AWARDS: Teens' Top Ten

Chabon, Michael. *The Amazing Adventures of Kavalier and Clay.* 656 p. TR. Picador. 978-0-312-28299-8. 2001. $16.00. TR. Random House Publishing Group. 978-0-679-45004-7. 2000. $27.95. CD. Brilliance Audio. 978-1-59737-157-5. 2005. $34.95. CASS. Brilliance Audio. 978-1-58788-123-7. 2000. $29.95.

Joe Kavalier, a young artist and magician, escapes pre-World War II Czecho-slovakia, making his way to the home of Sam Clay, his Brooklyn cousin. Sam dreams of making it big in the emerging comic book trade and sees Joe as the person to help him. As the cousins gain success with their masked superhero, the Escapist, Joe banks his earnings to bring his family from Prague and falls in love with Rosa Saks, daughter of an art dealer. But when the ship carrying his brother to America is torpedoed, Joe joins the navy and is posted to Antarctica. Half-insane, he returns to a wandering life that leads back to Rosa and now husband Sam. What results is a novel of love and loss, sorrow and wonder. Chabon encourages readers to ponder the ability of art to transcend the "harsh physics" of this world while giving us a magical glimpse of "the mys-terious spirit world beyond." Older teens, especially those in tune with the power of comic books, will do well to be exposed to this outstanding tale.

GRADES: 10–12

REVIEWS: *Booklist* 8/01/00, *Publishers Weekly* 8/18/00, *VOYA* 8/01

Chima, Cinda Williams. *The Warrior Heir.* 432 p. TR. Hyperion Books for Chil-dren. 978-0-7868-3916-2. 2006. $16.99. PB. Hyperion Press. 978-0-7868-3917-9. 2007. $8.99. EB. Recorded Books, LLC. 978-1-4294-0323-8. 2006. $1.00.

Jack's small town world in Ohio begins to unravel when he starts to unleash bursts of magical wizardry. The sixteen-year-old is one of "the Weir," a covert society of wizards, enchanters, and warriors. Jack's destiny is slowly defined until the setting switches to Great Britain where he learns he must fight a duel to the death with a mysterious opponent. Jack is a common, everyman sort of reluctant hero, but the battle scene is thrilling in a video game sort of way. His epic journey shows how a normal teenage American boy may have extraordi-nary powers. Other titles in the series include *The Wizard Heir* and *The Dragon Heir.*

GRADES: 7–12

REVIEWS: *Booklist* 4/01/06, *Kirkus* 4/01/06, *SLJ* 7/06, *VOYA* 2/06

Clare, Cassandra. *City of Bones* (*The Mortal Instruments* series). 496 p. TR. Simon & Schuster Children's Publishing. 978-1-4169-1428-0. 2007. $17.99. PB. Simon & Schuster Children's Publishing. 978-1-4169-5507-8. 2008. $9.99. EB. Simon & Schuster Children's Publishing. 978-1-4169-9575-3. 2009. $9.99. LP. Thorndike Press. 978-1-4104-0946-1. 2008. $23.95.

While at a New York City nightclub, fifteen-year-old Clary Fray notices several attractive teenagers following a blue-haired boy into a storage area. Soon he is dead and the body disappears. Clary is a mundie, meaning she can see Shadowhunters and the demons they hunt. When her mother is kidnapped she is adopted into the Shadowhunters to find her mother. There she also battles her feelings about her best friend Simon and a sexy Shadowhunter, Jace. Although thick in size, this fast-paced story will thrill fans of urban fantasy and adventure. Other titles in the series are *City of Ashes* (Teens' Top Ten), *City of Glass*, and *City of Fallen Angels*.

GRADES: 9–12

REVIEWS: *Publishers Weekly* 4/09/07, *SLJ* 5/07, *VOYA* 4/07

AWARDS: Teens' Top Ten

Clement-Moore, Rosemary. *Highway to Hell* (*Maggie Quinn: Girl vs. Evil* **series**). 368 p. TR. Random House Children's Books. 978-0-385-73463-9. 2009. $16.99. LB. Random House Children's Books. 978-0-385-90462-9. 2009. $19.99.

Maggie, who has a history of fighting demons, and her Dungeons-and-Dragons-loving friend Lisa, who is a practitioner of spells and magic, are on a spring-break trip to south Texas. Their jeep slams into a slaughtered cow on the highway and the two college freshmen girls become stranded in a small town. They are told by locals that a demon called El Chupacabra has been released from underground and is killing off livestock. Background information about the creature is believable to readers, but the story really takes off when Maggie and Lisa confront the demon in the desert. This tension-packed tale is not a cutesy fantasy, but one of bravery and resourcefulness and will appeal to mostly girls but boys may like hunting the gruesome Chupacabra. Other titles in the series are *Prom Dates from Hell* and *Hell Week*.

GRADES: 9–12

REVIEWS: *Booklist* 3/15/09, *SLJ* 4/09, *VOYA* 2/09

Colfer, Eoin. *Artemis Fowl*. 112 p. TR. Miramax Books. 978-0-7868-4881-2. 2007. $18.99. TR. Perfection Learning Corporation. 978-0-7569-0997-0. 2001. $15.65. PB. Hyperion Press. 978-1-4231-2452-8. 2009. $7.99. PB. Miramax Books. 978-0-7868-4882-9. 2007. $9.99. PLAY. Findaway World, LLC. 978-0-7393-7117-6. 2006. $44.99. EB. Random House Audio Publishing Group. 978-0-7393-6431-4. 2008. $46.75.

Artemis Fowl is a twelve-year-old son of an Irish crime lord, and he is a genius. He has confirmed the existence of underground fairies and quickly relieves them of the fairy holy book which is written in Gnommish. His nemesis is Captain Holly Short of the Lower Elements Police who is determined to stop Artemis from robbing the fairies of their gold fortune. Computerized gadgets and truly clever situations mark this first in a series. Several lively secondary characters such as Mulch Diggums and Foaly, a centaur, actually steal scenes. This title and series is a staple for middle school readers, especially boys. Other titles in the series are *The Arctic Incident*, *The Eternity Code*, *The Opal Deception*, *The Lost Colony*, *The Time Paradox*, *The Atlantis Complex*, and *The Artemis Fowl Files*. A graphic novel adaptation has been produced called *Artemis Fowl: The Graphic Novel.*

GRADES: 6–9

REVIEWS: *Booklist* 4/15/01, *Kirkus* 4/01/01, *Publishers Weekly* 4/09/01, *SLJ* 5/01

Collins, Suzanne. *Gregor the Overlander* (*The Underland Chronicles*). 320 p. TR. Scholastic, Incorporated. 978-0-439-43536-9. 2003. $17.99. LB. Perma-Bound Books. 978-0-605-02262-1. 2003. $6.99. RE. San Val, Incorporated. 978-1-4176-3767-6. 2004. $17.20. PB. Scholastic, Incorporated. 978-0-439-67813-1. 2004. $6.99. CD. Random House Audio Publishing Group. 978-0-307-28269-9. 2005. $39.00. EB. Random House Audio Publishing Group. 978-0-7393-4485-9. 2006. $42.50. LP. Thorndike Press. 978-0-7862-8085-8. 2005. $21.95.

Eleven-year-old Gregor tries to grab his two-year-old sister Boots before she falls down an air vent in their New York City apartment, but he also tumbles down the vent, sort of like Alice did way back when. What he discovers is an underground world called Underland, a place inhabited by violet-eyed humans, talking cockroaches, bats, spiders, and rats. Gregor becomes a reluctant warrior hero championed by these strange creatures, but all he wants to do is help his sister and return home. The underground world is thrilling and cleverly created. This title and series will attract a wide range of middle school readers. Other titles in the series are *The Prophecy of Bane, The Curse of the Warmbloods, The Marks of Secret,* and *The Code of Claw.*

GRADES: 9–12

REVIEWS: *Booklist* 11/01/03, *Publishers Weekly* 9/08/03, *SLJ* 11/03, *VOYA* 10/03

Cooper, Susan. *The Dark Is Rising* (*The Dark Is Rising Sequence*). 232 p. TR. Simon & Schuster Children's Publishing. 978-0-689-30317-3. 1973. $19.99. TR. Follett Library Resources. 978-0-7587-0253-1. 2002. $14.94. LB. Perma-Bound Books. 978-0-8479-2980-1. 1973. $8.99. RE. San Val, Incorporated. 978-0-613-90606-7. 1999. $16.00. PB. Simon & Schuster Children's Publishing. 978-1-4169-4969-5. 2007. $8.99. PB. Simon & Schuster Children's Publishing. 978-1-4169-4965-7. 2007. $8.99. CD. Random House Audio Publishing Group. 978-0-7393-5973-0. 2007. $37.00. CASS. Books on Tape, Incorporated. 978-0-7366-5121-9. 2000. $38.00. CASS. Random House Audio Publishing Group. 978-0-8072-8060-7. 1999. $46.00. EB. Simon & Schuster Children's Publishing. 978-0-689-84786-8. 2001. $5.99. EB. Random House Audio Publishing Group. 978-0-7393-6015-6. 2008. $68.00. LP. Thorndike Press. 978-0-7862-2920-8. 2001. $21.95.

Susan Cooper's work depicts the struggle between the forces of good, called The Light, and the forces of evil, known as The Dark. Will Stanton is an eleven-year-old boy who learns that he is an Old One, destined to wield the powers of The Light in an ancient struggle with The Dark. He must collect six signs that will become the Circle of Signs, which is one of the Things of Power. Tough duty for an eleven-year-old but Will discovers his inner strength to battle forces of The Dark. Other titles in the series are *Over Sea, Under Stone, Greenwitch, The Grey King* (Newbery Winner), and *Silver on the Tree.*

GRADES: 6–9

Cornish, D. M. *Monster Blood Tattoo: Foundling.* 434 p. TR. Perfection Learning Corporation. 978-0-7569-7957-7. 2007. $16.65. TR. Penguin Group (USA) Incorporated. 978-0-399-24638-8. 2006. $18.99. RE. San Val, Incorporated. 978-1-4177-8745-6. 2007. $19.65. CD. Random House Audio Publishing Group. 978-0-7393-4907-6. 2007. $45.00. CD. Random House Audio Publishing Group. 978-0-7393-5120-8. 2007. $55.00.

Rossamend Bookchild is an orphan living at Madam Opera's Estimable Marine Society for Foundling Boys and Girls, where instructors groom the orphans to serve in the Boschenberg Navy and other agencies. One day a stranger with odd eyes arrives and hires Rossamend as a "lamplighter" for the Emperor. En route to his new job, he is misled into boarding a doomed boat and winds up alone in a world where humans and monsters wage constant war. When a human kills a monster, he gets a "monster-blood tattoo," made from the beast's blood and bearing its likeness. Rossamend's journey is a vehicle to show-off Cornish's remarkable new world, the Half-Continent where danger awaits. The hefty page count may scare off reluctant readers, but teens ready for a challenge will be rewarded by Cornish's effort. The second title in the series is called *Lamplighter.*

GRADES: 10–12

REVIEWS: *Booklist* 4/01/06, *Publishers Weekly* 6/19/06, *SLJ* 7/06, *VOYA* 6/06

Cusick, Richie Tankersley. *The Harvest (Buffy the Vampire Slayer).* N/A. EB. Barnes & Noble Digital. 978-1-4014-9994-5. 2002. $5.99.

Perhaps more widely known as a television series, Buffy also appears in print. Something's wrong in Sunnydale, California, other than a bad hair day and since there are vampires, of course there must be a vampire slayer. Enter Buffy Summers, a sixteen-year-old who is not a normal teenager, but the slayer who is the hope for all mankind. She has come to this town, which is a center of energy threatening to release The Harvest, a night where the Master Vampire can break free into our world. Supernatural thriller with a kick-butt heroine, this series has many adaptations and will continue to thrill new generations of readers.

GRADES: 7–12

de Lint, Charles. *The Blue Girl.* 384 p. PB. Penguin Group (USA) Incorporated. 978-0-14-240545-1. 2006. $7.99.

Fifteen-year-old Imogene starts over at Redding High School, determined not to repeat the mistakes she made at her old school. She bonds with Maxine but then she sees Ghost, the school's lost soul. The girls enter an adventure that shifts between the confining social structure of high school and a terrifying netherworld of fairies, supernatural creatures, and anamithim—soul eaters attracted to Imogene's strong personality. Both Maxine and Imogene are strong female characters who are problem solvers in the face of evil. The tough background and ghoulish nature of the supernatural beings mark this urban fantasy more for older teens.

GRADES: 9–12

REVIEWS: *Booklist* 11/15/04, *Publishers Weekly* 12/20/04, *SLJ* 11/04, *VOYA* 12/04

Delaney, Joseph. *The Revenge of the Witch* (*The Last Apprentice*). 368 p. TR. HarperCollins Publishers. 978-0-06-076618-4. 2005. $16.99. LB. HarperCollins Publishers. 978-0-06-076619-1. 2005. $17.89. RE. San Val, Incorporated. 978-1-4177-7015-1. 2006. $18.40. LB. Perma-Bound Books. 978-0-605-02435-9. 2005. $7.99. CD. Recorded Books, LLC. 978-1-4193-8446-2. 2006. $49.75. CD. Harper Collins Publishers. 978-0-06-082402-0. 2005. $25.95. CASS. Recorded Books, LLC. 978-1-4193-8441-7. 2006. $49.75. EB. Recorded Books, LLC. 978-1-4356-7449-3. 2008. $46.00.

Twelve-year-old Thomas Ward, the seventh son of a seventh son, is apprenticed to the local Spook, Mr. Gregory. His job is to fight evil spirits and witches, and Thomas realizes this will become a dangerous life. What Thomas doesn't anticipate is that he may have to stand off against a powerful witch, Mother Malkin, alone. His new friend Alice may, or may not, be a help in this fight to the death. Geared to the younger end of young adult, Delaney's work is full of suspense with extreme gore mixed in. It has appeal for both boys and girls. Other titles in the series are *Curse of the Bane, Night of the Soul Stealer, Attack of the Fiend, Wrath of the Bloodeye, Clash of the Demons,* and *The Spook's Tale and Other Horrors.*

GRADES: 6–10

REVIEWS: *Booklist* 8/01/05, *Publishers Weekly* 10/10/05, *SLJ* 11/05, *VOYA* 10/05

Duane, Diane. *So You Want to Be a Wizard* (*Young Wizards* series). 336 p. TR. Houghton Mifflin Harcourt Trade & Reference Publishers. 978-0-15-204738-2. 2003. $16.95. RE. San Val, Incorporated. 978-0-613-36077-7. 2001. $17.15. PB. Houghton Mifflin Harcourt Trade & Reference Publishers. 978-0-15-204940-9. 2003. $6.95. CD. Recorded Books, LLC. 978-0-7887-4968-1. N/A. $69.00. EB. Recorded Books, LLC. 978-1-4237-2282-3. N/A. $1.00.

Nita Callahan, wishing to find a spot of solace from her school's bullies, checks out a book found in the children's section with the interesting title *So You Want to Be a Wizard*. On the way home, the bullies corner her, beat her up, and take a space pen given to her by her uncle. Before Nita goes to sleep, she takes the Wizard's Oath. The next morning she looks at her manual and sees her name in the wizards' list. Nita meets Christopher "Kit" Rodriquez and together they embark on an adventure involving spells and magic. Other titles in the series are *Deep Wizardry, High Wizardry, A Wizard Abroad, The Wizard's Dilemma, A Wizard Alone* (Teens' Top Ten), *Wizard's Holiday, Wizards at War* and *A Wizard of Mars*.

GRADES: 6–10

Duey, Kathleen. *Skin Hunger* (*A Resurrection of Magic:* **Book One**). 368 p. TR. Simon & Schuster Children's Publishing. 978-0-689-84093-7. 2007. $17.99. PB. Simon & Schuster Children's Publishing. 978-0-689-84094-4. 2008. $9.99. CASS. Recorded Books, LLC. 978-1-4361-1611-4. 2008. $67.75. EB. Recorded Books, LLC. 978-1-4356-9575-7. 2009. $86.00.

In this darkly atmospheric fantasy two teens live in a world in which the working of magic has a turbulent history. When her bitter father dies, Sadima, a young woman who can communicate with animals, keeps house for two renegade magicians at a time when magic has been outlawed. Her experiences alternate with Hahp, born years after Sadima, who attends a school of wizardry where students are starved to death if they cannot conjure up food. The truly alarming plot may be too intense for younger teens. The second title is called *Sacred Scars*.

GRADES: 9–12

REVIEWS: *Booklist* 6/01/07, *Publishers Weekly* 7/23/07, *SLJ* 11/07, *VOYA* 8/07

Eddings, David. *Pawn of Prophecy* (*The Belgariad* **series**). N/A. RE. San Val, Incorporated. 978-0-8085-8722-4. 1982. $17.20. PB. Random House Publishing Group. 978-0-345-46864-2. 2004. $6.99. PB. Random House Publishing Group. 978-0-345-33551-7. 1986. $7.99. EB. NetLibrary, Incorporated. 978-1-4294-6670-7. N/A. $51.95.

The book opens with the creation of the world by seven gods. One of the seven, Aldur, fashions an orb from stone and creates within it a living soul. This orb becomes known as the Orb of Aldur. One of the other gods, Torak, forcibly takes the Orb from Aldur and tries to make the magical stone submit to his will. The Orb retaliates, burning and maiming Torak throughout the left side of his body, and burning out his left eye. The Orb of Aldur is later recovered by Belgarath the Sorcerer, King Cherek, and his children. The Orb becomes the catalyst for a power struggle for control over the world. Other titles in the series are *Queen of Sorcery, Magician's Gambit, Castle of Wizardry,* and *Enchanter's End Game.*

GRADES: 9–12

Farmer, Nancy. *The Sea of Trolls.* 459 p. TR. Perfection Learning Corporation. 978-0-7569-7014-7. 2006. $17.65. TR. Simon & Schuster Children's Publishing. 978-0-689-86744-6. 2004. $17.95. LB. Perma-Bound Books. 978-0-605-01387-2. 2004. $9.99. PB. Simon & Schuster Children's Publishing. 978-0-689-86746-0. 2006. $9.99. CD. Recorded Books, LLC. 978-1-4025-9344-4. 2004. $29.99. EB. Simon & Schuster Children's Publishing. 978-1-4169-1432-7. 2005. $9.99. EB. Recorded Books, LLC. 978-1-4237-0893-3. N/A. $96.00. LP. Thorndike Press. 978-0-7862-7151-1. 2005. $23.95.

Set in AD 793 in Anglo-Saxon England, Scandinavia, and the mythical realm of Jotunheim, this title blends history and fantasy. Jack is accepted as the village bard's apprentice, but when Northmen invade his village, Jack and his sister Lucy are captured. He meets a young berserker, Thorgil. Throughout their epic quest Jack and Thorgil encounter many dangers, learn to make sacrifices for the sake of others, and eventually succeed in saving Lucy. Fans of in-depth fantasy will be engaged with Farmer's story. Other titles in the trilogy are *The Land of the Silver Apples* and *The Islands of the Blessed.*

GRADES: 7–10

REVIEWS: *Booklist* 11/01/04, *Publishers Weekly* 7/19/04, *SLJ* 10/04, *VOYA* 10/04

Fisher, Catherine. *Incarceron.* 448 p. TR. Penguin Group (USA) Incorporated. 978-0-8037-3396-1. 2010. $17.99. CD. Random House Audio Publishing Group. 978-0-307-70707-9. 2010. $48.00.

Inside the living prison of Incarceron, Finn keeps his wits about him while avoiding violent gangs and thieves. Outside the prison is Claudia, the pampered daughter of Incarceron's warden. With the aid of magical keys, Claudia communicates with Finn as he tries to escape the horrors of prison. Eventually both teens learn they are victims of centuries-old conspiracy and false identity. The lengthy work is highlighted by the clever secret setting of the prison, a living being that is truly a house of horrors. Both male and female readers will be drawn to the exciting escape from Incarceron.

GRADES: 7–12

REVIEWS: *Booklist* 1/01/10, *Publishers Weekly* 12/07/09, *SLJ* 2/10, *VOYA* 2/10

Fisher, Catherine. *The Oracle Betrayed (Oracle Prophecies* series). 332 p. TR. Perfection Learning Corporation. 978-0-7569-5269-3. 2005. $14.65. LB. HarperCollins Publishers. 978-0-06-057158-0. 2004. $17.89. RE. San Val, Incorporated. 978-

1-4177-0134-6. 2005. $17.20. PB. HarperCollins Publishers. 978-0-06-057159-7. 2005. $6.99.

Mirany, a shy girl, is one of the Nine, who serve the god-on-earth, Archon. The dying Archon secretly passes Mirany a message and now she must find the boy who is meant to take his place as god-on-earth. However many others would like to seize power and become the new Archon, and outwitting those who would seize power, ensure that he is proclaimed the new Archon. Mirany is a winning everygirl character who also wishes to end the extreme drought parching the land. The work targets younger teens who will also be interested in the other titles in the series, *Sphere of Secrets* and *Day of the Scarab*.

GRADES: 6–10

REVIEWS: *Booklist* 2/15/04, *Publishers Weekly* 1/26/04, *SLJ* 3/04, *VOYA* 4/04

Flanagan, John. *The Ruins of Gorlan (The Ranger's Apprentice).* 249 p. TR. Perfection Learning Corporation. 978-0-7569-6898-4. 2006. $15.65. TR. Penguin Group (USA) Incorporated. 978-0-399-24454-4. 2005. $15.99. LB. Perma-Bound Books. 978-0-605-02696-4. 2005. $7.99. PB. Penguin Group (USA) Incorporated. 978-0-14-240663-2. 2006. $7.99. CD. Recorded Books, LLC. 978-1-4193-9399-0. 2006. $74.75. CASS. Recorded Books, LLC. 978-1-4193-9394-5. 2006. $59.75. EB. Recorded Books, LLC. 978-1-4237-8636-8. 2006. $1.00.

Fifteen-year-old Will is nervous about Choosing Day at Castle Redmont, when each teen will be assigned to a different master for training. Though his dearest wish is to enter the Battleschool, his small stature prevents it. Instead, Will is apprenticed to the grim-faced, mysterious Ranger. Soon Will learns that becoming a ranger is more difficult, dangerous, and worthwhile than he had imagined. Will's world is threatened by an evil warlord and Will's learned Ranger skills are the kingdom's only hope. Other titles in the series are *The Burning Bridges, The Icebound Land, Oakleaf Bearers, The Sorcerer in the North, The Siege of Macindaw, Erak's Ransom, The Kings of Clonmel,* and *Halt's Peril.* All titles are terrific selections for middle school boys.

GRADES: 6–9

REVIEWS: *Booklist* 6/01/05, *Publishers Weekly* 10/03/05 *SLJ* 6/05, *VOYA* 12/05

Fünke, Cornelia Caroline. *Inkheart.* 544 p. TR. Scholastic, Incorporated. 978-0-439-53164-1. 2003. $24.99. LB. Perma-Bound Books. 978-0-605-02379-6. 2003. $10.99. RE. San Val, Incorporated. 978-1-4177-3397-2. 2005. $22.10. PB. Scholastic, Incorporated. 978-0-545-04626-8. 2009. $9.99. PB. Scholastic, Incorporated. 978-0-439-70910-1. 2005. $10.99. CD. Random House Audio Publishing Group. 978-0-307-28227-9. 2005. $34.99. PLAY. Findaway World, LLC. 978-0-7393-7495-5. 2006. $59.99. CASS. Random House Audio Publishing Group. 978-0-8072-

1951-5. 2004. $55.00. EB. Random House Audio Publishing Group. 978-0-7393-4489-7. 2006. $72.25. LP. Thorndike Press. 978-0-7862-8363-7. 2006. $11.95.

One dark night, a mysterious man called Dustfinger appears at the house where Meggie lives with her father, a bookbinder. The arrival begins a long, complicated chain of events involving a journey, fictional characters brought to life, dangerous secrets, evil deeds, and the triumph of courage. The close relationship between Meggie and her father are key components to this lightly magical, humorous, and fun story. Mild profanity makes this work not for the very young, but it will have wide appeal to many middle school readers. Other titles in the series are *Inkspell* and *Inkdeath*.

GRADES: 6–10

REVIEWS: *Booklist* 9/01/03, *Publishers Weekly* 7/21/03, *SLJ* 10/03, *VOYA* 12/03

AWARDS: Teens' Top Ten

Gaiman, Neil. *Anansi Boys.* 368 p. TR. HarperCollins Publishers. 978-0-06-134239-4. 2008. $14.95. TR. HarperCollins Publishers. 978-0-06-051518-8. 2005. $26.95. PB. HarperCollins Publishers. 978-0-06-051519-5. 2006. $7.99. CD. BBC Audiobooks America. 978-0-7927-3842-8. 2005. $49.95. CD. HarperCollins Publishers. 978-0-06-082384-9. 2005. $39.95. PLAY. Findaway World, LLC. 978-1-60252-939-7. 2007. $69.99. EB. HarperCollins Publishers. 978-0-06-089541-9. 2005. $19.95. LP. Thorndike Press. 978-0-7862-8510-5. 2006. $29.95.

Fat Charlie's life is about to be spiced up—his estranged father dies in a karaoke bar, and when the handsome brother he never knew shows up, his life becomes even more exciting. Soon Fat Charlie is being investigated by the police and he finds out his father was the god Anansi and that the beast gods of folklore are out for revenge on his bloodline. This fun book is marked with horror, mystery, magic, comedy, song, romance, ghosts, scary birds, and ancient grudges. Fans of this title should also seek out Gaiman's *American Gods.* Both titles are best suited for older teens.

GRADES: 10–12

REVIEWS: *Booklist* 8/01/05, *Publishers Weekly* 7/18/05, *SLJ* 1/06

AWARDS: Alex Award

Gaiman, Neil. *Coraline.* 192 p. TR. HarperCollins Publishers. 978-0-06-164970-7. 2008. $19.99. TR. HarperCollins Publishers. 978-0-06-082543-0. 2008. $18.99. LB. HarperCollins Publishers. 978-0-06-082544-7. 2008. $19.89. LB. HarperCollins Publishers. 978-0-06-623744-2. 2002. $17.89. PB. HarperCollins Publishers. 978-0-06-164969-1. 2008. $6.99. CD. HarperCollins Publishers. 978-0-06-166016-0. 2008. $9.95. EB. HarperCollins Publishers. 978-0-06-118750-6. 2002. $12.99. LP. Thorndike Press. 978-0-7862-5542-9. 2003. $25.95.

Coraline's parents are loving, but really too busy to play with her, so she amuses herself by exploring her family's apartment. A door seemingly against a brick wall opens to a horror that she doesn't expect. The young girl explores a parallel world with a mother similar to her own, but with an evil slant. Coraline becomes caught in this evil woman's realm, matching wits with the horrifying being that has stolen Coraline's parents and the souls of other children. A tension-packed, incredibly clever plot, and a gruesome climactic scene make this a top horror/fantasy novel. However, shy younger readers may find the story too intense.

GRADES: 6–12

REVIEWS: *Booklist* 8/01/02, *Kirkus* 6/15/02, *Publishers Weekly* 6/24/02, *SLJ* 8/02

Gaiman, Neil. *The Graveyard Book.* 320 p. TR. HarperCollins Publishers. 978-0-06-170912-8. 2008. $17.99. TR. HarperCollins Publishers. 978-0-06-053092-1. 2008. $17.99. LB. HarperCollins Publishers. 978-0-06-053093-8. 2008. $18.89. CD. HarperCollins Publishers. 978-0-06-155189-5. 2008. $29.95. CD. Recorded Books, LLC. 978-1-4361-5884-8. 2008. $76.75. CASS. Recorded Books, LLC. 978-1-4361-5879-4. 2008. $56.75. EB. HarperCollins Publishers. 978-0-06-170938-8. 2008. $17.99. EB. Recorded Books, LLC. 978-1-4356-9577-1. 2009. $68.00. LP. Thorndike Press. 978-1-4104-1441-0. 2009. $23.95.

While a highly motivated killer murders his family, a baby, ignorant of the horrific goings-on, pulls himself out of his crib, toddles out of the house and into the night. The baby was the killer's prime target and has escaped death. The child finds refuge in a crumbling graveyard. He is adopted by the denizens of this mysterious place and they name him Nobody, or Bod. Gaiman's creative take on an entire village pitching in to raise a child involves witches, vampires, ghosts and oh, yes, that murderer returns to finish his business. This is a top novel accented by creepy drawings that will thrill a wide range of readers, including adults.

GRADES: 6–12

REVIEWS: *Booklist* 9/15/08, *Publishers Weekly* 9/29/08, *SLJ* 10/08, *VOYA* 8/08

AWARDS: Newbery Winner, Teens' Top Ten

George, Jessica Day. *Sun and Moon, Ice and Snow.* 336 p. TR. Bloomsbury Publishing. 978-1-59990-109-1. 2008. $16.95. PB. Bloomsbury Publishing. 978-1-59990-328-6. 2009. $7.99.

A young girl from Norway with no name has a special gift enabling her to communicate with animals. She comes across a polar bear that may not be at all what he seems and who strikes a deal with her to stay in his palace for a year and a day. Her journey takes her along the four winds to the palace made of ice where she must defeat a troll queen and save a prince from an evil curse.

This part fairy tale, part fantasy story incorporates many words from the Old Norse language and will thrill middle school girls who treasure a happy ending.

GRADES: 6–9

REVIEWS: *Booklist* 2/01/08, *SLJ* 3/08, *VOYA* 4/08

Goodkind, Terry. *Stone of Tears* (*Sword of Truth* **series**). 560 p. TR. Tom Doherty Associates, LLC. 978-0-312-85706-6. 1995. $29.95. RE. San Val, Incorporated. 978-0-613-22447-5. 1996. $19.65. PB. Tom Doherty Associates, LLC. 978-0-8125-4809-9. 1996. $8.99. PB. Tom Doherty Associates, LLC. 978-0-614-98104-9. 1996. $6.99. CD. Brilliance Audio. 978-1-4233-2165-1. 2006. $44.95. CASS. Brilliance Audio. 978-1-59355-555-9. 2004. $39.95.

The quest of Richard Cypher, reluctant hero turned magical warrior, continues in this second volume of the series. Richard and his beloved Kahlan Amnell band together. Richard handles the magical part and Kahlan leads armies against the surviving forces of the dead mage, Darken Rahl. This is a big epic tale with plenty of action and many engaging characters. Other titles in the series are *Wizard's First Rule, Blood of the Fold, Temple of the Winds, Soul of the Fire, Faith of the Fallen, The Pillars of Creation, Naked Empire, Chainfire, Phantom,* and *Confessor.*

GRADES: 8–12

REVIEWS: *Booklist* 10/01/95, *Kirkus* 8/15/95, *Publishers Weekly* 9/25/95, *VOYA* 6/96

Goodman, Alison. *Eon: Dragoneye Reborn.* 544 p. TR. Penguin Group (USA) Incorporated. 978-0-670-06227-0. 2009. $19.99. CD. Brilliance Audio. 978-1-4233-7955-3. 2008. $36.99. PLAY. Findaway World, LLC. 978-1-60775-527-2. 2009. $70.00.

In this Asian-inspired fantasy world, political power belongs to the emperor, but also to the Dragoneyes. These are men who harness the power of the twelve energy dragons named for animals from the Chinese zodiac, and each year a new one comes to power. During the ceremony dragons choose the humans. Physically lame Eon is thought least likely to be chosen but also guards a secret: Eon is truly Eona, a sixteen-year-old girl. Eona thinks that all is lost until she sees a dragon no one has seen in 400 years, the Mirror Dragon. A strong female protagonist and an interesting world full of unique characters are components of Goodman's story that will engage readers of many ages.

GRADES: 6–12

REVIEWS: *Booklist* 12/15/08, *Publishers Weekly* 9/29/08, *SLJ* 1/09, *VOYA* 2/09

Haddix, Margaret Peterson. *Just Ella.* 218 p. TR. Perfection Learning Corporation. 978-0-7569-0505-7. 2001. $13.65. RE. San Val, Incorporated. 978-0-613-90928-0. 2001. $16.00. PB. Simon & Schuster Children's Publishing. 978-1-4169-3649-7. 2007. $5.99. PB. Simon & Schuster Children's Publishing. 978-0-689-84917-6. 2001. $4.99. EB. Recorded Books, LLC. 978-1-4356-6738-9. 2008. $1.00.

Fifteen-year-old Ella (Cinderella) discovers that life after the ball isn't necessarily lived happily ever after. Her prince is decidedly not charming, and castle life is cushy, but superficial and repressive. Then Ella meets tutor Jed Reston, a lively companion and social activist. Their relationship inspires her to rethink her wishes and priorities and to embark on a challenging quest to find true happiness in life and love. Instead of relying on magic in this fairy-tale world, Ella uses ingenuity and determination to find happiness. Teenage girls have flocked to this story for years and it never gets old.

GRADES: 6–10

REVIEWS: *Booklist* 9/01/99, *Kirkus* 8/15/99, *Publishers Weekly* 10/11/99, *SLJ* 9/99, *VOYA* 12/99

Hale, Shannon. *Book of a Thousand Days.* N/A. TR. Bloomsbury Publishing. 978-1-59990-051-3. 2007. $17.95. PB. Bloomsbury Publishing. 978-1-59990-378-1. 2009. $8.99. PLAY. Findaway World, LLC. 978-1-60514-680-5. 2008. $39.99. EB. Bloomsbury Publishing. 978-1-59990-411-5. 2008. $17.95. LP. Thorndike Press. 978-1-4104-0582-1. 2008. $23.95.

Orphaned Dashti lives in Central Asia and is a hardworking, pragmatic girl who grew up in the open, windswept steppes. She finds work in the city with a young noblewoman, Lady Saren. When Lady Saren refuses an advantageous marriage, she is punished. She's sentenced to seven years in a sealed tower along with Dashti. Written in diary form in Dashti's voice, the gripping tale follows the two young women through their imprisonment and their escape into a grim world of warring societies. Hale combines fantasy, romance, and thrilling adventure in her tale that will have wide appeal to younger teenage girls.

GRADES: 6–9

REVIEWS: *Booklist* 9/15/07, *Publishers Weekly* 9/24/07, *SLJ* 10/07, *VOYA* 10/07

Hale, Shannon. *Princess Academy.* 314 p. TR. Perfection Learning Corporation. 978-0-7569-8180-8. 2007. $15.60. TR. Bloomsbury Publishing. 978-1-58234-993-0. 2005. $17.99. LB. Perma-Bound Books. 978-0-605-02658-2. 2005. $16.95. PB. Bloomsbury Publishing. 978-1-59990-073-5. 2007. $7.95. PLAY. Findaway World, LLC. 978-1-60252-538-2. 2007. $49.99. EB. Bloomsbury Publishing. 978-1-59990-410-8. 2008. $7.95. LP. Thorndike Press. 978-0-7862-8733-8. 2006. $23.95.

Fourteen-year-old Miri would love to join her father and older sister as a miner in Mount Eskel's quarry producing the humble village's prize stone, linder. But when local girls are rounded up to compete for the hand of the kingdom's prince, Miri, the prize student in the Princess Academy, gets her chance to shine. In addition to her natural intelligence and spunk, she uses courage and intelligence to lead her classmates in the fight against being treated as social inferiors in the academy. This title about leadership and friendship with a feminist slant will appeal to middle school girls.

GRADES: 6–9

REVIEWS: *Booklist* 6/01/05, *Publishers Weekly* 8/08/05, *SLJ* 10/05, *VOYA* 8/05

AWARDS: Newbery Honor

Hartnett, Sonya. *Surrender.* 256 p. TR. Candlewick Press. 978-0-7636-2768-3. 2006. $16.99. PB. Candlewick Press. 978-0-7636-3423-0. 2007. $7.99.

A young man has changed his name to Gabriel and now reflects back on his tormented life as he approaches death. His youth was a series of terrible events that led to his mentally challenged brother's death. The only friends he has are a feral child named Finnegan and his dog, Surrender. Finnegan roams on the outskirts of the Australian town and may or may not be responsible for many arson incidents. This title is placed in the fantasy section due to the alternative world that Gabriel creates in his mind. Disturbing and powerful, this story is a commentary on good versus evil. Harsh and violent situations make it more suitable for mature readers.

GRADES: 10–12

REVIEWS: *Booklist* 2/01/06, *Publishers Weekly* 3/06/06, *SLJ* 3/06, *VOYA* 4/06

AWARDS: BBYA Top Ten, Printz Honor

Jackson, Shirley. *The Haunting of Hill House.* N/A. LB. Buccaneer Books, Incorporated. 978-0-89968-430-7. 1993. $25.95. LB. Amereon LTD. 978-0-89190-622-3. N/A. $22.95. CASS. American International Publishing Group. 978-1-59040-104-0. 2001. $25.00. EB. NetLibrary, Incorporated. 978-1-4356-7921-4. 2008. $32.95.

The story about Hill House, an eighty-year-old mansion, centers around three characters who are asked by Doctor Montague, a paranormal investigator, to stay there as his guests. Eleanor and Theodora accept along with a young man named Luke. All four of the inhabitants begin to experience strange events while in the house, including sounds and unseen spirits roaming the halls at night, "blood" spattered on walls, and other unexplained events. As the story progresses, it becomes clear to the characters that the house is beginning to possess Eleanor. Jackson's work has been tagged by Stephen King as one of the best horror stories of the twentieth century.

GRADES: 9–12

Jacques, Brian. *Redwall* (*Redwall* series). 352 p. TR. Penguin Group (USA) Incorporated. 978-0-399-24794-1. 2007. $23.99. LB. San Val, Incorporated. 978-0-8335-5260-0. 1998. $15.30. PB. Penguin Group (USA) Incorporated. 978-0-14-230237-8. 2002. $8.99. CD. Random House Audio Publishing Group. 978-0-307-28174-6. 2005. $39.95. CD. Random House Audio Publishing Group. 978-0-8072-2017-7. 2004. $55.25. CASS. Books on Tape, Incorporated. 978-0-7366-9097-3. 2000. $50.00. EB. Random House Audio Publishing Group. 978-0-7393-4987-8. 2007. $55.25. LP. Cengage Gale. 978-0-7862-3858-3. 2002. $25.95.

The peaceful life of the mice of Redwall Abbey is shattered by the onslaught of the fierce rat, Cluny the Scourge, and his army of rats, weasels, and other vermin. The mice and the other peaceful animals take refuge in the Abbey's strong walls while Cluny lays seige. Advantage is with the besieged and the Abbey defenders are able to withstand numerous attacks. Cluny cannot be completely defeated, however, until the sword of Martin, the legendary warrior who founded Redwall Abbey, can be found. A young novice, Matthias, embarks on a quest to find it. This epic fantasy series contains a subtle commentary on good versus evil and enjoys wide popularity, especially with middle school boys. Other titles in the series are *Mossflower, Mattimeo, Mariel of Redwall, Salamandastron, Martin the Warrior, The Bellmaker, Outcast of Redwall, The Pearls of Lutra, The Long Patrol, Marlfox, The Legend of Luke, Lord Brocktree, The Taggerung, Triss, Loamhedge, Rakkety Tam, High Rhulain, Eulalia!, Doomwyte,* and *The Sable Queen.*

GRADES: 6–9

REVIEWS: *Booklist* 6/01/87, *Publishers Weekly* 6/26/87, *SLJ* 8/87

Jenkins, A. M. *Repossessed.* 224 p. TR. HarperCollins Publishers. 978-0-06-083568-2. 2007. $16.99. LB. HarperCollins Publishers. 978-0-06-083569-9. 2007. $16.89. PB. HarperCollins Publishers. 978-0-06-083570-5. 2009. $8.99. EB. HarperCollins Publishers. 978-0-06-194801-5. 2009. $9.99. LP. Thorndike Press. 978-1-4104-0498-5. 2008. $22.95.

Bored and frustrated with his routine work in Hell, Kiriel takes over the body of seventeen-year-old Shaun. It's all about enjoyment and Kiriel finds that living inside a teenage boy's body is all about sex and anything else that is pleasurable. Jenkins writes an interesting take on growing up, but this coming-of-age tale can also be classified as a fantasy due to the spectral being arriving to live on earth. The sexual situations, although hilarious, are meant for a mature audience.

GRADES: 9–12

REVIEWS: *Publishers Weekly* 6/18/07, *SLJ* 12/07, *VOYA* 8/07

AWARDS: Printz Honor

Jinks, Catherine. *Evil Genius.* 496 p. TR. Houghton Mifflin Harcourt Trade & Reference Publishers. 978-0-15-205988-0. 2007. $17.00. LB. San Val, Incorporated. 978-0-606-10669-6. 2008. $18.40. PB. Houghton Mifflin Harcourt Trade & Reference Publishers. 978-0-15-206185-2. 2008. $7.95. EB. Random House Audio Publishing Group. 978-0-7393-5089-8. 2007. $85.00. LP. Thorndike Press. 978-1-4104-0295-0. 2007. $23.95.

When Cadel Piggott, a child genius, is expelled from his fancy school at age seven for computer hacking, his exasperated parents take him to see a child psychologist. By age thirteen, Cadel is placed in the top-secret Axis Institute where he is to earn a degree in World Domination. This is no private school with cute goblins and wizards. Strange and gruesome deaths befall members of the student body and Cadel tries to learn exactly why he has been added to the school's roster. This book is a bit on the long side, which will deter reluctant readers, but the intrigue will enthrall readers who like layered and fantastic plots. The sequel is titled *Genius Squad.*

GRADES: 7–10

REVIEWS: *Booklist* 5/15/07, *Publishers Weekly* 4/02/07, *SLJ* 7/07, *VOYA* 4/07

Jinks, Catherine. *The Reformed Vampire Support Group.* 368 p. TR. Houghton Mifflin Harcourt Trade & Reference Publishers. 978-0-15-206609-3. 2009. $17.00.

Nina Harrison has been fifteen years old since 1973, the year when she was bitten and turned into a vampire. She continues to live with her crabby mother but Nina is also a member of the Reformed Vampire Support Group, a group of vampires. Although they are part of the undead, they are not beautiful, strong, powerful, or rich. Their idle lives are interrupted when one of them is staked and the rest of the group fears a similar fate. Deciding to hunt down the killer, the dysfunctional group embarks on a journey that is witty, cunning, and hilarious. Jinks' very different take on the vampire theme will have strong appeal to many teens.

GRADES: 7–12

REVIEWS: *Booklist* 1/01/09, *Publishers Weekly* 1/26/09, *SLJ* 3/09, *VOYA* 10/09

AWARDS: BBYA Top Ten

Johnson, Maureen. *Devilish.* 272 p. PB. Penguin Group (USA) Incorporated. 978-1-59514-132-3. 2007. $8.99.

High school senior Jane Jarvis has a problem with her best friend Allison. There seems to be a weird connection between Allison and new girl Lanalee. It turns out Allison has sold her soul to junior devil Lanalee in exchange for popularity. Ally wants to back out, so Jane confronts Lanalee. Jane offers to take Ally's place and soon finds herself in a fight for her life. The joining of high school snarkiness with the supernatural will draw in many readers, especially high school girls.

GRADES: 9–12

REVIEWS: *Booklist* 10/15/06, *Publishers Weekly* 9/18/06, *SLJ* 10/06, *VOYA* 8/06

Jones, Diane Wynne. *Howl's Moving Castle.* 224 p. TR. HarperCollins Publishers. 978-0-688-06233-0. 1986. $16.95. RE. San Val, Incorporated. 978-0-613-37151-3. 2001. $17.20. PB. HarperCollins Publishers. 978-0-06-147878-9. 2008. $6.99. PB. HarperCollins Publishers. 978-0-06-441034-2. 2001. $6.99. EB. Recorded Books, LLC. 978-1-4356-8912-1. 2008. $1.00.

Sophie Hatter realizes as the eldest of three daughters she will probably lead a dull life running her family's hat shop. That is until she's turned into an old crone by the Witch of the Waste, a nasty and powerful witch who mistakes Sophie for her sister who is the current love of Wizard Howl. Finding work as the cleaning lady for Howl, Sophie learns he is not the cavalier person he pretends to be and the door to his castle is a portal opening to four different places. The Japanese animated film based on this work will help draw interest to this title, which is suitable for middle school readers.

GRADES: 6–10

Jordan, Robert. *The Eye of the World (The Wheel of Time* **series).** 688 p. TR. Tom Doherty Associates, LLC. 978-0-8125-0048-6. 1990. $14.95. RE. San Val, Incorporated. 978-0-613-17634-7. 1990. $17.20. PB. Tom Doherty Associates, LLC. 978-0-8125-1181-9. 1995. $6.99. CD. Macmillan Audio. 978-1-59397-432-9. 2004. $59.95. CD. The Publishing Mills, Incorporated. 978-1-57511-098-1. 2001. $69.95. CASS. Media Books, LLC. 978-1-57815-132-5. 2000. $7.95. CASS. The Publishing Mills, Incorporated. 978-1-879371-52-1. 1994. $16.95. EB. Tom Doherty Associates, LLC. 978-1-4299-5981-0. 1990. $15.00.

Jordan has constructed an epic tale on the concept that at the beginning of the dawn of time, a deity known as the Creator forged the universe and the Wheel of Time, which, as it turns, spins all lives. The Wheel has seven spokes, each representing an age, and it rotates under the One Power, which flows from the True Source. In this opening volume of the series, the peaceful villagers of Emond's Field pay little heed to rumors of war in the western lands until a savage attack by troll-like minions of the Dark One forces three young men to confront a destiny that has its origins in the time known as The Breaking of the World. Other titles in the series are *New Spring, The Great Hunt, The Dragon Reborn, The Shadow Rising, The Fires of Heaven, Lord of Chaos, A Crown of Swords, The Path of Daggers, Winter's Heart, Crossroads of Twilight, Knife of Dreams, The Gathering Storm, Towers of Midnight,* and *A Memory of Light.*

GRADES: 7–12

Kindl, Patrice. *Owl in Love.* 224 p. PB. Houghton Mifflin Harcourt Trade & Reference Publishers. 978-0-618-43910-2. 2004. $6.99. EB. Recorded Books, LLC. 978-1-4175-8878-7. N/A. $1.00.

Owl is fourteen years old and spends her nights hanging out in a tree near the home of her science teacher, Mr. Lindstrom. Owl is a wereowl who transforms each night living on a diet of rodents. She has a crush on Mr. Lindstrom, but her love is completely one-sided. The theme of teenage alienation is presented through a fantasy riff and the voice of Owl who alternates between witty and passionate narrations of her situation. Her blunt discussion of her desire for her teacher may alarm younger readers.

GRADES: 8–12

REVIEWS: *Booklist* 9/01/93, *Kirkus* 10/93, *Publishers Weekly* 9/06/93, *VOYA* 12/93

King, A. S. *The Dust of 100 Dogs.* 336 p. PB. Llewellyn Publications. 978-0-7387-1426-4. 2009. $9.95.

Seventeenth-century pirate Emer Morrisey, murdered and cursed to live the lives of one hundred dogs, rematerializes as Saffron Adams, a teenager living in the 1980s. Her only ambition is to reclaim a treasure buried in Jamaica, but her present-day parents are pushing her in a different direction. Chapters alternate between Saffron in the present day and descriptions of her former life on the high seas. The reincarnation theme will engage sophisticated readers of many ages, but the sexual situations of the revealed past mark this title for older readers.

GRADES: 10–12

REVIEWS: *Booklist* 2/15/09, *Publishers Weekly* 2/16/09, *VOYA* 4/09

Knox, Elizabeth. *Dreamhunter: Book One of the Dreamhunter Duet.* 365 p. TR. Farrar, Straus & Giroux. 978-0-374-31853-6. 2006. $19.00. PB. Square Fish. 978-0-312-53571-1. 2009. $8.99. LP. Thorndike Press. 978-0-7862-9621-7. 2007. $22.95.

Fifteen-year-old cousins Laura Hame and Rose Tiebold, only children of famous and successful dreamhunters, share a household at the turn of the twentieth century. Their lives will be determined by their tries at age sixteen, for only the gifted can enter The Place, which is invisible to all others. There they can capture dreams to sell at highest prices upon their return. The community, obsessed with dreaming as entertainment, has constructed a culture built around its dreamhunters, who enjoy pop-star status. But not everything is completely pleasant when one of the more powerful dreamhunters disappears. This sophisticated fantasy offers a theme on government control which makes it best suited for older teens.

GRADES: 10-12

REVIEWS: *Booklist* 4/01/06, *Publishers Weekly* 4/03/06, *SLJ* 3/06, *VOYA* 2/06

Knox, Elizabeth. *Dreamquake: Book Two of the Dreamhunter Duet.* 449 p. TR. Farrar, Straus & Giroux. 978-0-374-31854-3. 2007. $19.00. PB. Square Fish. 978-0-312-58147-3. 2009. $9.99.

This title begins where *Dreamhunter* left off, and is written in the same detailed, eloquent prose. Dreamhunter Laura Hame has inflicted the sleeping patrons at the Rainbow Opera dream palace with a nightmare that blows a government conspiracy wide open. Now that the government conspiracy is widely known, Laura and her family attempt to seek justice. The theme of seemingly everyday people confronting a huge government body will have appeal to older readers. The *Dreamhunter Duet* is top-notch fantasy highlighted by sophisticated writing.

GRADES: 10–12

REVIEWS: *Booklist* 1/01/07, *Publishers Weekly* 3/12/07, *SLJ* 6/07, *VOYA* 6/07

AWARDS: Printz Honor

Lackey, Mercedes. *The Black Gryphon (Mage Wars).* N/A. LB. San Val, Incorporated. 978-0-613-63017-7. 1995. $15.30. PB. Penguin Group (USA) Incorporated. 978-0-88677-643-5. 1995. $7.99.

The good archmage Urtho and his armies are locked in mortal combat with the evil Ma'ar. Urtho has created numerous races, most important the gryphons, a race of birds. Chief among them is the black-dyed mage, Skandranon, who is the leader. Lackey offers her take on the good battling evil theme, this time in a war fought by fantastic creatures. Fans of complicated fantasy plots will be drawn to this work. Other titles in the series are *The White Gryphon* and *The Silver Gryphon.*

GRADES: 8–12

REVIEWS: *Booklist* 12/15/93, *Kirkus* 11/15/93, *Publishers Weekly* 11/01/93, *VOYA* 4/94

Lanagan, Margo. *Tender Morsels.* 448 p. TR. Random House Children's Books. 978-0-375-84811-7. 2008. $16.99. LB. Random House Children's Books. 978-0-375-94811-4. 2008. $19.99. PB. Random House Children's Books. 978-0-375-84305-1. 2010. $11.99. CD. Brilliance Audio. 978-1-4233-9677-2. 2009. $29.99.

Liga lives with her sexually abusive father in a small cabin set apart from their poor village. When he dies, she is left alone to care for their newborn baby. A group of boys takes advantage of her isolation, and, pregnant again, Liga attempts to kill herself and the baby. Instead, magic takes her to a place where she can safely raise her daughters, Branza and Urdda, apart from the cruelty of the world. By combining a fantasy setting, Lanagan offers a commentary on the healing power of sisterhood and the plight of abused women. The intensity of the story places it in the older young adult readership category.

GRADES: 10–12

REVIEWS: *Booklist* 8/01/08, *Publishers Weekly* 9/08/08, *SLJ 11/08*, *VOYA* 10/08

AWARDS: Printz Honor

Larbalestier, Justine. *Magic or Madness.* 288 p. TR. Penguin Group (USA) Incorporated. 978-1-59514-022-7. 2005. $16.99. LB. Perma-Bound Books. 978-0-605-01450-3. 2005. $7.99.

After her mother is hospitalized with a nervous breakdown, fifteen-year-old Reason must now live with her grandmother Esmeralda (Mere). As she explores Mere's home, Reason discovers a key to a door which, when opened, transports her across the world to Manhattan where she is befriended by Jay-Tee, a teenager under the evil Jason Blake's control. Jay-Tee and Reason are torn between escaping from Blake and avoiding Mere who has come searching for Reason. Mere and Blake enter a showdown of powerful magic while Reason searches for an answer to her mother's madness.

GRADES: 9–12

REVIEWS: *Booklist* 3/15/05, *SLJ 3/05*, *VOYA* 2/05

Le Guin, Ursula. *A Wizard of Earthsea* (*Earthsea Cycle* series). N/A. RE. San Val, Incorporated. 978-0-88103-755-5. 1975. $18.40. PB. Random House Publishing Group. 978-0-553-26250-6. 1984. $7.99.

The Earthsea series begins with Ged who was the greatest sorcerer in Earthsea. But earlier he was known as Sparrowhawk, a reckless youth hungry for power and knowledge. He tampered with ancient secrets, letting loose a terrible shadow upon the world. *A Wizard of Earthsea* tells of his testing to make amends. Other titles in the series are *The Word of Unbinding, The Finder, Darkrose and Diamond, The Rule of Names, The Bones of Earth, The Tombs of Atuan, On the High Marsh, The Farthest Shore, Tehanu, Dragonfly, Tales from Earthsea,* and *The Other Wind.*

GRADES: 7–12

Leavitt, Martine. *Keturah and Lord Death.* 216 p. TR. Boyds Mills Press. 978-1-932425-29-1. 2006. $16.95. CD. Recorded Books, LLC. 978-1-4281-4649-5. 2007. $66.75. CASS. Recorded Books, LLC. 978-1-4281-4644-0. 2007. $56.75. EB. Recorded Books, LLC. 978-1-4294-7247-0. 2007. $1.00.

At age sixteen, Keturah is a poor peasant girl who worries about her future, especially being committed to finding a suitable husband. One day she follows a legendary hart deep into the forest and becomes lost. After three days she is about to die when Lord Death appears. Keturah sets a deal with Death to grant her a reprieve for one day, but she continues to delay the inevitable in hopes of finding true love. Leavitt's work is a romance with a completely different take on the figure of Death. Teenage girls hopelessly connected to romance will enjoy this story with a fantasy twist.

GRADES: 9–12

REVIEWS: *Booklist* 9/15/06, *Publishers Weekly* 11/20/06, *SLJ* 12/06, *VOYA* 12/06

Lee, Tanith. *The Birthgrave.* No formats available in print.

Birthgrave is set in a barbarian society, full of classic swordplay and sorcery. Uastis is one of the Lost Ones, a powerful race that enslaved humans years before but have since all but died off. Uastis grew from childhood to adulthood sleeping under a volcano and she fights like a man, with skill and strength, yet spends much of the book overpowered by men. She has terrifying powers, which she cannot use to help her or that desert her at the wrong times. *The Birthgrave* is out of print but other titles in the series include *Shadowfire* and *Quest for the White Witch.*

GRADES: 9–12

Lewis, C. S. *The Lion, the Witch and the Wardrobe* (*The Chronicles of Narnia* series). Page count varies with edition. There are significant formats currently available in print.

This classic and hugely popular fantasy tale is the story of four ordinary children—Peter, Susan, Edmund, and Lucy. They discover a wardrobe in Professor Digory Kirke's home that leads to the magical land of Narnia. There the children help Aslan, a talking lion, save Narnia from the evil White Witch who has reigned over the kingdom with a century of perpetual winter. Discussion has long taken place whether to read the series in order of publication or in chronological order. Nevertheless, other titles in the series are *The Magician's Nephew, Prince Caspian: The Return to Narnia, The Horse and His Boy, The Voyage of the Dawn Treader, The Silver Chair,* and *The Last Battle.*

GRADES: 6–12

Marillier, Juliet. *Wildwood Dancing.* 416 p. TR. Random House Children's Books. 978-0-375-83364-9. 2007. $16.99. LB. Random House Children's Books. 978-0-375-93364-6. 2007. $19.99. PB. Random House Children's Books. 978-0-375-84474-4. 2008. $9.99. CD. Random House Audio Publishing Group. 978-0-7393-7938-7. 2009. $50.00. CD. Random House Audio Publishing Group. 978-0-7393-7940-0. 2009. $75.00. EB. Random House Audio Publishing Group. 978-0-7393-7941-7. 2009. $63.75.

On the night of each full moon, the five Transylvanian sisters who reside in the castle Piscul Dracului don their finest gowns and raise their hands to create shadows against the wall. This action opens a portal to the Other Kingdom, where they will dance the night away with all manner of fantastical creatures. Among the creatures is a frog who may be more than he seems. The underlying theme is about human nature and choice. The complicated plot will be a hit with older teenage girls who will also be engaged with the decisions the sisters must make.

GRADES: 9–12

REVIEWS: *Booklist* 2/01/07, *Publishers Weekly* 1/22/07, *SLJ* 2/07, *VOYA* 2/07

Marr, Melissa. *Wicked Lovely.* 336 p. TR. HarperCollins Publishers. 978-0-06-121465-3. 2007. $16.99. LB. HarperCollins Publishers. 978-0-06-121466-0. 2007. $17.89. PB. HarperCollins Publishers. 978-0-06-121467-7. 2008. $8.99. CD. Recorded Books, LLC. 978-1-4281-6346-1. 2007. $97.75. CASS. Recorded Books, LLC. 978-1-4281-6341-6. 2007. $67.75. EB. HarperCollins Publishers. 978-0-06-185173-5. 2009. $9.99.

Seventeen-year-old Aislinn is told by her grandmother not to interact with the fey folk that she can see. Good advice except that when Keenan, the glorious Summer King, makes a play for her to be the next Summer Queen, Aislinn becomes involved in a dangerous relationship. Aislinn can move between two worlds, one where Keenan controls all women and another where she finds herself loving Seth, a protective human guy. Tension, sexual activity, and a truly gruesome climactic scene mark this title as a nice fit for older teens who like their urban fantasy on the edgy side. Companion books are *Ink Exchange, Fragile Eternity,* and *Radiant Shadows.*

GRADES: 9–12

REVIEWS: *Publishers Weekly* 4/30/07, *SLJ* 7/07, *VOYA* 6/07

McCaffrey, Anne. *Dragonflight* (*Dragonriders of Pern* series). 320 p. TR. Random House Publishing Group. 978-0-345-48426-0. 2005. $13.95. RE. San Val, Incorporated. 978-0-8085-2119-8. 1986. $18.40. PB. Random House Publishing Group. 978-0-345-33546-3. 1986. $7.99. PB. Random House Publishing Group. 978-0-345-45633-5. 2002. $6.99. CD. Brilliance Audio. 978-1-59737-948-9. 2005. $39.25. CD. Brilliance Audio. 978-1-59737-947-2. 2005. $24.95. CASS. Audio Literature. 978-1-57453-532-7. 2002. $25.00. CASS. Brilliance Audio. 978-1-59086-288-9. 2002. $29.95. EB. Adobe Systems, Incorporated. 978-1-59061-876-9. 2002. $6.99.

Dragonflight chronicles the story of Lessa, the sole survivor of the noble ruling family on the northern continent of Pern, a planet inhabited by humans. The flying, fire-breathing dragons have been harnessed by humans, which enables them to gain the upper hand in battles with the Thread in the skies over Pern. Lessa uses her psychic abilities to influence people, but she is also able to warn the people of Pern of the coming Thread reappearance, something they find hard to believe. Dragonflight is high fantasy that has been engaging readers for decades. Other titles in the series are *Dragonquest* and *The White Dragon*.

GRADES: 6–10

McKinley, Robin. *Beauty: A Retelling of the Story of Beauty and the Beast.* 247 p. TR. Perfection Learning Corporation. 978-0-8124-4280-9. 1993. $13.65. TR. Harper Collins Publishers. 978-0-06-024149-0. 1978. $16.99. LB. Perma-Bound Books. 978-0-8479-0919-3. 1978. $6.99. RE. San Val, Incorporated. 978-0-8085-6649-6. 1993. $16.00. PB. HarperCollins Publishers. 978-0-06-075310-8. 2005. $6.99. PB. HarperCollins Publishers. 978-0-06-440477-8. 1993. $5.99.

In the version offered by McKinley, Beauty is not as beautiful as her older sisters, who are both lovely and kind. However she takes pride in her intelligence and love of learning. When her father is financially ruined, Beauty agrees to inhabit the Beast's castle to spare her father's life. Magic abounds in the Beast's library where thousands of novels that haven't been written yet are shelved. This timeless tale is enhanced by McKinley's writing style.

GRADES: 9–12

REVIEWS: *Booklist* 6/01/88

McKinley, Robin, and Peter Dickinson. *Fire: Tales of Elemental Spirits.* 304 p. TR. Penguin Group (USA) Incorporated. 978-0-399-25289-1. 2009. $19.99.

The authors alternate stories and combine humor with creative fantasy. Each of the five stories in some way involves fire. The story "Phoenix" introduces readers to a boy living in a wooded area who when he was 100 years old found the Phoenix in a fire and now the boy has been growing younger ever since. In the story "Hellhound" an unusual dog with burning red eyes is adopted from the animal shelter and he turns out to be a blessing. Thrilling and cleverly written, this set of stories will appeal to readers who like their fantasy on the sophisticated side.

GRADES: 9–12

REVIEWS: *Booklist* 9/01/09, *SLJ* 9/09, *VOYA* 12/09

Mieville, China. *Un Lun Dun.* 474 p. TR. Perfection Learning Corporation. 978-1-60686-002-1. 2008. $16.65. PB. Random House Publishing Group. 978-0-345-45844-5. 2008. $9.95.

Un Lun Dun is a mirror image of the real London, but not exactly. It's more surreal. Readers follow the adventures of friends Zanna and Deeba as they wind up in this odd city filled with ghosts, zombies, walking garbage cans, and anthropomorphic umbrellas. Zanna is the chosen one to help the citizens defeat The Smog, a beast made from chemicals and poisons. Fate intervenes and Deeba becomes the story's reluctant hero. The clever setting and Deeba rising to the challenge carry this work marked by a thrilling climax.

GRADES: 8–12

REVIEWS: *Publishers Weekly* 2/12/07, *SLJ* 4/07, *VOYA* 2/07

Napoli, Donna Jo. *Breath.* N/A. LB. Perma-Bound Books. 978-0-605-01310-0. 2003. $5.99. LP. Thorndike Press. 978-0-7862-7420-8. 2005. $21.95.

Salz is a young man living in thirteenth-century Saxony. He suffers from fits of coughing that nobody in the village can explain. During this historical period, superstitions became the rationale for anything unknown. Also unexplained are why some children are unaffected by natural disasters that hit the town's crops and livestock. What Napoli cleverly offers is a completely different take on the fable of the Pied Piper of Hamlin. History and fantasy are mixed in a rewarding read for upper middle school students.

GRADES: 7–10

REVIEWS: *Booklist* 9/15/03, *SLJ* 11/03, *VOYA* 12/03

Nix, Garth. *Lirael.* 705 p. TR. Perfection Learning Corporation. 978-0-7569-1074-7. 2002. $15.65. LB. Perma-Bound Books. 978-0-605-01229-5. 2001. $7.99. RE. San Val, Incorporated. 978-0-613-62468-8. 2002. $18.40. PB. HarperCollins Publishers. 978-0-06-147434-7. 2008. $9.99. PB. HarperCollins Publishers. 978-0-06-000542-9. 2002. $7.99. CD. Random House Audio Publishing Group. 978-0-8072-2008-5. 2004. $80.00. EB. HarperCollins Publishers. 978-0-06-000549-8. 2001. $6.99. EB. Random House Audio Publishing Group. 978-0-7393-6081-1. 2008. $68.00.

Nix takes readers back to the complicated Old Kingdom: a world of necromancy, seers, dangerous monsters, and talking animals. The story is rich with relationships between the Kingdom's various realms and magic. Lirael is a member of a community of women who have "the Sight," the gift of being clairvoyant, which Lirael does not possess. Many subplots highlight this story that ultimately finds Lirael linking her destiny with handsome Prince Sameth. Readers drawn to layered plots flush with magic will enjoy this work. Other titles in the series are *Sabriel* and *Abhorsen* (Teens' Top Ten).

GRADES: 8–10

REVIEWS: *Booklist* 4/15/01, *Kirkus* 3/15/01, *Publishers Weekly* 3/19/01, *SLJ* 5/01, *VOYA* 8/01

AWARDS: BBYA Top Ten

Noel, Alyson. *Evermore (The Immortals series).* N/A. LB. San Val, Incorporated. 978-0-606-10569-9. 2009. $20.80. PB. St. Martin's Press. 978-0-312-53275-8. 2009.

$9.95. CD. Macmillan Audio. 978-1-4272-0840-8. 2009. $29.99. EB. St. Martin's Press. 978-1-4299-1868-8. 2009. $9.95.

Seventeen-year-old Ever survived the car crash that killed her parents, younger sister, and their dog. She lives with her aunt in Southern California and battles survivor guilt. Oddly enough, she also has the ability to hear the thoughts of everyone around her. By keeping her hoodie up and cranking her iPod, Ever keeps the distractions at bay, until cute new boy Damen encourages her to come out of her shell. What Ever comes to realize is that she may have control over her own immortality. Other titles in the Immortals series are *Blue Moon, Shadowland,* and *Dark Flame.*

GRADES: 8–12

REVIEWS: *Booklist* 2/01/09, *SLJ* 4/09, *VOYA* 2/09

Noyes, Deborah, ed. *Gothic: Ten Original Dark Tales.* N/A. LB. Perma-Bound Books. 978-0-605-01399-5. 2004. $8.99. RE. San Val, Incorporated. 978-1-4177-6927-8. 2006. $19.65. PB. Candlewick Press. 978-0-7636-2737-9. 2006. $8.99.

Joan Aiken, Neil Gaiman, Gregory Maguire, and Vivian Vande Velde are some of the authors who offer stories in this anthology that explores creepy happenings with a touch of humor. Vampires whine about the garlic in spaghetti sauce and shapeshifting witches eat Triscuits and use ATMs. This work explores the dark side of fantasy and will creep out the unwary reader who thinks all supernatural writing is just a lark. The content works well for both middle and high school students.

GRADES: 7–12

REVIEWS: *Booklist* 10/15/04, *Publishers Weekly* 11/01/04, *SLJ* 1/05, *VOYA* 8/04

Noyes, Deborah, ed. *The Restless Dead: Ten Original Stories of the Supernatural.* 272p. TR. Candlewick Press. 978-0-7636-2906-9. 2007. $16.99. PB. Candlewick Press. 978-0-7636-3671-5. 2009. $7.99.

M. T. Anderson, Holly Black, Libby Bray, and Annette Curtis Klause are featured authors in this anthology that mixes the macabre with the bizarre. Teen readers will laugh out loud at "The Wrong Grave" when a teenage boy digs up his girlfriend's corpse, only to find a different girl residing in the grave. Horror fans will appreciate the gruesomeness of the works, but there is something here for practically everyone, especially around Halloween. These ten stories have wide appeal for both boys and girls of all ages.

GRADES: 7–12

REVIEWS: *Booklist* 5/15/07, *SLJ* 9/07, *VOYA* 10/07

Paolini, Christopher. *Eragon* (*The Inheritance Cycle*). 544 p. TR. Random House Children's Books. 978-0-375-82668-9. 2003. $18.95. LB. Random House Children's Books. 978-0-375-92668-6. 2003. $20.99. RE. San Val, Incorporated. 978-1-4176-7552-4. 2005. $22.05. LB. Perma-Bound Books. 978-0-605-02167-9. 2003. $7.99. PB. Random House Children's Books. 978-0-440-24073-0. 2007. $7.99. PB. Random House Children's Books. 978-0-375-82669-6. 2005. $10.95. CD. Random House Audio Publishing Group. 978-1-4000-8624-5. 2004. $72.75. CD. Random House Audio Publishing Group. 978-1-4000-9068-6. 2004. $39.95. PLAY. Findaway World, LLC. 978-0-7393-7475-7. 2006. $54.99. CASS. Random House Audio Publishing Group. 978-0-8072-1963-8. 2004. $55.00. EB. Random House Audio Publishing Group. 978-0-7393-4480-4. 2006. $72.75.

> Eragon is a fifteen-year-old guy who is minding his own business when he discovers an odd blue gemstone. He soon learns it is a dragon egg that will come under his care during the hatching. Eragon develops a psychic connection with the newborn female dragon whom he names Saphira. Thus begins an epic adventure of boy and dragon as they battle warriors of evil King Galbatorix. This first title in the series launched Paolini (he was fifteen when he wrote the book) into a hugely popular author. Other titles in the series are *Eldest* (Teens' Top Ten) and *Brisingr*. *Eragon* is one of the teen publishing industries' most remarkable successes and has wide appeal to all ages of readers.

GRADES: 7–12

REVIEWS: *Booklist* 8/01/03, *Publishers Weekly* 7/21/03, *SLJ* 9/03, *VOYA* 8/03

AWARDS: Teens' Top Ten

Pattou, Edith. *East.* 507 p. TR. Perfection Learning Corporation. 978-0-7569-5054-5. 2005. $16.60. LB. Perma-Bound Books. 978-0-605-00563-1. 2005. $8.95. PB. Houghton Mifflin Harcourt Trade & Reference Publishers. 978-0-15-205221-8. 2005. $8.95. CASS. Random House Audio Publishing Group. 978-0-307-24666-0. 2005. $50.00.

> Rose is the youngest of seven children and when she is almost fifteen, a white bear appears at the door asking her father to turn over his youngest daughter. The huge animal carries her to a far off castle to live. Each night, a mysterious visitor climbs into her bed and hides under the covers. Her curiosity seals the fate of the visitor who is whisked away by the Troll Queen. Rose then begins a draining journey to right the wrong she committed. This title is fantasy of high drama and has special appeal to middle school girls.

GRADES: 7–10

REVIEWS: *Booklist* 9/01/03, *Publishers Weekly* 7/28/03, *SLJ* 12/03, *VOYA* 12/03

AWARDS: BBYA Top Ten

Pierce, Tamora. *Sandry's Book* (*The Circle of Magic*). 252 p. TR. Perfection Learning Corporation. 978-0-7807-9950-9. 1999. $14.65. RE. San Val, Incorporated. 978-0-613-17935-5. 1999. $17.20. PB. Scholastic, Incorporated. 978-0-590-55408-4. 1999. $6.99. PLAY. Findaway World, LLC. 978-1-59895-503-3. 2006. $39.99.

Four children—Daja, Briar, Tris, and Sandry—are brought to Winding Circle Temple for training in crafts and magic. While considered outcastes in their homeland, they are valued and respected for their powers in this magical place. Daja, the Trader girl, wants to be a metalworker, but making things is forbidden to traders. Briar, a streetwise thief, harbors a special affinity for plants, and Trisana, the Merchant girl, seems to have a direct line to the forces of nature. Other titles in the series are *Tris's Book, Daja's Book,* and *Briar's Book.* Pierce is known for creating strong female characters and this group will thrill middle school girls.

GRADES: 6–10

REVIEWS: *Booklist* 9/01/97, *Kirkus* 7/15/97, *Publishers Weekly* 6/23/97, *SLJ* 9/97

Pierce, Tamora. *Trickster's Choice* (*Daughter of the Lioness* series). 422 p. TR. Perfection Learning Corporation. 978-0-7569-5746-9. 2004. $16.60. LB. Perma-Bound Books. 978-0-605-01341-4. 2003. $6.99. PB. Random House Children's Books. 978-0-375-82879-9. 2004. $8.95. PB. Random House, Incorporated. 978-0-375-81472-3. 2003. $6.99. CASS. Random House Audio Publishing Group. 978-0-8072-1792-4. 2004. $46.00. EB. Random House Audio Publishing Group. 978-0-7393-4459-0. 2006. $59.50.

Sixteen-year-old Alianne, or Aly, wishes to become a spy like her father. When Aly is captured by slave traders in the Copper Isles, she fulfills her desire in unexpected ways. Making a wager with the Trickster god, Kyprioth, Aly contracts to safeguard two girls. Aly must create a secret spy network and fighting force to defend her charges from royal assassins. Pierce's layered plot will thrill readers as the smart and sassy Aly breaks away from her parents and carves out her own niche, a trait that will appeal to teenage girls. The second book in the series is called *Trickster's Queen.*

GRADES: 6–10

REVIEWS: *Booklist* 12/01/03, *Publishers Weekly* 9/15/03, *SLJ* 12/03, *VOYA* 10/03
AWARDS: Teens' Top Ten

Pratchett, Terry. *The Colour of Magic* (*Discworld* series). 272 p. TR. HarperCollins Publishers. 978-0-06-183310-6. 2009. $16.99. TR. HarperCollins Publishers. 978-0-06-168596-5. 2008. $24.95.

Twoflower is a naïve tourist who follows an incompetent and cynical wizard named Rincewind. They escape the city of Ankh-Morpork and begin a journey across the Disc. The do not realize their journey is controlled by the Gods playing a board game. There are thirty-eight titles in the *Discworld* series beginning with *The Colour of Magic* and ending with *I Shall Wear Midnight*. The series has been popular with middle school boys for decades.

GRADES: 6–10

Pullman, Philip. *The Golden Compass* (*His Dark Materials* **series**). 416 p. TR. Follett Library Resources. 978-1-4046-1654-7. 2002. $21.80. TR. Random House Children's Books. 978-0-679-87924-4. 1996. $20.00. LB. Perma-Bound Books. 978-0-605-02249-2. 1995. $7.50. RE. San Val, Incorporated. 978-0-613-81036-4. 2003. $17.85. PB. Random House Publishing Group. 978-0-345-91640-2. 1999. $5.99. PB. Random House Publishing Group. 978-0-345-91365-4. 1998. $5.99. CD. Random House Audio Publishing Group. 978-0-8072-0471-9. 2004. $29.95. CD. Random House Audio Publishing Group. 978-0-8072-1049-9. 2004. $60.00. PLAY. Findaway World, LLC. 978-0-7393-7483-2. 2007. $59.99. CASS. Books on Tape, Incorporated. 978-0-7366-9001-0. 2000. $50.00. CASS. Random House Audio Publishing Group. 978-0-8072-8143-7. 1999. $19.95. EB. Adobe Systems, Incorporated. 978-1-59061-391-7. 2001. $3.99. EB. Random House Audio Publishing Group. 978-0-7393-4512-2. 2006. $55.25. LP. Thorndike Press. 978-0-7862-4123-1. 2002. $25.95.

This fantasy yarn is firmly established as a young adult classic. The first establishment of *His Dark Materials* series keeps pages turning with horror and high adventure. The heroine, Lyra Belacqua, a young girl brought up in the cloistered world of Jordan College, Oxford, learns of the existence of Dust, a strange elementary particle believed to provide evidence for Original Sin. Lyra rescues Asriel, which launches a series of events that enable Lyra to discover her unusual powers and destiny. Flush with a Victorian-era tone, Pullman's masterwork has been examined by scholars and enjoyed by thousands of teen readers. Other titles in the series *The Subtle Knife* and *The Amber Spyglass*.

GRADES: 9–12

REVIEWS: *Booklist* 3/01/96, *Kirkus* 3/01/96, *Publishers Weekly* 2/19/96, *SLJ* 4/96

Reeve, Philip. *Here Lies Arthur.* 352 p. TR. Scholastic, Incorporated. 978-0-545-09334-7. 2008. $17.99.

Reeve breathes fresh life into the Authurian legend with his fable that gives a behind-the-scenes take on The Lady of the Lake myth. Gwyna narrates her adventures beginning when she is around nine years old and meets Myrddin who witnesses her swimming ability. Soon she is disguised as The Lady of the Lake and has a hand in Arthur's stunning exploits. Reeve offers that Arthur's life is a complete political spin with Myrddin's trickery as its cause. A strong heroine in Gwyna marks this work as an interesting treat for upper middle school and some high school readers.

GRADES: 7–10

REVIEWS: *Booklist* 8/01/08, *Publishers Weekly* 10/06/08, *SLJ* 12/08, *VOYA* 2/09

Riordan, Rick. *The Lightning Thief* (*Percy Jackson and the Olympians* series). 384 p. TR. Hyperion Press. 978-1-4231-2170-1. 2009. $25.00. TR. Disney Publishing Worldwide. 978-1-4231-3589-0. 2009. $17.99. LB. Perma-Bound Books. 978-0-605-02451-9. 2005. $7.99. RE. San Val, Incorporated. 978-1-4177-3247-0. 2006. $18.40. PB. Hyperion Press. 978-1-4231-3494-7. 2010. $7.99. CD. Random House Audio Publishing Group. 978-0-307-24530-4. 2005. $19.99. CD. Random House Audio Publishing Group. 978-0-307-24531-1. 2005. $51.00. PLAY. Findaway World, LLC. 978-0-7393-7113-8. 2008. $54.99. CASS. Random House Audio Publishing Group. 978-0-307-24529-8. 2005. $45.00. EB. Random House Audio Publishing Group. 978-0-7393-4514-6. 2006. $51.00. LP. Thorndike Press. 978-0-7862-8225-8. 2006. $22.95.

Librarians seeking fast-moving action in stories that will attract boy readers should acquire this must-have series. Percy Jackson is the son of a human mother and the god Poseidon, a fact that is revealed to him as monsters and demons seem to want to kill the young man. Clever characters abound as Percy has loyal friends—both male and female—who protect him. An added bonus is the delightful take on the Greek gods who reside at Camp Half-Blood Hill. The series features great storytelling, crackling action, and Percy is a conflicted and sympathetic character. There's something here for all readers. Other titles in the series are *The Sea of Monsters, The Titan's Curse, The Battle of the Labyrinth,* and *The Last Olympian.*

GRADES: 6–12

REVIEWS: *Booklist* 9/15/05, *Publishers Weekly* 7/18/05, *SLJ* 8/05, *VOYA* 8/05

Rowling, J. K. *Harry Potter and the Sorcerer's Stone.* 309 p. TR. Scholastic, Incorporated. 978-0-439-55493-0. 2003. $24.95. TR. Follett Library Resources. 978-0-7587-0016-2. 2002. $21.37. LB. Perma-Bound Books. 978-0-605-65644-4. 1998. $10.99. RE. San Val, Incorporated. 978-0-613-95992-6. 2001. $17.20. PB. Scholastic, Incorporated. 978-0-439-36213-9. 2001. $6.99. PB. Scholastic, Incorporated. 978-0-439-21116-1. 2000. $5.95. CD. Random House Audio Publishing Group. 978-0-8072-8600-5. 2004. $50.00. CD. Books on Tape, Incorporated. 978-0-7366-5092-2. 2000. $49.95. CASS. Random House Audio Publishing Group. 978-0-8072-8118-5. 2004. $40.00. CASS. Books on Tape, Incorporated. 978-0-7366-9000-3. 1999. $33.95. LP. Thorndike Press. 978-1-59413-000-7. 2003. $13.95.

Of course this series has to be in any list of recommended books for young adults. After all, Rowling's creation is a publishing giant unmatched in young adult literature and perhaps all literature. Harry Potter is an orphan raised by his dysfunctional aunt and uncle. What's worse is that he's the target of the evil Lord Voldemort, a wizard who killed Harry's parents and narrowly missed murdering Harry. All this is because Harry is a wizard with extraordinary powers yet uncovered. Soon he is enrolled in Hogwarts, a school for boys and girls with magical powers. The entire series is creative, imaginative and downright thrilling. There will always be an interest, especially when the movie versions are shown. For the record, the other series' titles are *Harry Potter and the Chamber of Secrets, Harry Potter and the Prisoner of Azkaban, Harry Potter and the Goblet of Fire, Harry Potter and the Order of the Phoenix* (Teens' Top Ten), *Harry Potter and the Half-Blood Prince* (Teens' Top Ten), and *Harry Potter and the Deathly Hallows* (Teens' Top Ten).

GRADES: 9–12

REVIEWS: *Booklist* 9/15/98, *Kirkus* 9/01/98, *Publishers Weekly* 7/20/98, *SLJ* 10/98, *VOYA* 12/98

Sage, Angie. *Magyk* (*Septimus Heap*). 564 p. TR. Perfection Learning Corporation. 978-0-7569-7760-3. 2006. $15.65. TR. HarperCollins Publishers. 978-0-06-057731-5. 2005. $17.99. LB. HarperCollins Publishers. 978-0-06-057732-2. 2005. $18.89. RE. San Val, Incorporated. 978-1-4177-3321-7. 2006. $18.40. PB. HarperCollins Publishers. 978-0-06-057733-9. 2006. $7.99. CD. HarperCollins Publishers. 978-0-06-156306-5. 2008. $14.95. EB. HarperCollins Publishers. 978-0-06-167193-7. 2008. $7.99.

In a tale involving magic and royal family intrigue, Septimus Heap is the seventh son of a seventh son. His destiny is to use awesome magical powers, but that may not happen. His father, Silas Heap, who is also a wizard, discovers a newborn baby girl in the snow. At the same time Septimus is whisked away from his mother by the midwife. Flashing forward ten years has a nasty wizard named DomDaniel trying to finish off the royal line. Fans of Harry Potter will seamlessly move to this intricate series of an underdog young magician confronted with evil. Other titles in the series include *Flyte, Physik, Queste,* and *Syren.*

GRADES: 6–10

REVIEWS: *Booklist* 3/15/05, *Kirkus* 1/15/05, *Publishers Weekly* 1/03/05, *SLJ* 4/05, *VOYA* 2/05

Scott, Michael. *The Alchemyst* (*The Secrets of the Immortal Nicholas Flamel*). 400 p. TR. Random House Children's Books. 978-0-385-73357-1. 2007. $16.99. LB. Random House Children's Books. 978-0-385-90372-1. 2007. $19.99. PB. Random House Children's Books. 978-0-385-73600-8. 2008. $8.99. CD. Random House Audio Publishing Group. 978-0-7393-5032-4. 2007. $40.00. CD. Random House Audio Publishing Group. 978-0-7393-5104-8. 2007. $60.00. EB. Random House

Audio Publishing Group. 978-0-7393-5105-5. 2007. $68.00. LP. Thorndike Press. 978-0-7862-9886-0. 2007. $23.95.

This fast-moving story takes place in one fantastic day as fifteen-year-old twins, Josh and Sophie Newman, are unknowingly drawn into an ancient battle between Nicholas Flamel and Dr. John Dee. They are immortal. Dr. Dee seeks the Book of Abraham the Mage, which holds the spell of nothing less than the destruction of all mankind. It seems the earth was populated with a race long before humans appeared. The book holds the key. Sophisticated readers of fantasy will be more likely to grasp references to ancient mythology, but this title has wide appeal for both boys and girls. Other titles in the series are *The Magician, The Sorceress,* and *The Necromancer.*

GRADES: 6–10

REVIEWS: *Booklist* 3/01/07, *Kirkus* 3/01/07, *Publishers Weekly* 3/05/07, *SLJ* 5/07, *VOYA* 7/07

Sedgwick, Marcus. *My Swordhand Is Singing.* 224 p. TR. Random House Children's Books. 978-0-375-84689-2. 2007. $15.99. PB. Random House Children's Books. 978-0-375-84690-8. 2009. $6.99.

Set in a time of seventeenth-century Europe, Peter lives with his alcoholic father Tomas. Isolated in their home surrounded by a forest, they cut wood for their neighbors. Two gruesome and bizarre murders alarm the citizens. Peter uncovers the horrifying truth: the Undead are rising from their graves to kill and recruit more humans. Tomas must rise from his stupor and wield an old sword to dispatch the zombie-vampires. A fine mix of horror and fantasy marks this title with appeal to older teens. Caveat emptor—a significant amount of blood is spilled throughout the pages.

GRADES: 9-12

REVIEWS: *Booklist* 11/15/07, *Kirkus* 9/15/07, *Publishers Weekly* 11/12/07, *SLJ* 11/07, *VOYA* 10/07

Shan, Darren. *Cirque du Freak: A Living Nightmare.* 272 p. TR. Little, Brown Books for Young Readers. 978-0-316-60340-9. 2001. $15.95. LB. Perma-Bound Books. 978-0-605-03763-2. 2000. $7.99. RE. San Val, Incorporated. 978-0-613-52592-3. 2002. $18.40. PB. Little, Brown Books for Young Readers. 978-0-316-60510-6. 2002. $7.99.

This series has become more than a cult phenomenon and has moved into a large driving publishing force geared to middle school readers. In the opening story, twelve-year-old Darren Shan and his friend Steve sneak out to attend a late-night freak show, where one of the performers is identified as a vampire. Through a series of horrifying events, Darren agrees to become the vampire's assistant, becoming a half-vampire, and the game is on. More plot driven than character driven, this series is heavy on action as Darren finds himself more and more involved with the bizarre and bloody world of vampires. Middle school readers, especially boys, simply love these books. Other titles in the series are *Tunnels of Blood, Vampire Mountain, Trials of Death, The Vampire Prince, Hunters of the Dusk, Allies of the Night, Killers of the Dawn, The Lake of Souls, Lord of the Shadows* and *Sons of Destiny.*

GRADES: 6–10

REVIEWS: *Booklist* 4/15/01, *Publishers Weekly* 2/26/01, *SLJ* 5/01, *VOYA* 4/01

Shusterman, Neal. *Everlost* (*The Skinjacker* series). 320 p. TR. Simon & Schuster Children's Publishing. 978-0-689-87237-2. 2006. $16.95. RE. San Val, Incorporated. 978-1-4178-1799-3. 2007. $17.20. PB. Simon & Schuster Children's Publishing. 978-1-4169-9749-8. 2009. $8.99. PB. Simon & Schuster Children's Publishing. 978-0-689-87238-9. 2007. $6.99. CD. Brilliance Audio. 978-1-4233-7314-8. 2009. $29.99. EB. Simon & Schuster Children's Publishing. 978-1-4391-0725-6. 2008. $6.99. LP. Thorndike Press. 978-0-7862-9365-0. 2007. $22.95.

Traveling along a lonely highway two cars collide. Teenagers Nick and Allie are both killed in the accident and they meet heading down a tunnel toward a light. Their weird journey ends up in the land of Everlost, a stopping place between the living and what waits at the end of the tunnel. There they learn they've become Afterlights and cannot be seen by the living. The teens are initially confused about this strange new world, but they do adjust and grow as they try to figure out their destiny. Shusterman's story includes questioning authority and understanding what is truly important in life. The next book in the series is *Everwild.*

GRADES: 8–12

REVIEWS: *Booklist* 9/15/06, *Kirkus* 10/01/06, *Publishers Weekly* 11/02/06, *SLJ* 10/06, *VOYA* 10/06

Shusterman, Neal. *Full Tilt.* 208 p. TR. Simon & Schuster Children's Publishing. 978-0-689-80374-1. 2003. $16.95. LB. San Val, Incorporated. 978-1-4176-3919-9. 2004. $17.20. PB. Simon & Schuster Children's Publishing. 978-1-4169-9748-1. 2009. $8.99. PB. Simon & Schuster Children's Publishing. 978-0-689-87325-6. 2004. $6.99.

Sixteen-year-old Blake is sucked into an alternate universe and must confront his deepest fears to escape. After riding an awesome roller coaster, Blake and his brother Quinn meet Cassandra, a mysterious girl who invited Blake to attend a midnight carnival. Soon Quinn has slipped into a coma and Blake realizes Cassandra is a key to Quinn's survival. At the midnight carnival, Blake is challenged to ride seven rides formed by Cassandra's probing Blake's mind. Each ride is based on his suppressed fears. Readers learn about Blake's past and the rides become increasingly terrifying. There are several psychological themes worked into the narrative, but the action carries the story and the book will appeal to many readers.

GRADES: 8–12

REVIEWS: *Booklist* 5/15/03, *Kirkus* 6/01/03, *Publishers Weekly* 6/23/03, *SLJ* 6/03, *VOYA* 10/03

Smith, Cynthia Leitich. *Tantalize.* 336 p. TR. Candlewick Press. 978-0-7636-2791-1. 2007. $16.99. PB. Candlewick Press. 978-0-7636-4059-0. 2008. $8.99. CD. Random House Audio Publishing Group. 978-0-7393-6400-0. 2007. $38.00. EB. Random House Audio Publishing Group. 978-0-7393-6401-7. 2008. $32.30.

Smith winks at the vampire/werewolf craze with her story about Quincie Morris, who is grieving her parents' accidental death. In this world supernatural beings interact with humans and Quincie dates Kieren, a werewolf hybrid with little self-control. Quincie's self-appointed mission is to reopen her family's Italian eatery as a vampire-themed restaurant. When her chef is brutally murdered, suspicion of a werewolf attack arises and the finger points to Kieren. There's a lighthearted tone to this story despite brutal murders threatening to stop the restaurant's opening. The companion book to this story is called *Eternal.*

GRADES: 8–12

REVIEWS: *Booklist* 3/01/07, *Kirkus* 2/15/07, *Publishers Weekly* 3/05/07, *SLJ* 5/07, *VOYA* 6/07

Stiefvater, Maggie. *Lament: The Faerie Queen's Deception.* 336 p. PB. Llewellyn Publications. 978-0-7387-1370-0. 2008. $9.95.

Sixteen-year-old Deirdre Monaghan, a gifted harpist who regularly plays for weddings, becomes physically ill with stage fright. While she's vomiting before a performance, Luke Dillon gently holds her hair. As a flautist, Luke accompanies Deirdre and a romance blossoms. Four-leaf clovers appear everywhere and Deirdre learns she is a cloverhand, a person who can see faeries. Danger abounds when Deirdre is targeted by the Faerie Queen to be killed. Celtic faerie lore meets modern America in this tension-packed tale of forbidden love. The complicated plot may be best appreciated by older teens.

GRADES: 9–12

REVIEWS: *Booklist* 12/01/08, *Publishers Weekly* 10/13/08, *VOYA* 12/08

Stiefvater, Maggie. *Shiver.* 400 p. TR. Scholastic, Incorporated. 978-0-545-12326-6. 2009. $17.99. CD. Scholastic, Incorporated. 978-0-545-16508-2. 2009. $79.95. CD. Scholastic, Incorporated. 978-0-545-16506-8. 2009. $39.95.

Seventeen-year-old Grace is fascinated by the wolves residing behind her Minnesota home. As a young child she was dragged from her swing by the pack, only to be rescued by one particular wolf. He is eighteen-year-old Sam, a guy leading a double life; wolf in the winter, boy in the summer. He longs for Grace but the wolf pack is his family. Grace is determined to save Sam following a gruesome murder of a town boy, but can Sam stay in human form and escape the vigilante group? The intricate back and forth of shape shifting may confuse younger middle school readers.

GRADES: 9–12

REVIEWS: *Publishers Weekly* 8/03/09, *SLJ* 10/09, *VOYA* 12/09

Stroud, Jonathan. *The Amulet of Samarkand* (*The Bartimaeus Trilogy*, **Book One**). 464 p. TR. Hyperion Books for Children. 978-0-7868-1859-4. 2003. $17.95. LB. Perma-Bound Books. 978-0-8000-9583-3. 2003. $8.99. CD. Random House Audio Publishing Group. 978-0-7393-5613-5. 2007. $50.00. CASS. Random House Audio Publishing Group. 978-0-8072-1954-6. 2004. $50.00. EB. Random House Audio Publishing Group. 978-0-7393-4455-2. 2007. $63.75.

At the age of twelve, Nathaniel is finally on his way to becoming a real magician. He summons a 5,000-year-old djinni named Bartimaeus who is ordered by Nathaniel to steal the valuable Amulet of Samarkand. London is in an uproar. Young Nathaniel isn't sure what to do and Bartimaeus is little help as he is snarky and rebellious. The narrative alternates between smart-mouth Bartimaeus and third-person descriptions of Nathaniel's dilemma. Plenty of action keeps this lengthy book moving. Other titles in the trilogy are *The Golem's Eye* and *Ptolemy's Gate*.

GRADES: 9–12

REVIEWS: *Booklist* 9/01/03, *Kirkus* 10/01/03, *Publishers Weekly* 7/21/03, *SLJ* 1/04, *VOYA* 12/03

AWARDS: BBYA Top Ten

Stroud, Jonathan. *Heroes of the Valley.* 496 p. TR. Hyperion Press. 978-1-4231-0966-2. 2009. $17.99. CD. Random House Audio Publishing Group. 978-0-7393-8220-2. 2009. $50.00. CD. Random House Audio Publishing Group. 978-0-7393-8222-6. 2009. $65.00. EB. Random House Audio Publishing Group. 978-0-7393-8223-3. 2009. $55.25.

Short and squat, Halli Sveinsson has never felt a part of his tall and handsome family. His knack for pranks backfires on him, setting in motion events that prompt him to leave home to avenge the murder of his uncle. His quest is accomplished with the help of Aud, a girl with tremendous fighting skills. Once home, Halli must lead his people to battle creatures called Trows who live behind a barrier protecting the village. The theme is one of living up to others' expectations, but that is secondary to the crackling action of the pitched battle on the wall against the Trows. This title is not for everyone and takes some time to get moving, but patient readers will be rewarded with the exciting climactic scene.

GRADES: 8–12

REVIEWS: *Booklist* 12/01/08, *Kirkus* 12/15/08, *Publishers Weekly* 11/24/08, *SLJ* 1/09, *VOYA* 2/09

Taylor, Laini. *Lips Touch: Three Times.* 272 p. TR. Scholastic, Incorporated. 978-0-545-05585-7. 2009. $17.99. PB. Scholastic, Incorporated. 978-0-545-05586-4. 2009. N/A.

The connecting thread to these three stories is kissing, whether it's one of seduction or a harsh show of power. Each tale begins somewhat innocently, but soon tension develops as humans and demons interact. Illustrations by Jim Di Bartolo, the author's husband, introduce the stories. Titles entice readers much like kisses entice the characters. They are *Goblin Fruit, Spicy Little Curses Such as These,* and *Hatchling.* Truly wonderful descriptions carry this outstanding work, but it requires a sophisticated reader to grasp the underlying subtleness of the work.

GRADES: 10–12

REVIEWS: *Booklist* 10/01/09, *Kirkus* 9/15/09, *Publishers Weekly* 9/21/09, *SLJ* 11/09, *VOYA* 12/09

AWARDS: BBYA Top Ten

Thompson, Kate. *The New Policeman.* 448 p. TR. HarperCollins Publishers. 978-0-06-117427-8. 2007. $16.99. LB. HarperCollins Publishers. 978-0-06-117428-5. 2007. $17.89. PB. HarperCollins Publishers. 978-0-06-117429-2. 2008. $8.99. CD. Recorded Books, LLC. 978-1-4281-4759-1. 2007. $66.75. CASS. Recorded Books, LLC. 978-1-4281-4754-6. 2007. $51.75. EB. HarperCollins Publishers. 978-0-06-183129-4. 2009. $9.99.

J. J. Liddy is fifteen years old when he ventures into an alternate fairy world. There he begins an epic quest dealing with dark family rumors and a cosmic time leak between his world and "the land of eternal youth." This novel is packed with Irish culture (including phrases defined in a glossary), interconnected mysteries, and sly questions about the stresses of contemporary life and the age-old frictions between religion and folklore. Fantasy readers will thrill with the recommendation, but non-fantasy readers are not likely to cross over to the story.

GRADES: 9–12

REVIEWS: *Booklist* 2/01/07, *Kirkus* 12/15/06, *Publishers Weekly* 12/11/06, *SLJ* 3/07, *VOYA* 2/07

Tolkien, J. R. R. *The Fellowship of the Ring (The Lord of the Rings trilogy).* Page count varies with edition. There are significant formats currently available.

Perhaps the most influential work of fantasy in all of literature, Tolkien's masterpiece is a must-have for all young adult collections. Although it is today mostly known as a trilogy, Tolkien intended it to be one volume of a two-volume set that was to include *The Silmarillion.* Here the Dark Lord Sauron has created the One Ring to rule the other Rings of Power and ultimately control all of Middle-earth. From their calm Shire, notable hobbits Frodo Baggins, Samwise Gamgee (Sam), Meriadoc Brandybuck (Merry) and Peregrin Took (Pippin) embark on an epic journey following the course of the War of the Ring. Recent movie versions have given the work a boost in popularity. Other titles in the trilogy are *The Two Towers* and *The Return of the King.*

GRADES: 9–12

Tolkien, J. R. R. *The Hobbit or, There and Back Again.* 330 p. TR. Houghton Mifflin Harcourt Publishing Company. 978-0-618-96863-3. 2007. $25.00. TR. Houghton Mifflin Harcourt Trade & Reference Publishers. 978-0-618-16221-5. 2001. $18.00. LB. San Val, Incorporated. 978-0-8085-2080-1. 1986. $16.45. PB. Houghton Mifflin Harcourt Trade & Reference Publishers. 978-0-618-26030-0. 2002. $10.00.

The Hobbit ushers readers into the fantasy realm of one Bilbo Baggins, a hobbit who is very comfortable in his home surroundings. His epic journey has him meeting different types of creatures created by Tolkien. By using his wits and common sense, the everyman character Bilbo matures and becomes competent in his actions. His hero's journey results in triumph. Tolkien raised the fantasy bar with his work and many of today's popular works can attribute their roots to Tolkien's genius. For all collections.

GRADES: 9–12

Turner, Megan Whalen. *A Conspiracy of Kings (The Queen's Thief series).* 336 p. TR. HarperCollins Publishers 978-0-06-187093-4. 2010. $16.99. LB. HarperCollins Publishers. 978-0-06-187094-1. 2010. $17.89.

Turner weaves a tale of plots, counterplots, battle tactics, political skullduggery, and the tension of betrayal in this fourth novel set in her semi-classical world. The focus is on Sophos, prince of Sounis who has been kidnapped by rebel barons. In order to establish his kingship, Sophos undergoes a period of extreme maturation. He becomes a slave, rescues his father from murderers, becomes king and falls in love. There's something here for practically all readers. Previous titles in the series are *The Thief, The Queen of Attolia* and *The King of Attolia* (BBYA Top Ten).

GRADES: 7–12

REVIEWS: *Booklist* 2/15/10, *Kirkus* 3/01/10, *Publishers Weekly* 2/15/10, *SLJ* 4/10

Vande Velde, Vivian. *Heir Apparent.* N/A. LB. Perma-Bound Books. 978-0-605-01322-3. 2002. $6.95. PB. Houghton Mifflin Harcourt Trade & Reference Publishers. 978-0-15-205125-9. 2004. $6.95. CASS. Recorded Books, LLC. 978-1-4193-2654-7. 2005. $64.75. EB. Recorded Books, LLC. 978-1-4237-3184-9. 2005. $1.00.

Set in a technologically advanced future, Vande Velde's work shows the implications of virtual reality gone awry. Intelligent but alienated Giannine celebrates her fourteenth birthday at a computer gaming center where she joins in on a virtual reality role-playing game set in medieval times. The game pulls Giannine into a time where she becomes an exiled princess who must stay alive until she can assume the throne. However Giannine also learns she must complete the game in the allotted time or die. The fantastic drama and intricate game details dovetail nicely with the tough girl protagonist Giannine. Many teens will be thrilled with the adventure even though the technological aspect may grow stale over the years as the gaming world advances.

GRADES: 6–10

REVIEWS: *Booklist* 2/01/03, *Kirkus* 9/15/02, *Publishers Weekly* 9/16/02, *SLJ* 10/02, *VOYA* 12/02

Werlin, Nancy. *Impossible.* 384 p. TR. Penguin Group (USA) Incorporated. 978-0-8037-3002-1. 2008. $17.99. CD. Brilliance Audio. 978-1-4233-7861-7. 2008. $72.97. CD. Brilliance Audio. 978-1-4233-7860-0. 2008. $29.99. PLAY. Findaway World, LLC. 978-1-60812-656-9. 2009. $54.99.

A nifty mix of magic, romance, and a family curse are highlights of this fairy tale set in present time. On the night of her prom, seventeen-year-old Lucy is raped by her date and becomes pregnant. What becomes clear is that similar fates have befallen the women in Lucy's family. Each has tried to solve the riddle of the ballad Scarborough Fair or they will go insane. Detemined to break the curse, Lucy, with the help of good friend Zach, works to solve the riddle challenge set forth by the Elfen Knight. There are tough topics in this romantic fairy tale such as rape, teen pregnancy, and mental illness. Still, it is a fine choice for all hopeless-romantic readers.

GRADES: 8–12

REVIEWS: *Booklist* 7/01/08, *Kirkus* 9/01/08, *Publishers Weekly* 7/28/08, *SLJ* 9/08, *VOYA* 9/08

Westerfeld, Scott. *Leviathan.* 448 p. TR. Simon & Schuster Children's Publishing. 978-1-4169-7173-3. 2009. $19.99. CD. Simon & Schuster Audio. 978-0-7435-8388-6. 2009. $29.99. EB. Simon & Schuster Children's Publishing. 978-1-4169-8706-2. 2009. $19.99.

Beginning with the political intrigue leading up to World War I, the Archduke Franz Ferdinand and his wife are assassinated. Their murders launch the world into a deadly conflict. That is fact, but Westerfeld takes the framework of World War I and inserts his own fantastic creations. The global conflict is waged between Clankers—who love their machines—and Darwinists—whose technology is based on the development of new species. The Leviathan is a massive biological airship that brings together Prince Aleksandar and Deryn Sharp, a girl disguised as a male airman on Leviathan. The action is broad and fast with the clever creation of a living organism molded into an airship. The fast-moving plot will attract many readers, especially middle school boys.

GRADES: 6–10

REVIEWS: *Booklist* 9/01/09, *Kirkus* 9/01/09, *Publishers Weekly* 8/24/09, *SLJ* 9/09, *VOYA* 10/09

Wrede, Patricia. *Dealing with Dragons* (*Enchanted Forest Chronicles*). 212 p. TR. Perfection Learning Corporation. 978-0-7807-1216-4. 2002. $13.60. LB. Perma-Bound Books. 978-0-7804-5131-5. 1990. $5.95. RE. San Val, Incorporated. 978-0-613-56300-0. 2002. $15.95. CASS. Random House Audio Publishing. 978-0-8072-7634-1. 1996. $32.00. EB. Random House Audio Publishing Group. 978-0-7393-3066-1. 2007. $32.30.

Princess Cimorene is a tough no-nonsense girl who shuns the traditions of her royalty. She wants nothing to do with the loser of a prince her parents have chosen for her. Instead she enters a career as a dragon's princess where she fends off nosy wizards and helps out hysterical princesses as she carves out her area in the dragon world. Fast moving and full of excitement, this tale will appeal to girls who like to march away from society's rules. Other books in the series are *Searching for Dragons, Calling on Dragons,* and *Talking to Dragons.*

GRADES: 6–9

REVIEWS: *SLJ* 12/90

Yancey, Rick. *The Monstrumologist.* 448 p. TR. Simon & Schuster Children's Publishing. 978-1-4169-8448-1. 2009. $17.99. EB. Simon & Schuster Children's Publishing. 978-1-4391-5261-4. 2009. $17.99. EB. NetLibrary, Incorporated. 978-1-4416-2686-8. 2009. $60.00.

Will Henry is a twelve-year-old orphan about to begin the most thrilling adventure he could ever imagine. Will is the apprentice to a strange "monstrumologist," Dr. Pellinore Warthrop, whose task is to hunt and kill anthropophagi. These creatures have astounding strength and speed, but their uniqueness is that they hunt and devour only humans. Written in the style of a journal from the late 1800s, this bloody and gruesome adventure will have readers glued to the pages. Lovers of supernatural horror of many ages will be transfixed.

GRADES: 8–12

REVIEWS: *Booklist* 9/01/09, *Kirkus* 9/01/09, *Publishers Weekly* 9/07/09, *SLJ* 11/01, *VOYA* 2/10

AWARDS: Printz Honor

Yolen, Jane. *The Devil's Arithmetic.* 176 p. TR. Follett Library Resources. 978-0-7587-9594-6. 2002. $16.66. TR. Peter Smith Publisher, Incorporated. 978-0-8446-7321-9. N/A. $23.25. LB. San Val, Incorporated. 978-1-4177-0488-0. 2004. $17.20. LB. San Val, Incorporated. 978-0-8335-4335-6. 1990. $14.15. PB. Penguin Group (USA) Incorporated. 978-0-14-240109-5. 2004. $6.99. PB. Penguin Group (USA) Incorporated. 978-0-14-034535-3. 1990. $6.99.

When Hannah Stern opens the door to symbolically welcome the prophet Elijah, she is transported back to the year 1941 when World War II was raging throughout Poland. The modern-day girl is caught up in the horrors of the Holocaust and Hannah (who is thought to be Chaya Abramowicz) is rounded up with other Jews and sent to a concentration camp. There the chilling induction process by the Nazis includes shaving their heads and applying tattoos. Historical fiction is mixed with the fantasy world of time travel as Hannah is seemingly trapped in the past. This is a fine work for schools with a heavy emphasis on Holocaust studies.

GRADES: 7–12

REVIEWS: *Publishers Weekly* 10/26/90

Zevin, Gabrielle. *Elsewhere.* 288 p. TR. Perfection Learning Corporation. 978-0-7569-8191-4. 2007. $14.60. TR. Farrar, Straus & Giroux. 978-0-374-32091-1. 2005. $16.00. PB. Square Fish. 978-0-312-36746-6. 2007. $6.95. CD. Random House Audio Publishing Group. 978-0-307-28240-8. 2005. $39.00. CD. Random House Audio Publishing Group. 978-0-307-28370-2. 2005. $42.50. EB. Random House Audio Publishing Group. 978-0-7393-4479-8. 2007. $42.50.

Fifteen-year-old Elizabeth "Liz" Hall is hit by a taxi and mysteriously awakens as a passenger on a cruise ship traveling an unidentified ocean. She's unable to recall how she boarded the ship or where she is going. She meets Thandi, a girl who seems to have been shot in the head. Liz learns she is dead and the ship docks in the port of Elsewhere, a place where humans and animals age backward until they are ready to be reincarnated. This unique take on what happens in the Afterlife will draw readers, and Liz's understanding of relationships is an important message.

GRADES: 8–12

REVIEWS: *Booklist* 8/01/05, *Kirkus* 8/15/05, *Publishers Weekly* 8/15/05

AWARDS: Teens' Top Ten

6

Graphic Novels

In the past decade graphic novels have become commonplace in teen areas in libraries and bookstores. No longer found only in comic book shops, this format is enjoying a robust popularity explosion among teenage readers. Many librarians find it an overwhelming challenge to keep up with the vast array of characters, plots, series, spin-off story lines and different publishers. To top it off, teens know what they want, probably much more so than an average librarian working in a public library.

The explosive interest and embracing of graphic novels comes with some myths about the format. I feel the need to emphasize that graphic novels are a format, not a genre. Graphic novels are produced in all genres from nonfiction to historical fiction. The titles are not exclusively adventure tales about superheroes; however, for ease of identification, graphic novels have their own section in this edition. A handful of graphic novels do appear in other sections of this work.

The titles and series included in this list are not to be viewed as comprehensive. Think of it as a starting point. Graphic novels, more than any other type of teen reading material, have their dedicated readers who know their favorite series inside and out. These dedicated readers can cite the different characters and the strengths and fatal flaws in each character. They know protagonists, antagonists, and all the secondary characters that pop in and out of the series. That is what literary purists want teens to be able to do, but many book people would rather have this passion for dissecting a story happen with traditional novels, or classic works of literature. These teen readers are achieving this knowledge on their own by voraciously reading graphic novels.

Of course, any teen collection that includes graphic novels should strive to contain both Western and manga titles. Refer to your teen readers. I've worked in libraries where manga titles were a complete mystery to the teens and in other places I've worked with teens that went out of their way to tell me when a new issue was due to be released.

Use this brief list as a starting point. There are examples of famous titles and other works that have made lists such as Best Books for Young Adults. Indeed, YALSA now recognizes graphic novels by having its own selection committee,

Great Graphic Novels for Teens. Many series involving graphic novel characters have not been included in the following list (The Hulk, The Fantastic Four, Hellboy, Wonder Woman). Listing superheroes and their extensive series would overwhelm users of this work. These exclusions make this list only a starting point for any library's core collection. Based on patrons' needs, your results may vary.

This edition offers only a very brief list, but the ever-changing world of graphic novels has a huge following on the Internet. Also, very dedicated graphic novel fans and librarians have written professional books loaded with information and title suggestions. The following list is a quick starting point allowing users to dig further into the world of graphic novels.

Books:

> Brenner, Robin. *Understanding Manga and Anime.* Libraries Unlimited. 2007. 978-1-5915-8332-5.
>
> Kannenberg, Gene. *500 Essential Graphic Novels: The Ultimate Guide.* Collins Design. 2008. 978-0-0614-7451-4.
>
> Pawuk, Michael. *Graphic Novels: A Genre Guide to Comic Books, Manga, and More* (Genreflecting Advisory Series). Libraries Unlimited. 2006. 978-1-5915-8132-1.
>
> Weiner, Steve. *The 101 Best Graphic Novels.* Nantier Beall Minoustchine Publishing. 2006. 978-1-5616-3443-9.

Websites:

> www.comicsworthreading.com
> www.comic-con.org/cci/cci_eisners_main.php (San Diego Comic Con International—Announcement of Eisner Awards)
> www.dccomics.com
> www.marvel.com
> www.noflyingnotights.com
> www.onemanga.com
> www.rightstuf.com
> www.tokyopop.com
> www.viz.com

Abadzis, Nick. *Laika.* 208 p. TR. Roaring Brook Press. 978-1-59643-101-0. 2007. $17.95.

The space race between the United States and the Soviet Union was marked by intense competition to be first in all aspects. The first dog in space was Laika, a mongrel pulled from the streets. This graphic novel contrasts the feelings of Laika's handler with scientists only concerned with the dog as an object to study without worrying about Laika's death sentence in space. Ironically Laika was chosen due to her willingness to please the humans. Illustrations add to the touching story as Laika's face is shown with almost human expression. A fine mix of history and storytelling in a graphic novel format.

GRADES: 7–12

REVIEWS: *Booklist* 9/01/07, *Kirkus* 8/01/07, *Publishers Weekly* 10/01/07, *SLJ* 11/07

AWARDS: Great Graphic Novels for Teens (Top Ten)

Arakawi, Hiromu. *Full Metal Alchemist* **(series).** Viz Media.

The Cartoon Network helps push this series' popularity. Two brothers, Edward and Alphonse Elric have explored the powers of alchemy, an advanced science in which objects can be created from other materials. The brothers dabbled in Human Transmutation, which is an attempt to modify a human being. Their actions left Alphonse's soul trapped in a body of armor and Edward's right arm is now a mechanical device. The brothers' relationship remains strong as they battle a variety of antagonists. Not only is the manga series hugely popular, but this series has spin-offs in DVDs, nonfiction books about the anime artwork, and video games.

GRADES: 6–12

REVIEWS: *Publishers Weekly* 5/02/05

AWARDS: Quick Picks Top Ten

Carey, Mike. *Re-Gifters.* 174 p. TR. DC Comics. 978-1-4012-0371-9. 2007. $9.99. RE. San Val, Incorporated. 978-1-4177-8429-5. 2007. $20.85.

Dixie decides to spend the entry fee of an upcoming hapkido competition on an elaborate birthday present for Adam, a classmate she is crushing on. The gift changes hands among an intricate group of friends, which allows Dixie to see them in a new light. The black-and-white illustrations give depth to the story and this work combines the drama of high school with thrilling martial arts scenes.

GRADES: 7–12

REVIEWS: *Booklist* 6/01/07, *Publishers Weekly* 6/04/07, *SLJ* 1/08

AWARDS: Great Graphic Novels for Teens (Top Ten)

Eisner, Will. *A Contract with God and Other Tenement Stories.* 208 p. TR. W. W. Norton & Company, Incorporated. 978-0-393-32804-2. 2006. $16.95. TR. Kitchen Sink Press, Incorporated. 978-0-87816-018-1. 1996. $11.95.

This groundbreaking work by Eisner is actually a set of short stories set in a Bronx tenement during the 1930s. Eisner draws heavily on his own childhood experiences dealing with the theme of immigration and first-generation

Americans. The stories explore the brutality and tenderness that human beings can inflict upon each other. A trivia note: this is the work Eisner described as a "graphic novel" when asked by a publisher what to call this type of format with a different appearance.

GRADES: 10–12

Gaiman, Neil. *Death: The High Cost of Living* **(series).** 104 p. TR. DC Comics. 978-1-56389-133-5. 1994. $12.99.

In this spin-off series from Gaiman's epic *Sandman* stories, Death appears as a teenage goth girl, Didi, who really, really cares about helping her clients cross over to the afterlife. She's allowed to walk the Earth one day each century, and in this work Didi runs across a young man named Sexton who is considering suicide. Didi bonds with Sexton and together they embark on an adventure for him to regain his self-esteem. What sets this graphic novel apart from other stories is the totally unique representation of Death. She's really kind of sexy in her goth way.

GRADES: 10–12

REVIEWS: *Publishers Weekly* 2/21/94

Gaiman, Neil. *The Sandman* **(series).** DC Comics.

This series involves the main character, Dream, who is also known by a variety of names, especially Morpheus. Morpheus has escaped from being held prisoner by an occult ritual for seventy years. He now sets about rebuilding his kingdom and exacting revenge on his captors. Gaiman himself summarizes the series plot as, "The Lord of Dreams learns that one must change or die, and makes his decision." Other titles in the series are *Preludes and Nocturnes, The Doll's House, Dream Country, Season of Mists, A Game of You, Fables and Reflections, Brief Lives, World's End, The Kindly Ones,* and *The Wake.*

GRADES: 10–12

REVIEWS: *Publishers Weekly* 10/24/94

Helfer, Andrew, and Randy DuBurke. *Malcolm X: A Graphic Biography.* 128 p. TR. Farrar, Straus & Giroux. 978-0-8090-9504-9. 2006. $15.95.

A powerful figure in African American history is brought to life in this biography presented in graphic novel format. By using only black-and-white coloring, the work is given an old look, much like comics from the 1940s. Before becoming Malcolm X, Malcolm Little was a hustler dodging the law. This work shows the harsh background of his life, but also progresses to his conversion to Islam and his subsequent assassination. The violent race relations of the 1960s are represented in realistic detail and this graphic novel is a fine way to introduce the biography of Malcolm X to high school students.

GRADES: 9–12

REVIEWS: *Booklist* 2/01/07, *Publishers Weekly* 12/04/06, *SLJ* 5/07, *VOYA* 4/07

Hino, Matsuri. *Vampire Knight* **(series).** Viz Media.

Schedules are complicated at Cross Academy. At night the classes are attended by vampires and the daytime classes must be protected from them without revealing the secret. Yuki Cross is one of the school's guardians and her task is to keep the two groups apart, no matter how attracted the Days are to the Nights. Yuki's mission is noble but also self-centered as she is fascinated by one particular vampire who rescued her years ago. This graphic novel series offers an interesting take on the flood of vampire titles in the young adult book world. Hugely popular, teens will clamor for additional volumes.

GRADES: 7–12

REVIEWS: *Publishers Weekly* 12/18/06

Kishimoto, Masashi. *Naruto* **(series).** Viz Media.

Naruto Uzumaki is a young boy who has the Nine-Tailed Demon Fox sealed within him. This demon attacked and slaughtered many people in the village of Konohagakure. The demon was sealed up in the body of Naruto and now villagers mistreat him as if he were the demon itself. Naruto grows up and becomes part of Team 7 whose task is to carry out orders given by the villagers. This is one of the most popular manga series in publication and has especially strong pull for male readers. This series has been adapted into video, CDs have been produced, and teenagers have been known to purchase Naruto merchandise, including the unique chrome headband.

GRADES: 6–10

Moore, Alan. *The League of Extraordinary Gentlemen.* 192 p. TR. DC Comics. 978-1-56389-858-7. 2002. $14.99. RE. San Val, Incorporated. 978-0-613-91294-5. 2002. $26.95.

Billed as a Justice League for Victorian England, this first volume in the series introduces the group of extraordinary individuals who will protect the interests of the Empire. Captain Nemo, Allan Quatermain, and Dr. Jekyll all play roles in this creative story about airship threats that need to be halted before mass destruction of Britain occurs. With a steampunk feel, this story is for the thinking reader with a background in the classic novels of the late 1800s and early 1900s.

GRADES: 10–12

Moore, Alan. *Watchmen.* 416 p. DC Comics. 978-0-930289-23-2. 1995. $19.99. RE. San Val, Incorporated. 978-0-613-91964-7. 1995. $33.05.

An aging superhero, Rorschach, is puzzled as to why one of his former colleagues has been murdered and he sets out to discover the truth. Set in a parallel world of America, this different country has been dramatically changed by the Vietnam War and Richard Nixon's presidency. The uniqueness of the story is that the superheroes rarely show superpowers, but are shown in a more human light. A subtle commentary on the United States' political situation of the 1980s is mixed in the fight against the evil superhero story line. This sophisticated story will be best appreciated by older teenagers. The film version released in 2009 generated huge interest in this graphic novel.

GRADES: 10–12

Ohba, Tsugumi. *Death Note* **(series).** Viz Media.

This intricate series is a more cerebral story but that is not to say it doesn't contain action or suspense. Light Yagami discovers a notebook dropped to Earth by a shinigami, a death god, named Ryuk. The holder of the notebook has the power to kill anyone simply by writing in the victim's name. Light wishes to cleanse the world of evil by killing off nasty criminals, but his actions are monitored by a young genius detective known as L. The mental tug of war between Light and L is a terrific story line as Ryuk looks on with interest. This also is a series that has a movie adaptation. High school students and sophisticated manga fans will love the layered story line.

GRADES: 9–12

AWARDS: Great Graphic Novels for Teens (Top Ten)

Petersen, David. *Mouse Guard* **(series).** Archaia Entertainment, LLC.

Snakes and crabs are only two of the dangers confronting the Mouse Guard in this medieval fantasy. Headquartered at the fortress of Lockhaven, the Mouse Guard is sworn to protect travelers from predators. Betrayal, adventure, and noble mice make this story come to life with crackling danger. The color illustrations accent the unique world created by David Peterson. This is a fine addition to any collection and will attract younger readers of fantasy stories to the graphic novel format.

GRADES: 6–9

REVIEWS: *Booklist* 9/01/07, *Publishers Weekly* 4/09/07

Satrapi, Marjane. *Persepolis: The Story of a Childhood.* 160 p. TR. Knopf Doubleday Publishing Group. 978-0-375-71457-3. 2004. $12.95. TR. Fantagraphics Books. 978-1-56097-516-8. 2002. $24.95.

This autobiography has been created by the great-granddaughter of Iran's last emperor, who was overthrown by the father of the shah who in turn was overthrown during the 1979 Islamic revolution. Details of the revolution come alive seen through the eyes of Satrapi between the ages of ten through fourteen as readers view political demonstrations, persecution of Jews, and the outbreak of the Iran-Iraq war. This graphic novel brought credibility to the format and is still important today with the unrest and American involvement in the region. This autobiography is for sophisticated readers.

GRADES: 10–12

REVIEWS: *Booklist* 5/01/03, *Publishers Weekly* 7/14/03, *SLJ* 8/03, *VOYA* 12/03

AWARDS: Alex Award

Satrapi, Marjane. *Persepolis 2: The Story of a Return.* 192 p. TR. Knopf Doubleday Publishing Group. 978-0-375-71466-5. 2005. $12.95.

Satrapi's autobiographical graphic novel continues when, at age fourteen, she was sent to Vienna. Arriving in a much freer country she made new friends (some very liberal and some quite conservative), had several relationships, became increasingly aware of the sexual freedom of her new milieu, and even dealt drugs for a boyfriend. Eventually, she ended up living on the streets. She struggles to get herself together and teens will recognize her feelings of alienation presented in the simplistic, but powerful, black-and-white illustrations. This story can be presented as part of a multicultural lesson in schools.

GRADES: 10–12

REVIEWS: *Booklist* 8/01/04, *Publishers Weekly* 6/21/04, *SLJ* 12/04

Shelley, Mary, and Gary Reed. *Frankenstein: The Graphic Novel.* 176 p. TR. Perfection Learning Corporation. 978-0-7569-5809-1. 2005. $18.65.

Graphic novels often showcase classic works of literature to give teenage, and maybe adult, readers a more lucid take on the classic's storyline. Here, Mary Shelley's horror novel appears with illustrations that help set the tone of the story. By using murky dark colors, readers sense the despair of the monster and Dr. Victor Frankenstein's descent into the dark madness of attempting to create life. Frankenstein is a work that established the horror genre and this graphic novel version helps a new generation of readers become familiar with the work.

GRADES: 8–12

REVIEWS: *Booklist* 3/15/05, *SLJ* 9/05, *VOYA* 8/05

Small, David. *Stitches: A Memoir.* 336 p. TR. W. W. Norton & Company, Incorporated. 978-0-393-06857-3. 2009. $24.95.

To counter the argument that graphic novels are only useful as an outlet for teenage fantasies about being stronger and larger than life, *Stitches* is a work that dispels that myth. David Small uses washed-out illustrations and bland colors to show the horror story that was his childhood. At age fourteen the boy undergoes throat surgery for the cancer his surgeon father subjected him to by exposing him to X-rays as a baby. His scar is a cover for his severed vocal cords. His home life was totally dysfunctional and this moving work will make an excellent companion story to teens fascinated with the abuse in *A Child Called It*. The alarming intensity of Small's childhood marks this title as a selection for high school readers.

GRADES: 9–12

REVIEWS: *Booklist* 7/01/09, *Kirkus* 6/15/09, *Publishers Weekly* 8/10/09, *SLJ* 9/09, *VOYA* 10/09

AWARDS: Alex Award, BBYA Top Ten

Smith, Jeff. *Bone* **(series).** Scholastic, Incorporated.

Jeff Smith's work introduces readers to Bone, a character drawn with simple lines that conveys his personality as an everyman figure. With his cousins, Bone stumbles into a valley full of strange creatures, magic, wild farmers, an exiled princess, and a huge, hilarious dragon. Secondary characters are quirky yet they become familiar to readers due to Smith's talent at giving everyone a variety of emotional facial expressions. It's an epic journey filled with humor and excitement. Titles in the series are *Out of Boneville, The Great Cow Race, Eyes of the Storm, The Dragonslayer, Rock Jaw: Master of the Eastern Border, Old Man's Cave, Ghost Circles, Treasure Hunters,* and *Crown of Horns*.

GRADES: 9–12

Spiegelman, Art. *Maus, A Survivor's Tale: My Father Bleeds History.* N/A. TR. Knopf Doubleday Publishing Group. 978-0-394-54155-6. 1991. $22.00 RE. San Val, Incorporated . 978-0-8085-9853-4. 1986. $23.45.

Spiegelman helped bring literary credibility to the graphic novel format with his brilliant story that is a combination of autobiography and social commentary. This Holocaust tale tells the story of Spiegelman's father's survival from a concentration camp. The characters act real but are depicted with heads of animals—Jews are mice and the Nazis are rats. By using only black and white colors, the illustrations suggest a contrast of good versus evil. This is a work of art plus literature and can be used in a variety of teaching possibilities from history to literature studies.

GRADES: 9–12

REVIEWS: *SLJ* 5/87

Spiegelman, Art. *Maus II, A Survivor's Tale: And Here My Troubles Began.* N/A. RE. San Val, Incorporated. 978-1-4178-1642-2. 1992. $26.90.

In this sequel to *Maus*, much of Spiegelman's narrative details his own struggle to encourage his father to remember the past, something the older man would like to forget. Tragedy follows the father after surviving Auschwitz and Dachau and the old man continues a cheap, miserly behavior later in life. He managed to survive the camps by bartering but now this behavior frustrates his son. Together these two works give a fascinating take on the Holocaust and due to their unique graphic format, they become standouts in the mass of Holocaust literature.

GRADES: 9–12

REVIEWS: *Booklist* 10/15/91, *Kirkus* 10/01/91, *Publishers Weekly* 9/27/91

Takahashi, Kazuki. *Yu-Gi-Oh!* (series). Viz Media.

Yu-Gi-Oh! is not only a graphic novel; it is a cultural phenomenon. A card game, anime videos, and video games are all spawns of the original story. Yugi Mutou is a shorter-than-average high school student who is given a piece of an Egyptian artifact by his grandfather. Once he pieces together the puzzle, the young boy is possessed by another personality who is the 3,000-year-old spirit of a pharaoh. Together with his friends, Yu-Gi-Oh embarks on adventures, attempting to piece together the pharaoh's lost memories. Younger teens love *Yu-Gi-Oh!*, perhaps more for the card game, but this lengthy manga series is a must have for public libraries.

GRADES: 6–9

Takahashi, Rumiko. *Ranma 1/2* (series). Viz Media.

As a result of an accident during marital arts training, sixteen-year-old Ranma Saotome is cursed to become a girl when splashed with cold water. Hot water will change him back to a boy. *Ranma 1/2* gained huge popularity during the 1990s and many role-playing games have adopted the cursed spring plot device that allows a quick transgender. This series is popular with younger readers of manga, perhaps due to the often hilarious situations Ranma encounters as he changes sex.

GRADES: 7–10

Takaya, Natsuki. *Fruits Basket* (series). TOKYOPOP, Incorporated.

In this manga romantic comedy humans can transform into animals. Tohru Honda is a homeless teenage girl living in a tent on the estate of Shigure and his family. He invites Tohru to their home where the family secret is revealed. When they are hugged by a member of the opposite sex, they transform into different animals of the Chinese zodiac calendar. This fast-moving series is a huge draw for middle school girls who enjoy reading about the awkward situations in which the effervescent Tohru finds herself.

GRADES: 6–9

REVIEWS: *Publishers Weekly* 3/08/04

AWARDS: Quick Picks Top Ten

Takeuchi, Naoko. *Sailor Moon* (series). TOKYOPOP, Incorporated.

The *Sailor Moon* series introduced the concept of a magical girl using her powers to fight evil. The strong female protagonist has become a standard archetype of manga. Indeed, the sailor outfit, used as a popular girls' school uniform in Japan, appears often in manga. In this series Sailor Senshi are teenage girls who can transform into heroines named for the moon and other planets thus becoming Sailor Moon, Sailor Mars, Sailor Mercury and so on. Once again, this manga series with positive female characters has strong appeal for younger teens, especially middle school girls.

GRADES: 6–9

Talbot, Bryan. *The Tale of One Bad Rat.* N/A. Book Wholesalers, Incorporated. 978-1-4046-2391-0. 2002. $23.19.

This graphic novel shows the story of a girl suffering from childhood sexual abuse and her journey to recovery. Helen Potter has run away from her abusive father. Along the way Helen meets characters who are symbolically derived from Beatrix Potter. Helen eventually decides to take responsibility for her own recovery, which will inspire readers undergoing similar circumstances. This work has potential for use by social work counselors involved with incarcerated teens who have experienced sexual abuse by family members.

GRADES: 9–12

REVIEWS: *Booklist* 9/15/95

Tamaki, Mariko, and Jillian Tamaki. *Skim.* 144 p. TR. Groundwood Books. 978-0-88899-964-1. 2010. $12.95. TR. Groundwood Books. 978-0-88899-753-1. 2008. $18.95.

Kimberly Keiko Cameron is also known as "Skim." She's struggling with her identity as a mixed-race teen and also her friends who seem to shun her. Skim searches for answers and turns to tarot cards and Wicca to make sense of her life. She becomes obsessive with her interest in free-spirited teacher Ms. Archer. Themes of rejection that lead to suicide are woven through this story accented by gorgeous black-and-white drawings. Teens experiencing confusion will connect with the realistic dialogue and the varied relationships Skim works through. Some are successful, others not so much. Mature themes make this graphic novel suitable for high school readers.

GRADES: 9–12

REVIEWS: *Booklist* 3/15/08, *Publishers Weekly* 2/04/08, *SLJ* 5/08, *VOYA* 6/08

AWARDS: BBYA Top Ten, Great Graphic Novels for Teens (Top Ten)

Tan, Shaun. *The Arrival.* 128 p. TR. Scholastic, Incorporated. 978-0-439-89529-3. 2007. $19.99.

This graphic novel made up of only illustrations without text conveys the confusion and awe that immigrants entering a different country experience. The author has created a fascinating new world where nothing is familiar and everything is a new experience. Younger readers will struggle to make sense of unusual creatures popping up in unexpected situations, but more sophisticated readers will be hand in hand with the unnamed character's journey.

GRADES: 10–12

REVIEWS: *Booklist* 9/01/07, *Kirkus* 9/01/07, *Publishers Weekly* 7/16/07, *SLJ* 9/07, *VOYA* 8/07

AWARDS: BBYA Top Ten, Great Graphic Novels (Top Ten)

Tan, Shaun. *Tales from Outer Suburbia.* 96 p. TR. Scholastic, Incorporated. 978-0-545-05587-1. 2009. $19.99.

Shaun Tan's collection of short stories groups words and mixed-media art, giving an effect that alternates between creepy and poignant. Readers' imaginations are challenged to find their own interpretation of these stories that are purposely left open-ended. Tan does not shy away from social commentary on the odd happenings in suburban settings, but he also inserts a story showing readers the dangers of arms buildup. Less sophisticated readers will say this work is truly "out there" but mature readers, especially those with an interest in art, will be enthused by Tan's work.

GRADES: 9–12

REVIEWS: *Booklist* 12/08, *Kirkus* 1/01/09, *Publishers Weekly* 11/03/08, *SLJ* 3/01/09, *VOYA* 6/09

Thompson, Craig. *Blankets.* 592 p. TR. Top Shelf Productions. 978-1-891830-43-3. 2003. $29.95. RE. San Val, Incorporated. 978-0-613-92595-2. 2003. $45.20.

In this autobiographical work, Thompson shows readers his struggles with his religious faith. He was attracted to the Church's message but he felt repelled by the Church. With softened lines, Thompson's illustrations tell a deeply moving story about growing up and finding one's self. Many illustrations seem bizarre with paisley fantasy feel, but the whole works. There are instances of full nudity and thus many libraries have shelved this title in the adult section. The library's decision of where to shelve this book should not lessen the power of the story.

GRADES: 9– 12

REVIEWS: *Booklist* 6/01/03, *Publishers Weekly* 8/18/03, *SLJ* 4/04, *VOYA* 4/04

AWARDS: BBYA Top Ten

Toriyama, Akira. *Dragon Ball* **(series).** Scholastic, Incorporated.

A monkey-tailed boy named Goku befriends a teenage girl named Bulma? Sounds like an improv manga skit, but in this series that refuses to lose its popularity, Bulma and Goku embark on a quest to find the seven magic Dragon Balls. Goku trains in martial arts in order to participate in the World Martial Arts Tournament, which features the most powerful fighters in the world. Villains, cool fight scenes, and a sympathetic character in Goku mark this as a very successful series for younger teens. It is a great introductory series into the world of manga and should be in all public libraries.

GRADES: 6–8

Ueda, Miwa. *Peach Girl* **(series).** TOKYOPOP, Incorporated.

Momo Adachi is a former member of the swim team who tans easily and her hair is bleached out. These traits have given her a stereotype of ignorant by her classmates. She has one friend, Sae, but unknown to Momo, Sae loves to spread nasty rumors. Love interest Toji plays baseball, but both Momo and Sae have their sights on the boy athlete. Younger teen readers will instantly connect with the relationship drama in this older manga series.

GRADES: 6–9

Various Authors. *Batman* **(series).** DC Comics.

The villains are almost as great as Batman. The Joker, The Riddler, The Penguin all battle Batman. As a hero without actual superpowers, Bruce Wayne has dedicated his life to fighting crime as Batman, or the Dark Knight. Several spin-offs are quite violent, but the film industry has whetted the appetites for teen readers.

GRADES: 7–12

Various Authors. *Spiderman* **(series).** Marvel Enterprises, Incorporated.

Spiderman is not a teenager, but his personal life has many issues that teens will identify with. He has relationship issues with Mary Jane Watson, his boss yells at him, and he knows he is better than his Peter Parker identity. Librarians will find it difficult to keep up with all the series titles (*Amazing Spiderman, Ultimate Spiderman, Spectacular Spiderman*), but that doesn't matter; acquire titles with Spiderman on the cover and teens will appreciate the purchase.

GRADES: 7–12

Various Authors. *Superman* **(series).** DC Comics.

Yep, the Man of Steel rules. He's been thrilling teen readers since the 1930s and all libraries should have copies of his adventures on the shelves. Think of it—Superman is noble, powerful, he can fly, and he fights evil. These are traits all teenage boys dream of having one day. Well, maybe not the flying thing. American graphic novels about superheroes are a must for a teen section and these three traditional series are a great place to start.

GRADES: 7–12

Various Authors. *Teen Titans* **(series).** DC Comics.

In this series teenage superheroes patterned after the actual heroes fight evil just like the grownups. Batman's sidekick Robin seems to be the main force in the series that has a stable of heroes ranging from Nightwing and Beast Boy to Cyborg. There are many spin-offs of this concept, beginning in the 1960s. Librarians will want to keep up with the series that began in 2008 written by Judd Winick. Teen patrons do not want to read about the same character their dad or granddad read about.

GRADES: 7–12

Vaughan, Brian K. *Ex Machina* **(series).** DC Comics.

What if the mayor of New York was a superhero? Mitchell Hundred is a civil engineer working under the Brooklyn Bridge when a glowing light gives him the power to talk to machines. After performing as a superhero, Hundred is now mayor but is suffering through a series of political problems. Forbidden to talk about his powers, Hundred must deal with issues ranging from a crippling blizzard to a serial killer who is killing the snowplow drivers. This graphic novel that mixes superhero themes with realistic political maneuverings will appeal to older readers.

GRADES: 10–12

REVIEWS: *Publishers Weekly* 2/14/05

Vaughan, Brian K. *Runaways* **(series).** Marvel Enterprises, Incorporated.

What happens when a group of teenagers who think their parents are evil learn that their parents actually are evil? Worse yet, they are evil supervillains plotting mass murder. The teens escape into Los Angeles but find out that hiding is difficult as their parents have connections throughout the city. Characters at first glance seem to be stock profiles, but each plays his or her role very well. What's extra cool is the betrayal the teen group must deal with as they realize someone is ratting them out. This is a great bridge book as an introductory story for teens unfamiliar with graphic novels.

GRADES: 7–12

REVIEWS: *Publishers Weekly* 6/28/04

AWARDS: BBYA Top Ten

Whedon, Joss. *Astonishing X-Men* **(series).** Marvel Enterprises, Incorporated.

The film series brings this series to the front of the pack making it a must-have for libraries. The characters are powerful and unique including Emma Frost, Wolverine, and Beast. Teens will connect with these somewhat renegade superheroes who have left the X-Men over a conflict with Professor X. Savvy librarians will display these titles with a movie connection.

GRADES: 7–12

Winick, Judd. *Pedro and Me: Friendship, Loss, and What I Learned.* 192 p. TR. Henry Holt & Company. 978-0-8050-6403-2. 2000. $16.99. TR. Henry Holt & Company. 2009. 978-1-4420-2533-2. RE. San Val, Incorporated. 978-0-613-31574-6. 2000. $29.35.

Themes of friendship and education about HIV-positive young people are presented in this powerful graphic novel. Winick relates his story of how he landed a role in MTV's *The Real World* in order to live rent-free in San Francisco for six months. Once in the house, he meets Pedro Zamora, a Cuban immigrant who developed HIV as a teenager. Pedro and Winick become close friends as Pedro gives informational workshops about HIV. As his health declines and leads to Pedro's death, Winick shows readers his period of grieving and recovery. There will always be a place for this work as it shows the tragedy of the AIDS virus in an accessible format.

GRADES: 9–12

REVIEWS: *Booklist* 9/15/00, *Kirkus* 9/01/00, *Publishers Weekly* 9/18/00, *SLJ* 10/00

7

Historical Fiction

As a genre, historical fiction for young adults presents a mixed bag for many librarians. Through casual conversation, many of my colleagues working as teen librarians in metropolitan library systems emphatically stated that historical fiction was one of their most difficult "sells" to teenagers. Yet, other librarians in rural or suburban libraries report that the genre is thriving in popularity.

So what is historical fiction? Simply put, it is a fictional story set in a historical period. To attract teens, that historical period should have some degree of notability. Perhaps the mixed reaction is due to the different styles in which historical fiction may be packaged.

Historical fiction titles may feature actual figures from history depicted in their youth. These yet-to-be-famous characters may be placed in a situation occurring during a time before gaining fame as an adult. In another instance, the historical story may center on an actual event such as a famous battle or the unveiling of an invention. In this case the characters may or may not be actual persons from history. A third type of historical novel is simply set in an era and the author creates an atmospheric feel of that era. The characters then deal with conflicts created by the author. There may or may not be a single notable historical event, or a notable person from history, in the story.

At times historical fiction may feel extremely "dry" to teens if the author neglects pacing and plotting in favor of excruciating detail and dialogue from an era hundreds of years ago. On the other hand, twenty-first century slang used in a story from a time such as the seventeenth century comes off as a joke to today's teens.

Adding to the task of "selling" historical fiction is the fact that teens may prefer to read a nonfiction book about the historical event. Teenage male readers tend to gravitate to the nonfiction books on a topic such as World War II, rather than a fictional story about a teen caught up in a battle.

Historical fiction must stay true to the era. Stories set in the past incorporating time-travel or insertions of modern technology fall into the realm of fantasy.

Yet skilled authors annually produce thrilling stories set in a historical period. The research is correct, the characters are intriguing, and the story moves. In this section, I've included titles that have a distinct feel to a particular era, and the teen characters are placed in a conflict that reflects the nature of the time.

Ambrose, Stephen E. *This Vast Land: A Young Man's Journal of the Lewis and Clark Expedition.* 265 p. LP. Thorndike Press. 978 0-7862-6139-0. 2004. $22.95.

At age eighteen, George Shannon was the youngest member of the Lewis and Clark Corps of Discovery. Presented in the form of his diary, George expresses his thoughts, fears, and concerns about the grueling journey. Ambrose gives George a human side by including his romance with an Indian girl. However, the historical backdrop of one of the greatest journeys of the nineteenth century is the fascinating component of this work. As history is made, George matures from teen to a man—a solid theme for any young adult novel. The depth and intricate writing indicates that this is a work for upper middle school readers.

GRADES: 8–10

REVIEWS: *Booklist* 9/01/03, *Kirkus* 8/01/03, *Publishers Weekly* 8/25/03, *SLJ* 9/03, *VOYA* 12/03

Anderson, Laurie Halse. *Chains.* 320 p. TR. Simon & Schuster. 978-1-4169-0585-1. 2008. $16.99. CD. Brilliance Audio. 978-1-4233-6730-7. 2008. $29.99. PLAY. Findaway World. 978-1-60640-588-8. 2008. $54.99. EB. Brilliance Audio. 978-1-4233-6735-2. 2008. $39.25. LP. Thorndike Press. 978-1-4104-1425-0. 2009. $23.95.

Anderson sets her story at the beginning of the Revolutionary War in New York City. Although led to believe they would be freed upon the death of their owner, Isabel and her sister become the property of a cruel Loyalist family. Told in Isabel's voice, readers are shown the conflict beneath the surface of the common historical facts of the era. Prisoners are treated horribly and spies are everywhere. Isabel's involvement with Loyalists and the rebels mirrors her own desire for freedom. Her compelling story is well paced and presents readers a little-known view of the Revolutionary struggle.

GRADES: 7–10

REVIEWS: *Booklist* 11/01/08, *Kirkus* 9/01/08, *Publishers Weekly* 9/01/08, *SLJ* 10/08, *VOYA* 10/08

Anderson, Laurie Halse. *Fever 1793.* 256 p. TR. Simon & Schuster. 978-0-689-83858-3. 2000. $17.99. RE. San Val, Inc. 978-0-613-45039-3. 2002. $17.20. LB. Perma-Bound Books. 978-0-605-00990-5. 2000. $12.99. PB. Simon & Schuster. 978-0-689-84891-9. 2002. $6.99. CASS. Random House Audio. 978-0-8072-8718-7. 2004. $32.00. CASS. Random House Audio. 978-0-8072-8719-4. 2004. $38.00.

EB. Random House Audio. 978-0-7393-5609-8. N/A. $38.25. LB. Thorndike Press. 978-0-7862-3408-0. 2001. $22.95.

Matilda Cook, age fourteen, grudgingly faces her bleak work in a coffeehouse owned by her mother. Soon enough the city of Philadelphia comes under the grip of the deadly yellow fever disease. In the chaos and death throughout the city, Mattie and her mother become separated and the young girl is thrust into a battle for her own survival. Readers will become caught up in the struggle and Anderson includes an admirable historical sidebar when the Free African Society takes on the noble task of burying bodies and assisting the sick. This work will appeal to a wide range of teens both by age and gender.

GRADES: 7–10

REVIEWS: *Booklist* 10/01/00, *Kirkus* 6/15/00, *Publishers Weekly* 7/31/00, *SLJ* 8/00, *VOYA* 12/00

Anderson, M. T. *The Astonishing Life of Octavian Nothing, Traitor to the Nation: The Pox Party.* 353 p. TR. Candlewick Press. 978-0-7636-2402-6. 2006. $17.99. PB. Candlewick Press. 978-0-7636-3679-1. 2008. $10.99. CD. Random House Audio. 978-0-7393-3862-9. 2007. $45.00. CD. Random House Audio. 978-0-7393-4846-8. 2007. $55.00. EB. Books on Tape, Incorporated. 978-0-7393-5161-1. 2007. $46.75. LP. Thorndike Press. 978-0-7862-9552-4. 2007. $23.95.

Anderson's sophisticated writing reveals a concept that is both disturbing and fascinating. Octavian Nothing and his mother, an African princess, are kept at an estate in a time before the Revolutionary War. He slowly realizes that he is the subject of an experiment conducted by a household of philosophers attempting to determine the intellectual guile of Africans. Octavian is a prodigy with the violin until he runs off following a gruesome experiment with the pox disease. Later captured, he's forced to wear an iron mask. Anderson's work reveals uncomfortable secrets that have been swept under the rug over the course of time. An intricate writing style marks this title for upper high school readers. The sequel is called *The Astonishing Life of Octavian Nothing, Traitor to the Nation, Vol. 2: The Kingdom on the Waves.*

GRADES: 10–12

REVIEW: *Booklist* 9/01/06, *Kirkus* 9/15/06, *Publishers Weekly* 9/18/06, *SLJ* 10/06, *VOYA* 10/06

AWARDS: BBYA Top Ten, Printz Honor

Avi. *Crispin: The Cross of Lead.* 262 p. TR. Hyperion. 978-0-7868-0828-1. 2002. $15.99. PB. Hyperion. 978-0-7868-1658-3. 2004. $7.99. LB. Paw Prints. 978-1-4352-3483-3. $16.99. LB. Turtleback Books. 978-0-613-74965-7. $18.40. LB. Perfection Learning. 978-0-7569-3187-2. 2002. $16.85. LP. Thorndike. 978-0-7862-5501-6. 2003. $25.95.

Crispin has lived as a peasant his entire life, but now at age thirteen, following his mother's death and subsequent accusations against him, he flees his village. Initially he has very few skills and no self-confidence, but during his travels with Bear and by the end of the story he becomes a proud young man. Although Crispin doesn't realize it, he is the illegitimate son of Lord Furnival. Crispin is also deeply religious and prays to his patron saint, St. Giles. Avi writes accurately of the Middle Ages and provides a strong plot that will interest middle school boys. The sequel is called *Crispin: At the Edge of the World.*

GRADES: 6–8

REVIEWS: *Booklist* 5/15/02, *Kirkus* 6/15/02, *Publishers Weekly* 6/03/02, *SLJ* 6/02, *VOYA* 6/02

AWARDS: Newbery Winner

Avi. *The Fighting Ground.* 157 p. TR. HarperCollins. 978-0-397-32074-5. 1984. $16.89. PB. Trophy. 978-0-06-440185-2. 1987. $5.99. LB. San Val/Turtleback. 978-0-8085-9452-9. 1987. $16.00. LB. Perfection Learning. 978-0-7569-8461-8. 2008. $14.85. LB. Paw Prints. 978-1-4420-1709-2. 2009. $14.99.

Jonathan, a thirteen-year-old son of a farmer, leaves home against his father's wishes to join the Revolutionary army. He is given a rifle by a local tavern keeper and becomes involved in a skirmish with Hessian soldiers near Trenton, New Jersey. In the battle's aftermath, he is captured by three Hessian soldiers and experiences the reality of war in a thrilling twenty-hour period that changes his life. Middle school boys will love this fast-paced story that portrays the Revolution from the perspectives of participants from both sides and provides food for thought about war and its consequences.

GRADES: 6–8

Avi. *The True Confessions of Charlotte Doyle.* 337 p. TR. Peter Smith Publisher Incorporated. 978-0-8446-7235-9. 2003. $20.75. LB. Perma-Bound Books. 978-0-7804-2319-0. 1990. $12.99. LB. San Val, Incorporated. 978-0-8335-9372-6. 1992. $14.15. RE. San Val, Incorporated. 978-0-613-82985-4. 1992. $17.20. PB. McDougal Littell Incorporated. 978-0-395-87477-6. 2004. $10.50. CASS. Recorded Books, LLC. 1999. $44.00. LP. Thorndike Press. 978-0-7862-7252-5. 2005. $10.95.

In the early 1800s, Charlotte Doyle finds herself as the only female aboard the good ship *Seahawk.* The teen must earn her keep as part of the crew, an existence that is a far cry from the high-class privileged life she once led. The tension mounts as Charlotte becomes involved in an uprising against the captain and is accused of murder. This title has long been a staple of middle school reading lists and is still offered to readers. The plucky heroine will not disappoint them.

GRADES: 6–9

REVIEWS: *Publishers Weekly* 9/14/90, *SLJ* 9/90

Bagdasarian, Adam. *Forgotten Fire.* 304 p. LB. Perma-Bound Books. 978-0-605-24456-6. 2000. $12.99. RE. San Val, Incorporated. 978-0-613-49414-4. 2002. $17.20. PB. Random House. 978-0-440-22917-9. 2002. $7.50.

In a brief preface Bagdasarian paraphrases Adolf Hitler with this statement, "Who does now remember the Armenians?" We all should. Based on the true story of a young boy who witnessed members of his family and thousands of fellow Armenians murdered by the Turks in 1915, this story will captivate readers. The violence is gruesome and random. Scenes of rape, sexual abuse, and indiscriminate killing occur throughout the book. This novel is a perfect bibliographic companion to any lessons presented about the World War II Holocaust. Although the narrator begins the story at age twelve, this work is geared for older readers due to the stunning violence.

GRADES: 8–12

REVIEWS: *Booklist* 7/01/00, *Kirkus* 10/01/00, *Publishers Weekly* 10/09/00, *SLJ* 12/00, *VOYA* 12/00

AWARDS: BBYA Top Ten

Bartoletti, Susan Campbell. *The Boy Who Dared.* 192 p. TR. Scholastic. 978-0-439-68013-4. 2008. $16.99. CD. Random House Audio. 978-0-7393-7405-4. 2009. $28.00.

Bartoletti wrote the 2005 nonfiction book *Hitler Youth: Growing Up in Hitler's Shadow* and this companion title is a fictionalized account of Helmuth Hübener. In 1942, awaiting his execution in a prison, Helmuth recalls his early life as Hitler came to power. The teenage boy secretly listened to BBC radio and finally dared to write and distribute pamphlets calling for resistance. For his acts, he paid with his life. Any discussion about the importance of questioning absolute power and decisions for civil disobedience should include this title about a single teenager.

GRADES: 8–12

REVIEWS: *Booklist* 2/15/08, *Kirkus* 1/15/08, *Publishers Weekly* 2/08/08, *SLJ* 5/08, *VOYA* 4/08

Blackwood, Gary. *The Shakespeare Stealer.* 216 p. TR. Perfection Learning Corporation. 978-0-7807-9977-6. 2000. $14.65. LB. San Val, Incorporated. 978-0-613-28638-1. 2000 . $14.15. PB. Penguin Group. 978-0-14-130595-0. 2000. $6.99. CD. Recorded Books, LLC. 978-1-4025-1970-3. N/A. $48.00. EB. Penguin Group. 978-1-4295-3094-1. N/A. $6.99.

Widge is only fourteen, but the young man has been trained in an early form of shorthand. His skill catches the eye of his master who concocts a plan to have Widge copy the script of *Hamlet,* the Globe Theater's closely guarded play. Blackwood incorporates a behind-the-curtain view of early Elizabethan theater and the struggle experienced by the actors, especially young boys. A wholesome story, this title is suitable for both middle and high school readers.

GRADES: 6–10

REVIEWS: *Booklist* 6/01/98, *SLJ* 6/98, *VOYA* 8/98

Blackwood, Gary L. *The Year of the Hangman.* 261 p. TR. Perfection Learning Corporation. 978-0-7569-4274-8. 2004. $14.65. LB. Perma-Bound Books. 978-0-605-33797-8. 2002. $13.99. CD. Recorded Books, LLC. 978-1-4025-5063-8. 2003. EB. Recorded Books, LLC. 978-1-4356-0815-3. N/A. $1.00

Set in 1777, this title offers an alternate history on the premise that British forces have trounced the Continental Army and captured General Washington. Fifteen-year-old Creighton is shipped to America. His uncle's ship is attacked by a ragtag group of American rebels led by Benedict Arnold. Taken to New Orleans, Creighton befriends Benjamin Franklin and a group plotting against the British. This clever take on history encourages teens to ask, "What if . . . ?"

GRADES: 7–10

REVIEWS: *Booklist* 8/01/02, *Kirkus* 8/15/02, *Publishers Weekly* 9/16/02, *SLJ* 9/02, *VOYA* 10/02

Blundell, Judy. *What I Saw and How I Lied.* 288 p. TR. Scholastic. 978-0-439-90346-2. 2008. $16.99.

This title can be argued as being more of a coming-of-age novel, but I am placing it here due to its rich atmosphere set in 1947 Florida. Fifteen-year-old Evie is whisked on a road-trip vacation and finds it incredibly boring. That is until she meets Peter, an older guy who happened to be from the same World War II army unit as Evie's stepfather. Her loss of innocence is slowly unraveled as she becomes aware that Peter, and her parents, have agendas other than entertaining a lonely teenager. This work is a perfect example of historical fiction lacking a notable event or actual famous person. Yet the historical details place the reader right with Evie as she practices smoking with candy cigarettes. This layered story of betrayal will be better appreciated by older teens.

GRADES: 9–12

REVIEWS: *Booklist* 11/01/08, *Kirkus* 10/01/08, *Publishers Weekly* 9/29/08, *SLJ* 12/08, *VOYA* 2/09

Boyne, John. *The Boy in the Striped Pajamas.* 224 p. TR. Random House. 978-0-385-75106-3. 2006. $15.95. RE. San Val, Incorporated. 978-1-4178-1823-5. 2007. $19.65. PB. Random House. 978-0-385-75189-6. 2008. $8.99. CD. Random House

Audio. 978-0-7393-3705-9. 2006. $24.95. CD. Random House Audio. 978-0-7393-3774-5. 2006. $32.30. EB. Random House Audio. 978-0-7393-4828-4. N/A. $32.30. LP. Thorndike Press. 978-0-7862-9425-1. 2007. $23.95.

Although the main character here is only nine years old, this title will resonate with teens. Bruno is the son of a camp commandant who is proud of his ability to follow orders during "The Fury." Bruno wanders to the concentration camp fence and meets Shmuel, a boy who lives in the camp. The two boys discover they share the same birthday and a friendship is formed. The power of the story is Bruno set as a victim of his own innocence. Although more of an allegory than a realistic story, Boyne's work will fit nicely into any curriculum study of the Holocaust.

GRADES: 7–12

REVIEWS: *Booklist* 7/01/06, *Kirkus* 8/15/06, *Publishers Weekly* 7/17/06, *SLJ* 9/06, *VOYA* 12/06

Bruchac, Joseph. *Code Talker: A Novel About the Navajo Marines of World War Two.* 240 p. TR. Penguin Group. 978-0-8037-2921-6. 2005. $16.99. TR. Perfection Learning Corporation. 978-0-7569-6707-9. N/A. $15.45. RE. San Val, Incorporated. 978-1-4177-6105-0. 2006. $18.40. LB. Perma-Bound Books. 978-0-605-00009-4. 2005. $14.99. CASS. Recorded Books, LLC. 978-1-4193-5121-1. 2006. $39.75. EB. Recorded Books, LLC. 978-1-4294-6293-8. N/A. $1.00.

Bruchac brings to light the murky history of the Navajo men who volunteered to construct an unbreakable communication code during World War II. Only Navajos can speak their language with complete fluency and the Japanese were bewildered when hearing the communications. Bruchac's character Ned Begay relates his life before the war in the harsh mission schools, then to being recruited by the United States military. Scenes taking place in brutal battles in the Pacific find Ned lucky to survive. The human interest hook of serving a country that shunned their ancestors will engage teen readers in this realistic and informative story about a little-known slice of World War II.

GRADES: 7–10

REVIEWS: *Booklist* 2/15/05, *Kirkus* 1/15/05, *SLJ* 5/05, *VOYA* 4/05

Chevalier, Tracy. *Girl with a Pearl Earring.* 233 p. TR. Santillana USA Publishing Company, Incorporated. 978-84-204-4236-5. 2005. $22.95. TR. Penguin Group. 978-0-452-28493-7. 2003. $15.00. LB. Perma-Bound Books. 978-0-8000-3177-0. 1999. $23.00. RE. San Val, Incorporated. 978-1-4177-4829-7. 2003. $25.75. CD. Recorded Books, LLC. 978-1-4193-1176-5. 2004. $24.95. CD. HighBridge Company. 978-1-56511-497-5. 2001. $26.95. CASS. Recorded Books, LLC. 978-0-7887-6044-0. 2004. $25.95. EB. Penguin Group. 978-0-7865-0711-5. N/A. $12.00.

A young peasant girl finds herself more and more involved with the famous painter Vermeer. Based on a painting by the same title, this story evolves around sixteen-year-old Griet who advances from a servant girl to something of Vermeer's assistant. She mixes paints, cleans his studio, and stands in for models. Of course the increased closeness to the artist causes jealousy with Vermeer's wife and rumors fly about the town. Chevalier centers her novel on the mysterious girl who modeled for the famous painting. This title has wide appeal for older teenage girls and also adults. This book is perfect for a mother/daughter book club.

GRADES: 10–12

REVIEWS: *Booklist* 12/01/99, *Kirkus* 10/15/99, *Publishers Weekly* 10/01/99, *SLJ* 6/00, *VOYA* 8/00

AWARDS: Alex Award, BBYA Top Ten

Choldenko, Gennifer. *Al Capone Does My Shirts.* 240 p. TR. Penguin Group. 978-0-399-23861-1. 2004. $16.99. LB. Perma-Bound Books. 978-0-605-50449-3. 2004. $13.99. RE. San Val, Incorporated. 978-1-4177-3231-9. 2006. $17.20. CD. Recorded Books, LLC. 978-1-4193-1789-7. 2004. $48.75. CASS. Recorded Books, LLC. 978-1-4025-6409-3. 2004. $54.75.

The unique historical backdrop of Alcatraz prison in 1935 will draw readers to this story about twelve-year-old Moose Flanagan. Moose's father works as a guard in the prison, a grim and isolated place housing famous criminals of the day, including gangster Al Capone. Choldenko adds flavor to the historical novel with Moose's sister Natalie, a girl who is autistic. Teen themes of being alone resound in this story as Moose's mother focuses on Natalie's needs and his father works long hours. Moose finds a friend in Piper, the irresistible daughter of the warden. Middle school readers will find this coming-of-age novel set in a famous prison thoroughly engaging. The sequel is called *Al Capone Shines My Shoes.*

GRADES: 6–9

REVIEWS: *Booklist* 2/01/04, *Kirkus* 3/01/04, *Publishers Weekly* 2/02/04, *SLJ* 3/04, *VOYA* 4/04

AWARDS: Newbery Honor

Chotjewitz, David. *Daniel Half Human: And the Good Nazi.* 304 p. Simon & Schuster. 978-0-689-85747-8. 2004. $18.99. LB. San Val, Incorporated. 978-1-4177-4013-0. 2006. $10.25. PB. Simon & Schuster Children's Publishing. 978-0-689-85748-5. 2006. $6.99.

In an extended flashback following Germany's defeat in World War II, Daniel Kraushaar relates his life story between the years 1933 through 1939. Hitler has come to power and anyone with Jewish blood is ostracized. Daniel learns his mother is Jewish, thus he's labeled "half human." His friend Armin continues on to join Hitler's youth movement. He's full blooded and the "good Nazi." This story is an intriguing commentary on friendship and loyalty set against the horrors of war and gives another viewpoint of the Holocaust.

GRADES: 7–10

REVIEWS: *Booklist* 9/15/04, *Kirkus* 9/15/04, *Publishers Weekly* 9/15/04, *SLJ* 12/04, *VOYA* 12/04

Collier, James Lincoln, and Christopher Collier. *Jump Ship to Freedom.* 198 p. TR. Perfection Learning Corporation. 978-0-8124-5090-3. 1987. $13.65. LB. San Val, Incorporated. 978-0-8085-9126-9. 1987. $13.55. LB. Perma-Bound Books. 978-0-8000-1789-7. 1981. $12.50. PB. Random House Children's Books. 978-0-440-91158-6. 1996. $5.99.

Young Daniel Arabus and his mother are slaves and are considered property of Captain Ivers of Stratford, Connecticut. Since Daniel's father fought in the Revolutionary War, by law they should be freed from Ivers's Connecticut estate. However, the soldier's notes to buy their freedom are taken by Ivers's wife, but Daniel steals them back. His punishment is to be put on a ship bound for the West Indies and certain slavery. Daniel's determination and bravery will thrill middle school readers and at the same time inform them of the struggles to be free in a time well before the Civil War.

GRADES: 6–9

REVIEWS: *SLJ* 2/87

Crowe, Chris. *Mississippi Trial, 1955.* 240 p. TR. Penguin Group. 978-0-8037-2745-8. 2002. $17.99. LB. San Val, Incorporated. 978-0-613-86522-7. 2003. $14.15. LB. Perma-Bound Books. 978-0-605-34005-3. 2002. $12.99.

Centered on the gruesome death of Emmett Till, Chris Crowe offers a coming-of-age story that places readers alongside the extreme racism of the South in 1955. Hiram is spending the summer in Mississippi with his admired grandfather. He befriends African American Emmett Till who is also visiting from Chicago. Following a minor confrontation with whites, Emmett is kidnapped, tortured, and killed. The ensuing trial puts a spotlight on the racial tension of the small community and Hiram learns that people he respects may be hiding terrifying secrets. Crowe's admirable research is woven into a story of a teenager learning that adults cannot always be trusted.

GRADES: 7–10

REVIEWS: *Booklist* 2/15/02, *Kirkus* 4/01/02, *Publishers Weekly* 6/17/02, *SLJ* 5/02, *VOYA* 4/02

Cullen, Lynn. *I Am Rembrandt's Daughter.* 320 p. TR. Bloomsbury Publishing. 978-1-59990-046-9. 2007. $16.95.

Cornelia has a contemptuous relationship with her father, the volatile and famous painter Rembrandt. Believing God tells him what to paint, the artist lags far behind in completing works. His brash personality keeps patrons away and his bastard daughter tries to keep the household together. Cornelia is a sympathetic character who following her mother's death is forced to grow up and shoulder adult responsibilities too early in life, a theme today's teens will embrace.

GRADES: 7–10

REVIEWS: *Booklist* 4/15/07, *Publishers Weekly* 6/25/07, *SLJ* 8/07, *VOYA* 6/07

Curtis, Christopher Paul. *Bud, Not Buddy.* 256 p. TR. Book Wholesalers, Incorporated. 978-1-4046-1884-8. 2002. $14.17. TR. Random House Children's Books. 978-0-385-32306-2. 1999. $16.95. LB. San Val, Incorporated. 978-0-613-36783-7. 2002. $14.15. LB. Perma-Bound Books. 978-0-605-77252-6. 1999. $13.50. PB. Random House Children's Books. 978-0-553-49410-5. 2004. $6.99. CD. Random House Audio. 978-0-7393-3179-8. 2006. $19.95. CD. Random House Audio. 978-0-8072-1045-1. 2004. $40.00. CASS. Random House Audio. 978-0-8072-8209-0. 2004. $30.00. CASS. Books on Tape, Incorporated. 978-0-7366-9016-4. 2000. $24.00. EB. Random House Audio. 978-0-7393-4438-5. N/A. $38.25. LP. Thorndike Press. 978-0-7862-6191-8. 2003. $10.95.

Young Bud Caldwell (the ten-year-old hates being talked down to as "Buddy") lives in a Flint, Michigan, orphanage in the middle of the Great Depression. The year is 1936 and Bud is fed up with the hassles of being in a foster home. He sets out to find his father whom he has never met. His only clue is a fading flyer his mother owned about Herman E. Calloway and the Dusky Devastators of the Depression. Bud's charming personality and dogged determination to discover his heritage makes this a totally engaging yarn suitable for all middle school readers.

GRADES: 6–9

REVIEWS: *Booklist* 9/01/99, *Publishers Weekly* 8/09/99, *SLJ* 9/99, *VOYA* 2/00

AWARDS: Newbery Winner

Curtis, Christopher Paul. *The Watsons Go to Birmingham, 1963.* 224 p. TR. Book Wholesalers, Incorporated. 978-0-7587-0328-6. 2002. $14.47. TR. Random House Children's Books. 978-0-385-32175-4. 1995. $16.95. LB. San Val, Incorporated. 978-0-613-85111-4. 2000. $14.15. CD. Random House Audio. 978-0-307-24317-1. 2005. $19.95. CD. Random House Audio. 978-0-8072-1777-1. 2004. $32.30. PLAY. Findaway World, LLC. 978-0-7393-7565-5. 2006. $39.99. CASS. Random House Audio. 978-0-8072-8334-9. 2004. $32.00. CASS. Random House Audio.

978-0-8072-0880-9. 2002. $17.99. EB. Adobe Systems, Inc. 978-1-59061-404-4. 2001. $3.99.

Kenny Watson is a typical teenager in Flint, Michigan, trying to please his hard-working parents while getting into trouble with his older brother, Byron. The decision is made to place troublemaker Byron in the Alabama home of their strict grandmother. The entire family, including younger sister Joetta, pile into the family car for a road trip. Once in the South, things are okay until Joetta attends a church targeted to be bombed by racists. Author Curtis mixes in a sly brand of humor while relating a grim historical situation that sent shock waves across the country. This title is often picked as a class read by a variety of schools. Teens will not be disappointed in the selection.

GRADES: 6–10

REVIEWS: *Booklist* 8/01/95, *Kirkus* 9/15/95, *SLJ* 10/95

Cushman, Karen. *Catherine, Called Birdy.* 224 p. TR. Book Wholesalers, Incorporated. 978-0-7587-0246-3. 2002. $15.00. TR. Pathways Publishing. 978-1-58303-085-1. 2000. $19.95. LB. Perma-Bound Books. 978-0-605-07553-5. 1994. $13.50. RE. San Val, Incorporated. 978-0-7857-6149-5. 1995. $17.20. CD. Recorded Books, LLC. 978-0-7887-9520-6. N/A. $58.00. CASS. Books on Tape, Incorporated. 978-0-7366-9031-7. 2000. $18.00. EB. Recorded Books, LLC. 978-1-4175-8719-3. N/A. $1.00.

Set in the late 1200s of Medieval England, Catherine is asked to begin writing a journal. The thirteen-year-old describes the activities of the time—embroidery, making soap, and doctoring the sick. Soon her father begins searching for a wealthy suitor for his daughter and she ends up spoken for by a truly despicable man, Shaggy Beard. Although set in a time hundreds of years ago, this story of a girl trying to gain control of her own life will continue to draw in middle school girls.

GRADES: 6–9

REVIEWS: *Publishers Weekly* 4/11/94, *SLJ* 6/94

AWARDS: Newbery Honor

Donnelly, Jennifer. *A Northern Light.* 396 p. TR. Perfection Learning Corporation. 978-0-7569-3614-3. 2004. $16.60. LB. Perma-Bound Books. 978-0-605-59501-9. 2003. $15.95. RE. San Val, Incorporated. 978-1-4176-3718-8. 2004. $19.60. CD. Random House Audio. 978-0-8072-1787-0. 2004. $51.00. CASS. Random House Audio. 978-0-8072-0896-0. 2004. $40.00. EB. Random House Audio. 978-0-7393-5380-6. N/A. $51.00.

Mattie Gokey faces her sixteenth year with a yearning to leave the poverty of her upstate New York farm and find her fortune in New York City. But her job as a worker in a resort hotel brings her into the middle of a murder. The same crime that inspired Theodore Dreiser's *An American Tragedy* is mined as the catalyst influencing Mattie's decisions. Donnelly inserts many sidebars about feminism, friendship versus love, and taking control of one's own destiny. The atmosphere of early 1900s rural life is sharply contrasted with the lavish wealth of hotel guests. A sophisticated writing style marks this title for older readers.

GRADES: 9–12

REVIEWS: *Booklist* 5/15/02, *Kirkus* 3/15/03, *Publishers Weekly* 3/03/03, *SLJ* 5/03, *VOYA* 4/03

AWARDS: BBYA Top Ten, Printz Honor

Fitzgerald, F. Scott. *The Great Gatsby.* Page count varies with edition. There are significant formats currently available in print.

Set in 1922, Fitzgerald's venerable novel sets the tragedy of Jay Gatsby's life against the backdrop of the wealth and excess of the Roaring 1920s. The interaction of the complex characters, each heavily flawed, is examined and related by everyman Nick Carraway. This title, written in 1925, has earned the status of one of the top American novels of the twentieth century. It is almost a certainty that the majority of teenagers will be required to read this book sometime during their academic careers

GRADES: 11–12

Fletcher, Christine. *Ten Cents a Dance.* 356 p. TR. Bloomsbury Publishing. 978-1-59990-164-0. 2008. $16.95.

The desperation of earning money during the latter stages of the Great Depression is the setting of Fletcher's story of fifteen-year-old Ruby Jacinski. Ruby quits her awful job at a Chicago meatpacking factory but her family still needs her to bring in money. She finds a chance to make big money by dancing at the Starlight Dance Academy. In the club, girls known as taxi dancers charge lonely men for each dance and maybe more. Ruby is a spunky girl who stands up for what she believes in. Struggles with boyfriends, creepy men, and her own family will connect with today's teenage female readers. Sexual situations make this title more suited for upper middle and high school teens.

GRADES: 8–12

REVIEWS: *Booklist* 7/01/08, *Publishers Weekly* 4/21/08, *SLJ* 4/08, *VOYA* 8/08

AWARDS: BBYA Top Ten

Forbes, Esther. *Johnny Tremain.* Page count varies with edition. There are significant formats currently available in print.

This classic story of a teenage boy in pre-Revolutionary Boston spans the Boston Tea Party, the blockade of Boston harbor by the British, and Paul Revere's ride. Mixed in are the battles of Lexington and Concord. Johnny, a fourteen-year-old silversmith apprentice, finds his career ended by a horrible accident that maims his hand, the result of a trick by a jealous fellow apprentice. No longer able to work as a silversmith, he eventually goes to work for *The Boston Observer*, a Whig newspaper, where he is befriended by Rab Silsbee, an older teenager and ardent Patriot. Johnny becomes involved in the exciting world of the Sons of Liberty and experiences the intrigue of the Boston Tea Party and the excitement of the first battles of the Revolution. *Johnny Tremain* has been a constant winning title for middle school readers for decades.

GRADES: 6–8

AWARDS: Newbery Winner

Gardner, Sally. *The Red Necklace.* 384 p. TR. Penguin Group. 978-0-8037-3100-4. 2008. $17.99. CD. Random House Audio. 978-0-7393-5648-7. 2008. $50.00. EB. Penguin Group. 978-1-4362-2370-6. 2008. $16.99. EB. Random House Audio. 978-0-7393-6232-7. N/A. $42.50. LP. Thorndike Press. 978-1-4104-1016-0. 2008. $23.95.

Yann Margoza, a fourteen-year-old magician's assistant who can read minds, has his life disrupted on the eve of the French Revolution. The performers Yann accompanies arrive at the chateau of a debt-ridden marquis and during their act, a murder occurs. Yann becomes involved with the marquis' twelve-year-old daughter, a dangerous situation due to the treachery of Count Kalliovski. The intrigue between the characters is combined with the exploding horrors of the revolution. Gardner stirs in elements of the supernatural with the historical accuracy of peasants storming the homes of aristocrats.

GRADES: 9–12

REVIEWS: *Booklist* 4/15/08, *Kirkus* 4/01/08, *Publishers Weekly* 5/26/08, *SLJ* 5/08, *VOYA* 8/08

Geras, Adele. *Troy.* 368 p. LB. Perma-Bound Books. 978-0-605-92082-8. 2000. $13.95. RE. San Val, Incorporated. 978-0-613-55224-0. 2002. $17.15. PB. Houghton Mifflin Harcourt Trade & Reference Publishers. 978-0-15-204570-8. 2002. $6.95. CASS. Random House Audio. 978-0-8072-0599-0. 2004. $40.00. EB. Random House Audio. 978-0-7393-6758-2. N/A. $51.00.

Geras retells the saga of the Trojan War from a feminist point of view. Two sisters, Xanthe and Marpessa, are the focal point of the story. Xanthe is the caretaker of Andromache's child but also helps out in the blood room where injured soldiers are taken. Marpessa is Helen's assistant and can see the gods. As the siege becomes more desperate, the two sisters become attracted to the same boy, Alastor. By combining figures from history with common everyday folks, Geras has created an intriguing viewpoint of the ancient legend. A necessary familiarity with the legend and a violent climactic scene indicates this title is more appropriate for high school readership.

GRADES: 9–12

REVIEWS: *Booklist* 4/01/01, *Publishers Weekly* 5/07/01, *SLJ* 7/01, *VOYA* 6/01

Gratz, Alan M. *Samurai Shortstop.* 288 p. TR. Penguin Group. 978-0-8037-3075-5. 2006. $17.99. CD. Random House Audio. 978-0-7393-3639-7. 2006. $39.00. CD. Random House Audio. 978-0-7393-3624-3. 2006. $50.00. CASS. Random House Audio. 978-0-7393-3629-8. 2006. $40.00. EB. Random House Audio. 978-0-7393-6083-5. N/A. $42.50.

Toyo Shimada is a sixteen-year-old caught between two worlds of Japan in the 1890s. The emperor has decided to open Japan to the Western world and Toyo's father and uncle desperately wish to hang on to the traditional samurai beliefs of bushido, or the warrior's code. Toyo wins a place on his school's besuboro (or baseball) team, but hanging over his head is his father's request to be his second in his planned ritual suicide or seppuku. Toyo is a teen determined to experience new things, but to do so he must defy his father. Gratz's work shows a country emerging from the medieval world to one of modern complications.

GRADES: 7–10

REVIEWS: *Booklist* 4/15/06, *Kirkus* 4/15/06, *Publishers Weekly* 5/22/06, *SLJ* 7/06, *VOYA* 6/06

AWARDS: BBYA Top Ten

Greene, Bette. *Summer of My German Soldier.* 230 p. TR. Penguin Group. 978-0-8037-2869-1. 2003. $18.99. TR. Peter Smith Publisher, Incorporated. 978-0-8446-7144-4. 2000. $20.50. CD. Recorded Books, LLC. 978-1-4025-2339-7. N/A. $69.00. LP. Thorndike Press. 978-0-7862-7361-4. 2005. $10.95.

Patty Bergen is a twelve-year-old Jewish girl living in Jenkensville, Arkansas. Her somewhat typical life becomes complicated when a group of World War II German prisoners are brought to her small town. Anton, one of the prisoners, escapes, and Patty immediately helps him. By doing so she defies her parents, her friends, and her religion. This title, which has been introduced to teens for decades, still causes readers to ponder doing the right thing even though the popular feeling is different. The atmosphere of small town America during the war is sharply contrasted by Patty's worldly decisions.

GRADES: 6–9

Grey, Christopher. *Leonardo's Shadow: Or, My Astonishing Life as Leonardo da Vinci's Servant.* 400 p. TR. Simon & Schuster Children's Publishing. 978-1-4169-0543-1. 2006. $16.95. PB. Simon & Schuster Children's Publishing. 978-1-4169-0544-8. 2008. $8.99.

Giacomo is an everyman servant for the great Leonardo. He performs his duties and does what is asked of him, but he realizes Leonardo spends much of his time making excuses for delays in completing commissioned works. Giacomo becomes the behind-the-scenes string puller who knows that Leonardo must complete his masterpiece, *The Last Supper*, in order for artist and servant to get paid and survive. The late fourteenth-century comes alive with this intriguing "what-if" solution for present-day questions behind one of the most treasured paintings of all time.

GRADES: 7–9

REVIEWS: *Booklist* 8/01/06, *Publishers Weekly* 1/01/07, *SLJ* 10/06, *VOYA* 8/06

Hesse, Karen. *Out of the Dust.* 160 p. TR. Book Wholesalers, Incorporated. 978-0-7587-0207-4. 2002. $13.19. TR. Scholastic, Incorporated. 978-0-590-36080-7. 1997. $16.95. LB. Perma-Bound Books. 978-0-605-67693-0. 1997. $13.99. RE. San Val, Incorporated. 978-0-613-11953-5. 1999. $17.20. PB. Scholastic, Incorporated. 978-0-590-37125-4. 1999. $6.99. CD. Random House Audio. 978-0-307-28403-7. 2006. $13.00. CASS. Books on Tape, Incorporated. 978-0-7366-9096-6. 2000. $18.00. CASS. Random House Audio. 978-0-8072-8012-6. 1998. $23.00. EB. Random House Audio. 978-0-7393-5990-7. N/A. $20.40.

Thirteen-year-old Billie Jo finds solace in playing the piano, but after a tragic accident burns her hands she may never find pleasure in playing again. Set in the midst of the Great Depression's Dust Bowl, Billie Jo hops a train heading west but comes to realize there is no real escaping her Oklahoma home. Presented in verse format, this title's descriptions of the hardship during dust storms of the 1930s will fascinate and also stun teenage readers.

GRADES: 6–10

REVIEWS: *Booklist* 10/01/97, *Kirkus* 9/15/97, *Publishers Weekly* 8/25/97, *SLJ* 9/97

AWARDS: Newbery Winner

Hesse, Karen. *Witness.* N/A. TR. Scholastic, Incorporated. 978-0-439-27199-8. 2001. $16.95. LB. Perma-Bound Books. 978-0-605-02944-6. 2001. $12.99. RE. San Val, Incorporated. 978-0-613-62503-6. 2003. $16.00. PB. Scholastic, Incorporated. 978-0-439-27200-1. 2003. $5.99. EB. Random House Audio. 978-0-7393-3804-9. N/A. $20.40.

Hesse details a small part of American history with a town in Vermont dealing with racism threatening to pull the community apart. Distinct voices speak, each revealing a part of themselves through their words. Hesse again uses the verse format to bring each character to life. The Ku Klux Klan arrives and tries to convince the townspeople an African American child and a young Jewish girl have no place with the other citizens. This novel gives a glimpse of how easily love and hate can be heavily influenced by outside forces.

GRADES: 7–10

REVIEWS: *Booklist* 10/01/01, *Kirkus* 8/01/01, *Publishers Weekly* 8/20/01, *VOYA* 10/01

Hughes, Dean. *Soldier Boys.* 176 p. TR. Perfection Learning Corporation. 978-0-7569-4566-4. 2003. $14.65. TR. Simon & Schuster Children's Publishing. 978-0-689-81748-9. 2001. $16.95. LB. San Val, Incorporated. 978-0-613-66437-0. 2003. $13.00.

Two teenage boys get caught up with the patriotic fervor of World War II and enlist in their respective military forces. Spence Morgan leaves his small Utah town and enters basic training as a paratrooper. Dieter Hedrick joins the German Hitler youth. Both teens are thrust into the gripping violence of battle. Their paths converge in the freezing backdrop of The Battle of the Bulge. Hughes shifts his story in a single page to a stunning climax and teens, especially boys, will be drawn to the bravery shown in war.

GRADES: 7–10

REVIEWS: *Kirkus* 11/01/01, *Publishers Weekly* 12/03/01, *SLJ* 11/01

Janeczko, Paul B. *Worlds Afire.* 112 p. LB. Perma-Bound Books. 978-0-605-01393-3. 2004. $22.99.

The circus fire that happened in Hartford, Connecticut, on July 6, 1944, killed 167 people. Janeczko's series of poems construct events before, during, and after the tragedy. Voices range from an animal trainer, an usher, a nurse, and a police detective. Janeczko's use of multiple characters gives a comprehensive portrait of a gruesome event while capturing the flavor of 1940s America.

GRADES: 7–10

REVIEWS: *Booklist* 1/01/04, *Publishers Weekly* 3/19/07, *VOYA* 4/04

Jocelyn, Marthe. *How It Happened in Peach Hill.* 240 p. TR. Random House Children's Books. 978-0-375-83701-2. 2007. $15.99. PB. Random House Children's Books. 978-0-375-83702-9. 2009. $6.99.

Fifteen-year-old Annie and her mother, the flamboyant Madame Caterina, travel small towns on the eastern coast. Their scam is to feast on the simple townsfolks' desire to communicate with dead loved ones and relieve them of their cash. Annie must pretend to be dim-witted to glean gossip, but fed up with milking honest people out of their savings, Annie refuses to cooperate. This novel set in the 1920s captures how people embraced the little known spiritualist movement and gives an interesting snapshot of small town life.

GRADES: 6–9

REVIEWS: *Booklist* 1/01/07, *Publishers Weekly* 3/19/07, *SLJ* 4/07, *VOYA* 12/07

Kass, Pnina Moed. *Real Time.* N/A. TR. Houghton Mifflin Harcourt Trade & Reference Publishers. 978-0-618-44203-4. 2004. $15.00. PB. Houghton Mifflin Harcourt Publishing Company. 978-0-618-69174-6. 2006. $7.99.

The Middle East conflict is detailed in this novel presented from varying points of view. Thomas Wanninger is a sixteen-year-old German youth who travels to Israel to discover the truth about his grandfather. Other characters give insight about the tension including a suicide bomber's thoughts as he attempts to blow up a crowded bus near Jerusalem. Although not history from the far past, this novel gives gripping testimony to life in a contemporary historical location.

GRADES: 9–12

REVIEWS: *Booklist* 2/01/05, *Publishers Weekly* 11/22/04, *SLJ* 10/04, *VOYA* 2/05

Keith, Harold. *Rifles for Watie.* 332 p. PB. Trophy. 978-0-06-447030-8. 1987. $6.99. LB. Perfection Learning. 978-0-8124-5548-9. 1988. $15.85. LB. HarperCollins. 978-0-690-04907-7. 1991. $18.89. LB. Paw Prints. 978-1-4420-3666-6. 2009. $15.99.

This Civil War tale is set in Kansas where a teenager sees the war from both sides. Jefferson Bussey, a sixteen-year-old from Kansas, joins the Union army and fights in Oklahoma Indian Territory, where Cherokee Indian chief, Stand Watie, is raiding Union lines for the Confederacy. Jeff experiences the war from both sides when he ends up in the Confederate army as a Union spy and falls in love with a Rebel girl. History comes alive for middle school boys with this thrilling tale.

GRADES: 6–8

AWARDS: Newbery Winner

Lawrence, Iain. *The Buccaneers.* 244 p. TR. Perfection Learning Corporation. 978-0-7569-1454-7. 2003. $13.65. RE. San Val, Incorporated. 978-0-613-64433-4. 2003. $16.00. PB. Random House Children's Books. 978-0-440-41671-5. 2003. $5.99. EB. Recorded Books, LLC. 978-1-4237-2264-9. N/A. $1.00. LP. Thorndike Press. 978-0-7862-3464-6. 2001. $23.95.

Opening with *The Wreckers,* bridged by the book *The Smugglers* and ending with *The Buccaneers,* this seagoing trilogy is packed with action from the sailing ship era. John Spencer, now sixteen years old, is once again on a voyage when a lifeboat is spotted. The occupant, Mr. Horn, joins the ship's crew but the superstitious crew considers him a "Jonah" who will bring misfortune to the journey. Soon enough piracy, storms, and the danger of crashing into rocks all befall the hapless ship. This story is a fitting end to the trilogy that brings to life the thrill of surviving on the high seas of the nineteenth century.

GRADES: 6–9

REVIEWS: *Booklist* 5/15/01, *Kirkus* 5/15/01

Lawrence, Iain. *The Wreckers*. 196 p. TR. Perfection Learning Corporation. 978-0-7807-9987-5. 1999. $14.65. RE. San Val, Incorporated. 978-0-613-22807-7. 1999. $16.60. PB. Random House Children's Books. 978-0-440-41545-9. 1999. $6.99. CD. Recorded Books, LLC. 978-0-7887-4654-3. 2000. $48.00.

London teen John Spencer sets sail on his father's merchant ship. The year is 1799 and a storm destroys the vessel. The fourteen-year-old John washes up on the beach only to discover that the ship was a victim of "wreckers" who lure ships to dangerous shores so they will wreck and the cargo can be looted. But the goods cannot be claimed if there are any survivors. John searches for a way to escape, but learns his father may also be alive.

GRADES: 6–9

REVIEWS: *Booklist* 6/15/98, *Kirkus* 5/01/98, *Publishers Weekly* 6/01/98, *SLJ* 6/98, *VOYA* 2/99

Lester, Julius. *Day of Tears: A Novel in Dialogue*. 177 p. TR. Hyperion. 978-0-7868-0490-0. 2005. $15.99. RE. San Val, Incorporated. 978-1-4177-7242-1. 2007. $18.45. LB. Perma-Bound Books. 978-0-605-00011-7. 2005. $14.99. PB. Hyperion Books for Children. 978-1-4231-0409-4. 2007. $7.99. CD. Recorded Books, LLC. 978-1-4193-6811-0. 2006. $29.75. CASS. Recorded Books, LLC. 978-1-4193-6806-6. 2006. $19.75. EB. Recorded Books, LLC. 978-1-4237-6526-4. N/A. $1.00.

Lester's research into the biggest slave auction in history helps bring this novel in verse to life. The event took place in Savannah in 1859 with the owner selling his "property" to pay off gambling debts. The dehumanizing process of selling humans becomes very disturbing when reading of different characters describing the situation. Runaways, family members, and an abolitionist all share their viewpoints. The metaphor of rain symbolizing tears as families are torn apart brings a sobering touch to the narrative.

GRADES: 7–12

REVIEWS: *Booklist* 2/01/05, *Publishers Weekly* 5/16/05, *SLJ* 3/05, *VOYA* 6/05

Lester, Julius. *The Guardian.* 160 p. TR. HarperCollins Publishers. 978-0-06-155890-0. 2008. $16.99. LB. HarperCollins Publishers. 978-0-06-155891-7. 2008. $17.89.

A pair of fourteen-year-old boys experience racism's grim reality in their small Southern town during 1946. Ansel Anderson is white and his friend, Willie Benton, is black. When a white girl is murdered, Ansel's father helps the lynch mob that captures and executes Willie's father. Ansel knows the identity of the actual killer but is powerless to stop the violence. Lester's concise writing style heightens the horror by giving readers an almost observer's account of the lynching. Lester's work is an examination of the power of friendship coming against the prevailing mind-set of racism and will engage readers of various ages.

GRADES: 7–12

REVIEWS: *Booklist* 9/15/08, *Publishers Weekly* 11/03/08, *SLJ* 11/08, *VOYA* 2/09

Mazer, Harry. *The Last Mission.* 188 p. TR. Perfection Learning Corporation. 978-0-8124-3089-9. 1981. $14.15. LB. Perma-Bound Books. 978-0-8479-5080-5. 1979. $12.50. RE. San Val, Incorporated. 978-0-8085-1692-7. 1992. $16.60. PB. Random House Children's Books. 978-0-440-94797-4. 1981. $6.99. CASS. Recorded Books, LLC. 978-1-55690-596-4. 1992. $35.00. CASS. Random House Audio. 978-0-8072-1822-8. 1985. $15.98.

In 1944, fifteen-year-old Jack Raab has visions of being a war hero. Swept up with the nationwide feeling of patriotism, Jack uses a false ID and enlists in the military. He becomes a gunner on a bomber that flies missions over Europe. After flying twenty-four missions, the plane is shot down on the last mission and Jack is taken prisoner. The horrors of flying in combat are lessened by what the Jewish teenager discovers on the ground. This title has been an engaging action story for decades. Boys are especially drawn to Jack's heroism as a teenager.

GRADES: 6–9

Meyer, Carolyn. *Mary, Bloody Mary.* 227 p. TR. Perfection Learning Corporation. 978-0-7569-0514-9. 2001. $14.60. LB. San Val, Incorporated. 978-0-613-35461-5. 2001. $14.15. PB. Harcourt Trade Publishers. 978-0-15-201905-1. 2001. $6.00.

Presented in the first person narrative of Mary's voice, this novel focuses on the life of Mary Tudor who went from princess to servant. As Henry VIII's oldest daughter, Mary lives a life of lavish wealth, until Henry becomes obsessed with having a male heir. Mary witnesses Henry's affair with Anne Boleyn, whom he marries. This marriage changes history as well as Mary's life and now she enters a struggle to merely survive. This period of violent royal maneuvering is presented through the eyes of a teenager and will engage older middle school readers, especially girls.

GRADES: 7–10

REVIEWS: *Booklist* 9/15/99, *Kirkus* 8/15/99, *Publishers Weekly* 9/27/99, *SLJ* 10/99, *VOYA* 2/00

AWARDS: BBYA Top Ten

Morpurgo, Michael. *Private Peaceful.* 208 p. TR. Scholastic, Incorporated. 978-0-439-63648-3. 2004. $16.95. LB. Perma-Bound Books. 978-0-605-56133-5. 2003. $13.99. RE. San Val, Incorporated. 978-1-4177-6923-0. 2006. $17.20. CD. Recorded Books, LLC. 978-1-4193-5614-8. 2005. $51.75. CASS. Recorded Books, LLC. 978-1-4193-2977-7. 2005. $39.75.

Two English brothers are caught in the horror of trench warfare of World War I. Thomas, age fifteen, has lied about his age to join his admired older brother, Charles, who is fighting in France. Thomas now sits in the dark marking time until a punishment at dawn will be dealt. In extended flashbacks readers become aware of the simple farm life the brothers left behind in England, along with the girl both of them loved. The ending is grim and provides insight into a little-known aspect of military life during the Great War. The sobering narrative will be best appreciated by older teens.

GRADES: 8–12

REVIEWS: *Booklist* 10/01/04, *Publishers Weekly* 12/06/04, *SLJ* 11/04, *VOYA* 12/04

AWARDS: BBYA Top Ten

Myers, Walter Dean. *Fallen Angels.* TR. Perfection Learning Corporation. 978-0-7569-8797-8. 2008. $14.65. TR. Book Wholesalers, Incorporated. 978-0-7587-0353-8. 2002. $13.19. RE. San Val, Incorporated. 978-0-7383-0736-7. 2008. $17.20. PB. Scholastic, Incorporated. 978-0-545-05576-5. 2008. $6.99.

At age seventeen Richie Perry figures his future is pretty bleak, so to buy time while considering his future he enlists into the military. In Southeast Asia, at the height of the Vietnam War, Richie and his fellow soldiers are thrust into the horror of battle. He witnesses his mates gunned down, women and children killed, and experiences periods of boredom alternating with terror. The intensity of the battles is contrasted by Richie's despair that he will not survive either guerilla raids or his racist officers. Although recommended to be read by a wide range of ages, this title also contains harsh language and extreme violence.

GRADES: 7–12

REVIEWS: *Kirkus* 5/01/88, *Publishers Weekly* 5/13/88, *SLJ* 6/88

Myers, Walter Dean. *Here in Harlem: Poems in Many Voices.* 96 p. TR. Holiday House, Incorporated. 978-0-8234-1853-4. 2004. $16.95. LB. Perma-Bound Books. 978-0-605-01400-8. 2004. $23.95. PB. Holiday House, Incorporated. 978-0-8234-2212-8. 2008. $8.95.

Myers gathers many voices in this poetic salute to his beloved home of Harlem. The featured voices are designed to provide the look and feel of Harlem during various times, and people from all walks of life give their insight. We hear from students, old folks, a hairdresser, and a hustler. While each poem varies in length, all give an interesting insight into the history and complexity of Harlem, a place today that seems to be known only as a cliché. The emphasis on diversity will enhance any multicultural lesson.

GRADES: 8–12

REVIEWS: *Booklist* 11/01/04, *Publishers Weekly* 11/15/04, *SLJ* 12/04, *VOYA* 2/05

Napoli, Donna Jo. *Bound.* 192 p. TR. Simon & Schuster Children's Publishing. 978-0-689-86175-8. 2004. $16.95. LB. Perma-Bound Books. 978-0-605-56663-7. 2004. $12.99. RE. San Val, Incorporated. 978-1-4177-7177-6. 2006. $17.20. PB. Simon & Schuster Children's Publishing. 978-0-689-86178-9. 2006. $6.99.

Napoli explores layered themes of freedom and captivity in this powerful survival story set in China during the Ming dynasty. Xing Xing is the stepdaughter who tends to her stepmother and stepsister after her father dies. Her stepsister has begun binding her feet and due to the pain can barely walk. Patterning her novel after the traditional Cinderella story, Napoli weaves a tale based on the subversive position of women during Chinese history. Incorporating fantasy aspects of her dead mother's spirit alongside the realistic pain of binding feet, this title is a unique portrayal of a culture vastly different from Western traditions.

GRADES: 8–12

REVIEWS: *Booklist* 12/01/04, *Publishers Weekly* 11/08/04, *SLJ* 11/04, *VOYA* 2/05

O'Brien, Tim. *The Things They Carried.* 272 p. TR. Broadway Books. 978-0-7679-0289-2. 1998. $14.95. LB. Perma-Bound Books. 978-0-7804-3349-6. 1990. $21.95. PB. Spark Publishing Group. 978-1-58663-827-6. 2002. $5.95. CD. Recorded Books, LLC. 978-1-4025-7369-9. 2004. $24.99. EB. Recorded Books, LLC. 978-1-4175-9236-4. N/A. $1.00.

O'Brien's work is not a memoir, but a novel based on recollections of his own Vietnam experience as a foot soldier. By describing the various items each soldier of the small platoon carries into battle, the author gives insight into each character. Often the same event is repeated, but told from another character's point of view. Although the items carried are physical, O'Brien's extended metaphor becomes the emotional burden soldiers carry into and out of war. The grim aspect of war violence and layered meanings captured in the narrative mark this story as a great fit for college-bound students.

GRADES: 10–12

REVIEWS: *SLJ* 2 /91

Olmstead, Robert. *Coal Black Horse.* TR. Algonquin Books of Chapel Hill. 978-1-56512-601-5. 2008. $13.95. TR. Algonquin Books of Chapel Hill. 978-1-56512-521-6. 2007. $23.95. EB. Recorded Books, LLC. 978-1-4356-0231-1. N/A. $1.00. LP. Thorndike Press. 978-1-59413-237-7. 2008. $13.95.

In 1863, fourteen-year-old Robey Childs is sent away by his mother. His task is to find his father, a Civil War soldier Robey's mother senses has been injured in battle. He borrows a magnificent coal black horse, an animal that carries him to the hell of the aftermath of the battle of Gettysburg where his father lays dying. Along the way Robey witnesses the grim nastiness of humanity from rape, to grave robbing, to lingering death. The horse becomes the vehicle to carry Robey to hell and return him to civilization. Following his journey, Robey changes from an observer to almost an avenging angel, righting the wrongs he witnessed. The harsh reality of war carnage and the layered plot places this book into the upper end of young adult reading.

GRADES:10–12

REVIEWS: *Booklist* 1/01/07, *Publishers Weekly* 10/23/06, *SLJ* 6/07, *VOYA* 10/07

Park, Linda Sue. *A Single Shard.* 192 p. TR. Houghton Mifflin Harcourt Trade & Reference Publishers. 978-0-395-97827-6. 2001. $15.00. PB. Random House Children's Books. 978-0-440-41851-1. 2003. $6.99. CD. Random House Audio Publishing Group. 978-1-4000-8495-1. 2004. $14.99. CD. Random House Audio Publishing Group. 978-0-8072-1607-1. 2004. $30.00. CASS. Random House Audio Publishing Group. 978-0-8072-0702-4. 2004. $30.00. EB. Houghton Mifflin Harcourt Trade & Reference Publishers. 978-0-618-23238-3. N/A. $15.00.

Orphan Tree-ear and his guardian Crane-man are homeless and eat only what they can find in the garbage. When he reaches age twelve, Tree-ear becomes an assistant to a potter, Min. Tree-ear must gain the trust of the harsh taskmaster while attempting to carry two valuable pots across miles of unknown territory. The pots meet disaster and only a single shard remains available to show at journey's end. Park's novel provides insight into twelfth-century Korean society, an era readers will find different from Western history.

GRADES: 6–9

REVIEWS: *Booklist* 4/01/01, *Kirkus* 1/15/01, *Publishers Weekly* 3/05/01, *SLJ* 5/01

AWARDS: Newbery Winner

Peck, Richard. *The River Between Us.* 176 p. TR. Penguin Group (USA) Incorporated. 978-0-8037-2735-9. 2003. $16.99. RE. San Val, Incorporated. 978-1-4176-6931-8. 2005. $17.20. LB. Perma-Bound Books. 978-0-7804-3929-0. 2003. $13.99. PB. Penguin Group (USA) Incorporated. 978-0-14-240310-5. 2005. $6.99. CD. Random House Audio Publishing Group. 978-1-4000-8982-6. 2004. $32.30. CD. Random House Audio Publishing Group. 978-0-307-28250-7. 2005. $30.00. CASS. Random House Audio Publishing Group. 978-1-4000-8626-9. 2004. $32.00. EB. Random House Audio. 978-0-7393-4520-7. N/A. $32.30.

Peck's story opens in 1915 as Grandma Tilly begins a narrative of life in Grand Tower during April 1861. Grand Tower is located on the Mississippi River at the southern tip of Illinois. Arriving by riverboat are two women from New Orleans, Delphine and a woman assumed to be her slave, Calinda. The women bring an unknown air of sophistication to Grand Tower and spark thoughts in young Tilly that a much more interesting life exists outside her small town. The secrets the two woman guard will reveal a little-known part of the racial positioning before the Civil War.

GRADES: 9–12

REVIEWS: *Booklist* 9/15/03, *Publishers Weekly* 7/14/03, *SLJ* 9/03, *VOYA* 10/03

Peck, Robert Newton. *A Day No Pigs Would Die.* 160 p. TR. Pathways Publishing. 978-1-58303-093-6. 1999. $15.95. LB. San Val, Incorporated. 978-0-7857-1352-4. 1974. $13.55. PB. Random House Children's Books. 978-0-679-85306-0. 1994. $6.99. CD. Audio Bookshelf. 978-1-883332-59-4. 1993. $29.95. PLAY. Findaway World, LLC. 978-1-60514-767-3. 2008. $34.99. CASS. Random House Audio Publishing Group. 978-0-8072-8507-7. 1989. $30.00. EB. Random House Audio Publishing Group. 978-0-7393-7221-0. N/A. $25.00.

Robert's Shaker family lives on a Vermont farm raising pigs to be slaughtered to earn money. Robert's father teaches lessons on hard work and doing his chores the correct way. Soon Robert adopts a pig, Pinky, as a pet that even wins a prize at the fair for Best-Behaved Pig. Trouble arises when the fall harvest comes in weak and the family becomes desperate for food and money. Pinky becomes expendable. Robert slowly begins to understand his father's harsh exterior and what it takes to become a man. Peck's descriptions of life in a rural twentieth-century farm will engage readers' senses, especially when dealing with cold temperatures and smells of animals being butchered.

GRADES: 6–10

Peet, Mal. *Tamar: A Novel of Espionage, Passion, and Betrayal.* 432 p. TR. Candlewick Press. 978-0-7636-3488-9. 2007. $17.99. PB. Candlewick Press. 978-0-7636-4063-7. 2008. $8.99. CD. Candlewick Press. 978-0-7636-4121-4. 2008. $50.00.

The behind-enemy-lines tension of espionage agents is presented in Peet's layered novel set in two time frames. Fifteen-year-old Tamar is the present-day granddaughter of a resistance fighter. After her grandfather commits suicide, Tamar is determined to find out the historical truth. The story flips back to Holland in the years 1944 through 1945 when two men, Dart and Tamar, pair up in resistance fighting against the Germans. Alongside them is Marijke, a woman both men love. The intrigue mounts as jealousy, loyalty, and love become conflicted during the dangers of German occupation. The dual time-line and intricate plotting place interest for this title mostly with older teens.

GRADES: 10–12

REVIEWS: *Booklist* 2/01/07, *Publishers Weekly* 1/15/07, *SLJ* 4/07, *VOYA* 4/07

AWARDS: BBYA Top Ten

Rees, Celia. *Witch Child.* 261 p. TR. Perfection Learning Corporation. 978-0-7569-1892-7. 2001. $16.65. LB. Perma-Bound Books. 978-0-605-92111-5. 2000. $15.99. RE. San Val, Incorporated. 978-0-613-60740-7. 2002. $19.65. PB. Candlewick Press. 978-0-7636-4228-0. 2009. $8.99. CASS. Random House Audio Publishing Group. 978-0-8072-0628-7. 2004. $32.00. EB. Random House Audio Publishing Group. 978-0-7393-6760-5. N/A. $38.25. LP. Cengage Gale. 978-0-7862-3896-5. 2002. $22.95.

Presented as the false diary of Mary Newbery, the attitudes and suspicions against witchcraft come alive in the year 1659. Mary is given passage with Puritans leaving England bound for the New World. During the voyage, Mary, who is somewhat of a healer, saves a baby from being stillborn. Immediately she is suspected of using witchcraft, or using the devil's breath, to save the child by blowing air into its lungs. Arriving in Salem, Mary continues to be an outsider and becomes a scapegoat for girls accused of playing at witchcraft. The cruel physical atmosphere of the fifteenth century and strict religious beliefs of the time highlight this story. The sequel is called *Sorceress*.

GRADES: 8–12

REVIEWS: *Booklist* 10/15/01, *Kirkus* 5/15/01, *Publishers Weekly* 6/25/01, *SLJ* 8/01, *VOYA* 10/01

Remarque, Erich Maria. *All Quiet on the Western Front.* 128 p. TR. Random House Publishing Group. 978-0-449-91149-5. 1996. $15.00. LB. Buccaneer Books, Incorporated. 978-0-89966-292-3. 1981. $21.95. RE. San Val, Incorporated. 978-0-88103-982-5. 1995. $17.20. LB. Perma-Bound Books. 978-0-8479-1202-5. N/A. $13.99. PB. Random House Publishing Group. 978-0-449-21394-0. 1987. $6.99. CD. Recorded Books, LLC. 978-0-7887-3441-0. 2000. $54.00. CD. Recorded Books, LLC. 978-1-4025-2234-5. N/A. $34.95. CASS. Recorded Books, LLC.

978-1-55690-960-3. 1994. $42.00. CASS. Recorded Books, LLC. 978-1-4025-1659-7. N/A. $19.95.

First published in book form in 1929, this war novel gives a sobering view of soldiers caught in the slaughter of World War I, but is told from the German perspective. Paul Baumer is eighteen years old when he joins the army with several of his classmates. Their loss of innocence parallels the devastating physical and psychological damage done to each of them. The realistic horror of war is the backdrop of how youth is left behind and humans in combat lose their individuality. This title has long been a staple of upper grade high school reading lists.

GRADES: 10–12

Rinaldi, Ann. *The Coffin Quilt: The Feud Between the Hatfields and the McCoys.* 228 p. TR. Perfection Learning Corporation. 978-0-7569-0557-6. 2001. $14.60. RE. San Val, Incorporated. 978-0-613-35451-6. 2001. $17.15. PB. Holt McDougal. 978-0-03-073522-6. 2002. $4.80.

The legendary nineteenth-century feud between the West Virginia Hatfields and the Kentucky McCoys is shown through the eyes of the youngest McCoy, Fanny. Beginning over a dispute about a hog, the feud turned increasingly deadly. In Rinaldi's work, the catalyst for the most violent episode is Roseanna McCoy's affair with Johnse Hatfield. After spending several months living with Johnse, Roseanna returns with an unborn baby and an unfinished coffin quilt chronicling Hatfield family births and deaths. This novel offers details about the feud most readers recognize by name but know little of the factual background.

GRADES: 7–10

REVIEWS: *Booklist* 9/01/99, *Publishers Weekly* 11/29/99, *SLJ* 5/00, *VOYA* 8/99

Ryan, Pam Muñoz. *Esperanza Rising.* 307 p. TR. Scholastic, Incorporated. 978-0-439-12041-8. 2000. $17.99. LB. Perma-Bound Books. 978-0-605-06929-9. 2000. $12.99. RE. San Val, Incorporated. 978-0-613-53807-7. 2002. $17.20. PB. Scholastic, Incorporated. 978-0-439-12042-5. 2007. $6.99. CD. Random House Audio Publishing Group. 978-0-7393-3896-4. 2007. $25.00. CD. Random House Audio Publishing Group. 978-0-8072-1769-6. 2004. $35.00. CASS. Random House Audio Publishing Group. 978-0-8072-8862-7. 2004. $30.00. EB. Random House Audio Publishing Group. 978-0-7393-3061-6. N/A. $32.30.

Following her father's death, fourteen-year-old Esperanza and her mother move to the United States where they find work in farming camps. Set during the Great Depression, Esperanza leaves a life of privilege and now must learn household chores and the harsh labor of migrant life. The young girl witnesses strikes and injustice forced on the workers by the government. The struggle to survive on low wages will hit home with teens who may have experienced similar economic hardships.

GRADES: 6–8

REVIEWS: *Booklist* 12/01/00, *Kirkus* 10/01/00, *Publishers Weekly* 10/09/00, *SLJ* 8/01, *VOYA* 12/00

AWARDS: BBYA Top Ten

Sáenz, Benjamin Alire. *Sammy and Juliana in Hollywood.* 304 p. TR. Cinco Puntos Press. 978-0-938317-81-4. 2004. $19.95. LB. Perma-Bound Books. 978-0-605-01360-5. 2004. $14.99. RE. San Val, Incorporated. 978-1-4177-3187-9. 2006. $19.65. CD. Random House Audio Publishing Group. 978-0-307-28592-8. 2006. $60.00. CASS. Random House Audio Publishing Group. 978-0-307-28591-1. 2006. $45.00. EB. Random House Audio Publishing Group. 978-0-7393-6065-1. N/A. $51.00.

Life in the barrio during the 1960s is told by sixteen-year-old Sammy Santos. He relates how he loves his friends, family, and neighbors. He especially loves his girlfriend, Juliana Rios. But his love cannot save her from being murdered by her crazed father. Sammy's inner goodness and generosity carry him through his grief. Sáenz offers a view of the barrio in Las Cruces, New Mexico, and how the Latino experience has been a part of American culture long before the 1969 timeframe. Older teens, especially those in a bilingual environment, will be taken with Sammy's poignant narrative.

GRADES: 10–12

REVIEWS: *Booklist* 10/01/04, *SLJ* 9/1/04, *VOYA* 12/04

AWARDS: BBYA Top Ten

Salisbury, Graham. *Eyes of the Emperor.* 240 p. TR. Random House Children's Books. 978-0-385-72971-0. 2005. $15.95. RE. San Val, Incorporated. 978-1-4177-6903-2. 2007. $17.20. PB. Random House Children's Books. 978-0-440-22956-8. 2007. $6.99. CD. Recorded Books, LLC. 978-1-4193-8486-8. 2006. $49.75. CASS. Recorded Books, LLC. 978-1-4193-8481-3. 2006. $39.75. EB. Recorded Books, LLC. 978-1-4237-6882-1. N/A. $1.00.

Eddie Okubo feels the pull of patriotism and is anxious to join the military to help his country. He is a Japanese-American youth living in Hawaii at the time of the Pearl Harbor attack. Eddie and his friends join the United States Army and they're upset by having to endure forced marches and perform unskilled labor tasks. Salisbury relates the shocking experiment where the Japanese-American soldiers are forced to hide from military dogs that are being trained to attack when smelling the so-called Japanese body odor. This novel relates a little known ugly racial practice during the grim days on the World War II homefront.

GRADES: 7–10

REVIEWS: *Booklist* 5/15/05, *Publishers Weekly* 9/05/05, *SLJ* 9/05, *VOYA* 8/05

Schmidt, Gary D. *Lizzie Bright and the Buckminster Boy.* 224 p. TR. Houghton Mifflin Harcourt Trade & Reference Publishers. 978-0-618-43929-4. 2004. $15.00. LB. Perma-Bound Books. 978-0-605-00037-7. 2004. $13.50. RE. San Val, Incorporated. 978-1-4177-3378-1. 2006. $16.60. PB. Random House Children's Books. 978-0-375-84169-9. 2008. $6.99. PB. Random House Children's Books. 978-0-553-49495-2. 2006. $6.99. CD. Random House Audio Publishing Group. 978-0-307-28183-8. 2005. $34.00. CD. Random House Audio Publishing Group. 978-0-307-28185-2. 2005. $42.50. CASS. Random House Audio Publishing Group 978-0-307-20725-8. 2005. $40.00. EB. Random House Audio Publishing Group. 978-0-7393-4493-4. N/A. $42.50.

Schmidt weaves his story around the destruction of an island community in 1912. Turner Buckminster arrives in Phippsburg, Maine, and soon shoulders a huge dislike for his new home. He feels friendless and his status as the new preacher's son doesn't help. But spending time with Lizzie Bright Griffin, an African American living in a poor community of freed and escaped slaves, provides him with interesting and new experiences. Racism leads to removal of the people and they are sent to a home for feeble-minded, but a terrible tragedy occurs. Schmidt writes of the ignorance and power of racism, but also shows nobility in standing up to do what is right.

GRADES: 6–9

REVIEWS: *Booklist* 5/15/04, *SLJ* 5/04, *VOYA* 8/04

AWARDS: Printz Honor, Newbery Honor

Selznick, Brian. *The Invention of Hugo Cabret.* 544 p. TR. Scholastic, Incorporated. 978-0-439-81378-5. 2007. $24.99. CD. Scholastic, Incorporated. 978-0-545-00363-6. 2007. $29.95. PLAY. Findaway World, LLC. 978-1-60252-612-9. 2007. $44.99.

By combining a narration with illustrations positioned in a cinematic format, Selznick offers what very well may be the bridgework that shifts emphasis from novels to graphic novels. In the early twentieth century, Hugo's recently deceased father worked in a museum where he discovered an automaton—a human-like figure that is actually a robot. Hugo becomes obsessed with the inventor's notebooks, writings that lead him to a toymaker who is the key to the whole mystery. A piece of history comes alive in intricate black-and-white illustrations and Selznick's narrative will engage readers. This title could easily be placed in multiple genres, but it has landed here due to the revealing of a little-known moment of history.

GRADES: 6–9

REVIEWS: *Booklist* 1/01/07, *Publishers Weekly* 1/01/07, *SLJ* 3/07, *VOYA* 2/07

AWARDS: BBYA Top Ten

Sharenow, Robert. *My Mother the Cheerleader.* 352 p. TR. HarperCollins Publishers. 978-0-06-114896-5. 2007. $16.99. LB. HarperCollins Publishers. 978-0-06-114897-2. 2007. $17.89. PB. HarperCollins Publishers. 978-0-06-114898-9. 2009. $8.99. EB. HarperCollins Publishers. 978-0-06-185133-9. 2009. $9.99.

The cheerleader in the title is thirteen-year-old Louise's mother, a woman who during the push to New Orleans integration of 1960 stood outside a school and chanted racist remarks at first-grader Ruby Bridges—the first African American to enter an all-white school. Louise observes her mother's actions but becomes involved in the political drama when a border arrives, Morgan Miller, a Jewish journalist from New York. Author Sharenow presents the story of a young girl going against her mother's wishes during a very turbulent time during the civil rights era.

GRADES: 7–10

REVIEWS: *Booklist* 7/01/07, *Publishers Weekly* 5/28/07, *SLJ* 7/07

Sheth, Kashmira. *Keeping Corner.* 304 p. TR. Hyperion Press. 978-0-7868-3860-8. 2009. $5.99.

Opening in 1918 India, twelve-year-old Leela enjoys the pampering of her parents and in-laws, whose house she will enter after her anu ceremony. But following the death of her husband, the young widow enters a different fate. She must give up her jewelry, shave her head, and remain indoors for a year, or "keep corner." Against the backdrop of India's drive for social change, Leela grows from a self-centered girl to an intelligent young woman. This novel examines the treatment of women in the Indian culture of the early twentieth century.

GRADES: 7–10

REVIEWS: *Booklist* 10/15/07, *Publishers Weekly* 11/05/07, *SLJ* 12/07, *VOYA* 12/07

Smith, Roland. *Elephant Run.* 356 p. TR. Hyperion Press. 978-1-4231-0402-5. 2007. $15.99. PB. Hyperion Press. 978-1-4231-0401-8. 2009. $5.99.

Sent to live with his father, Nick Freestone arrives in a Burma teak plantation on the eve of the Japanese takeover during 1941. The tension of living under oppression during World War II confronts Nick when his father is taken prisoner. Determined to help his father, Nick enlists the aid of Mya and trained elephants to help with the rescue. The historical setting is realistic and the elephants become heroes. Refreshingly, the Japanese soldiers are not depicted as stereotypes but emerge as complex characters. The action scenes mark this title as a middle school read.

GRADES: 6–9

REVIEWS: *Booklist* 2/15/08, *SLJ* 2/08, *VOYA* 12/07

Speare, Elizabeth George. *The Sign of the Beaver.* 135 p. TR. Houghton Mifflin Harcourt. 978-0-395-33890-2. 1983. $16.00. LB. Perfection Learning Prebound. 978-0-8124-1281-9. 1984 $15.85. PB. Yearling. 978-0-440-47900-0. 1997 $6.99. CASS. Listening Library. 978-0-8072-7959-5. 1998. $23.00. CD. Listening Library. 978-1-4000-8497-5. 2004. $14.99.

A twelve-year-old boy journeys with his father to Maine in 1768 to build a cabin. Matt has to hold the claim while his father goes back to Massachusetts to bring the rest of the family. Matt encounters problems but eventually is befriended by an Indian chief, who asks Matt to teach his grandson to read. The Indian boy, Attean, and Matt eventually form a strong friendship, but if Matt's family does not return on schedule he faces a winter alone in the wilderness. The outdoors hook will interest middle school boys.

GRADES: 6–8

AWARDS: Newbery Honor

Spillebeen, Geert. *Kipling's Choice.* 147 p. TR. Perfection Learning Corporation. 978-0-7569-8061-0. 2007. $15.65. PB. Houghton Mifflin Harcourt Trade & Reference Publishers. 978-0-618-80035-3. 2007. $7.99.

In this story set during World War I, Rudyard Kipling is portrayed as a flawed father who pushes his son to be a war hero. Lt. John Kipling is severely wounded on the front in France. During his last hours, he flashes back to scenes from his youth and his relationship with his famous father. This novel, which could be classified as a fictionalized biography, captures the horror of war while examining a complicated father/son relationship.

GRADES: 7–10

REVIEWS: *Booklist* 5/15/05, *Publishers Weekly* 4/18/05, *SLJ* 6/05, *VOYA* 12/05

Steinbeck, John. *The Grapes of Wrath.* Page count varies with edition. There are significant formats currently available in print.

The economic downturn of 2008–2009 may very well bring renewed interest in this classic novel of a family desperately trying to survive during the Great Depression of the 1930s. Considered a shocking novel when it was first published in 1939, Steinbeck's work chronicles the Joad family's journey west from the Dustbowl of Oklahoma to the promised land of California. The family endures death and hardship while trying to scrap together enough money to eat consistently. The backdrop of the Depression becomes a vehicle for a sophisticated commentary on the strength of the human spirit. *The Grapes of Wrath* has earned its place on many high school recommended reading lists.

GRADES: 10–12

Taylor, Mildred. *Roll of Thunder, Hear My Cry.* Page count varies with edition. There are significant formats currently available in print.

In 1933 young Cassie Logan begins her first day of school with her siblings. They are children of an African American couple living on 400 acres of land in rural Mississippi. The family is struggling to maintain ownership of the land and not relinquish it to Mr. Granger, whose family owned it during the slavery era. Based on the author's own family, this story describes the hardship of being self-sufficient while dealing with racism during the first half of the twentieth century. Other titles in the series are *The Land* (a prequel and a BBYA Top Ten), *Let the Circle Be Unbroken, The Road to Memphis, Mississippi Bridge, The Friendship, Song of the Trees,* and *The Well: David's Story.*

GRADES: 6–9

REVIEWS: *Booklist* 3/01/88

AWARDS: Newbery Winner

Venkatraman, Padma. *Climbing the Stairs.* 256 p. TR. Penguin Group (USA) Incorporated. 978-0-399-24746-0. 2008. $16.99.

Fifteen-year-old Vidya finds her life in Bombay, India, to be in direct contrast with her relatives. In 1941, the tradition of entering an arranged marriage, then having babies, and serving a husband is expected of a girl. It is her only option. Yet Vidya has a goal of attending college. Her dreams are shattered when her father is beaten by British police and suffers extreme brain damage. Paralleling her own country's struggle for independence, Vidya is determined to break away from traditional expectations of young girls.

GRADES: 10–12

REVIEWS: *Booklist* 4/15/08, *Publishers Weekly* 4/28/08, *SLJ* 5/08, *VOYA* 6/08

Wilder, Laura Ingalls. *The Long Winter.* 334 p. TR. Harper Row. 978-0-06-026460-4. 1953. $16.99. PB. Trophy. 978-0-06-440006-0. 1953. $6.99. PB. HarperTorch. 978-0-06-058185-5. 2004. $8.99. LB. HarperCollins. 978-0-06-026461-1. 1953. $18.89. LB. Perfection Learning. 978-0-7807-7162-8. 1995. $18.85. LB. Paw Prints. 978-1-4352-0776-9. 2007. $17.99. CD. HarperCollins. 978-0-06-056502-2. 2005. $25.95.

A title more suited for young girls finds thirteen-year-old Laura Ingalls and her family trying to avoid starvation in this exciting story of survival in DeSmet, South Dakota, during the 1870s. Her class is caught in a blizzard coming home from school. The trains can't get through to bring food and fuel, and the whole town is facing starvation. This is one of the forever popular *Little House on the Prairie* series titles. Other titles in the series are *Little House in the Big Woods, Farmer Boy, Little House on the Prairie, On the Banks of Plum Creek* (Newbery Honor), *By the Shores of Silver Lake* (Newbery Honor), *Little Town on the Prairie* (Newbery Honor), *These Happy Golden Years* (Newbery Honor), *The First Four Years, On the Way Home, West from Home,* and *A Little House Traveler.*

GRADES: 6–8

AWARDS: Newbery Honor

Wolff, Virginia Euwer. *Bat 6.* 240 p. TR. Perfection Learning Corporation. 978-0-7569-0463-0. 2000. $13.65. TR. Scholastic, Incorporated. 978-0-590-89799-0. 1998. $16.95. RE. San Val, Incorporated. 978-0-613-28413-4. 2000. $16.00. PB. Scholastic, Incorporated. 978-0-590-89800-3. 2000. $5.99. CASS. Random House Audio Publishing Group. 978-0-8072-8221-2. 2004. $30.00. CASS. Books on Tape, Incorporated. 978-0-7366-9021-8. 2000. $24.00.

A sixth grade softball game in 1949 becomes the catalyst for racial tension. Two small Oregon towns compete, but the game becomes ugly when a player, whose father was killed at Pearl Harbor, slams her elbow into the face of a Japanese American. Wolff provides a look at small-town life that is slow to change even following the horrible carnage of World War II. Players from both teams offer their voices and opinions about the underlying racism in small-town America. *Bat 6* is a solid introductory title for school lessons about suppressing racial prejudice.

GRADES: 6–9

REVIEWS: *Booklist* 5/01/98, *Kirkus* 5/01/98, *Publishers Weekly* 4/20/98, *SLJ* 5/98

Zusak, Markus. *The Book Thief.* 560 p. TR. Perfection Learning Corporation. 978-0-7569-8440-3. 2007. $19.65. LB. Random House Children's Books. 978-0-375-93100-0. 2006. $18.99. PB. Random House Children's Books. 978-0-375-84220-7. 2007. $11.99. CD. Random House Audio Publishing Group. 978-0-7393-3800-1. 2006. $63.75. EB. Random House Audio Publishing Group. 978-0-7393-4834-5. N/A. $63.75. LP. Thorndike Press. 978-0-7862-9021-5. 2006. $24.95.

Zusak's work could easily be placed in a variety of genre sections. Historical fiction seems correct as the book is set during World War II in Molching, Germany. Liesel Meminger grows up during the war while her family deteriorates. Liesel has stolen a book and her foster father reads from it to lull her to sleep. The family is also harboring a Jewish refugee. The tension of their situation is alternated with the narrative voice of Death who describes events as he waits to gather those who will die. Zusak's work will be examined and talked about for years and fits nicely in any college prep reading list.

GRADES: 10–12

REVIEWS: *Booklist* 1/01/06, *Publishers Weekly* 1/30/06, *SLJ* 3/06, *VOYA* 6/06

AWARDS: BBYA Top Ten, Printz Honor

8

Humorous Novels

There are problems with young adult novels billed by publicists as humorous. For any given scene or story line that's thought to be hilarious, there is a reader who may think the exact opposite. One of the more challenging reader's advisory queries to teen librarians is to give the reader "something funny."

Teen humor is not the same thing as adult humor. Indeed, there are all kinds of funny stories. Dry wit, black humor, slapstick, sarcasm, or a droll character may all be considered funny, but probably not by all readers.

So what's a librarian to do? With the heavy emphasis on standardized testing, many teens are turning to reading as an escape from the drudgery of school lessons. Humorous stories can fill that need quite easily, if the librarian is lucky enough to place the right book in the right hands.

Teen novels can be laugh-out-loud funny but the ones that stand out from the pack are those that deftly mix comedy with poignant scenes where the character moves from being a clown to a character who shows a caring soul.

The roller coaster ride is much like everyday teen life. Teens ride a wave of extreme emotions from one moment to the next and a key catalyst for these wide emotional swings is the opposite sex.

Face it, a large chunk of the teenage years is about figuring out what makes the opposite sex tick. First-time relationships usually do not finish with a flourish, but are often awkward slapstick moments. Skilled young adult authors capture these moments in their stories and teen readers will nod in agreement in a "been there, done that" kind of way.

What follows are title suggestions that have been received as funny. They range from middle school locker room humor to older teens obsessed with sex and partying. Interestingly, many of these titles have fleeting publishing runs. Perhaps what was funny just five years ago is not so funny now? Maybe the many pop culture references have grown dated. At any rate, when teens ask for a funny story, whip out this list and direct them to a great read.

Abdel-Fattah, Randa. *Does My Head Look Big in This?* 368 p. TR. Scholastic, Incorporated. 978-0-439-91947-0. 2007. $16.99. TR. Scholastic, Incorporated. 978-1-4287-4610-7. 2007 N/A. PB. Scholastic, Incorporated. 978-0-439-92233-3. 2008. $8.99.

Amal enters eleventh grade as a smart student and a loyal friend. She's also a devout Muslim who decides to wear the hijab, or head covering, full time. Amal has a wild number of issues from a mad crush on a guy to helping a friend whose mother wants her to leave school and get married. The humorous tone is a pleasant break from multicultural titles that have a preachy tone. Here, through everyday teen life, readers learn why so many Muslim women choose to wear the hijab.

GRADES: 7–10

REVIEWS: *Booklist* 7/01/07, *Kirkus* 4/15/07, *Publishers Weekly* 5/21/07, *SLJ* 6/07, *VOYA* 8/07

Anderson, M. T. *Burger Wuss.* 188 p. RE. San Val, Incorporated. 978-1-4178-1910-2. 2008. $18.45. PB. Candlewick Press. 978-0-7636-3178-9. 2008. $7.99.

By presenting a series of bizarre situations, Anderson offers a parody of the fast-food industry, which is a staple of the teenager job market. Anthony catches his girlfriend in a passionate embrace with Turner, a worker at O'Dermott (which is very much like McDonald's). Determined to gain revenge, Anthony steals a display from the rival place, Burger Queen, hoping the crime will be pinned on Turner. This work is filled with quirky characters including graffiti artists who correct grammar on highway signs. Fast-paced and wild, this work has strong middle school appeal.

GRADES: 7–10

REVIEWS: *Booklist* 11/15/99, *Kirkus* 8/01/99, *Publishers Weekly* 8/02/99, *SLJ* 11/99, *VOYA* 12/99

Bauer, Joan. *Squashed.* 194 p. TR. Perfection Learning Corporation. 978-0-7569-5781-0. 2005. $15.65. PB. Penguin Group (USA) Incorporated. 978-0-14-240426-3. 2005. $7.99.

A teenage girl bonding with her pumpkin and encouraging him to grow to win first prize for biggest pumpkin grown in Iowa seems like something out of an improv skit. But here is sixteen-year-old Ellie Morgan doing just that with her protégé pumpkin, Max. Rival farmer Cyril Pool is also in the contest and Ellie figures Max has to reach 611 pounds so she sets to pampering her orange friend. Ellie is a witty and likeable character who learns about adults not being honest while she depends on the help of boyfriend Wes. This is a funny and wholesome novel with wide appeal despite the strange story line.

GRADES: 6–10

REVIEWS: *Kirkus* 10/15/92, *Publishers Weekly* 10/19/92, *SLJ* 9/92

Black, Jonah. *The Black Book: Diary of a Teenage Stud,* **Vol. I:** *Girls, Girls, Girls.* N/A. EB. HarperCollins Publishers. 978-0-06-118730-8. N/A. $6.50.

If these mass-market paperback titles are still residing on your library shelves, please do not discard them. They are tremendously funny and probe into the mind of a teenage boy who is obsessed with girls. Think of the wild times in the movie *Superbad* and that is pretty much what goes on in these books. Jonah Black is forced to repeat his junior year and has unrequited love for Posie, a girl who is his best friend. He also has a vivid fantasy sex life that he can slip into at any time. Of course his fantasy life and real life often intersect in weird, weird ways. Other titles in the series: *Stop, Don't Stop, Run, Jonah, Run,* and *Faster, Faster, Faster*

GRADES: 9–12

REVIEWS: *Booklist* 10/15/01, *Kirkus* 7/01/01, *Publishers Weekly* 10/01/01, *SLJ* 8/01

Cabot, Meg. *All-American Girl*. 398 p. RE. San Val, Incorporated. 978-1-4178-2386-4. 2008. $18.40. PB. HarperCollins Publishers. 978-0-06-147989-2. 2008. $7.99. PB. HarperCollins Publishers. 978-0-06-447277-7. 2003. $6.99. CD. Random House Audio Publishing Group. 978-0-8072-1597-5. 2004. $42.50. CASS. Random House Audio Publishing Group. 978-0-8072-0902-8. 2004. $36.00. EB. HarperCollins Publishers. 978-0-06-118727-8. 2002. $6.99. EB. Random House Audio Publishing Group. 978-0-7393-3027-2. 2007. $42.50. LP. Thorndike Press. 978-0-7862-6986-0. 2004. $10.95.

Samantha Madison is bored with her Washington, DC, high school and cannot wait to be free and in college. One day, she skips her after-school art class and by circumstance finds herself as the bystander who prevents an assassination of the president of the United States. Immediately she is the darling of the national media and her high school's popular crowd adores her. And even more weird is the president's son showing romantic interest. The theme of outsider girl thrust into the spotlight in a bizarre way will appeal to younger girls who find themselves on the outskirts of the popular crowd.

GRADES: 7–10

REVIEWS: *Booklist* 10/01/02, *Kirkus* 8/15/02, *Publishers Weekly* 6/24/02, *SLJ* 10/02, *VOYA* 10/02

Calame, Don. *Swim the Fly*. 352 p. TR. Candlewick Press. 978-0-7636-4157-3. 2009. $16.99. PB. Candlewick Press. 978-0-7636-4776-6. 2010. $7.99. CD. Brilliance Audio. 978-1-4418-1487-6. 2010. $24.99.

During the summer Matt Gratton and his friends Sean and Coop make the vow to see a girl naked. The fifteen-year-old guys are willing to go to any lengths to meet their goal, some of them on the slapstick side of crazy. Matt's other summer challenge is to swim the butterfly stroke in a local competition. Gross-out humor featuring vomiting, bowel movements, and calculated "accidents" involving public nudity mark this title that borders on over-the-top situations. Yet guys will flock to this work as the all-too-normal friends try their best to catch a glimpse of the female anatomy. This book is geared toward middle school, especially for guy readers.

GRADES: 6–9

REVIEWS: *Booklist* 3/15/09, *Kirkus* 3/01/09, *Publishers Weekly* 4/20/09, *SLJ* 4/09, *VOYA* 8/09

Carter, Ally. *I'd Tell You I Love You, but Then I'd Have to Kill You* (*Gallagher Girls* series). N/A. RE. San Val, Incorporated. 978-1-4177-7199-8. 2007. $19.65. PB. Hyperion Press. 978-1-4231-0004-1. 2007. $8.99. CD. Brilliance Audio. 978-1-4233-1182-9. 2006. $39.25. CD. Brilliance Audio. 978-1-4233-1181-2. 2006. $24.95.

Cammie Morgan is a student at Gallagher Academy, a top-secret boarding school for girls who are spies in training. The curriculum includes covert operations, advanced encryption, and Cammie speaks fourteen languages. She's all that but her troubles begin when she falls for Josh, a local boy who has no clue about her real identity. Cammie ends up in bizarre situations trying to keep her double life active while guarding her spy part from Josh. Other titles in the series are *Cross My Heart and Hope to Spy, Don't Judge a Girl by Her Cover,* and *Only the Good Spy Young.*

GRADES: 6–10

REVIEWS: *Publishers Weekly* 5/15/06, *SLJ* 7/06, *VOYA* 10/06

Doyle, Larry. *I Love You, Beth Cooper.* 272 p. TR. HarperCollins Publishers. 978-0-06-123617-4. 2007. $19.95. PB. HarperCollins Publishers. 978-0-06-174485-3. 2009. $7.99. CD. HarperCollins Publishers. 978-0-06-177207-8. 2009. $19.99.

Denis Cooverman has the honor of giving the valedictorian's speech at his high school graduation. Instead of playing it safe and giving advice about the future and making something of oneself, Denis publicly blurts out his undying love for Beth Cooper. She is furious. What follows is a wild night of sex, violence, and out-of-control partying. Denis and his buddy Rich become involved is a series of slapstick scenes with drunken girls finally paying attention to these geeks. The humor centers around sex, making this title more for older teens.

GRADES: 9–12

REVIEWS: *Booklist* 4/15/07, *Kirkus* 4/15/07, *SLJ* 8/07

Ehrenhaft, Daniel. *The After Life*. No formats available in print.

An out-of-control road trip brings together three teens as they try to cash in on their father's inheritance. Twins Kyle and Liz, and their half-brother Will, find themselves in Florida watching a DVD of their dead father giving instructions for them to acquire $2 million dollars. The trio has to drive their father's old Volvo from Miami to New York City in 48 hours to collect the cash. During the trip the teens find out things about themselves, and the whole journey is drenched with booze and drugs, making for hilarious situations. The underage drinking and drug use (including Ecstasy) marks this title for an older readership.

GRADES: 9–12

REVIEWS: *Kirkus* 9/01/06, *Publishers Weekly* 10/30/06, *VOYA* 4/07

Elish, Dan. *Born Too Short: The Confessions of an Eighth-Grade Basket Case*. No formats available in print.

Matt Greene is thirteen years old and stands five-feet, one inch tall. Yet Matt is a solid guitarist. His best friend Keith is the school's jock, has stunning good looks, and girls worship him. However, when Keith announces he will write a rock musical, Matt fumes with jealousy. Angry, he explodes in a tirade of wishes against his best friend. A homeless guy appears and says, "Better be careful. Wishes that strong can come true." Unfortunate events begin to happen to Keith, and Matt desperately hunts for the homeless guy to reverse the curse. Middle school readers will be drawn to Matt's attempt to level the popularity playing field.

GRADES: 6–9

REVIEWS: *Booklist* 1/01/02, *Kirkus* 1/01/02, *Publishers Weekly* 1/14/02, *SLJ* 2/02

Geerling, Marjetta. *Fancy White Trash*. 272 p. TR. Penguin Group (USA) Incorporated. 978-0-670-01082-0. 2008. $16.99.

Fifteen-year-old Abby Savage lives with her family, which seems to be a group straight off the Jerry Springer stage. Her sisters, Shelby and Kait, both became pregnant as teens. Now her mother announces she is also pregnant, by the same rock musician who is the father of Kait's baby! Abby has an anchor in next-door-neighbor Cody, but there are complications there also, especially when Cody's brother Jackson returns home. The drama is nonstop and this train wreck of a family is hilarious as they attempt to become normal. Good luck with that. The sexual situations mark this title as a high school read.

GRADES: 9–12

REVIEWS: *Publishers Weekly* 5/19/08, *SLJ* 10/08, *VOYA* 8/08

Jaffe, Michele. *Bad Kitty.* 268 p. TR. HarperCollins Publishers. 978-0-06-078108-8. 2006. $16.99. PB. HarperCollins Publishers. 978-0-06-078110-1. 2007. $8.99. EB. HarperCollins Publishers. 978-0-06-183698-5. 2009. $9.99.

Seventeen-year-old Jasmine (Jas) has a nose for trouble. She's wanted to be a detective since the first grade and now during her family's summer vacation to Las Vegas, she finds the city to be a great place to fight crime. The mystery Jas uncovers involves a famous model and a three-legged cat. Jas, who is not above dusting for fingerprints with eye shadow, is a likeable narrator and her first-person point of view gives quick-witted comments as she solves the crime.

GRADES: 7–10

REVIEWS: *Booklist* 1/01/06, *Kirkus* 2/15/06, *Publishers Weekly* 1/30/06, *SLJ* 2/06, *VOYA* 2/06

AWARDS: Teens' Top Ten

Korman, Gordon. *No More Dead Dogs.* N/A. RE. San Val, Incorporated. 978-0-613-61850-2. 2002. $16.00. PB. Hyperion Books for Children. 978-0-7868-1601-9. 2002. $5.99. CD. Recorded Books, LLC. 978-0-7887-6162-1. N/A. $39.00.

Wallace Wallace is an eighth grader who becomes an instant hero to his class-mates when he mouths off about his true feelings about reading a story (*Old Shep, My Pal*) where the dog dies. His civil disobedience earns him a detention that boots him off the football team and to the auditorium where another production of *Old Shep, My Pal* is being formed. Wallace offers suggestions and soon the play becomes a rock musical. Toss in girlfriend interest, Rachel Turner, and Korman's work is a breath of fresh air to all middle school readers who are tired of reading depressing books.

GRADES: 6–8

REVIEWS: *Booklist* 10/01/01, *VOYA* 12/00

Korman, Gordon. *Son of the Mob.* 262 p. TR. Hyperion Books for Children. 978-0-7868-2616-2. 2002. $16.49. RE. San Val, Incorporated. 978-1-4176-2754-7. 2004. $18.40. PB. Hyperion Books for Children. 978-0-7868-1593-7. 2004. $7.99. CASS. Random House Audio Publishing Group. 978-0-8072-0971-4. 2004. $30.00. EB. Random House Audio Publishing Group. 978-0-7393-5572-5. N/A. $32.30.

Vince Luca is seventeen years old and really just wants to be a normal teen-ager and maybe find a girl who likes him. The problem is he's the son of a ma-jor crime lord and nobody wants to risk offending the family. Thus Vince is a loner, that is, until he meets Kendra. Sparks fly, but the problem is Kendra's father is an FBI agent determined to take down Vince's father. The star-crossed romance struggles to get off the ground as a stable of quirky charac-ters has the story zooming. Although marketed as a middle school read, this fast-moving story has also been embraced by high school readers. The sequel is called *Son of the Mob 2: Hollywood Hustle.*

GRADES: 7–12

REVIEWS: *Booklist* 11/01/02, *Kirkus* 9/01/02, *Publishers Weekly* 10/28/02, *SLJ* 11/02, *VOYA* 2/03

AWARDS: BBYA Top Ten, Quick Picks Top Ten

Limb, Sue. *Girl, 15, Charming but Insane.* N/A. RE. San Val, Incorporated. 978-1-4177-8538-4. 2007. $16.00. PB. Random House Children's Books. 978-0-440-23896-6. 2007. $5.99. CD. Random House Audio Publishing Group. 978-1-4000-9482-0. 2005. $38.25. CASS. Random House Audio Publishing Group. 978-1-4000-9110-2. 2005. $32.00. EB. Random House Audio Publishing Group. 978-0-7393-3081-4. 2007. $38.25.

British chick lit comes alive when readers are introduced to Jess Jordan. Jess ponders who is the right boy for her, dreamy Brad or her good friend, Fred? Horoscopes play a big role in the story and introduce each chapter. Issues of body image, popularity, and insecurity are all fair game with Jess and her friends. Jess, worried about her smaller breasts (tagged with the names Bonnie and Clyde) decides plastic bags of minestrone soup will enhance what Mother Nature neglected. Other titles in the series are *Girl, (Nearly) 16: Absolute Torture* and *Girl, Going on 17: Pants on Fire.*

GRADES: 7–10

REVIEWS: *Booklist* 9/15/04, *Kirkus* 7/15/04, *Publishers Weekly* 8/16/04, *SLJ* 9/04, *VOYA* 8/04

Lubar, David. *Sleeping Freshmen Never Lie.* 160 p. TR. Penguin Group (USA) Incorporated. 978-0-525-47311-4. 2005. $16.99. PB. Penguin Group (USA) Incorporated. 978-0-14-240780-6. 2007. $7.99. PLAY. Findaway World, LLC. 978-1-59895-943-7. 2007. $44.99.

Ninth-grader Scott Hudson begins his school year very uncertain of what will happen. Girls have bloomed over the summer (in a good way) but that joy is contrasted with nasty gym classes and being relieved of his lunch money. His home life is crazy as his mother announces her pregnancy, prompting Scott to write sarcastic letters to his unborn sibling. His year is full of ups and downs, but Scott triumphs in the end. This title has appeared on many recommended reading lists for schools and is an excellent choice for a coming-of-age tale with a humorous slant.

GRADES: 8–12

REVIEWS: *Booklist* 5/15/05, *Kirkus* 6/15/05, *Publishers Weekly* 11/01/05, *SLJ* 7/05, *VOYA* 6/05

Madison, Bennett. *Lulu Dark Can See Through Walls.* No formats available in print.

Lulu Dark loses her purse while out clubbing and she wants it back. Inside is gorgeous Alfy Romero's phone number. What starts as a simple track-down of the missing purse becomes a wild caper of identity theft and homicide. Lulu Dark is flip, snarky, and clever as she is challenged by rumors about herself that could not possibly be true. The sequel to this lighthearted mystery is called *Lulu Dark and the Summer of the Fox.*

GRADES: 9–12

REVIEWS: *Booklist* 5/01/05, *SLJ* 6/05, *VOYA* 8/05

Paulsen, Gary. *How Angel Peterson Got His Name and Other Outrageous Tales About Extreme Sports.* N/A. RE. San Val, Incorporated. 978-1-4176-1987-0. 2004. $16.00. PB. Random House Children's Books. 978-0-440-22935-3. 2004. $5.99.

This short story collection is based on events from Paulsen's own youth and it's quite a wild ride. Geared to readers around age thirteen, the reasons for peeing on an electric fence and other weird things boys do are presented. No video gamers, these stories show guys believing they can do anything from wrestling bears to flying large army surplus kites (think of predecessors to hang-gliding) and landing in a chicken coup. The action takes place fifty or so years ago, but readers will come away shaking their heads about the insanity of the adolescent mind.

GRADES: 6–8

REVIEWS: *Booklist* 12/15/02, *Kirkus* 12/01/02, *Publishers Weekly* 1/20/03, *SLJ* 2/03, *VOYA* 4/03

Payne, C. D. *Youth in Revolt: The Journals of Nick Twisp.* 544 p. TR. Broadway Books. 978-0-7679-3124-3. 2009. $17.99.

Nick Twisp writes in his journal about his obsession with losing his virginity, an act he hopes to accomplish with the girl of his dreams, Sheeni. Unfortunately she's run off to Paris, and to win her Nick concocts a series of events that includes trying to get thrown out of his mother's house so he can move in with his father and thus be closer to Sheeni. Nick cannot let her go and he digs himself into a deeper and more bizarre hole trying to just get near Sheeni. This title was made into a movie in 2009, a fact that did not hurt interest. The pursuit of sex will be a strong connection with older readers.

GRADES: 9–12

REVIEWS: *Publishers Weekly* 3/06/95

Powell, Randy. *Is Kissing a Girl Who Smokes Like Licking an Ashtray?* N/A. LB. San Val, Incorporated. 978-0-613-71864-6. 2003. $14.10. CASS. Recorded Books, LLC. 978-0-7887-0201-3. 1997. $35.00.

Now eighteen years old, Biff has spent almost two years crushing on the girl of his dreams, Tommie Isaac. He obsessively drives past her house, but cannot bring himself to talk to her. He sets aside his crush for another girl, fifteen-year-old Heidi, who is quick with wisecracks and is a fierce smoker. Together Heidi and Biff travel around Seattle and Biff's past is revealed. He also realizes he is very comfortable being around Heidi. A nice blend of poignant storytelling laced with humor marks this as a work that will definitely be revisited by a new generation of readers.

GRADES: 9–12

REVIEWS: *Publishers Weekly* 6/22/92, *SLJ* 6/92

Pratchett, Terry. *The Amazing Maurice and His Educated Rodents.* 340 p. TR. Perfection Learning Corporation. 978-0-7569-1458-5. 2003. $14.65. RE. San Val, Incorporated. 978-0-613-65757-0. 2003. $17.20. PB. HarperCollins Publishers. 978-0-06-001235-9. 2003. $6.99. EB. HarperCollins Publishers. 978-0-06-137657-3. N/A. $6.99.

Pratchett introduces his bizarre Discworld to younger readers in this first book geared to this age group. The Amazing Maurice is a cat who cons Keith into playing a flute (like the pied-piper) and run scams on several towns. Along on the caper is a hoard of rats. This crew meets their match in the village of Bad Blintz where the mayor's daughter is something of a conniver herself. Mayhem ensues as rat catchers have formed an evil scheme in tunnels and sewers beneath the town. The fast-paced story is filled with danger and comic relief. This title will appeal to many ages due to the author's solid reputation.

GRADES: 6–12

REVIEWS: *Booklist* 1/01/02, *Kirkus* 10/15/01, *Publishers Weekly* 11/5/01, *SLJ* 12/01, *VOYA* 2/02

Rallison, Janette. *All's Fair in Love, War, and High School.* 192 p. PB. Walker & Company. 978-0-8027-7725-6. 2005. $7.99.

Samantha scored really low on her SAT, so she figures why not run for student body president? Unfortunately Samantha shoots sarcastic remarks at almost all of her classmates. Logan, a former boyfriend, makes a bet that Samantha cannot say anything critical to any classmate for two weeks. It's a tough task, made worse when Samantha's presidential opponent launches a smear campaign. Can Samantha keep her mouth shut? Will she be able to snag a date to the prom? Light in tone and with an enjoyable peek into the workings of high school mark this book as a fine summer read for teens entering high school.

GRADES: 8–10

REVIEWS: *Kirkus* 10/15/03, *Publishers Weekly* 11/24/03, *SLJ* 9/03, *VOYA* 6/04

Rees, Douglas. *Vampire High.* 240 p. TR. Random House Children's Books. 978-0-385-73117-1. 2008. $15.99. RE. San Val, Incorporated. 978-1-4176-9928-5. 2005. $16.00. PB. Random House Children's Books. 978-1-55212-608-0. 2001. $19.95.

Cody is washing out of school. Hoping for a fresh start, he's forced into choosing between two new schools: Our Lady of Perpetual Homework or Vlad Dracul Magnet School. He picks Vlad Dracul and enrolls in an institution where students are vampires, except for a few like Cody who are brought in as athletes, specifically water polo players, because vampires cannot swim. Soon Cody works to earn his grades and even decides to give his own blood to save a friend. This is a humorous take on the vampire craze geared for the younger end of young adult readership. The sequel is called *Vampire High: Sophomore Year.*

GRADES: 6–9

REVIEWS: *Booklist* 8/01/03, *Kirkus* 9/01/03, *Publishers Weekly* 8/04/03, *SLJ* 11/03, *VOYA* 2/04

Rennison, Louise. *Angus, Thongs and Full-Frontal Snogging: Confessions of Georgia Nicolson.* 247 p. TR. Perfection Learning Corporation. 978-0-7569-0459-3. 2001. $16.65. LB. HarperCollins Publishers. 978-0-06-028871-6. 2000. $17.89. RE. San Val, Incorporated. 978-0-613-35897-2. 2001. $19.65. LB. San Val, Incorporated. 978-0-613-71444-0. 2003. $15.30. PB. HarperCollins Publishers. 978-0-06-447227-2. 2001. $8.99. CD. Recorded Books, LLC. 978-1-4025-0465-5. N/A. $48.00. CASS. Recorded Books, LLC. 978-1-4025-0866-0. 2004. $14.99.

For readers on the American side of the Atlantic, full-frontal snogging means making out in a serious way. Fourteen-year-old Georgia Nicolson is quite keen on finding a guy to snog with. Life at home is turned upside down when her father takes off to New Zealand for a better job and her pet cat Angus is a vicious beast that torments the neighbor's poodle. Robbie is a seventeen-year-old older man that Georgia has her eye on but he is dating Lindsay, who (gasp) wears a thong. Georgia has misadventures on every other page, but they are hilarious and teenage girls will be nodding in agreement with this madcap British teen. Other titles in the series are *On the Bright Side, I'm Now the Girlfriend of a Sex God; Knocked Out by My Nunga-Nungas; Dancing in My Nuddy-Pants; Away Laughing on a Fast Camel; Then He Ate My Boy-Entrancers; Startled by His Furry Shorts; Love Is a Many Trousered Thing; Stop in the Name of Pants!;* and *Are These my Basoomas I See Before Me?*

GRADES: 6–12

REVIEWS: *Booklist* 7/01/00, *Publishers Weekly* 4/23/01, *SLJ* 7/00, *VOYA* 6/00

AWARDS: Printz Honor, Quick Picks Top Ten

Schmidt, Gary D. *The Wednesday Wars.* 272 p. TR. Houghton Mifflin Harcourt Trade & Reference Publishers. 978-0-618-72483-3. 2007. $16.00. LB. San Val, Incorporated. 978-0-606-10573-6. 2009. $17.20. PB. Houghton Mifflin Harcourt Trade & Reference Publishers. 978-0-547-23760-2. 2009. $6.99. CD. Scholastic, Incorporated. 978-0-439-92501-3. 2007. $34.95. PLAY. Findaway World, LLC. 978-1-60252-706-5. 2007. $49.99.

> On Wednesday afternoons, while his Catholic and Jewish schoolmates attend religious instruction, Holling Hoodhood, the only Presbyterian in his seventh grade, is alone in the classroom with his teacher, Mrs. Baker. Without much else to do, Holling is assigned to read Shakespeare's plays and his summaries of the plots are a hoot. Mrs. Baker is something of a mystery woman who has connections to the New York Yankees and is a former Olympic runner. What carries the story is Holling's voice of a seventh grader who is becoming aware of the world around him and sees it with a comedian's eye. Both humorous and poignant, this story is a great recommendation for all middle school collections.

GRADES: 6–9

REVIEWS: *Booklist* 6/01/07, *Kirkus* 5/15/07, *Publishers Weekly* 4/16/07, *SLJ* 7/07, *VOYA* 6/07

Shaw, Tucker. *Flavor of the Week.* No formats available in print.

> Cyril Bartholomew loves cooking and is something of a prodigy, but is extremely overweight. His two passions are food and a girl named Rose. With a nod to Cyrano de Bergerac, Cyril's handsome best friend decides to get close to Rose by passing off Cyril's culinary creations as his own. Cyril goes along with the scheme thinking this is the only way Rose will sample his cooking. This romantic comedy is marked by actual recipes provided throughout the book making it a light romp for readers in the mid-range of the young adult audience.

GRADES: 7–10

REVIEWS: *Booklist* 11/15/03, *Publishers Weekly* 10/06/03, *SLJ* 12/03, *VOYA* 2/04

Sheldon, Dyan. *Planet Janet.* 240 p. TR. Candlewick Press. 978-0-7636-2048-6. 2003. $14.99. PB. Candlewick Press. 978-0-7636-2556-6. 2004. $6.99.

> Janet Foley Bandry is sixteen years old and decides to embark on the dark phase of her life by exploring her creative side and nurturing her passionate

soul. Of course to accomplish these tasks, she must wear only black and purple. The self-absorbed teen enters into long conversations with best friend Disha about the mess of their lives. As with all good comedies, some sadness is mixed in when Janet's parents separate, forcing the young drama queen to become a bit more compassionate. Teens marching to a different drummer will connect with Janet's voice.

GRADES: 9–12

REVIEWS: *Booklist* 3/15/03, *Kirkus* 1/15/03, *Publishers Weekly* 1/06/03, *SLJ* 5/03

Vizzini, Ned. *Be More Chill.* N/A. RE. San Val, Incorporated. 978-1-4176-7627-9. 2005. $18.40.

Why not take a pill to make you cool? That's the hook of Vizzini's novel that has readers following Jeremy as he emerges from dork to someone who can walk, talk, and dress cool. Guiding him is a microchip called a squip that has Jeremy hooking up with the hottest girls in school, maybe. Jeremy really longs for Christine and the squib plots strategy to win her over. But we all know technology can go on the blink at any time and the squip abandons Jeremy in his moment of need. A cool premise and a hip techno-hook mark this story for older teens who longingly wish to be super cool.

GRADES: 9–12

REVIEWS: *Booklist* 8/01/04, *Kirkus* 6/01/04, *Publishers Weekly* 6/28/04, *SLJ* 6/04, *VOYA* 6/04

Whytock, Cherry. *My Cup Runneth Over: The Life of Angelica Cookson Potts.* 192 p. PB. Simon & Schuster Children's Publishing. 978-0-689-86551-0. 2004. $5.99.

Angelica Cookson Potts has a dream of graduating high school and moving on to become a chef. Unfortunately the larger girl endures criticism from her former model mother and she knows she hardly has a chance with Adam, the love of her life. Angelica's voice constantly pokes fun at herself while her mother nags her about what she eats. With a British accent, Angelica is a winning character that younger teen girls will bond with and they will also hope she comes out on top. Angelica's recipes (and how to enjoy them) spice up this story for middle school readers.

GRADES: 7–10

REVIEWS: *Booklist* 11/15/03, *Kirkus* 8/15/03, *Publishers Weekly* 9/01/03, *SLJ* 9/03, *VOYA* 12/03

Wizner, Jake. *Spanking Shakespeare.* 304 p. TR. Random House Children's Books. 978-0-375-84085-2. 2007. $15.99. PB. Random House Children's Books. 978-0-375-85594-8. 2008. $7.99. CD. Random House Audio Publishing Group. 978-0-

7393-6325-6. 2007. $45.00. EB. Random House Audio Publishing Group. 978-0-7393-6326-3. 2008. $38.25.

Shakespeare Shapiro uses his senior memoir-writing class to summarize his life as a series of dark and comedic humiliations. Nothing is off limits when Shakespeare is insulted by his father about body functions and Shakespeare's obsession with sex. The young man also has the misfortune to be born on Hitler's birthday, a situation that prompts his father to call him Adolf when angry. Constantly horny and falling into slapstick situations, Shakespeare's descriptions of his bawdy senior year will have older teens chuckling and nodding in agreement.

GRADES: 10–12

REVIEWS: *Booklist* 10/15/07, *Kirkus* 9/01/07, *Publishers Weekly* 9/24/07, *SLJ* 11/07, *VOYA* 10/07

Yoo, David. *Girls for Breakfast.* No formats available in print.

After what has to be the worst night of his life, Nick Park looks back on his lousy social life in suburbia. He admits to being girl-crazy and sexually obsessive with the white girls in his neighborhood. As the only Asian kid, he figures he stands no chance in scoring with these gorgeous creatures. Throughout the humorous book are passages of sadness and anger as Nick relates how he has been misjudged by teachers and his fellow classmates.

GRADES: 9–12

REVIEWS: *Kirkus* 5/01/05, *SLJ* 5/05, *VOYA* 6/05

9

Inspirational Fiction

With the wide range of eye-raising topics presented in young adult fiction, it is easy to overlook inspirational fiction as a lesser genre. It is also a genre that figuratively walks on eggshells, as any representation of religion, even in a fictional format, may cause controversy.

That said, there are several titles that need to be included in young adult collections. Many of them are individual titles in a series that show the characters' faith being challenged by a variety of outside influences. The teenage years are times of questioning authority and finding one's own direction in life. For many teens, finding their own direction means either embracing religious beliefs or shunning them.

But to me the theme of "inspiration" does not necessarily have to be totally focused on religious beliefs. Teens may draw inspiration from their peers, their families, or a whole community. In my experience it seems teenagers would rather read a fiction story about a controversial topic (such as questioning religious values or dealing with a social issue) than a nonfiction work that puts out dry facts about that topic.

Most teen librarians field the question of adult caregivers asking for appropriate books or "clean" titles. Often these earnest adults are not sure what they want for their young readers, but they know they do not want their teenagers reading books with the big three social controversies: sex, swearing, or violence. These selections may provide a go-to list of titles that are wholesome, inspiring, and also contain story lines that are interesting to teen readers.

Billingsley, ReShonda Tate. *Blessings in Disguise. (Good Girlz* **series).** 192 p. TR. Simon & Schuster. 978-1-4165-2561-5. 2007. $11.00. EB. Simon & Schuster. 978-1-4165-4820-1. 2007. N/A.

> Four friends—Camille, Alexis, Jasmine, and Angel—bond by participating with their faith-based after-school group, yet two of the group struggle with family problems as their parents are splitting up. Alexis and Jasmine are tempted to shoplift to attract attention to themselves, but that will only lead to more trouble and they need to regain Camille and Angel's trust. In this series,

the girls' lives are guided by their faith. Other titles in the series are *Nothing But Drama, With Friends Like These, Getting Even,* and *Fair-Weather Friends.*

GRADES: 7–10

Brande, Robin. *Evolution, Me, and other Freaks of Nature.* N/A. LB. Random House Children's Books. 978-0-375-94349-2. 2007. $18.99. PB. Random House Children's Books. 978-0-440-24030-3. 2009. $7.99. CD. Random House Audio Publishing Group. 978-0-7393-5134-5. 2007. $45.00. EB. Random House Audio Publishing Group. 978-0-7393-5135-2. N/A. $38.25.

Mena Reece has been kicked out of her church after writing a letter that prompted a lawsuit. Now her science teacher introduces a unit on evolution and members of Mena's former Christian youth group rebel and refuse to participate, which has the community in an uproar. With her quirky and brilliant lab partner, Casey Conner, Mena struggles to rise above the fray. Robin Brande has created a sympathetic character in Mena who goes about being a typical teenager, but finds that path blocked by outside forces that challenge her beliefs.

GRADES: 8–12

REVIEWS: *Booklist* 6/01/07, *Publishers Weekly* 8/06/07, *SLJ* 10/07, *VOYA* 8/07

Byrd, Sandra. *Island Girl (Friends for a Season series).* 240 p. TR. Bethany House Publishers. 978-0-7642-0020-5. 2005. $10.99.

Thirteen-year-old Meg is spending the summer on her grandparents' Oregon berry farm. But this year things are different. Meg's mother and her husband are about to have a baby, and Meg's dad, an army colonel, may be leaving the service, causing Meg to wonder if she should move and live with him. Having conversations with God allows Meg to understand and cope with her situation. Other titles in this series are *Chopstick, Red Velvet,* and *Daisy Chains.*

GRADES: 8–10

REVIEWS: *Booklist* 10/1/05

Carlson, Melody. *Diary of a Teenage Girl: Becoming Me, By Caitlin O'Conner.* 256 p. TR. The Doubleday Religious Publishing Group. 978-1-57673-735-4. 2000. $12.99.

Caitlin is the focus of this series and she's a girl who loves cool clothes and thumbing through glossy fashion magazines. She believes that with God, she can learn to accept people for who they really are, but that proves to be problematic. Her classmates are dealing with pregnancy, divorcing parents, and drug problems. Caitlin steers her friends to prayer sessions, hoping to straighten them out. Other titles in the series are *It's My Life, Who I Am, On My Own,* and *I Do.*

GRADES: 8–12

REVIEWS: *SLJ* 6/01

Carlson, Melody. *The Last Dance* (*The Carter House Girls* **series**). 208 p. TR. Zondervan. 978-0-310-71495-8. 2010. $9.99.

The drama seems unending for the Carter House girls as they struggle with college visits, choosing the correct prom dress, and boyfriend issues that are piling up. This last title in the series has the girls' time at Carter House coming to an end as they try to patch up differences or leave as enemies. Only God can help them. Other titles in the series are *Mixed Bags, New York Debut, Viva Vermont, Lost in Las Vegas, Homecoming Queen, Spring Breakdown,* and *Stealing Bradford.*

GRADES: 9–12

Cushman, Karen. *The Loud Silence of Francine Green.* 240 p. TR. Houghton Mifflin Harcourt Trade & Reference Publishers. 978-0-618-50455-8. 2006. $16.00. PB. Random House Children's Books. 978-0-375-84117-0. 2008. $6.99. EB. Random House Audio Publishing Group. 978-0-7393-4806-2. 2007. $38.25.

Francis Green is attending school at the All Saints School for Girls in Los Angeles between 1949 and 1950. A new student, Sophie Bowman, enters the school and sets off controversy when she questions the nuns' comments about "Godless" communists. Sophie's expulsion prompts Francine to question her own values, stand up to the authoritative principal, and exercise her own freedom of speech. Historically accurate, this title will appeal to teenagers confused about being forced to do the "right things."

GRADES: 7–10

REVIEWS: *Booklist* 7/1/06, *Kirkus* 7/1/06, *Publishers Weekly* 6/26/06, *SLJ* 8/06, *VOYA* 6/06

Dekker, Ted. *Chosen* (*The Lost Book* **series**). 136 p. TR. Thomas Nelson Incorporated. 978-1-59554-859-7. 2010. $9.99. TR. Thomas Nelson Incorporated. 978-1-59554-359-2. 2008. $14.99. CD. Oasis Audio. 978-1-60814-456-3. 2008. $22.99. EB. Thomas Nelson Incorporated. 978-1-4185-7700-1. N/A. $15.99.

A football game is played to select four leaders who have joined the Forest Guard to fight against the Horde—disfigured creatures created when people fail to bathe in sacred lake waters. Johnis becomes one of the four and finds that he can communicate with mythical creatures and realizes there is another mission with greater urgency. There are subplots of good versus evil here that will appeal to teens of varied faiths. Other titles in the series are *Infidel, Renegade, Chaos, Lunatic,* and *Elyon.*

GRADES: 9–12

REVIEWS: *Booklist* 3/15/08

Gallo, Donald, ed. *Owning It: Stories About Teens with Disabilities.* 224 p. TR. Candlewick Press. 978-0-7636-3255-7. 2008. $17.99.

Inspiration may be drawn from instances other than religion affiliations. In this collection of short stories, various authors for young adults offer their takes on teenagers taking responsibility for their own disabilities and the actions stemming from those situations. The stories show teens becoming their own source of inspiration. The stable of authors includes high level names such as Gail Giles, Chris Crutcher, David Lubar, and Ron Koertge. A perfect fit for classroom discussion, these stories read easily without becoming overbearing.

GRADES: 8–12

REVIEWS: *SLJ* 5/08, *VOYA* 8/08

Gallo, Donald, ed. *Sixteen: Short Stories by Outstanding Writers for Young Adults.* 192 p. PB. Random House Children's Books. 978-0-440-97757-5. 1985. $6.99. CASS. Random House Audio Publishing Group. 978-0-8072-3026-8. 1987. $44.98.

Written for a 1980s audience, these short stories represent a variety of themes including friendship, social turmoil, love, and decisions about their lives and futures. The topics are interesting and thought provoking, making this collection a nice fit for teachers who wish to inspire their students to take a big-picture look at the lives of other teenagers. Authors included are some of the more famous names in young adult literature such as Richard Peck, Harry Mazer, and Robert Cormier. Back matter includes a section of questions designed to inspire readers to think more deeply about the issues.

GRADES: 8–12

Gunn, Robin Jones. *Summer Promise* (*Christy Miller* series). 496 p. TR. The Doubleday Religious Publishing Group. 978-1-59052-584-5. 2005. $14.99.

After moving across the country, Christy begins her sophomore year of high school uncertain of how she will fit in. She experiences ups and downs as the year progresses. Friendships are forged, a job challenges her, and Christy has high expectations for the prom. Throughout it all, Christy and friends rely on their love for God and they stay true, and find strength, in identity with Christ. Libraries with a strong Christian population would do well to have this series on the shelves. Other titles in the series are *A Whisper and A Wish, Yours Forever, Surprise Endings, Island Dreamer, A Heart Full of Hope, True Friends, Starry Night, Seventeen Wishes, A Time to Cherish, Sweet Dreams,* and *A Promise Is Forever.*

GRADES: 8–12

Holt, Kimberly Willis. *When Zachary Beaver Came to Town.* 240 p. TR. Henry Holt & Company. 978-0-8050-6116-1. 1999. $17.99. RE. San Val, Incorporated. 978-0-613-72251-3. 2003. $17.20. PB. Random House Children's Books. 978-0-440-23841-6. 2003. $6.99. CD. Random House Audio Publishing Group. 978-0-7393-3734-9. 2006. $28.00. CASS. Random House Audio Publishing Group. 978-0-8072-8393-6. 2004. $30.00. EB. Random House Audio Publishing Group. 978-0-7393-6138-2. 2008. $32.30. LP. Thorndike Press. 978-0-7862-2515-6. 2000. $22.95.

> Toby Wilson is thirteen years old and is marking time in dot-on-the-map Antler, Texas, during the hot summer of 1971. Excitement stirs when Zachary Beaver, a 600-pound teenager comes to town billed as "the fattest man in the world." Zachary is a sideshow but is abandoned by his manager, allowing Toby and his friends to get to know Zachary. They find him a conflicted teen. There are many tender moments in this story. Toby's best friend Cal learns his older brother has been killed in Vietnam. The teenagers band together to help Zachary who wishes to be baptized, only to discover it's a tough task to transport a 600-pound body. Teens of a wide range of ages will be fascinated by the quirkiness and also the tenderness of this novel.

GRADES: 7–10

REVIEWS: *Booklist* 9/15/99, *Kirkus* 9/15/99, *SLJ* 11/99, *VOYA* 12/99

AWARDS: BBYA Top Ten

Konigsburg, E. L. *The Outcasts of 19 Schuyler Place.* 296 p. TR. Perfection Learning Corporation. 978-0-7569-6307-1. 2005. $13.65. TR. Simon & Schuster Children's Publishing. 978-0-689-86636-4. 2004. $16.95. PB. Simon & Schuster Children's Publishing. 978-0-689-86637-1. 2005. $5.99. CD. Random House Audio Publishing Group. 978-1-4000-8609-2. 2004. $38.25. CASS. Random House Audio Publishing Group. 978-0-8072-2326-0. 2004. $32.00. EB. Random House Audio Publishing Group. 978-0-7393-4976-2. 2007. $38.25. LP. Thorndike Press. 978-0-7862-8090-2. N/A. $10.95.

> Twelve-year-old Margaret returns home from a lousy experience at summer camp. She's shocked to learn that her beloved but eccentric uncles are upset that their Tower Garden, a monument made of steel and glass, is ordered by the city to be demolished. Margaret begins a campaign of civil disobedience to stop the city's actions. Margaret is an inspiring character who throws herself into meaningful action based on her love of art and her fondness for her uncles. Younger teens sensing injustices in the world around them will bond with the effervescent Margaret.

GRADES: 6–10

REVIEWS: *Booklist* 12/15/03, *Kirkus* 12/15/03, *Publishers Weekly* 1/12/04, *SLJ* 1/04, *VOYA* 6/04

LaHaye, Tim, and Jerry B. Jenkins. *Left Behind: A Novel of the Earth's Last Days.* 320 p. TR. Tyndale House Publishers. 978-0-8423-2912-5. 1996. $14.99. RE. San Val, Incorporated. 978-0-613-13825-3. 1995. $26.95. CD. Recorded Books, LLC. 978-0-7887-4973-5. 2004. $39.95. CD. Tyndale House Publishers. 978-0-8423-4323-7. 2000. $19.99. CASS. Recorded Books, LLC. 978-0-7887-4972-8. 2004. $34.95. EB. Recorded Books, LLC. 978-1-4175-9029-2. 1998. $1.00.

The first book in this series sets the tone for the authors' take on prophecies from the biblical books of Revelation, Isaiah, and Ezekiel. Marketed for an adult audience, these titles are often requested by teens. The story line involves a politician, Nicolae Jetty Carpathia, who promises to restore peace to all nations following the end times. What is revealed is that Nicolae is actually the Antichrist. The heavy religious message of the series is geared to an adult audience, but older teens may be drawn to the works. Other titles in the series are *The Rising, The Regime, The Rapture, Tribulation Force, Nicolae, Soul Harvest, Apollyon, Assassins, The Indwelling, The Mark, Desecration, The Remnant, Armageddon, Glorious Appearing,* and *Kingdom Come.*

GRADES: 9–12

Mackall, Dandi Daley. *Crazy in Love.* 240 p. PB. Penguin Group (USA) Incorporated. 978-0-14-241157-5. 2008. $6.99.

Mary Jane Ettermeyer is torn between what she feels are her two personalities: Plain Jane, her good-girl inner voice, wants her to follow the rules; But MJ, her red-lipstick-loving inner wild woman, wants her to do just the opposite. She's attracted to hottie Jackson House and Mary Jane has a decision to make about going all the way, or should she wait for marriage? The angel/devil temptation will ring true for girl readers who just might find themselves in a similar situation and may applaud Mary Jane's values.

GRADES: 8–12

REVIEWS: *SLJ* 2/07, *VOYA* 2/07

Mackall, Dandi Daley. *Eva Underground.* 256 p. TR. Houghton Mifflin Harcourt Trade & Reference Publishers. 978-0-15-205462-5. 2006. $17.00.

Eva Lott, high school senior from Chicago, travels with her English professor father to Poland in 1978. The Iron Curtain still covers the country and the underground movement is a dangerous activity. Eva is a spoiled American teen who becomes aware of the political activism swirling throughout the country, including instances in Catholic churches. Eva slowly begins to get involved, especially since her love interest, Tomek, is behind the printing of information about the cause. Eva's involvement in a social cause that is initially not her own is an inspiring story for older teens who may know of the unrest in Poland thirty years ago.

GRADES: 9–12

REVIEWS: *Booklist* 3/01/06, *Kirkus* 2/15/06, *SLJ* 6/06, *VOYA* 6/06

Marshall, Catherine. *Christy.* 558 p. TR. Perfection Learning Corporation. 978-0-8124-1800-2. 1976. $15.65. LB. Buccaneer Books, Incorporated. 978-1-56849-309-1. 1994. $35.95. RE. San Val, Incorporated. 978-0-8085-6647-2. 1968. $18.40. PB. HarperCollins Publishers. 978-0-380-00141-5. 1976. $7.99.

While attending a Christian revival meeting, nineteen-year-old Christy Huddleston is fascinated by the founder of an Appalachian mission program. Christy plunges into volunteerism for poverty-stricken mountain people and becomes a teacher for students in a remote area. Christy connects with minister David Grantland to teach the local people alternatives to family feuds, which has led to a cycle of revenge for decades. Christy is an inspiring character with her selfless acts of helping others and the religious mission theme will inspire teen readers considering a similar path.

GRADES: 9–12

McDaniel, Lurlene. *Angels in Pink: Raina's Story.* 240 p. TR. Random House Children's Books. 978-0-385-73156-0. 2004. $10.95.

Raina has convinced her best friends, Kathleen and Holly, to spend their summer as "pink angels" in Parker-Sloan General Hospital's summer volunteer program. Kathleen is reluctant to do it because she's needed at home caring for her sick mother. But when she meets Carson, a cute and flirty fellow volunteer, she is happy that she joined the program. Carson's "old friend" Stephanie keeps showing up and Kathleen's mother insists she needs help at home. Kathleen is able to realize that helping others also allows you to help yourself, an inspiring message for teenage girls. Other titles in the series are *Holly's Story* and *Kathleen's Story.*

GRADES: 7–10

Montgomery, Lucy Maud. *Anne of Green Gables.* Page count varies with edition. There are significant formats currently available in print.

Marilla and Matthew Cuthbert are brother and sister who live together at Green Gables, a farm in the village of Avonlea on Prince Edward Island in Canada. They decide to adopt a boy from an orphan asylum in Nova Scotia as a helper on their farm. Through a series of mishaps, the person who ends up under their roof is a precocious girl of eleven named Anne Shirley. Anne is bright, quick, eager to please and talkative, but dissatisfied with her name, her pale countenance dotted with freckles, and with her long braids of red hair. Although wishing she was named Cordelia, she insists that Anne be spelled with an "e." Anne is a talkative but wholesome girl and a safe role model for today's younger girls. Other titles in the series are *Anne of Avonlea, Anne of the Is-*

land, Anne of Windy Poplars, Anne of Windy Willows, Anne's House of Dreams, Anne of Ingleside, Rainbow Valley, Rilla of Ingleside, and *The Blythes Are Quoted.*

GRADES: 6–8

Moore, Stephanie Perry. *Prime Choice (Perry Skky Jr.* **series).** 208 p. PB. Kensington Publishing Corporation. 978-0-7582-1863-6. 2007. $9.95.

This series by Stephanie Perry Moore is the male counterpart to the Payton Skky stories. Perry Skky is a senior star football player who is torn between his desire to please God and his need for sex. His girlfriend is not ready to take their relationship to the next level due to her Christian beliefs. Her decision forces Perry into a re-evaluation of his own values and his own religious commitment. Other titles in the series are *Pressing Hard, Problem Solved,* and *Prayed Up.*

GRADES: 8–12

Moore, Stephanie Perry. *Staying Pure (Payton Skky* **series).** 200 p. TR. Moody Publishers. 978-0-8024-4236-9. 2000. $7.99. RE. San Val, Incorporated. 978-0-613-90878-8. 2000. $18.40. EB. Moody Publishers. 978-1-57567-782-8. 2000. $5.99.

Payton Skky is a teenage girl who has a problem. The African American girl is with Dakari Graham, the most popular boy in school, who wants Payton to start a more physical relationship with him. Payton is interested but struggles with her commitment to God and tries to find a balance between her love for God and her love for Dakari. The *Payton Skky* series is a great go-to series when African American readers are seeking an inspirational novel with real teen issues. Other titles in the series are *Sober Faith, Saved Race,* and *Sweetest Gift.*

GRADES: 8–12

Peck, Richard. *On the Wings of Heroes.* 160 p. TR. Penguin Group (USA) Incorporated. 978-0-8037-3081-6. 2007. $16.99. PB. Penguin Group (USA) Incorporated. 978-0-14-241204-6. 2008. $6.99. CD. Random House Audio Publishing Group. 978-0-7393-3883-4. 2007. $27.00. CD. Random House Audio Publishing Group. 978-0-7393-4860-4. 2007. $38.00. EB. Random House Audio Publishing Group. 978-0-7393-5500-8. 2007. $30.00. LP. Thorndike Press. 978-0-7862-9703-0. 2007. $23.95.

Set in a small town during World War II, this story shows how the people in a village come together to lend one another support. The 1940s atmosphere comes alive with plenty of item placements such as victory gardens, ration coupons, and scrap collections. But what pushes this work to an inspiring tale is how adults comfort youngsters who are searching for heroes and find them within their own family. This story fits well into school libraries or as a selection for multigenerational community reads.

GRADES: 6–9

REVIEWS: *Booklist* 12/01/06, *Kirkus* 1/01/07, *Publishers Weekly* 1/08/07, *SLJ* 4/07, *VOYA* 4/07

Peck, Richard. *A Season of Gifts.* 176 p. TR. Penguin Group (USA) Incorporated. 978-0-8037-3082-3. 2009. $16.99. CD. Random House Audio Publishing Group. 978-0-7393-8546-3. 2009. $25.00. CD. Random House Audio Publishing Group. 978-0-7393-8548-7. 2009. $30.00. LP. Thorndike Press. 978-1-4104-2409-9. 2010. $23.95.

Set in 1958, Peck's story takes readers to a simpler time where television has just begun to take over living rooms. Grandma Dowdel is approaching ninety but is still able to put a positive influence on local youth. Narrated by twelve-year-old Bob Barnhardt, this story shows how an unassuming young boy learns to appreciate the power of helping others. Set in Illinois during the Christmas season, Grandma Dowdel manipulates the townsfolk by showing the way with her generosity, which is in contrast to her gruff personality. The positive message Peck delivers will be especially inspiring to readers seeking a sweet holiday tale.

GRADES: 6–9

REVIEWS: *Booklist* 8/01/09, *Kirkus* 8/01/09, *Publishers Weekly* 7/13/09, *SLJ* 10/09, *VOYA* 12/09

Peck, Richard. *The Teacher's Funeral.* 208 p. TR. Penguin Group (USA) Incorporated. 978-0-8037-2736-6. 2004. $16.99. RE. San Val, Incorporated. 978-1-4177-2798-8. 2001. $17.20. PB. Penguin Group (USA) Incorporated. 978-0-14-240507-9. 2006. $6.99. EB. Random House Audio Publishing Group. 978-0-7393-4523-8. 2006. $32.30.

Again Richard Peck takes readers back in history to small-town America around the turn of the twentieth century. In a rural area, Miss Myrt Arbuckle suddenly keels over dead. Narrator Russel Culver hopes that will be the end of school, but little does he know that his older sister Tansy will become the schoolmarm. Many homilies are scattered throughout Peck's writing, which will bring smiles to many readers. Perhaps more wholesome than inspiring, this is a tame story suitable for libraries with a strong conservative population.

GRADES: 6–9

REVIEWS: *Booklist* 10/01/04, *Kirkus* 10/01/04, *Publishers Weekly* 11/01/04, *SLJ* 11/04, *VOYA* 12/04

Peretti, Frank. *Hangman's Curse.* 288 p. TR. Thomas Nelson Incorporated. 978-1-59554-445-2. 2008. $12.99. LB. San Val, Incorporated. 978-0-613-77934-0. 2003. $18.40. PB. Thomas Nelson Incorporated. 978-1-4003-1016-6. 2008. $7.99.

Peretti's story is a thriller about evils brought on by bullying and intolerance. Athletes of a Washington State high school are stricken by hallucinations, prompting the Springfield family to investigate the mystery. The Springfields have a mobile home dubbed the Holy Roller and are guided by their Judeo-Christian faith to seek the truth behind the strange occurrences. They discover a legend about a boy who hung himself in a school during the 1930s and now shows his ghostly presence. More of a thriller than a preachy tale, Peretti's work will draw teens who have a strong Christian background.

GRADES: 7–10

REVIEWS: *Publishers Weekly* 5/14/01, *SLJ* 7/01

Sniegoski, Thomas E. *The Fallen.* 272 p. PB. Simon & Schuster Children's Publishing. 978-1-4169-3877-4. 2006. $6.99. EB. Simon & Schuster Children's Publishing. 978-0-689-85577-1. 2003. N/A.

On his eighteenth birthday Aaron Corbet learns he is one of the Nephilim who are children of angels and mortal women. Soon he's pressed into a battle against the Powers, angels who have made it their mission to destroy Nephilim. Believing Aaron is the figure of a 1,000- year-old prophecy, the fallen angels protect Aaron. Not as heavy-handed as other teen novels with a religious slant, this work is more action oriented rather than a message-driven tale.

GRADES: 8–12

REVIEWS: *Publishers Weekly* 2/3/03, *SLJ* 5/03, *VOYA* 4/03

Weinheimer, Beckie. *Converting Kate.* 288 p. TR. Penguin Group (USA) Incorporated. 978-0-670-06152-5. 2007. $16.99.

After her father dies, Kate Anderson undergoes a year of change. Her mother and Kate relocate from Maine to Phoenix, Arizona, and move into Aunt Katherine's bed and breakfast. Kate renounces the Holy Divine Church, her mother's place of worship, and begins to attend a different church run by a liberal-thinking pastor. Kate's beliefs are challenged when she learns of her new minister's sexual orientation and she struggles to reestablish her identity. The different views of religious tolerance will be best appreciated by older readers.

GRADES: 9–12

REVIEWS: *Kirkus* 2/1/07, *SLJ* 4/07, *VOYA* 2/07

Young, William P. *The Shack.* 272 p. TR. Windblown Media. 978-0-9647292-4-7. 2008. $24.99. CD. Oasis Audio. 978-1-59859-419-5. 2008. $27.99. PLAY. Findaway World, LLC. 978-1-60640-151-4. 2009. $59.99. EB. Windblown Media. 978-0-9647292-9-2. 2008. $9.99.

This story from a rags-to-riches author has been marketed to adults but the story line has great teen potential. Four years after his daughter is abducted, evidence of her murder is found in an abandoned shack. Mackenzie Allen Philips returns to the shack in response to a note claiming to be from God. During a wintry night Philips arrives at the shack and what he finds there enables him to embrace God's grace and the weekend will change his life forever. The unique take on God speaking to a man will be best appreciated by older readers.

GRADES: 10–12

10

Problem Novels

It's not an outlandish statement to say that the majority of young adult novels published are in some way problem novels. The teenage years are a period of growth, discovering limits, and learning of the world outside of one's own self-interest. It makes sense that a teenager undergoing these changes and experiences may run into a few bumps in the road.

But let's give a quick explanation of what I consider criteria for a "problem novel."

First, the problem (usually some sort of situation recognized by society as a detriment to young adult emotional growth) is created by some outside action. This action leads to a problem that directly affects the teen character's life. I separated these titles from cautionary tales based on the perception that the problem in problem novels is not a direct result of the teen character's acts.

Problem novels are frequently written in the first person with the teen as the narrator. Thus readers get the main character's point of view as they work through the problem, hopefully toward a resolution. Often a variety of problems are placed in the teen's lap. This can be both a draw and a turn-off, depending on the reader. Many teens thrive on reading about serious problems and may see their own lives reflected in the writing. Other teen readers may feel that the story is too over-the-top and no one person is confronted with a huge list of multiple problems.

Teen characters often are presented as more mature people than surrounding adults in many problem novels. For example, parents may have alcohol or drug use issues and the teen refuses to get involved with drinking or using illegal substances. Poverty often plays a role in the setting, which could be rural, suburban, or inner city. Lack of money leading to a desperate financial situation is often a catalyst for the main problem confronting the teen character.

Whatever the problem, the true inner strength of the character comes forth. He or she overcomes a stacked deck and grows throughout the course of the story. These problem novels may very well be the titles librarians must constantly replace due to demand, or wear and tear on the bindings.

Alexie, Sherman. *The Absolutely True Diary of a Part-Time Indian.* 230 p. TR. Perfection Learning Corporation. 978-1-60686-072-4. 2009. $16.65. TR. Little, Brown Books for Young Readers. 978-0-316-01368-0. 2007. $16.99. PB. Little, Brown Books for Young Readers. 978-0-316-01369-7. 2009. $8.99. CD. Recorded Books, LLC. 978-1-4281-8297-4. 2008. $46.75. CASS. Recorded Books, LLC. 978-1-4281-8292-9. 2008. $33.75. EB. Recorded Books, LLC. 978-1-4356-3355-1. N/A. $1.00. LP. Thorndike Press. 978-1-4104-0499-2. 2008. $23.95.

Arnold Spirit finds himself as a teenager moving between two worlds and feels out of place in both. While growing up on a Spokane Indian reservation, he feels loyalty to his people and his best friend Rowdy, yet when a teacher encourages him to attend the white school, Arnold grabs the chance to gain a high-quality education. His decision comes with problems as he is shunned by Rowdy and becomes an outsider to his own family. Alexie's humor is biting but carries a powerful message of stereotyping a group of people. Language issues and hard-hitting realism mark this title more for high school readers.

GRADES: 9–12

REVIEWS: *Booklist* 8/01/07, *Publishers Weekly* 8/20/07, *SLJ* 9/07, *VOYA* 8/07

AWARDS: BBYA Top Ten

Alexie, Sherman. *Flight.* N/A. RE. San Val, Incorporated. 978-1-4177-8848-4. 2007. $25.75. CD. Blackstone Audio, Incorporated. 978-1-4332-0869-0. 2008. $40.00. CD. Blackstone Audio, Incorporated. 978-1-4332-0870-6. 2007. $29.95. CASS. Blackstone Audio, Incorporated. 978-1-4332-0868-3. 2008. $24.95. EB. Blackstone Audio, Incorporated. 978-1-4332-4644-9. N/A. $39.95.

This rough title is about a teenage boy who has problems fitting in with society. As a so-called half-breed, fifteen-year-old Heck has a history of abuse and his face is so broken out with acne, he goes by the nickname Zits. By utilizing a time travel sequence, Alexie shows readers how Heck is transformed by shape-shifting into bodies of a white FBI agent confronting Indian activists, an Indian boy at the Battle of Little Big Horn, and a homeless Indian drunk. Violent, disturbing, and hard to put down, this title addresses the anger roiling inside teens who do not neatly fit into society.

GRADES: 10–12

REVIEWS: *Booklist* 3/01/07, *Publishers Weekly* 2/26/07, *SLJ* 8/07, *VOYA* 8/07

Anderson, Laurie Halse. *Catalyst.* 240 p. TR. Penguin Group (USA) Incorporated. 978-0-670-03566-3. 2002. $17.99. TR. Perfection Learning Corporation. 978-0-7569-1532-2. 2001. $15.65. LB. Perma-Bound Books. 978-0-8000-8695-4. 2002. $14.99. LB. San Val, Incorporated. 978-0-613-70575-2. 2003. $15.30. PB. Penguin Group (USA) Incorporated. 978-0-14-240001-2. 2003. $7.99. CASS.

Random House Audio Publishing Group. 978-0-8072-0940-0. 2004. $32.00. EB. Random House Audio Publishing Group. 978-0-7393-5983-9. N/A. $42.50.

Kate Malone has put herself on a one way course to MIT, but outside influences disrupt her lifelong goal. Following her mother's death, she has shouldered the responsibility of taking care of her minister father and her brother. Bully Teri Litch carries a rage that threatens everyone, but when she becomes homeless, Kate's father takes her under his wing. The conflict between Kate and Teri crackles throughout the story, but a stunning tragedy shows Kate that some people have more serious problems than trying to be accepted by a prestigious university. Teri and Kate's arguments will appeal to most high school students who find themselves victims of verbal and emotional abuse.

GRADES: 9–12

REVIEWS: *Booklist* 9/15/02, *Kirkus* 9/01/02, *Publishers Weekly* 7/22/02, *SLJ* 10/02, *VOYA* 12/02

AWARDS: BBYA Top Ten

Anderson, Laurie Halse. *Speak.* N/A. TR. Peter Smith Publisher, Incorporated. 978-0-8446-7292-2. 2006. $24.50. TR. Book Wholesalers, Incorporated. 978-1-4046-1072-9. 2002. $14.89. LB. San Val, Incorporated. 978-1-4177-5081-8. 2008. $13.90. LB. Perma-Bound Books. 978-0-605-81331-1. 1999. $17.00. PB. Penguin Group (USA) Incorporated. 978-0-14-240732-5. 2006. $10.00. CD. Random House Audio Publishing Group. 978-0-7393-3672-4. 2006. $30.00. CD. Random House Audio Publishing Group. 978-1-4000-8998-7. 2004. $35.00. CASS. Random House Audio Publishing Group. 978-0-8072-8403-2. 2004. $30.00. CASS. Random House Audio Publishing Group. 978-0-8072-8404-9. 2004. $36.00. EB. Random House Audio Publishing Group. 978-0-7393-4453-8. N/A. $38.25. LP. Thorndike Press. 978-0-7862-2525-5. 2000. $20.95.

Melinda has a problem. She refuses to speak to anyone in her school as she enters her freshman year. It seems she was the one who called the police to break up a summer drinking party. She had good reason—a popular senior guy raped her at the party. What carries this story is Melinda's achingly authentic voice of a teenager lashing out at the hypocrisy of high school while trying to cope with her own secrets. This title flew to the top of young adult literature when it was first published and has remained a staple of many recommended reading lists. I predict that twenty years from now, teenagers will still thrill at the power of this novel.

GRADES: 8–12

REVIEWS: *Booklist* 9/15/99, *Kirkus* 9/15/99, *Publishers Weekly* 9/13/99, *SLJ* 10/99, *VOYA* 12/99

AWARDS: BBYA Top Ten, Printz Honor

Anderson, Laurie Halse. *Twisted.* 272 p. TR. Penguin Group (USA) Incorporated. 978-0-670-06101-3. 2007. $16.99. CD. Random House Audio Publishing Group. 978-0-7393-4884-0. 2007. $35.00. CD. Random House Audio Publishing Group. 978-0-7393-5102-4. 2007. $45.00. EB. Random House Audio Publishing Group. 978-0-7393-5103-1. N/A. $38.25. LP. Thorndike Press. 978-0-7862-9885-3. 2007. $23.95.

Tyler Miller used to be a footnote in his high school hierarcy. But a summer of work has added muscle to his frame and girls have taken notice. Struggling to move from video gamer to a popular attraction for girls, Tyler also deals with his Type-A father and dysfunctional home life. Anderson deftly details the rage and despair of a teenage boy quickly growing into manhood. The high school party scene is totally realistic and this title is a fine example of showing, not telling, how a guy feels when he's expected to do more than he is able to provide. Language and sexual suggestions set this title more for high school readers.

GRADES: 9–12

REVIEWS: *Booklist* 1/01/07, *Publishers Weekly* 1/15/07, *SLJ* 5/07, *VOYA* 4/07

AWARDS: Teens' Top Ten

Anonymous. *Go Ask Alice.* 192 p. TR. Simon & Schuster Children's Publishing. 978-0-671-66458-9. 1971. $16.95. LB. Perma-Bound Books. 978-0-8479-1425-8. 1971. $14.99. RE. San Val, Incorporated. 978-1-4177-3474-0. 2006. $20.85. PB. Simon & Schuster Children's Publishing. 978-1-4169-1463-1. 2005. $9.99. EB. Recorded Books, LLC. 978-1-4237-0846-9. N/A. $46.00.

Using the technique of a journal of a girl telling her own story about using drugs, this novel was originally published in 1971 but still brings requests from twenty-first-century teens. The now familiar story line of a young teen being unwittingly pulled into using drugs and then progressing to harder substances was a new sensation when this title hit the market. The unnamed narrator describes using the drugs, undergoing a pregnancy scare, and how dating a dealer keeps her in the loop of drug use. Crowded with many social issues, this title set the bar for many future stories about teens becoming drug addicted.

GRADES: 9–12

Bauer, Joan. *Hope Was Here.* 186 p. TR. Book Wholesalers, Incorporated. 978-1-4046-0748-4. 2002. $13.19. TR. Perfection Learning Corporation. 978-0-7569-5777-3. 2001. $15.65. LB. Perma-Bound Books. 978-0-605-23385-0. 2000. $14.99. RE. San Val, Incorporated. 978-1-4176-8744-2. 2005. $18.40. PB. Penguin Group (USA) Incorporated. 978-0-14-240424-9. 2005. $7.99. CD. Random House Audio Publishing Group. 978-1-4000-8615-3. 2004. $30.00. CASS. Random House Audio Publishing Group. 978-0-8072-1698-9. 2004. $30.00. EB. Random House Audio Publishing Group. 978-0-7393-5998-3. N/A. $34.00. LP. Thorndike Press. 978-0-7862-3258-1. 2001. $22.95.

Hope Yancey has been on the move for a number of years with her Aunt Addie. Hope works as a waitress and Addie lends her talent as a cook to various diners. When the pair leaves a diner, sixteen-year-old Hope marks with a pen somewhere on the premises, "Hope was Here." However, the town of Mulhoney, Wisconsin, captures her heart and leaves a mark on Hope. Bauer's story is about a girl confronted with other people's problems. She learns not to escape them but becomes trusting in her relationships with others. Bauer's wit springs from the pages, but this is Hope's story of overcoming her fears.

GRADES: 8–12

REVIEWS: *Booklist* 9/15/00, *Kirkus* 9/01/00, *Publishers Weekly* 9/04/00, *SLJ* 11/00, *VOYA* 2/01

AWARDS: BBYA Top Ten, Newbery Honor

Bauer, Joan. *Rules of the Road.* 208 p. TR. Penguin Group (USA) Incorporated. 978-0-399-23140-7. 1998. $20.99. LB. Perma-Bound Books. 978-0-8479-8799-3. 1998. $14.99. PB. Penguin Group (USA) Incorporated. 978-0-14-240425-6. 2005. $7.99.

Sixteen-year-old Jenna Boller is thrilled with her job at Gladstone's Shoe Store. But when she is tapped by Mrs. Madeline Gladstone, the company's matriarch, to drive her from Chicago to Dallas, Jenna gets an education from many angles. She learns about corporate greed versus loyalty as Mrs. Gladstone's son is trying to push his mother aside in running the company. Jenna also has issues of her own ranging from her alcoholic father to an ailing grandmother. Bauer's story takes a teen on a journey of change, both physically and emotionally. This novel about an earnest girl being exposed to a variety of problems is a strong choice for multiple grade levels and libraries.

GRADES: 8–12

REVIEWS: *Booklist* 2/01/98, *Publishers Weekly* 2/23/98, *SLJ* 3/98

Block, Francesca Lia. *Weetzie Bat.* N/A. RE. San Val, Incorporated. 978-1-4176-6985-1. 2004. $19.65. PB. HarperCollins Publishers. 978-0-06-440818-9. 1999. $7.99. PB. HarperCollins Publishers. 978-0-06-073625-5. 2004. $8.99. CASS. Recorded Books, LLC. 978-0-7887-0601-1. 1997. $19.00.

Weetzie loves being around the Hollywood atmosphere and is not afraid to embrace an avant-garde lifestyle. She meets Dirk and they slamdance their way into Los Angeles clubs. Dirk tells Weetzie he's gay and soon Dirk finds his ideal surfer blond crush while Weetzie falls for her Secret Agent Lover Man. They all move in together and a baby is born. This groundbreaking story of an offbeat search for love, and valuing love above everything else, will resonate with teens searching for a novel that describes living outside society's rules.

GRADES: 9–12

REVIEWS: *Booklist* 1/15/90, *Kirkus* 4/01/89, *Publishers Weekly* 4/05/91, *SLJ* 4/89

Bloor, Edward. *Tangerine.* 320 p. TR. Houghton Mifflin Harcourt Trade & Reference Publishers. 978-0-15-201246-5. 1997. $17.00. LB. Perma-Bound Books. 978-0-605-65257-6. 1997. $13.95. RE. San Val, Incorporated . 978-1-4177-5356-7. 2006. $17.15. PB. Houghton Mifflin Harcourt Trade & Reference Publishers. 978-0-15-205780-0. 2006. $6.95. PB. Scholastic, Incorporated. 978-0-590-43277-1. 1998. $4.99. CD. Recorded Books, LLC. 978-1-4025-1967-3. N/A. $89.00. EB. Recorded Books, LLC. 978-1-4237-3182-5. N/A. $1.00.

Paul needs thick glasses to see well enough to do things other kids do, but he's able to "see" the facade of Tangerine County, Florida. His family has moved there and Paul has to adjust to this new place while working at his soccer game. What is slowly revealed is the truth behind Erik, his disturbed and menacing older brother, and the secret of what happened to Paul several years ago. Lightning strikes the town each day and a sinkhole envelopes the school's portable classrooms, but Paul's voice reveals the injustice of his new community. Paul's noble sense of self-worth contrasts with the amoral characters surrounding him.

GRADES: 8–10

REVIEWS: *Booklist* 5/15/97, *Kirkus* 2/01/97, *Publishers Weekly* 3/24/97, *SLJ* 4/97

Booth, Coe. *Kendra.* 320 p. TR. Scholastic, Incorporated. 978-0-439-92536-5. 2008. $16.99.

Fourteen-year-old Kendra Williamson is waiting for Renee, her twenty-eight-year-old mom, to finish school so they can get their own place. But Renee feels this is her time to be free and moves into a Harlem apartment leaving Kendra under her strict grandmother's rules. Kendra not only deals with absentee Renee, she also falls into a jealousy trap with her best friend Adonna. Teens will be engaged with Kendra's dilemma of breaking free from the adult mess while trying to be a normal teenager. Kendra's feelings of abandonment and betrayal are the strengths of this story set in the inner city.

GRADES: 10–12

REVIEWS: *Booklist* 11/01/08, *SLJ* 10/08, *VOYA* 10/08

Booth, Coe. *Tyrell.* 320 p. TR. Scholastic, Incorporated. 978-0-439-83879-5. 2006. $16.99. RE. San Val, Incorporated. 978-1-4177-9361-7. 2007. $18.40. PB. Scholastic, Incorporated. 978-0-439-83880-1. 2007. $7.99.

Fifteen-year-old Tyrell has problems he tries to work out. His mother is satisfied to stay on welfare forcing them to live in a roach-infested Brooklyn shelter. At the shelter, Tyrell tries to take care of his seven-year-old brother, but soon hooks up with Jasmine. That conflicts with his girlfriend Novisha who lives in a middle-class area of the city. Tyrell is determined to stay clean as he agonizes over creating a new life for his family, but the only money solution seems to be to take over his incarcerated father's business. Raw street slang and blunt sex scenes mark this realistic novel of the streets as Tyrell tries to sort out problems while moving through two different economic worlds.

GRADES: 10–12

REVIEWS: *Booklist* 11/15/06, *Publishers Weekly* 11/20/06, *SLJ* 11/06, *VOYA* 2/07

Brothers, Meagan. *Debbie Harry Sings in French.* 240 p. TR. Henry Holt & Company. 978-0-8050-8080-3. 2008. $16.95.

Fresh out of rehab, seventeen-year-old Johnny is a recovering alcoholic and is sent to live with his march-to-a-different-drummer uncle. Johnny has a retro fascination with singer Debbie Harry, which moves to a desire to look like her—tough and beautiful. Johnny's prep-school classmates assume he is gay and taunt him. Johnny's status as a transvestite is compounded when others are unable to differentiate between cross-dressing and being gay. Partnering with Maria, the pair discusses music and what it means to be an outcast. Yet, by entering a cross-dressing competition, Johnny discovers things about himself and others like him. The transvestite theme is handled with respect by the author but may be too avant garde for middle school readers.

GRADES: 10–12

REVIEWS: *Booklist* 4/01/08, *Publishers Weekly* 4/28/08, *SLJ* 9/08

Buckhanon, Kalisha. *Upstate.* 256 p. TR. St. Martin's Press. 978-0-312-33269-3. 2006. $12.95. RE. San Val, Incorporated. 978-1-4177-6143-2. 2006. $24.45. PB. St. Martin's Press. 978-0-312-33269-3. 2006. $12.95. CASS. BBC Audiobooks America. 978-0-7927-3427-7. 2005. $39.95.

Antonio and Natasha, two Harlem teenagers, are deeply in love with each other until their love is challenged when Antonio is sentenced to jail for killing his father. Buckhanon presents this moving story in epistolary fashion as the two lovers grow over time while sending each other letters exposing their feelings. Natasha moves on with her life, but Antonio cannot due to his incarceration. Antonio seems to be an unlikable character until a sudden twist reveals an explanation for his crime. The sophisticated style that lacks dialogue may not connect with younger teens, but experienced readers will be moved by Antonio and Natasha's relationship.

GRADES: 10–12

REVIEWS: *Booklist* 12/15/04, *Publishers Weekly* 11/22/04

AWARDS: Alex Award, BBYA Top Ten

Burg, Anne E. *All the Broken Pieces.* 224 p. TR. Scholastic, Incorporated. 978-0-545-08092-7. 2009. $16.99.

Twelve-year-old Matt Pin is the son of a Vietnamese woman and an American soldier. He was airlifted out of the war zone and now lives in the United States. Opening in 1977, this story shows a loving couple who try to help Matt through the horrible memories of what Matt was forced to leave behind in Vietnam. Burg's choice for a verse format makes the story move quickly and Matt deals with racism of adults who take one look at his face and immediately blame him for tragedies resulting from the war. Readers learn that war creates more than just physical broken pieces.

GRADES: 8–10

REVIEWS: *Booklist* 2/15/09, *Publishers Weekly* 4/13/09, *SLJ* 5/09

Caletti, Deb. *The Fortunes of Indigo Skye.* 304 p. TR. Simon & Schuster Children's Publishing. 978-1-4169-1007-7. 2008. $15.99. PB. Simon & Schuster Children's Publishing. 978-1-4169-1008-4. 2009. $9.99.

Receiving a gift of $2.5 million seems too good to be true for Indigo Skye, a high school senior who works as a waitress. In return for her small kindness, a stranger leaves her the astronomical tip. Indigo struggles to remain true to herself, but all around her the negative side effects of instant wealth spring forth. The theme of money as the ultimate corrupter works well, but what carries the story is Caletti's quirky cast of characters who all clamor for a piece of the action. Most readers will be engaged with this money-as-the-root-of-all-evil story.

GRADES: 9–12

REVIEWS: *Booklist* 4/01/08, *Publishers Weekly* 2/11/08, *SLJ* 4/08

Cassidy, Anne. *Looking for JJ.* 336 p. TR. Houghton Mifflin Harcourt Trade & Reference Publishers. 978-0-15-206190-6. 2007. $17.00. PB. Scholastic, Incorporated. 978-0-439-97717-3. 2005. N/A.

Seventeen-year-old Alice Tully finally has things in place and her outlook is positive. She has a boyfriend, a job, a place to live, and plans to attend college. The problem is that Alice has not always been Alice. Six years earlier she was Jennifer Jones, a girl with boiling rage, about being deserted by her mother, that resulted in a young playmate dead. Now the painful past resurfaces as the media rehashes the crime and speculates about Jennifer's current life. This is an interesting story about a teenager who cannot escape her past due to the sensationalism of the event.

GRADES: 9–12

REVIEWS: *Booklist* 10/01/07, *Publishers Weekly* 10/29/07, *SLJ* 8/07, *VOYA* 10/07

Castellucci, Cecil. *Beige.* 320 p. TR. Candlewick Press. 978-0-7636-3066-9. 2007. $16.99. TR. Candlewick Press. 978-1-4287-4767-8. 2007. N/A. PB. Candlewick Press. 978-0-7636-4232-7. 2009. $8.99.

Fourteen-year-old Katy has to move in with her father when her mother leaves Montreal to head off on an archaeological dig. Her father is The Rat, a legendary drummer for the punk rock band, Suck. Arriving in Los Angeles, Katy feels very plain and beige next to her father's flamboyant friends and lifestyle. Katy has trouble fitting in until Lake, a girl her father bribes to befriend Katy, lands her a job selling merchandise at Suck's gigs. Teen readers into music, especially retro punk, will nod in time with Katy's emergence as she claims her place as part of the band.

GRADES: 9–12

REVIEWS: *Booklist* 10/01/07, *Publishers Weekly* 6/18/07, *SLJ* 8/07, *VOYA* 6/07

Chbosky, Stephen. *The Perks of Being a Wallflower.* 213 p. TR. Simon & Schuster. 978-0-671-02734-6. 1999. $14.00. LB. Perma-Bound Books. 978-0-605-16592-2. 1999. $21.00. RE. San Val, Incorporated. 978-0-613-23752-9. 1999. $25.75. CD. Recorded Books, LLC. 978-1-4193-8724-1. 2006. $19.99. CASS. Books on Tape, Incorporated. 978-0-7366-4936-0. 2001. $24.95. CASS. Books on Tape, Incorporated. 978-0-7366-4904-9. 2000. $40.00.

Fifteen-year-old Charlie pens letters to a never-identified person but his stream of consciousness will resonate with readers. Charlie observes—his take on high school life involves sex, drug use, and regular participation in Rocky Horror Picture Show screenings. He grows to learn how to become a friend rather than someone who is pushed around. But first he must come to grips with the secret of what happened between him and his deceased Aunt Helen. This title has appeal for teens who consider high school a strange place they would rather not attend. The realistic use of drugs and straightforward discussions of sex mark this book more suitable for older high school readers.

GRADES: 10–12

REVIEWS: *Booklist* 2/15/99, *Kirkus* 1/15/99, *Publishers Weekly* 1/25/99, *SLJ* 6/99, *VOYA* 12/99

Cohn, Rachel. *Gingerbread.* N/A. LB. Perma-Bound Books. 978-0-605-96875-2. 2002. $13.99. PB. Simon & Schuster Children's Publishing. 978-0-689-84337-2. 2002. $15.95. CD. Recorded Books, LLC. 978-1-4193-3032-2. 2005. $51.75. CASS. Recorded Books, LLC. 978-1-4193-5133-4. 2005. $37.75.

Back home in San Francisco, after being thrown out of boarding school for sexual indiscretions, sixteen-year-old Cyd Charisse is in hot water with her parents because of her open defiance of their curfew ordinance. Fed up with her attitude, her parents decide to let Cyd's biological father deal with the situation. In New York, she meets her stepsibs and begins to ponder the meaning of family. When she reconnects with her mother, Cyd's secrets come forth and she can begin to heal. Sex and pregnancy are up-front issues in this book with more appeal to high school over middle school students despite the innocent-sounding title. The sequel is called *Shrimp*.

GRADES: 10–12

REVIEWS: *Kirkus* 1/15/02, *Publishers Weekly* 1/21/02, *SLJ* 2/02, *VOYA* 4/02

AWARDS: Quick Picks Top Ten

Cooney, Caroline B. *The Face on the Milk Carton.* 192 p. TR. Random House Children's Books. 978-0-385-32328-4. 1996. $15.95. LB. San Val, Incorporated. 978-0-8335-6470-2. 1994. $14.15. LB. Perma-Bound Books. 978-0-7804-2723-5. 1990. $13.50. PB. Random House Children's Books. 978-0-440-22065-7. 1991. $6.99. PB. Random House Children's Books. 978-0-440-91009-1. 1994. $4.99. CD. Recorded Books, LLC. 978-0-7887-3447-2. 2000. $45.00. CASS. Recorded Books, LLC. 978-0-7887-2463-3. 1998. $49.24. LP. Thorndike Press. 978-0-7862-8930-1. 2006. $10.95.

Three-year-old Jennie Spring was kidnapped twelve years earlier, but when fifteen-year-old Janie Johnson sees the photo, she knows she is that child. Her parents believe that she is really their grandchild, the child of their long-missing daughter who had joined a cult. The curiosity about having been adopted or even kidnapped may sound intriguing to readers, but the decisions Janie must face become painful and complex. She experiences denial, anger, and guilt while trying to come to grips with her own identity. With horrific true media stories in the twenty-first century about kidnapped girls, this book will continue to draw readers of many ages.

GRADES: 8–10

REVIEWS: *SLJ* 2/89

Cormier, Robert. *After the First Death.* N/A. TR. Peter Smith Publisher, Incorporated. 978-0-8446-7215-1. 2002. $23.00. RE. San Val, Incorporated. 978-0-8085-1612-5. 1991. $17.20. PB. Random House Children's Books. 978-0-440-20835-8. 1991. $6.99.

In a title way ahead of its time, Kate Forrester is a high school student filling in as a bus driver for her uncle. Heading for a day camp in Massachusetts, a team of four terrorists hijack the bus and make Kate park it on an abandoned railway bridge. The stalemate intensifies when a Delta force anti-terrorism unit is called in. The terrorists will accept the $10 million ransom money only if delivered by the sixteen-year-old son of Delta's general. Grim and tension-packed, this book will hit hard for twenty-first-century readers who read about terrorism each day.

GRADES: 9–12

REVIEWS: *Booklist* 10/15/88

Coy, John. *Crackback.* 201 p. TR. Perfection Learning Corporation. 978-0-7569-8274-4. 2007. $14.65. TR. Scholastic, Incorporated. 978-0-439-69733-0. 2005. $16.99. RE. San Val, Incorporated. 978-1-4177-9279-5. 2007. $17.20. PB. Scholastic, Incorporated. 978-0-439-69734-7. 2007. $6.99.

Miles Manning enters his junior year psyched to be the starting cornerback for his high school football team. More of a think-and-react player than a smash-'em-in-the-mouth force, Miles finds himself in the coach's doghouse. When his teammate Zach begins taking steroids, Miles has to re-evaluate his team's win-at-all-costs mind-set. Coy paints a realistic picture of high school athletes that swagger above the rules. The realistic football scenes will attract many male readers and they will not be disappointed. Rough language and locker room talk about sex marks this book for high school readers.

GRADES: 9–12

REVIEWS: *Booklist* 9/01/05, *SLJ* 12/05, *VOYA* 12/05

Creech, Sharon. *Walk Two Moons.* 288 p. TR. Book Wholesalers, Incorporated. 978-0-7587-0223-4. 2002. $15.00. TR. HarperCollins Publishers. 978-0-06-023334-1. 1994. $16.99. LB. HarperCollins Publishers. 978-0-06-023337-2. 1994. $17.89. RE. San Val, Incorporated. 978-0-613-81971-8. 2004. $17.20. LB. Perma-Bound Books. 978-0-605-18128-1. 1994. $13.99. PB. HarperCollins Publishers. 978-0-06-056013-3. 2004. $6.99. PB. Pathways Publishing. 978-1-58303-067-7. 1998. $15.95. CD. HarperCollins Publishers. 978-0-06-171909-7. 2009. $14.99. CD. Random House Audio Publishing Group. 978-0-8072-2012-2. 2004. $40.00. PLAY. Findaway World, LLC. 978-1-60252-803-1. 2007. $39.99. CASS. Books on Tape, Incorporated. 978-0-7366-5023-6. 2000. $30.00. CASS. Random House Audio Publishing Group. 978-0-8072-7871-0. 1997. $32.00. EB. HarperCollins Publishers. 978-0-06-178689-1. 2008. $9.99. LP. Thorndike Press. 978-0-7862-2773-0. 2000. $21.95.

Thirteen-year-old Sal Hiddle has trouble dealing with her mother who has removed herself from Sal's life. Her mother, Sugar, is in Idaho and Mr. Hiddle has taken up with a woman named Mrs. Cadaver. Sal is taken on a road trip with her grandparents to Idaho. Along the journey, Sal relates the story of Phoebe, a friend who receives mysterious messages and has to cope with the disappearance of her mother. The problems Sal faces become obvious, but the message in this title is one of finally accepting a situation beyond your control.

GRADES: 6–9

REVIEWS: *Booklist* 11/15/94, *Kirkus* 6/15/94, *SLJ* 10/94, *VOYA* 2/95

AWARDS: Newbery Winner

Crist-Evans, Craig. *Amaryllis.* N/A. RE. San Val, Incorporated. 978-1-4177-6941-4. 2006. $18.40.

Brothers Frank and Jimmy Staples love to surf the waves created by the shipwreck of the *Amaryllis.* But the year is 1967 and Vietnam looms. Eighteen-year-old Frank enlists in the army to escape his abusive father. Jimmy is left behind to grow up on his own. Letters from Frank reveal his disintegrating mental condition and Jimmy is powerless to help his brother. Crist-Evans' sophisticated style of writing will attract readers seeking a challenge, thus making this title more appealing to high school students.

GRADES: 10–12

REVIEWS: *Booklist* 11/01/03, *Publishers Weekly* 12/15/03, *SLJ* 11/03, *VOYA* 12/03

Crutcher, Chris. *Staying Fat for Sarah Byrnes.* N/A. LB. Perma-Bound Books. 978-0-605-02777-0. 1993. $13.99. RE. San Val, Incorporated. 978-0-613-61464-1. 1993. $19.65. PB. HarperCollins Publishers. 978-0-06-009489-8. 2003. $8.99.

Sarah Byrnes' only friend is Eric Calhoun, an overweight classmate nicknamed Moby. When she was three years old Sarah's face and hands were horribly burned in a home "accident." Her abusive father refused reconstructive surgery and now Sarah lies in a catatonic state in a hospital. Eric learns she is there to escape her father and tries to help but Sarah's father threatens to kill Eric unless he reveals Sarah's location. A long list of problems is hurled at readers, but this title works with the power of friendship. The gripping truth about Sarah's abusive father is fascinating but may be too intense for middle school readers.

GRADES: 9–12

REVIEWS: *Booklist* 3/15/93, *Kirkus* 3/15/93, *Publishers Weekly* 3/29/93, *VOYA* 8/93

Crutcher, Chris. *Whale Talk.* 224 p. TR. HarperCollins Publishers. 978-0-688-18019-5. 2001. $16.99. LB. Perma-Bound Books. 978-0-605-01250-9. 2001. $13.50. RE. San Val, Incorporated. 978-0-613-61739-0. 2002. $17.20. PB. HarperCollins Publishers. 978-0-06-177131-6. 2009. $8.99. PB. Random House Children's Books. 978-0-440-22938-4. 2002. $6.99. CD. Random House Audio Publishing Group.

978-0-8072-1778-8. 2004. $45.00. EB. Random House Audio Publishing Group. 978-0-7393-7981-3. N/A. $42.50. LP. Thorndike Press. 978-0-7862-7916-6. 2005. $10.95.

T. J. Jones is a superior athlete but refuses to participate in the regimentation of high school sports. His cool English teacher needs to form a swim team and asks T. J. to help out. He is reluctant until Chris, a brain-challenged student, is bullied by jocks for wearing his brother's varsity jacket. T. J. is determined to help Chris earn his own letter. Soon a weird swim team of misfits is formed. They bond over long bus trips and each carries the weight of their own dysfunctional home life. Each situation is more alarming then the previous, but T. J.'s nobility carries the book as he becomes a champion in more ways than one. The characters' abusive backgrounds and the complications brought forth by parents will be better appreciated by high school readers.

GRADES: 9–12

REVIEWS: *Booklist* 4/01/01, *Kirkus* 3/01/01, *Publishers Weekly* 3/12/01, *SLJ* 5/01

AWARDS: BBYA Top Ten

Cummings, Priscilla. *Red Kayak.* 209 p. TR. Penguin Group (USA) Incorporated. 978-0-7569-7019-2. 2006. $14.65. TR. Penguin Group (USA) Incorporated. 978-0-525-47317-6. 2004. $15.99. LB. Perma-Bound Books. 978-0-605-56551-7. 2004. $13.99. RE. San Val, Incorporated. 978-1-4177-2955-5. 2007. $17.20. EB. Penguin Group (USA) Incorporated. 978-1-4295-3110-8. N/A. $6.99.

The Chesapeake Bay area is where Brady, J. T., and Digger live with their working-class families. Jealous of rich summer families, Brady has to determine if J. T. and Digger sabotaged a new kayak of Mrs. DiAngelo and her two-year-old son, Ben. When the kayak overturns and young Ben dies due to hypothermia, thirteen-year-old Brady faces a moral decision if his friends are the direct cause of the tragedy. Themes of betrayal and grief are brought forth through the voices of boys just entering their teenage years. This story will have wide appeal for multiple grade levels.

GRADES: 9–12

REVIEWS: *Booklist* 9/01/04, *SLJ* 9/04, *VOYA* 10/04

Curtis, Christopher Paul. *Bucking the Sarge.* 272 p. LB. Random House Children's Books. 978-0-385-90159-8. 2004. $17.99. RE. San Val, Incorporated. 978-1-4177-4847-1. 2006. $17.20. LB. Perma-Bound Books. 978-0-605-55751-2. 2004. $13.50. PB. Random House Children's Books. 978-0-440-41331-8. 2006. $6.99. CD. Random House Audio Publishing Group. 978-1-4000-9097-6. 2004. $30.00. CD. Random House Audio Publishing Group. 978-1-4000-9484-4. 2004. $45.00. CASS. Random House Audio Publishing Group. 978-1-4000-9036-5. 2004. $35.00. EB. Random House Audio Publishing Group. 978-0-7393-6007-1. N/A. $42.50. LP. Thorndike Press. 978-0-7862-8928-8. 2006. $10.95.

Fifteen-year-old Luther Farrell exists under the iron hand of his mother, nick-named "The Sarge." Always looking for a get-rich scheme in their Flint, Michigan, neighborhood, the Sarge has Luther taking care of four men in her Rehab Center. Meanwhile she milks poor families living in her slum housing. Christopher Paul Curtis blends humor and sorrow into Luther's life as he tries to maintain a sunny attitude even though he hates his vicious mother. But Luther has some schemes of his own as he plots revenge on his mother's fiefdom. The conflict between mother and son will resonant with many high school and middle school readers who may be living with a dominant parent.

GRADES: 8–10

REVIEWS: *Booklist* 7/01/04, *Publishes Weekly* 7/19/04, *SLJ* 9/04, *VOYA* 10/04

AWARDS: BBYA Top Ten

De la Peña, Matt. *Ball Don't Lie.* N/A. RE. San Val, Incorporated. 978-1-4177-8131-7. 2007. $18.40. PB. Random House Children's Books. 978-0-385-73425-7. 2007. $7.99.

Travis Reichard, who goes by the street name Sticky, lives to hoop in this tale of inner-city desperation. Bounced around in the foster care system, six-teen-year-old Sticky feels more at home on the sweat-stained court of the Lincoln Rec, a Los Angeles mecca for pickup basketball games. Chapters alternate between on-the-court action as Sticky triumphs in a school varsity game and flashbacks to his alarming youth that eventually explains his obsessive-compulsive disorder. Sticky is a kid of the streets and like many real-life inner-city teens, he makes rash decisions that have tragic consequences. Sex and extremely rough language make this title a definite upper high school selection.

GRADES: 10–12

REVIEWS: *Booklist* 11/15/05, *Publishers Weekly* 11/07/05, *SLJ* 11/ 05, *VOYA* 10/05

AWARDS: Quick Picks Top Ten

De la Peña, Matt. *We Were Here.* 368 p. TR. Random House Publishing Group. 978-0-385-73667-1. 2009. $17.99. LB. Random House Publishing Group. 978-0-385-90622-7. 2009. $20.99.

Miguel Casteneda, age sixteen, breaks out of his California group home and with two other troubled teens, Mong and Rondell, begins a journey to Mexico. The three homeless boys form an unsteady friendship as they steal, work, fight, and care for each other. Each carries the emotional burden kept hidden from the others. This is a survival story not set in the wilderness, but in the concrete jungle. De la Peña nails inner-city teen slang and their conversations make the characters leap from the pages. Rough profanity pushes this title for upper high school, but the story will be intriguing to a wide variety of ages.

GRADES: 10–12

REVIEWS: *Booklist* 9/01/09, *Kirkus* 9/01/09

Dessen, Sarah. *This Lullaby.* 304 p. TR. Penguin Group (USA) Incorporated. 978-0-670-03530-4. 2002. $16.99. LB. Perma-Bound Books. 978-0-605-34134-0. 2002. $14.99. RE. San Val, Incorporated. 978-1-4176-1852-1. 2004. $19.65. PB. Penguin Group (USA) Incorporated. 978-0-670-03530-4. 2002. $16.99. CD. Penguin Group (USA) Incorporated. 978-0-14-314467-0. 2009. $29.95.

> When Remy meets Dexter the summer after she graduates from high school, she breaks her cardinal rule: never get involved with a musician. Her father was a musician and he wrote a song for her, "This Lullaby." A line says, "I will let you down." He does. Remy falls in love making this title a romance, but she also has to deal with problems of her wandering stepfather, her smitten bother, and all the problems of her friends. Wishing to stay in control of her relationships, Remy finds that falling in love muddles that wish. Girls of many ages flock to Sarah Dessen's novels and this is one of her best.

GRADES: 9–12

REVIEWS: *Booklist* 4/01/02, *Kirkus* 4/15/02, *Publishers Weekly* 5/20/02, *SLJ* 4/02, *VOYA* 6/02

Deuker, Carl. *High Heat.* 288 p. TR. Houghton Mifflin Harcourt Trade & Reference Publishers. 978-0-618-31117-0. 2003. $16.00. RE. San Val, Incorporated. 978-1-4176-6942-4. 2005. $17.20. PB. HarperCollins Publishers. 978-0-06-057248-8. 2005. $6.99.

> Shane Hunter can bring heat to late innings of a baseball game. He seems to be a can't-miss prospect sure to go pro right out of high school. That is, until his father is caught laundering money. After his father commits suicide, Shane and his mother must adapt to living in public housing. Shane still plays baseball, but on a much more humble scale. His frustration with his life accumulates into a deliberate beaning of a rival batter. Deuker shows that sports often cover up larger problems teenagers are experiencing. The raw power of how Shane unravels and his journey to redemption will interest male readers of high school age.

GRADES: 9–12

REVIEWS: *Booklist* 8/01/03, *Publishers Weekly* 5/19/03, *SLJ* 6/03, *VOYA* 8/03

Deuker, Carl. *Night Hoops.* 224 p. TR. Houghton Mifflin Harcourt Trade & Reference Publishers. 978-0-395-97936-5. 2000. $15.00. LB. Perma-Bound Books. 978-0-8479-5827-6. 2000. $13.99. RE. San Val, Incorporated. 978-0-613-61919-6. 2001. $17.20. PB. HarperCollins Publishers. 978-0-06-447275-3. 2001. $6.99. EB. NetLibrary, Incorporated. 978-0-585-36795-8. 2000. $15.00.

Nick Abbott is desperate to live up to his father's expectations of him as a basketball player. One-on-one games with neighbor Trent Dawson enable each boy to improve their skills. But basketball ends up being an escape from much larger issues for each boy. Trent is avoiding a life of crime. Nick is removing himself from the emotional pain of his parents' divorce. Deuker understands sports. His descriptions of game action are spot on, making this book appealing to male readers of a variety of ages.

GRADES: 9–12

REVIEWS: *Booklist* 5/01/00, *SLJ* 5/00

Duncan, Lois. *I Know What You Did Last Summer.* N/A. LB. Perma-Bound Books. 978-0-8479-5010-2. 1973. $12.99. RE. San Val, Incorporated. 978-0-88103-516-2. 1999. $16.60. PB. Random House Children's Books. 978-0-440-22844-8. 1999. $6.50. PB. Simon & Schuster Children's Publishing. 978-0-671-63970-9. 1986. N/A.

During the previous summer, four teenagers became involved in an act that could forever change their lives—if they let the secret be known. They bury the truth but later someone knows what really happened last summer. And that someone is delivering notes written in block letters stating, "I know what you did last summer." This title has long been a favorite of teenagers who thrill to reading about a problem that manifests itself into a more desperate situation.

GRADES: 8–10

Duncan, Lois. *Killing Mr. Griffin.* N/A. LB. Perma-Bound Books. 978-0-8479-4333-3. 1978. $12.99. RE. San Val, Incorporated. 978-0-88103-514-8. 1981. $17.20. PB. Random House Children's Books. 978-0-440-94515-4. 1990. $6.99. EB. Recorded Books, LLC. 978-1-4237-2152-9. N/A. $1.00.

An impromptu prank goes terribly wrong when a group of teenagers who despise Mr. Griffin's teaching style and his personality decide to kidnap him and give him a scare. What they do not count on is that Mr. Griffin's weak heart giving out and he dies. Lies are quickly formed to cover up the tragedy, but the question is if everyone is on board to keep the situation secret. This suspenseful story has appeared on recommended reading lists for a variety of ages for years. It still packs a punch for all teens who may find themselves disliking a teacher they see every day.

GRADES: 8–10

Efaw, Amy. *After.* 304 p. TR. Penguin Group (USA) Incorporated. 978-0-670-01183-4. 2009. $17.99. CD. Penguin Group (USA) Incorporated. 978-0-14-314505-9. 2009. $34.95.

Fifteen-year-old Devon Davenport is literally covering up a lie in the beginning of this sobering story. Parked on her davenport, Devon is covered with a blanket. A baby has been found in a dumpster near her apartment. It's Devon's child. She is covering up the blood from the birthing and is in danger of bleeding to death. In total denial of the situation, Devon slowly comes to realize she will be put on trial for murder. The child lives but Devon's other problems have just begun. The opening scene grabs readers and reading about the blood coating Devon may be too intense for middle school readers.

GRADES: 10–12

REVIEWS: *Booklist* 8/01/09, *Publishers Weekly* 8/03/09, *SLJ* 9/09

Flake, Sharon G. *The Skin I'm In.* 176 p. TR. Hyperion Press. 978-0-7868-0444-3. 1999. $14.95. PB. Hyperion Books for Children. 978-1-4231-0385-1. 2007. $7.99. EB. Recorded Books, LLC. 978-1-4175-8802-2. N/A. $1.00. LP. Thorndike Press. 978-0-7862-2179-0. 1999. $20.95.

Seventh-grader Maleeka Madison is miserable and undergoing feelings that happen to many children of color. She hates her dark skin. Her new teacher, Miss Saunders, is self-assured but also has a white birthmark across her black skin. Maleeka endures taunts about her skin but finds solace in writing, an action suggested by Miss Saunders. Maleeka's problem is twofold; accepting herself and also learning how to cope with a clique of nasty girls. This title is a huge favorite of middle school readers and teachers. After reading it, impromptu discussions often spring forward about acceptance of others.

GRADES: 7–9

REVIEWS: *Booklist* 9/01/98, *SLJ* 11/98

Flinn, Alex. *Nothing to Lose.* 288 p. TR. HarperCollins Publishers. 978-0-06-051750-2. 2004. $16.99. LB. HarperCollins Publishers. 978-0-06-051751-9. 2004. $17.89. RE. San Val, Incorporated. 978-1-4176-8540-0. 2005. $18.40. LB. Perma-Bound Books. 978-0-605-01359-9. 2004. $13.99. PB. HarperCollins Publishers. 978-0-06-051752-6. 2005. $7.99.

Michael Daye has been living under an assumed name and traveling around the South with a carnival. The carnival's loop brings him back to Miami just at the time his mother is to stand trial for murdering her abusive husband, who was Michael's stepfather. Michael's secret is easy to guess, but that is not the point of the story. It is about Michael owning up for what he did and stepping forward to do the right thing. Discussions about the problem of sacrifice should be offered to teens reading this title as a group.

GRADES: 9–12

REVIEWS: *Booklist* 3/15/04, *Publishers Weekly* 3/29/04, *SLJ* 3/04, *VOYA* 6/04

Forman, Gayle. *If I Stay.* 208 p. TR. Penguin Group (USA) Incorporated. 978-0-525-42103-0. 2009. $16.99. CD. Penguin Group (USA) Incorporated. 978-0-14-314445-8. 2009. $29.95.

Mia can remember being in a car with her younger brother and her parents. But she's confused about why she is now outside the car watching her brother being worked on by paramedics. She's taken to a hospital and while her body is in a coma, her mind asks many questions, including if she has the fight to live. This is the ultimate problem: the question of living or dying and what quality of life awaits for survivors of a tragedy. Readers will naturally take stock of their own lives after reading Mia's gripping narrative. The intense car wreck may not be for very young readers, but the story will engage a wide age range.

GRADES: 8–12

REVIEWS: *Booklist* 12/15/08, *Publishers Weekly* 3/02/09, *SLJ* 5/09, *VOYA* 2/09

Frank, E. R. *Life Is Funny.* 272 p. PB. Penguin Group (USA) Incorporated. 978-0-14-230083-1. 2002. $7.99 RE. San Val, Incorporated. 978-0-613-88345-0. 2002. $18.40. LB Perma-Bound Books. 978-0-605-89616-1. 2000. $14.99.

Eleven teenagers from Brooklyn contribute their opinions about their lives in this volume of interlocking stories. Spanning seven years of their adolescence, readers see how each teen grows and deals with a variety of life situations. Some handle their problems and blossom into adulthood. Others never truly break away from negative issues that dominate their lives. Abuse, drug addiction, pregnancy, suicide, and sexual relationships are all shown with a straightforward tone that holds nothing back. Older teens, especially those living in an inner city, will be drawn to the power of this narrative.

GRADES: 10–12

REVIEWS: *Booklist* 3/15/00, *Publishers Weekly* 3/13/00, *SLJ* 5/00, *VOYA* 6/00

AWARDS: Quick Picks Top Ten

Garsee, Jeannine. *Say the Word.* 368 p. TR. Bloomsbury Publishing. 978-1-59990-333-0. 2009. $16.99.

Seventeen-year-old Shawna Gallagher has a whole set of problems that are fired at her salvo after salvo. Her mother has died, but Shawna has not lived with her for years. Her mother left the family to enter a lesbian relationship ten years ago. Shawna's high-powered physician father demands that the boy being raised by the lesbian couple should now fall under his custody. Shawna becomes the voice of reason in this legal battle of wills, but she also has her own personal problems that cause her to believe she is something of a split personality—the good Shawna and the evil Shawna. Sexual situations mark this title for high school readers.

GRADES: 9–12

REVIEWS: *Booklist* 4/01/09, *Publishers Weekly* 2/23/09, *SLJ* 6/09, *VOYA* 6/09

Giles, Gail. *What Happened to Cass McBride.* 211 p. TR. Perfection Learning Corporation. 978-0-7569-8178-5. 2007. $15.65. TR. Little, Brown Books for Young Readers. 978-0-316-16638-6. 2006. $16.99. RE. San Val, Incorporated. 978-1-4177-8067-9. 2007. $18.40. PB. Little, Brown & Company. 978-0-316-01703-9. 2006. $16.99. EB. Little, Brown Books for Young Readers. 978-0-316-05511-6. 2008. $7.99.

Cass McBride is the type of high school girl that others dislike. Her attitude conveys that she is special and that leads to jealousy and hatred. But when she refuses to attend a dance with David, the shunned guy commits suicide. His older brother, Kyle, kidnaps Cass and puts her through the psychological trap of being buried alive. Cass has the problem of escaping, but the more interesting character is Kyle with his inner hate that makes him believe he is getting revenge for the "harm" Cass put upon his brother. Although this is a clean story as far as sex and language, the very creepy situation makes it more suitable for high school readers.

GRADES: 9–12

REVIEWS: *Booklist* 1/01/07, *SLJ* 2/07, *VOYA* 12/06

AWARDS: Quick Picks Top Ten

Green, John. *Paper Towns.* 320 p. TR. Penguin Group (USA) Incorporated. 978-0-525-47818-8. 2008. $17.99. CD. Brilliance Audio. 978-1-4233-4422-3. 2008. $29.99. PLAY. Findaway World, LLC. 978-1-60640-601-4. 2008. $54.99. EB. Brilliance Audio. 978-1-4233-8002-3. 2008. $24.99.

Ever since seventeen-year-old Quentin Jacobsen was a young boy, he's carried a crush for his next-door neighbor, the effervescent Margo Roth Spiegelman. After a night of revenge on Margo's boyfriend, Quentin believes Margo is sending messages to him that she would like to date him. The exact opposite happens. Margo disappears, leaving only scant clues for Quentin to determine where she went. His obsession prompts a road trip with his quirky friends, a trip that becomes a journey of self discovery. Green's talent shines in this story about unrequited love and the lessons learned while growing up. The complex plot will entice sophisticated older readers.

GRADES: 10–12

REVIEWS: *Booklist* 6/01/08, *Publishers Weekly* 9/08/08, *SLJ* 10/08, *VOYA* 8/08

AWARDS: Teens' Top Ten

Grimes, Nikki. *Bronx Masquerade.* 176 p. TR. Penguin Group (USA) Incorporated. 978-0-8037-2569-0. 2001. $16.99. LB. San Val, Incorporated. 978-0-613-81701-1. 2003. $14.15. LB. Perma-Bound Books. 978-0-8037-2569-0. 2002. $12.99. CASS. Recorded Books, LLC. 978-1-4193-9475-1. 2006. $29.75.

Mr. Ward's inner-city English class is very different. His passion for poetry is conveyed through the writing and voices of eighteen different students. Although meant to study the Harlem Renaissance, the teenager's poems reveal more about their own personal lives. Constructing his classroom like an open mic coffeehouse, Mr. Ward encourages his students to express themselves in a way not likely duplicated in any other part of the school. This title is an excellent choice for classroom teachers intending to launch a poetry unit and will interest a wide range of readers.

GRADES: 8–12

REVIEWS: *Booklist* 2/15/02, *Kirkus* 11/01/01, *Publishers Weekly* 12/17/01, *SLJ* 1/02, *VOYA* 2/02

Haddix, Margaret Peterson. *Don't You Dare Read This, Mrs. Dunphrey.* N/A. LB. Perma-Bound Books. 978-0-605-02146-4. 1996. $11.99. RE. San Val, Incorporated. 978-1-4176-2771-4. 2004. $16.00. PB. Simon & Schuster Children's Publishing. 978-0-689-87102-3. 2004. $5.99.

Tish Bonner is sixteen years old and hides out in the back row of Mrs. Dunphrey's English class. Tish's homelife is bleak with her parents being both unstable and combative. Their dysfunctional life often ends up with Tish and her younger brother home alone. Encouraged to write about what is going on in her life, the young student describes her home life under the promise that Mrs. Dunphrey will not read a section if asked not to. Tish's journal shows the struggle of a teenager asked to take over adult responsibilities at a very young age. Tish's narrative will grab reader's attention and not let go.

GRADES: 8–10

REVIEWS: *Booklist* 10/15/96, *Kirkus* 9/01/96, *Publishers Weekly* 8/12/96, *SLJ* 10/96, *VOYA* 12/96

Haddon, Mark. *The Curious Incident of the Dog in the Night-Time: A Novel.* 240 p. TR. The Doubleday Religious Publishing Group. 978-0-385-51210-7. 2003. $26.00. LB. Perma-Bound Books. 978-0-605-01314-8. 2003. $19.95. RE. San Val, Incorporated. 978-1-4176-2208-5. 2004. $25.70. CD. Recorded Books, LLC. 978-1-4025-6885-5. 2004. $24.99. CD. Recorded Books, LLC. 978-1-4025-5980-8. 2003. $45.00. CASS. Recorded Books, LLC. 978-1-4025-5598-5. 2004. $19.99. CASS. Recorded Books, LLC. 978-1-4025-5978-5. 2003. $45.00.

Christopher Boone is a fifteen-year-old autistic savant who is fascinated by primary numbers and his personal hero, Sherlock Holmes. He also is unable to cope with anything outside of his normal routine. When a neighbor's dog is killed, Christopher channels his inner hero to solve the crime. What he discovers are other mysteries that he may not want to dissect too closely. The analytical tone and sophisticated phrasing makes this an excellent choice for older high school readers.

GRADES: 10–12

REVIEWS: *Booklist* 4/01/03, *Publishers Weekly* 4/07/03, *SLJ* 10/03, *VOYA* 12/03

AWARDS: Alex Award, BBYA Top Ten

Harmon, Michael. *Last Exit to Normal.* 288 p. TR. Alfred A. Knopf Incorporated. 978-0-375-84098-2. 2008. $15.99. LB. Alfred A. Knopf Incorporated. 978-0-375-94098-9. 2008. $18.99.

Michael Harmon crowds many social issues into one volume, but it all comes together. Ben Campbell often finds himself in trouble. His missteps include smoking pot and the usual bad-boy wrongdoings. Ben's father and Ben's father's partner, Edward, make the decision to move Ben to new surroundings. Transplanted to Montana Big Sky country, Ben is initially out of place and issues of homophobia, bullying, and falling for a girl are dealt with in this tidy novel. Teens experiencing a blended home life will be very interested in Ben's story.

GRADES: 9–12

REVIEWS: *Publishers Weekly* 2/18/08, *SLJ* 4/08, *VOYA* 6/08

Headley, Justina Chen. *North of Beautiful.* 384 p. TR. Little, Brown Books for Young Readers. 978-0-316-02505-8. 2009. $16.99. EB. Little, Brown Books for Young Readers. 978-0-316-04078-5. 2009. $16.99.

Terra is a high school student who is driven to achieve. Her grades are outstanding and she exercises to keep her killer body toned. But she also spends time applying heavy makeup to cover a port-wine birthmark on her cheek. Her face makes her feel like an outsider. A trip away from her small town prompts a chance meeting with Jacob, a goth guy with a cleft-palate scar. This is a story of breaking away from unreal expectations upheld by family members or boyfriends. Terra is an artist working with the collage medium, which becomes a perfect metaphor for her journey of self-discovery. The romance between Jacob and Terra will appeal to high school girls.

GRADES: 9–12

REVIEWS: *Booklist* 2/15/09, *Publishers Weekly* 12/01/08, *SLJ* 2/09, *VOYA* 6/09

Hernandez, David. *No More Us for You.* 288 p. TR. HarperCollins Publishers. 978-0-06-117333-2. 2009. $16.99. LB. HarperCollins Publishers. 978-0-06-117334-9. 2009. $17.89. EB. HarperCollins Publishers. 978-0-06-176134-8. 2009. $16.99.

Carlos and Isabel are two seventeen-year-olds who narrate their story in alternating chapters. Isabel is grieving her boyfriend who died a year before, but now her new love interest is Carlos. However, Carlos and his best friend become involved with drinking and driving, a rash act with tragic consequences. The authentic teen dialogue that never feels strained or forced sets this title apart. Both Carlos and Isabel relate the many problems they have while letting readers know they are attracted to each other. Intense situations and profanity make this story more suitable for older high school readers.

GRADES: 10–12

REVIEWS: *Booklist* 1/01/09, *SLJ* 7/09, *VOYA* 2/09

Hernandez, David. *Suckerpunch.* 224 p. TR. HarperCollins Publishers. 978-0-06-117330-1. 2008. $16.99. LB. HarperCollins Publishers. 978-0-06-117331-8. 2008. $17.89. EB. HarperCollins Publishers. 978-0-06-176166-9. 2009. $16.99.

Known as Nub because of a severed index finger, Marcus Mendoza narrates his story about his abusive father. Several comments about sex and getting high practically smack readers hard in the opening pages. The story focuses on Enrique, Marcus's younger brother, who steps into the spotlight. Enrique has suffered years of physical beatings from their father, a man who bolted to Monterey, California. The brothers embark on a road trip intent on revenge. This is a tough guy's book, and a perfect choice for reluctant male readers. Profanity and blunt conversations about sex mark it for upper high school.

GRADES: 10–12

REVIEWS: *Booklist* 4/15/08, *Kirkus* 1/01/08, *Publishers Weekly* 1/28/08, *SLJ* 8/08, *VOYA* 4/08

Hinton, S. E. *The Outsiders.* Page count varies with edition. There are significant formats currently available in print.

S. E. Hinton laid the groundwork for thousands of young adult problem novels to follow her 1967 classic story. Before *The Outsiders* there was no fiction addressing teenagers with a wide variety of problems. Ponyboy Curtis and his brothers Sodapop and Darry live on the wrong side of the tracks. Called Greasers, they are part of a tough, angry, and unforgiving group of teenagers. Their opposite set is the well-to-do Socs (short for Socials). Since their parents died in a car crash, the brothers try to steer Ponyboy to a better path than that of their gang friends. Over forty years after initial publication, this story still rings true for many teens realizing the injustices in society.

GRADES: 8–12

Hinton, S. E. *That Was Then, This Is Now.* 160 p. TR. Penguin Group (USA) Incorporated. 978-0-670-69798-4. 1971. $17.99. LB. Perma-Bound Books. 978-0-8479-1011-3. 1971. $14.99. PB. Penguin Group (USA) Incorporated. 978-0-14-038966-1. 1998. $9.99.

Written in 1971, S. E. Hinton's novel is a portrait of two boys arriving at a crossroads in their friendship. Mark has been living with Bryon since his parents died and the two boys have formed a brotherhood stronger than a friendship. But something is driving a wedge between Mark and Bryon. Readers are teased if it is Bryon's girlfriend Cathy or something else leading to jealousy. Mark lives to street fight but also seems to have lots of cash. The theme of protecting a friend versus doing what is right is a problem that will resonate with a wide variety of readers.

GRADES: 8–12

Howell, Simmone. *Everything Beautiful.* 320 p. TR. Bloomsbury Publishing. 978-1-59990-042-1. 2008. $16.99.

Various views of religion and teens coming to terms with their beliefs are the pivotal points in this Australian novel with a main character who is an atheist. Riley is a sixteen-year-old girl who narrates her disgust of being sent by her father and stepmother to a Christian summer camp. She considers having sex with a gorgeous counselor. However, she becomes more fed up with the hypocrisy she sees and plans a getaway road trip with a disabled camper, Dylan. Frank talk about having sex, and the raucous and sexy tone of the novel make it one more appealing for high school readers.

GRADES: 9–12

REVIEWS: *Booklist* 10/10/08, *SLJ* 1/09

Hrdlitschka, Shelley. *Dancing Naked.* N/A. RE. San Val, Incorporated. 978-0-613-60545-8. 2002. $19.60. PB. Orca Book Publishers USA. 978-1-55143-210-6. 2002. $9.95.

Sixteen-year-old Kia's life changes when she learns that she is pregnant. She has to mix in the feelings of her parents and also her church group. Her irresponsible boyfriend talks her into having an abortion, but Kia refuses to go through with the act. As Kia progresses through her pregnancy, she dreams of raising a child with a guy and becomes attracted to a twenty- three-year-old guy who is gay. The teen issue of course is the harsh message that giving birth is vastly different from becoming a parent. The sensitive issues of abortion and teenage sex make this novel a choice for mature readers.

GRADES: 9–12

REVIEW: *Booklist* 3/15/02, *SLJ* 3/02, *VOYA* 4/02

Johnson, Kathleen Jeffrie. *Target.* N/A. LB. Perma-Bound Books. 978-0-605-01339-1. 2003. $13.50.

Grady West is a sixteen-year-old terrified that his friends and outsiders will discover that he was savagely raped and assaulted by two men. Enrolling in a new school, Grady slowly forms a small circle of friends, including a wannabe investigative reporter, Gwendolyn. Grady struggles to move on with his life, but his path to healing is interrupted when it is revealed that Grady is the guy who was the victim of a rape reported in a nearby town. The grim reality of rape and the questioning that Grady undergoes regarding his sexuality make this title more appropriate for older readers.

GRADES: 10–12

REVIEWS: *Booklist* 11/15/03, *Publishers Weekly* 11/03/03, *SLJ* 12/03, *VOYA* 2/0

Klass, David. *You Don't Know Me.* N/A. LB. Perma-Bound Books. 978-0-8000-3793-2. 2001. $13.99. RE. San Val, Incorporated. 978-0-613-53336-2. 2002. $19.65. PB. HarperCollins Publishers. 978-0-06-447378-1. 2002. $8.99. EB. Macmillan. 978-0-374-70583-1. 2002. $18.00.

John is a fourteen-year-old who seems to be two different people. At high school he has several buddies and spends time worshipping a hot girl. But readers soon realize that John suffers daily abuse from his soon-to-be-stepfather. Told in John's voice, we as readers become part of the story as John's voice mocks the people who know his secret. This novel shows how abuse can be kept secret and victims become experts at leading a somewhat normal life outside the home. John's somewhat complicated and unreliable narrative will be best appreciated by older teens.

GRADES: 9–12

REVIEWS: *Publishers Weekly* 8/05/02, *VOYA* 10/02

Koertge, Ron. *Margaux with an X.* N/A. LB. Perma-Bound Books. 978-0-605-01382-7. 2004. $13.99.

Margaux may be popular and beautiful, but she is covering up a miserable home life. Her mother is addicted to the shopping channel and her father has his own vice—gambling. Intelligent and witty, Margaux keeps other teens at bay with sarcasm. This plan goes well until she meets Danny, who is a social outcast. Their unlikely friendship strengthens when Danny reveals his own family problems. Their release becomes checking up on people who have adopted dogs from a humane shelter. Danny is determined to see the dogs are given a loving life. The odd relationship shows Margaux what a healthy family life should be like. Koertge's writing is powerful as Margaux's voice leaps from the pages.

GRADES: 9–12

REVIEWS: *Publishers Weekly* 11/13/06

Koertge, Ron. *Strays.* 176 p. TR. Candlewick Press. 978-0-7636-2705-8. 2007. $16.99.

Ted is a sophomore who has problems adjusting to a foster home. He lives with the Rafters and it is far different from his birth home. His biological parents ran a pet shop and Ted believed they cared more for the animals than they cared for him. Ted is socially awkward and his foster brothers try to help him get on with his life. However, it is Ted's ability to communicate with animals that sets him on the path to recovery. This slim volume is a story about recovery and healing from emotional disaster. Older readers who like quirky happenings in their reading will be drawn to Ted's conversations with a variety of animals.

GRADES: 10–12

REVIEWS: *Booklist* 5/01/07, *Publishers Weekly* 5/28/07, *SLJ* 7/07, *VOYA* 8/07

Koja, Kathe. *Buddha Boy.* 117 p. TR. Perfection Learning Corporation. 978-0-7569-3117-9. 2004. $13.65. TR. Farrar, Straus & Giroux. 978-0-374-30998-5. 2003. $16.00. RE. San Val, Incorporated. 978-1-4176-8572-1. 2004. $16.00. LP. Cengage Gale. 978-0-7862-6012-6. 2003. $24.95.

Justin is having a hard time understanding the new transfer student, Michael Martin. Michael has shaved his head and is a practicing Buddhist. The unlikely pair begins a relationship that is not exactly friendship. Michael goes by his spiritual name "Jinsen" and during a joint effort on a classroom project Justin learns the basics of being a Buddhist. He also begins to emerge as his own person. Problems arise when "Jinsen" is taunted and physically threatened by classmates, a situation that has Justin making a decision to help out. The important theme of religious acceptance has merit for a wide range of readers.

GRADES: 9–12

REVIEWS: *Booklist* 2/15/03, *Kirkus* 1/01/03, *Publishers Weekly* 1/06/03, *SLJ* 2/03, *VOYA* 4/03

Konigsburg, E. L. *Silent to the Bone.* 272 p. TR. Simon & Schuster Children's Publishing. 978-0-689-83601-5. 2001. $23.95. LB. Perma-Bound Books. 978-0-605-21710-2. 2000. $12.99. RE. San Val, Incorporated. 978-0-613-73424-0. 2004. $16.00. PB. Simon & Schuster Children's Publishing. 978-0-689-86715-6. 2004. $6.99. PB. Simon & Schuster Children's Publishing. 978-0-689-83602-2. 2002. $5.99. CASS. Random House Audio Publishing Group. 978-0-8072-8740-8. 2004. $32.00. LP. Thorndike Press. 978-0-7862-3169-0. 2001. $23.95.

Conner Kane's best friend, Branwell Zamborska, refuses to speak and his silence lands him in a facility for troubled teens. Branwell witnessed his baby half-sister Nikki dropped and abused. She's in critical condition and Branwell is accused of being the one who harmed her. The truth will not be revealed if he continues to hold his tongue. Conner stands by his friend and devises a system of flash cards of names and places, hoping Branwell will react to the prompts. His "interviews" with Branwell will slowly uncover what really happened. Branwell is a victim of false accusation and Conner comes to realize the power of friendship. Both middle and younger high school students will be intrigued by the two boys' determination to solve Branwell's situation.

GRADES: 7–10

REVIEWS: *Publishers Weekly* 3/25/02

AWARDS: BBYA Top Ten

Koss, Amy Goldman. *Side Effects.* 144 p. TR. Roaring Brook Press. 978-1-59643-294-9. 2006. $16.95. TR. Roaring Brook Press. 978-1-4287-0203-5. 2006. N/A.

Isabella begins this novel as a typical fourteen-year-old who worries about school, friends, and gaining weight. A discovery of enlarged neck glands leads to a diagnosis of Hodgkin's lymphoma, changing Isabella's innocent world to one dominated by cancer. Her friends fade away and chemotherapy, hair loss, and nausea become daily events in her life. Throughout her battle, Isabella's voice rings honest and frank, a trait that will engage most readers.

GRADES: 9–12

REVIEWS: *Booklist* 9/15/06, *Kirkus* 9/01/06, *Publishers Weekly* 2/11/06, *SLJ* 9/06, *VOYA* 10/06

Krech, Bob. *Rebound.* 271 p. TR. Marshall Cavendish Corporation. 978-0-7614-5319-2. 2006. $16.99.

A racially divided town has a pre-determined concept of what activities are available to different teenagers. When seventeen-year-old Ray Wisniewski tries out for varsity basketball, he is told that white Polish kids should be wrestling. It's an unwritten "rule" that basketball is for the black kids and a sprinkling of players from the rich white neighborhood. Krech's story shows a way that racism can worm its way to subtle acceptance, until Ray challenges the status quo. This problem novel involving sports will appeal to high school teens, especially boys.

GRADES: 9–12

REVIEWS: *Booklist* 9/01/06, *Kirkus* 9/15/06, *SLJ* 12/06, *VOYA* 12/06

Larbalestier, Justine. *Liar.* 384 p. TR. Bloomsbury Publishing. 978-1-59990-305-7. 2009. $16.99. CD. Brilliance Audio. 978-1-4418-0200-2. 2009. $29.95.

Short-haired Micah is mistaken for a boy, a situation that allows her to interact with boys differently. Micah is an accomplished runner but is also a prolific liar. She has after-school hookups with Zach, a boy who is later found brutally murdered. Micah tells a story that pivots on a specific twist turning it into a deep fantasy tale, or not. It all depends on whether readers believe Micah. Remember, she is a liar. Teenage girls will be thrilled with Micah's issues, but the violence steers this title toward high school readership.

GRADES: 9–12

REVIEWS: *Booklist* 9/01/09, *Publishers Weekly* 8/24/09, *SLJ* 10/09, *VOYA* 12/09

Levine, Kristine. *The Best Bad Luck I Ever Had.* 272 p. TR. Penguin Group (USA) Incorporated. 978-0-399-25090-3. 2009. $16.99.

It's 1917 and in the rural Alabama town of Moundville a new postmaster is due to arrive. Twelve-year-old Harry "Dit" Sims hopes a boy his age will be part of the new family. What happens is that an African American man comes to town and with this new mailman is his daughter Emma Walker. Dit and Emma begin a friendship that challenges the racial mind-set of the times. This deceiving story begins as a right of passage to adolescence, but also packs a punch when adults assert their racial prejudices in an ugly way. This is a fine example of a story in which young teens are the more logical and level-headed characters. This is an important book to introduce to middle school readers.

GRADES: 6–8

REVIEWS: *Booklist* 11/15/08, *Kirkus* 12/08, *Publishers Weekly* 2/15/08, *SLJ* 1/09, *VOYA* 4/09

Lockhart, E. *The Disreputable History of Frankie Landau-Banks.* 502 p. TR. Thorndike Press. 978-1-4104-1439-7. 2009. $23.95. TR. Hyperion Press. 978-0-7868-3818-9. 2008. $16.99. PB. Hyperion Press. 978-0-7868-3819-6. 2009. $8.99. CD. Brilliance Audio. 978-1-4233-6680-5. 2008. $29.95. PLAY. Findaway World, LLC. 978-1-60640-890-2. 2008. $64.99. CASS. Brilliance Audio. 978-1-4233-6679-9. 2008. $16.99. EB. Brilliance Audio. 978-1-4233-6684-3. 2008. $24.95.

Frankie Landau-Banks is a girl who decides to challenge the old boys' network at her school, Alabaster Prep. During the summer between her freshman and sophomore years, Frankie's body blossoms and her newly developed figure attracts the attention of Matthew. He is a member of the Loyal Order of the Basset Hounds, an all-male secret society. An old mystery intrigues Frankie and she begins a guerilla assault on the Order and turns the tables on the guys with a series of elaborate pranks. Woven throughout the story are themes of economic privilege, gender, and power.

GRADES: 9–12

REVIEWS: *Booklist* 1/08, *Kirkus* 2/01/08, *Publishers Weekly* 1/07/08, *SLJ* 3/08, *VOYA* 12/07

AWARDS: Printz Honor, Teens' Top Ten

Lockhart, E. *Dramarama.* 320 p. TR. Hyperion Books for Children. 978-0-7868-3815-8. 2007. $15.99. TR. Hyperion Press. 978-1-4287-4612-1. 2007. N/A. PB. Hyperion Press. 978-0-7868-3817-2. 2008. $7.99. CD. Brilliance Audio. 978-1-4233-6724-6. 2008. $29.99. PLAY. Findaway World, LLC. 978-1-60640-786-8. 2008. $59.99. EB. Brilliance Audio. 978-1-4233-6729-1. 2008. $39.25.

Sadye and Demi (a.k.a. Sarah and Douglas) are best friends and the only people in their small Ohio town who know and appreciate theater. When they latch onto a summer camp for the performing arts, they both feel they will take over the camp and grab the spotlight. What the aggressive and intolerant Sadye doesn't realize is that her talent is limited and the quieter Demi is the one who shines. The problem is Sadye's refusal to be joyous for her supposedly best friend Demi's success. Several sexual situations nudge this title toward high school readers.

GRADES: 9–12

REVIEWS: *Booklist* 4/01/07, *Publishers Weekly* 4/30/07, *SLJ* 7/07, *VOYA* 6/07

MacCready, Robin. *Buried.* 208 p. TR. Penguin Group (USA) Incorporated. 978-0-525-47724-2. 2006. $16.99.

Set in a rural area of Maine, seventeen-year-old Claudine shares a trailer with her alcoholic mother. Her party-minded mom has gone off somewhere and Claudine wakes up to a filthy trailer. She begins an obsessive need to keep things in order and completely clean. Claudine feels pulled in many directions and her usual good work at school begins to unravel. Adults in the town are curious as to how much longer her mother will be away and if Claudine's obsessive-compulsive behavior will lead to exhaustion. Teens of a wide range of ages will be riveted by Claudine's problem and MacCready's plot will keep readers guessing until the last few pages.

GRADES: 7–10

REVIEWS: *Booklist* 10/01/06, *Kirkus* 7/15/06, *SLJ* 11/06, *VOYA* 10/06

Marchetta, Melina. *Jellicoe Road.* 432 p. TR. HarperCollins Publishers. 978-0-06-143183-8. 2008. $17.99. LB. HarperCollins Publishers. 978-0-06-143184-5. 2008. $18.89.

An Australian community is the setting of a conflict between three factions struggling for control over the area. Taylor Markham is the heir to the Underground Community, which is one of the three groups struggling for control. Pitted against the Cadets and the Townies, the conflict becomes a serious negotiation of land and property. Eventually Taylor finds information about her mother who left Taylor when she was eleven. The involved saga is complicated but will appeal to older readers willing to accept a challenge in their reading.

GRADES: 9–12

REVIEWS: *Booklist* 11/01/08, *Kirkus* 8/01/08, *SLJ* 12/08, *VOYA* 12/08

AWARDS: Printz Winner

Marchetta, Melina. *Saving Francesca.* 256 p. TR. Random House Children's Books. 978-0-375-82982-6. 2004. $15.95. LB. Random House Children's Books. 978-0-375-92982-3. 2004. $17.99. RE. San Val, Incorporated. 978-1-4177-6440-2. 2006. $19.60. LB. Perma-Bound Books. 978-0-605-01361-2. 2003. $15.95. LP. Thorndike Press. 978-0-7862-7309-6. 2005. $22.95.

> After transferring to a former all-boys school, sixteen-year-old Francesca struggles with adapting to the new atmosphere. Balanced with humorous scenes of both the guys and girls adjusting to a co-ed situation is Francesca's concern with her mother's depression. Marchetta's Australian backdrop comes alive when Francesca begins a journey to find herself and also understand her father's distress over her mother's seemingly hopeless situation. Both middle school and high school girls will feel a bond with Francesca as she tries to sort out her life.

GRADES: 9–12

REVIEWS: *Booklist* 10/01/04, *Kirkus* 9/01/04, *Publishers Weekly* 9/06/04, *SLJ* 9/04, *VOYA* 10/04

AWARDS: BBYA Top Ten

McCaughrean, Geraldine. *The White Darkness.* 373 p. TR. HarperCollins Publishers. 978-0-06-089035-3. 2007. $16.99. TR. HarperCollins Publishers. 978-0-06-089036-0. 2007. $18.89. PB. HarperCollins Publishers. 978-0-06-089037-7. 2009. $8.99. CD. BBC Audiobooks America. 978-1-4056-5557-6. 2006. $69.95.

> Symone has a hearing disability and shuns contact with boys. In fact, her only "friend" is Captain Laurence "Titus" Oates, a dead victim of Scott's 1912 expedition to the South Pole. When Symone's Uncle Victor tricks Symone into accompanying him on their own expedition to Antarctica, the girl agrees. What she doesn't know is her uncle's psychopathic determination to delve deep into the brutal cold of the continent. Symone is challenged to survive the elements and can rely only on advice from Titus to guide her. This thrilling tale will appeal to many teens, both male and female.

GRADES: 9–12

REVIEWS: *Booklist* 12/01/06, *Kirkus* 12/01/06, *Publishers Weekly* 1/22/07, *SLJ* 4/07, *VOYA* 2/07

AWARDS: Printz Winner

McDonald, Janet. *Spellbound.* 144 p. TR. Farrar, Straus & Giroux. 978-0-374-37140-1. 2001. $16.00. LB. Perma-Bound Books. 978-0-605-01245-5. 2001. $12.99. RE. San Val, Incorporated. 978-0-613-86523-4. 2003. $16.00.

Raven Jefferson finds her plans to get out of the projects after her high school graduation derailed. After a one-night stand with a guy, she is now a new mother changing diapers instead of planning her future. When her older sister hears about "Spell Success" she encourages Raven to enter the contest. Raven buckles down to study and is determined to win the scholarship awarded to the winner. McDonald's story shows the layered challenges facing many inner-city teens. Adults working with African American youth should consider this novel as a group read for multiple ages.

GRADES: 7–10

REVIEWS: *Kirkus* 11/15/01, *Booklist* 11/01/01, *Publishers Weekly* 11/19/01, *SLJ* 9/01, *VOYA* 10/01

McNamee, Graham. *Acceleration.* N/A. LB. Perma-Bound Books. 978-0-605-01305-6. 2003. $13.50. RE. San Val, Incorporated. 978-1-4176-7555-5. 2005. $16.60. PB. Random House Children's Books. 978-0-440-23836-2. 2005. $6.99. CD. Random House Audio Publishing Group. 978-0-605-01305-6. 2005. $45.00. CASS. Random House Audio Publishing Group. 978-0-307-20732-6. 2005. $35.00.

Duncan lives in Toronto and the seventeen-year-old is totally bored with his summer job at the lost and found office of the subway system. When the lost diary of a serial killer comes to his attention, Duncan feels he must intervene and save a woman's life. The police offer no help, so Duncan stalks the killer by himself. This title could easily fit into a suspense category, but it is placed as a problem novel because of Duncan's past resurfacing and his urge to save someone . . . if he can. If adults want teens to be engaged with a novel, this is a sure bet.

GRADES: 9–12

REVIEWS: *Kirkus* 9/15/03, *Publishers Weekly* 11/10/03, *SLJ* 11/03, *VOYA* 12/03

McNamee, Graham. *Hate You.* No formats available in print.

Seventeen-year-old Alice had her life changed ten years ago when her father grabbed her by the throat and squeezed so hard her voice is now permanently damaged. Her mother kicked him out and the pair now lives a satisfying life with zero contact from Alice's father. Out of the blue, her father's girlfriend calls and asks Alice to meet him. He's dying of cancer. McNamee's slim novel is all about forgiveness versus revenge. Alice's conflict to decide about reconnecting with her father is one sure to interest teenage girls from blended families who will understand alienation from a biological parent.

GRADES: 8–12

REVIEWS: *Booklist* 2/01/99, *Kirkus* 12/01/99, *Publishers Weekly* 1/11/99, *SLJ* 3/99, *VOYA* 4/99

Mowry, Jess. *Babylon Boyz.* 192 p. TR. Simon & Schuster Children's Publishing. 978-0-689-80839-5. 1997. $28.00. PB. Simon & Schuster Children's Publishing. 978-0-689-82592-7. 1999. $10.95.

Dante and his crew navigate the tough inner-city streets of Oakland, California. When the fourteen-year-old and his friends have a suitcase packed with cocaine literally land at their feet, a decision must be made. Should they sell the stuff and make money? That would further destroy their neighborhood. They have to decide what to do quickly as the adults will stop at nothing to get the product back. The gritty dialogue matches perfectly with the situation. Dante and his homeless friends rely on each other, and their intricate plan of revenge is sure to make older readers keep turning the pages.

GRADES: 9–12

REVIEWS: *Booklist* 2/15/97, *Kirkus* 4/15/97, *Publishers Weekly* 2/03/97, *SLJ* 9/97, *VOYA* 3/97

Na, An. *A Step from Heaven.* 160 p. PB. Penguin Group (USA) Incorporated. 978-0-14-250027-9. 2003. $7.99. CD. Random House Audio Publishing Group. 978-0-8072-1612-5. 2004. $35.00. EB. Random House Audio Publishing Group. 978-0-7393-6000-2. N/A. $38.00.

When she was only four years old, Young Ju and her parents emigrated from Korea to California by plane and the child believed she was flying to heaven. Now as a young woman about to enter college, the American dream is something short of heavenly. Problems facing immigrants such as language barriers, dealing with the government bureaucracy. and working to make ends meet are commonplace. The realism portrayed is the abusive and alcoholic father frustrated about not providing for his family. Sophisticated writing sets this title for high school readers.

GRADES: 9–12

REVIEWS: *Booklist* 6/01/01, *Publishers Weekly* 4/02/01, *SLJ* 5/01, *VOYA* 6/01

AWARDS: Printz Winner

Osa, Nancy. *Cuba 15.* 288 p. LB. Random House Children's Books. 978-0-385-90086-7. 2003. $17.99. RE. San Val, Incorporated. 978-1-4177-3377-4. 2005. $19.65. PB. Random House Children's Books. 978-0-385-73233-8. 2005. $8.99.

Violet Paz, a sophomore living near Chicago, spends most of a year preparing for her quincea-ero, the celebration of her womanhood. Violet uses humor to fend off problems of her father not acknowledging their Cuban culture while her grandmother insists the family stick to tradition. Violet is a teen with each foot in two very different cultures and she has problems accepting a place in either of them. Nancy Osa creates a witty voice in Violet that will engage younger readers while showing them problems families have when leaving their homelands and settling in the United States.

GRADES: 7–10

REVIEWS: *Booklist* 7/01/03, *Kirkus* 6/01/03, *Publishers Weekly* 6/23/03, *SLJ* 6/03, *VOYA* 6/03

Paterson, Katherine. *Jacob Have I Loved.* 224 p. TR. HarperCollins Publishers. 978-0-690-04078-4. 1980. $16.99. LB. Perma-Bound Books. 978-0-8479-7650-8. 1980. $13.50. RE. San Val, Incorporated. 978-0-88103-923-8. 1999. $17.20. LB. HarperCollins Publishers. 978-0-690-04079-1. 1980. $17.89. PB. HarperCollins Publishers. 978-0-06-440368-9. 1990. $6.99. PB. HarperCollins Publishers. 978-0-380-56499-6. 1981. $2.95. CD. Recorded Books, LLC. 978-0-7887-4217-0. 2000. $45.00. PLAY. Findaway World, LLC. 978-1-60252-759-1. 2007. $34.99. EB. Harper Collins Publishers. 978-0-06-183276-5. 2009. $6.99. LP. LRS. 978-1-58118-073-2. 2000. $29.95.

Louise and Caroline are twin sisters who are very different. Louise is older while Caroline is the beloved and pampered younger sister. Life on the tiny island is harsh with very little money. Still, their parents make sure Caroline has her music classes and her education. Louise retreats into herself and builds a defense against the hurt from the attention Caroline gathers. Katherine Paterson's story often appears on recommended school reading lists for middle school readers and up.

GRADES: 8–10

AWARDS: Newbery Winner

Pearsall, Shelley. *All of the Above.* 234 p. TR. Perfection Learning Corporation. 978-0-7569-8144-0. 2008. $13.65. PB. Little, Brown Books for Young Readers. 978-0-316-11526-1. 2008. $5.99. EB. Little, Brown Books for Young Readers. 978-0-316-05590-1. 2008. $5.99.

A group of poverty-stricken inner-city teenagers finds themselves challenged by their math teacher to construct the world's largest tetrahedron structure. Alternating voices reveal the cast of teens who initially have no hope but do buy into the vision that gives them goals and hope for their futures. This novel is based on an actual situation that happened in Cleveland schools. For African American students in that school district, this will be a classic for many years.

GRADES: 6–12

REVIEWS: *Booklist* 9/01/06, *Kirkus* 7/15/06, *SLJ* 9/06

Pearson, Mary E. *A Room on Lorelei Street.* 272 p. TR. Henry Holt & Company. 978-0-8050-7667-7. 2005. $16.95. PB. Square Fish. 978-0-312-38019-9. 2008. $7.99.

Zoe is seventeen and fed up with being responsible for her alcoholic mother. She figures it's time to make it on her own and takes money from her waitress job and rents a room in an old house on Lorelei Street. She wants to be alone and independent, but that is not so easy. Like any teen, Zoe makes poor decisions but her acts are compounded by her self-supporting situation. This is a story about survival, not against nature but against family problems that may be too severe for one person to handle, no matter how independent she is. Harsh language and an alarming sexual encounter will pull in high school readers.

GRADES: 9–12

REVIEWS: *Booklist* 6/01/05, *Kirkus* 5/15/05, *SLJ* 8/05, *VOYA* 6/05

Pfeffer, Susan Beth. *The Year Without Michael.* CASS. Recorded Books, LLC. 978-0-7887-1112-1. 1997. $35.00.

Sixteen-year-old Jody Chapman's younger brother, Michael, has disappeared. He never made it home from a softball field and now the family is disintegrating before Jody's eyes. Her parents barely speak to each other and her sister is angry and bitter. Jody's friends have adopted a hands-off attitude. All they seem to be able to do is wait and hope that Michael returns. But Jody's need to find him leads to a last-ditch effort that she hopes will keep her family together. This heart-breaking story is not explicit but still gives a strong emotional slam to the heart.

GRADES: 8–12

Picoult, Jodi. *My Sister's Keeper.* 448 p. TR. Simon & Schuster. 978-0-7434-5453-7. 2005. $16.00. TR. Simon & Schuster. 978-0-7434-5452-0. 2004. $26.95. RE. San Val, Incorporated. 978-1-4176-7598-2. 2005. $28.20. CD. Recorded Books, LLC. 978-1-4193-6437-2. 2005. $29.99. CASS. Recorded Books, LLC. 978-1-4025-7321-7. 2004. $34.99.

Although marketed as an adult novel, *My Sister's Keeper* had tremendous teen appeal. Kate Fitzgerald has a rare form of leukemia and her younger sister Anna was conceived to provide a donor match to keep Kate alive. Now age thirteen, Anna no longer wishes to fulfill her assigned role and refuses to donate a kidney to Kate. This emotional tale will have teens reading long into the night to discover why Anna has made her decision. Secondary characters are equally as fascinating and the story explodes on the very last page. This book is for mature readers.

GRADES: 9–12

REVIEWS: *Booklist* 1/01/04, *Kirkus* 1/15/04, *Publishers Weekly* 2/16/04, *SLJ* 1/05, *VOYA* 12/04

AWARDS: Alex Award, Teens' Top Ten

Plum-Ucci, Carol. *The Body of Christopher Creed.* N/A. RE. San Val, Incorporated. 978-0-613-49392-5. 2001. $17.20. PB. Houghton Mifflin Harcourt Trade & Reference Publishers. 978-0-15-206386-3. 2008. $6.95. PB. Hyperion Books for Children. 978-0- 7868-1641-5. 2001. $6.99. CASS. Recorded Books, LLC. 978-1-4025-0956-8. N/A. $54.00. EB. Recorded Books, LLC. 978-1-4237-3338-6. N/A. $1.00.

When class freak Chris Creed suddenly disappears, his classmates seem to be only mildly curious. Did he run away, commit suicide, or is he a victim of a crime? Sixteen-year-old Torey Adams stews about the disappearance and feels guilty because he failed to stop the bullying directed at Chris. Determined to find the truth, Torey takes several chances and finds himself the subject of vicious gossip. The problem of what happened to Chris Creed eats at Torey until he finally embarks on a stunning late-night search for the body. This problem novel is about carrying guilt and feeling remorseful after a situation has occurred. The story's intensity marks it as one for the high school crowd.

GRADES: 9–12

REVIEWS: *Kirkus* 5/15/00, *Publishers Weekly* 5/22/00, *SLJ* 7/00, *VOYA* 8/00

AWARDS: Printz Honor

Porter, Connie. *Imani All Mine.* 224 p. TR. Houghton Mifflin Harcourt Trade & Reference Publishers. 978-0-618-05678-1. 2000. $12.95. TR. Perfection Learning Corporation. 978-0-7569-3390-6. 2000. $20.60. RE. San Val, Incorporated. 978-0-613-23730-7. 2000. $24.45.

Tasha is fifteen years old and an honors student living in the Buffalo projects. She dreams of attending college and escaping the bleak conditions of her apartment home. That is, until an awful situation falls into place and Tasha is raped and then gives birth to her daughter Imani. The young mother is determined she will give her baby a good future in spite of the poverty, drugs, gangs, and ignorance surrounding her. But these problems are too large even for Tasha's generous heart. Violence, harsh language, and gritty street realism are elements of this book with wide appeal to high school students living in the inner cities of America.

GRADES: 9–12

REVIEWS: *Booklist* 1/01/99, *Kirkus* 12/01/98, *Publishers Weekly* 11/15/98, *SLJ* 1/00

AWARDS: Alex Award, BBYA Top Ten

Portman, Frank. *King Dork.* 368 p. PB. Random House Children's Books. 978-0-385-73450-9. 2008. $8.99. CD. Random House Audio Publishing Group. 978-0-7393-3113-2. 2006. $48.00. CD. Random House Audio Publishing Group. 978-0-7393-3125-5. 2006. $55.00. EB. Random House Audio Publishing Group. 978-0-7393-6006-4. N/A. $85.00.

Sophomore Tom Henderson's problem is that he's bored with pseudo-AP classes. To engage his mind he enlists the help of his best friend to invent bands including a name, songs, cover art, and so forth. This is slacker fiction about a guy who just doesn't fit in and that is a "problem" that will resonate with many teen readers. Mature situations and casual sexual experiences suggest an older teen audience.

GRADES: 10–12

REVIEWS: *Booklist* 5/15/06, *Kirkus* 5/15/06, *Publishes Weekly* 3/13/06, *SLJ* 4/06, *VOYA* 4/06

Rapp, Adam. *33 Snowfish.* N/A. LB. Perma-Bound Books. 978-0-605-01340-7. 2003. $13.99. RE. San Val, Incorporated. 978-1-4177-2732-2. 2006. $17.20.

This is a dark tale about a group of runaways who are more understanding of hatred and violence than love. Custis is an orphan fleeing his "owner," a producer of pornography. Custis is accompanied by Curl, a child prostitute, and her boyfriend, Boobie, who has just murdered his parents and kidnapped his baby brother to sell on the streets. The loose band travels from town to town stealing and scavenging. This startling story shows the disturbing results of adult abuse and exploitation thrust upon young people. This powerful book is definitely for a high school and older audience.

GRADES: 9–12

REVIEWS: *Kirkus* 2/01/03, *Publishers Weekly* 1/13/03, *SLJ* 4/03, *VOYA* 4/03
AWARDS: BBYA Top Ten

Rapp, Adam. *Under the Wolf, Under the Dog.* 320 p. TR. Candlewick Press 978-0-7636-1818-6. 2004. $16.99. LB. Perma-Bound Books. 978-0-605-64427-4. 2004. $23.99. PB. Candlewick Press. 978-0-7636-3365-3. 2007. $8.99.

Sixteen-year-old Steve Nugent has endured a variety of problems. His mother's death, his older brother's suicide, and his father's depression have all contributed to his erratic behavior. In Rapp's novel, Steve tells readers of all these events that brought him to Burnstone Grove, a therapeutic facility for teens with substance abuse issues and suicidal tendencies. Steve is a teen dealing with all these issues while trying to grow up as normal as possible. Rapp's work is realistic and the narrative doesn't flinch when describing gruesome scenes, especially when Steve finds his brother's body. Certainly not a book for everyone, but teens may very well find someone with more serious problems than their own in Steve Nugent.

GRADES: 10–12

REVIEWS: *Booklist* 11/15/04, *Kirkus* 9/15/04, *SLJ* 10/04, *VOYA* 12/04

AWARDS: BBYA Top Ten

Resau, Laura. *Red Glass.* 288 p. TR. Random House Children's Books. 978-0-385-73466-0. 2007. $15.99. LB. Random House Children's Books. 978-0-385-90464-3. 2007. $18.99. PB. Random House Children's Books. 978-0-440-24025-9. 2009. $8.99. CD. Random House Audio Publishing Group. 978-0-7393-7976-9. 2009. $45.00.

A Mexican refugee, Pablito, brings to motion a series of life-changing events for sixteen-year-old Sophie. Sophie becomes attached to Pablito, a five-year-old whose parents died during their illegal border crossing. Sophie suffers from anxiety attacks, but her relationship and determination to help the little boy has her gaining confidence. Silent since arriving at Sophie's home, Pablito finally utters the name of his home village, prompting Sophie to take the boy back to find his relatives. Sophie's problems are both emotional and physical and her battle to overcome them is the strength of the story. Teens will also become aware of the plight of young people entering the country without a family network.

GRADES: 8–12

REVIEWS: *Booklist* 9/15/07, *Kirkus* 8/15/07, *Publishers Weekly* 10/01/07, *SLJ* 10/07, *VOYA* 8/07

Resau, Laura. *What the Moon Saw.* 272 p. PB. Random House Children's Books. 978-0-440-23957-4. 2008. $5.99. LP. Thorndike Press. 978-0-7862-9278-3. 2007. $22.95.

Fourteen-year-old Clara Luna journeys to rural Mexico for a summer visit with her grandparents whom she has never met. During her stay, Clara discovers a strong connection to her heritage. Clara's father had entered the United States as an illegal immigrant years before and never told his daughter about the rural life he left behind. Throughout the story, Clara becomes aware of her connection to her grandmother and finds joy in the simple rural lifestyle. She also becomes fond of Pedro, a neighboring goat herder. Clara is a teen facing the problem of her hidden past, a task that will engage younger readers.

GRADES: 7–10

REVIEWS: *Booklist* 10/15/06, *Kirkus* 9/01/06, *SLJ* 9/06, *VOYA* 10/06

Runyon, Brent. *Surface Tension: A Novel in Four Parts.* 208 p. TR. Alfred A. Knopf Incorporated. 978-0-375-84446-1. 2009. $16.99. LB. Alfred A. Knopf Incorporated. 978-0-375-94446-8. 2009. $19.99.

Spread over four summers, this novel shows the maturing process of Luke, initially a fourteen-year-old guy who each summer spends a two-week vacation with his parents. The lake cottage shifts from a world of natural wonders to something that is corny and an interruption of Luke's independence. Luke rebels against his parents and becomes interested in his childhood friend, Claire, who is also growing up. The story shows rather than tells how a boy can change from an angst-ridden brat to a heroic young man when a tragedy occurs. The sophisticated style will be better appreciated by older teens.

GRADES: 9–12

REVIEWS: *Booklist* 2/15/09, *Kirkus* 2/01/09, *Publishers Weekly* 2/23/09, *SLJ* 4/09, *VOYA* 8/09

Sachar, Louis. *Holes.* 272 p. TR. Farrar, Straus & Giroux. 978-0-374-33266-2. 2008. $18.00. TR. Book Wholesalers, Incorporated. 978-0-7587-0192-3. 2002. $15.00. LB. San Val, Incorporated. 978-0-613-87297-3. 2001. $14.75. RE. San Val, Incorporated. 978-0-613-87800-5. 2003. $17.20. LB. Perma-Bound Books. 978-0-605-81560-5. 1998. $13.50. PB. Random House Children's Books. 978-0-440-41946-4. 2003. $6.99. PB. Random House Children's Books. 978-0-440-22859-2. 2001. $6.99. CD. Random House Audio Publishing Group. 978-0-7393-3176-7. 2006. $19.95. CD. Random House Audio Publishing Group. 978-0-8072-8611-1. 2004. $32.30. CASS. Books on Tape, Incorporated. 978-0-7366-9104-8. 2000. $24.00. EB. Random House Audio Publishing Group. 978-0-7393-4442-2. N/A. $32.30. LP. Thorndike Press . 978-0-7862-6190-1. 2003. $10.95.

Holes is a title that has become an instant classic. Teachers and adults working with teens recommend this title as it fits such a wide range of readers. Stanley Yelnats has been sentenced to a camp for juvenile defenders for a crime he did not commit. The camp is a front that covers for adults determined to locate a treasure rumored to be hidden somewhere nearby. The young inmates are forced to dig a series of holes that resemble graves, but they are actually unknowingly probing the ground for treasure. Of course the problem here is false accusation and abusive adults. Laced with humor and also a thrilling mystery, this title hits on all cylinders for both male and female readers of a wide span of ages.

GRADES: 6–10

REVIEWS: *Booklist* 6/01/98, *Kirkus* 6/98, *Publishers Weekly* 7/15/98, *SLJ* 9/98, *VOYA* 12/08

AWARDS: Newbery Winner

Sapphire. *Push.* 192 p. TR. Knopf Doubleday Publishing Group. 978-0-679-76675-9. 1997. $12.95. TR. San Val, Incorporated. 978-1-4176-2627-4. 1997. $23.30.

Precious Jones endures a grim life by being bullied by her sexually abusive mother, Clareece. Overweight and HIV-positive, Precious is pregnant for the second time with her father's child. Her voice is moving and powerful. She names her first child Mongo, "...short for Mongoloid Down Sinder, which is what she is; sometimes what I feel I is. I feel so stupid sometimes. So ugly, worth nuffin." Hope finally comes from a social worker but Precious faces an uphill struggle each day. Sexual abuse and alarming abusive behavior designates this story strictly for mature teen readers.

GRADES: 11–12

REVIEWS: *Kirkus* 4/15/96, *Publishers Weekly* 4/22/96

Scott, Elizabeth. *Living Dead Girl.* 176 p. TR. Simon & Schuster Children's Publishing. 978-1-4169-6059-1. 2008. $16.99. CD. Brilliance Audio. 978-1-4233-9750-2. 2009. $19.99. CD. Brilliance Audio. 978-1-4233-9751-9. 2009. $49.97.

Elizabeth Scott's slim novel is a moving and powerful story of a teenage girl who has existed as a sex slave for the past five years. Now called Alice, the girl who used to be known as Kyla, is in fear of doing something wrong and attracting the negative attention of Ray, the guy who routinely rapes her and wants her to remain a pre-adolescent girl. Alice's dilemma is that Ray, who doesn't care for Alice's developing body, orders her to find a replacement sex partner for him. Alice's voice is clinical and without emotion, making the narrative even more horrifying. This simple story has a complicated ending and will be emotionally wrenching for younger readers.

GRADES: 9–12

REVIEWS: *Kirkus* 8/15/08, *Publishers Weekly* 9/08/08, *SLJ* 10/08, *VOYA* 2/09

Scott, Elizabeth. *Stealing Heaven.* 320 p. TR. HarperCollins Publishers. 978-0-06-112280-4. 2008. $16.99. LB. HarperCollins Publishers. 978-0-06-112281-1. 2008. $17.89. PB. HarperCollins Publishers. 978-0-06-112282-8. 2009. $8.99.

Danielle has led a secret life for years. Always on the move from town to town with her sexy mother, the pair stakes out expensive homes and schemes to steal the silver. Her mother uses her sexuality to gain information about the locals, but Danielle is fed up with the danger. When they hit the small resort town of Heaven, Danielle feels it is time to settle down. Using the name "Sydney" she makes friends with the town cop, against the specific rules laid down by her mother. This problem novel shows a girl ready to break away from her dysfunctional mother, yet she still feels loyal to her. Some mild comments about sex are mentioned early on, but both middle and high school readers will be fascinated by Danielle's struggle for independence.

GRADES: 9–12

REVIEWS: *Booklist* 4/15/08, *Kirkus* 5/15/08, *SLJ* 8/08

Sebold, Alice. *The Lovely Bones.* 336 p. TR. Little, Brown & Company. 978-0-316-66634-3. 2002. $21.95. LB. Perma-Bound Books. 978-0-605-55816-8. 2002. $20.95. RE. San Val, Incorporated. 978-1-4176-2234-4. 2004. $25.75. CD. Hachette Audio. 978-1-60024-068-3. 2007. $24.98. CD. Recorded Books, LLC. 978-1-4025-3290-0. 2004. $29.99. CASS. Recorded Books, LLC. 978-1-4025-2115-7. 2002. $29.99. EB. Little, Brown & Company. 978-0-316-01549-3. 2007. $16.99.

Fourteen-year-old Suzy Salmon is murdered in this novel's first chapter. She will forever remain that age. The rest of the story is told through Suzy's eyes as a ghost who observes her family grieve. She also watches the boy who she kissed for the first time, who now represents her lost hopes. Suzy is the only character who can identify her killer. This novel was written for adults, but also has tremendous teen appeal. It is a coming-of-age story about a girl unable to grow up. It shows the problems of family grief and Suzy's longing to return to Earth. The sophisticated plot marks this title as one for high school readers.

GRADES: 9–12

REVIEWS: *Booklist* 5/01/02, *Kirkus* 5/01/02, *Publishers Weekly* 6/17/02, *SLJ* 10/02, *VOYA* 12/02

Sones, Sonya. *One of Those Hideous Books Where the Mother Dies.* 272 p. TR. Simon & Schuster Children's Publishing. 978-0-689-85820-8. 2004. $16.95. RE. San Val, Incorporated. 978-1-4176-9517-1. 1989. $18.40. PB. Simon & Schuster Children's Publishing. 978-1-4169-0788-6. 2005. $7.99.

Fifteen-year-old Ruby Milliken is on a journey flying to meet with her father whom she really doesn't know that well. Her mother has died and she is unsure of her future with her father who happens to be a famous movie star in California. Ruby pours out her feelings in e-mails to her best friend, her boyfriend, and especially to her deceased mother. Ruby's voice is authentic and teens of a wide age range will embrace her feelings of self-doubt.

GRADES: 8–12

REVIEWS: *Booklist* 5/01/04, *Publishers Weekly* 6/21/04, *SLJ* 8/04, *VOYA* 10/04

Sones, Sonya. *Stop Pretending: What Happened When My Big Sister Went Crazy.* N/A. LB. San Val, Incorporated. 978-0-613-34979-6. 2001. $15.25. LB. HarperCollins Publishers. 978-0-06-028386-5. 1999. $14.89. PB. HarperCollins Publishers. 978- 0-06-446218-1. 2001. $7.99.

Thirteen-year-old Cookie relates the events of her older sister's nervous breakdown. Presented as a novel in verse, Cookie tells of the effects on her parents and herself of her sister being placed in an institution. She fears she also will have a breakdown. Believing something is terribly wrong, Cookie's friends shun her and her parents' marriage begins to crumble under the strain. The problems here are serious and Sones' novel shines a light on the often ignored families of the mentally ill.

GRADES: 9–12

REVIEWS: *Booklist* 11/15/99, *Kirkus* 10/01/99, *SLJ* 10/99

AWARDS: Quick Picks Top Ten

Spinelli, Jerry. *Maniac Magee.* N/A. TR. Book Wholesalers, Incorporated. 978-0-7587-0201-2. 2002. $13.15. TR. Pathways Publishing. 978-1-58303-050-9. 1998. $15.95. LB. Perma-Bound Books. 978-0-7804-2316-9. 1990. $13.99. RE. San Val, Incorporated. 978-0-8335-8556-1. 1990. $17.20. PB. Little, Brown Books for Young Readers. 978-0-316-80906-1. 1999. $6.99. PB. Scholastic, Incorporated. 978-0-590-36644-1. 1997. $3.95. CD. Random House Audio Publishing Group. 978-0-307-24318-8. 2005. $19.95. CD. Random House Audio Publishing Group. 978-0-8072-1166-3. 2004. $32.30. CASS. Pharaoh Audiobooks. 978-1-882209-10-1. N/A. $15.95. EB. Random House Audio Publishing Group. 978-0-7393-4449-1. N/A. $32.30. LP. Thorndike Press. 978-0-7862-6356-1. 2004. $10.95.

Jeffrey Magee is a homeless youth who has left the troubled home of his aunt and uncle. His yearlong flight becomes stuff of legend. Because of his extraordinary athletic ability and his knack of suddenly popping into situations, he's nicknamed Maniac. Spinelli's parable shows readers that Maniac's fame allows him to cross over between two strictly segregated areas of town. He makes friends and enemies but he has the ability and charisma to soften the lines of racism. Maniac Magee is an extended metaphor about overcoming segregation and beginning to practice acceptance. This title is geared to younger adult readers.

GRADES: 6–8

REVIEWS: *Kirkus* 5/01/90, *Publishers Weekly* 5/11/90, *SLJ* 6/90

AWARDS: Newbery Winner

Spinelli, Jerry. *Stargirl.* 199 p. TR. EMC/Paradigm Publishing. 978-0-8219-2504-1. N/A. $12.99. TR. Random House Children's Books. 978-0-679-88637-2. 2000. $16.99. LB. Random House Children's Books. 978-0-679-98637-9. 2000. $17.99. RE. San Val, Incorporated. 978-1-4176-5661-5. 2004. $17.20. LB. Perma-Bound

Books. 978-0-8000-1545-9. 2000. $13.99. PB. Random House Children's Books. 978-0-440-41677-7. 2004. $6.99. PB. Random House Children's Books. 978-0-375-82233-9. 2002. $8.95. CD. Random House Audio Publishing Group. 978-0-7393-3897-1. 2007. $25.00. CD. Random House Audio Publishing Group. 978-0-8072-1048-2. 2004. $32.30. EB. Adobe Systems, Incorporated. 978-1-59061-403-7. 2001. $3.99. EB. Random House Audio Publishing Group. 978-0-7393-3062-3. N/A. $32.30. LP. Thorndike Press. 978-0-7862-6187-1. 2004. $10.95.

Stargirl Caraway brings excitement with her when she enters Arizona's Mica High School. Sure she's eccentric but always comes across with a certain charm. She serenades the cafeteria with her ukulele and demonstrates random acts of kindness. Alas, her individuality cannot last and the student body begins to ridicule her. That is except Leo, a guy who is attracted to her zany behavior and weird style of clothes. Leo's problem is age-old: will he cave to peer pressure and remain part of the group or join Stargirl in celebrating individuality? Younger teen readers, especially girls, worship Stargirl, both the character and the book. The sequel is called *Love, Stargirl.*

GRADES: 7–10

REVIEWS: *Booklist* 6/01/00, *Kirkus* 6/15/00, *Publishers Weekly* 6/26/00, *SLJ* 8/00, *VOYA* 10/00

AWARDS: BBYA Top Ten

Strasser, Todd. *Give a Boy a Gun.* N/A. RE. San Val, Incorporated. 978-0-613-73375-5. 2002. $17.20. PB. Simon & Schuster Children's Publishing. 978-0-689-84893-3. 2002. $6.99. CD. Recorded Books, LLC. 978-1-4025-1966-6. N/A. $32.00. EB. Recorded Books, LLC. 978-1-4237-0917-6. N/A. $27.00.

Unfolding in a series of interviews by a college student following a shooting massacre at Middletown High School, this novel relates the story of the shooters. Readers discover that the two boys were bullied and labeled outcasts during their formative middle school years. The shooting scenario will sound familiar as the boys go on their rampage in the gym and the school library. The puzzle is pieced together with the help of recollections of the boys' peers. The problem of school shooting is obvious, but Strasser also allows readers to understand that all actions have consequences.

GRADES: 8–10

REVIEWS: *Booklist* 10/01/00, *Kirkus* 7/01/00, *Publishers Weekly* 8/25/00, *SLJ* 9/00, *VOYA* 10/00

Stratton, Allan. *Chanda's Secrets.* N/A. LB. Perma-Bound Books. 978-0-605-58601-7. 2004. $15.95. PB. Polyglot Press, Incorporated. 978-1-4115-2052-3. 2004. $8.95.

Africa becomes the setting of this teen novel that deals with the AIDS epidemic. Sixteen-year-old Chanda's baby dies, and her siblings are told that she "went on a trip." There is complete denial of AIDS, which is happening throughout Chanda's city. The social shame of having AIDS is so strong that Chanda cannot help her mother, who is weakening from the disease. Chanda's problem is to battle the social taboo of the disease even while her immediate family needs her attention. Stratton presents the powerful topic in a respectful way, making the book accessible for younger teens. The sequel is called *Chanda's Wars*.

GRADES: 8-10

REVIEWS: *Booklist* 7/01/04, *Kirkus* 5/15/04, *SLJ* 7/04, *VOYA* 12/04

AWARDS: Printz Honor

Summers, Courtney. *Cracked Up to Be*. 224 p. PB. St. Martin's Press. 978-0-312-38369-5. 2008. $9.95. EB. St. Martin's Press. 978-1-4299-4810-4. 2008. $9.95.

What has caused high-school senior Parker Fadley, who used to be the most popular girl at her Catholic school, to suddenly quit cheerleading and show up at school drunk? Something awful happened at a summer party, an event that caused her to break up with her boyfriend. Parker is carrying tremendous guilt that she covers up with sarcasm and lashes out at anyone who tries to help her. Parker's voice is rough and cuts deep at her fellow classmates. She seems to be on the path to totally ruining her life and her many problems are exactly what will draw older readers to this novel.

GRADES: 9–12

REVIEWS: *Kirkus* 12/15/08, *SLJ* 1/09, *VOYA* 4/09

Tharp, Tim. *Knights of the Hill Country*. 240 p. LB. Random House Children's Books. 978-0-375-93653-1. 2006. $18.99. PB. Random House Children's Books. 978-0-553-49513-3. 2008. $6.99.

Two high school football stars find their friendship challenged during their senior year. The Kennishaw Knights of Oklahoma hill country spend time playing football, drinking beer, and talking about sex. They have a chance to achieve immortality by having an undefeated season for the fifth straight year. Linebacker Hampton Green and running back Blaine Keller find their bond loosening over a girl and Blaine's desperate attempt at on-field glory. Jealousy, rage, and tenderness all emerge from this novel about sports that showcases teen problems.

GRADES: 9–12

REVIEWS: *Booklist* 10/01/06, *Kirkus* 7/01/06, *SLJ* 9/06

Trueman, Terry. *Inside Out.* 128 p. TR. HarperCollins Publishers. 978-0-06-623962-0. 2003. $15.99. LB. HarperCollins Publishers. 978-0-06-623963-7. 2003. $16.89. RE. San Val, Incorporated. 978-1-4176-4052-2. 2004. $18.40. LB. Perma-Bound Books. 978-0-605-01323-0. 2003. $13.99. PB. HarperCollins Publishers. 978-0-06-447376-7. 2004. $8.99.

A coffee shop holdup goes terribly wrong and ends up being a standoff between two teenage brothers and the police. Inside the shop is sixteen-year-old Zach who was waiting for his mother. Zach suffers from a psychotic condition and needs his meds. During the hostage situation he begins to hear voices telling him awful things. This is an action story that shows several problems. The robbers are teens trying to gain cash because they are worried about their single mother's unemployment and cancer. Zach is a sympathetic innocent caught in a situation that is way beyond his control and as the clock ticks, his lack of medicine has his problems multiplying.

GRADES: 9–12

REVIEWS: *Booklist* 9/01/03, *Kirkus* 7/15/03, *Publishers Weekly* 8/18/03, *SLJ* 9/03, *VOYA* 10/03

AWARDS: Quick Picks Top Ten

Trueman, Terry. *Stuck in Neutral.* 128 p. LB. HarperCollins Publishers. 978-0-06-028518-0. 2000. $16.89. RE. San Val, Incorporated. 978-0-613-44419-4. 2001. $19.65. LB. Perma-Bound Books. 978-0-605-21266-4. 2000. $13.99. PB. Harper Collins Publishers. 978-0-06-447213-5. 2001. $8.99. CD. Recorded Books, LLC. 978-1-4025-1486-9. 2000. $29.00.

Perhaps the ultimate teen problem is coming to realize your biological father is planning to kill you. Shawn McDaniel is a fourteen-year-old with cerebral palsy. He's unable to speak or control his body movements. He is also a genius that can remember everything he hears. Through intuition, he realizes his father wants to put him "out of his misery." Trapped in his body, Shawn has no way of communicating his fears to other members of his family. This tension-packed story enlightens readers to the plight of handicapped teens. It also will make readers become aware of their own and lesser problems.

GRADES: 9–12

REVIEWS: *Booklist* 7/01/00, *Kirkus* 6/01/00, *Publishers Weekly* 7/11/00, *SLJ* 7/00, *VOYA* 12/00

AWARDS: Printz Honor

Vizzini, Ned. *It's Kind of a Funny Story.* 444 p. TR. Miramax Books. 978-0-7868-5196-6. 2006. $16.95. RE. San Val, Incorporated. 978-1-4178-1818-1. 2007. $19.65.

Partying and drugs fail to help fifteen-year-old Craig Gilner cope with the pressure of his prestigious Manhattan high school. He is battling depression and as his illness intensifies, he finds help through a therapist. Events lead to him entering an adult psychiatric wing of a hospital. Contrasting Craig's efforts to get well are unsure thoughts about sex, friendship, and his future. This title's in-depth presentation of depression is geared to older teens who may be feeling their own form of outside pressure.

GRADES: 9–12

REVIEWS: *Booklist* 2/01/06, *Kirkus* 4/01/06, *Publishers Weekly* 4/10/06, *SLJ* 4/06, *VOYA* 4/06

Voight, Cynthia. *Izzy Willy Nilly.* 336 p. Simon & Schuster Children's Publishing. 978-1-4169-0340-6. 2005. $17.95. LB. Perma-Bound Books. N/A. $14.65. RE. San Val, Incorporated. 978-1-4176-9701-4. 2005. $17.20. PB. Simon & Schuster Children's Publishing. 978-1-4169-0339-0. 2005. $6.99. CASS. Random House Audio Publishing Group. 978-0-8072-8762-0. 2004. $40.00.

Izzy Lingard loses the lower part of her right leg in an auto accident and is forced to take a look at her life from a different perspective. Not only does she have to cope with her physical change, but she also deals with her friends' sudden shift in attitude. Izzy comes to relay on a network of new friends and her supportive family to carry her through the change of living with only one lower limb. This older title remains one of the few teen novels dealing with amputation but Izzy's emotional problems will be recognized by a wide range of teen readers, especially girls.

GRADES: 9–12

REVIEWS: *Kirkus* 8/01/86, *Publishers Weekly* 4/25/86, *SLJ* 4/86

Volponi, Paul. *Rooftop.* 199 p. TR. Perfection Learning Corporation. 978-0-7569-7958-4. 2007. $14.65. TR. Penguin Group (USA) Incorporated. 978-0-670-06069-6. 2006. $15.99. LB. Perma-Bound Books. 978-0-605-01648-4. 2006. $13.99.

With a plot torn from almost any major city's newspaper headline, Paul Volponi presents a teen with a huge problem. Clay is busy trying to gain a GED but his cousin Addison is still selling drugs. The cousins spot a dude that owes Addison money and chase him to the rooftop of a building. Chasing them is a cop, and not knowing this, Addison pretends he has a gun. He is shot and Clay feels responsible for the tragedy. What Clay also has trouble coming to terms with is how politicians embrace Addison's death for their own selfish gains. This hard-hitting novel is about standing up for yourself and speaking your mind, something many teens dream about doing but lack the courage to act.

GRADES: 9–12

REVIEWS: *Booklist* 4/15/06, *Kirkus* 6/01/06, *Publishers Weekly* 9/04/06, *SLJ* 8/06, *VOYA* 8/06

Wallace, Rich. *Playing Without the Ball.* N/A. LB. Perma-Bound Books. 978-0-605-20491-1. 2000. $12.50. RE. San Val, Incorporated. 978-0-613-62400-8. 2002. $16.00.

Jay McLeod has worked very hard to make his senior year a successful time on the basketball court. Unfortunately a dictatorial coach cuts the young man. Jay tries to continue his joy for hoops in a community league. He also has a list of problems that are challenging. His mother left when he was nine and his father took off to California to "find himself." Living alone in a small apartment above a bar, Jay works at the bar and deals with the rough themes of sex, drug use, and his increasing loneliness. The basketball scenes are excellent, but what moves this title is Jay's struggles to get his life on track. Mature themes mark it as a high school read.

GRADES: 9–12

REVIEWS: *Booklist* 9/01/00, *Publishers Weekly* 8/21/00, *SLJ* 10/00, *VOYA* 10/00

Wallace, Rich. *Wrestling Sturbridge.* N/A. LB. Perma-Bound Books. 978-0-605-02952-1. 1996. $12.99. RE. San Val, Incorporated. 978-0-613-02559-1. 1997. $16.60. PB. Random House Children's Books. 978-0-679-88555-9. 1997. $6.50.

Sturbridge High School is in the middle of a depressed Pennsylvania region but everyone cheers the wrestling team, which is on track to win a state championship. Ben is a great 135-pound wrestler, but the best wrestler in the state is in the same weight class and also attends Sturbridge. Wrestling becomes an extended metaphor for the struggles of the community and also Ben coming to grips with what he knows is an injustice. Problems of questioning rules, being loyal to friends, and finding one's own moral compass are woven through this novel that has several outstanding wrestling scenes. Issues of teenage drinking move this title to the high school level.

GRADES: 9–12

REVIEWS: *Booklist* 9/01/96, *Publishers Weekly* 6/03/96, *SLJ* 10/96

Werlin, Nancy. *The Killer's Cousin.* 240 p. TR. Penguin Group (USA) Incorporated. 978-0-8037-3370-1. 2009. $16.99. LB. San Val, Incorporated. 978-0-613-23909-7. 2000. $13.00. CD. Brilliance Audio. 978-1-4233-8078-8. 2009. $54.97. CD. Brilliance Audio. 978-1-4233-8076-4. 2009. $26.99. LP. Thorndike Press. 978-0-7862-2188-2. 1999. $21.95.

David has been acquitted of murdering his girlfriend and is now focused on completing high school. He moves in with Massachusetts relatives and his tiny attic apartment may be haunted by the ghost of the family's daughter who committed suicide four years earlier. But why is the remaining daughter, Lily, harassing him? Werlin's tale is a web of mystery, tension, and deception. David's problems stem from more than just being accused of murder. The intricate plot steers this title to a high school readership.

GRADES: 9–12

REVIEWS: *Booklist* 9/01/98, *Publishers Weekly* 10/19/98, *SLJ* 11/98, *VOYA* 10/98

Werlin, Nancy. *The Rules of Survival.* 273 p. TR. San Val, Incorporated. 978-1-4178-1801-3. 2008. $17.55. TR. Penguin Group (USA) Incorporated. 978-0-8037-3001-4. 2006. $16.99. CD. Random House Audio Publishing Group. 978-0-7393-4908-3. 2007. $30.00. CD. Random House Audio Publishing Group. 978-0-7393-5115-4. 2007. $38.00. EB. Random House Audio Publishing Group. 978-0-7393-5116-1. N/A. $32.30.

Seventeen-year-old Matt knows what the problem is in his family so he writes an extended letter to his youngest sister, Emmy. The letter recalls their childhood with their sadistic and mentally unbalanced mother. When Matt was thirteen, he witnessed a stranger stepping in to stop a father from abusing his small son. Matt figures he needs that guy in his own life and a few months later Murdoch enters their lives by dating Matt's mother. The adults in this story are contrasting good and evil as Matt's mother ramps up her disturbing abuse. Matt's letter looks back on the situation while offering an explanation to Emmy. This novel is a riveting read about teens overcoming problems of abuse and taking steps to solve the situation.

GRADES: 9–12

REVIEWS: *Booklist* 8/01/06, *Publishers Weekly* 9/11/06, *SLJ* 9/06, *VOYA* 10/06

AWARDS: BBYA Top Ten

Wiess, Laura. *Such a Pretty Girl.* N/A. RE. San Val, Incorporated. 978-1-4177-8306-9. 2007. $24.55. PB. Simon & Schuster. 978-1-4165-2183-9. 2007. $13.00. CD. Recorded Books, LLC. 978-1-4281-6717-9. 2007. $51.75. CASS. Recorded Books, LLC. 978-1-4281-6712-4. 2007. $41.75. EB. Recorded Books, LLC. 978-1-4294-8727-6. N/A. $1.00.

Fifteen-year-old Meredith has a problem that may be unfixable. She's marking time until she graduates and then can move on. Good reason: her father has been released from prison after being sentenced for molesting his own daughter. Now he returns to live in the condo complex, frighteningly close to Meredith. Her mother is thrilled he's back and will do anything to keep her man. Although her paraplegic friend Andy is sympathetic, Meredith knows she will have to take matters into her own hands. Gritty and terrifying, this novel will chill even the most hardened high school readers.

GRADES: 10–12

REVIEWS: *Booklist* 4/15/07, *Kirkus* 9/01/06, *VOYA* 12/06

Williams, Carol Lynch. *The Chosen One.* 224 p. TR. St. Martin's Press. 978-0-312-55511-5. 2009. $16.95. CD. Macmillan Audio. 978-1-4272-0706-7. 2009. $24.99.

Kyra Leigh Carlson is fourteen and is horrified that she has been tagged to become the seventh wife of her father's brother, a much older church apostle. Kyra is part of a polygamist compound and lives with her father, three mothers, and twenty-one brothers and sisters. She has been secretly seeing a boy her own age and hopes to marry him, which would be against the wishes of the men controlling the church. This novel shows the dilemma of a teen desperate to break away from adult control and establish her own life. Although several scenes are high on the creepy scale, this title fits for a wide range of ages.

GRADES: 8–12

REVIEWS: *Booklist* 2/15/09, *Kirkus* 4/01/09, *Publishers Weekly* 5/25/09, *SLJ* 7/09, *VOYA* 6/09

Williams-Garcia, Rita. *Jumped.* 176 p. TR. HarperCollins Publishers. 978-0-06-076091-5. 2009. $16.99. LB. HarperCollins Publishers. 978-0-06-076092-2. 2009. $17.89. EB. HarperCollins Publishers. 978-0-06-176729-6. 2009. $16.99.

Trina is a girly-girl who unknowingly is being targeted for a beat down when school ends at 2:45. Dominique is a tough basketball player who is bringing anger issues to school and when Trina cuts her off in the hallway, Dominique's anger begins to boil. Overseeing this drama is Leticia, a gossipy girl who knows what is going on but chooses to remain an observer. Williams-Garcia writes a tense minute-by-minute buildup to the confrontation. Trina is a self-centered teen, but her problem is that she cannot see trouble coming. Realistic scenes of an inner-city high school bring this title to life.

GRADES: 9–12

REVIEWS: *Booklist* 2/01/09, *Kirkus* 2/15/09, *Publishers Weekly* 2/02/09, *SLJ* 3/09, *VOYA* 8/09

Williams-Garcia, Rita. *Like Sisters on the Homefront.* N/A. LB. San Val, Incorporated. 978-0-613-05373-0. 1997. $14.15. LB. Perma-Bound Books. 978-0-605-29925-2. 1995. $12.99.

When fourteen-year-old Gayle finds she is pregnant for the second time, her mother flips out, takes her to an abortion clinic, and then ships her to live with family on a rural Southern farm. Gayle is headstrong and wants to skip out from the farm and make her way back to New York and her man. When she's asked to watch over her ancient great-grandmother, Gayle finds a connection with the old woman and her own family's history. This story's theme is about re-inventing one's self and becoming aware of the world. Gayle goes looking for problems until her great-grandmother shows her the power of love. A sharply intense scene about the abortion is a landmine that librarians may wish to tiptoe around.

GRADES: 9–12

REVIEWS: *Publishers Weekly* 7/01/95, *SLJ* 10/95

Williams-Garcia, Rita. *No Laughter Here.* 144 p. TR. HarperCollins Publishers. 978-0-688-16247-4. 2004. $15.99. LB. Perma-Bound Books. 978-0-605-00220-3. 2004. $22.99. LB. HarperCollins Publishers. 978-0-688-16248-1. 2004. $16.89. EB. HarperCollins Publishers. 978-0-06-176737-1. 2009. $6.99.

Akilah eagerly awaits the start of fifth grade. Her best friend, Victoria, has been in Nigeria for the whole summer, but when she returns she is physically unwell and unable to laugh. Victoria has survived female circumcision and swears Akilah to secrecy about the FGM (female genital mutilation) that Victoria's family is keeping secret. There are several problems presented here. There's pressure to keep a secret from adults and other adults condoning a situation that puts their own daughter at risk. Even though the characters are young in age, this title and subject matter fits better for older readers.

GRADES: 8–10

REVIEWS: *Booklist* 12/01/03, *Kirkus* 11/15/03, *Publishers Weekly* 12/22/03, *SLJ* 2/04, *VOYA* 4/04

Wolff, Virginia Euwer. *Make Lemonade (Make Lemonade Trilogy).* 208 p. TR. Henry Holt & Company. 978-0-8050-2228-5. 1993. $17.95. PB. Henry Holt & Company. 978-0-8050-8070- 4. 2006. $7.99. CD. Random House Audio Publishing Group. 978-0-7393-8228-8. 2009. $27.00. CASS. Random House Audio Publishing Group. 978-0-8072-0689- 8. 2004. $30.00. EB. Random House Audio Publishing Group. 978-0-7393-7206- 7. N/A. $25.50.

Determined to start putting away money for college, fourteen-year-old LaVaughn accepts a job babysitting. Set in an urban environment, nothing is as easy as it seems. The babysitting job is appalling. LaVaughn meet Jolly, a seventeen-year-old single parent who lives with two small children in squalor. LaVaughn shoulders the responsibility of helping Jolly, which becomes a growing problem. Jolly is a mess and themes of sexual harassment, abuse, and parental love are laced throughout this intriguing novel. The realism of trying to make a life as a teenage mother will resonate with teens who may be experiencing a similar situation. Other titles in the series are *True Believer* (A Printz Honor title and a BBYA Top Ten) and *Full House.*

GRADES: 9–12

REVIEWS: *Booklist* 6/01/93, *Kirkus* 5/01/93, *Publishers Weekly* 5/31/93, *SLJ* 7/93

Woodson, Jacqueline. *Hush.* 192 p. TR. Penguin Group (USA) Incorporated. 978-0-399-23114-8. 2002. $15.99. LB. Perma-Bound Books. 978-0-605-93535-8. 2002. $12.99. RE. San Val, Incorporated. 978-1-4177-5739-8. 2006. $16.00. CD. Recorded Books, LLC. 978-1-4025-5375-2. N/A. N/A. EB. Recorded Books, LLC. 978-1-4175-8646-2. N/A. $1.00.

Toswiah Green's family is forced to enter the federal witness protection program following her father's testimony against two fellow police officers who killed an innocent boy. The move causes extreme loneliness for Toswiah as she does a complete makeover and must reinvent a life for herself. The twelve-year-old narrates her journey from loneliness to hope, but also describes the effect that events have on her family. This moving book is tame in the sense that there are no taboos broken, but Toswiah's problems will connect with younger readers.

GRADES: 7–10

REVIEWS: *Kirkus* 12/01/01, *Publishers Weekly* 12/10/01, *SLJ* 2/02, *VOYA* 2/02

Woodson, Jacqueline. *Locomotion.* 100 p. TR. San Val, Incorporated. 978-1-4176-4275-5. 2005. $15.25. TR. Penguin Group (USA) Incorporated. 978-0-399-23115-5. 2003. $15.99. LB. Perma-Bound Books. 978-0-605-65839-4. 2003. $12.99. CASS. Recorded Books, LLC. 978-1-4025-3949-7. 2003. $10.00. EB. Recorded Books, LLC. 978-1-4175-8649-3. N/A. $1.00.

Young Lonnie Collins Motion, a.k.a. Locomotion, has his sad situation enhanced by a teacher who encourages him to write poetry. Through Locomotion's series of poems readers become aware of what has caused Lonnie's despair. At age seven, his parents died in a fire leaving him and his younger sister orphaned. The separation of the siblings and how Lonnie figures out a way to visit her is uplifting. However, the power of this novel in verse is Locomotion's growing maturity and his ability to find himself through writing, which sets him on the path of emotional healing. The sequel is called *Peace, Locomotion.*

GRADES: 6–9

REVIEWS: *Booklist* 2/15/03, *Kirkus* 11/15/02, *Publishers Weekly* 11/25/02, *SLJ* 1/03, *VOYA* 2/03

Wyatt, Melissa. *Funny How Things Change.* 208 p. TR. Farrar, Straus & Giroux. 978-0-374-30233-7. 2009. $16.95. EB. Farrar, Straus & Giroux. 978-1-4299-4702-2. 2009. $16.95.

High school has ended for Remy Walker. His girlfriend Lisa is buzzed about her plans to leave Dwyer, their backwoods West Virginia town. She is ready to find herself at college and wants Remy to find a job there and they'll live to-gether. Remy is torn as he feels loyalty to the mountains where his family has lived for generations. Further complicating his mind is flirty Dana, an outgo-ing girl visiting Dwyer to paint a mural. Remy struggles with the problem of being loyal to a concept versus trying to make his future work in another loca-tion. This is a subtle novel about making a decision as a teenager that will for-ever change one's life. Older high school readers will recognize the unravel-ing of Remy and Lisa's love.

GRADES: 9–12

REVIEWS: *Booklist* 3/15/09, *Kirkus* 3/15/09, *SLJ* 4/09, *VOYA* 6/09

Wynne-Jones, Tim. *The Uninvited.* 368 p. TR. Candlewick Press. 978-0-7636-3984-6. 2009. $16.99.

College student Mimi Shapiro has bolted from New York University and is on the road to find an isolated farmhouse owned by her biological father. She is running away from an affair with a professor and seeks to lose herself in the wild. What she discovers at the farmhouse is a twenty-two-year-old musician al-ready living there. He's her half-brother, someone she's never met. Wynne-Jones cranks up the tension by including a third voice, an anonymous stalker who is watching Mimi...and she knows it. The combination of the tension of being stalked with flashes of sexual attraction between the half-siblings makes an interesting read for older teens.

GRADES: 10–12

REVIEWS: *Booklist* 5/09, *Kirkus* 4/15/09, *Publishers Weekly* 5/04/09, *VOYA* 6/09

Zarr, Sara. *Story of a Girl.* 192 p. TR. Little, Brown Books for Young Readers. 978-0-316-01453-3. 2007. $16.99. RE. San Val, Incorporated. 978-1-4178-1306-3. 2008. $18.40. CD. Random House Audio Publishing Group. 978-0-7393-7133-6. 2008. $38.00. EB. Little, Brown Books for Young Readers. 978-0-316-02917-9. 2008. $7.99. EB. Random House Audio Publishing Group. 978-0-7393-7134-3. N/A. $32.30.

When Deanna was thirteen, her father caught her having sex with Tommy, a seventeen-year-old bad boy of the school. Three years later she still feels out-cast and labeled as the school slut. Surrounding Deanna are more problems. Her older brother lives with his girlfriend and their baby in a basement room. Her mother is numb to it all and her father is constantly angry and depressed. When Deanna lands a job at a pizza joint, she is shocked to discover Tommy is also an employee. This story of the working poor and their struggle to be a family is very realistic. Teenage girls will immediately latch on to Deanna's problem of breaking away from a permanent label. Sexual situations steer this one to mature high school readers.

GRADES: 9–12

REVIEWS: *Booklist* 3/01/07, *Kirkus* 12/15/06, *Publishers Weekly* 1/29/07, *SLJ* 1/07, *VOYA* 2/07

Zevin, Gabrielle. *Memoirs of a Teenage Amnesiac.* 271 p. TR. Farrar, Straus & Giroux. 978-0-374-34946-2. 2007. $17.00. PB. Square Fish. 978-0-312-56128-4. 2009. $8.99. CD. Random House Audio Publishing Group. 978-0-7393-6130-6. 2007. $50.00. EB. Random House Audio Publishing Group. 978-0-7393-6131-3. N/A. $51.00.

Sixteen-year-old Naomi Porter's problem seems initially to be just a physical one. She fell down a flight of steps at school and now cannot remember the last four years of her life. She has to detective-style piece together her life, including her relationship with her divorced parents and a boyfriend who expects to pick up where they left off before the accident. While Naomi must deal with problems, the amnesia allows her to re-invent herself and try untested activities like landing a role in the school play. This is an interesting take on the problems of coming of age...for the second time. A wide range of high school readers will like Naomi.

GRADES: 9–12

REVIEWS: *Booklist* 9/01/07, *Kirkus* 8/15/07, *Publishers Weekly* 8/06/07, *SLJ* 10/07, *VOYA* 10/07

11

Readable Nonfiction

Nonfiction is essential to any core collection in a teen area whether the collection resides in a public or a school library. Librarians have a great desire to tailor their collections to their patron population. Nowhere is this trait more evident than in the nonfiction area.

There are two philosophies to consider when choosing nonfiction titles. First, is the goal of your teen area to support a school curriculum? The answer is an easy yes if you work in a school library. However, it may take some time to become familiar with recurring assignments. During my school librarian years, several teachers were methodical in planning their teaching units. I knew exactly when *Hamlet* would be taught or when the ninth-graders would need criticism sources on *Lord of the Flies*.

Yet public librarians working in a teen area may not have the luxury of consistency in school lessons. Of course there are libraries that serve the community in a one school, one public library situation. I've always worked in public libraries that drew teen patrons from quite a few different school districts. The budget was never big enough to have a satisfactory number of titles on any given subject. It always seemed to happen that the first teen that came in requested titles on a topic and checked out the three best sources. The next twenty-five teens were out of luck as many teachers at that time did not approve of resources found in online databases; they wanted the information to come from a book.

I found that circulation for nonfiction increased when I concentrated on ordering readable nonfiction, that is, titles of high interest based on pop culture. For my population, assignments requiring the book collection were fading fast. The Internet changed many things, including the need for the public library to include a wide range of books on many curriculum topics.

There's also the frustration of changing curriculum topics. One teacher gave me an extensive list of titles on the French Revolution, a sophomore topic for the whole school. I purchased the titles. Things went okay. The following year nobody asked for French Revolution books. The topic was not assigned. The teacher did not want students copying the previous year's efforts.

The titles in this section are focused on pop culture and are arranged in Dewey number order. I jotted down titles shelved in a suburban library noticing which volumes seemed to be more worn than others. Call it something of a field test. Other titles were "hits" during booktalks. Be aware, however, that books reflecting pop culture may lack professional reviews and go out of print rather quickly.

Many of the titles included in this list are merely samples of a topic. There are probably many more titles on any given topic than are offered in this limited space. Some are no-brainers, so the annotations will be brief, focusing more on why this title should be included rather than a summary of information inside the book.

001.942   **Davis, Barbara J.** *The Kids' Guide to Aliens.* 32 p. TR. Capstone Press, Incorporated. 978-1-4296-3369-7. 2009. $25.32.

Younger teens love the mystery of aliens and visitors from outer space. Throw in the mystery of Roswell, New Mexico, and there will speculative discussion for hours. Why not also include books on UFOs?

GRADES: 6–10

006   **Duggan, Michael.** *Web Comics for Teens.* 240 p. TR. Course Technology. 978-1-59863-467-9. 2008. $29.99. EB. Course Technology. 978-1-59863-668-0. 2008. $29.99.

The next step for drawing on scrap paper, a teen guy hobby since the beginning of study hall, is to upload their creativity to an online site. Sharing their artwork is a great component of MySpace or Facebook.

GRADES: 9–12

006.7   **Mezrich, Ben.** *The Accidental Billionaires: The Founding of Facebook: A Tale of Sex, Money, Genius and Betrayal.* 272 p. TR. Knopf Doubleday Publishing Group. 978-0-7679-3155-7. 2010. $15.95. TR. Knopf Doubleday Publishing Group. 978-0-385-52937-2. 2009. $25.00. CD. Random House Audio Publishing Group. 978-1-4159-6565-8. 2009. $70.00.

Speaking of Facebook, this work tells the background of how a college student took an idea and made it into a multibillion-dollar phenomenon. And he's only in his mid-twenties. This is a great example of semi-biography of a pop culture figure who currently dominates the news. Plus many teens log onto their Facebook pages multiple times each day.

GRADES: 10–12

016   **Dimery, Robert, ed.** *1001 Albums You Must Hear Before You Die.* 960 p. Universe Publishing. 978-0-7893-2074-2. 2010. $36.95. TR. Universe Publishing. 978-0-7893-2074-2. 2010. $36.95.

What's on your iPod? Let the debate begin as to whether the music of the 1950s, 1960s, or today is the best that must be heard. Or does disco rule? Teenagers are huge consumers of music and a large chunk of new music is geared to the older teen audience.

GRADES: 9–12

016.791   **Maltin, Leonard.** *Leonard Maltin's Movie Guide* **(annual).** Penguin Group (USA) Incorporated.

Before ordering the next round of DVDs from Netflix for the weekend, maybe teens would wish to view something great. Each year Maltin gives his take on hundreds of movie titles. It's research, really it is.

GRADES: 6–12

031   *Guinness World Records* **(annual).** Guinness World Records Ltd.

Outrageous, funny, alarming . . . it's all that and more. Based on super-latives (fastest, oldest, biggest, etc.) this annual production is a teen-age boy browsing delight. Girls too, but mostly I have seen boys with their noses stuck inside the pages. The glossy color photographs ap-proach website attractiveness. Buy several copies.

GRADES: 6–12

031.02   *Ripley's Believe It or Not! Planet Eccentric!* 256 p. TR. Ripley Entertain-ment, Incorporated. 978-1-893951-10-5. 2005. $27.95.

Guinness's twisted cousin here, but has perhaps even more browsing potential. Full of odd things, some that are really gross, this title will have younger teens buzzing about the entries with their friends.

GRADES: 6–12

REVIEWS: *Publishers Weekly* 1/02/06, *SLJ* 1/06

031.02   **Tibballs, Geoff.** *Ripley's Believe It or Not! Seeing Is Believing.* 256 p. TR. Ripley Entertainment, Incorporated. 978-1-893951-45-7. 2009. $28.95.

The annual version of Ripley's focuses on the weird and is divided into categories that will grab readers' attention. Crazy creatures, incredible science, and amazing feats are just a few of the work's enticements.

GRADES: 9–12

133.3   **Morningstar, Sally.** *How to Tell the Future: Discover and Shape Your Future Through Palm-Reading, Tarot, Astrology, Chinese Arts, I Ching, Signs, Symbols and Listening to Your Dreams.* 256 p. TR. Anness Publishing. 978-1-84476-162-3. 2006. $18.99.

The teenage years are full of uncertainty and many teens grab on to the idea that mysterious forces are guiding them through these difficult times. It is hard to judge which of these topics is the most alluring, but interpreting dreams is always a top draw.

GRADES: 6–12

133.3   **Reading, Mario.** *The Complete Prophecies of Nostradamus.* 340 p. TR. Sterling Publishing Co., Inc. 978-1-84293-180-6. 2006. $14.95.

Still popular? Yep, and with the Internet fueling rumors about conspiracy on almost any news item, this title will fascinate teens who wonder if their future has already been planned for them.

GRADES: 8–12

133.4   **Anson, Jay.** *The Amityville Horror.* 256 p. PB. Simon & Schuster. 978-1-4165-0769-7. 2005. $7.99. EB. Blackstone Audio, Incorporated. 978-1-4417-2718-3. N/A. $39.95.

Sure, it has been around for awhile, but c'mon. Walls bleeding, harsh voices telling the family to "get out"? Totally creepy and who cares if it is real or not? This is the stuff that stirs up middle school sleepovers.

GRADES: 7–12

133.4   **Ravenwolf, Silver.** *Teen Witch: Wicca for a New Generation.* 288 p. TR. Llewellyn Publications. 978-1-56718-725-0. 1998. $14.95

All I know is Silver Ravenwolf's books were *always* checked out of my collection. Nobody ever asked for them, but managed to find them in the catalog. Wicca fascinates teens who may be disillusioned with traditional religions.

GRADES: 8–12

133.4   **Steer, Dugald.** *Wizardology: A Guide to Wizards of the World.* 40 p. TR. Candlewick Press. 978-0-7636-3710-1. 2007. $14.99.

This is an example of the power of nonfiction. The book is very interactive with pullouts, flaps, and attractive coloring. Geared to a younger audience, it is a great browsing item, especially for middle school readers just getting into fantasy titles.

GRADES: 6–10

133.5   **Crawford, Saffi.** *The Power of Birthdays, Stars, & Numbers: The Complete Personology Reference Guide.* 840 p. TR. Random House Publishing Group. 978-0-345-41819-7. 1998. $26.95.

Another example of a book about teens believing their futures are out of their hands. Can the stars really guide them to success? Or even true love? Always, always, always have astrology books in your teen collection.

GRADES: 6–12

REVIEWS: *SLJ* 4/99

133.9   **Willin, Melvyn.** *Ghosts Caught on Film: Photographs of the Paranormal.* 156 p. TR. David & Charles Publishers. 978-0-7153-2728-9. 2007. $16.99.

A staple question during every campout or sleepover: "Do you believe in ghosts?" This books makes one believe as it's pretty convincing. I mean, a picture is worth a thousand words, right?

GRADES: 6–12

AWARDS: Quick Picks Top Ten

158.1   **Canfield, Jack.** *Chicken Soup for the Teenage Soul on Tough Stuff: Stories of Tough Times and Lessons Learned.* 400 p. TR. Health Communications, Incorporated. 978-1-55874-942-9. 2001. $14.95. TR. Health Communications, Incorporated. 978-1-55874-943-6. 2001. $24.00. CD. Health Communications, Incorporated. 978-1-55874-944-3. 2001. $11.95. CASS. Health Communications, Incorporated. 978-1-55874-945-0. 2001. $9.95.

The *Chicken Soup* line is thriving with many titles focused on teenagers. The short entries are not challenging to read and teenagers love reading about other teens going through similar situations such as those they are experiencing (although they will not admit it to an adult).

GRADES: 6–12

158.1   **Kirberger, Kimberly.** *No Body's Perfect: Stories by Teens About Body Image, Self-Acceptance, and the Search for Identity.* 304 p. TR. Scholastic, Incorporated. 978-0-439-42638-1. 2003. $12.95.

Teens need assurance that they are not alone in this crazy journey of adolescent growth changes. Perhaps an anonymous checkout of this title will put their minds at ease.

GRADES: 6–10

170.84   **Harper, Hill.** *Letters to a Young Brother: MANifest Your Destiny.* 192 p. TR. Penguin Group (USA) Incorporated. 978-1-59240-249-6. 2007. $14.00.

Many African American teenage boys are deemed at risk, especially those living in inner cities. Indeed, my experiences booktalking in juvenile detention centers showed me that about 95 percent of the incarcerated teens were African American males. This title gives them hope to set their lives straight. A companion book for girls is *Letters to a Young Sister: Define Your Destiny* also by Hill Harper.

GRADES: 6–12

REVIEWS: *Booklist* 4/15/06

200   **Breuilly, Elizabeth.** *Religions of the World: The Illustrated Guide to Origins, Beliefs, Customs & Festivals.* 160 p. TR. Facts On File, Incorporated. 978-0-8160-6258-4. 2005. $29.95.

Adults tend to forget that teenagers are seeking stability in their lives and many wish to find structure through religion. This title gives the basic outline of the various religions in the world, making it a handy book for older teens leaving their own communities and entering colleges with diverse populations.

GRADES: 8–12

REVIEWS: *SLJ* 2/01/06, *VOYA* 6/06

204   **Walsch, Neale Donald.** *Conversations with God for Teens.* 256 p. TR. Hampton Roads Publishing Company, Incorporated. 978-1-57174-263-6. 2001. $19.95. PB. Scholastic, Incorporated. 978-0-439-31389-6. 2002. $7.99.

Teens wishing to find out about other teenagers with devotion to God will do well to thumb through this book that examines the power of prayer. They just need reassurance that their faith is not something unique to them.

GRADES: 9–12

220.5   **Barnhill, Carla, ed.** *Teen Devotional Bible: New International Version.* 1600 p. TR. Zondervan. 978-0-310-91654-3. 1999. $22.99.

A teen-friendly Bible is a solid addition to any public library. This work takes Bible lessons and applies them to everyday circumstances confronting teens. It also focuses on tough situations for teens with conversations from youth leaders.

GRADES: 7–12

292   **Hamilton, Edith.** *Mythology: Timeless Tales of Gods and Heroes.* 352 p. PB. Grand Central Publishing. 978-0-446-60725-4. 1999. $7.99.

This title has been a staple in libraries for decades, but still is relevant because many schools emphasize study of the ancient myths. I've found out that middle school is where this teaching unit takes place.

GRADES: 8–12

297.5   **Hafiz, Dilara.** *The American Muslim Teenager's Handbook.* 192 p. TR. Simon & Schuster Children's Publishing. 978-1-4169-8578-5. 2009. $11.99. EB. Simon & Schuster Children's Publishing. 978-1-4169-8657-7. 2009. N/A.

It's all about sticking to your beliefs and still managing to be accepted. This title gives practical advice from other Muslim teens and young adults about handling yourself as a Muslim in situations where you may be in the minority.

GRADES: 8–12

REVIEWS: *Booklist* 4/01/09, *VOYA* 6/09

305.235   **Bowman, Robin.** *It's Complicated: The American Teenager.* 153 p. TR. Umbrage Editions. 978-1-884167-69-0. 2007. $40.00.

Armed with her camera and a list of questions, Bowman toured the United States interviewing and photographing teens in their world. The moving pictures show the diversity of teens. Some are optimistic and others are distrustful about their future.

GRADES: 9–12

AWARDS: BBYA Top Ten

306   **Wright, Richard.** *Black Boy.* 448 p. TR. HarperCollins Publishers. 978-0-06-144308-4. 2008. $16.95. TR. HarperCollins Publishers. 978-0-06-113024-3. 2007. $14.99. LB. San Val, Incorporated. 978-0-8085-1052-9. 1998. $22.25. CD. HarperCollins Publishers. 978-0-06-076352-7. 2005. $39.95. EB. HarperCollins Publishers. 978-0-06-193548-0. 2009. $16.99.

It was necessary to grow up restrained and submissive in Southern white society and to endure torment and abuse, and Richard Wright's parents made sure he would survive in the Jim Crow South. This work is part autobiography and part fiction, but will definitely resonate with today's teens as they become aware of race issues in their own lives.

GRADES: 9–12

306.4   **Gay, Kathlyn.** *Body Image and Appearance: The Ultimate Teen Guide.* 158 p. TR. Scarecrow Press, Incorporated. 978-0-8108-6645-4. 2009. $40.00. EB. Scarecrow Press, Incorporated. 978-0-8108-6646-1. 2009. N/A.

Teenage girls may have weird opinions about their bodies, a trait that may lead to serious problems such as anorexia or bulimia. This title sets them on track about ranges of what is normal and what is beyond expectations.

GRADES: 9–12

REVIEWS: *SLJ* 5/10, *VOYA* 2/10

306.708 **Feinstein, Stephen.** *Sexuality and Teens: What You Should Know About Sex, Abstinence, Birth Control, Pregnancy and STDs.* 104 p. TR. Enslow Publishers, Incorporated. 978-0-7660-3312-2. 2009. $31.93.

The question of to have or not to have sex is daunting enough, but nobody takes time to consider all the possible situations that may arise. This title offers advice and a game plan for teenagers who are considering having sex. Works on this topic should populate every teen area.

GRADES: 9–12

REVIEWS: *SLJ* 3/10

306.76 **Huegel, Kelly.** *GLBTQ: The Survival Guide for Queer and Questioning Teens.* 240 p. TR. Free Spirit Publishing, Incorporated. 978-1-57542-126-1. 2003. $15.99.

During my years as a teen librarian, I do not recall being asked for books about teens who may be considering their homosexuality, yet they were often checked out. This volume has been a go-to title for gay teens for several years.

GRADES: 9–12

REVIEWS: *Booklist* 10/01/03, *SLJ* 12/03, *VOYA* 12/03

306.89 **Lamotte, Elisabeth J.** *Overcoming Your Parents' Divorce: 5 Steps to a Happy Relationship.* 224 p. TR. New Horizon Press Publishers, Incorporated. 978-0-88282-329-4. 2008. $14.95.

Divorce strikes many teens' lives and many find it hard to cope with a split home life. This title assures teens that it is not the end of the world, and a healthy relationship can still be achieved with both parents.

GRADES: 8–12

323.092 **Hoose, Phillip.** *Claudette Colvin: Twice Toward Justice.* 144 p. TR. Farrar, Straus & Giroux. 978-0-374-31322-7. 2009. $19.95. CD. Brilliance Audio. 978-1-4418-0236-1. 2009. $19.99. EB. Farrar, Straus & Giroux. 978-1-4299-4821-0. 2009. $19.95.

This National Book Award winner of 2009 details the life of Claudette Covin, a sixteen-year-old African American girl who refused to ride in the back of a bus months before Rosa Parks. This honest and moving story not only focuses on her role in the civil rights movement but also her own personal life as a teenager with several issues, including pregnancy.

GRADES: 7–12

REVIEWS: *Booklist* 2/01/09, *Kirkus* 1/15/09, *Publishers Weekly* 2/02/09, *SLJ* 2/09, *VOYA* 2/09

323.119   **McWhorter, Diane.** *A Dream of Freedom: The Civil Rights Movement from 1954 to 1968.* TR. Scholastic, Incorporated. 978-0-439-57678-9. 2004. $19.99.

This oversized book includes striking photographs of the civil rights movement and gives a concise explanation of the dangers and triumphs of the people involved.

GRADES: 7–12

REVIEWS: *Booklist* 11/15/04, *Kirkus* 10/01/04, *Publishers Weekly* 11/22/04, *SLJ* 12/04, *VOYA* 4/05

331.702   ***Young Person's Occupational Outlook Handbook.*** 160 p. TR. JIST Publishing. 978-1-59357-743-8. 2010. $19.95. LB. San Val, Incorporated. 978-0-613-27661-0. 2001. $30.35. EB. JIST Publishing. 978-1-59357-414-7. 2007. $19.95.

Teens work just like adults. They're also concerned about a career and how much money they can expect to make. This title tells all that and also outlines the necessary qualifications for all jobs. The information can also be found online at the Bureau of Labor Statistics website at: www.bls.gov/oco

GRADES: 9–12

332.024   **Kiyosaki, Robert T.** *Rich Dad, Poor Dad for Teens: The Secrets About Money—That You Don't Learn in School!* 128 p. TR. Running Press Book Publisher. 978-0-7624-3654-5. 2009. $4.95.

Call it money management. Call it staying out of debt. Older teens without a clue about credit cards and debit cards may find themselves in a financial hole difficult to climb out of before they are twenty-five years old. This title gives sound advice about money and similar titles should be shelved in teen sections.

GRADES: 10–12

362.29   **Assael, Shaun.** *Steroid Nation: Juiced Home Run Totals, Anti-aging Miracles, and a Hercules in Every High School: The Secret History of America's True Drug Addiction.* 368 p. TR. ESPN Enterprises. 978-1-933060-37-8. 2007. $24.95.

Not just Olympians or professional athletes consider taking performance-enhancing drugs. Many high school jocks also find themselves under extreme pressure to perform, and look for any competitive edge they can find. This title gives straightforward information about the effects of steroid use.

GRADES: 9–12

364.1   **Bugliosi, Vincent.** *Helter Skelter: The True Story of the Manson Murders.* 736 p. TR. W. W. Norton & Company, Incorporated. 978-0-393-32223-1. 2001. $14.95.

The crime that shook the United States more than forty years ago still draws teen fascination. Teens are also riveted to the fact that many members of Manson's family were barely out of their teens. True crime always draws readership and this is a classic examination of a horrific set of murders.

GRADES: 10–12

364.15   **Larson, Erik.** *The Devil in the White City: Murder, Magic, and Madness at the Fair That Changed America.* 464 p. TR. Crown Publishing Group. 978-0-609-60844-9. 2003. $26.95. TR. Knopf Doubleday Publishing Group. 978-0-375-72560-9. 2004. $15.00. CD. Random House Audio Publishing Group. 978-0-7393-4381-4. 2007. $34.95. EB. Books on Tape, Incorporated. 978-0-7393-5301-1. 2007. $83.30.

History meets serial killer. H. H. Holmes preyed on young women drawn to the World's Columbian Exposition of 1893 held in Chicago. Contrasting the horror Holmes brought to women is the hope for a bright future at the Exposition held just blocks away.

GRADES: 10–12

REVIEWS: *Booklist* 2/15/03, *Kirkus* 11/15/02, *Publishers Weekly* 12/16/02

373.126   **Rockowitz, Murray, PhD.** *Barron's GED: High School Equivalency Exam.* 936 p. TR. Barron's Educational Series, Incorporated. 978-0-7641-4463-9. 2010. $18.99.

Not every teen goes to college and many opt out of high school. This study guide to help obtain a GED should be on all teen shelves. In fact, have multiple copies available.

GRADES: 10–12

378   **Kaplan, Inc.** *Kaplan 12 Practice Tests for the SAT.* No formats available in print.

This work will not circulate all year long, but it is a must-have, especially in communities where there is extreme pressure to get high SAT scores and enter the best college available.

GRADES: 10–12

378   **Princeton Review.** *Complete Book of Colleges* **(annual).** Unicol, Incorporated.

Information about universities and colleges is all over the Internet, but often those websites are more promotional than informative. This work gives equal information on all institutions without any bias.

GRADES: 10–12

378.1   **Ehrenhaft, George.** *Writing a Successful College Application Essay.* N/A. TR. Barron's Educational Series, Incorporated. 978-0-7641-3637-5. 2008. $13.99.

Various colleges place a huge emphasis on the application essay. Make titles about planning, outlining, and constructing the essay available to teens.

GRADES: 10–12

REVIEWS: *VOYA* 6/08

378.1   **Kaplan, Inc.** *Kaplan ACT 2010: Strategies, Practice, and Review.* 528 p. TR. Kaplan Publishing. 978-1-4195-5326-4. 2010. $19.99.

Have this one on your shelves also, along with SAT guides. Librarians should take the guesswork out of which colleges require the SAT and which ones prefer the ACT. Purchase both in multiple copies.

GRADES: 10–12

378.1   **Korn, Rachel.** *How to Survive Getting into College: By Hundreds of Students Who Did.* 240 p. TR. Hundreds of Heads Books, Incorporated. 978-1-933512-05-1. 2006. $13.95. EB. Hundreds of Heads Books, Incorporated. 978-1-933512-41-9. 2006. $13.95.

Teenagers are unsure of the college experience and may be suspicious about the advice adults provide. This title gives practical advice on how to organize your life before entering college and have a more rewarding college experience.

GRADES: 9–12

394.1   **Schlosser, Eric.** *Chew On This: Everything You Don't Want to Know About Fast Food.* 320 p. TR. Houghton Mifflin Harcourt Trade & Reference Publishers. 978-0-618-59394-1. 2007. $9.99.

Eric Schlosser exposes how fast food is made, why it tastes so good, and the reasoning behind handing out toys with meals. Full of alarming facts, this book will open teens' eyes to the reality of consumerism. Who knew that McDonald's is the biggest toy company in the world?

GRADES: 9–12

REVIEWS: *Publishers Weekly* 4/16/07

394.1   **Schlosser, Eric.** *Fast Food Nation: The Dark Side of the All-American Meal.* 368 p. TR. Houghton Mifflin Harcourt Trade & Reference Publishers. 978-0-395-97789-7. 2001. $26.00. TR. HarperCollins Publishers. 978-0-06-083858-4. 2005. $14.99. CD. Random House Audio Publishing Group. 978-0-7393-1250-6. 2004. $34.95. EB. Houghton Mifflin Harcourt Trade & Reference Publishers. 978-0-618-23240-6. 2001. $25.00. LP. Cengage Gale. 978-0-7838-9502-4. 2001. $30.95.

Teenagers eat fast food. They are employed at fast food restaurants. They love buying their meals at drive-through windows. What they may not know is the workings of the industry are not always in the patrons' best interest. This book explains the process behind the cheery exteriors of fast food establishments.

GRADES: 9–12

REVIEWS: *Booklist* 1/01/01, *Kirkus* 12/01/00

398.2   **Lynette, Rachel.** *Urban Legends.* 48 p. TR. Cengage Gale. 978-0-7377-4049-3. 2007. $27.00.

Teens love these stories about the strange and bizarre. But are they true? Alligators in the sewers, purposely tainted food, and nothing good happens to hitchhikers—the draw is the toe-curling possibility that any of these things could randomly happen to any teenager.

GRADES: 6–12

398.24   **Steer, Dugald.** *Dr. Ernest Drake's Dragonology: The Complete Book of Dragons.* 32 p. TR. Candlewick Press. 978-0-7636-2329-6. 2003. $19.99.

There must be hundreds of fantasy novels involving dragons. Why not display all those fiction books with this eye-catching title that examines the history of dragons and legends behind the creatures? The work is tactile in the way of a child's board book. Readers can "feel" the dragon's skin.

GRADES: 6–10

REVIEWS: *Booklist* 3/21/04, *Publishers Weekly* 12/22/03, *SLJ* 4/04, *VOYA* 8/04

413   **Merriam-Webster.** *Webster's Thesaurus.* N/A. PB. Federal Street Press. 978-1-59695-094-8. 2010. $3.39.

The ability to write involves communicating thoughts without being repetitive. A solid thesaurus is a handy tool when searching for the right word. It's a must-have title.

GRADES: 6–12

419   **Riekehof, Lottie L.** *The Joy of Signing: The Illustrated Guide for Mastering Sign Language and the Manual Alphabet.* 352 p. TR. Gospel Publishing House. 978-0-88243-520-6. 1987. $23.99.

Although the percentage of deaf and mute teens in any given population may not be large, this title is fun to browse while being informative. The manual alphabet is shown along with common phrases to use. Teens will be fascinated by this different language and a librarian never knows which teenager has a family member needing this skill to communicate.

GRADES: 6–12

423   *The American Heritage High School Dictionary.* 1636 p. TR. Houghton Mifflin Harcourt Trade & Reference Publishers. 978-0-618-71487-2. 2007. $26.00.

Many schools still teach dictionary skills lessons. There are online dictionaries but the savvy librarians have multiple copies of a solid print dictionary on their shelves. *The American Heritage High School Dictionary* is an excellent choice for teenagers.

GRADES 6–12

463   **Merriam-Webster.** *Webster's Spanish-English Dictionary for Students.* N/A. TR. Perfection Learning Corporation. 978-1-60686-079-3. N/A. $11.85. LB. San Val, Incorporated. 978-0-613-68550-4. 2003. $10.65.

This may be more of a regional work to have in libraries in the South and Southwest where Latino populations thrive. However, Spanish-speaking teens may be found anywhere in the United States. It's a safe bet this work will be used.

GRADES: 6–12

500   **Sandvold, Lynnette Brent.** *Time for Kids Super Science Book.* 128 p. TR. Time, Incorporated Home Entertainment. 978-1-60320-812-3. 2009. $11.99.

Science fair anyone? Not all teens have to take part in a science fair, but this rite of passage is thriving in many regions. Stock up on books that contain a variety of topics. There are also many titles that specialize in science areas like weather or marine biology.

GRADES: 6–9

546   **Gray, Theodore.** *The Elements: A Visual Exploration of Every Known Atom in the Universe.* 240 p. TR. Black Dog & Leventhal Publishers, Incorporated. 978-1-57912-814-2. 2009. $29.95.

This title is one of the more visually stunning works of the past few years. The whole periodical chart of the elements is given with examples of each element presented. Set against a black background, each page shows the history of the element and extremely interesting trivia.

GRADES: 8–12

567.9   **Brusatte, Steve.** *Dinosaurs.* 144 p. TR. Book Sales, Incorporated. 978-1-84916-006-3. 2009. $14.99.

It seems dinosaurs have taken over the juvenile book world, but there is still call for a quality title about these beasts in the teen area. Flush with colorful illustrations, this work emphasizes the evolutionary process and speculates on the fate of the dinosaurs.

GRADES: 6–10

REVIEWS: *Publishers Weekly* 4/05/10

576.8   **Heiligman, Deborah.** *Charles and Emma: The Darwins' Leap of Faith.* 272 p. TR. Henry Holt & Company. 978-0-8050-8721-5. 2009. $18.95. CD. Random House Audio Publishing Group. 978-0-307-74603-0. 2010. $34.00. EB. Random House Audio Publishing Group. 978-0-7393-8050-5. 2009. $42.50.

Focusing on Darwin's *Origin of the Species*, this well-researched work is actually a pair of biographies about Charles Darwin and his wife Emma. Not only does the author detail the debate about evolution, but Deborah Heiligman also shows the love between the couple even though Emma was deeply religious and Charles fretted that his theory would conflict with her beliefs.

GRADES: 10–12

REVIEWS: *Booklist* 1/01/09, *Kirkus* 12/15/08, *Publishers Weekly* 12/15/08, *SLJ* 1/09, *VOYA* 12/08

AWARDS: Printz Honor

600   **MacAulay, David.** *The New Way Things Work.* 400 p. TR. Houghton Mifflin Harcourt Trade & Reference Publishers. 978-0-395-93847-8. 1998. $35.00

This title is an excellent curriculum support tool due to the simple drawings and lucid explanations of such simple machines' concepts as the screw, levers, and pulleys.

GRADES: 6–12

REVIEWS: *Booklist* 12/01/98, *SLJ* 12/9

600   **Woodford, Chris.** *Cool Stuff Exploded: Get Inside Modern Technology.* 256 p. TR. Dorling Kindersley Publishing Staff. 978-0-7566-4028-6. 2008. $24.99.

The fascinating world of technology comes alive in this work with color illustrations that show the inner workings of machines such as the dishwasher, the spacesuit, the electric guitar, and the inkjet printer. I always wondered how dishes don't break from the jet spray in a dishwasher.

GRADES: 6–9

612   **MacAulay, David.** *The Way We Work.* 336 p. TR. Houghton Mifflin Harcourt Trade & Reference Publishers. 978-0-618-23378-6. 2008. $35.00.

The amazing world inside the human body is shown in different sections as cells divide to create the different organs and components of the body. How the body works to breathe, circulate blood, and send signals through the nervous system is explained in easy-to-understand wording.

GRADES: 6–12

REVIEWS: *Booklist* 10/15/08, *Kirkus* 9/15/08, *Publishers Weekly* 10/27/08, *SLJ* 10/08, *VOYA* 10/08

612.8   **Seckel, Al.** *Optical Illusions: The Science of Visual Perception.* 312 p. TR. Firefly Books, Limited. 978-1-55407-151-7. 2006. $24.95.

Optical illusions captivate younger teens as they can be observed turning the book this way and that trying to figure out what they are seeing. When they finally connect with the optical illusion, the ah-ha moment is priceless.

GRADES: 6–12

613.9   **Madaras, Lynda.** *The "What's Happening to My Body?" Book for Boys.* 272 p. TR. Newmarket Press. 978-1-55704-765-6. 2007. $12.95.

Changes in a boy's body are explained with focus on the body's changing size and shape, the growth spurt, the reproductive organs, voice changes, romantic and sexual feelings, and how puberty affects girls.

GRADES 6–10

REVIEWS: *VOYA* 12/07

613.9   **Madaras, Lynda.** *The "What's Happening to My Body?" Book for Girls.* 288 p. TR. Newmarket Press. 978-1-55704-768-7. 2007. $24.95.

The physical changes of puberty are explained with straight talk on the sensitive topics of the menstrual cycle, reproductive organs, breasts, and emotional changes, puberty in boys, body hair, pimples, and masturbation.

GRADES: 6–10

613.9071   **Howard-Barr, Elissa.** *The Truth About Sexual Behavior and Unplanned Pregnancy.* 240 p. TR. Facts On File, Incorporated. 978-0-8160-7634-5. 2009. $35.00. EB. Facts On File, Incorporated. 978-0-8160-6865-4. 2009. $35.00.

Divided into sections, the topics are presented from A through Z in a nonjudgmental way. The information here is relevant to teens. For example, in the section on sexual behavior the text includes discussions about contraception, abortion, sexual orientation, STDs, and violence against women.

GRADES: 9–12

614   **Walker, Sally M.** *Written in Bone: Buried Lives of Jamestown and Colonial Maryland.* 144 p. TR. Lerner Publishing Group. 978-0-8225-7135-3. 2009. $19.95.

This work is a browser's delight for fans of television's CSI series with a nod to forensic anthropology, history, and archaeology. Skeletons are exhumed in burial sites in and about the Jamestown colony. They're examined in detail and conclusions are drawn about the health and social status of the population.

GRADES: 8–12

REVIEWS: *Booklist* 2/01/09, *Kirkus* 2/01/09, *SLJ* 2/09, *VOYA* 4/09

AWARDS: BBYA Top Ten

621.3845   **Levitus, Bob.** *Incredible iPhone Apps for Dummies.* 240 p. TR. John Wiley & Sons, Incorporated. 978-0-470-60754-1. 2010. $16.99. EB. John Wiley & Sons, Incorporated. 978-0-470-63261-1. 2010. $16.99.

With the rapid pace in which cell phone technology changes, this title will need an update by the time this edition of *A Core Collection* is printed. Cell phones dominate the everyday lives of teenagers. Why not provide useful information about their favorite things in the whole world?

GRADES: 9–12

621.389   **Kelby, Scott.** *The iPod Book: How to Do Just the Useful and Fun Stuff with Your iPod and iTunes Book.* 256 p. TR. Peachpit Press. 978-0-321-64906-5. 2009. $19.99.

The hook here is iTunes, the concept that has revolutionized the recording industry and is causing compact disc sales to plummet. Teens know all about technology, but they also are eager to learn time-and cost-saving shortcuts.

GRADES: 9–12

641.300   **Menzel, Peter.** *What the World Eats.* 160 p. TR. Ten Speed Press. 978-1-58246-246-2. 2008. $22.99. TR. Ten Speed Press. 978-1-58008-869-5. 2007. $24.95.

The title emphasizes the diversity of eating habits of different populations around the world. Each region or continent is represented by a group or family gathered around stacks of food that they normally eat. It is fascinating to compare the eating habits of the United States to other countries in the world.

GRADES: 9–12

REVIEWS: *Booklist* 7/01/08, *Kirkus* 7/15/08, *Publishers Weekly* 9/01/08, *SLJ* 7/08

646   *inStyle* **Magazine.** *The New Secrets of Style: Your Complete Guide to Dressing Your Best Every Day.* 208 p. TR. Time, Incorporated Home Entertainment. 978-1-60320-082-0. 2009. $29.95.

Magazines are great browsing items for any teen area and *inStyle* fascinates teenage girls with its trendy styles. This work shows exactly what the title states; it guides girls on dressing with style, which of course is important throughout the teen years and beyond.

GRADES: 9–12

739.27   **Campbell, Jean.** *Steampunk-Style Jewelry: Victorian, Fantasy, and Mechanical Necklaces, Bracelets, and Earrings.* 144 p. TR. Quayside. 978-1-58923-475-8. 2010. $24.99.

Full disclosure here: I had no idea about this title until online patron requests came through asking my library to purchase it. Immediately reserves starting building. For those of us who don't know, steampunk jewelry makers are often master metalsmiths who combine found objects with fine metals to create elaborate pieces. The stuff looks cool.

GRADES: 6–12

741.2   **Scott, Damion.** *How to Draw Hip-Hop.* 144 p. TR. Watson-Guptill Publications, Incorporated. 978-0-8230-1446-0. 2006. $19.95.

Do guys who visit your library ask for scrap paper from the printer so they can simply draw? Include as many how-to-draw books as your budget allows. Hip-hop is the pop culture driving force for many African American teens and this title shows different techniques. It's much more than graffiti.

GRADES: 6–12

REVIEWS: *SLJ* 7/06

741.5   **Dougall, Alastair.** *The Marvel Encyclopedia: A Definitive Guide to the Characters of the Marvel Universe.* 400 p. TR. Dorling Kindersley Publishing, Incorporated. 978-0-7566-5530-3. 2009. $40.00.

The history, background, origin, alternate names, and all the Marvel characters are in this single volume. Included are The Hulk, Captain America, Spiderman, and other lesser-known, but just as cool, superheroes and villains.

GRADES: 6–12

741.5   **Estudio, Joso.** *The Monster Book of Manga: Draw Like the Experts.* 384 p. TR. HarperCollins Publishers. 978-0-06-082993-3. 2006. $24.99.

There are many spin-offs from this title: titles for boys, girls, fairies, and magical creatures. In this work, Estudio shows how to create manga boys, girls, samurais, and monsters, all items common in manga stories.

GRADES: 6–12

741.5   **Flores, Irene.** *Shojo Fashion Manga Art School: How to Draw Cool Looks and Characters.* 144 p. TR. F&W Media, Incorporated. 978-1-60061-180-3. 2009. $22.99.

This drawing book will attract girls with an interest in manga and the cute fashions the shojo girls wear. Along with explaining how to draw parts of the body, included are instructions on how to create skin tones, makeup, hair, facial expressions, clothes, and accessories.

GRADES: 6–12

741.5   **Hart, Christopher.** *Manga Mania Occult and Horror: How to Draw the Elegant and Seductive Characters of the Dark Side.* 144 p. TR. Watson-Guptill Publications, Incorporated. 978-0-8230-1422-4. 2007. $19.95.

There are many Christopher Hart books on how to draw a variety of topics. This one on manga occult and horror caught my eye and without a doubt will be a guy-magnet in any library.

GRADES: 6–12

741.5   **Watterson, Bill.** *The Essential Calvin and Hobbes: A Calvin and Hobbes Treasury.* 256 p. TR. Andrews McMeel Publishing. 978-0-8362-1805-3. 1988. $16.99. RE. San Val, Incorporated. 978-0-8335-5455-0. 1988. $29.40.

There are many comic-strip anthologies published but none as sophisticated, insane, and funny as Calvin and Hobbes. When my son joined the Air Force at age eighteen, his copy of this title from his high school days went with him wherever he was stationed, including Honduras and the Middle East. There's a pretty good testimonial.

GRADES: 6–12

745.594   **Rogge, Hannah.** *Hardwear: Jewelry from a Toolbox.* No formats available.

Create your own version of jewelry from hardware store items such as pins, clips, washers, nuts, and bolts. It's a great ice-breaking program for teen groups in public libraries and the creations shown here are definitely unique.

GRADES: 9–12

REVIEWS: *SLJ* 10/06

782.421   **Garofoli, Wendy.** *Hip-Hop History.* 48 p. LB. Capstone Press, Incorporated. 978-1-4296-4018-3. 2010. $29.32.

Hip-hop is all over the lives of teens, but how did it start? Was it planned or spontaneous? Are any of the originators still alive? Still performing? There are many other histories of hip-hop, but this title is one of the more recent and is accessible for a wide range of readers.

GRADES: 6–10

791.45   **Golden, Christopher.** *Buffy the Vampire Slayer: The Watcher's Guide.* 304 p. TR. Simon & Schuster Children's Publishing. 978-0-671-02433-8. 1998. $17.95.

Before Bella there was Buffy. Vampires, demons, witches, zombies, mummies, werewolves, shape shifters, ghosts that appeared on the hit television series are described along with samples of scripts. Buffy totally rocked and probably ushered in the latest vampire pop culture craze.

GRADES: 6–12

793.93   **Buckell, Tobias.** *Halo Encyclopedia: The Definitive Guide to the Halo Universe.* 352 p. TR. Dorling Kindersley Publishing, Incorporated. 978-0-7566-5549-5. 2009. $40.00.

Boys will drool over this complete history of the video game. Included are backgrounds of the major characters, the different sides of the conflict, and the ultra-cool weapons section. Boys will flip to that area first and gasp in awe.

GRADES: 9–12

796   **Blumenthal, Karen.** *Let Me Play: The Story of Title IX: The Law That Changed the Future of Girls in America.* 160 p. TR. Simon & Schuster Children's Publishing. 978-0-689-85957-1. 2005. $19.99. TR. DIANE Publishing Company. 978-1-4379-6649-7. 2009. $18.00.

Those girls who play soccer, volleyball, basketball, softball, and run track in high school and college didn't always have these opportunities. This title explains the history behind the Title IX law that opened doors to many females.

GRADES: 8–12

REVIEWS: *Booklist* 7/01/05, *Kirkus* 1/01/06, *Publishers Weekly* 9/12/05, *SLJ* 7/05, *VOYA* 8/05

796.22   **Sohn, Emily.** *Skateboarding: How It Works.* 48 p. LB. Capstone Press, Incorporated. 978-1-4296-4024-4. 2010. $29.32. PB. Capstone Press, Incorporated. 978-1-4296-4877-6. 2010. $9.95.

I've seen many signs posted near library entrances stating "No Skateboarding." Yet skateboarders need library love too. This title gives background to the hobby/sport that attracts thousands of teenagers to do amazing feats.

GRADES: 6–10

REVIEWS: *SLJ* 4/10

796.357   **Wendel, Tim.** *Far from Home: Latino Baseball Players in America.* 160 p. TR. National Geographic Society. 978-1-4262-0216-2. 2008. $28.00.

Professional baseball players from a variety of countries are shown competing, but the work also shows their teenage backgrounds. But this work is a not an athletic biography. Color photographs of teens and pre-teens playing baseball in parks and streets of Latin America set it apart from other baseball books.

GRADES: 9–12

796.52 **Krakauer, Jon.** *Into Thin Air: A Personal Account of the Mt. Everest Disaster.* 368 p. TR. Knopf Doubleday Publishing Group. 978-0-385-49478-6. 1999. $15.00. PB. Knopf Doubleday Publishing Group. 978-0-307-47525-1. 2009. $7.99. CD. Random House Audio Publishing Group. 978-0-7393-4379-1. 2007. $29.95.

Jon Krakauer was part of a climbing party caught in a storm on Everest that resulted in five deaths. This story, which is part explanation, part adventure, and part justification, shows man challenged by nature with a sobering outcome.

GRADES: 10–12

REVIEWS: *Booklist* 4/01/97, *Publishers Weekly* 3/17/97, *SLJ* 11/97

796.81203 **Shields, Brian.** *WWE Encyclopedia: The Definitive Guide to World Wrestling Entertainment.* 300 p. TR. Dorling Kindersley Publishing, Incorporated. 978-0-7566-4190-0. 2009. $45.00.

With over 350 pages, nearly 1,000 superstars, and more than 1,500 images, this is the book for all WWE fans, especially teenage boys. It has a steep price tag, but it is a wonderful addition to a teen collection.

GRADES: 6–12

808 **Silverstein, Shel.** *Where the Sidewalk Ends.* 192 p. TR. HarperCollins Publishers. 978-0-06-057234-1. 2004. $18.99. LB. HarperCollins Publishers. 978-0-06-058653-9. 2004. $19.89. CASS. HarperCollins Publishers. 978-0-694-00048-7. N/A. $11.95.

Silverstein reaches young readers with silly words and simple pen-and-ink drawings. Who can resist a poem called "Dancing Pants" or "The Dirtiest Man in the World"? This classic work will encourage younger teens to become interested in poetry.

GRADES: 6–12

REVIEWS: *Publishers Weekly* 3/08/04 (30th Anniversary Edition)

811 **Dickinson, Emily.** *Collected Poems of Emily Dickinson.* 400 p. PB. Barnes & Noble, Incorporated. 978-1-59308-050-1. 2003. $5.95.

Poetry may be dense to many teens and they immediately turn away from lengthy poems. Emily Dickinson wrote powerful poems with a minimal word count. Her observations about life and death, love and nature, and solitude and society continue to resonate with today's teens.

GRADES: 9–12

811   **Frost, Robert.** *The Poetry of Robert Frost: The Collected Poems.* 640 p. TR. Henry Holt & Company. 978-0-8050-6986-0. 2002. $21.99. CASS. New Millennium Entertainment. 978-1-59007-034-5. 2004. $15.00.

Frost's appreciation of common folks and his wonderful understanding of the human condition make his poems easily accessible for teenagers. His work is easy to comprehend and worthy of classroom discussion.

GRADES: 9–12

813   **Gresh, Lois H.** *The Twilight Companion: The Unauthorized Guide to the Series.* 272 p. TR. St. Martin's Press. 978-0-312-59450-3. 2009. $12.99. EB. St. Martin's Press. 978-1-4299-4046-7. 2009. $12.99.

After all, it is the publishing hit following Harry Potter and it created a huge push for anything vampire. Merchandise touting Edward and Jacob has flooded the market. Of course fans need to know the background and relationships formed throughout the series.

GRADES: 6–12

REVIEWS: *VOYA* 4/09

822.3   **Dominic, Catherine C.** *Shakespeare for Students: Volumes I and II.* No formats available in print.

This two-volume set is no longer in print, but hang on to your copy. It is one of the more concise and clear-cut analyses of Shakespeare's plays and includes character, plot, and language explanations.

GRADES: 9–12

REVIEWS: *Booklist* 9/15/97

823   **Kronzek, Allan Zola.** *The Sorcerer's Companion: A Guide to the Magical World of Harry Potter.* 352 p. TR. Broadway Books. 978-0-7679-1944-9. 2004. $15.95.

For now the Harry Potter craze has waned, but just wait until the next movie comes out on DVD. Not just a pop culture fad, the Harry Potter books are creative, well constructed, and thrilling.

GRADES: 6–12

REVIEWS: *Publishers Weekly* 9/10/01, *SLJ* 12/01, *VOYA* 2/02

902.02   **National Geographic Society (U. S.).** *Visual History of the World.* 656 p. TR. National Geographic Society. 978-0-7922-3695-5. 2005. $35.00.

A time line found at the bottom of every page pinpoints key events, names, and dates corresponding to the page's content that includes events from the past 4,000 years. The work is chock-full of information from facts, biographies of famous people, and key ideas from different historical eras. History comes alive!

GRADES: 7–12

REVIEWS: *Booklist* 2/15/06

910.4 **Andrew, Ian P.** *Pirateology: The Pirate Hunter's Companion.* 32 p. TR. Candlewick Press. 978-0-7636-3143-7. 2006. $19.99. TR. DIANE Publishing Company. 978-1-4379-6914-6. 2009. $20.00.

Although the story line here is geared to younger readers, topics such as ocean navigation, tying sailor's knots, weaponry, battle tactics, and the Jolly Roger will also draw teen readers. Items look like worn parchments and are chock-full of sidebars, maps to unfold, and packets of gold dust to examine. I suppose we have Johnny Depp's character Captain Jack Sparrow to thank for this book's popularity.

GRADES: 6–10

REVIEWS: *Publishers Weekly* 4/16/07

917.9804 **Krakauer, Jon.** *Into the Wild.* 224 p. TR. Random House Publishing Group. 978-0-679-42850-3. 1996. $23.00. LB. San Val, Incorporated. 978-0-613-03357-2. 1997. $14.95. CD. Random House Audio Publishing Group. 978-0-7393-5804-7. 2007. $19.99. EB. Books on Tape, Incorporated. 978-1-4159-4489-9. 2007. $57.00. LP. Thorndike Press. 978-0-7838-8334-2. 1997. $28.95.

Teenagers are fascinated by Christopher McCandless deciding to trade in his future for death by starvation in an abandoned bus in the Alaskan woods. This nonfiction work reads like a novel and will spark discussion for teens who may be fed up with society's pressures and want to get away from it all.

GRADES: 10–12

REVIEWS: *Kirkus* 10/01/95, *Publishers Weekly* 11/06/95

929.4 **Astoria, Dorothy.** *The Name Book: Over 10,000 Names—Their Meanings, Origins, and Spiritual Significance.* 320 p. TR. Bethany House Publishers. 978-0-7642-0566-8. 2008. $12.99.

All teens want to know if their name has a noble meaning or is something their parents pulled out of a hat. The other reality is that pregnant teens also need a source to search out baby names.

GRADES: 6–12

940.54 **Hersey, John.** *Hiroshima.* 160 p. TR. Knopf Doubleday Publishing Group. 978-0-679-72103-1. 1989. $7.50. LB. San Val, Incorporated. 978-0-88103-025-9. 1999. $17.85. CD. Audio Partners Publishing Corporation. 978-1-57270-840-2. 2007. $25.95. PLAY. Findaway World, LLC. 978-1-60252-837-6. 2007. $74.99. EB. Recorded Books, LLC. 978-1-4356-6815-7. 2008. $46.00.

Today's teens live under a cloud of threatening nuclear war that may occur in the Middle East. This work provides personal testimonials of the aftermath of a nuclear bomb. Over sixty years later, the story is both horrifying and poignant.

GRADES: 8–12

943.086 **Bartoletti, Susan Campbell.** *Hitler Youth: Growing Up in Hitler's Shadow.* 176 p. TR. Scholastic, Incorporated. 978-0-439-35379-3. 2005. $19.95. EB. Random House Audio Publishing Group. 978-0-7393-4835-2. 2007. $32.30.

By incorporating oral histories, diaries, letters, and interviews with Holocaust survivors, Hitler Youth, and political resisters, Bartoletti paints a fascinating picture of what it was like being a teenager under the horrific situations of the Nazi regime.

GRADES: 7–12

REVIEWS: *Booklist* 4/15/05, *Kirkus* 4/01/05, *Publishers Weekly* 5/23/05, *SLJ* 6/05, *VOYA* 8/05

AWARDS: BBYA Top Ten, Newbery Honor

967.7305 **Bowden, Mark.** *Black Hawk Down: A Story of Modern War.* 496 p. TR. Penguin Group (USA) Incorporated. 978-0-451-20393-9. 2001. $7.99. CD. BBC Audiobooks America. 978-0-7927-2661-6. 2002. $49.95. EB. Grove/Atlantic, Incorporated. 978-1-55584-604-6. 2007. $11.00. LP. Thorndike Press. 978-0-7838-8983-2. 2000. $28.95.

This narrative of the actual battle fought in Mogadishu, Somalia, will resonate with older teenagers who may be considering joining the military after high school graduation. The work is an extended snapshot of war in a single battle with an aftermath that has influenced the United States' foreign policy since 1993.

GRADES: 10–12

REVIEWS: *Booklist* 1/01/99, *Kirkus* 1/15/99, *Publishers Weekly* 2/01/99

973 **Gonick, Larry.** *The Cartoon History of the United States.* 400 p. TR. HarperCollins Publishers. 978-0-06-273098-5. 1991. $17.99.

Don't make the mistake of dismissing this title as a fluff piece. It actually gives a detailed explanation of the historical events that occurred in the United States from the first English colony to the Gulf War. The bonus is that the work is in comic format, a draw for reluctant readers.

GRADES: 7–12

12

Romance Novels

Ah, romance. Some would say that is what the teenage years are all about, yet teenage romance is not always a young couple clutching each other on top of a windblown cliff with waves crashing underneath as she tilts her chin to accept his kiss. The setting is more likely to be inside a fast-food restaurant.

In real life, and romance novels that reflect real life, there are awkward moments that can be heartbreaking, hilarious, or disturbing, or perhaps all in succession. In teen love novels, the attraction to the opposite sex can be told from either the guy's or girl's point of view. Authors can also adapt the technique of alternating voices of narrators to compare and contrast what each character is feeling.

Teen romance novels are not all about falling in love and living happily ever after. Often these works relate more of the thorns of a rose rather than the soft petals. An incredible amount of emotional pain is found in the pages of a teenage romance novel. At times the pain moves to tragedy and wise readers have tissues handy.

Most often, but certainly not always, romance novels target female readers and for the most part the titles in this section reflect that trait. However, I took the liberty of including romance and attraction of teens of the same sex in this section. Many great romance titles show the ups and downs of falling in love and the characters are gay. I see no reason to separate those titles from heterosexual romance.

Each year dozens of titles are produced that are more in line with the light-hearted side of romance. Often they are produced in paperback and are dated with trendy pop culture name-droppings that will quickly fade in popularity. I've tried to avoid including these titles in this section. My intent is to list titles that have more universal staying power and will be relevant to the next generation of teen readers. Several titles listed here are the first in a series. I've included other titles in the series following the annotation.

Nevertheless, teen readers will always flock to a good romance story. Savvy librarians will include many of the following titles in their library's collection.

Abbott, Hailey. *Summer Boys.* N/A. RE. San Val, Incorporated. 978-0-613-72220-9. 2004. $19.65. PB. Scholastic, Incorporated. 978-0-439-75540-5. 2005. $8.99.

When Jamie and her extended family arrive at their Maine summer vacation home, she is determined to rekindle her romance with Ethan. She met him the previous summer and they have kept in touch. Soon Ethan lets Jamie know he would rather just be friends. She's devastated. Meanwhile her cousins are all about hooking up and there is a certain amount of intricate boyfriend stealing going on. The cousins have different tastes in boys and this sexy novel shows how teen romance can diverge into many problems. It's sexy and has definite high school appeal. Other titles in the series are *Next Summer, After Summer, Last Summer,* and *Summer Girls.*

GRADES: 9–12

REVIEWS: *Publishers Weekly* 8/02/04, *SLJ* 11/04. *VOYA* 2/05

Austen, Jane. *Pride and Prejudice.* Page count varies with edition. There are significant formats currently available in-print.

The social scene of nineteenth-century England is the backdrop of Jane Austen's novel that may be the most influential title for all modern-day romance novels. Elizabeth Bennet meets Mr. Darcy at a dance where Elizabeth and her sisters are showcased for prospective husbands. Mr. Darcy, being somewhat socially unpolished, immediately insults her appearance. Later he notices her sharp mind and becomes attracted to her, but she refuses all advances. The rolling give-and-take between Elizabeth and Mr. Darcy has intrigued readers for generations. Recent movie adaptations will not harm this classic title's popularity.

GRADES: 9–12

Blume, Judy. *Forever.* 208 p. TR. Simon & Schuster. 978-1-4169-5391-3. 2007. $14.00. TR. Simon & Schuster Children's Publishing. 978-0-689-84973-2. 2002. $17.99. LB. Perma-Bound Books. 978-0-605-02212-6. 1975. $13.99. PB. Simon & Schuster. 978-1-4169-3400-4. 2007. $8.99. PB. Simon & Schuster Children's Publishing. 978-1-4169-4738-7. 2007. $7.99.

During her senior year Katherine finds herself attracted to Michael. As their relationship progresses, the issue of sex comes up. Michael has had sex and Katherine has not. Despite advice from friends that doesn't really help, they do have sex on the floor of Michael's sister's bedroom. They feel the act will seal the deal and they will be in love "forever." However summer employment separates the young lovers and Katherine becomes attracted to Theo and realizes the limitations of her relationship with Michael. Blume's work was groundbreaking in the 1970s and set the stage to include realistic situations about sex in more teen novels.

GRADES: 9–12

Bradley, Alex. *24 Girls in 7 Days.* N/A. RE. San Val, Incorporated. 978-1-4177-0022-6. 2006. $17.20.

Because Jack Grammer is shy and has never even kissed a girl, his prospects for a prom date are slim. That's where his friends Natalie and Percy step in and post his situation on the school's website. More than 150 girls respond and Jack has to pick twenty-four to put on The List. His task is to go out with all of them in seven days and then make his selection. This romp of a romance has some depth when Jack realizes not all of the girls are attracted to him but are there due to Natalie and Percy's work. More fun than sexy, this title will be embraced by younger teens.

GRADES: 8–10

REVIEWS: *Publishers Weekly* 3/20/06

Brooks, Geraldine. *Year of Wonders: A Novel of the Plague.* 336 p. TR. Penguin Group (USA) Incorporated. 978-0-14-200143-1. 2002. $15.00. TR. Perfection Learning Corporation. 978-0-7569-3392-0. 2002. $21.65. CD. HighBridge Company. 978-1-56511-489-0. 2001. $34.95. CASS. Books on Tape, Incorporated. 978-0-7366-7166-8. 2001. $56.00. LP. Thorndike Press. 978-0-7838-9682-3. 2001. $30.95.

This novel was marketed for adults but will have appeal to older teens. It is based on the historical events of 1666 that happened in the English village of Eyam. The plague struck swiftly and a young priest convinces the villagers to sequester themselves and prevent the disease from spreading. Told through the eyes of Anna Frith, the priest's young maid, readers witness the destruction of the community. Despite the horror, Anna falls in love with the priest. The allure of forbidden love set against the backdrop of gruesome deaths is a shift from teen romance novels. Yet this story has a powerful narrative of a young woman who falls in love under extremely difficult circumstances.

GRADES: 9–12

REVIEWS: *Kirkus* 6/15/01, *Publishers Weekly* 6/25/01, *SLJ* 11/01

AWARDS: Alex Award

Burd, Nick. *The Vast Fields of Ordinary.* 320 p. TR. Penguin Group (USA) Incorporated. 978-0-8037-3340-4. 2009. $16.99.

Dade Hamilton is set to leave his suburban Midwestern home for college. But until August, he's unsure of his future and deals with a boring job at Foodworld. His parents' marriage is failing, but what really rocks his mind is his on-and-off sexual relationship with Pablo. Pablo refuses to accept his homosexuality, but has no problems using Dade for sex and their on the down-low relationship leaves Dade feeling stranded. Entering his life is the dangerous and sexy Alex, who adores Dade and does not hide his feelings. Themes of unrequited love along with Dade's complex situation mark this book as a solid read for older teens.

GRADES: 9–12

REVIEWS: *Booklist* 5/01/09, *Publishers Weekly* 5/11/09, *SLJ* 6/09

Cabot, Meg. *The Princess Diaries.* 240 p. TR. HarperCollins Publishers. 978-0-380-97848-9. 2000. $16.99. LB. San Val, Incorporated. 978-0-613-37165-0. 2001. $15.30. LB. HarperCollins Publishers. 978-0-06-029210-2. 2000. $17.89. PB. HarperCollins Publishers. 978-0-06-147993-9. 2008. $8.99. PB. HarperCollins Publishers. 978-0-380-81402-2. 2001. $6.99. CD. Random House Audio Publishing Group. 978-0-307-28585-0. 2006. $45.00. CD. Random House Audio Publishing Group. 978-0-307-24326-3. 2005. $19.99. CASS. Random House Audio Publishing Group. 978-0-8072-0514-3. 2004. $32.00. EB. HarperCollins Publishers. 978-0-06-119759-8. 2002. $6.99. EB. Random House Audio Publishing Group. 978-0-7393-4458-3. N/A. $38.25. LP. Cengage Gale. 978-0-7862-4058-6. 2002. $24.95.

The prolific Meg Cabot struck the book jackpot when she created insecure Mia Thermopolis who at age fourteen is told that she is actually Princess Amelia Mignonette Grimaldi Thermopolis Renaldo of Genovia. Mia has sort-of normal teen problems with school and friends, but her divorced mother begins dating her teacher, which creeps her out. Still, her father and grandmother give lessons to the new princess on how to be a royal. The comedy moves to a romantic interest when Mia meets Michael Moscovitz to whom she is attracted throughout the series. This modern-day fairy tale has wide appeal to many teenage girls. Other titles in the series are *Princess in the Spotlight, Princess in Love, Princess in Waiting, Project Princess, Princess in Pink* (Teens' Top Ten), *Princess in Training, The Princess Present, Party Princess, Sweet Sixteen Princess, Valentine Princess, Princess on the Brink, Princess Mia,* and *Forever Princess.*

GRADES: 9–12

REVIEWS: *Booklist* 10/15/00, *Publishers Weekly* 10/09/00, *SLJ* 10/00, *VOYA* 4/01

AWARDS: Quick Picks Top Ten

Cart, Michael, ed. *Love & Sex: Ten Stories of Truth.* 240 p. TR. Simon & Schuster Children's Publishing. 978-0-689-85668-6. 2003. $13.95. RE. San Val, Incorporated. 978-0-613-60696-7. 2003. $16.45.

This short story collection is all about the ups and downs of different aspects of teen romance. As the title suggests, there is more than a first glance attraction. Some entries are on the extreme fringe. There are thoughts of heterosexual sex, mulling over why a lesbian feels attracted to a transsexual. Other tales settle back to traditional presentations of adolescent curiosity about the opposite sex. Interracial relationships, one-sided crushes, and romantic obsession all come together in this volume. Teens will snatch this book up by title. Educators will view it with a raised eyebrow.

GRADES: 9–12

REVIEWS: *Booklist* 5/01/01, *Kirkus* 5/01/01, *Publishers Weekly* 5/28/01, *SLJ* 6/01, *VOYA* 6/01

Castellucci, Cecil. *Boy Proof.* 208 p. TR. Candlewick Press. 978-0-7636-2333-3. 2005. $15.99. PB. Candlewick Press. 978-0-7636-2796-6. 2006. $7.99. EB. Recorded Books, LLC. 978-1-4294-2549-0. N/A. $1.00.

Victoria Jurgen is a senior at Melrose Prep in Hollywood. She dominates any conversation about science fiction or fantasy, aces all her AP tests and is on track to be valedictorian. A devoted fan of the movie *Terminal Earth*, Victoria shaves her head and calls herself "Egg." Her mother labels her appearance boy proof. Egg is her own person until Max enters Melrose Prep. He's her intellectual rival and she grudgingly respects him in spite of herself. Castellucci's work shows a driven girl who is off the charts in IQ points dealing with an everyday thing called love. Older teens will embrace Egg's frank narrative.

GRADES: 9–12

REVIEWS: *Booklist* 2/15/05, *Publishers Weekly* 2/21/05, *SLJ* 4/05, *VOYA* 4/05

Cohn, Rachel, and David Levithan. *Nick and Norah's Infinite Playlist.* 183 p. TR. Perfection Learning Corporation. 978-0-7569-7949-2. 2007. $16.65. TR. Random House Children's Books. 978-0-375-83531-5. 2006. $16.95. PB. Random House Children's Books. 978-0-375-84614-4. 2008. $7.99. PB. Random House Children's Books. 978-0-375-83533-9. 2007. $8.99.

When he spots Norah in a packed bar, under-aged bass player Nick asks her to be his girlfriend for the next five minutes. This great opening hook launches an all-night steamy lustfest throughout Manhattan. Told in alternating chapters, readers gain insight as to what both Nick and Norah think of each other. Their long journey into the night is edgy, sexual, and profane. Yep, it's all that and more. Nick and Norah are two of the best teenage lovers created for teen readers in the opening decade of the twenty-first century. Liberal use of the "F" word may steer school librarians away, but teens will find a way to access this novel. The pair of authors also teamed up on *Naomi and Ely's No Kiss List*.

GRADES: 9–12

REVIEWS: *Booklist* 4/01/06, *Publishers Weekly* 5/01/06, *SLJ* 5/06, *VOYA* 4/06

AWARDS: Quick Picks Top Ten

Cross, Shauna. *Derby Girl.* 240 p. TR. Henry Holt & Company. 978-0-8050-8023-0. 2007. $17.99. PB. Square Fish. 978-0-312-53599-5. 2009. $8.99.

Blue-haired Bliss Cavendar is stuck in tiny Bodeen, Texas. She barely tolerates her high school and is bored by her dead-end job at the local barbeque place, The Oink Joint. Compounding her despair is her mother's wish that Bliss will follow in her footsteps and be crowned Miss Bluebonnet. Shunning the beauty queen pageantry, Bliss happens upon the roller derby. Soon she adopts the persona Babe Ruthless and feels free when flying around the track. But her love life is put on hold when she finds that her musician boyfriend is not totally loyal. This is a kitchy-cool novel with frank talk about sex, but high school girls seeking thrills will love it. A paperback version of this work goes by the title *Whip It,* which is also the title of the movie adaptation.

GRADES: 9–12

REVIEWS: *Publishers Weekly* 9/10/07, *SLJ* 12/07, *VOYA* 10/07

Davidson, Dana. *Jason and Kyra.* N/A. RE. San Val, Incorporated. 978-1-4177-7781-5. 2005. $16.00. PB. Hyperion Books for Children. 978-0-7868-3653-6. 2005. $5.99.

Kyra is known as a brainiac, so why is star hooper Jason Vincent hanging around? By chance Jason and Kyra are assigned a school group project and soon their study sessions lead to mutual attraction. But is Jason just playing with Kyra? Is he still involved with his ultra-sexy girlfriend, Lisa? Two likeable but opposite characters find love in this uplifting work. The road is rocky, but readers will keep flipping pages to see if love overcomes all hardships. Several steamy sexual situations mark this title more suited for high school readers.

GRADES: 9–12

REVIEWS: *Booklist* 6/01/04, *Publishers Weekly* 6/07/04, *SLJ* 7/04, *VOYA* 6/04

Davidson, Dana. *Played.* 240 p. TR. Hyperion Books for Children. 978-0-7868-3690-1. 2005. $16.99. RE. San Val, Incorporated. 978-1-4177-9858-2. 2007. $19.65. PB. Hyperion Books for Children. 978-0-7868-3691-8. 2007. $8.99.

Ian Striver is on the fast track to be accepted into the FBI, an exclusive fraternity at Cross High School. Before his acceptance becomes official, he has to achieve one last challenge. He must convince Kylie Winship, an obvious virgin, to give it up and also must prove she has fallen in love with him. Ian goes about his challenge, but what he discovers is he's the one falling in love with Kylie. The question of course is: Will Kylie figure out Ian's ploy or will he abandon his game and be straight up with her? Once again, Davidson explores the power of love and respect. Sexual talk and situations are sprinkled throughout the story.

GRADES: 9–12

REVIEWS: *Booklist* 12/15/05, *Publishers Weekly* 12/19/05, *SLJ* 6/06, *VOYA* 10/05

AWARDS: Quick Picks Top Ten

de la Cruz, Melissa. *The Au Pairs.* 304 p. TR. Simon & Schuster Children's Publishing. 978-0-689-87066-8. 2004. $14.95. PB. Simon & Schuster Children's Publishing. 978-0-689-87319-5. 2005. $8.99. LP. Thorndike Press. 978-0-7862-8291-3. 2006. $21.95.

> Summertime is hot, hot, hot, for three sixteen-year-old girls who score summer jobs as au pairs in the Hamptons. Mara, Eliza, and Jacqui have taken different routes to their summer employment and their work with children of wealthy families is only a sideline. Their main focus is to party and be right on target for finding hot guys. There are hook ups, but the sex is not graphically described. What adds depth to their adventures is how the girls grow to rely on each other through both good times and bad. Fluffy, sure, but there is no denying this series' popularity for high school readers. Other titles in the series are *Skinny-Dipping, Sun-Kissed,* and *Crazy Hot.*

GRADES: 9–12

REVIEWS: *Booklist* 7/01/04, *Publishers Weekly* 6/21/04, *SLJ* 6/04, *VOYA* 10/04

Dessen, Sarah. *Dreamland.* 280 p. TR. Penguin Group (USA) Incorporated. 978-0-670-89122-1. 2000. $16.99. LB. Perma-Bound Books. 978-0-605-21367-8. 2000. $14.99. RE. San Val, Incorporated. 978-1-4176-2676-2. 2004. $19.65. PB. Penguin Group (USA) Incorporated. 978-0-14-240175-0. 2004. $8.99. CD. Penguin Group (USA) Incorporated. 978-0-14-314469-4. 2009. $29.95.

> Caitlin O'Koren has felt she should follow in the footsteps of her almost perfect older sister, Cassandra, yet Cassandra has run away to be with her boyfriend. Caitlin tries to fill her shoes by being named to the cheerleading squad. Soon her life is sidetracked when she meets the mysterious and sexy Rogerson Biscoe, the major drug dealer of the school. Their relationship is something of a convenience for Rogerson as he makes Caitlin carry his product while on deliveries. He also becomes demanding and abusive. This is not a fairy tale romance, but does examine obsessive love and how teens can fall into wrong relationships. Scenes of date violence mark it as a high school read.

GRADES: 9–12

REVIEWS: *Booklist* 11/01/00, *Kirkus* 8/01/00, *Publishers Weekly* 9/04/00, *SLJ* 9/00

Draper, Sharon M. *Romiette and Julio.* 240 p. TR. Simon & Schuster Children's Publishing. 978-0-689-82180-6. 1999. $18.99. RE. San Val, Incorporated. 978-0-613-33723-6. 2001. $17.20. PB. Simon & Schuster Children's Publishing. 978-1-

4169-5514-6. 2009. $8.99. PB. Simon & Schuster Children's Publishing. 978-0-689-84209-2. 2001. $6.99.

Borrowing from Shakespeare's play, Romeo and Juliet, this is a story of two modern-day inner-city teens battling misconceptions about each other's support group. Romiette Capelle is an African American girl and Julio Montague is Hispanic. They first meet in a chat room and realize they attend the same Cincinnati high school. Like the star-crossed lovers of Shakespeare, a local gang steps in to keep Romiette away from the "foreigner" and stay with her own people. Draper captures the tension and working of an inner-city high school where gangs control much of the goings on. This story without offensive language or sexual issues will appeal to a wide range of readers.

GRADES: 7–12

REVIEWS: *Booklist* 9/15/99, *Kirkus* 7/15/99, *SLJ* 9/99, *VOYA* 12/99

Ferris, Jean. *Eight Seconds.* N/A. LB. Perma-Bound Books. 978-0-605-01221-9. 2000. $24.00.

John Ritchie attends rodeo camp during the summer of his eighteenth year. He comes back enthused about tips he learned on bull riding from Kit, an instructor from college. When he is told Kit is gay, John worries about his own sexuality and his possible attraction to Kit. He doesn't handle it well and picks fights with other guys who lump John and Kit together. This story is more about friendship than outright romance, but it is an excellent story about issues confronting gay teens. John's journey is one of accepting himself and discovering the difference between friendship and love.

GRADES: 9–12

REVIEWS: *Booklist* 10/02/00, *Publishers Weekly* 11/13/00, *SLJ* 12/01

Freymann-Weyr, Garret. *My Heartbeat.* 160 p. TR. Houghton Mifflin Harcourt Trade & Reference Publishers. 978-0-618-14181-4. 2002. $15.00. LB. Perma-Bound Books. 978-0-605-45718-8. 2002. $14.99. RE. San Val, Incorporated. 978-0-613-81700-4. 2003. $18.40. CD. Random House Audio Publishing. 978-0-8072-1599-9. 2004. $30.00. CASS. Random House Audio Publishing. 978-0-8072-1243-1. 2004. $30.00.

Fourteen-year-old Ellen is close to her older brother Link and his best friend James. Set in the privileged atmosphere of Manhattan, Ellen struggles with her love for her older brother and her own feelings for James. She wonders if James and her brother are lovers, but when Link begins dating a girl, Ellen and James try to find out what they mean to each other without Link. Ellen's emerging sexuality comes with many questions as her relationship with James becomes physical. She learns love can be confusing and sex further muddies the waters. Freymann-Weyr's beautiful and sophisticated writing may be lost to younger teens.

GRADES: 9–12

REVIEWS: *Booklist* 6/01/02, *Kirkus* 4/01/02, *Publishers Weekly* 3/18/02, *SLJ* 4/02, *VOYA* 4/02

AWARDS: Printz Honor

Galloway, Gregory. *As Simple As Snow.* N/A. RE. San Val, Incorporated. 978-1-4177-7200-1. 2006. $25.75. CD. Blackstone Audio, Incorporated. 978-0-7861-8285-5. 2005. $29.95. EB. Blackstone Audio, Incorporated. 978-0-7861-3805-0. N/A. $39.95.

The voice of an unnamed narrator shows the power of sexual attraction in this open-ended story that can easily be classified as a mystery. Anna is interested in the paranormal and spends her free time writing sample obituaries. She hooks up with the book's narrator and he falls heavily for her sexuality. When she suddenly goes missing, he cannot accept her death as a suicide or an accident. She seemingly has fallen through ice into a lake, but there is no body. His search for clues will intrigue readers who must ultimately form their own conclusions. Driving the narrator's search are his strong emotional feelings for Anna and the connection they had. Galloway's complicated plot will intrigue older readers.

GRADES: 9–12

REVIEWS: *Booklist* 1/01/05, *Publishers Weekly* 2/07/05, *SLJ* 5/05

AWARDS: Alex Award

Garden, Nancy. *Annie on My Mind.* N/A. LB. San Val, Incorporated. 978-0-8085-8756-9. 1984. $14.10. RE. San Val, Incorporated. 978-1-4177-9311-2. 2007. $18.45. PB. Farrar, Straus & Giroux. 978-0-374-40011-8. 2007. $8.00. CD. Random House Audio Publishing Group. 978-0-7393-6745-2. 2008. $55.00. EB. Random House Audio Publishing Group. 978-0-7393-6746-9. N/A. $46.75.

First published in 1982, Garden's story was one of the first young adult novels to explore a lesbian love affair. Meeting at the Metropolitan Museum of Art, Anna and Liza feel an instant connection that develops into something more emotionally complex. The girls' relationship is threatened by circumstances at Liza's school, but Garden steers the plot to a happy ending. *Annie on My Mind* was a controversial sensation for many years, but today's readers may consider it tame. Still, it is an important book about sexual attraction and love in a multi-layered situation. This title is for all ages.

GRADES: 9–12

REVIEWS: *Booklist* 2/15/88, *Booklist* 7/01/07 (25th Anniversary Edition)

Giovanni, Nikki. *Love Poems.* 96 p. TR. HarperCollins Publishers. 978-0-688-14989-5. 1997. $14.00. TR. HarperCollins Publishers. 978-0-614-20397-4. 1997. $12.00. EB. HarperCollins Publishers. 978-0-06-179004-1. 2008. $13.99.

Giovanni's poetry is smart and to the point. In this compilation her poems speak of a variety of loves. She writes of the love of a daughter and mother, and a woman's deep love for a man that outlasts the initial euphoric romance. African American teens will be deeply interested in her work *All Eyez on U*, written for Tupac Shakur. Her writing is bold and also erotic, but will resonate with older teenagers who enjoy poetry over prose.

GRADES: 10–12

REVIEWS: *Booklist* 1/01/97

Green, John. *An Abundance of Katherines.* 256 p. TR. Penguin Group (USA) Incorporated. 978-0-525-47688-7. 2006. $16.99. LB. Perma-Bound Books. 978-0-605-01777-1. 2006. $23.99. CD. Brilliance Audio. 978-1-4233-2452-2. 2006. $24.95. CD. Brilliance Audio. 978-1-4233-2450-8. 2006. $29.95. PLAY. Findaway World, LLC. 978-1-60514-809-0. 2008. $69.99. EB. Brilliance Audio. 978-1-4233-2454-6. 2006. $24.95.

Colin Singleton has graduated as a valedictorian with a talent for creating anagrams. Unfortunately he's been recently dumped by his girlfriend. It seems odd, but all his girlfriends have been named Katherine. To ease his emotional pain, good buddy Hassan loosely plans a road trip from Chicago to Tennessee. Along the way, they meet a girl who is not named Katherine. Lindsey helps Colin work out a mathematical theorem that will predict the duration of romantic relationships. Older characters and sophisticated humor steers this title to older high school readers.

GRADES: 9–12

REVIEWS: *Booklist* 8/01/06, *Publishers Weekly* 9/04/06, *SLJ* 9/06, *VOYA* 10/06

AWARDS: Printz Honor

Hartinger, Brent. *The Geography Club.* 240 p. TR. HarperCollins Publishers. 978-0-06-001221-2. 2003. $17.99. RE. San Val, Incorporated. 978-0-613-71366-5. 2004. $18.40. PB. HarperCollins Publishers. 978-0-06-001223-6. 2004. $8.99.

Russel Middlebrook, a sophomore at Goodkind High School, feels he has to keep his sexuality a secret or he'll be a total outcast in his small town. He's gay but through social networking in chat rooms, he discovers a handful of classmates who also are gay. They form an after-school club under the cover name of The Geography Club figuring nobody would want to discuss maps. Russel's comfort is disrupted by his attraction to Kevin, a baseball jock who refuses to go public with their relationship. Russel juggles his feelings of love and desire, then suffers betrayal. Hartinger's tender tale is laced with humor but does send a message of being honest while in a relationship.

GRADES: 9–12

REVIEWS: *Booklist* 4/01/03, *Kirkus* 12/15/02, *Publishers Weekly* 2/03/03, *SLJ* 2/03, *VOYA* 4/03

Johnson, Angela. *The First Part Last*. 132 p. TR. Perfection Learning Corporation. 978-0-7569-3925-0. 2005. $14.65. TR. Simon & Schuster Children's Publishing. 978-0-689-84922-0. 2003. $15.95. LB. Perma-Bound Books. 978-0-605-01170-0. 2003. $12.99. PB. Simon & Schuster Children's Publishing. 978-0-689-84923-7. 2004. $6.99. CD. Random House Audio Publishing Group. 978-1-4000-9065-5. 2004. $19.99. CD. Random House Audio Publishing Group. 978-1-4000-9115-7. 2004. $20.40. CASS. Random House Audio Publishing Group. 978-1-4000-9066-2. 2004. $15.00. EB. Random House Audio Publishing Group. 978-0-7393-4511-5. N/A. $20.40. LP. Thorndike Press. 978-0-7862-7379-9. 2005. $10.95.

Angela Johnson's story about teenage pregnancy has become one of the cornerstones of twenty-first-century young adult literature. Bobby turns sixteen and is informed by his girlfriend Nia that he is to be a father. Although his parents are supportive, the struggles to be a teen parent are daunting. Told in alternating chapters of Then and Now, readers will be riveted by the circumstances that have Bobby endeavoring to raise his child alone. This serious topic is handled with respect and grace by the author and should be read by almost all young adults.

GRADES: 8–12

REVIEWS: *Booklist* 9/01/03, *Publishers Weekly* 6/13/03, *SLJ* 6/03, *VOYA* 6/03
AWARDS: BBYA Top Ten, Printz Winner, Quick Picks Top Ten

Johnson, Maureen. *The Bermudez Triangle*. 370 p. RE. San Val, Incorporated. 978-1-4176-9398-6. 2005. $18.45.

Mel, Avery, and Nina, a.k.a the Bermudez Triangle, have been inseparable friends since their childhood. During the summer before their senior year—while Nina is away at a college leadership institute—Mel and Avery develop feelings that go beyond simple friendship. Each member of the three-sided friendship struggles with the budding romance. Mel tries to come to grips with her homosexuality, Avery is confused about what she really wants, and Nina is hurt by being on the sidelines looking in. Maureen Johnson shows how a teen romance can send ripple effects away from the two lovers.

GRADES: 9–12

REVIEWS: *Booklist* 9/01/04, *Publishers Weekly* 12/06/04, *SLJ* 11/04, *VOYA* 9/04

Juby, Susan. *Another Kind of Cowboy.* 344 p. TR. HarperCollins Publishers. 978-0-06-076517-0. 2007. $16.99. LB. HarperCollins Publishers. 978-0-06-076518-7. 2007. $17.89. EB. HarperCollins Publishers. 978-0-06-195837-3. 2009. $16.99.

Alex Ford has always been a horse guy. His problem is that he really doesn't want to be part of the rough–and-tumble rodeo that his father favors. Alex dreams of being part of the pageantry of dressage and soon by luck he has his chance. He meets Cleo, a rebellious girl with money, and the story alternates between the two characters. Alex knows he is gay and has spent most of his teen years trying to accept who he is but is concerned his family will never understand. Cleo and Alex struggle through their share of romantic problems but this title shows hope that each teen will move on to happiness.

GRADES: 9–12

REVIEWS: *Booklist* 12/01/07, *SLJ* 2/08, *VOYA* 4/08

Katcher, Brian. *Playing with Matches.* 304 p. TR. Random House Children's Books. 978-0-385-73544-5. 2008. $15.99. LB. Random House Children's Books. 978-0-385-90525-1. 2008. $18.99. PB. Random House Children's Books. 978-0-385-73545-2. 2009. $7.99. EB. Sony Connect, Incorporated. 978-1-60504-234-3. 2008. $3.50.

Leon Sanders is seventeen years old and sort of a dork who pushes lame jokes onto his classmates. His dream is to date the gorgeous and popular Amy Green. However, he chats up his locker neighbor, Melody Henno, an outcast girl with a horribly burned face. He realizes that beneath the scars Melody has a keen mind and loves Monty Python and Leon's lousy jokes. The two begin seeing each other, but when Leon has a chance to date Amy Green, he takes it. Katcher's theme is obvious—that beauty is only skin deep as Amy turns out to be a shallow chain-smoker. But has Leon done too much damage? This title will appeal to a wide variety of ages.

GRADES: 9–12

REVIEWS: *Booklist* 8/01/08, *SLJ* 10/08, *VOYA* 10/08

Kerr, M. E. *Deliver Us from Evie.* 177 p. TR. Perfection Learning Corporation. 978-0-7807-5127-9. 1995. $14.65. TR. San Val, Incorporated. 978-0-7857-7638-3. 1995. $14.15. PB. HarperCollins Publishers. 978-0-06-447128-2. 1995. $6.99. EB. HarperCollins Publishers. 978-0-06-190936-8. 2009. $6.99.

Seventeen-year-old Evie Burrman is a top-notch mechanic and farmer who is falling in love, but not with Cord Whittle, who her family assumes will be able to keep the farm going. Evie is attracted to the daughter of the man holding the mortgage on their farm. Told from a point of view of Evie's brother Parr, Evie's secret is safe until Parr explodes with the truth, not just to their parents, but to the whole town. Kerr writes of how a teenage romance can complicate an entire family's situation.

GRADES: 9–12

REVIEWS: *Booklist* 9/15/94, *Kirkus* 11/15/94, *Publishers Weekly* 10/03/94, *SLJ* 11/94, *VOYA* 10/94

Klause, Annette Curtis. *The Silver Kiss.* 198 p. TR. Perfection Learning Corporation. 978-0-7807-1684-1. 1992. $14.65. LB. Random House Children's Books . 978-0-385-90435-3. 2007. $11.99. RE. San Val, Incorporated. 978-0-8335-9378-8. 1999. $17.20. PB. Random House Children's Books. 978-0-375-85782-9. 2009. $8.99. PB. Random House Children's Books. 978-0-385-73422-6. 2007. $8.99.

Before Stephenie Meyer burst onto the young adult scene with her hugely successful *Twilight* series, Annette Curtis Klause introduced readers to a romance between a vampire and a human girl in *The Silver Kiss.* Seventeen-year-old Zoe meets Simon when she is vulnerable about her mother's imminent death due to cancer. Simon is on a mission to kill his younger vampire brother. Zoe's attraction to Simon is set aside as the pair come up with a plan to kill the vampire. The story moves and teens will thrill to Zoe's dilemma of loving a handsome stranger with a disturbing past. Gruesome violence marks this title for high school readers.

GRADES: 9–12

REVIEWS: *Booklist* 10/15/90, *Publishers Weekly* 7/27/90, *SLJ* 9/90

Koja, Kathe. *The Blue Mirror.* 128 p. TR. Farrar, Straus & Giroux. 978-0-374-30849-0. 2004. $16.00. CASS. Recorded Books, LLC. 978-1-4025-9933-0. 2004. $28.75. LP. Thorndike Press. 978-0-7862-6960-0. 2004. $21.95.

Maggie is a sixteen-year-old with a lot going against her. She has an alcoholic mother, a missing father, and could not care less about school. She spends time practicing sketching in an urban diner where she meets a street youth, Cole. When he shows an interest in her drawing, she believes he's the one guy who will love her. Cole is a manipulative and charismatic leader of a crew of teens who work for him as shoplifters. Maggie is encouraged to join in, and ignoring the danger, joins Cole's group. This title shows how loneliness can lead to falling into a dysfunctional relationship. It is a solid read for teens interested in reading about life on the dirty and dangerous streets.

GRADES: 9–12

REVIEWS: *Booklist* 2/15/04, *Publishers Weekly* 2/9/04, *SLJ* 3/04, *VOYA* 4/04

Krovatin, Christopher. *Heavy Metal and You.* 192 p. TR. Scholastic, Incorporated. 978-0-439-73648-0. 2005. $16.95. RE. San Val, Incorporated. 978-1-4177-7161-5. 2006. $18.40. PB. Scholastic, Incorporated. 978-0-439-74399-0. 2006. $7.99.

Sam Markus gets wasted with his friends, favors spiked bracelets, and has total recall of all heavy metal music. Along with his buddies, he cuts school and wanders New York City getting high or drunk or both, that is, until he meets Melissa who is a straight arrow. It doesn't matter that she seems to be the exact opposite of Sam; he falls for her. In fact he tells Melissa the only things he cares about are "heavy metal and you." But can opposites hold an attraction? This title is chock-full of heavy metal bands, lyrics, and more. Be warned, it also has raw sexual talk. Call it love on the edgy side.

GRADES: 10–12

REVIEWS: *Booklist* 8/01/05, *SLJ* 10/05, *VOYA* 10/05

Levithan, David. *Boy Meets Boy.* N/A. LB. Perma-Bound Books. 978-0-605-01309-4. 2003. $15.95. RE. San Val, Incorporated. 978-1-4176-9400-6. 2005. $19.60. PB. Random House Children's Books. 978-0-375-83299-4. 2005. $8.95. PLAY. Findaway World, LLC. 978-1-60252-601-3. 2007. $44.99. EB. St. Martin's Press. 978-0-312-26446-8. N/A. $12.95.

Paul meets Noah in the bookstore and they fall in sweet, realistic teenage love. Their school is a gaytopia where boys come out of the closet and become class president and the gay-straight alliance has more members than the football team. Paul and Noah's relationship is unhampered by gay-bashing, parental rejection, or identity crises. Paul becomes a cerebral teen's dream narrator—reflective and insightful, occasionally snarky, and consistently hilarious. Levithan offers a refreshing take on two boys in love.

GRADES: 9–12

REVIEWS: *Booklist* 8/01/03, *Publishers Weekly* 10/06/03, *SLJ* 9/03, *VOYA* 10/03

AWARDS: BBYA Top Ten

Levithan, David. *The Realm of Possibility.* No formats available in print.

Written in free-verse poetry, this title examines different aspects of high school romance. Each character begins his section with some link to previous narrators. There are many powerful phrases throughout this work—"He holds me and it's that drowning kind of holding." The poems tell of relationships of all kinds: lovers, family, self, and friends. Levithan's random choice of characters is brilliant and readers will identify them as teenagers resembling people walking the halls of their own school. The sophisticated writing requires a mature audience.

GRADES: 10–12

REVIEWS: *Booklist* 9/01/04, *Publishers Weekly* 9/06/04, *SLJ* 9/04, *VOYA* 8/04

AWARDS: BBYA Top Ten

Lockhart, E. *The Boyfriend List: 15 Guys, 11 Shrink Appointments, 4 Ceramic Frogs and Me, Ruby Oliver.* 240 p. TR. Random House Children's Books. 978-0-385-73206-2. 2005. $15.95. PB. Random House Children's Books. 978-0-385-73207-9. 2006. $8.95. CD. Random House Audio Publishing Group. 978-0-307-20686-2. 2005. $38.25. CASS. Random House Audio Publishing Group. 978-1-4000- 9888-0. 2005. $35.00 EB. Random House Audio Publishing Group. 978-0-7393-2935-1. N/A. $38.25.

Ruby Oliver is fifteen and is in the middle of a tough year at Tate Prep. She has lost friends and her own dignity. Her stress leads to panic attacks, prompting Ruby to spend some couch time with a psychologist. At her doctor's urging, she begins a list of all her past boyfriends and the document teaches things about her inner person. Ruby is a winning character with a snarky voice that many teenage girls will adore, but that love thing also presents its share of problems. Other titles in the series are *The Boy Book: A Study of Habits and Behaviors, Plus Techniques for Taming Them* and *The Treasure Map of Boys: Noel, Jackson, Finn, Hutch, Gideon—and Me, Ruby Oliver.*

GRADES: 8–12

REVIEWS: *Booklist* 4/01/05, *Publishers Weekly* 2/28/05, *SLJ* 4/05, *VOYA* 4/05

Lyga, Barry. *The Astonishing Adventures of Fanboy and Goth Girl.* 320 p. TR. Houghton Mifflin Harcourt Publishing Company. 978-0-618-72392-8. 2006. $16.95. RE. San Val, Incorporated. 978-1-4177-9948-0. 2007. $19.65. PB. Houghton Mifflin Harcourt Trade & Reference Publishers. 978-0-618-91652-8. 2007. $8.99. CD. Random House Audio Publishing Group. 978-0-7393-3904-6. 2007. $50.00. CD. Random House Audio Publishing Group. 978-0-7393-4861-1. 2007. $60.00. EB. Random House Audio Publishing Group. 978-0-7393-5501-5. N/A. $51.00.

Fifteen-year-old Fanboy hates school and has a home life that is pretty lousy. His mother is pregnant and he refers to her new husband as the "step-facist." Entering the picture is Goth Girl. Kyra is an odd girl who witnesses the bullying abuse Fanboy endures. What they have in common is a love of comic books and Fanboy is storyboarding his own creation. He's also carrying a bullet and keeps a list of his abusers. Lyga writes a realistic story of a teen escaping his life through art and how two mismatched teens may, or may not, begin a love relationship. Harsh language and blunt talk about sex, mostly from Goth Girl, makes this title more suitable for the high school set.

GRADES: 9–12

REVIEWS: *Booklist* 9/01/06, *Publishers Weekly* 10/23/06, *SLJ* 11/06, *VOYA* 10/06

Lyga, Barry. *Goth Girl Rising.* 400 p. TR. Houghton Mifflin Harcourt Trade & Reference Publishers. 978-0-547-07664-5. 2009. $17.00.

Fanboy and Goth Girl's relationship continues…sort of. Told from Kyra's point of view, readers find an angry girl who spent six months in rehab without a single contact from Fanboy. She plots revenge. She's appalled that during her absence, Fanboy has gained enough confidence to publish his comic creation in the school's literary journal. Goth Girl now has mixed feelings about Fanboy: "God, I just want to tear his head off. And throw him down on the bed." Goth Girl is profane, sexy, and exciting and older teens will love her voice, and be amazed about her earlier life.

GRADES: 9–12

REVIEWS: *Publishers Weekly* 10/12/09

Madigan, L. K. *Flash Burnout*. 336 p. TR. Houghton Mifflin Harcourt Trade & Reference Publishers. 978-0-547-19489-9. 2009. $16.00.

A different take on teenage romance is found in this title. Presented in the voice of a fifteen-year-old guy, the confusion, raging lust, and sappiness of falling in love is spot on. Blake has two girls in his life: his hotter than hot girlfriend, Shannon, and his photography buddy, Marissa. His relationship with Marissa gets more involved than he would like, but he admires her spunk with her difficult situation at home with a methhead mother. What sets this story apart is Blake's straightforward attitude about sex and thinking exactly like a fifteen-year-old boy. The narrative is laced with humor but goes deeper while examining emotions involved with love versus lust.

GRADES: 9–12

REVIEWS: *Booklist* 9/15/09

McCafferty, Megan. *Sloppy Firsts (Jessica Darling Novels)*. 304 p. TR. Crown Publishing Group. 978-0-609-80790-3. 2001. $13.95. RE. San Val, Incorporated. 978-0-613-56939-2. 2001. $25.70.

Sixteen-year-old Jessica Darling is devastated when her best friend moves away from Pineville, New Jersey. She is left alone to battle teen issues such as shopping, her dad's obsession with her track meets, and the drama swirling around her older sister's wedding. To top it off, Jessica has completely mixed-up feelings about Marcus Flutie, a mysterious and intelligent guy who has worked his way into her heart. Other titles in the series are *Second Helpings, Charmed Thirds, Forth Comings,* and *Perfect Fifths.*

GRADES: 10–12

REVIEWS: *VOYA* 4/02

AWARDS: Quick Picks Top Ten

McCants, William D. *Much Ado About Prom Night.* No formats available in print.

When the budget ax falls on her high school, senior Becca decides to organize a Peer Counseling Network (PCN) for those in need. Unfortunately Becca has some problems of her own: her boyfriend is all over a ninth grader and the only date she can snag to the prom is a slimebag who has her as tenth on his list. To top off her problems, the gorgeous Jeff is determined to put the PCN out of action. The weirdness of high school romance and sex is mixed in with the crush of peer pressure. It is light-hearted, but unfortunately out of print. If a copy haunts your shelves, keep it; this is a fun book.

GRADES: 9–12

REVIEWS: *Kirkus* 6/15/95, *Publishers Weekly* 6/26/95, *SLJ* 6/95

McDaniel, Lurlene. *I'll Be Seeing You.* 195 p. TR. Perfection Learning Corporation. 978-0-7807-6565-8. 1996. $13.65. RE. San Val, Incorporated. 978-0-7857-9988-7. 1996. $16.60. PB. Random House Children's Books. 978-0-553-56718-2. 1996. $6.50.

Two teens with their features altered by accidents meet in a hospital. So begins a tear-jerker by Lurlene McDaniel. Kyle is a handsome guy but has been blinded by a chemistry experiment. Carley's face has been disfigured by cancer surgery. There is a happy ending after all that drama, which comes complete with a valentine finale. Carley is courageous and worries if their romance will vanish when he regains his sight and sees her scars. Lurlene McDaniel is all about romance mixed with tragedy. Steer teens who don't mind weeping to all of her books.

GRADES: 8–12

REVIEWS: *Booklist* 7/01/96, *SLJ* 12/96

Meyer, Stephenie. *Twilight: A Novel.* 544 p. TR. Little, Brown Books for Young Readers. 978-0-316-16017-9. 2005. $19.99. LB. San Val, Incorporated. 978-1-4177-5591-2. 2006. $13.50. PB. Little, Brown Books for Young Readers. 978-0-316-03837-9. 2008. $7.99. CD. Random House Audio Publishing Group. 978-0-307-28090-9. 2005. $29.99. CASS. Random House Audio Publishing Group. 978-0-307-28295-8. 2005. $55.00. EB. Little, Brown Books for Young Readers. 978-0-316-00744-3. 2007. $10.99. EB. Random House Audio Publishing Group. 978-0-7393-4530-6. N/A. $63.75. LP. Thorndike Press. 978-1-4104-1356-7. 2008. $25.95.

Of course one of the publishing industry's runaway successes of the twenty-first century must be included in any core collection. This is a title, and series, worshiped by millions of teenagers. Bella Swan is a girl who is lonely after moving to Forks, Washington. There she meets the gorgeous but angry Edward Cullen. He's a vampire and their romance becomes palpable. Edward is first attracted by Bella's scent, and ironically, Bella is repelled when she sees blood. Be sure to include paperback copies with movie tie-in covers. This series is a sure thing. Other titles in the series are *New Moon* (Teens' Top Ten), *Eclipse* (Teens' Top Ten), *Breaking Dawn* (Teens' Top Ten) and *The Short Second Life of Bree Tanner.*

GRADES: 7–12

REVIEWS: *Booklist* 11/15/05, *Publishers Weekly* 7/18/05, *SLJ* 10/05, *VOYA* 10/05

AWARDS: BBYA Top Ten, Quick Picks Top Ten, Teens' Top Ten

Murdock, Catherine. *Dairy Queen.* 288 p. TR. Houghton Mifflin Harcourt Publishing Company. 978-0-618-68307-9. 2006. $16.00. RE. San Val, Incorporated. 978-1-4177-7979-6. 2007. $19.65. PB. Houghton Mifflin Harcourt Trade & Reference Publishers. 978-0-618-86335-8. 2007. $8.99. CD. Random House Audio Publishing Group. 978-0-7393-3547-5. 2006. $30.00. CD. Random House Audio Publishing Group. 978-0-7393-3612-0. 2006. $38.25. CASS. Random House Audio Publishing Group. 978-0-7393-3611-3. 2006. $35.00. EB. Random House Audio Publishing Group. 978-0-7393-3087-6. N/A. $38.25.

Fifteen-year-old D. J. Schwenk works on a Wisconsin farm but rather than being a hick, she's a totally winning character. Her brothers were football heroes but now with her dad's injury, D. J. may have to give up her own athletic career to work the farm. Helping out with chores is a rival school's quarterback who asks for D. J.'s help in training. After all, she did work out with her brothers. Once school starts, D. J. decides to try out for her small school's football team. Of course the big game comes down to her on defense and guess who is the opposing quarterback? Romance on the field of play has never been better. Readers will love D. J.'s voice and her spunk. Other titles in the series are *The Off Season* and *Front and Center.*

GRADES: 8–12

REVIEWS: *Booklist* 4/01/06, *Publishers Weekly* 5/15/06, *SLJ* 4/06, *VOYA* 6/06

Myers, Walter Dean. *Street Love.* 144 p. TR. Perfection Learning Corporation. 978-0-7569-8102-0. 2007. $16.65. TR. HarperCollins Publishers. 978-0-06-028079-6. 2006. $15.99. LB. HarperCollins Publishers. 978-0-06-028080-2. 2006. $16.89. LB. Perma-Bound Books. 978-0-605-01776-4. 2006. $14.99. PB. HarperCollins Publishers. 978-0-06-440732-8. 2007. $8.99. EB. HarperCollins Publishers. 978-0-06-178342-5. 2008. $9.99. LP. Thorndike Press. 978-0-7862-9629-3. 2007. $22.95.

Damien Battle and Junice Ambers both live in Harlem but come from very different worlds. Damien is a star hooper and has been accepted to Brown University. He goes against his parents' wishes and falls in love with Junice, a sixteen-year-old girl whose mother has been sentenced to twenty-five years for possession and drug dealing. Presented in free verse poetry, this title has a rhythm that is in step with the teenagers' love.

GRADES: 9–12

REVIEWS: *Booklist* 10/01/06, *Publishers Weekly* 10/09/06, *SLJ* 11/06, *VOYA* 12/06

Myracle, Lauren. *Kissing Kate.* N/A. LB. Perma-Bound Books. 978-0-605-06054-8. 2003. $12.99.

Lissa and Kate are high school sophomores and have been inseparable friends since seventh grade. During a party, and after drinking alcohol, they tumble into each other's arms and share a first kiss. Lissa is totally into it and replays the scene over and over in her mind and cannot wait to see Kate on Monday. Unfortunately Kate is in denial and avoids Lissa at school. This is a story of a romance that fails to leave the ground despite the fact that Lissa worships Kate and Kate returned the kiss. The pain of rejection compounded with Kate's homophobia makes for a powerful story for mature readers.

GRADES: 9–12

REVIEWS: *Booklist* 8/01/03, *Publishers Weekly* 3/17/03, *SLJ* 4/03, *VOYA* 4/03

Niffenegger, Audrey. *The Time Traveler's Wife.* 460 p. TR. MacAdam/Cage Publishing, Incorporated. 978-1-931561-46-4. 2003. $25.00. PB. Houghton Mifflin Harcourt Trade & Reference Publishers. 978-0-15-602943-8. 2004. $14.95. CD. HighBridge Company. 978-1-59887-737-3. 2008. $39.95. PLAY. Findaway World, LLC. 978-1-59895-157-8. 2006. $64.99.

Henry and Clare Detamble seem to be a normal couple living in Chicago's Lincoln Park neighborhood. Henry works at a library and Clare creates abstract art, but the reality is that Henry is a prisoner of time. He is swept from present to past at time's leisure with no regard to where he is or what he is doing. Henry was dropped naked into Clare Detamble's parents' meadow when she was six. When Clare was growing up, Henry was a perfect gentleman as he dropped in and out of her young life. Romance across time? It will intrigue older readers willing to accept a challenging read.

GRADES: 10–12

REVIEWS: *Booklist* 9/01/03, *Publisher's Weekly* 8/04/03

AWARDS: Alex Award

Peters, Julie Anne. *Keeping You a Secret.* N/A. RE. San Val, Incorporated. 978-1-4176-9403-7. 2005. $18.40. PB. Little, Brown Books for Young Readers. 978-0-316-00985-0. 2005. $7.99. EB. Little, Brown Books for Young Readers. 978-0-316-02575-1. 2007. $7.99.

Holland Jaeger has things going on. She is dating a cute guy and is on the fast track to be accepted at an Ivy League school. Into her life walks a new student, the out-and-proud Cece Goddard. There is an instant attraction and the two girls begin a sexual affair. Holland wonders why Cece doesn't want her to tell anyone about their relationship, but when she does, old friends drift away and her hysterical mother changes the locks on their doors. Peters has written a moving and credible story about romance that is challenged by many people in the characters' lives. Older teens will recognize the realistic situations and homophobic slurs that hamper the romance.

GRADES: 9–12

REVIEWS: *Booklist* 6/01/03, *Publishers Weekly* 4/21/03, *SLJ* 5/03, *VOYA* 6/03

Plummer, Louise. *A Dance for Three.* No formats available in print.

Fifteen-year-old Hannah Ziebarth is crushing over popular Milo. Unfortunately he doesn't have the same feelings and only uses her for his selfish pleasure. When Hannah becomes pregnant, she imagines Milo will come around and support her. Wrong. He verbally and physically abuses her. This is a story of deep and one-sided love going completely wrong. Hannah is so stunned by Milo's behavior that she ends up hospitalized. Themes of responsibility and consequences of actions are laced throughout this powerful story. Sadly it is listed as out of print by *Books in Print.* Hang on to your copy; older teens will feel Hannah's pain.

GRADES: 9–12

REVIEWS: *Booklist* 5/01/00, *Kirkus* 12/15/99, *Publishers Weekly* 2/14/00, *SLJ* 2/00, *VOYA* 4/00

Plummer, Louise. *The Unlikely Romance of Kate Bjorkman.* 192 p. TR. Random House Children's Books. 978-0-375-89521-0. 1997. $15.00. LB. San Val, Incorporated. 978-0-613-87807-4. 1997. $24.60.

A surprise Christmas visit from her older brother and a former neighbor, Richard, who is Kate's dream guy, has Kate Bjorkman living the life of a torrid bodice ripper novel. Feeling that she is gawky and homely, Kate considers herself a socially inept teenager. When Kate's best friend, Ashley, moves in on Richard, Kate paints her as the perfect romance novel villain. Of course everything works out in the end of Plummer's rags-to-riches tale of an unlikely girl finding true love, at least for a little while. This title will have wide age appeal.

GRADES: 8–10

REVIEWS: *Publishers Weekly* 10/13/97, *SLJ* 10/95, *VOYA* 12/95

Ryan, Sara. *Empress of the World.* 192 p. TR. Penguin Group (USA) Incorporated. 978-0-670-89688-2. 2001. $14.99. LB. San Val, Incorporated. 978-0-613-67491-1. 2003. $16.45. LB. Perma-Bound Books. 978-0-605-01222-6. 2001. $14.99.

On the very first day of a summer program in archaeology, Nicola feels an attraction to another girl. Not wishing to be labeled as a lesbian, Nic moves on to her other physical attraction, which is to boys. Over the summer Nicola learns things about herself as she is willing to explore her sexuality with a girl and also a boy in the same summer term. The relationships are hampered by the summer winding down and the closed setting of the workshop community. Teens unsure of their own sexuality will be drawn to this title.

GRADES: 9–12

REVIEWS: *Booklist* 7/01/01, *Kirkus* 6/15/01, *Publishers Weekly* 7/23/01, *SLJ* 7/01, *VOYA* 8/01

Sanchez, Alex. *Rainbow Boys.* 256 p. TR. Simon & Schuster Children's Publishing. 978-0-689-84100-2. 2001. $17.00. LB. Perma-Bound Books. 978-0-605-01237-0. 2001. $14.99. RE. San Val, Incorporated. 978-0-613-66434-9. 2003. $19.65. PB. Simon & Schuster Children's Publishing. 978-0-689-85770-6. 2003. $8.99.

Sanchez's novel chronicles the senior year of Nelson, Kyle, and Jason, three gay teens struggling with a variety of serious social issues when an HIV scare is contrasted with coming out to a first love. Nelson and Kyle confront their school principal over the right to form a gay-straight alliance. After meeting a stranger online, Nelson has dangerous unprotected sex. Meanwhile Kyle's relationship with closeted jock Jason progresses, which leads to an awkward friendship between the three boys. Mixed messages, and fear of what others think about a relationship are strong themes in this novel. Other titles in the series are *Rainbow High* and *Rainbow Road.*

GRADES: 9–12

REVIEWS: *Booklist* 11/01/01, *Kirkus* 10/15/01, *Publishers Weekly* 11/26/01, *SLJ* 10/01, *VOYA* 12/01

Sanchez, Alex. *So Hard to Say.* 240 p. TR. Simon & Schuster Children's Publishing. 978-0-689-86564-0. 2004. $16.99. PB. Simon & Schuster Children's Publishing. 978-1-4169-1189-0. 2006. $9.99.

Xio is head over heels crushing on new boy Frederick. The quiet guy is from Wisconsin and Latina Xio is certain he is just unsure of himself, having been relocated to their Southern California school. Xio befriends him and ushers the cute guy into her circle of friends but Frederick is more interested in soccer and the guys on the soccer team. He slowly becomes aware of the effervescent Xio's agenda—she wants him as her first boyfriend. Sanchez casts a humorous light on first love and the issues that may not be noticeable on the surface of any relationship.

GRADES: 8–10

REVIEWS: *Booklist* 9/15/04, *Publishers Weekly* 11/01/04, *SLJ* 11/04, *VOYA* 12/04

Schreiber, Ellen. *Vampire Kisses (Vampire Kisses* series). 208 p. TR. HarperCollins Publishers. 978-0-06-009334-1. 2003. $16.99. RE. San Val, Incorporated. 978-1-4177-0071-4. 2005. $16.00. PB. HarperCollins Publishers. 978-0-06-009336-5. 2005. $5.99. EB. HarperCollins Publishers. 978-0-06-172333-9. 2008. $5.99. LP. Thorndike Press. 978-1-4104-0727-6. 2008. $22.95.

Raven is a goth girl who has a hard time fitting into her school or town, a place she calls Dullsville. When a new family moves into the town's old mansion, Raven becomes convinced the teen boy in the family, Alexander, is a vampire. There's an attraction and Raven drops big hints that she wouldn't mind joining the ranks of the undead. Although she's into vampire lore, Raven is also a teenage girl in small-town America and deals with relationships that swirl around her school. Other titles in the series are *Kissing Coffins, Vampireville, Dance with a Vampire, The Coffin Club,* and *Royal Club.* The series is also presented in manga format as *Blood Relatives I, II,* and *III.*

GRADES: 7–10

REVIEWS: *Booklist* 11/15/03, *Publishers Weekly* 8/04/03, *SLJ* 8/03, *VOYA* 2/04

Sloan, Brian. *A Really Nice Prom Mess.* 272 p. TR. Simon & Schuster Children's Publishing. 978-0-689-87438-3. 2005. $14.95. PB. Simon & Schuster Children's Publishing. 978-1-4169-5389-0. 2008. $8.99.

Cameron reluctantly agrees to go on a double date to prom with Virginia McKinley, a redhead with stunning beauty. He would much rather be paired up with Shane Wilson, his football playing boyfriend. Shane is going to the dance with Jane, a move designed to keep his relationship with Cameron on the down low. Problems arise when Cameron picks up Virginia, who knows he is gay and has drowned her sorrows with large amounts of booze. Thus begins a night to remember, or forget. The comedy is hilarious but underneath the raucous night's events is an underlying theme of unrequited love. Drinking and blunt talk about sex make this title a cool read for mature readers.

GRADES: 10–12

REVIEWS: *Publishers Weekly* 10/03/05, *SLJ* 8/05, *VOYA* 10/05

Sones, Sonya. *What My Mother Doesn't Know.* 259 p. TR. Perfection Learning Corporation. 978-0-7569-4268-7. 2003. $15.65. LB. Perma-Bound Books. 978-0-605-01251-6. 2001. $13.99. RE. San Val, Incorporated. 978-0-613-61828-1. 2003.

$18.40. PB. Simon & Schuster Children's Publishing. 978-0-689-85553-5. 2003. $7.99. CD. Brilliance Audio. 978-1-4233-6574-7. 2008. $39.25. CD. Brilliance Audio. 978-1-4233-6571-6. 2008. $19.95. CASS. Brilliance Audio. 978-1-4233-6570-9. 2008. $44.25.

Sophie is trying really hard to find true love. The fifteen-year-old tries to establish a relationship through the Internet but finds the guy to be an older pervert. Later during a Halloween dance, a mysterious masked guy captures her heart. All this time there's Murphy, an outcast teen boy, waiting in the wings to be noticed by Sophie. When she strikes up a conversation with him, she's surprised to learn he is actually very interesting. But can she date an outcast and still be accepted by the cool kids at school? And what about that masked guy? The novel in verse format makes for a brisk read that will appeal to readers debating on who will be their own true love.

GRADES: 8–10

REVIEWS: *Booklist* 11/01/01, *Kirkus* 9/15/01, *Publishers Weekly* 10/15/01, *SLJ* 10/01, *VOYA* 10/01

AWARDS: Quick Picks Top Ten

Sparks, Nicholas. *The Notebook.* 224 p. TR. Grand Central Publishing. 978-0-446-52080-5. 1996. $20.00. RE. San Val, Incorporated. 978-0-613-26424-2. 1998. $18.40. PB. Grand Central Publishing. 978-0-446-60523-6. 2004. $7.99. CD. Hachette Audio. 978-1-60024-256-4. 2007. $14.98. CD. Recorded Books, LLC. 978-0-7887-3841-8. 1999. $46.00. CASS. Hachette Audio. 978-1-57042-134-1. 1997. N/A. CASS. Recorded Books, LLC. 978-0-7887-1000-1. 1997. $49.00. EB. Grand Central Publishing. 978-0-446-19977-3. 2007. $13.99. LP. Thorndike Press. 978-1-4104-0462-6. 2008. $30.95.

Marketed as an adult romance, this title that has also been made into a movie has wide teen appeal. At age eighty, Noah Calhoun reads from a notebook about the love between Noah and Allie. Readers learn of their teenage love and their fourteen-year separation and reunion that happens just weeks before Allie is to marry another man. Sadly in the present time, Allie is suffering from Alzheimer's and Noah reads the notebook hoping that the power of love will reach her. This is a title that needs accompanying tissues. Older girls will devour the story.

GRADES: 10–12

REVIEWS: *Booklist* 8/01/96, *Kirkus* 7/15/96, *Publishers Weekly* 7/22/96

Sparks, Nicholas. *A Walk to Remember.* 256 p. TR. Grand Central Publishing. 978-0-446-52553-4. 1999. $35.00. RE. San Val, Incorporated. 978-0-613-28129-4. 2000. $18.40. PB. Grand Central Publishing. 978-0-446-60895-4. 2000. $7.99. CD. Recorded Books, LLC. 978-0-7887-4209-5. 2000. $36.00. CASS. Recorded Books,

LLC. 978-0-7887-3745-9. 1999. $35.00. CASS. Books on Tape, Incorporated. 978-0-7366-4683-3. 1999. $32.00. EB. Grand Central Publishing. 978-0-7595-1786-8. 2006. $13.99. LP. Random House Large Print. 978-0-375-72800-6. 2000. $20.00.

Another Nicholas Sparks adult book comes with definite teen appeal. Landon Carter is gliding through his senior year in Beaufort, South Carolina. When his congressman father insists he do something to counteract his bad grades, Landon runs for class president and wins. One of his new responsibilities is to attend school dances. Since he isn't dating anyone, he decides to ask Jamie Sullivan. They have a good time and a relationship blossoms. Landon is falling in love, but walks home will reveal a secret Jamie is guarding. The film version of this title, plus the heartbreaking ending, become magnets for readers who don't mind shedding a tear or three in their reading.

GRADES: 10–12

REVIEWS: *Booklist* 8/01/99, *Kirkus* 8/15/99, *Publishers Weekly* 8/23/99

Van Draanen, Wendelin. *Confessions of a Serial Kisser.* 304 p. TR. Random House Children's Books. 978-0-375-84248-1. 2008. $15.99. LB. Random House Children's Books. 978-0-375-94248-8. 2008. $18.99.

A steamy novel called *A Crimson Kiss* is the prompt for Evangeline to establish a goal in her life—she wants to experience a perfect kiss of her own. The reason for this quest is because Evangeline has witnessed her parents' marriage fall apart during the past two months. Unfortunately Evangeline's spontaneous smooches with her classmates are not exactly heart-stopping. The hot-pink cover and the hunt-for-romance plotline suggest chick lit, but Van Draanen moves beyond formula with her poignant portrayal of a teen dealing with parental separation.

GRADES: 8–10

REVIEWS: *Booklist* 7/01/08, *Publishers Weekly* 5/05/08, *SLJ* 6/08, *VOYA* 6/08

Whitcomb, Laura. *A Certain Slant of Light.* 288 p. PB. Houghton Mifflin Harcourt Trade & Reference Publishers. 978-0-618-58532-8. 2005. $8.99. CD. Random House Audio Publishing Group. 978-0-7393-3575-8. 2006. $55.00. CASS. Random House Audio Publishing Group. 978-0-7393-3574-1. 2006. $40.00. EB. Random House Audio Publishing Group. 978-0-7393-6085-9. N/A. $51.00.

It could be that romance knows no limits and *A Certain Slant of Light* affirms that thought. Helen perished 130 years ago, but her soul still roams the earth. She latches onto humans who share her love of literature. When she meets James, another being who is also "Light," she encourages him to enter the body of an "empty" teenager. Helen poses as the daughter of fundamentalist Christians but is determined to be with James. When Helen and James rediscover the pleasures of taste and touch, the sparks are supernatural and extremely sensual. The sexual descriptions are borderline erotic, marking this title for mature teens.

GRADES: 10–12

REVIEWS: *Booklist* 11/15/05, *Publishers Weekly* 8/22/05, *SLJ* 9/05, *VOYA* 2/06

Wittlinger, Ellen. *Hard Love*. N/A. LB. Perma-Bound Books. 978-0-8479-3566-6. 1999. $15.99. RE. San Val, Incorporated. 978-0-613-34759-4. 2001. $19.65. PB. Simon & Schuster Children's Publishing. 978-0-689-84154-5. 2001. $8.99. CASS. Random House Audio Publishing Group. 978-0-8072-8866-5. 2004. $30.00. EB. Random House Audio Publishing Group. 978-0-7393-6459-8. N/A. $32.30.

Zine writer John is a high school junior who feels lost and confused due to his difficult family life. He meets Marisol, a self-proclaimed "Puerto Rican Cuban Yankee Cambridge, Massachusetts, rich spoiled lesbian private-school gifted-and-talented writer virgin looking for love." John finds himself falling for Marisol, but she cannot, and will not, return his feelings. Wittlinger's story is in many ways typical of the harsh reality of high school romance, but her different take on unrequited love provides an engaging read for most readers.

GRADES: 9–12

REVIEWS: *Booklist* 10/01/99, *Kirkus* 6/15/99, *Publishers Weekly* 6/21/99, *SLJ* 7/99, *VOYA* 8/99

AWARDS: Printz Honor

Woodson, Jacqueline. *Behind You*. 128 p. TR. Penguin Group (USA) Incorporated. 978-0-399-23988-5. 2004. $15.99. LB. Perma-Bound Books. 978-0-605-51446-1. 2004. $12.99. RE. San Val, Incorporated. 978-1-4177-6897-4. 2006. $16.00.

In this sequel to *If You Come Softly*, Miah and Ellie pick up where the first book left off with a stunning climactic scene. Multiple voices tell of the tragedy facing the lovers and how they feel about the situation. Friends and family lend their opinions on how Ellie and Miah should continue and move on. The backdrop of a failed romance exposes the characters' hope that they will grow from the tragedy. It is possible for this title to stand alone, but it is meant to be savored after reading Woodson's *If You Come Softly*.

GRADES: 9–12

REVIEWS: *Booklist* 2/15/04, *SLJ* 6/04, *VOYA* 6/04

Woodson, Jacqueline. *If You Come Softly*. 181 p. TR. Perfection Learning Corporation. 978-0-7569-6769-7. 2006. $14.65. TR. Penguin Group (USA) Incorporated. 978-0-399-23112-4. 1998. $17.99. LB. Perma-Bound Books. 978-0-605-

80838-6. 1998. $12.99. RE. San Val, Incorporated. 978-1-4177-4884-6. 2006. $17.20.

Jeremiah (Miah) and Elisha (Ellie) are fifteen-year-olds who meet during their first year at an exclusive New York prep school. Their relationship is challenged by Miah being black and Ellie white. Both of their home lives are in disarray: Miah's father has left for another woman and Ellie's mom has abandoned her family twice in the past. As a mixed-race couple, Miah and Ellie must handle bigotry as their love builds. Told through alternating voices, the story projects a shared contentment by the teens. Reader alert: prepare yourself for a stunning ending.

GRADES: 9–12

REVIEWS: *Booklist* 10/01/98, *Kirkus* 6/01/98, *Publishers Weekly* 6/22/98, *SLJ* 12/98, *VOYA* 12/98

Zarr, Sara. *Sweethearts.* 228 p. TR. Little, Brown Books for Young Readers. 978-0-316-01455-7. 2008. $16.99. PB. Little, Brown Books for Young Readers. 978-0-316-01456-4. 2009. $7.99. CD. Random House Audio Publishing Group. 978-0-307-70603-4. 2009. $30.00. CD. Random House Audio Publishing Group. 978-0-7393-6776-6. 2008. $45.00. EB. Little, Brown Books for Young Readers. 978-0-316-02926-1. 2008. $7.99. EB. Random House Audio Publishing Group. 978-0-7393-6775-9. N/A. $38.25.

Jennifer Harris and Cameron Quick were each other's best friend and support system during their elementary school years. Suddenly Cameron disappeared following a creepy encounter with his abusive father and nobody really knew where he ended up, or even if he was still alive. Jennifer felt lost without him, but managed to transform herself into a popular high school senior. She is understandably shocked when she sees Cameron sitting in her homeroom one morning. Should they revisit their shared childhood memories and relationship? Zarr's moving story is all about the staying power of love and will appeal to many high school readers.

GRADES: 9–12

REVIEWS: *Booklist* 1/01/08, *Publishers Weekly* 12/24/07, *SLJ* 4/08, *VOYA* 4/08

Zindel, Paul. *My Darling, My Hamburger.* N/A. LB. Perma-Bound Books. 978-0-8479-1363-3. 1969. $11.50. RE. San Val, Incorporated. 978-1-4177-3589-1. 2005. $17.20. PB. HarperCollins Publishers. 978-0-06-075736-6. 2005. $6.99. PB. Random House, Incorporated. 978-0-553-20759-0. 1999. N/A.

Set in the late 1960s, Zindel's classic tale focuses on four friends: Liz Carstensen, Sean Collins, Maggie Tobin, and Dennis Holowitz. The unlikely foursome, seniors in high school, face some dramatic life changes as their lives transition into adulthood. The four teenagers find themselves caught between desire and the fear of intimacy. Liz and Sean, misunderstood by their parents, have an affair that ends shatteringly. Maggie and Dennis, who are confused about their relationship, take their first steps toward understanding the demands life makes on everyone. As with many teen romances, there are no easy answers. This title has appeared on school reading lists for decades.

GRADES: 9–12

13

Science Fiction

Science fiction, a cornerstone of fictional literature for generations, provides wide teenage appeal. The genre can trace its roots back to the 1800s with the work of Jules Verne and H. G. Wells. These pioneering authors established many of the traditional science fiction themes still in use today.

A general theme deals with humans venturing into scientific realms where they encounter forces too powerful to control. H. G. Wells used this technique with his work, *The Invisible Man.* Another common theme involves encounters with other beings that are more powerful, clever, ruthless, and smarter than humans. Again, H. G. Wells brought us *The War of the Worlds* that mined this theme.

This section of the second edition of *A Core Collection for Young Adults* features many classic titles from the 1800s, 1950s, and 1960s. Names are familiar: Jules Verne, Robert Louis Stevenson, Ray Bradbury, Andre Norton, and Isaac Asimov. That is not to say all science fiction was created more than fifty years ago. Modern writers such as Nancy Werlin, Scott Westerfeld, Geraldine McCaughrean, and Cory Doctorow have made outstanding contributions to the genre.

Of course science fiction involves science. The science hook does not necessarily have to be spaceships or machinery. Often biology takes center stage and recently genetic engineering has become a common theme. But then we again remember H. G. Wells and his classic story, *The Island of Dr. Moreau.*

Many titles were published during the time of the cold war in the late 1950s and 1960s. Society was unsure where science was taking us and the science fiction world reflected that. There are many stories about government control and loss of human individuality.

My choice of titles included in this section features many that were marketed for adults and the stories lack a teen character. That does not mean they are without teen appeal. In fact, I believe that science fiction is one of the more accessible crossover genres between adult and young adult readership.

Since science is not exact, many things can go wrong in a science fiction tale. In fact, a large number of titles listed here can easily be grouped into horror or problem novels. But I feel that all the titles listed have some connection back to science and its many satellite topics.

Adams, Douglas. *The Hitchhiker's Guide to the Galaxy.* 272 p. TR. Crown Publishing Group. 978-1-4000-5292-9. 2004. $15.00. RE. San Val, Incorporated. 978-0-613-06405-7. 1997. $25.70. CASS. Books on Tape, Incorporated. 978-0-7366-2681-1. 1994. $30.00. EB. RosettaBooks. 978-0-7953-2821-3. 2003. $7.20.

Arthur Dent is a mild-mannered kind of guy who is more on the drifty side. One day he's whisked from Earth by his newfound friend Ford Perfect moments before the planet is destroyed to make way for a hyper-space bypass. Ford is a researcher for the revised edition of *The Hitchhiker's Guide to the Galaxy* and the pair set out on a hilarious jaunt through time and space. Douglas Adams' work has been a hit for older young adult readers for decades and has a loyal following of readers. It is a perfect fit for teens who like the insanity of Monty Python and also works for teens who march to a different drummer. Other titles in the series are: *The Restaurant at the End of the Universe; Life, the Universe and Everything; So Long, and Thanks for All the Fish;* and *Mostly Harmless.*

GRADES: 9–12

Asimov, Isaac. *I, Robot.* 240 p. TR. Random House Publishing Group. 978-0-553-80370-9. 2004. $24.00. TR. Random House Publishing Group. 978-0-553-38256-3. 2008. $14.00. LB. San Val, Incorporated. 978-0-7857-7338-2. 1991. $15.90. PB. Random House Publishing Group. 978-0-553-29438-5. 1991. $7.99. EB. Barnes & Noble Digital. 978-1-4014-0038-5. 2001. $4.95. EB. Books on Tape, Incorporated. 978-0-7393-4627-3. 2007. $68.85.

I, Robot contains a series of tales, published throughout the 1940s in various pulp magazines, in which Asimov introduced three basic laws of robotics in science fiction literature. Number one: A robot may not injure a human being or through inaction, allow a human being to come to harm. Number two: A robot must obey orders given to it by human beings except where such orders would conflict with the First Law. Number three: A robot must protect its own existence as long as such protection does not conflict with the First or Second Law. A film by the same title produced in 2004 sparked a rebirth of interest in Asimov's work. His book is a classic of science fiction and is suited for serious readers.

GRADES: 9–12

Atwood, Margaret. *The Handmaid's Tale.* 392 p. TR. Knopf Doubleday Publishing Group. 978-0-307-26460-2. 2006. $25.00. TR. Knopf Doubleday Publishing Group. 978-0- 385-49081-8. 1998. $14.95. LB. Perma-Bound Books. 978-0-8000-2446-8. 1986. $21.95. RE. San Val, Incorporated. 978-0-8085-9829-9. 1987. $26.90. CD. BBC Audiobooks America. 978-0-563-52463-2. 2004. $39.95. CASS. Durkin Hayes Publishing Ltd. 978-0-88646-214-7. 1987. $16.99.

Atwood's novel is marketed as an adult book but has strong appeal for mature readers. In her work, Offred is a Handmaid in the Republic of Gilead (which was once the United States). In this society women are oppressed. They are no longer allowed to read and their only value is for reproduction. Offred must lie on her back once a month and pray that the Commander makes her pregnant, because in an age of declining births, the Handmaids are valued only if their ovaries are viable. Once Offred lived with her husband, protected her daughter, and had a job, but all of that is now gone. Atwood gives a riveting look into an unsettling dystopian society.

GRADES: 9–12

REVIEWS: *Booklist* 3/01/87

Bechard, Margaret. *Spacer and Rat.* 192 p. TR. Roaring Brook Press. 978-1-59643-058-7. 2005. $16.95.

Jack has spent his whole life in space and is about to leave his apprenticeship. On his way back from the spaceport, he runs into an Earthie named Kit. She is considered a rat, a term the Spacers use to refer to anyone who doesn't contribute to society, especially children abandoned by their parents. Kit has in her possession a modified "maintenance bot" that is a highly intelligent being. Jack's views about his future and his attitudes shift as he and Kit must protect the bot from others trying to possess the device. Part adventure, part science fiction, this title has appeal to both middle and high school readers.

GRADES: 8–12

REVIEWS: *Booklist* 9/01/05, *SLJ* 11/05, *VOYA* 10/05

Bradbury, Ray. *Fahrenheit 451.* Page count varies with edition. There are significant formats currently available in print.

Fahrenheit 451 is a novel that takes place far in the future. Bradbury takes readers to a society where intelligence is altered by people who fear the knowledge gained from books. Firemen no longer put fires out but start them, burning everything along the path to former knowledge found in books. A ruined romance between a fireman named Montag and his wife is the book's focus as she does unspeakable things to the man after he shows her a secret stash of books that destroys his life forever. The alternate universe where minds and free thinking are suppressed is presented in Bradbury's chilling masterpiece. *Fahrenheit 451* has been listed on high school recommended reading lists for decades.

GRADES: 9-12

Brooks, Terry. *Star Wars, Episode I: The Phantom Menace.* N/A. Random House Publishing Group. 978-0-345-43754-9. 1999. N/A. PB. Random House Publishing Group. 978-0-345-43411-1. 2000. $7.99.

The Jedi Knight Qui-Gon Jinn and his apprentice, young Obi-Wan Kenobi, are charged with the protection of Amidala, the young Queen of Naboo. Amidala wishes to end the siege of her planet by Trade Federation warships. In the city of Tatooine is a shop where the slave boy Anakin Skywalker toils and dreams of finding a way to win freedom for himself and his beloved mother. Amidala's wishes bring Qui-Gon, Obi-Wan, and one of the Queen's young handmaidens to Anakin. There they discover he has a gift of understanding the rightness of things. Teen readers will be drawn to this title and the many other spin-offs of the Star Wars legend.

GRADES: 8–10

REVIEWS: *Booklist* 6/15/99

Burgess, Anthony. *A Clockwork Orange.* N/A. TR. W. W. Norton & Company, Incorporated. 978-0-393-31283-6. 1995. $13.95. LB. Buccaneer Books, Incorporated. 978-1-56849-511-8. 1996. $31.95. RE. San Val, Incorporated. 978-0-8085-8194-9. 1995. $25.70. CD. HarperCollins Publishers. 978-0-06-117062-1. 2007. $34.95. CASS. Spoken Arts, Incorporated. 978-0-8045-1120-9. N/A. $10.95. EB. Recorded Books, LLC. 978-1-4356-7193-5. 2008. $68.00. LP. Thorndike Press. 978-0-7862-4644-1. 2002. $28.95.

The violence and disturbing look at a dystopian society in *A Clockwork Orange* marks this classic work a read for sophisticated and mature readers. In Britain's future, society is divided into two groups—the well-offs who live in mansions surrounded with security, and the have-nots who struggle to survive day to day. Burgess's character is an unlawful youth belonging to a gang that rapes girls, fights other gangs, and terrorizes peaceful souls. He reaches a stage where his humanity is in question and attempts to rehabilitate him occur. Burgess is probing the fundamentals of moral choice and free will offering the question to readers, "Is a person necessarily good if he is incapable of choosing evil?"

GRADES: 10–12

Burgess, Melvin. *Bloodsong.* 354 p. RE. San Val, Incorporated. 978-1-4178-2373-4. 2007. $18.45. PB. Simon & Schuster Children's Publishing. 978-1-4169-3616-9. 2007. $7.99.

This sequel to Burgess's *Bloodtide* stands alone and pushes the envelope of defining young adult literature. By bringing together science fiction and Viking mythology this story focuses on fifteen-year-old Sigurd, son of *Bloodtide*'s Sigmund. Organic machines roam war-torn futuristic England and Sigurd tries to reclaim his royal lineage. Burgess pulls no punches in his dark dystopian world. Classic themes of heroism, love, and betrayal are illustrated with violent imagery that is shocking. Obviously not for all readers, but this title refuses to leave the stage and there are readers who will be enthralled with the story line.

GRADES: 10-12

REVIEWS: *Booklist* 9/01/07, *Publishers Weekly* 7/30/07, *VOYA* 8/07

Burgess, Melvin. *Bloodtide.* N/A. RE. San Val, Incorporated. 978-0-613-92618-8. 2002. $17.20. PB. Simon & Schuster Children's Publishing. 978-1-4169-3615-2. 2007. $7.99.

It seems odd to suggest that a novel based on a thirteenth-century Icelandic saga will appeal to teenagers, but *Bloodtide* is that kind of book. Post-apocalyptic London is populated by halfmen and humans. The halfmen are slaves—composites of people and animals, achieved through genetic engineering. The humans are prejudiced, power-hungry rulers, crippled by economic depression. Alternating narrations by various characters and also by an omniscient narrator may challenge less-proficient readers. However, Burgess's bleak and horrific vision of a ruthless society will engage sophisticated readers. This book is a bloody, profane page-turner.

GRADES: 10–12

REVIEWS: *Booklist* 10/15/01, *Kirkus* 8/15/01, *Publishers Weekly* 11/26/01, *VOYA* 12/01

Butler, Octavia. *Kindred.* N/A. TR. Beacon Press. 978-0-8070-8369-7. 2004. $15.00. TR. Beacon Press. 978-0-8070-8310-9. N/A. $24.95. LB. Perma-Bound Books. 978-0-605-06613-7. 1979. $21.00. RE. San Val, Incorporated. 978-1-4176-2941-1. 2004. $26.95. EB. Beacon Press. 978-0-8070-8370-3. 2003. $12.95.

Dana is snatched abruptly from her home in California and transported to the antebellum South to save a young boy named Rufus. The problem is that Dana is a twenty-six-year-old black woman from California and Rufus is a small white child living on his father's plantation in Maryland. Rufus and his parents treat her as a slave. Her modern mind-set puts her in great danger, especially her ability to read and write. She learns that Rufus is the key to her heritage and her goal is to help Rufus survive until he fathers her great-great-grandmother. *Kindred* has been recognized as a groundbreaking title about race but it also is an example of high-quality science fiction. Older readers in a diverse setting will appreciate being introduced to this classic title.

GRADES: 10–12

Butler, Octavia. *Parable of the Sower.* N/A. TR. Grand Central Publishing. 978-0-446-67550-5. 2000. $13.99. RE. San Val, Incorporated. 978-1-4177-3869-4. 2000. $25.75.

In the year 2025, Lauren Olamina, a young black woman, flees her Los Angeles neighborhood when the paints, who are desperate homeless scavengers and violent pyromaniac addicts, overrun her community. She heads north with thousands of other refugees seeking a better life. The world is in full decline due to global warming, pollution, and racial and ethnic tensions. Lauren suffers from hyperempathy, a genetic condition that causes her to feel the pain of others. Her journey is one of hope to discover a better world and leave this one of cruelty and hunger. Octavia Butler's writing is geared to an adult audience but her use of current themes mixed with a science fiction background will appeal to older and more proficient teen readers.

GRADES: 10–12

REVIEWS: *Booklist* 11/15/03, *Kirkus* 10/15/93, *Publishers Weekly* 12/06/93, *SLJ* 7/94

Card, Orson Scott. *Ender's Game.* 368 p. TR. Tom Doherty Associates, LLC. 978-0-312-93208-4. 1985. $27.95. LB. Perma-Bound Books. 978-0-8479-2854-5. 1977. $12.99. RE. San Val, Incorporated. 978-0-613-82422-4. 2002. $16.00. PB. Tom Doherty Associates, LLC. 978-0-7653-4229-4. 2002. $5.99. PB. Tom Doherty Associates, LLC. 978-0-8125-2358-4. 1994. $6.99. CD. Macmillan Audio. 978-1-4272-0526-1. 2008. $39.95. CASS. BBC Audiobooks America. 978-0-7927-3358-4. N/A. $59.95. EB. Tom Doherty Associates, LLC. 978-1-4299-6393-0. 1985. $14.00.

This is the story of child genius Ender Wiggin, a six-year-old who advances from being the smartest, smallest boy in Battle School to savior of humankind. In order to prepare for an impending war with a murderous insectoid race, various earth children are selected to train on "The Battle Game." Ender quickly rises to the top of Battle School but also has to navigate the land mines his fellow students set for him in the boarding school. Many titles have been spun off *Ender's Game* including *Speaker for the Dead, Xenocide, Children of the Mind, A War of Gifts,* and *Ender in Exile.*

GRADES: 8–12

REVIEWS: *Booklist* 12/15/87

Card, Orson Scott. *Ender's Shadow.* 384 p. TR. Tom Doherty Associates, LLC. 978-0-312-86860-4. 1999. $24.95. CD. Macmillan Audio. 978-1-59397-664-4. 2005. $49.95. EB. Tom Doherty Associates, LLC. 978-1-4299-6398-5. 1999. $14.00.

Ender's Shadow is a stand-alone parallel novel to *Ender's Game.* Here the focus is on superhuman child Bean. The child prodigy was raised on the streets and was in danger of dying from starvation. His genius is discovered and he's sent to the Battle School where he becomes Ender's ally. The strength of Card's writing is in his child characters who are both conflicted and noble. Both *Ender's Game* and *Ender's Shadow* maintain devoted readers bordering on cult status and the story lines remain creatively fresh to a new generation of readers. Other titles stemming from *Ender's Shadow* are *Shadow of the Hegemon, Shadow Puppets,* and *Shadow of the Giant.*

GRADES: 8–12

REVIEWS: *Booklist* 7/01/99, *Publishers Weekly* 7/05/99

AWARDS: Alex Award, BBYA Top Ten

Cart, Michael, ed. *Tomorrowland: Ten Stories About the Future.* 208 p. TR. Scholastic, Incorporated. 978-0-590-37678-5. 1999. $15.95. PB. Scholastic, Incorporated. 978-0-590-37679-2. 2001. $4.99.

Ten prominent children's and young adult writers have created stories that reveal their vision of the future. Authors include Jon Scieszka, Gloria Skurzynski, and Rodman Philbrick. Their tales include hints of humor, sadness, loss, and hope. Characters explore the reason why the world is the way it is, from explaining the disappearance of Neanderthal man to an allegory of Cain and Abel on Mars. There is an emphasis on the strength of relationships among family and friends. Although released in time with the millennium change, these short stories will appeal to students pondering their own individual futures.

GRADES: 8–10

REVIEWS: *Booklist* 8/01/99, *Publishers Weekly* 9/20/99, *SLJ* 9/99, *VOYA* 12/99

Clarke, Arthur C. *2001: A Space Odyssey.* 296 p. TR. Perfection Learning Corporation. 978-0-7569-0678-8. 2000. $15.65. LB. Buccaneer Books, Incorporated. 978-1-56849-417-3. 1994. $24.95. CD. Brilliance Audio. 978-1-4233-3662-4. 2008. $14.99. CD. Brilliance Audio. 978-1-58788-179-4. 2000. $57.25. CASS. Harper Collins Publishers. 978-0-89845-220-4. 1984. $8.98. LP. Thorndike Press. 978-0-8161-7486-7. 1994. $23.95.

Clarke's masterpiece explores man's connection to technology, its rapid advancement, and the danger of being reliant on machines. The peril here is the computer HAL 9000 of which man does not fully comprehend its inner workings. Dr. David Bowman is the sole human left to confront HAL who is malfunctioning and disobeys Bowman's orders. The suspense of man versus machine is intense as Bowman realizes HAL is a murderer. Clarke is sending a warning message about dependency on technology and it is very interesting to realize this title was written before the United States placed a man on the moon. This classic tale is a solid fit for older, advanced readers. Other titles spun off the original work are: *2010: Odyssey Two, 2061: Odyssey Three, 3001: The Final Odyssey.*

GRADES: 9–12

Clements, Andrew. *Things Not Seen.* 251 p. TR. Perfection Learning Corporation. 978-0-7569-2599-4. 2004. $14.65. TR. Penguin Group (USA) Incorporated. 978-0-399-23626-6. 2002. $16.99. LB. Perma-Bound Books. 978-0-605-95278-2. 2002. $13.99. RE. San Val, Incorporated. 978-1-4176-0978-9. 2004. $17.20. PB. Penguin Group (USA) Incorporated. 978-0-14-240076-0. 2004. $6.99. CD. Random House Audio Publishing Group. 978-0-307-28251-4. 2005. $39.00. EB. Books on Tape, Incorporated. 978-0-7393-4536-8. 2007. $38.25.

Clements's work is about the adventure of Bobby Phillips, who wakes up one morning to find that somehow he has turned invisible. Readers are encouraged to ponder the benefits and drawbacks of suddenly being invisible, but Bobby has fears of being alone and unable to talk to friends. He reaches out to a blind girl, Alicia Van Dorn, and together they try to find a solution to his weird situation. An additional conflict arises when Bobby is labeled a victim of foul play and his parents are threatened to be tossed in jail. The funny situation that turns scary is a nice blend of teen conflict and science fiction. This title is on the cute side rather than alarming and has potential appeal for middle school readers.

GRADES: 7–9

REVIEWS: *Kirkus* 2/01/02, *Publishers Weekly* 1/28/02, *SLJ* 3/02, *VOYA* 2/02

Colfer, Eoin. *The Supernaturalist.* 272 p. TR. Hyperion Books for Children. 978-0-7868-5148-5. 2004. $16.95. PB. Hyperion Books for Children. 978-0-7868-5149-2. 2005. $7.99. CD. Random House Audio Publishing Group. 978-0-7393-7137-4. 2008. $39.00. EB. Random House Audio Publishing Group. 978-0-7393-3017-3. 2007. $42.50.

Fourteen-year-old Cosmo is rescued from near death following his escape from a nasty orphanage. His benefactors are three streetwise people on a mysterious mission. Led by Stefan, the trio includes a Latina teen with awesome mechanical skills and a child-size adult who is a paramedic. They are hunting evil parasites that no one else, except Cosmo, can see. Colfer's fast-paced story is as thrilling as a video game and includes plenty of speculative technology used to destroy the parasites. With strong appeal for boys, this plot-driven story is a nice fit for middle school techno-geeks.

GRADES: 6–9

REVIEWS: *Booklist* 8/01/04, *Publishers Weekly* 4/19/04, *SLJ* 7/04, *VOYA* 8/04

Cormier, Robert. *Fade.* N/A. TR. Peter Smith Publisher, Incorporated. 978-0-8446-7216-8. 2002. $20.50. LB. Perma-Bound Books. 978-0-605-02175-4. 1988. $14.95. PB. Random House Children's Books. 978-0-385-73134-8. 2004. $7.99.

Cormier offers a different take on the invisible character theme. Thirteen-year-old Paul learns that he can make himself invisible, a power handed down through generations in his family. The ability to "fade" and come back at first seems to be incredibly cool, but Paul is shown dark secrets about people he encounters. Sex (including incest), violence (even murder) and monstrosities in relatives and friends are revealed. Paul swears to never use the fade, but the power is repeated in the next generation when Paul confronts his thirteen-year-old nephew who is vandalizing and killing in a small town. Cormier's talent bursts forth in the climactic scene of uncle and nephew wrestling for a knife. The grim topics revealed while invisible may shock younger readers.

GRADES: 9–12

REVIEWS: *Booklist* 9/01/88, *Publishers Weekly* 9/30/88, *SLJ* 10/88

Crichton, Michael. *The Andromeda Strain.* 331 p. TR. Perfection Learning Corporation. 978-0-8124-1506-3. 2003. $15.65. LB. Buccaneer Books, Incorporated. 978-1-56849-066-3. 1991. $21.95. RE. San Val, Incorporated. 978-1-4177-7978-9. 2003. $17.55. PB. HarperCollins Publishers. 978-0-06-170315-7. 2008. $9.99.

The United States government becomes aware that returning space probes may be contaminated. This warning is given by several top biophysicists in the country, but the warnings are not acted upon for two years. A satellite sent to outer space to collect organisms for study falls to earth in a remote area of the Arizona desert. Twelve miles away is the small town of Piedmont. There a shocking discovery is made: the streets are littered with the dead, as if they dropped in midstride. Crichton's novel is a gripping reminder for humans not to mess with forces greater than themselves. Although written for an adult audience, this title deserves a place on young adult library shelves.

GRADES: 10–12

Crichton, Michael. *Timeline.* 464 p. Knopf Doubleday Publishing Group. 978-0-679-44481-7. 1999. $26.95. LB. Perma-Bound Books. 978-0-605-23182-5. 1999. $14.99. RE. San Val, Incorporated. 978-0-613-33633-8. 2000. $18.40. PB. Random House Publishing Group. 978-0-345-41762-6. 2000. $7.99. EB. Adobe Systems, Incorporated. 978-1-58945-590-0. 2000. $7.99.

Crichton's action-packed story combines time travel with archaeological exploration and involves a power struggle in medieval France. ITC is a company at the forefront of quantum technology and has developed the means to transport humans back in time. A message from a Professor Johnson stating "Help me" is uncovered at the remains of a medieval castle in France. A rescue effort of five people is launched but two ITC escorts are immediately killed when they arrive in the year 1357. The survivors try to find the missing professor and are in a race against time to return to their own era. This title, marketed for adults, is a fine example of man abusing technology.

GRADES: 10–12

REVIEWS: *Booklist* 11/15/99, *Kirkus* 11/01/99, *Publishers Weekly* 11/08/99, *SLJ* 4/00

Dickinson, Peter. *Eva.* 220 p. TR. Peter Smith Publisher, Incorporated. 978-0-8446-7274-8. 2005. $21.50. TR. Perfection Learning Corporation. 978-0-8124-8923-1. 1990. $14.65. LB. San Val, Incorporated. 978-0-8335-6146-6. 1990. $14.15. PB. Random House Children's Books. 978-0-440-20766-5. 1990. $6.99.

Eva is fourteen years old and has been involved in a terrible car crash. She awakens from a strange dream and finds herself in a hospital bed. Medical science has allowed doctors to transplant her functioning brain from her crushed body and place it in an able body of a chimpanzee. Eva is able to communicate with a voice synthesizer and grows comfortable with her new self. Dickinson's story has a political slant about animal rights and placing chimps back into the wild, yet, the story is a fascinating take on science's place in determining the fate of living things. The complicated story line is more appropriate for high school students.

GRADES: 9–12

REVIEWS: *Booklist* 5/01/89, *Publishers Weekly* 2/10/89, *SLJ* 4/89

DuPrau, Jeanne. *The City of Ember* (*Books of Ember* **series**). 288 p. TR. Random House Children's Books. 978-0-375-82273-5. 2003. $16.99. LB. Random House Children's Books. 978-0-375-92274-9. 2003. $19.99. RE. San Val, Incorporated. 978-1-4176-3594-8. 2004. $16.00. LB. Perma-Bound Books. 978-0-605-02073-3. 2003. $12.99. PB. Random House Children's Books. 978-0-385-73628-2. 2008. $6.99. PB. Random House Children's Books. 978-0-375-82274-2. 2004. $5.99. CD. Random House Audio Publishing Group. 978-0-7393-3167-5. 2006. $30.00. CD. Random House Audio Publishing Group. 978-1-4000-8983-3. 2004. $45.00. PLAY. Findaway World, LLC. 978-0-7393-7097-1. 2008. $44.99. CASS. Random House Audio Publishing Group. 978-0-8072-2076-4. 2004. $32.00. EB. Random House Audio Publishing Group. 978-0-7393-4508-5. 2006. $42.50.

Ember is a doomed city that is more than 200 years old and surrounded by a dark unknown. Humans live here but instructions on how to escape have been lost. Everyone knows to stay in the city and cross their fingers as the rickety electricity continues to power the lights. Lina Mayfleet and Doon Harrow, a pair of twelve-year-olds, acquire jobs on Assignment Day. Soon the youngsters realize that due to a lack of food the public will panic, causing the city to die. The story becomes a race against time to discover how to escape Ember. Middle school readers will love how Doon and Lina become heroes for Ember's population. Other titles in the series are *The People of Sparks, The Prophet of Yonwood,* and *The Diamond of Darkhold.*

GRADES: 6–9

REVIEWS: *Booklist* 4/15/03, *SLJ* 5/03, *VOYA* 6/03

Farmer, Nancy. *The House of the Scorpion.* 400 p. TR. Simon & Schuster Children's Publishing. 978-0-689-85222-0. 2002. $17.95. LB. Perma-Bound Books. 978-0-605-45908-3. 2002. $14.99. RE. San Val, Incorporated. 978-1-4176-1900-9. 2004. $20.85. PB. Simon & Schuster Children's Publishing. 978-0-689-85223-7. 2004. $9.99. CD. Simon & Schuster Audio. 978-0-7435-7246-0. 2008. $39.99. CASS. Recorded Books, LLC. 978-1-4025-4173-5. 2004. $29.99. LP. Thorndike Press. 978-0-7862-5048-6. 2003. $24.95.

Young Matteo (Matt) Alacran lives because he is a clone of the original Matteo Alacran, a.k.a El Patron, the ruler of an opium farm bordering the United States. El Patron is 142 years old, surviving by harvesting necessary organs from his stable of clones. Matt is given perks but he's not allowed to forget his life's purpose. Farmer's plot incorporates a coming-of-age story with a horrifying misuse of science. The intensity of Matt's life and death situation will be better appreciated by mature readers.

GRADES: 9–12

REVIEWS: *Booklist* 9/15/02, *Kirkus* 7/01/02, *Publishers Weekly* 7/08/02, *SLJ* 9/02

AWARDS: BBYA Top Ten, Newbery Honor, Printz Honor

Finney, Jack. *Time and Again.* 400 p. TR. Simon & Schuster. 978-0-684-80105-6. 1995. $14.95. LB. Buccaneer Books, Incorporated. 978-0-89968-403-1. 1995. $25.95. RE. San Val, Incorporated. 978-0-613-16436-8. 1995. $26.90. CASS. Recorded Books, LLC. 978-1-4025-2494-3. N/A. $39.95.

Time and Again is more of a cerebral story than an action tale about time travel and was originally marketed to an adult audience. The United States government has discovered a method to travel back in time strictly by mental means. A young artist, Si Morely, is picked to first travel back in time. He discovers the experience affects him and realizes he is falling in love with a woman from another time. He also is determined to solve a mystery but ponders if he should interfere and disrupt history. The complicated theme of time travel and a more adult story tone places this book into the upper young adult interest area.

GRADES: 10–12

Goodman, Alison. *Singing the Dogstar Blues.* N/A. LB. Perma-Bound Books. 978-0-7804-5926-7. 1998. $13.99. PB. Penguin Group (USA) Incorporated. 978-0-14-240246-7. 2004. $7.99.

Joss is a wild, fun-loving girl who plays the harmonica and is also a student of time travel. Her life turns upside down when Mavkel, the first Chorian to visit Earth, comes to study time travel and selects Joss to be his roommate and study partner. Joss's carefree lifestyle is disrupted but there is plenty of excitement with Mavkel. However, when he becomes ill and is near death, Joss has to break a strict rule and travel back in time to save her alien friend. Goodman mixes adventure, mystery, and humor with science fiction to create a fast-paced yarn suitable for a wide range of young adult ages.

GRADES: 8–12

REVIEWS: *Booklist* 4/15/03, *Publishers Weekly* 3/03/03, *SLJ* 4/03, *VOYA* 2/03

Gould, Stephen. *Jumper.* 352 p. TR. Tom Doherty Associates, LLC. 978-0-312-85272-6. 1992. $21.95. PB. Tom Doherty Associates, LLC. 978-0-7653-5769-4. 2008. $7.99.

Gould's story about teleportation has only one character able to perform the feat. He doesn't use chambers or worry about having his DNA scrambled. Instead he has no idea how he does it. David Rice is seventeen and first "jumps" to escape his abusive father. He is now a very unique runaway and is able to set up a comfortable life in New York City. Eventually the authorities corner him; they want to understand his powers and for him to go to work for them. This story will make teens wonder, "What would I do if . . . ?"

GRADES: 9–12

REVIEWS: *Kirkus* 6/02/92, *Kirkus* 7/01/92, *Publishers Weeky* 7/06/92

Grant, Michael. *Gone.* 576 p. TR. HarperCollins Publishers. 978-0-06-144876-8. 2008. $17.99. LB. HarperCollins Publishers. 978-0-06-144877-5. 2008. $18.89. EB. HarperCollins Publishers. 978-0-06-190966-5. 2009. $9.99.

Everyone over the age of thirteen had disappeared from Perdido Beach, California. The children left behind find themselves battling hunger, fear, and each other. Without adult authority leaders, both good and evil emerge to control the town. They discover a dome has been placed over a twenty-mile radius, preventing any hope of escape. Worse yet, freakish mutations show up in animals and when anyone turns fourteen, he or she disappears. There is a creepy gruesomeness to the work as the children are intent on killing each other. A climactic scene ends just in time to set up a sequel. The work targets younger readers, but passages are quite intense. Other titles in the series are *Hunger: A Gone Novel* and *Lies: A Gone Novel.*

GRADES: 8–10

REVIEWS: *Booklist* 5/15/08, *SLJ* 8/08, *VOYA* 4/08

Haddix, Margaret Peterson. *Among the Hidden* (*Shadow Children* series). 160 p. TR. Perfection Learning Corporation. 978-0-7569-0553-8. 2000. $14.65. TR. Simon & Schuster Children's Publishing. 978-0-689-81700-7. 1998. $17.99. LB. San Val, Incorporated. 978-0-613-23618-8. 2000. $13.00. LB. Fitzgerald Books. 978-1-4242-0395-6. 2000. $20.00. PB. Simon & Schuster Children's Publishing. 978-0-689-82475-3. 2000. $6.99. CASS. Recorded Books, LLC. 978-1-4025-7617-1. 2004. $24.95. EB. Recorded Books, LLC. 978-1-4294-6596-0. 2007. $1.00. LP. Thorndike Press. 978-0-7862-3051-8. 2000. $20.95.

Luke Garner is twelve years old and must hide from the government. He lives on a farm with his mother, father, and two brothers. That makes Luke the family's third child, which makes him illegal. Isolated from the world, he peeks outside a small vent in his upstairs room and realizes the neighbors also have a third child. He recklessly leaves his house to meet thirteen-year-old Jen Talbot. Together they challenge the Population Police by organizing a rally. The results are shockingly tragic. Haddix writes about a dystopia that has fallen under a government's abusive power and her story has wide appeal for middle school readers. Other titles in the series are *Among the Impostors, Among the Betrayed, Among the Barons, Among the Brave, Among the Enemy,* and *Among the Free.*

GRADES: 6–9

REVIEWS: *Kirkus* 7/15/98, *Publishers Weekly* 8/10/98, *SLJ* 9/98, *VOYA* 10/98

AWARDS: Quick Picks Top Ten

Halam, Ann. *Dr. Franklin's Island.* N/A. TR. Peter Smith Publisher, Incorporated. 978-0-8446-7282-3. 2006. $21.75. LB. Perma-Bound Books. 978-0-605-01272-1. 2002. $12.50. RE. San Val, Incorporated. 978-0-613-72267-4. 2003. $17.20. PB. Random House Children's Books. 978-0-440-23781-5. 2003. $6.99.

Semirah and two other survivors find themselves stranded on a remote island following a horrific plane crash. Semirah's companions are the brave Miranda and the whiny Arnie. The three teens try to form a survival plan, but Arnie wanders off. Semirah and Miranda find him but also locate the compound of a mad scientist, Dr. Franklin. He is researching trans-species genetic engineering and plucks the teens as his first experiments. His cool abuse in the name of science is terrifying and there seems to be no escape for Semirah, Miranda, and Arnie. This tension-packed tale will appeal to many teens, both male and female.

GRADES: 8–12

REVIEWS: *Booklist* 7/01/02, *Publishers Weekly* 5/06/02, *SLJ* 5/02, *VOYA* 10/02

Halam, Ann. *Siberia.* 233 p. TR. DIANE Publishing Company. 978-1-4379-6445-5. 2008. $25.00.

Wild animals have become extinct in Halam's metaphorical Siberia. In this icy environment, thirteen-year-old Sloe has grown up with her mother, an exiled scientist who nurtured genetically engineered life forms. These forms may develop into lost species. When her mother is arrested, Sloe takes responsibility for the "Lindquist kits" and protects them from frostbite, hunger, bandits, and government patrols. Sloe is an engaging teen determined to correct the wrongs of society despite the overwhelming odds she faces. Halam's novel will cause her readers to believe in the redemptive value of science.

GRADES: 9–12

REVIEWS: *Booklist* 6/01/05, *Kirkus* 6/01/05, *SLJ* 6/05, *VOYA* 6/05

Hautman, Pete. *Rash*. 256 p. TR. Simon & Schuster Children's Publishing. 978-0-689-86801-6. 2006. $16.99. PB. Simon & Schuster Children's Publishing. 978-0-689-86904-4. 2007. $9.99. CD. Recorded Books, LLC. 978-1-4281-1103-5. 2006. $66.75. CASS. Recorded Books, LLC. 978-1-4281-1098-4. 2006. $39.75. EB. Recorded Books, LLC. 978-1-4294-1259-9. 2006. $1.00.

Hautman begins his tale with a tongue-in-check situation. In 2076 verbal abuse and dangerous activities are against the law in the United Safer States of America. Technology has advanced for the sole reason of protecting everyone, including athletes, from injury. For Bo Marsten, the punishment for allegedly spreading a rash throughout his school is a prison sentence for lack of self-control. His jail is located in the frozen north tundra where he's forced to play a nasty game of football. Clever gadgetry comes in handy when Bo decides to escape. The satire and extensive use of technology may be lost on younger readers, but older readers will enjoy the blend of science and humor.

GRADES: 8–12

REVIEWS: *Booklist* 5/15/06, *Publishers Weekly* 5/08/06, *SLJ* 8/06, *VOYA* 6/06

Heinlein, Robert. *Stranger in a Strange Land*. 448 p. TR. Penguin Group (USA) Incorporated. 978-0-441-78838-5. 1991. $16.95. TR. Amereon LTD. 978-0-8488-0522-7. 1976. $16.95. LB. Perma-Bound Books. 978-0-8479-0987-2. 1961. $14.99. RE. San Val, Incorporated. 978-0-8085-2087-0. 1987. $18.40. CD. Blackstone Audio, Incorporated. 978-0-7861-7430-0. 2006. $32.95. CD. Blackstone Audio, Incorporated. 978-0-7861-8848-2. 2004. $59.95. CASS. Blackstone Audio, Incorporated. 978-0-7861-4406-8. 2006. $32.95. CASS. Blackstone Audio, Incorporated. 978-0-7861-9356-1. 2006. $24.95. EB. Penguin Group (USA) Incorporated. 978-1-4295-3732-2. 2007. $7.99. EB. Blackstone Audio, Incorporated. 978-1-4417-1050-5. 2009. $49.95.

Heinlein's Hugo Award-winning story features Valentine Michael Smith, a human raised by Martians on the planet Mars. He returns to Earth in his early adulthood and the book details in interaction with Earth culture. Since Smith is unaccustomed to the atmosphere and gravity of Earth, he is confined at Bethesda Hospital. Eventually he earns his freedom and the story moves to political commentary about various traditions of churches. Smith is truly a stranger in a strange land as science brings him from his comfortable world of Mars to the seemingly odd traditions of Earth. Heinlein's sophisticated themes are meant to be appreciated by mature readers.

GRADES: 9–12

Heinlein, Robert. *Tunnel in the Sky.* 272 p. TR. Simon & Schuster. 978-1-4165-0551-8. 2005. $15.00. PB. Random House Publishing Group. 978-0-345-46623-5. 2003. $6.99.

This classic science fiction story examines the theme of sending Earth's excess population to colonize other planets. Rod Walker is a high school student who dreams of becoming a professional colonist. The final test of his Advanced Survival class is to stay alive on an unfamiliar planet for between two and ten days. Things go terribly wrong and Rod ends up stranded on a planet where he becomes the leader of a community. Heinlein's tale is an example of a science fiction theme of man overreaching his own world and exploring other locations. This book is for sophisticated and true fans of old-school science fiction.

GRADES: 9–12

Herbert, Frank. *Dune* (*Dune Chronicles*). 528 p. TR. Penguin Group (USA) Incorporated. 978-0-441-00590-1. 1999. $29.95. LB. Perma-Bound Books. 978-0-8479-0998-8. 1965. $14.99. RE. San Val, Incorporated. 978-0-88103-636-7. 1996. $18.40. PB. Penguin Group (USA) Incorporated. 978-0-441-01062-2. 2002. $9.99. PB. Penguin Group (USA) Incorporated. 978-0-441-17271-9. 1990. $7.99. CD. Macmillan Audio. 978-1-4272-0143-0. 2007. $59.95. CD. Macmillan Audio. 978-1-4272-0236-9. 2007. $34.95. CASS. Books on Tape, Incorporated. 978-0-7366-8959-5. 2002. $36.00. EB. NetLibrary, Incorporated. 978-1-4001-9361-5. 2009. $54.99.

Herbert's classic science fiction work is set far in the future with the human race scattered throughout countless planetary systems. Science and technology have advanced despite the prohibition of computers and artificial intelligence. In this expansive world, Dune is the only planet that can grow spice and becomes the focal point for political maneuverings. Herbert incorporates many themes into his work by giving an interesting portrayal of the downfall of a galactic empire, exploring environmentalism and ecology and the role of gender in society. His characters are heroic and the work is epic in scale, which may intimidate novice readers. The *Dune* series includes many titles such as *Children of Dune, Dune Messiah, God Emperor of Dune,* and *Heretics of Dune.*

GRADES: 9–12

Hoffman, Mary. *Stravaganza: City of Masks.* 344 p. TR. San Val, Incorporated. 978-1-4176-2440-9. 2004. $17.50.

Fifteen-year-old Lucien is suffering from cancer and his father gives him a small notebook to help communicate his thoughts. The notebook is a talisman enabling Lucien to "stravagate," or travel, between contemporary London and sixteenth-century Talia, an alternate world resembling Italy. There Lucien is physically healthy, but he becomes involved with the politics of this alternate world. Using time travel as a device to underscore historical detail, Hoffman's work will interest older readers who enjoy a magical setting. Other titles in the series are *City of Stars, City of Flowers,* and *City of Secrets.*

GRADES: 9–12

REVIEWS: *Booklist* 10/15/02, *Kirkus* 9/15/02, *Publishers Weekly* 9/30/02, *SLJ* 11/02, *VOYA* 12/02

Huxley, Aldous. *Brave New World.* Page count varies with edition. There are significant formats currently available in print.

Although the novel is set sometime in the future, Huxley modeled the setting from America. He uses his classic science fiction novel to express the fear of losing individual identity in an increasingly fast-paced world. In his futuristic society, all members of society are conditioned in childhood to hold the values that the World State idealizes. Constant consumption is the bedrock of stability for the World State. In an early trip to the United States, Huxley was outraged by the culture of youth, commercial cheeriness, and sexual promiscuity. He incorporates these themes in his novel. His social commentary is meant for adult consideration, but mature teens should be exposed to this legendary novel.

GRADES: 10–12

Keyes, Daniel. *Flowers for Algernon.* N/A. LB. Perma-Bound Books. 978-0-8479-1054-0. 1966. $14.99. RE. San Val, Incorporated. 978-1-4176-7080-2. 2005. $24.45. LB. Buccaneer Books, Incorporated. 978-0-89968-345-4. 1993. $18.95. PB. Harcourt Trade Publishers. 978-0-15-603576-7. 2009. $7.99. PB. Spark Publishing Group. 978-1-58663-514-5. 2002. $5.95. CASS. Walberg Publishing. 978-1-886392-04-5. 1995. $24.00. LP. Thorndike Press. 978-0-7838-1412-4. 1995. $22.95.

Charlie Gordon has an IQ of 68 and works a menial job. He also attends reading and writing classes to improve himself and comes to the attention of researchers who seek a human subject on whom they can test experimental surgery to increase intelligence. The surgery has already been done on a mouse named Algernon. When Charlie's IQ reaches 185 he's able to discover flaws in the researchers' theory and he observes Algernon beginning to behave erratically, lose his intelligence, and die. Charlie realizes this will also be his fate. This heartbreaking story points out dangers of science conducting experimental scientific theories on living organisms, treating them as objects, not life. The scientific concepts can be understood by both middle and high school students.

GRADES: 8–12

King, Stephen. *Firestarter.* 401 p. TR. Perfection Learning Corporation. 978-0-8124-3057-8. 1981. $15.65. RE. San Val, Incorporated. 978-0-88103-725-8. 2003. $18.40.

During his college years, Andrew McGee participated in an experiment dealing with "Lot 6," a drug with hallucinogenic effects. Years later his daughter Charlie has developed frightening pyrokinetic abilities. Government agents, not knowing the full extent of Charlie's ability, attempt to capture the father and daughter. Charlie's rage ignites an entire farm and kills several agents, forcing Andrew and Charlie to flee with the shadow government agency determined to stop them. King's story is a classic snapshot of innocent people manipulated by faulty science with tragic results. King's work is ultra-violent and profane and is geared to a mature audience.

GRADES: 10–12

King, Stephen. *The Stand.* N/A. RE. San Val, Incorporated. 978-0-88103-722-7. 1999. $19.65. PB. Penguin Group (USA) Incorporated. 978-0-451-16953-2. 1991. $8.99.

Originally published in 1978, this large tome was re-released in 1990 with an additional 400 pages. Needless to say the book's length may be a challenge for many teen readers, but those who tackle it will come away with a rewarding experience. A man-made biological weapon, a superflu know as "Project Blue," has been released. It kills 99.94% of the human population. *The Stand* shows the total breakdown of society with widespread violence. What also emerges is an epic showdown of good versus evil for the control of the surviving population. Grim scenes of death will startle younger readers.

GRADES: 10–12

REVIEWS: *Publishers Weekly* 4/05/91

Klass, David. *Firestorm: The Caretaker Trilogy.* 304 p. TR. Farrar, Straus & Giroux. 978-0-374-32307-3. 2006. $17.99. CD. Recorded Books, LLC. 978-1-4281-3472-0. 2007. $97.75. CASS. Recorded Books, LLC. 978-1-4281-3467-6. 2007. $67.75.

Jack Danielson finds himself on the run and in danger of being killed. He doesn't know why; all he knows is that his parents sacrificed their lives to save him. Jack must change from a jock teenage football player to become the last hope of a long line of planetary caregivers. He is expected to save the world, one environmental aspect at a time. With training and advice from sultry Eco and a psychic shaggy dog named Gisco, Jack prepares for a showdown over a mysterious orb called Firestorm. Klass has produced a fast-moving thriller that sends a message of how Earth's environment is being abused. Blunt talk about sex sends up a flag making this title a better fit for more mature readers. Other titles in the series are *Whirlwind* and *Timelock.*

GRADES: 8–12

REVIEWS: *Booklist* 9/15/06, *Publishers Weekly* 10/09/06, *SLJ* 9/06, *VOYA* 10/06

Koontz, Dean. *Watchers.* N/A. RE. San Val, Incorporated. 978-0-613-57487-7. 2003. $18.40. CD. Brilliance Audio. 978-1-59355-330-2. 2004. $42.95. PLAY. Findaway World, LLC. 978-1-60812-695-8. 2009. $79.99. CASS. Brilliance Audio. 978-1-59355-328-9. 2004. $29.95. EB. Penguin Group (USA) Incorporated. 978-1-4362-1525-1. 2008. $14.00.

When Travis Cornell encounters a stray dog while hiking, he quickly realizes that the animal is most unusual. He also realizes something terrifying has frightened the dog and is stalking them both. The dog is named Einstein and is the result of a genetic experiment gone wrong. The stalker is a murderous hybrid called "The Outsider." Travis and Einstein, along with romantic interest Nora Devon, are on the run to save their lives. However, they all know a confrontation with The Outsider must happen. This story is a truly frightening tale but also one that has Einstein stealing every scene. High school readers, and dog lovers, will be thrilled.

GRADES: 10–12

REVIEWS: *SLJ* 7/87

Kostick, Conor. *Epic.* 384 p. TR. Penguin Group (USA) Incorporated. 978-0-670-06179-2. 2007. $17.99. RE. San Val, Incorporated. 978-1-4178-2018-4. 2008. $20.85. PB. Penguin Group (USA) Incorporated. 978-0-14-241159-9. 2008. $9.99.

Kostick's story is set in New Earth where violence has been banned for generations. Instead of face-to-face confrontations, arguments and conflicts are settled by playing the fantasy computer game, Epic. Erik and his friends feel their parents have been treated unfairly and set out to put an end to Epic's domination. Erik adopts the persona of a beautiful swashbuckler named Cindella and is threatened with death in the fantasy game, and possibly outside the game. The connection between a fantasy gaming world and reality will surely hook a wide range of readers, especially those who are gamers in real life. The sequel to *Epic* is called *Saga.*

GRADES: 8–12

REVIEWS: *Booklist* 3/01/07, *Publishers Weekly* 5/21/07, *SLJ* 5/07, *VOYA* 6/07

L'Engle, Madeleine. *A Wrinkle in Time.* Page count varies with edition. There are significant formats currently available in print.

Meg Murry is a high-school-aged girl who is transported through time and space to rescue her father. Along with her younger brother Charles Wallace and her friend Calvin O'Keefe, the trio travels by means of tesseract, a fifth-dimensional phenomenon similar to folding the fabric of space and time. Her father, a gifted scientist, is being held prisoner by evil forces on another planet called Camazotz, whose inhabitants are under a form of mind control that also threatens the children. Meg must find a way to battle the mind control and bring everyone back home safely. This classic tale is one of the foundation works of young adult literature and will appeal to many ages.

GRADES: 7–10

AWARDS: Newbery Winner

Lowry, Lois. *The Giver.* 192 p. TR. Houghton Mifflin Harcourt Trade & Reference Publishers. 978-0-395-64566-6. 1993. $17.00. RE. San Val, Incorporated. 978-0-613-72266-7. 2002. $17.20. PB. Random House Children's Books. 978-0-385-73255-0. 2006. $8.95. PB. Spark Publishing Group. 978-1-58663-816-0. 2003. $5.95. CD. Random House Audio Publishing Group. 978-0-8072-8609-8. 2004. $32.30. CD. Random House Audio Publishing Group. 978-0-8072-6203-0. 2001. $28.00. CASS. Random House Audio Publishing Group. 978-0-8072-8312-7. 2004. $32.00. CASS. Books on Tape, Incorporated. 978-0-7366-9042-3. 2000. $30.00. EB. Random House Audio Publishing Group. 978-0-7393-4456-9. 2006. $32.30. LP. Thorndike Press. 978-0-7862-7154-2. 2004. $23.95.

The setting of *The Giver* at first seems to be a peaceful utopian community where pain and confusion have been eliminated. A Council of Elders assigns each twelve-year-old a job that he or she will perform for the rest of his or her life. The main character, Jonas, is one of these young people. Rules apply in the community and if a serious infraction is committed three times, that person is punished by "release." Jonas comes to realize that this society is void of technology, and uses lethal injection as a routine method of population control. *The Giver* has been a selection for assigned readings for a wide variety of ages since it was first published. Companion novels are *Gathering Blue* and *Messenger.*

GRADES: 7–10

REVIEWS: *Kirkus* 3/01/93, *Publishers Weekly* 2/15/93, *SLJ* 5/93, *VOYA* 8/93

AWARDS: Newbery Winner

MacHale, D. J. *Merchant of Death* (*The Pendragon* series). 384 p. TR. Simon & Schuster Children's Publishing. 978-1-4169-3625-1. 2007. $17.99. RE. San Val, Incorporated. 978-0-613-52144-4. 2002. $19.65. PB. Simon & Schuster Children's Publishing. 978-1-4169-5080-6. 2008. $9.99. CD. Brilliance Audio. 978-1-

4233-9896-7. 2009. $49.97. CD. Brilliance Audio. 978-1-4233-9895-0. 2009. $19.99. PLAY. Findaway World, LLC. 978-1-60775-515-9. 2009. $60.00. CASS. Brilliance Audio. 978-1-59737-235-0. 2005. $29.95.

Bobby Pendragon discovers he can travel through flumes to a parallel universe called Denduron. There he becomes a hero-in-training to help resolve a civil war because an evil shape-shifter is set to grab ultimate power and control. Bobby must learn how to fight and becomes more confident in his abilities. The story has a video game riff as there are clear-cut good versus evil scenes leaving no doubt who is evil. The technique of moving between two worlds by means of a South Bronx subway stop will engage the targeted audience of middle school boys. Other titles in this series are *The Lost City of Faar, The Never War, The Reality Bug, Black Water, The Rivers of Zadaa, The Quillan Games, The Pilgrims of Rayne, Raven Rise,* and *The Soldiers of Halla.*

GRADES: 6–9

REVIEWS: *SLJ* 11/02, *VOYA* 12/02

Matheson, Richard. *I Am Legend.* 320 p. TR. Tom Doherty Associates, LLC. 978-0-312-86504-7. 1997. $14.95. LB. Buccaneer Books, Incorporated. 978-0-89966-838-3. 1991. $27.95. RE. San Val, Incorporated. 978-0-613-25618-6. 1997. $26.90. PB. Tom Doherty Associates, LLC. 978-0-8125-2300-3. 1995. $4.99. CD. Blackstone Audio, Incorporated. 978-1-4332-0331-2. 2007. $19.95. CD. Blackstone Audio, Incorporated. 978-1-4332-0332-9. 2007. $29.95. PLAY. Findaway World, LLC. 978-1-60252-869-7. 2007. $74.99. CASS. Blackstone Audio, Incorporated. 978-1-4332-0330-5. 2007. $19.95. EB. Tom Doherty Associates, LLC. 978-0-7653-1874-9. 2007. $14.95.

Robert Neville is the sole uninfected survivor of a pandemic that results in vampirism. In Los Angeles, Neville attempts to comprehend and possibly cure the disease that killed mankind. He copes against losing his humanity by going about a daily routine, but each night a vampire hoard lays siege to his home. He is shocked to find an uninfected woman (maybe) in the daylight. Neville comes across the seemingly uninfected woman, Ruth, abroad in the daylight and captures her. This classic tale is a combination of science trying to find a cure for a horror plot staple—vampires attacking humans.

GRADES: 9–12

Miller, Kirsten. *Kiki Strike: Inside the Shadow City.* N/A. TR. Bloomsbury Publishing. 978-1-58234-960-2. 2006. $16.95. RE. San Val, Incorporated. 978-1-4178-0812-0. 2007. $18.40. PB. Bloomsbury Publishing. 978-1-59990-092-6. 2007. $7.95.

Narrator Ananka Fishbein reveals her adventures as sidekick to Kiki Strike who bills herself as a girl detective. The girls meet in a private school when they are twelve years old. They have discovered a Shadow City, a group of tunnels fifty feet below Manhattan's Chinatown. The tunnels were once used to smuggle illegal goods but now hide gold, cash, and cadavers guarded by huge rats. Ananka and Kiki team up with a troupe of four other girls—with specialties in chemistry, forgery, disguise, and mechanics—and name themselves the Irregulars. The science hook is how the Irregulars incorporate scientific know- how to solve the mystery. Middle school girls who are intelligent readers will love Kiki Strike. The sequel is titled *The Empress's Tomb.*

GRADES: 6–9

REVIEWS: *Booklist* 7/01/06, *Kirkus* 5/15/06, *Publishers Weekly*, 6/12/06, *SLJ* 6/06 *VOYA* 8/06

Ness, Patrick. *The Knife of Never Letting Go* (*Chaos Walking* **series**). 496 p. RE. Candlewick Press. 978-0-7636-3931-0. 2008. $18.99. PB. Candlewick Press. 978-0-7636-4576-2. 2009. $9.99.

Todd Hewitt lives on another planet from Earth where a war has killed all the women and a germ has infected the males enabling their thoughts to be heard by all. The sound is called the Noise and it is accepted by members of Todd's settlement. When Todd discovers a break in the Noise, that is, silence, he realizes he lives in a unique world. Able to communicate with his dog, Todd flees his settlement and is on the run chased by a madman preacher and the rest of the town. The inventiveness of the story makes for a fast-moving plot with many cliffhanging chapters. Both boys and girls will be absorbed into this story of a society gone terribly wrong. Other titles in the series are *The Ask and the Answer* and *Monster of Men.*

GRADES: 8–10

REVIEWS: *Booklist* 9/01/08, *SLJ* 11/08, *VOYA* 10/08

Nix, Garth. *Mister Monday* (*The Keys to the Kingdom* **series**). 361 p. TR. Perfection Learning Corporation. 978-0-7569-1580-3. 2003. $14.65. RE. San Val, Incorporated. 978-0-613-67341-9. 2003. $18.40. PB. Scholastic, Incorporated. 978-0-439-55123-6. 2003. $6.99. CASS. Random House Audio Publishing Group. 978-0-8072-1657-6. 2004. $40.00. EB. Random House Audio Publishing Group. 978-0-7393-4966-3. 2007. $46.75.

Arthur Penhaligon's first day at a new school is marked by a nearly fatal asthma attack, but a key shaped like the minute hand of a clock somehow helps him breathe. Soon, strange-looking people pursue Arthur and a mysterious plague breaks out. He enters a house (that only he can see) searching for a clue to stop the plague and finds the enigmatic Mister Monday. The house holds a weird collection of beings including robot-like Commissionaires and other evil mechanical creatures. Nix's work is a fine blend of science fiction and fantasy that has huge appeal, especially for younger boys. Other titles in the series are *Grim Tuesday, Drowned Wednesday, Sir Thursday, Lady Friday, Superior Saturday,* and *Lord Sunday.*

GRADES: 6–9

REVIEWS: *SLJ* 12/03, *VOYA* 2/04

Norton, Andre. *Voodoo Planet* (*Solar Queen* **series**). 112 p. TR. Wildside Press. 978-1-4344-0505-0. 2009. $19.99. PB. Wildside Press. 978-1-4344-0504-3. 2009. $9.99.

Andre Norton certainly deserves a spot on any list of science fiction stories. *Voodoo Planet* is an interesting tale that combines religion, racial commentary, and science fiction and appears in the third installment in Norton's *Solar Queen* series. In *Voodoo Planet,* three crew members of the Solar Queen are invited to a safari on a planet colonized by people from Africa; whites are the minority and they are stalked by a voodoo priest who tries to block the travelers from returning to civilization. Norton is considered a groundbreaking innovator of science fiction writing. Other titles in the series are *Sargasso of Space, Plague Ship, Postmarked the Stars, Redline the Stars, Derelict for Trade,* and *A Mind for Trade.*

GRADES: 10–12

O'Brien, Robert C. *Z for Zachariah.* 249 p. TR. Perfection Learning Corporation. 978-0-7569-8098-6. 2007. $15.65. TR. Book Wholesalers, Incorporated. 978-0- 7587-4827-0. 2002. $13.40. LB. San Val, Incorporated. 978-0-8085-9337-9. 1987. $13.00. RE. San Val, Incorporated. 978-1-4177-9219-1. 2007. $18.40. LB. Perma- Bound Books. 978-0-8000-1684-5. 1974. $13.99. PB. Simon & Schuster Children's Publishing. 978-1-4169-3921-4. 2007. $7.99. PB. Simon & Schuster Children's Publishing. 978-0-689-84453-9. 2001. $4.99. CD. Recorded Books, LLC. 978-0-7887-4216-3. 2000. $54.00. EB. Recorded Books, LLC. 978-1-4237-3115-3. 2005. $1.00. LP. LRS. 978-1-58118-105-0. 2002. $32.95.

Following a nuclear war that seems to have made much of Earth's land uninhabitable, sixteen-year-old Ann Burden lives alone in a small town in the eastern United States. She believes she is the only one left alive in the world, until she observes a stranger coming to her valley dressed in a plastic radiation protection suit. He bathes in a stream, but is soon contaminated by the radioactive water. Ann nurses him back to health and finds out that he was a scientist before the war. The teen and adult begin an uneasy companionship that is filled with tension. Teens will be intrigued by Ann's situation and serious issues including rape mark this book for mature readers.

GRADES: 8–10

REVIEWS: *Booklist* 7/01/88, *Publishers Weekly* 4/10/87

Patterson, James. *Maximum Ride: The Angel Experiment.* 422 p. TR. Perfection Learning Corporation. 978-0-7569-8272-0. 2007. $15.65. TR. Little, Brown Books for Young Readers. 978-0-316-15556-4. 2005. $16.99. RE. San Val, Incorporated. 978-1-4177-5029-0. 2006. $18.40. CD. Little, Brown Books for Young Readers. 978-1-60024-226-7. 2008. $9.98. CD. Recorded Books, LLC. 978-1-4193-3844-1. 2005. $69.75. CASS. Recorded Books, LLC. 978-1-4193-3629-4. 2005. $62.75. EB. Yen Press. 978-0-7595-2991-5. 2009. $10.99. LP. Thorndike Press. 978-1-4104-1517-2. 2006. $11.95.

Max, a fourteen-year-old girl, is the leader of a group of genetically enhanced kids who have unique talents including the ability to fly. Her troupe was created in a laboratory called "The School" and a sympathetic scientist helped them escape. Now a group called The Erasers have orders to kill them and are led by Ari who was Max's childhood friend. Patterson's fast-moving plot will thrill young adult readers of many ages, especially the battle scenes fought high above the ground. Other titles in the series are *Maximum Ride: School's Out Forever* (Teens' Top Ten), *Maximum Ride: Saving the World and Other Extreme Sports* (Teens' Top Ten), *Maximum Ride: The Final Warning*, *MAX: A Maximum Ride Novel,* and *Fang: A Maximum Ride Novel.* This series has also been adapted into graphic novel format.

GRADES: 7–12

REVIEWS: *Booklist* 2/01/05, *Publishers Weekly* 3/21/05, *SLJ* 5/05, *VOYA* 4/05

AWARDS: Teens' Top Ten

Pfeffer, Susan Beth. *Life as We Knew It* (*The Last Survivors* series). 347 p. TR. Perfection Learning Corporation. 978-1-60686-060-1. 2008. $14.60. TR. Houghton Mifflin Harcourt Trade & Reference Publishers. 978-0-15-205826-5. 2006. $17.00. RE. San Val, Incorporated. 978-1-4178-1541-8. 2008. $17.15. PB. Houghton Mifflin Harcourt Trade & Reference Publishers. 978-0-15-206154-8. 2008. $6.95. CD. Random House Audio Publishing Group. 978-0-7393-3683-0. 2006. $45.00. CD. House Audio Publishing Group. 978-0-7393-3789-9. 2006. $46.75. EB. Random House Audio Publishing Group. 978-0-7393-4810-9. 2007. $46.75.

Natural disasters disrupt the earth following a collision between an asteroid and the moon. Sixteen-year-old Miranda witnesses climate changes on Earth and realizes things she took for granted will never be the same. The electrical grid near her Pennsylvania home is iffy and volcanic ash blocks the sun, causing weird weather patterns, including unseasonable cold. This is a survival tale caused by an outer space disaster. Pfeffer includes explanation as to why the climate has changed but the book's focus is on Miranda's determination to survive with little food or warm shelter. Companion titles are *The Dead and the Gone* and *The World We Live In.*

GRADES: 9–12

REVIEWS: *Booklist* 9/01/06, *Publishers Weekly* 10/16/06, *SLJ* 10/06, *VOYA* 10/06

AWARDS: Teens' Top Ten

Philbrick, Rodman. *The Last Book in the Universe.* 223 p. TR. Perfection Learning Corporation. 978-0-7569-1004-4. 2002. $14.65. LB. Perma-Bound Books. 978-0-605-21724-9. 2000. $12.99. RE. San Val, Incorporated. 978-0-613-45598-5. 2002. $17.20. PB. Scholastic, Incorporated. 978-0-439-08759-9. 2002. $6.99. CASS. Random House Audio Publishing Group. 978-0-8072-8843-6. 2004. $30.00. EB. Random House Audio Publishing Group. 978-0-7393-8090-1. 2009. $32.30.

Philbrick's title is set in an alternate world where poverty reigns and nearly everyone is illiterate. Spaz is an epileptic boy who encounters an elderly man called Ryter. The old man believes in the power of books and the two make a daring visit to Eden, a place with fresh air and technological marvels. Once in Eden Spaz is determined to find Bean, his foster sister. Despite the noble quest, all is not well in this dystopian world. Death occurs and the story is left without a fairy-tale ending. This title has appeared on many recommended school reading lists and will draw readers from the older middle school range.

GRADES: 8–10

REVIEWS: *Booklist* 11/15/00, *Kirkus* 11/01/00, *Publishers Weekly* 11/27/00, *SLJ* 11/00, *VOYA* 12/00

Price, Susan. *The Sterkarm Handshake.* 448 p. TR. HarperCollins Publishers. 978-0-06-028959-1. 2000. $17.95. TR. HarperCollins Publishers. 978-0-06-029392-5. 2000. $18.89.

There's much to like about a book that combines time travel, romance, and rip-roaring action. A British company, FUP, has developed a time tube that leads back to the sixteenth century when the land was ruled by the primitive Sterkarm clan. High-ups in FUP decide to make the area a tourist destination and at the same time rob it of its natural resources. An FUP employee, Andrea, becomes caught up in the Sterkarm world and is concerned about the company's plan. Her actions spark a war between the two worlds and nobody should dismiss the violence warriors from the sixteenth century can create. Bloodshed and a romantic slant mark this title for older young adult readers.

GRADES: 10–12

REVIEWS: *Booklist* 10/01/00, *Kirkus* 10/15/00, *Publishers Weekly* 11/27/00, *SLJ* 12/00, *VOYA* 12/00

Reeve, Philip. *Mortal Engines* (*The Hungry City Chronicles*). 373 p. TR. Perfection Learning Corporation. 978-0-7569-3246-6. 2004. $14.65. LB. Perma-Bound Books. 978-0-605-50862-0. 2001. $13.99. RE. San Val, Incorporated. 978-1-4176-8581-3. 2004. $17.20. PB. HarperCollins Publishers. 978-0-06-008209-3. 2004. $6.99.

Tom Natsworthy is a low-ranking employee with the London Museum. This London is set in the far future and is now a Traction City, one that roams over the world on huge treads scooping up smaller cities and towns. Tom is not worried about enslaving these citizens, but when a scavenger girl tries to assassinate Head Historian Thaddeus Valentine, Tom prevents the murder. He finds himself ejected from London and now travels the destroyed countryside trying to determine who Valentine really is and what plot he is hatching. Clever use of gadgets and steampunk machines keep this story flowing as Tom is the only one who can stop a war from occurring. Some violence and death happens in Reeve's story, but most teenagers will be able to handle the action. Other titles in the series are *Predator's Gold, Infernal Devices, A Darkling Plain, Fever Crumb* (a prequel) and *A Web of Air.*

GRADES: 7–10

REVIEWS: *Booklist* 11/01/03, *Publishers Weekly* 10/27/03, *SLJ* 12/03, *VOYA* 12/03

Ryan, Carrie. *The Forest of Hands and Teeth.* 320 p. TR. Random House Publishing Group. 978-0-385-73681-7. 2009. $16.99. LB. Random House Publishing Group. 978-0-385-90631-9. 2009. $19.99.

At the center of Ryan's story about a zombie apocalypse is a young girl named Mary who is of marrying age. A massive infection has all but wiped out her world, leaving only the handful of people surviving in her village. They're surrounded by zombies craving their flesh. When the protective fence collapses, only Mary and a few other teenagers survive the slaughter. These teens are in a race for their lives as they try to escape the hoard of moaning flesheaters. Ryan's book is an extreme example of science recklessly unleashed with horrifying results. High tension, violence, and gruesome death will probably be too intense for very young readers. The sequel is called *The Dead-Tossed Waves.*

GRADES: 9–12

REVIEWS: *Booklist* 1/01/09, *Publishers Weekly* 2/02/09, *SLJ* 5/09

Shusterman, Neal. *Unwind.* 352 p. TR. Simon & Schuster Children's Publishing. 978-1-4169-1204-0. 2007. $16.99. PB. Simon & Schuster Children's Publishing. 978-1-4169-1205-7. 2009. $8.99. CD. Brilliance Audio. 978-1-4233-7307-0. 2009. $29.99.

Conner Lassiter is sixteen years old and has been assigned to be unwound, which means the incorrigible youth is to have his organs harvested and transplanted into other people. He escapes his fate and meets with other teens also assigned to be unwound. In this futuristic society, parents can assign their offspring to be unwound before they turn eighteen simply by signing a paper. An underground network helps Conner avoid capture, but he is not aware he will be betrayed. Shusterman's work hits high on the creepy factor and is much too intense for younger teens. Older readers will be thrilled.

GRADES: 9–12

REVIEWS: *Booklist* 10/15/07, *Publishers Weekly* 11/26/07, *SLJ* 1/08, *VOYA* 10/07

AWARDS: Quick Picks Top Ten

Skurzynski, Gloria. *Virtual War* **(*Virtual War Chronologs*).** 188 p. PB. Simon & Schuster Children's Publishing. 978-1-4169-7577-9. 2008. $10.99.

One of the early teen novels featuring a video game slant, *Virtual War* has an interesting story line. Fourteen-year-old Corgan has been genetically engineered to fight a virtual reality war for one of the few places left on Earth to live. His team includes rebellious Sharla and ten-year-old Brig who are code-breaker and strategist, respectively. As Corgan prepares for the battle, he comes to realize that he is involved in something more than a game. This title's concept was many years ahead of its time, but still remains a riveting, fast-paced read for middle school teens. Other titles in the series are *The Clones, The Revolt,* and *The Choice.*

GRADES: 6–9

REVIEWS: *Booklist* 8/01/97, *Kirkus* 5/15/97, *Publishers Weekly* 5/19/97, *SLJ* 7/97

Sleator, William. *House of Stairs.* TR. Peter Smith Publisher, Incorporated. 978-0-8446-7186-4. 2001. $20.75. LB. San Val, Incorporated. 978-0-8335-5985-2. 1994. $14.15. LB. Perma-Bound Books. 978-0-605-02326-0. 1974. $12.99. PB. Penguin Group (USA) Incorporated. 978-0-14-034580-3. 1991. $5.99.

In a dystopian America set in the future, five sixteen-year-olds are taken from orphanages and placed inside a strange building. The building has no walls, no ceiling, and no floor. It is an endless complex of stairs that lead nowhere. The five teenagers must learn to live with lack of privacy and are dependent on a strange machine that feeds them only if the teens perform certain feats. They are being conditioned to respond to the machine's actions, but suddenly it stops feeding them altogether. Sleator's novel speaks to the sinister side of science fiction with humans being controlled by technology and will appeal to many readers.

GRADES: 7–10

Sleator, William. *Interstellar Pig.* N/A. TR. Peter Smith Publisher, Incorporated. 978-0-8446-6898-7. 1996. $23.00. TR. Perfection Learning Corporation. 978-0-8124-4933-4. 1995. $14.65. LB. Perma-Bound Books. 978-0-605-01107-6. 1984. $13.99. RE. San Val, Incorporated. 978-0-8085-6615-1. 1995. $17.20.

Zena, Manny, and Joe move into the cottage next door, and their presence intrigues Barney. To him, they lead a glamorous lifestyle. When Zena introduces Barney to their favorite pastime, a board game called Interstellar Pig,

Barney is even more fascinated. The goal is to finish the card with the Piggy card in hand. What Barney slowly comes to realize is that Zena, Manny, and Joe are aliens and playing Interstellar Pig is for real. Sleator's novel explores the traditional science fiction theme of humans encountering aliens, but the twist here is that both sides are guarding secrets. Middle school and younger high school teens will become absorbed by this title. The sequel is called *Parasite Pig*.

GRADES: 8–10

Stahler, David. *Doppelganger.* 272 p. TR. HarperCollins Publishers. 978-0-06-087232-8. 2006. $16.99. LB. HarperCollins Publishers. 978-0-06-087233-5. 2006. $17.89. PB. HarperCollins Publishers. 978-0-06-087234-2. 2008. $8.99.

A young man becomes fed up with abuse at the hands of his mother, so he leaves home and decides to make his way into the world. He is a doppelganger, a shape-shifter destined to stalk and kill humans. Unable to control his natural urges, he kills a drunk and a belligerent high school football player and assumes that life. This brooding story of literally stepping into someone else's shoes combines romance, horror, and angst to create a distinctive story of redemption. There's a hint of Frankenstein's monster to the story although the doppelganger is a natural creation, not one made by science. High school students will absorb the fresh take on high school social life seen by an outsider.

GRADES: 9–12

REVIEWS: *Publishers Weekly* 1/10/06, *SLJ* 6/06, *VOYA* 4/06

Stevenson, Robert Louis. *The Strange Case of Dr. Jekyll and Mr. Hyde.* N/A. TR. 1st World Publishing, Incorporated. 978-1-4218-0666-2. 2005. $26.95. PB. Simon & Schuster. 978-1-4165-0021-6. 2005. $3.95. EB. B & R Samizdat Express. 978-1-102-00771-5. 2008. $.99.

Stevenson's masterwork created a traditional character theme for literature by introducing the split personality that battles between a good side and an evil side. Set in the Victorian era, Dr. Jekyll was a humanitarian who performed good work. His other side is Mr. Hyde. The science aspect comes from the use of potions to change from Jekyll to Hyde and back. Through this work Stevenson created the theme of men tempted by the power of science, even though it leads to evil—in this case murder by Mr. Hyde. This classic work is well worth examining by today's teens.

GRADES: 9–12

Verne, Jules. *20,000 Leagues Under the Sea.* Page count varies with edition. There are significant formats currently available in print.

This story begins in 1866 with the depths of the ocean as a great unknown. A sea monster is sighted after damaging an ocean liner, which prompts an expedition to be assembled. Included on board is the book's narrator, Professor Pierre Aronnax. Following an accident, Aronnax and two others find themselves on board the *Nautilus,* a submarine commanded by Captain Nemo. The vessel is powered by electricity and is carrying out marine biology research. Nemo informs Aronnax that he will never be allowed to leave the submarine as Nemo demands secrecy. Verne created this story about science underwater well before actual submarines were invented. The image of the *Nautilus* attacked by the giant squid is a brand of science fiction adventure.

GRADES: 9–12

Verne, Jules. *A Journey to the Center of the Earth.* 224 p. TR. The Editorium. 978-1-4341-0249-2. 2009. $13.95. PB. Waldman Publishing Corporation. 978-0-86611-960-3. 1990. $9.95. PLAY. Findaway World, LLC. 978-1-59895-857-7. 2007. $59.99. EB. B & R Samizdat Express. 978-1-102-01729-5. 2008. $.99. EB. Blackstone Audio, Incorporated. 978-1-4332-4384-4. 2008. $39.95.

The science here is mainly geology but on their fantastic journey, German Professor Von Hardwigg and his nephew Axel also encounter prehistoric animals. Although today's science has a better idea of what the interior of the Earth looks like, at the time Verne wrote this novel it was a feat of creative imagination. As the explorers journey deeper into the earth, the geological formations are older as are the animals they encounter. *A Journey to the Center of the Earth* is pure adventure pitting man against nature, but also incorporates science into the narrative. It can be viewed as one of the grandfathers of the science fiction genre.

GRADES: 8–12

Vonnegut, Kurt. *Slaughterhouse-Five or The Children's Crusade: A Duty-Dance with Death.* 288 p. TR. Random House Publishing Group. 978-0-385-33384-9. 1999. $15.00. LB. Perma-Bound Books. 978-0-8479-3913-8. 1969. $14.99. RE. San Val, Incorporated. 978-0-613-64788-5. 1999. $25.75. PB. Random House Publishing Group. 978-0-440-18029-6. 1991. $7.99. CD. Blackstone Audio, Incorporated. 978-1-4332-6968-4. 2009. $59.95. CD. HarperCollins Publishers. 978-0-06-057377-5. 2003. $29.95. CASS. HarperCollins Publishers. 978-0-06-056492-6. 2003. $25.95. CASS. Durkin Hayes Publishing Ltd. 978-0-88646-495-0. 1999. $16.99. EB. RosettaBooks. 978-0-7953-0260-2. 2002. $8.99. LP. Thorndike Press. 978-0-7838-8370-0. 1998. $26.95.

Billy Pilgrim, an American soldier, is captured by the Germans during the Battle of the Bulge and taken to a prison in Dresden. The Germans put Billy and his fellow prisoners in a disused slaughterhouse, known as "Slaughterhouse number 5." Hiding in a deep cellar, the POWS and German guards are some of the few survivors of the firestorm bombing of Dresden in World War II. Billy has come "unstuck in time" and experiences past and future events out of sequence. He is kidnapped by extraterrestrial aliens from the planet Tralfamadore who exhibit him in a zoo with B-movie starlet Montana Wildhack as his mate. Billy is a time traveler who becomes aware of the exact moment of his death. Advanced English classics have often tagged Vonnegut's work as a recommended read and it is a good fit for college-bound students.

GRADES: 10–12

Wells, H. G. *The Invisible Man.* Page count varies with edition. There are significant formats currently available in print.

One of the great scenes in science fiction is the arrival of The Invisible Man at the local inn in West Sussex, England. He wears a long coat and gloves with his face entirely hidden by bandages. He demands to be left alone, but mysterious burglaries occur in the village. He is later confronted by an innkeeper and he demonstrates how he is invisible. Horrified she flees and the police are called in but the stranger throws off his clothes and escapes. He begins what he calls a Reign of Terror and the townspeople rally to destroy him. Wells' work incorporates the theme of a lone, mentally unbalanced person manipulating science for his own gain, but with tragic results.

GRADES: 8–12

Wells, H. G. *The Island of Dr. Moreau.* Page count varies with edition. There are significant formats currently available in print.

An upper-class gentleman named Edward Prendick finds himself shipwrecked in the ocean. A passing ship takes him aboard and Prendick is informed they are bound for an unnamed island. After many problems, Prendick arrives at the island and is introduced to Dr. Moreau, a cold man who conducts research on the island. Exploring the island Prendick discovers a hybrid species that is a combination of animal and man. He realizes Moreau has been doing gruesome experiments by vivisecting humans. There seems to be no escape from his fate as Moreau's next subject. This imaginative story is an early example of the mad scientist theme using humans to alter life and being confronted by an innocent individual.

GRADES: 8–12

Wells, H. G. *The Time Machine.* Page count varies with edition. There are significant formats currently available in print.

An English scientist and inventor, identified by the narrator as the Time Traveler, is this novel's protagonist. The Traveler informs people that time is merely a fourth dimension and reveals he has built a machine to travel through time. The device is tested by traveling far into the future where he meets the Eloi, members of a peaceful society resulting from humanity conquering nature with technology. He discovers his machine has been moved and The Traveler is approached by menacing Morlocks. He then realizes the human race has evolved into two species, which interact much like ranchers and cattle. Wells' work is the key link to all stories about time travel that followed its publication.

GRADES: 8–12

Wells, H. G. *The War of the Worlds.* Page count varies with edition. There are significant formats currently available in print.

Wells brought the threat-from-other-worlds theme to literature with his novel *The War of the Worlds.* A cylinder lands near London and Martians emerge. They have trouble with Earth's atmosphere and retreat inside the cylinder. Humans close in but the Martians incinerate them with a heat-ray weapon. So begins an epic struggle of humans versus Martians with the aliens in their mobile tripod machines dominating the fight. The narrator witnesses much death and destruction and also how humans react to the crisis. Many of the science fiction themes that emerged in later novels and popular culture can be traced back to Wells' masterpiece.

GRADES: 8–12

Werlin, Nancy. *Double Helix.* 244 p. TR. Penguin Group (USA) Incorporated. 978-0-8037-2606-2. 2004. $16.99. LB. Perma-Bound Books. 978-0-605-50450-9. 2004. $13.99. RE. San Val, Incorporated. 978-1-4176-9396-2. 2005. $17.20. PB. Penguin Group (USA) Incorporated. 978-0-14-240327-3. 2005. $6.99. CD. Recorded Books, LLC. 978-1-4193-1830-6. 2004. $69.75.

Eighteen-year-old Eli Samuels is stoked to be hired at the Wyatt Transgenics Lab. His father is against him taking the job due to past issues between the lab's owner Dr. Quincy Wyatt and Eli's mother. Once on the job, Eli meets Kayla Matheson who resembles a younger version of Eli's mother. Slowly, Eli unravels the truth behind Wyatt's genetic-engineering experiments and how they're closely tied to Eli's parents. The science fiction theme of adults manipulating science to alter humans is a sure hook and Werlin's title has broad appeal for both middle and high school students.

GRADES: 8–12

REVIEWS: *Booklist* 2/01/04, *Publishers Weekly* 2/16/04, *SLJ* 3/04, *VOYA* 4/04

Westerfeld, Scott. *Peeps.* 320 p. TR. Penguin Group (USA) Incorporated. 978-1-59514-031-9. 2005. $16.99. RE. San Val, Incorporated. 978-1-4177-6225-5. 2006. $19.65. PB. Penguin Group (USA) Incorporated. 978-1-59514-083-8. 2006. $8.99.

Peeps stands for parasite positives, which are infected cannibals that cause illness. College freshman Cal was somewhat lucky—he caught the sexually transmitted disease during a one-night stand, but it never materialized in its full-blown form. Now he works for an underground bureau in Manhattan tracking down peeps. There is much science about parasitology in the story but what is more interesting, and terrifying, is the peeps' burning desire to reproduce to accelerate the evolutionary scale. Westerfeld combines science and horror legends in a truly frightening novel. Blunt commentary about sex marks this title for older teens. The sequel to *Peeps* is titled *The Last Days.*

GRADES: 9–12

REVIEWS: *Booklist* 8/01/05, *Publishers Weekly* 10/03/05, *SLJ* 10/05, *VOYA* 10/05

AWARDS: BBYA Top Ten, Teens' Top Ten

Westerfeld, Scott. *The Secret Hour* **(*Midnighters* series).** 304 p. TR. HarperCollins Publishers. 978-0-06-051951-3. 2004. $16.99. LB. HarperCollins Publishers. 978-0-06-051952-0. 2004. $17.89. RE. San Val, Incorporated. 978-1-4177-0101-8. 2005. $19.65. PB.. HarperCollins Publishers. 978-0-06-051953-7. 2005. $8.99. EB. Harper Collins Publishers. 978-0-06-195455-9. 2009. $9.99. LP. Thorndike Press. 978-1-4104-0781-8. 2008. $22.95.

A creative hook marks this story about a group of high school students with unique powers. Fifteen-year-old Jessica Day enters a new school and bizarre events occur. She realizes she's part of the Midnighters—teens who can move about in a secret twenty-fifth hour where all other time practically stands still. Also roaming around that hour are slithers and darklings, creatures that are violent and aggressive. The paranormal activity has a science background and the teens' duty is to kill the night creatures. Westerfeld's writing has wide appeal to many ages of teens. Other titles in the series are *Touching Darkness* and *Blue Noon.*

GRADES: 9–12

REVIEWS: *Publishers Weekly* 3/22/04, *SLJ* 6/04, *VOYA* 4/04

Westerfeld, Scott. *Uglies* **(*Uglies* series).** 448 p. PB. Simon & Schuster Children's Publishing. 978-0-689-86538-1. 2005. $8.99. LP. Thorndike Press. 978-0-7862-9705-4. 2007. $23.95.

Tally Youngblood is a somewhat normal teenager except she's living in a world hundreds of years in the future. She is waiting for her sixteenth birthday because at that time everyone receives the gift of plastic surgery transforming them into gorgeous creatures. Before she's transformed, she ventures into New Pretty Town to see her former friend and realizes there's more changed in the teens than just outward appearances. Tally bolts with Shay to a renegade settlement, but the government is not above blackmail to get what they want. Westerfeld incorporates many clever techie gadgets such as magnetic surfing in the air by following iron train tracks. Science used to alter a teenager's future is a big hook and Tally is a winning character who appeals to many girl readers. Other titles in the series are *Pretties, Specials,* and *Extras* (Teen's Top Ten).

GRADES: 7–12

REVIEWS: *Booklist* 3/15/05, *Publishers Weekly* 3/15/05, *SLJ* 3/05, *VOYA* 6/05

Wooding, Chris. *The Haunting of Alaizabel Cray.* 304 p. TR. Scholastic, Incorporated. 978-0-439-54656-0. 2004. $16.95. PB. Scholastic, Incorporated. 978-0-439-59851-4. 2005. $7.99.

Set in an alternative Victorian London, a new plague has occurred. Demonic creatures known as wych-kin are roaming around and seventeen-year-old Thaniel Fox reduces their number by using magic, superstition, and good ol' gunslinging. Thaniel happens upon Alaizabel, a girl who has escaped from a cult called the Fraternity. This is a classic gothic horror, but loosely falls to science fiction due to the alternative world that has a steampunk riff. Serial killers, creatures drawn from legend and lore, a mysterious cult, and can-do characters both male and female make this work a crackling read. The story is intense but many ages of teens will be thrilled.

GRADES: 8–12

REVIEWS: *Booklist* 8/01/04, *Publishers Weekly* 9/13/04, *SLJ* 8/04, *VOYA* 10/04

Yolen, Jane, and Bruce Coville. *Armageddon Summer.* 266 p. TR. Perfection Learning Corporation. 978-0-7569-0460-9. 1999. $14.60. LB. San Val, Incorporated. 978-0-613-19505-8. 1999. $14.15. LB. Perma-Bound Books. 978-0-605-80619-1. 1998. $12.99. PB. Houghton Mifflin Harcourt Trade & Reference Publishers. 978-0-15-202268-6. 1999. $6.95.

Yolen and Coville have co-authored this story giving voice to a pair of teens concerned about the world coming to an end and its religious consequences. The parents of Marina and Jed have joined a millennialist cult whose members call themselves "The Believers." Reverend Beelson leads his flock and informs them the world will end on July 27 in the year 2000. Only the disciples who have fled up to Mount Weeupcut in western Massachusetts will be saved. Parental neglect, family relationships, medical care, hypocrisy, news media behavior, cults, and abortion are all part of this story. I place it here in science fiction due to the fuzzy science about the world coming to an end. Serious situations shift this work to the upper end of young adult readership.

GRADES 9–12

REVIEWS: *Booklist* 8/01/98, *Kirkus* 7/01/98, *Publishers Weekly* 6/15/98, *SLJ* 10/98, *VOYA* 10/98

14

Putting It All Together

This second edition of *A Core Collection for Young Adults* is designed to be a helpful collection development tool. It certainly is not the final word for recommending young adult titles. In the upcoming year, another Printz winner will be announced. The new BFYA (Best Fiction for Young Adults) committee will make their selections plus a top ten. The Great Graphic Novels committee, Quick Picks for Reluctant Young Adult Readers and all the other book selection committees will continue to perform their outstanding service. In no time at all, a new wave of young adult titles will hit the bookshelves in libraries and bookstores.

Any core collection is exactly that, a core. Titles can be taken away or added at any time from these suggested titles. Are titles or authors left out of this edition? Certainly, but this starting point gives a librarian faced with creating a teen collection a leg up on the task.

A young adult collection can be formed in two ways. It can be built from scratch with zero titles, or an old, tired collection with lots of middle-aged sag can be weeded to make room for new, lively and fresh titles. The second edition of *A Core Collection for Young Adults* will assist a librarian faced with either task. I purposely left in several titles that are out of print believing they are enticing reads and it is possible they still lurk on some library's shelves. Of course it is up to librarians to make the final call as to titles included in their collection.

I am looking forward to seeing what new titles will be published in the upcoming years. Without a doubt, this work will need updating within the next five years. Now truly are the golden years of young adult books with the best yet to come.

Appendixes

Appendix A

John Newbery Medal Winners and Honor Books

Year	Title (winner first, in bold)	Author/Illustrator
2010	**When You Reach Me**	**Stead, Rebecca**
	Claudette Colvin: Twice Towards Justice	Hoose, Phillip
	The Evolution of Calpurnia Tate	Kelly, Jacqueline
	Where the Mountain Meets the Moon	Lin, Grace
	The Mostly True Adventures of Homer P. Figg	Philbrick, Rodman
2009	***The Graveyard Book**	**Gaiman, Neil**
	The Underneath	Appelt, Kathi
	The Surrender Tree: Poems of Cuba's Struggle for Freedom	Engle, Margarita
	Savvy	Law, Ingrid
	*After Tupac and D Foster	Woodson, Jacqueline
2008	**Good Masters! Sweet Ladies! Voices from a Medieval Village**	**Schlitz, Laura Amy**
	Elijah of Buxton	Curtis, Christopher Paul
	The Wednesday Wars	Schmidt, Gary D.
	Feathers	Woodson, Jacqueline
2007	**The Higher Power of Lucky**	**Patron, Susan**
	Penny from Heaven	Holm, Jennifer L.
	Hattie Big Sky	Larson, Kirby
	Rules	Lord, Cynthia
2006	**Criss Cross**	**Perkins, Lynne Rae**
	Whittington	Armstrong, Alan
	*Hitler Youth: Growing Up in Hitler's Shadow	Bartoletti, Susan Campbell
	Princess Academy	Hale, Shannon
	Show Way	Woodson, Jacqueline
2005	**Kira-Kira**	**Kadohata, Cynthia**
	*Al Capone Does My Shirts	Choldenko, Gennifer
	The Voice That Challenged a Nation: Marian Anderson and the Struggle for Equal Rights	Freedman, Russell
	*Lizzie Bright and the Buckminster Boy	Schmidt, Gary D.

*Asterisk indicates that the title has an annotation in the text of this book.

Year	Title (winner first, in bold)	Author/Illustrator
2004	**The Tale of Despereaux**	**DiCamillo, Kate**
	Olive's Ocean	Henkes, Kevin
	An American Plague: The True and Terrifying Story of the Yellow Fever Epidemic of 1793	Murphy, Jim
2003	***Crispin: The Cross of Lead**	**Avi**
	*The House of the Scorpion	Farmer, Nancy
	Pictures of Hollis Woods	Giff, Patricia Reilly
	*Hoot	Hiaasen, Carl
	A Corner of the Universe	Martin, Ann M.
	Surviving the Applewhites	Tolan, Stephanie S.
2002	***A Single Shard**	**Park, Linda Sue**
	Everything on a Waffle	Horvath, Polly
	Carver: A Life in Poems	Nelson, Marilyn
2001	**A Year Down Yonder**	**Peck, Richard**
	*Hope Was Here	Bauer, Joan
	The Wanderer	Creech, Sharon
	*Because of Winn Dixie	DiCamillo, Kate
	Joey Pigza Loses Control	Gantos, Jack
2000	***Bud, Not Buddy**	**Curtis, Christopher Paul**
	Getting Near to Baby	Couloumbis, Audrey
	26 Fairmount Avenue	DePaola, Tomie
	Our Only May Amelia	Holm, Jennifer L.
1999	***Holes**	**Sachar, Louis**
	A Long Way from Chicago	Peck, Richard
1998	***Out of the Dust**	**Hesse, Karen**
	Lily's Crossing	Giff, Patricia Reilly
	Ella Enchanted	Levine, Gail Carson
	Wringer	Spinelli, Jerry
1997	**The View from Saturday**	**Konigsburg, E. L.**
	*A Girl Named Disaster	Farmer, Nancy
	The Moorchild	McGraw, Eloise
	The Thief	Turner, Megan Whalen
	Belle Prater's Boy	White, Ruth
1996	**The Midwife's Apprentice**	**Cushman, Karen**
	What Jamie Saw	Coman, Carolyn
	*The Watsons Go to Birmingham: 1963	Curtis, Christopher Paul
	Yolanda's Genius	Fenner, Carol
	The Great Fire	Murphy, Jim
1995	***Walk Two Moons**	**Creech, Sharon**
	*Catherine, Called Birdy	Cushman, Karen
	The Ear, the Eye and the Arm	Farmer, Nancy
1994	***The Giver**	**Lowry, Lois**
	Crazy Lady	Conly, Jane Leslie
	Eleanor Roosevelt: A Life of Discovery	Freedman, Russell
	Dragon's Gate	Yep, Laurence

Year	Title (winner first, in bold)	Author/Illustrator
1993	**Missing May**	**Rylant, Cynthia**
	What Hearts	Brooks, Bruce
	The Dark-Thirty: Southern Tales of the Supernatural	McKissack, Patricia
	Somewhere in the Darkness	Myers, Walter Dean
1992	**Shiloh**	**Naylor, Phyllis Reynolds**
	*Nothing But the Truth: A Documentary Novel	Avi
	The Wright Brothers: How They Invented the Airplane	Freedman, Russell
1991	****Maniac Magee***	**Spinelli, Jerry**
	* The True Confessions of Charlotte Doyle	Avi
1990	**Number the Stars**	**Lowry, Lois**
	Afternoon of the Elves	Lisle, Janet Taylor
	The Winter Room	Paulsen, Gary
	Shabanu, Daughter of the Wind	Staples, Suzanne Fisher
1989	**Joyful Noise: Poems for Two Voices**	**Fleischman, Paul**
	In the Beginning: Creation Stories from Around the World	Hamilton, Virginia
	Scorpions	Myers, Walter Dean
1988	**Lincoln: A Photobiography**	**Freedman, Russell**
	After the Rain	Mazer, Norma Fox
	*Hatchet	Paulsen, Gary
1987	**The Whipping Boy**	**Fleischman, Sid**
	On My Honor	Bauer, Marion Dane
	Volcano: The Eruption and Healing of Mount St. Helens	Lauber, Patricia
	A Fine White Dust	Rylant, Cynthia
1986	**Sarah, Plain and Tall**	**MacLachlan, Patricia**
	Commodore Perry In the Land of the Shogun	Blumberg, Rhoda
	*Dogsong	Paulsen, Gary
1985	**The Hero and the Crown**	**McKinley, Robin**
	The Moves Make the Man	Brooks, Bruce
	One-Eyed Cat	Fox, Paula
	Like Jake and Me	Jukes, Mavis
1984	**Dear Mr. Henshaw**	**Cleary, Beverly**
	The Wish Giver	Brittain, Bill
	Sugaring Time	Lasky, Kathryn
	* The Sign of the Beaver	Speare, Elizabeth George
	A Solitary Blue	Voigt, Cynthia
1983	**Dicey's Song**	**Voigt, Cynthia**
	Graven Images	Fleischman, Paul
	Homesick: My Own Story	Fritz, Jean
	Sweet Whispers, Brother Rush	Hamilton, Virginia
	Doctor De Soto	Steig, William
1982	**A Visit to William Blake's Inn: Poems for Innocent and Experienced Travelers**	**Willard, Nancy**
	Ramona Quimby, Age 8	Cleary, Beverly
	The Blue Sword	McKinley, Robin

Year	Title (winner first, in bold)	Author/Illustrator
	Upon the Head of the Goat: A Childhood in Hungary 1939–1944	Siegal, Aranka
1981	***Jacob Have I Loved***	**Paterson, Katherine**
	The Fledgling	Langton, Jane
	A Ring of Endless Night	L'Engle, Madeleine
1980	***A Gathering of Days: A New England Girl's Journal***	**Blos, Joan W.**
	The Road from Home: The Story of an Armenian Girl	Kherdian, David
1979	****The Westing Game***	**Raskin, Ellen**
	The Great Gilly Hopkins	Paterson, Katherine
1978	****Bridge to Terabithia***	**Paterson, Katherine**
	Ramona and Her Father	Cleary, Beverly
	Anpao: An American Indian Odyssey	Highwater, Jamake
1977	****Roll of Thunder, Hear My Cry***	**Taylor, Mildred D.**
	A String in the Harp	Bond, Nancy
	Abel's Island	Steig, William
1976	***The Grey King***	**Cooper, Susan**
	The Hundred Penny Box	Mathis, Sharon Bell
	Dragonwings	Yep, Laurence
1975	****M. C. Higgins, the Great***	**Hamilton, Virginia**
	My Brother Sam Is Dead	Collier, James Lincoln, and Christopher Collier
	Philip Hall Likes Me, I Reckon Maybe	Greene, Bette
	The Perilous Gard	Pope, Elizabeth Marie
	Figgs & Phantoms	Raskin, Ellen
1974	***The Slave Dancer***	**Fox, Paula**
	* *The Dark Is Rising*	Cooper, Susan
1973	***Julie of the Wolves***	**George, Jean Craighead**
	Frog and Toad Together	Lobel, Arnold
	The Upstairs Room	Reiss, Johanna
	The Witches of Worm	Snyder, Zilpha Keatley
1972	***Mrs. Frisby and the Rats of NIMH***	**O'Brien, Robert C.**
	Incident at Hawk's Hill	Eckert, Allan W.
	The Planet of Junior Brown	Hamilton, Virginia
	The Tombs of Atuan	Le Guin, Ursula K.
	Annie and the Old One	Miles, Miska
	The Headless Cupid	Snyder, Zilpha Keatley
1971	***The Summer of the Swans***	**Byars, Betsy**
	Knee-Knock Rise	Babbitt, Natalie
	Enchantress from the Stars	Engdahl, Sylvia
	Sing Down the Moon	O'Dell, Scott
1970	****Sounder***	**Armstrong, William H.**
	Our Eddie	Ish-Kishor, Sulamith
	The Many Ways of Seeing: An Introduction to the Pleasures of Art	Moore, Janet Gaylord
	Journey Outside	Steele, Mary Q.

Year	Title (winner first, in bold)	Author/Illustrator
1969	**The High King**	Alexander, Lloyd
	To Be a Slave	Lester, Julius
	When Shlemiel Went to Warsaw and Other Stories	Singer, Isaac Bashevis
1968	**From the Mixed-Up Files of Mrs. Basil E. Frankweiler**	Konigsburg, E. L.
	Jennifer, Hecate, Macbeth, William McKinley, and Me, Elizabeth	Konigsburg, E.L.
	The Black Pearl	O'Dell, Scott
	The Fearsome Inn	Singer, Isaac Bashevis
	The Egypt Game	Snyder, Zilpha Keatley
1967	**Up a Road Slowly**	Hunt, Irene
	The King's Fifth	O'Dell, Scott
	Zlateh the Goat and Other Stories	Singer, Isaac Bashevis
	The Jazz Man	Weik, Mary Hays
1966	**I, Juan de Pareja**	de Trevino, Elizabeth Borton
	The Black Cauldron	Alexander, Lloyd
	The Animal Family	Jarrell, Randall
	The Noonday Friends	Stolz, Mary
1965	**Shadow of a Bull**	Wojciechowska, Maia
	*Across Five Aprils	Hunt, Irene
1964	**It's Like This, Cat**	Neville, Emily
	Rascal	North, Sterling
	The Loner	Wier, Ester
1963	***A Wrinkle in Time**	L'Engle, Madeleine
	Men of Athens	Coolidge, Olivia
	Thistle and Thyme: Tales and Legends from Scotland	Leodhas, Sorche Nic
1962	**The Bronze Bow**	Speare, Elizabeth George
	The Golden Goblet	McGraw, Eloise Jarvis
	Belling the Tiger	Stolz, Mary
	Frontier Living	Tunis, Edwin
1961	**Island of the Blue Dolphins**	O'Dell, Scott
	America Moves Forward: A History for Peter	Johnson, Gerald W.
	Old Ramon	Schaefer, Jack
	The Cricket in Times Square	Selden, George
1960	**Onion John**	Krumgold, Joseph
	*My Side of the Mountain	George, Jean Craighead
	America Is Born: A History for Peter	Johnson, Gerald W.
	The Gammage Cup	Kendall, Carol
1959	***The Witch of Blackbird Pond**	Speare, Elizabeth George
	The Family Under the Bridge	Carlson, Natalie Savage
	Along Came a Dog	DeJong, Meindert
	Chucaro: Wild Pony of the Pampa	Kalnay, Francis
	The Perilous Road	Steele, William O.
1958	***Rifles for Watie**	Keith, Harold
	Gone-Away Lake	Enright, Elizabeth
	Tom Paine, Freedom's Apostle	Gurko, Leo

Year	Title (winner first, in bold)	Author/Illustrator
	The Great Wheel	Lawson, Robert
	The Horsecatcher	Sandoz, Mari
1957	***Miracles on Maple Hill***	**Sorensen, Virginia**
	Black Fox of Lorne	de Angeli, Marguerite
	The House of Sixty Fathers	DeJong, Meindert
	*Old Yeller	Gipson, Fred
	Mr. Justice Holmes	Judson, Clara Ingram
	The Corn Grows Ripe	Rhoads, Dorothy
1956	***Carry On, Mr. Bowditch***	**Latham, Jean Lee**
	The Golden Name Day	Lindquist, Jennie
	The Secret River	Rawlings, Marjorie Kinnan
	Men, Microscopes, and Living Things	Shippen, Katherine
1955	***The Wheel on the School***	**DeJong, Meindert**
	The Courage of Sarah Noble	Dalgliesh, Alice
	Banner in the Sky	Ullman, James
1954	***. . . And Now Miguel***	**Krumgold, Joseph**
	All Alone	Bishop, Claire Huchet
	Magic Maize	Buff, Mary and Conrad
	Hurry Home, Candy	DeJong, Meindert
	Shadrach	DeJong, Meindert
	Theodore Roosevelt, Fighting Patriot	Judson, Clara Ingram
1953	***Secret of the Andes***	**Clark, Ann Nolan**
	The Bears on Hemlock Mountain	Dalgliesh, Alice
	Birthdays of Freedom, Vol. 1	Foster, Genevieve
	Moccasin Trail	McGraw, Eloise Jarvis
	Red Sails to Capri	Weil, Ann
	Charlotte's Web	White, E.B.
1952	***Ginger Pye***	**Estes, Eleanor**
	Americans Before Columbus	Baity, Elizabeth
	The Apple and the Arrow	Buff, Mary and Conrad
	Minn of the Mississippi	Holling, Holling C.
	The Defender	Kalashnikoff, Nicholas
	The Light at Tern Rock	Sauer, Julia
1951	***Amos Fortune, Free Man***	**Yates, Elizabeth**
	Better Known as Johnny Appleseed	Hunt, Mabel Leigh
	Gandhi, Fighter Without a Sword	Eaton, Jeanette
	Abraham Lincoln, Friend of the People	Judson, Clara Ingram
	The Story of Appleby Capple	Parrish, Anne
1950	***The Door in the Wall: Story of Medieval London***	**de Angeli, Marguerite**
	Tree of Freedom	Caudill, Rebecca
	The Blue Cat of Castle Town	Coblentz, Catherine
	George Washington	Foster, Genevieve
	Song of the Pines: A Story of Norwegian Lumbering in Wisconsin	Havighurst, Walter and Marion

Year	Title (winner first, in bold)	Author/Illustrator
	Kildee House	Montgomery, Rutherford George
1949	***King of the Wind***	**Henry, Marguerite**
	Story of the Negro	Bontemps, Arna
	My Father's Dragon	Gannett, Ruth S.
	Seabird	Holling, Holling C.
	Daughter of the Mountain	Rankin, Louise
1948	***The Twenty-One Balloons***	**du Bois, William Pène**
	The Quaint and Curious Quest of Johnny Longfoot	Besterman, Catherine
	Pancakes-Paris	Bishop, Claire Huchet
	The Cow-Tail Switch, and Other West African Stories	Courlander, Harold
	Misty of Chincoteague	Henry, Marguerite
	Li Lun, Lad of Courage	Treffinger, Carolyn
1947	***Miss Hickory***	**Bailey, Carolyn Sherwin**
	Wonderful Year	Barnes, Nancy
	Big Tree	Buff, Mary and Conrad
	The Avion My Uncle Flew	Fisher, Cyrus
	The Hidden Treasure of Glaston	Jewett, Eleanor
	The Heavenly Tenants	Maxwell, William
1946	***Strawberry Girl***	**Lenski, Lois**
	Justin Morgan Had a Horse	Henry, Marguerite
	The Moved-Outers	Means, Florence Crannell
	New Found World	Shippen, Katherine
	Bhimsa, the Dancing Bear	Weston, Christine
1945	***Rabbit Hill***	**Lawson, Robert**
	The Silver Pencil	Dalgliesh, Alice
	Lone Journey: The Life of Roger Williams	Eaton, Jeanette
	The Hundred Dresses	Estes, Eleanor
	Abraham Lincoln's World	Foster, Genevieve
1944	****Johnny Tremain***	**Forbes, Esther**
	Rufus M.	Estes, Eleanor
	Fog Magic	Sauer, Julia
	These Happy Golden Years	Wilder, Laura Ingalls
	Mountain Born	Yates, Elizabeth
1943	***Adam of the Road***	**Gray, Elizabeth Janet**
	The Middle Moffat	Estes, Eleanor
	Have You Seen Tom Thumb?	Hunt, Mabel Leigh
1942	***The Matchlock Gun***	**Edmonds, Walter D.**
	George Washington's World	Foster, Genevieve
	Down Ryton Water	Gaggin, Eva Roe
	Indian Captive: The Story of Mary Jemison	Lenski, Lois
	Little Town on the Prairie	Wilder, Laura Ingalls
1941	***Call It Courage***	**Sperry, Armstrong**
	Young Mac of Fort Vancouver	Carr, Mary Jane
	Blue Willow	Gates, Doris
	Nansen	Hall, Anna Gertrude

Year	Title (winner first, in bold)	Author/Illustrator
	*The Long Winter	Wilder, Laura Ingalls
1940	**Daniel Boone**	**Daugherty, James**
	Boy with a Pack	Meader, Stephen W.
	Runner of the Mountain Tops: The Life of Louis Agassiz	Robinson, Mabel
	The Singing Tree	Seredy, Kate
	By the Shores of Silver Lake	Wilder, Laura Ingalls
1939	**Thimble Summer**	**Enright, Elizabeth**
	Nino	Angelo, Valenti
	Mr. Popper's Penguins	Atwater, Richard and Florence
	Hello the Boat!	Crawford, Phyllis
	Leader by Destiny: George Washington, Man and Patriot	Eaton, Jeanette
	Penn	Gray, Elizabeth Janet
1938	**The White Stag**	**Seredy, Kate**
	Pecos Bill: The Greatest Cowboy of All Time	Bowman, James Cloyd
	Bright Island	Robinson, Mabel
	On the Banks of Plum Creek	Wilder, Laura Ingalls
1937	**Roller Skates**	**Sawyer, Ruth**
	The Golden Basket	Bemelmans, Ludwig
	The Codfish Musket	Hewes, Agnes
	Whistler's Van	Jones, Idwal
	Phoebe Fairchild: Her Book	Lenski, Lois
	Audubon	Rourke, Constance
	Winterbound	Williams, Margery
1936	**Caddie Woodlawn**	**Brink, Carol Ryrie**
	Young Walter Scott	Gray, Elizabeth Janet
	The Good Master	Seredy, Kate
	All Sail Set: A Romance of the Flying Cloud	Sperry, Armstrong
	Honk, the Moose	Stong, Phil
1935	**Dobry**	**Shannon, Monica**
	Davy Crockett	Rourke, Constance
	Pageant of Chinese History	Seeger, Elizabeth
	Day on Skates: The Story of a Dutch Picnic	van Stockum, Hilda
1934	**Invincible Louisa: The Story of the Author of Little Women**	**Miegs, Cornelia L.**
	Winged Girl of Knossos	Berry, Erik
	Big Tree of Bunlahy: Stories of My Own Countryside	Colum, Padraic
	ABC Bunny	Gág, Wanda
	Glory of the Seas	Hewes, Agnes
	Apprentice of Florence	Kyle, Ann
	New Land	Schmidt, Sarah
	Swords of Steel	Singmaster, Elsie
	The Forgotten Daughter	Snedeker, Caroline
1933	**Young Fu of the Upper Yangtze**	**Lewis, Elizabeth Foreman**

Year	Title (winner first, in bold)	Author/Illustrator
	Children of the Soil: A Story of Scandinavia	Burglon, Nora
	Swift Rivers	Meigs, Cornelia
	The Railroad to Freedom: A Story of the Civil War	Swift, Hildegarde
1932	**Waterless Mountain**	**Armer, Laura Adams**
	Jane's Island	Allee, Marjorie Hill
	Truce of the Wolf and Other Tales of Old Italy	Davis, Mary Gould
	Calico Bush	Field, Rachel
	The Fairy Circus	Lathrop, Dorothy P.
	Out of the Flame	Lownsbery, Eloise
	Boy of the South Seas	Tietjens, Eunice
1931	**The Cat Who Went to Heaven**	**Coatsworth, Elizabeth**
	Mountains Are Free	Adams, Julie Davis
	Garram the Hunter: A Boy of the Hill Tribes	Best, Herbert
	Meggy MacIntosh	Gray, Elizabeth Janet
	Spice and the Devil's Cave	Hewes, Agnes
	Queer Person	Hubbard, Ralph
	Ood-Le-Uk the Wanderer	Lide, Alcie and Margaret Johansen
	The Dark Star of Itza: The Story of a Pagan Princess	Malkus, Alida
	Floating Island	Parrish, Anne
1930	**Hitty, Her First Hundred Years**	**Field, Rachel**
	Vaino, A Boy of New Finland	Adams, Julia Davis
	A Daughter of the Seine: The Life of Madame Roland	Eaton, Jeanette
	The Jumping-Off Place	McNeely, Marian Hurd
	Pran of Albania	Miller, Elizabeth
	Little Blacknose: The Story of a Pioneer	Swift, Hildegarde
	The Tangle-Coated Horse and Other Tales	Young, Ella
1929	**The Trumpeter of Krakow**	**Kelly, Eric P.**
	The Pigtail of Ah Lee Ben Loo	Bennett, John
	Millions of Cats	Gág, Wanda
	The Boy Who Was	Hallock, Grace
	Clearing Weather	Meigs, Cornelia
	Runaway Papoose	Moon, Grace
	Tod of the Fens	Whitney, Elinor
1928	**Gay Neck: The Story of a Pigeon**	**Mukerji, Dhan Gopal**
	Downright Dencey	Snedeker, Caroline
	The Wonder Smith and His Son	Young, Ella
1927	**Smoky, the Cowhorse**	**James, Will**
1926	**Shen of the Sea**	**Chrisman, Arthur Bowie**
	The Voyagers: Being Legends and Romance of Atlantic Discovery	Colum, Padraic
1925	**Tales from Silver Lands**	**Finger, Charles J.**
	Nicholas: A Manhattan Christmas Story	Moore, Annie Carroll
	The Dream Coach	Parrish, Anne
1924	**The Dark Frigate**	**Hawes, Charles Boardman**
1923	**The Voyages of Doctor Dolittle**	**Lofting, Hugh**

Year	Title (winner first, in bold)	Author/Illustrator
1922	***The Story of Mankind***	**Van Loon, Henrik Willem**
	The Old Tobacco Shop: A True Story of What Befell a Little Boy in Search of Adventure	Bowen, William
	The Golden Fleece and the Heroes Who Lived Before Achilles	Colum, Padraic
	The Great Quest	Hewes, Charles
	Cedric the Forester	Marshall, Bernard
	The Windy Hill	Meigs, Cornelia

Appendix B

Michael L. Printz Award Winners and Honor Books

Year	Title (winner first, in bold)	Author/Illustrator
2010	***Going Bovine***	**Bray, Libba**
	*Tales of the Madman Underground (An Historical Romance, 1973)	Barnes, John
	*Charles and Emma: The Darwins' Leap of Faith	Heiligman, Deborah
	*Punkzilla	Rapp, Adam
	*The Monstrumologist	Yancey, Rick
2009	***Jellicoe Road***	**Marchetta, Melina**
	*The Astonishing Life of Octavian Nothing, Traitor to the Nation, Vol. 2: The Kingdom on the Waves	Anderson, M. T.
	*Tender Morsels	Lanagan, Margo
	*The Disreputable History of Frankie Landau-Banks	Lockhart, E.
	*Nation	Pratchett, Terry
2008	***The White Darkness***	**McCaughrean, Geraldine**
	*One Whole and Perfect Day	Clarke, Judith
	Your Own, Sylvia: A Verse Portrait of Sylvia Plath	Hemphill, Stephanie
	*Repossessed	Jenkins, A. M.
	*Dreamquake: Dreamhunter Duet, Book 2	Knox, Elizabeth
2007	***American Born Chinese***	**Yang, Gene Luen**
	*The Astonishing Life of Octavian Nothing, Traitor to the Nation, Vol. 1: The Pox Party	Anderson, M. T.
	*An Abundance of Katherines	Green, John
	*Surrender	Hartnett, Sonya
	*The Book Thief	Zusak, Markus
2006	***Looking for Alaska***	**Green, John**
	Black Juice	Lanagan, Margo
	A Wreath for Emmett Till	Nelson, Marilyn
	John Lennon: All I Want Is the Truth, a Photographic Biography	Partridge, Elizabeth
	*I Am the Messenger	Zusak, Markus

*Asterisk indicates that the title has an annotation in the text of this book.

Year	Title (winner first, in bold)	Author/Illustrator
2005	***how i live now***	**Rosoff, Meg**
	Airborn	Oppel, Kenneth
	Lizzie Bright and the Buckminster Boy	Schmidt, Gary D.
	Chanda's Secrets	Stratton, Allan
2004	***The First Part Last***	**Johnson, Angela**
	A Northern Light	Donnelly, Jennifer
	Keesha's House	Frost, Helen
	Fat Kid Rules the World	Going, K. L.
	The Earth, My Butt, and Other Big Round Things	Mackler, Carolyn
2003	***Postcards from No Man's Land***	**Chambers, Aidan**
	The House of the Scorpion	Farmer, Nancy
	My Heartbeat	Freymann-Weyr, Garret
	Hole in My Life	Gantos, Jack
2002	***A Step from Heaven***	**Na, An**
	Heart to Heart: New Poems Inspired by Twentieth-Century American Art	Abrams, Jan Greenberg
	The Ropemaker	Dickinson, Peter
	Freewill	Lynch, Chris
	True Believer	Wolff, Virginia Euwer
2001	***Kit's Wilderness***	**Almond, David**
	Many Stones	Coman, Carolyn
	The Body of Christopher Creed	Plum-Ucci, Carol
	Angus, Thongs, and Full Frontal Snogging: Confessions of Georgia Nicolson	Rennison, Louise
	Stuck in Neutral	Trueman, Terry
2000	***Monster***	**Myers, Walter Dean**
	Skellig	Almond, David
	Speak	Anderson, Laurie Halse
	Hard Love	Wittlinger, Ellen

Appendix C

Best Books for Young Adults Top Ten 2000–2010

Year	Title	Author/Illustrator
2010	*The Demon's Lexicon	Brennan, Sarah Rees
	*The Orange Houses	Griffin, Paul
	*The Great Wide Sea	Herlong, M. H.
	*The Reformed Vampire Support Group	Jinks, Catherine
	Alligator Bayou	Napoli, Donna Jo
	*Stitches: A Memoir	Small, David
	When You Reach Me	Stead, Rebecca
	*Marcelo in the Real World	Stork, Francisco X.
	*Lips Touch: Three Times	Taylor, Laini
	*Written in Bone: Buried Lives of Jamestown and Colonial Maryland	Walker, Sally M.
2009	*It's Complicated: The American Teenager	Bowman, Robin
	*The Hunger Games	Collins, Suzanne
	*Waiting for Normal	Conner, Leslie
	Mexican WhiteBoy	de la Peña, Matt
	*Bog Child	Dowd, Siobhan
	*Ten Cents a Dance	Fletcher, Christine
	*Baby	Monninger, Joseph
	*Nation	Pratchett, Terry
	*Skim	Tamaki, Mariko, and Jillian Tamaki
2008	*The Absolutely True Diary of a Part-Time Indian	Alexie, Sherman
	A Long Way Gone: Memoirs of a Boy Soldier	Beah, Ishmael
	*Before I Die	Downham, Jenny
	Your Own, Sylvia: A Verse Portrait of Sylvia Plath	Hemphill, Stephanie
	*Mister Pip	Jones, Lloyd
	Skulduggery Pleasant	Landy, Derek
	*Tamar: A Novel of Espionage, Passion, and Betrayal	Peet, Mal

*Asterisk indicates that the title has an annotation in the text of this book.

Year	Title	Author/Illustrator
	American Shaolin: Flying Kicks, Buddhist Monks and the Legend of Iron Crotch: An Odyssey in the New China	Polly, Matthew
	*The Invention of Hugo Cabret: A Novel	Sleznick, Brian
	*The Arrival	Tan, Shaun
2007	**The Astonishing Life of Octavian Nothing, Traitor to the Nation, Vol. 1: The Pox Party*	Anderson, M. T.
	*Samurai Shortstop	Gratz, Alan
	*Surrender	Hartnett, Sonya
	*Sold	McCormick, Patricia
	Anahita's Woven Riddle	Sayres, Meghan Nuttall
	*The Trap	Smelcer, John
	The King of Attolia	Turner, Megan Whalen
	*The Rules of Survival	Werlin, Nancy
	*American Born Chinese	Yang, Gene Luen
	*The Book Thief	Zusak, Markus
2006	*Come Back to Afghanistan: A California Teenager's Story*	Akbar, Said Hyder and Susan Burton
	*Hitler Youth: Growing Up in Hitler's Shadow	Bartoletti, Susan Campbell
	*Upstate	Buckhannon, Kalisha
	*Looking for Alaska	Green, John
	*Inexcusable	Lynch, Chris
	*Twilight: A Novel	Meyer, Stephenie
	Runaways: Vol. 1	Vaughan, Brian K.
	*Peeps	Westerfeld, Scott
	Poison	Wooding, Chris
	*I Am the Messenger	Zusak, Markus
2005	*The Unthinkable Thoughts of Jacob Green*	Braff, Joshua
	*Bucking the Sarge	Curtis, Christopher Paul
	The Race to Save Lord God Bird	Hoose, Phillip M.
	*The Realm of Possibility	Levithan, David
	*Saving Francesca	Marchetta, Melina
	*Private Peaceful	Morpurgo, Michael
	*Airborn	Oppel, Kenneth
	*Under the Wolf, Under the Dog	Rapp, Adam
	*Sammy and Juliana in Hollywood	Sáenz, Benjamin Alire
	*So B. It: A Novel	Weeks, Sarah
2004	**True Confessions of a Heartless Girl*	Brooks, Martha
	*A Northern Light	Donnelly, Jennifer
	*The Curious Incident of the Dog in the Night-Time: A Novel	Haddon, Mark
	*The First Part Last	Johnson, Angela
	*Boy Meets Boy	Levithan, David
	*The Usual Rules	Maynard, Joyce
	*East	Pattou, Edith
	*33 Snowfish	Rapp, Adam

Year	Title	Author/Illustrator
	*The Amulet of Samarkand: Bartimaeus Trilogy, Book One	Stroud, Jonathan
	*Blankets: An Illustrated Novel	Thompson, Craig
2003	*Catalyst	Anderson, Laurie Halse
	*Feed	Anderson, M. T.
	*The House of the Scorpion	Farmer, Nancy
	*America	Frank, E. R.
	*Son of the Mob	Korman, Gordon
	The Lightkeeper's Daughter	Lawrence, Iain
	Lamb: The Gospel According to Biff, Christ's Childhood Pal	Moore, Christopher
	Left for Dead: A Young Man's Search for Justice for the USS Indianapolis	Nelson, Peter
	19 Varieties of Gazelle: Poems of the Middle East	Nye, Naomi Shihab
	This Land Was Made for You and Me: The Life & Songs of Woody Guthrie	Partridge, Elizabeth
2002	*The Sisterhood of the Traveling Pants	Brashares, Ann
	The Rag and Bone Shop	Cormier, Robert
	*Whale Talk	Crutcher, Chris
	*Breathing Underwater	Flinn, Alex
	*Damage	Jenkins, A. M.
	Zazoo	Mosher, Richard
	*Lirael	Nix, Garth
	The Land	Taylor, Mildred
	Every Time a Rainbow Dies	Williams-Garcia, Rita
	True Believer	Wolff, Virginia Euwer
2001	*Forgotten Fire	Bagdasarian, Adam
	*Hope Was Here	Bauer, Joan
	*Girl with a Pearl Earring	Chevalier, Tracy
	Geeks: How Two Boys Rode the Internet Out of Idaho	Katz, Jon
	*Silent to the Bone	Konigsburg, E. L.
	The Beet Fields	Paulsen, Gary
	*Esperanza Rising	Ryan, Pam Muñoz
	*Stargirl	Spinelli, Jerry
	Homeless Bird	Whelan, Gloria
	Memories of Summer	White, Ruth
2000	*Speak	Anderson, Laurie Halse
	*Ender's Shadow	Card, Orson Scott
	*When Zachary Beaver Came to Town	Holt, Kimberly Willis
	The Raging Quiet	Jordan, Sherryl
	Crooked	McNeal, Laura and Tom
	*Mary, Bloody Mary	Meyer, Carolyn
	*Monster	Myers, Walter Dean
	Ties That Bind, Ties That Break	Namioka, Lensey
	*Imani All Mine	Porter, Connie

Quick Picks for Reluctant Young Adult Readers Top Ten 2000–2010

Year	Title	Author/Illustrator
2010	*Street Art Book: 60 Artists in Their Own Words*	Blackshaw, Ric, and Liz Farrelly
	The Naked Truth: Young, Beautiful and (HIV) Positive	Brown, Marvelyn
	Perfect Chemistry	Elkeles, Simone
	Jumping Off Swings	Knowles, Jo
	*Dope Sick	Myers, Walter Dean
	The Vampire Book	Regan, Sally
	Lockdown: Escape from Furnace	Smith, Alexander Gordon
	Show Me How: 500 Things You Should Know Instructions for Life from the Everyday to the Exotic	Fagerstrom, Derek, and Lauren Smith
	High Voltage Tattoo	Von D, Kat
	The Paranormal Caught on Film	Willin, Melvyn
2009	*Life Sucks*	Abel, Jessica, and Gabriel Soria
	One Hundred Young Americans	Franzini, Michael
	Permanence	Fulbeck, Kip
	No Choirboy: Murder, Violence and Teenagers on Death Row	Kuklin, Susan
	Wake	McMann, Lisa
	Body Drama	Redd, Nancy Amanda
	Skulls	Scalin, Noah
	Retaliation	Shiraz, Yasmin
	Custom Kicks	Smits, Kim, and Matthijs Maat
	*Ghosts Caught on Film: Photographs of the Paranormal	Willin, Melvyn
2008	*Class Pictures*	Bey, Dawoud

*Asterisk indicates that the title has an annotation in the text of this book.

Year	Title	Author/Illustrator
	Quaking	Erskine, Kathryn
	Thin	Greenfield, Lauren
	Graffiti L. A.: Street and Art	Grody, Steve, and James Prigoff
	Glass	Hopkins, Ellen
	Tupac Shakur Legacy	Jamal, Joesph
	Safe	Shaw, Susan
	*Unwind	Shusterman, Neal
	Homeboyz	Sitomer, Alan L.
	Thalia: ¡Belleza!: Lessons in Lipgloss and Happiness	Thalia
2007	**Nick and Norah's Infinite Playlist*	Cohn, Rachel, and David Levithan
	*Played	Davidson, Dana
	Blue Bloods	de la Cruz, Melissa
	*What Happened to Cass McBride	Giles, Gail
	Emily the Strange: The Lost Issue	Gruner, Jessica, and Buzz Parker
	Body Type: Intimate Messages Etched in Flesh	Saltz, Ina
	Optical Illusions: The Science of Visual Perception	Seckel, Al
	The Sleeper Conspiracy: Part 1, Sleeper Code; Part 2, Sleeper Agenda	Sniegoski, Tom
	Street Pharm	van Diepen, Allison
	PostSecret: Extraordinary Confessions from Ordinary Lives	Warren, Frank
2006	*From Pieces to Weight: Once Upon a Time in Southside, Queens*	50 Cent
	*Full Metal Alchemist, Vols. 1–4	Arakawa, Hiromu
	It's Happy Bunny: Life, Get One	Benton, Jim
	*Ball Don't Lie	de la Peña, Matt
	*Twilight: A Novel	Meyer, Stephenie
	Bling Bling: Hip Hop's Crown Jewels	Oh, Minya
	Bat Boy Lives! The Weekly World News Guide to Politics, Culture, Celebrities, Alien Abductions, and the Mutant Freaks That Shape Our World	Perel, David
	Lord Loss	Shan, Darren
	*Black and White	Volponi, Paul
	Boy Kills Man	Whyman, Matt
2005	**Who Am I Without Him? A Collection of Stories about Girls and the Boys in Their Lives*	Flake, Sharon
	In the Paint: Tattoos of the NBA and the Stories Behind Them	Gottlieb, Andrew
	The Official Movie Plot Generator: 27,000 Hilarious Movie Plot Combinations	Heimberg, Jason, and Justin Heimberg
	VX: 10 Years of Vibe Photography	Kenner, Rob, and George Pitts
	Monster Garage: How to Customize Damn Near Everything	Klancher, Lee

Year	Title	Author/Illustrator
	The Book of Bunny Suicides	Riley, Andy
	Confessions of a Backup Dancer	Shaw, Tucker
	The Boy Who Couldn't Die	Sleator, William
	*Fruits Basket, Vols. 1–5	*Takaya, Natsuki*
	Emako Blue	Woods, Brenda
2004	*Foolish/Unfoolish: Reflections on Love*	Ashanti
	Dead Girls Don't Write Letters	Giles, Gail
	Skeleton Key: An Alex Rider Adventure	Horowitz, Anthony
	Boards: The Art + Design of the Skateboard	Hoye, Jacob, ed.
	*The First Part Last	Johnson, Angela
	Dropping in with Andy Mac: Life of a Pro Skateboarder	Macdonald, Andy
	Only the Strong Survive: The Odyssey of Allen Iverson	Platt, Larry
	Odd Jobs: Portraits of Unusual Occupations	Schiff, Nancy Rica
	Jesse James: The Man and His Machines	Seate, Mike
	*Inside Out	Trueman, Terry
2003	**Gingerbread*	Cohn, Rachel
	E.A.R.L.: The Autobiography of DMX	Fontaine, Smokey D.
	Oh My Goddess! Wrong Number	Fujishima, Kosuke
	Anime Mania: How to Draw Characters for Japanese Animation	Hart, Christopher
	Between Boardslides and Burnout: My Notes from the Road	Hawk, Tony
	Point Blank: An Alex Rider Adventure	Horowitz, Anthony
	*Son of the Mob	Korman, Gordon
	*Sloppy Firsts	McCafferty, Megan
	Alphabetical Hookup List A–J	McPhee, Phoebe
	*Gossip Girl	Von Ziegesar, Cecily
2002	**Darkness Before Dawn*	Draper, Sharon M.
	Vatos	Galvez, Jose
	Manga Mania: How to Draw Japanese Comics	Hart, Christopher
	The Brimstone Journals	Koertge, Ron
	The Mad Gross Book	Meglin, Nick, and John Ficarra, eds.
	This Book Is about Sex	Shaw, Tucker, and Fiona Gibb
	*What My Mother Doesn't Know	Sones, Sonya
	Thrasher: Insane Terrain	*Thrasher Magazine*
	Sweep (series): *Book of Shadows, The Coven, Blood Witch, Dark Magic, Awakening*	Tiernan, Cate
	Hip Hop Divas	*Vibe Magazine*
2001	**The Princess Diaries*	Cabot, Meg
	Deal with It: A Whole New Approach to Your Body, Brain, and Life as a gURL	Drill, Esther, Heather McDonald, and Rebecca Odes
	You Hear Me? Poems and Writing by Teenage Boys	Franco, Betsy
	*Life Is Funny	Frank, E. R.

Year	Title	Author/Illustrator
	The Girls	Koss, Amy Goldman
	*Cut	McCormick, Patricia
	The Worst-Case Scenario Survival Handbook	Piven, Joshua, and David Borgenicht
	*Angus, Thongs, and Full-Frontal Snogging: Confessions of Georgia Nicolson	Rennison, Louise
	The Art of Optical Illusions	Seckel, Al
	The Rose That Grew from Concrete	Shakur, Tupac
2000	*The Concrete Wave (The History of Skateboarding)*	Brooke, Michael
	*Among the Hidden	Haddix, Margaret Petersen
	Spiders in the Hairdo: Modern Urban Legends	Holt, David, and Bill Mooney
	Seen and Heard: Teenagers Talk About Their Lives	Kalergis, Mary Motley
	Man Eating Bugs: The Art and Science of Eating Bugs	Menzel, Peter, and Faith D'Aluisio
	Star Wars, Episode 1: Incredible Cross-Sections	Reynolds, David West
	The Fairies: Photographic Evidence of the Existence of Another World	Scalora, Suza
	Rewind	Sleator, William
	*Stop Pretending: What Happened When My Sister Went Crazy	Sones, Sonya
	Rats	Zindel, Paul

Appendix E

Alex Awards 2000–2010

Year	Title	Author/Illustrator
2010	*Soulless: An Alexia Tarabotti Novel*	Carriger, Gail
	Everything Matters!	Currie, Ron
	The Good Soldiers	Finkel, David
	The Magicians	Grossman, Lev
	The Boy Who Harnessed the Wind: Creating Currents of Electricity and Hope	Kamkwamba, William, and Bryan Mealer
	My Abandonment	Rock, Peter
	The Bride's Farewell	Rosoff, Meg
	Stitches: A Memoir	Small, David
	The Kids Are All Right: A Memoir	Welch, Diana and Liz, with Amanda and Dan Welch
	Tunneling to the Center of the Earth	Wilson, Kevin
2009	*City of Thieves*	Benioff, David
	Sharp Teeth	Barlow, Toby
	The Oxford Project	Bloom, Stephen G.
	Finding Nouf	Ferraris, Zoë
	Mudbound	Jordan, Hillary
	Just After Sunset: Stories	King, Stephen
	Three Girls and Their Brother	Rebeck, Theresa
	The Dragons of Babel	Swanwick, Michael
	The Good Thief	Tinti, Hannah
	Over and Under	Tucker, Todd
2008	*A Long Way Gone: Memoirs of a Boy Soldier*	Beah, Ishmael
	Genghis: Birth of an Empire	Iggulden, Conn
	Mister Pip	Jones, Lloyd
	The God of Animals	Kyle, Aryn
	Tales from the Farm: Essex County, Vol. 1	Lemire, Jeff
	The Spellman Files	Luts, Lisa
	The Night Birds	Maltman, Thomas

*Asterisk indicates that the title has an annotation in the text of this book.

Year	Title	Author/Illustrator
	American Shaolin: Flying Kicks, Buddhist Monks, and the Legend of Iron Crotch: An Odyssey in the New China	Polly, Matthew
	The Name of the Wind	Rothfuss, Patrick
	Bad Monkeys	Ruff, Matt
2007	*The Book of Lost Things*	Connolly, John
	The Whistling Season	Doig, Ivan
	Eagle Blue: A Team, A Tribe, and a High School Basketball Season in Arctic Alaska	D'Orso, Michael
	Water for Elephants	Gruen, Sara
	Color of the Sea	Hamamura, John
	The Floor of the Sky	Joern, Pamela Carter
	The Blind Side: Evolution of a Game	Lewis, Michael
	Black Swan Green	Mitchell, David
	The World Made Straight	Rash, Ron
	The Thirteenth Tale	Setterfield, Diane
2006	*Midnight at the Dragon Café*	Bates, Judy Fong
	Upstate	Buckhanon, Kalisha
	Anansi Boys	Gaiman, Neil
	As Simple As Snow	Galloway, Gregory
	Never Let Me Go	Ishiguro, Kazuo
	Gil's All Fright Diner	Martinez, A. Lee
	The Necessary Beggar	Palwick, Susan
	My Jim	Rawles, Nancy
	Jesus Land: A Memoir	Scheeres, Julia
	The Glass Castle: A Memoir	Walls, Jeannette
2005	*Candyfreak: A Journey through the Chocolate Underbelly of America*	Almond, Steve
	Swimming to Antarctica: Tales of a Long-Distance Swimmer	Cox, Lynn
	Donorboy	Halpin, Brendan
	Shadow Divers	Kurson, Robert
	Work of Wolves	Meyers, Kent
	Truth & Beauty: A Friendship	Patchett, Ann
	My Sister's Keeper	Picoult, Jodi
	Thinner Than Thou	Reed, Kit
	Project X	Shepard, Jim
	Rats: Observations on the History and Habitat of the City's Most Unwanted Inhabitants	Sullivan, Robert
2004	*Wonder When You'll Miss Me*	Davis, Amanda
	The Curious Incident of the Dog in the Night-Time: A Novel	Haddon, Mark
	The Kite Runner	Hosseini, Khaled
	The Time Traveler's Wife	Niffenegger, Audrey
	Drinking Coffee Elsewhere	Packer, Z. Z.
	Stiff	Roach, Mary
	True Notebooks	Salzman, Mark

Year	Title	Author/Illustrator
	Persepolis	Satrapi, Marjane
	Maisie Dobbs	Winspear, Jacqueline
	Leave Myself Behind	Yates, Bart
2003	*One Hundred Demons*	Barry, Lynda
	My Losing Season	Conroy, Pat
	Seeing in the Dark: How Backyard Stargazers Are Probing Deep Space and Guarding Earth from Interplanetary Peril	Ferris, Timothy
	The Eyre Affair	Fforde, Jasper
	Crow Lake	Lawson, Mary
	The Year of Ice	Malloy, Brian
	When the Emperor Was Divine	Otsuka, Julie
	The Dive from Clausen's Pier	Packer, Ann
	The Fall of Rome	Southgate, Martha
	10th Grade	Weisberg, Joseph
2002	*Year of Wonders: A Novel of the Plague*	Brooks, Geraldine
	An American Insurrection: The Battle of Oxford, Mississippi, 1962	Doyle, William
	Gabriel's Story	Durham, David
	Nickel and Dimed: On (Not) Getting by in Boom-Time America	Ehrenreich, Barbara
	Peace Like a River	Enger, Leif
	The Wilderness Family: At Home with Africa's Wildlife	Kruger, Kobie
	Kit's Law	Morrissey, Donna
	The Rover	Odom, Mel
	Motherland	Vijayaraghavan, Vineeta
	Black, White, and Jewish: Autobiography of a Shifting Self	Walker, Rebecca
2001	*Flags of Our Fathers*	Bradley, James, and Ron Powers
	The Sand-Reckoner	Bradshaw, Gillian
	Girl with a Pearl Earring	Chevalier, Tracy
	Counting Coup: A True Story of Basketball and Honor on the Little Big Horn	Colton, Larry
	Soldier: A Poet's Childhood	Jordan, June
	Daughter of the Forest	Marillier, Juliet
	In the Heart of the Sea: The Tragedy of the Whaleship Essex	Philbrick, Nathaniel
	The Man Who Ate the 747	Sherwood, Ben
	Chang and Eng	Strauss, Darin
	Diamond Dogs	Watt, Alan
2000	*High Exposure: An Enduring Passion for Everest and Unforgiving Places*	Breashears, David
	Ender's Shadow	Card, Orson Scott
	River, Cross My Heart	Clarke, Breena
	Educating Esmé: Diary of a Teacher's First Year	Codell, Esmé Raji
	The Reappearance of Sam Webber	Fuqua, Jonathon Scott

Year	Title	Author/Illustrator
	Stardust	Gaiman, Neil
	The Hungry Ocean: A Swordboat Captain's Journey	Greenlaw, Linda
	Barefoot Heart: Stories of a Migrant Child	Hart, Elva Trevino
	Plainsong	Haruf, Kent
	*Imani All Mine	Porter, Connie

Appendix F

Great Graphic Novels for Teens Top Ten 2007–2010

Year	Title	Author/Illustrator
2010	*The Helm*	Hardison, Jim, and Bart Sears
	Children of the Sea, Vol. 1	Igarashi, Daisuke
	Pinocchio: Vampire Slayer	Jensen, Van, and Dusty Higgins
	I Kill Giants	Kelly, Joe, and J. M. Ken Nimura
	Omega the Unknown	Lethem, Jonathan, and Farel Dalrymple
	Bayou, Vol. 1	Love, Jeremy
	A.D.: New Orleans after the Deluge	Neufeld, Josh
	Gunnerkrigg Court, Vol. 1: Orientation	Siddell, Tom
	Pluto	Urasawa, Naoki, and Takashi Nagasaki
	Ooku: The Inner Chambers, Vol. 1	Yoshinaga, Fumi
2009	*Life Sucks*	Abel, Jessica, Gabriel Soria, and Warren Pleece
	Sand Chronicles, Vols. 1–3	Ashihara, Hinako
	Atomic Robo: Atomic Robo and the Fightin' Scientists of Tesladyne	Clevinger, Brian, and Steve Wegener
	Real, Vols. 1–2	Inoue, Takehiko
	Uzumaki, Vol. 1	Ito, Junki
	Pitch Black	Landowne, Youme, and Anthony Horton
	Japan Ai: A Tall Girl's Adventures in Japan	Steinberger, Aimee Major
	*Skim	Tamaki, Mariko, and Jilliam Tamaki
	Umbrella Academy: Apocalypse Suite	Way, Gerard, and Gabriel Ba

*Asterisk indicates that the title has an annotation in the text of this book.

Year	Title	Author/Illustrator
	Cairo	Wilson, G. Willow, and M. K. Perker
2008	*Laika*	Abadzis, Nick
	Re-Gifters	Carey, Mike
	The Magical Life of Long Tack Sam	Fleming, Ann Marie
	Blue Beetle: Shell-Shocked Blue Beetle: Road Trip	Giffen, Keith
	King of Thorn, Vols. 1–2	Iwahara, Yuji
	Sidescrollers	Loux, Matthew
	After School Nightmare, Vols. 1-5	Mizushiro, Setona
	Emma, Vols. 1–5	Mori, Kaoru
	The Wall: Growing Up Behind the Iron Curtain	Sis, Peter
	The Arrival	Tan, Shaun
2007	*Nextwave: Agents of H.A.T.E.*	Ellis, Warren, and Stuart Immonen
	Sloth	Hernandez, Gilbert, and Jared K. Fletcher
	Castle Waiting	Medley, Linda
	Identity Crisis	Meltzer, Brad, and Rags Morales
	Death Note, Vols. 1–3	Ohba, Tsugumi, and Takeshi Obata
	Runaways, Vols. 4–5	Vaughan, Brian K., and Adrian Alphona
	Pride of Baghdad	Vaughan, Brian K., and Niko Henrichon
	Death, Jr.	Whitta, Gary, and Ted Naifeh
	Demo: The Collection	Wood, Brian, and Becky Cloonan
	American Born Chinese	Yang, Gene Luen

Appendix G

Teens' Top Ten 2003–2009

Year	Rank	Title	Author/Illustrator
2009	1.	*Paper Towns*	Green, John
	2.	*Breaking Dawn*	Meyer, Stephenie
	3.	*The Hunger Games*	Collins, Suzanne
	4.	*City of Ashes*	Clare, Cassandra
	5.	*Identical*	Hopkins, Ellen
	6.	*The Graveyard Book*	Gaiman, Neil
	7.	*Wake*	McMann, Lisa
	8.	*Untamed*	Cast, P. C., and Kristin Cast
	9.	*The Disreputable History of Frankie Landau-Banks*	Lockhart, E.
	10.	*Graceling*	Cashore, Kristin
2008	1.	*Eclipse*	Meyer, Stephenie
	2.	*Harry Potter and the Deathly Hallows*	Rowling, J. K.
	3.	*Diary of a Wimpy Kid*	Kinney, Jeff
	4.	*Vampire Academy*	Mead, Richelle
	5.	*Maximum Ride: Saving the World and Other Extreme Sports*	Patterson, James
	6.	*City of Bones*	Clare, Cassandra
	7.	*The Sweet Far Thing*	Bray, Libba
	8.	*Extras*	Westerfeld, Scott
	9.	*Before I Die*	Downham, Jenny
	10.	*Twisted*	Anderson, Laurie Halse
2007	1.	*New Moon*	Meyer, Stephenie
	2.	*Just Listen*	Dessen, Sarah
	3.	*How to Ruin a Summer Vacation*	Elkeles, Simone
	4.	*School's Out—Forever: Maximum Ride, Book 2*	Patterson, James
	5.	*Firegirl*	Abbott, Tony
	6.	*All Hallows' Eve: 13 Stories*	Velde, Vivian Vande
	7.	*Life as We Knew It*	Pfeffer, Susan Beth
	8.	*River Secrets*	Hale, Shannon
	9.	*Bad Kitty*	Jaffe, Michele

*Asterisk indicates that the title has an annotation in the text of this book.

Year	Rank	Title	Author/Illustrator
	10.	*Road of the Dead*	Brooks, Kevin
2006	1.	*Harry Potter and the Half-Blood Prince*	Rowling, J. K.
	2.	*Twilight: A Novel*	Meyer, Stephenie
	3.	*Eldest*	Paolini, Christopher
	4.	*Rebel Angels*	Bray, Libba
	5.	*Peeps*	Westerfeld, Scott
	6.	*13 Little Blue Envelopes*	Johnson, Maureen
	7.	*Poison*	Wooding, Chris
	8.	*Captain Hook: The Adventures of a Notorious Youth*	Hart, J. V.
	9.	*If I Have a Wicked Stepmother, Where's My Prince?*	Kantor, Melissa
	10.	*Elsewhere*	Zevin, Gabrielle
2005	1.	*Girls in Pants: The Third Summer of the Sisterhood*	Brashares, Ann
	2.	*The Truth about Forever*	Dessen, Sarah
	3.	*Looking for Alaska*	Green, John
	4.	*My Sister's Keeper*	Picoult, Jodi
	5.	*Drums, Girls & Dangerous Pie*	Sonnenblick, Jordan
	6.	*Maximum Ride: The Angel Experiment*	Patterson, James
	7.	*The Gangsta Rap*	Zephaniah, Benjamin
	8.	*Teen Idol*	Cabot, Meg
	9.	*The Garden*	Eidinoff, Elise
	10.	*How I Paid for College: A Novel of Sex, Theft, Friendship & Musical Theater*	Acito, Marc
2004	1.	*Harry Potter and the Order of the Phoenix*	Rowling, J. K.
	2.	*Eragon*	Paolini, Christopher
	3.	*Pirates!*	Rees, Celia
	4.	*Trickster's Choice*	Pierce, Tamora
	5.	*Inkheart*	Fünke, Cornelia
	6.	*A Great and Terrible Beauty*	Bray, Libba
	7.	*The Goose Girl*	Hale, Shannon
	8.	*Princess in Pink*	Cabot, Meg
	9.	*The Earth, My Butt, and Other Big Round Things*	Mackler, Carolyn
	10.	*Curse of the Blue Tattoo*	Meyer, L. A.
2003	1.	*A Wizard Alone (Young Wizards, Book 6)*	Duane, Diane
	2.	*The Second Summer of the Sisterhood*	Brashares, Ann
	3.	*Tithe: A Modern Faerie Tale*	Black, Holly
	4.	*The Thief Lord*	Fünke, Cornelia
	5.	*The True Meaning of Cleavage*	Fredericks, Mariah
	6.	*Abhorsen*	Nix, Garth
	7.	*The Book of Wizardry: The Apprentice's Guide to the Secrets of the Wizards' Guild*	Rumstuckle, Cornelius
	8.	*Dead Girls Don't Write Letters*	Giles, Gail
	9.	*True Confessions of a Heartless Girl*	Brooks, Martha
	10.	*America*	Frank, E. R.

Title Index

Boldface page numbers indicate annotations.

Author Index

About the Author

Rollie Welch has been employed as a librarian for thirty years, mostly working directly with young adults. His career started with working as a school librarian, responsible for everything going on in the library, in various Ohio districts. After eighteen years, Rollie migrated to public libraries first as a teen librarian and currently as Cleveland Public Library's Collection Manager. At each stop, the focus was connecting young adults to great books. Rollie has served on several YALSA book selection committees: Quick Picks for Reluctant Young Adult Readers, Best Books for Young Adults, and the Michael L. Printz Award. As a reviewer, Rollie currently writes for *The Cleveland Plain Dealer* and *Library Journal*. He also co-authors a column for VOYA called *Man Up!* Rollie's thirty years of experience has put him in tune with thousands of young adult books, which was a direct influence for his writing this second edition of *A Core Collection for Young Adults*.